Gower
HANDBOOK
of
TEAMWORKING

GOWER
HANDBOOK
OF
TEAMWORKING

edited by
Roger Stewart

Gower

Published by
Gower Publishing Limited
Gower House
Croft Road
Aldershot
Hampshire GU11 3HR
England

Gower
Old Post Road
Brookfield
Vermont 05036
USA

British Library Cataloguing in Publication Data
Gower handbook of teamworking
   1. Teams in the workplace
   I. Stewart, Roger   II. Handbook of teamworking
   658.4'02

   ISBN 0 566 07968 2

Library of Congress Cataloging-in-Publication Data
Gower handbook of teamworking/edited by Roger Stewart.
      p.   cm.
   Includes index.
   ISBN 0–566–07968–2 (hardcover)
   1. Teams in the workplace.   I. Stewart, Roger, 1949–   .
II. Gower Publishing Company.
HD66.G68   1998
658.3'128—dc21   98–25002
                                                              CIP

Phototypeset in Cheltenham 10 on 12 pt by Intype London Ltd
and printed in Great Britain by MPG Books Ltd, Bodmin

Contents

PART I   TEAMS AND THE ORGANIZATION

1   The business environment   7
George Blair and Sandy Meadows
Organizational considerations – Lessons learnt from implementing
Total Quality Management, re-engineering and empowerment –
Overcoming initiative fatigue – Why do you want to establish
teams? – Does your organizational culture support teams? –
How far do you want to go? – Having the best of both worlds –
New paradoxes – References – Recommended reading – Useful
organization

2   The flexible organization   24
Valerie Garrow and Linda Holbeche
Rhetoric versus reality – Types of team – Power-distance – Enabling
teamworking – Leadership – New manager roles – Supporting
structures – Conclusion – References

PART II UNDERSTANDING TEAMS

PART IV   TEAMS AND TECHNOLOGY

List of figures

List of tables

List of boxes

List of charts

Preface

Recent years have seen a series of rapid changes in economies and markets, the result of which is that organizations have altered the way in which they structure their operations and modified their attitudes as to what constitutes employment. For example, the concept of a job for life in a single organization, with career progression based on merit and experience, has largely disappeared. Flexible work packages, project-based employment and short-term contracts are becoming the norm for large groups of individuals. This is due in no small way to the strategy of many organizations in adopting structures, such as flat, federalist or decentralized, designed to make them more responsive to market conditions and more efficient in their operations. Downsizing, rightsizing and outsourcing have all affected the size of the workforce and the nature of the work that is performed.

An integral part of these structural changes is the creation and operation of teams in order to achieve the flexibility required by their market place and customers. While in certain types of organization, such as the military, emergency services and healthcare provision, teams have always been a key feature, the awareness of the importance of teams in commercial organizations has increased substantially in recent times. The behaviour of teams is perceived as a critical factor in the success of the organization as a whole.

The understanding of what makes a team tick, the setting of team objectives and the management of team performance are therefore important in the restructuring and management of the process of change. However, it is not only economies and market places that have changed; technology has also developed rapidly, enabling different modes of operation and supporting new work practices.

Against this background it is clear that a great many people are interested in and involved with teams. There is no shortage of published material on teams and teamworking. Many excellent books are available on the various *xvii* aspects of teams and organizations, such as organizational structure, general management, behavioural psychology and organizational development. However, most of them, dealing as they do with one particular theme, are necessarily limited. By way of contrast the *Handbook of Teamworking* sets out to cover the whole spectrum in a single volume. The thirty contributors are drawn, deliberately, from a wide variety of backgrounds, and they represent a range of viewpoints.

The text is arranged in four main parts.

PART I   TEAMS AND THE ORGANIZATION

Part I looks at teams in an organizational context. It deals with the market place pressures that have caused businesses to restructure themselves in a team-based form, and the cultural changes necessary in organization to be successful with teams. Different types of structures are examined and there is discussion of the problems with existing business process-changes. Structures make up one component of the organization; another component, that of team needs and roles within teams, is also covered in this part.

PART II   UNDERSTANDING TEAMS

The structuring of organizations and the establishing of teams is the start. However, to make the running of teams successful requires an understanding of what constitutes a team as opposed to a group of individuals. This Part explores the nature of teams and covers: teams within the organization; teams processes; team behaviour and individual behaviour.

PART III   MANAGING TEAMS

The previous two Parts have examined the organizational reasons for teams, and what makes a team. Part III deals with the process of managing teams, often the starting point for organizations, despite not having undertaken any prior work on understanding what teams are or why they have them. It encompasses: the operational cycle of designing, building and managing teams; the training of teams; and why teams fail and what can be done to prevent this happening.

PART IV   TEAMS AND TECHNOLOGY

Modern technology has dramatically affected the way organizations operate internally and on a global basis. This Part looks at the 'technology effect' on teamworking, team behaviour and cultural change. The final two chapters adopt a wider perspective, with technology being only one part, but nevertheless an important part.

This handbook has been written for the widest possible audience, not just for line managers and HRD professionals. As readers will come from organizations with a variety of structures, their concept and use of teams will differ. Some organizations will have extensive experience of team operation, and others will be in the process of setting up team operation. The structure of the book reflects these different interests and needs.

The book may be approached in different ways. For example, a reader could start at the beginning and read to the end. The flow of the book takes the reader through: why organizations perceive teamworking as important; understanding what happens in teams and why they fail; the management of teams from the initial design and creation of teams to running very experienced teams; the impact of technology.

It is more likely, however, that a reader has some experience of teamworking but wishes to know more about a particular area of team operation. For example, developing a deeper understanding of the development of teams or managing a particular stage of teamworking. In this case a particular part will be of most relevance.

The handbook will also interest readers who have extensive experience in teamworking but wish to expand their knowledge of a specific topic such as psychometrics or failure analysis. However you may use this book, good luck with the teams you are in or manage.

Roger Stewart

Notes on contributors

George Blair (*The business environment*) is a managing consultant with substantial experience of implementing organizational change both within the UK and internationally. He has advised private and public organizations and governments. His previous career spans marketing and human resource management. George is a director of the Manpower Society and associate editor of *Health Manpower Management*. He is, with Sandy Meadows, joint author of *Winning at Change*, published by Pitman (1996) and *A Real Life Guide to Organizational Change*, published by Gower (1997).

Hugh Brawley (*Developing strategic team leaders*) is Leadership and Organization Development Manager at EMEA, PCS, Motorola, Scotland. He is currently researching individual and organization learning, linked to change management for his PhD thesis. Initially, he commenced his career as an electrical engineer, moving through middle to senior management and Human Resources roles in manufacturing and service industries, such as the NHS, British Aerospace, Thorn EMI and Babcock Rosyth Defence Ltd.

Wendy Briner (*Teams and the learning organization; The superteam approach*) is a founder member of New Organization Consulting, using a combination of organizational teamworking, executive development and project ways of working to enable organizations to learn how to sustain improved performance. Prior to this she was a Business Director at Ashridge Management College, developing their consulting services in organizational change and project leadership. She continues to work as an associate for Ashridge, concentrating on senior executive one-to-one feedback and development. Wendy is currently interested in project-based organizations and has published *Project Leadership* (2nd edition, 1996) which outlines her interest in projects as vehicles for organizational change. She speaks regularly at conferences and has published articles on project management and organizational change. Currently she is a visiting lecturer at City University Business School, involved with their management MBA, working with managers on their in-company strategic projects that enhance organizational learning, as well as contribute to the individual's personal development. Wendy offers individual development support to executives encountering personally challenging situations. She designs and facilitates small group learning sets, as well as one-to-one mentoring activities to generate self-managed learning. She is also a counsellor in systemic family therapy, working in a Social Services Unit in London. She seeks to draw on the relationship focus of systemic thinking in her organizational development work with individuals, teams and whole systems in handling complex change. Her clients include Anglian Water, Allied Domecq, J. Sainsbury, British Airways, NHS-Executive, Pfizer, EDAW Planning, TOPS in Berlin, Theseus Institut in France and the World Health Organization.

Jane Cranwell-Ward (*Managing stress for optimum performance*) is Director of the Henley Learning Partnership, a Client Director at Henley Management College, and also works as a freelance consultant. She specializes in team building, managing change, stress management, interpersonal skills and personal and managerial effectiveness. She regularly runs workshops in the private and public sector, and speaks at conferences. Prior to working at Henley, Jane was a senior lecturer in Psychology and Organizational Behaviour at Kingston Polytechnic, now Kingston University, and was initially employed at Harrods. She has a BSc in Botany and Psychology from Exeter University, and an MPhil. from the University of Surrey. She is a Fellow of the Institute of Personnel and Development. Jane is the author of *Managing Stress* (1987) and *Thriving on Stress* (1990), and is also editor of a Self-Development Series for managers published by Routledge and International Thomson.

Malcolm Crockford (*Team selection, psychometrics and feedback; Designing and facilitating team development*) is an independent consultant working in the area of individual, team and leadership development. He has spent over thirty years working for household name companies (Mobil Oil, Burroughs Machines, IBM and Prudential) in Human Resource Development, specializing in management and executive development. At IBM he was Management Development Manager for the UK company and a member of the Management Development Board for IBM Europe, Middle East and Africa. He supported the development of leadership and culture change programmes for IBM Managers worldwide, and ran senior team development programmes in the UK and Europe for IBM and its customers. At Prudential, as Human Resource Development Manager, Malcolm was responsible for strategic Management Development programmes, including Leadership and Team Development. Malcolm has a Cambridge degree in Classics and is a Fellow of the Institute of Personnel and Development.

Quentin de la Bedoyere (*Leading team meetings; Solving problems face-to-face*) is a consultant in financial communications for IQ Productions, having retired in 1997 as Managing Director, Sun Life of Canada Unit Managers Ltd. Books he has written include *Managing People and Problems*, Gower (1988); *How to Get Your Own Way in Business*, Gower (1990); *Getting What You Want*, Piatkus (1994); *The Remaking of Marriages*, Liverpool Institute; and *Choices in Sex*, PDG. Quentin writes for, among others, *The Sunday Times, Sunday People, New Woman, Tablet, The Month, Catholic Herald* and *Universe*, and has contributed poems to *The Poetry of Business Life* (1994). He is married, with five children and 12 grandchildren.

Maggie Dunn (*Negotiating teams in industrial relations*) is Senior National Officer with UNISON, the public sector union. She joined NUPE (one of the founder unions which merged to form UNISON) in 1982. Before joining NUPE she qualified as a nurse, then went on to study labour relations at Ruskin College, Oxford and economics at the London School of Economics. More recently she became a Fellow of the Royal Society of Arts. Maggie's main responsibilities within UNISON are for negotiations and industrial relations within the Health Group. She is the lead negotiator for nurses, midwives, health visitors and ambulance personnel on the Joint Union National Staff Side. Author of numerous articles, she has addressed conferences and contributed to courses in the USA, Cuba, Nicaragua, France, Belgium, Czech Republic, Russia, South Africa and the UK.

Chris Elgood (*Choosing, joining and leaving teams*; *Using management games*) has wide experience of teaching and training in colleges and major companies. After gaining a BA degree (Hons) from Cambridge University, and working in administration, he became Lecturer in Practical Administration, Staff Training College, Lusaka, Zambia, to then go on to work as Training Officer with Standard Telephones & Cables Ltd. Following his post as Group Training Executive with Guest, Keen & Nettlefolds Ltd, he was Senior Civilian Tutor (Management Studies) at the Police Staff College, Bramshill from 1975–1980. Up to 1997, Chris has been an independent consultant and author of Management Games, Training Exercises and Simulations, and is Managing Director of Chris Elgood Associates Ltd. He is a member of AMED, having served for five years on the Executive. Chris is the author of several books, including *The Handbook of Management Games*, Sixth Edition, Gower (1997); *Using Management Games*, Gower (1996); *The New Manager* (formerly *Who's in Charge?*), Pitman Publishing (1996). He is also the author of 'Venture – the International Strategic Management Game', and has written numerous articles in industrial training journals. Chris has produced about 30 packaged games and simulations and has custom-made others for clients such as Touche Ross, Esso Chemical, British Printing Industries Federation and Guinness plc. He has also carried out training and teambuilding assignments for organizations such as Ampex, British Telecom, Wessex Training Services and Hoskyns Group plc. Chris is married, with one daughter.

Dr Joyce Fortune *(A systems approach to team effectiveness)* is a Senior Lecturer in the Faculty of Technology at The Open University. Her teaching specialisms are systems thinking and quality management, although she has also written distance teaching materials in areas such as project management and the impact of new technology on work. Her main research interest is the application of systems thinking to the study of failures, and the use of lessons from failures to prevent future failures and promote organizational learning. She has published widely in this area.

Nancy Foy *(Using team roles)* author of *Empowering People at Work*, Gower (1994, paperback edition 1997), still speaks with a Californian accent, but her vocabulary is rich in Scots vernacular. Other books include *The Sun Never Sets on IBM*, and *People at Work*, about the Volvo experience in the 1970s. Since her landmark study of the future of management education (which led to *The Yin and Yang of Organisations*), Nancy has worked on team development, employee communications, and HR development strategies inside a number of major organizations – many moving from a public-service culture to the stringent atmosphere of the private sector. She has been involved with BT's employee and consumer communications, and her client list includes ScotRail and BR, as well as the BAA, BAe, British Gas, and a number of Scottish hospitals. Nancy lives on top of a breezy brae in the centre of Scotland and runs a second-hand bookshop in Blair Atholl in her 'spare' time.

Valerie Garrow *(The flexible organization)* is a Researcher at Roffey Park Management Institute. Valerie graduated from Lancaster University in French Studies and Sociology and has a Masters degree in Organizational Behaviour from London University. She began her career as a social worker in Paris. Since returning to the UK she has worked mainly in Customer Services in the airline industry. Since joining Roffey Park in 1993, Valerie has carried out research on a variety of projects including equal opportunities, mergers and acquisitions, self-directed teams and, most recently, 360 Degree Feedback.

Terry Gillen *(Managing teams assertively)* is a consultant trainer and author with over 20 years experience in people development in industries as diverse as financial services, ship building, pharmaceuticals, leisure, retail and scientific research. He has six books and training manuals published to date (one with Professor John Adair) which, together, have been translated into over twelve languages. He has consulted on, and appeared in, three videos on interpersonal skills, and been interviewed live on national radio on the subject of politicians' body language. As well as running courses for clients throughout the UK, he has taught in Cyprus, Singapore, Malaysia and Hong Kong.

Gisela Hagemann *(Motivating teams)* is an economist (University of Zürich   *xxiii* and Bonn) and has more than 15 years experience as an independent management consultant and trainer. She has led major projects in Germany, Norway, Sweden, Austria and Italy – helping companies to motivate staff in situations of change. She lives in Berlin where she leads her own company, Gisela Hagemann Innovationsconsulting, dealing mainly with creativity and innovation. Gisela is author of *The Motivation Manual*, published in England by Gower, and also in Germany, Norway, Sweden, Finland, Italy, The Czech Republic and Indonesia. Her second book, *Die Hohe Schule der Führung*, has been published in three countries, and her third book, *Å vinne fremtiden*, has been published in Norway. Gisela is certified in Edward de Bono's methods 'Six Thinking Hats' and 'Lateral Thinking', and she has a degree from Tony Buzan in 'Mind Mapping'.

Colin Hastings (*Creating a team-based organization*) was brought up in East Africa and educated in the UK, where he gained a BA Hons degree from Sussex University. He spent nine years as a manager with the Delta Metal Group, both in Tanzania and the UK, and then gained an MSc and PhD in Organizational Psychology at Birkbeck College, London University. Colin joined Ashridge Management College, becoming Head of the Organization Behaviour faculty, working on open and tailor-made General Management and Human Resource programmes. He started up Ashridge Teamworking Services, from which came the Ashridge Consulting Group. Since 1988, Colin, with two other colleagues, has been a partner in New Organization Consulting. They undertake consultancy, training and research in multidisciplinary teamworking, the project approach in organizations, the development of partnerships, alliances, and new forms of organization, action-based learning/development processes and the effective management of change. He has worked at Board level, consulting and coaching both senior teams and individuals for clients such as WHO, The Bank for International Settlements (Basle), Rank Xerox Europe, Novo Nordisk Engineering (Denmark) and Shell Research Laboratories (Amsterdam and The Hague), BP Engineering and Research, Safeway, Prudential Corporation, AMEC Process and Energy and Kvaerner Oil and Gas. Colin is a well-known writer, conference presenter and workshop facilitator and the co-author of *Superteams*, 6th edn, Fontana (1986) and *Project Leadership*, 2nd edn, Gower (1996). He has also written *The New Organization: growing the culture of organizational networking*, McGraw-Hill Europe (1993). He was instrumental in commissioning and directing the 'Developing the Developers' research project on behalf of AMED. Based in north London, Colin is married to Helen, who is a therapist and novelist, and they have two sons.

Robin Hirsch (*Making the most of new technology*) has worked in technology strategy and benchmarking since 1976, when he became European Corporate Planner and later Finance Director of National Semiconductor in Germany, and later when he became Group Accounting Manager (deputy controller) at Sun Alliance in the UK. In 1985, he moved into consultancy, spending six years at A.T. Kearney and then founding Kingdom Technology, which provided IT and corporate strategy advice to electricity companies, mines, banks and central government. In 1992, he became a Senior Associate at Imperial College and in 1997 was made responsible for the IC Civil Engineering Benchmarking Initiative. This provides process benchmarking services for the European Construction Institute, whose membership consists of about 60 of Europe's largest construction clients and contractors. Robin Hirsch was part of the founding team at Imperial College's Railway Technology Strategy Centre which benchmarked British Rail's R&D practices against other national railways and against industries which had been transformed by an increase in competition. Clients for technology, research and competition strategy projects included the UK Secretary of Transport and the Commission of the European Union. In 1994, five large metro railways founded a benchmarking group of which he was the project manager. It will now include all of the world's nine largest metros, while a second group is being launched under the aegis of the UITP, the world public transport umbrella organization based in Brussels, to which he is also a consultant. His academic background includes the design and management of a course at INSEAD on 'Computers and Management', articles such as 'Getting the Ratios Right' (*Management Today*, April 1990) 'Profit-Driven Technology Strategy' and other methodologies. He lectures on MSc courses at Imperial College (Transport Studies), Sheffield University (Railway Systems Engineering) and Kingston University (Information Systems Design). He is an MA of Oxford University, an MBA from INSEAD, a Chartered Management Accountant and a Chartered Secretary. He is currently writing a book on 'Benchmarking and beyond – creating radical change and supporting continuous improvement'.

Linda Holbeche (*The flexible organization*) graduated from Durham University in French and also has masters degrees in Languages and Education. Linda worked in marketing and publishing before qualifying as a teacher. She held a variety of senior teaching positions in London before joining American Express as a management training consultant. Linda joined Roffey Park Management Institute in 1994 and is now Director of Research. Key research topics include 'Career Development in Flatter Structures' and 'International Leadership'. She has produced several major research reports and published articles on peer mentoring, strategic leadership and career development. Linda's special areas of interest include designing and delivering programmes on senior management development, coaching and counselling, performance management, team skills, management of change and a wide variety of personal and career development methods. A frequent speaker at conferences, Linda has addressed international gatherings on topics such as leadership, evaluation and innovative development centres.

Chris Hutchison (*Computer-supported cooperative work; Virtual teams*) has taught at Kingston University since 1988. His main research interests are in *xxv* intelligent multimedia interfaces for teaching and learning, computer support for collaborative learning, and intelligent agents in virtual environments. He has received a number of grants from the European Commission to undertake projects in these areas, and has presented at several EC-sponsored conferences and seminars. He is a member of the ACM and of the Groupe Ampère, a European think-tank on IT in education under the auspices of DG XIII of the European Commission.

Patrick Keane *(IT teams in the London Borough of Richmond Upon Thames)* is the head of IT for the London Borough of Richmond Upon Thames. He has been with the authority for over ten years, joining as an analyst in 1987. The opportunity arose to undertake a masters degree at Kingston Polytechnic (as it was called at the time) and this proved an invaluable experience. Since becoming the head of IT the authority has gone through major organizational change which has given IS/IT a much higher profile. Patrick's background has not always been in IT and he came to it late in life through a re-training scheme. He is married with three children.

Ronnie Lessem *(Turning teamwork into knowledge creation)* is currently Reader in International Management at City University Business School in London, where he has been teaching and researching for 27 years, and Director of the Four Worlds Institute. He also acts as learning strategist for Anglian Water, for the Surrey Police and for Virgin Direct and is a Director of his family business in Zimbabwe. Born in Zimbabwe, he gained an economics degree there, taking his masters degree, in the economics of industry, at the London School of Economics. After acquiring his MBA from Harvard Business School, he took his PhD at City University, in the area of action learning focused on enterprise development. Ronnie began his business career as a corporate planner with Fisons, in South Africa, before becoming managing director of a small chain of retailers. Thereafter he helped to develop business consultancies in social auditing (Intermatrix Group), urban and economic development and intrapreneurship (URBED), organizational learning and knowledge creation (New York Ventures) and transcultural management (Four Worlds Institute), based worldwide. He has had visiting professorships at IMD, in Lausanne, and at Wits Graduate Business School in Johannesburg. Ronnie is also the author or co-author of some 20 books including *Enterprise Development and Intrapreneurship*; *Business as a Learning Community and Total Quality Learning*; *African, European and Global Business*; *Managing in Four Worlds*; *Management Development through Cultural Diversity* and, prospectively, *The Evolving Ecology of Organizations*. Finally, Ronnie has developed the SMTI (Spectral Management Type Inventory), the general concept of the 'global businessphere' and the specific video on the Southern African Businessphere.

Dennis Lock *(Organizing for project work)*, after qualifying in applied physics, began his career as an electronics engineer. His subsequent experience has been long, successful and exceptionally wide, with management positions in engineering industries ranging from electronics to heavy machine tools and international mining. Dennis is a Fellow of the Institute of Management Services, Fellow of the Association for Project Management and a Member of the Institute of Management. He has carried out consultancy assignments in Europe and America and is now a freelance writer and lecturer. He has written or edited many management books, mainly for Gower, including the best-selling *Project Management*.

Nigel MacLennan *(Corporate alignment and cultural realignment; Coaching and mentoring teams)* is one of that rare species, an entrepreneur who is also an author and business professor. After selling out of a healthcare business which he founded and grew, he set up his own management consultancy organization and started writing. So far his books include: *Opportunity Spotting*, Gower (1994); *Coaching and Mentoring*, Gower (1995); *Counselling for Managers*, Gower (1996); *Opportunity Spotting* (revised edition), Gower (1997); *Awesome Purpose*, Gower (1998). Nigel is Visiting Professor of Management at the University of Southern Europe in Monaco. USE consistently performs in the top one or two per cent in the worldwide major field test of business schools. Nigel's civic responsibilities include being a Director (Council Member) of the Institute of Management. He currently splits his time between growing another business and management consultancy work.

Sandy Meadows *(The business environment)*, joint Director of Personnel at the University College London Hospitals NHS Trust, is a versatile, general management and human resource professional with over 20 years experience in the NHS. She possesses significant board level experience in the public and private sector not only as an executive director, but also in an advisory capacity as an external consultant. This rare combination of roles has involved leading and developing strategic human resource strategy and capability in a number of diverse settings working alongside boards, Trade Union representatives and other significant stakeholders. She is also co-author, with George Blair, of *Winning at Change*, published by Pitman (1996) and *A Real Life Guide to Organizational Change*, published by Gower (1997).

Tony Molony *(Transient teams and organizational structure)* joined the Royal Engineers in 1973 and enjoyed a varied and active career which took him to most parts of the world. He was selected to lead a diving expedition to Papua New Guinea with Operation Drake, the scientific and youth development exercise, sponsored by the Prince of Wales. He qualified as an Army Diving Supervisor and became the Inspector of Diving for the Army. This role included liasion with the Health and Safety Executive, formulating Diving Regulations for UK-wide application. Having survived the university of life, Tony studied for a BSc (Hons) with the Open University and then gained an MSc (Distinction) in Information Systems at Kingston University. He has now *xxvii* left the Army and works as the Business Change Manager (IS) for a leading firm of solicitors.

Christopher Moore (*Intra-team communication*) spent the first few years of his career in mechanical engineering principally in the field of research and development. Prior to taking up a position in 1980 as a staff development consultant, he held the position of Training Manager. Since 1989 he has run his own management development consultancy specializing in the development of management teams and the management of change. Client companies have included those from pharmaceuticals, chemical, mechanical and electronics engineering, aerospace, retail, leisure and transport industries. In 1992 he accepted the position of part-time Associate Lecturer with the Open University and now lectures in 'Systems Behaviour', 'Managing in Organisations' and 'Creative Management'. In 1996 he became course tutor for the Certificate in Management course 'The Capable Manager' and in June 1997 he accepted an additional role as Part-Time Assistant Senior Counsellor, South East Region. Christopher has sat on a number of advisory and organizing committees such as the Association for Management Education and Development (South East) and The Open University Systems Society, and since 1983 has been a member of the Chemical Industries Training Organisation. Over the years Christopher has obtained qualifications in Engineering, Science, Technology, Education and Psychology, being awarded the degrees of Bachelor of Science (honours), Bachelor of Arts and a Diploma in Management Studies, and is a member of both the Institute of Personnel and Development and the Institute of Management. His consultancy work includes the presentation of training courses, focused workshops, individual and group projects, individual coaching and counselling. Techniques to stimulate individual creativity are significant elements in all his work.

Alan Mumford (*How groups and teams learn*) BA, D. Litt., is a specialist in Director and Management Development, whose experience has included periods with John Laing & Sons, IPC Magazines, International Computers Ltd and the Chloride Group. In 1983 he was appointed Professor of Management Development at International Management Centres, and is now Visiting Professor there. His main work is on improving management performance, especially through effective learning processes, with senior managers and directors and developers in a variety of organizations including Ford of Europe, Pilkington, the Post Office and Unison (the UK's largest Trade Union). He has worked with organizations in Australia, South Africa and the United States. His publications include: *The Manual of Learning Styles*, 3rd edn (1992); *The Manual of Learning Opportunities*(1989); *Developing Top Managers*, Gower (1988); *Management Development: Strategies for Action*, IPM, 3rd edn (1997); *How Managers Can Develop Managers*, Gower, (1993); *Learning at the Top*, McGraw Hill (1995); *Effective Learning*, IPD (1995); *How to Manage Your Learning Environment*, Honey (1996); *How to Choose the Right Development Method*, Honey (1997).

Julia Pokora (*Teams and the learning organization*; *The superteam approach*) is a founder of New Organisation Consulting. She has a BSc in Psychology from Birmingham University, and an MSc in Occupational Psychology from the University of London, also gaining an accredited Graduate Diploma in Counselling. Prior to starting independent practice in 1985, Julia worked in organizational development for Exxon Chemical Ltd. She has 15 years consulting experience, working on organization and management development assignments with a range of organizations including Neste Oy (Finland), Shell International (Holland), AMEC, Safeway, Coca Cola Schweppes Beverages, the BBC and UK National Health Service. Julia has designed and delivered development programmes for senior executives and career professionals, and is interested in the relationship between individual and organization change. She is experienced in psychometrics and one-to-one feedback in executive development, and has been involved in these with Marconi. She is currently involved in a leadership development initiative to a UK consortium, and has designed a mentoring programme for senior executives in the largest UK hospital trust. She has trained staff in both mentoring and facilitation skills. Until New Organisation Consulting became a full-time commitment, she was an associate of Ashridge Management College, involved in Project Leadership and Leadership for Women Executives programmes, as well as tailored consultancy work. Julia has also written articles for books, journals and postgraduate teaching material. She is an occasional lecturer to postgraduate students, and an associate of York University Department of Health Studies. She has a counselling practice for executives seeking help with personal and professional development, and also works as a counsellor in Primary Care in a GP health centre. Julia is married, with two children.

Tudor Rickards (*Creativity in teams*) is Professor of Creativity and Organisational Change at The Manchester Business School where he directs The Creativity Research Unit. He is Alex Osborn visiting Professor at The SUNY, Buffalo, and has been a visiting Professor at University of Keil. He founded and co-edits *Creativity and Innovation Management Journal*. His awards include The Partnership Trust prize for teaching creativity in 1995. Tudor has written various popular and scholarly books and numerous other published articles. His area of interest concerns the direct stimulation of creativity in industrial organizations through teaching and action research.

Leslie Rae (*Team needs analysis*) is a management and trainer training consultant, and author of management and training books with more than 25 titles to his name, including the best-selling *Techniques of Training*, Third Edition, Gower; *How to Measure Training Effectiveness*, Third Edition, Gower; *Assessing Trainer Effectiveness*, Gower; *Let's Have a Meeting*, McGraw-Hill; *The Trainer Development Programme*, Kogan Page; *Using Activities in Training and Development*, Kogan Page. He is a regular contributor to the professional training press and has been a reviewer of training and management books   *xxix* with the *Training Officer* for 15 years. His career has spanned teaching, soldiering, television presenting, careers advice, photography, personnel management, training and training management, and he has been an internal and external consultant in local and national government and a wide range of industries.

Roger Stewart, BA(Hons), PhD. MBCS, FRSA (Editor, *Information systems and cultural change*) is Reader in Systems Management at Kingston University. Currently he is an external examiner at the Open University, Lincolnshire and Humberside University and Glasgow Caledonian University. He is a past chairman of the UK Systems Society. His previous career was in the computer industry where he held a variety of management positions in international accounts, technical education, sales training and user relations. His interest in teams and teamworking has led him to work with a wide spread of organizations including the Royal Navy, police, healthcare and Formula One racing. The breadth of his previous publications reflect the diversity of his interests. These embrace: systems behaviour, organizational communication analysis, teamworking and project management.

Chris Wills (*Negotiating teams in industrial relations*) was educated at Ruskin College and Brunel University; and is a Principal Lecturer in Information Systems at Kingston University. Prior to entering academia ten years ago, he worked in the field of industrial relations and general management consultancy. Latterly, he has pursued research and consultancy interests in the areas of information systems requirements engineering, socio-technical systems design, and human factors in civil and military command and control systems. For much of the last five years, he has been engaged in various projects for the Defence Evaluation Research Agency.

PART I
TEAMS AND THE ORGANIZATION

Introduction to Part I

The chapters in this first Part of the Handbook reflect the need to understand the organizational context in which teams operate. Teams do not operate in isolation and their design and functioning will be affected by the other parts of the business, and indeed by the markets in which the organization operates. Teams are also affected by the structures that they choose to adopt, organization and business analysis, and the roles assigned to them. The three main dimensions are: Business environments; Structures; and Relationships.

BUSINESS ENVIRONMENTS

In their chapter on the business environment, George Blair and Sandy Meadows consider the influences in the business climate faced by organizations that cause them to change from more traditional structures and manage themselves differently. The authors then discuss what happens inside the organization and examine the role that teams and teamwork play in Total Quality Management, Re-engineering and empowerment. The lessons drawn from these experiences lead to a review of issues that must be dealt with, such as initiative fatigue, organizational culture and development plans, if teamworking is to be successful in an organization.

The following chapter takes a particular type of organizational change, considering the theory and challenges to teamworking presented by 'flat' flexible organizations and teams. Valerie Garrow and Linda Holbeche propose that in this kind of environment various types of team emerge, together with barriers to successful operation. These are identified, as are the development processes of team learning, appraisal systems, reward systems and career development.

Changes to organizations are not just a matter of adjusting the structures:

there are associated cultural changes. Nigel MacLennan examines the alignment of the corporate purpose and values and changes to the prevailing culture of the organization and the teams that work within the organization. He provides a corporate alignment model and looks at 'the nine Rs' that are needed to create any lasting change or alignment in a team or company.

STRUCTURES

Given that an organization has decided to adopt structures that emphasize the use of teams in order to be more effective, it needs to consider how teamworking will work within the organization. In his chapter Colin Hastings looks at the role of senior management and the creation of high-performance teams. Aspects of a team's functioning, such as negotiating success criteria, managing the outside, planning the 'what' and leading the team, are also included together with ways of dealing with consultants in a team environment.

In the following chapter Dennis Lock looks at how organizations adopt a project-based organizational structure in order to adjust to rapidly changing environments. He considers the advantages and disadvantages of project teams, and their roles in functional matrix, project services, balanced, and contract matrix structures. Finally he discusses the characteristics of the project manager in this environment.

RELATIONSHIPS

Organizations embark on many different kinds of change programme and the relationship of teams to the organization is obviously an important component. The chapters that follow discuss some of the issues that arise when team-based operation is used.

One of the most common change programmes is Business Process Reengineering, which frequently involves the development of team values and beliefs. Hugh Brawley argues that, for BPR or any other change initiative to succeed, it needs commitment from the people involved. This chapter describes a long-term modular programme that deals with the people side of the business in order to overcome the deficiencies seen in many change programmes and the development of strategic team leaders.

Following on from this, Julia Pokora and Wendy Briner develop the theme that the organization must learn from team operation. The creation of linkages between individual, team and organizational learning enables a strong base of organization knowledge to be established. By using both individual learning and organizational learning, contrasting different types of learning in organizations, and by the use of case studies, the authors come to the conclusion that a teamworking organization gives both scope and opportunities to individuals and teams to learn, but that for the organization to learn, there must be an awareness of its existing mental model and a readiness to modify it.

However, there may be more than one type of structure operating in an organization and conflict between the structures may result. The chapter by Tony Molony on transient teams and organizational structure takes an example of where structures within teams can conflict with the overall structure of an organization. Using Army teams as an example, the chapter highlights some of the problems involved, describes how they were resolved and draws some conclusions for organizations in general.

1 The business environment

George Blair and Sandy Meadows

You may be fired up to implement teams and team building because some of your key competitors have just done so. Perhaps your CEO, taking his philosophy from sportswear manufacturers, has told you 'just do it'. While you may have certainly heard that most change initiatives fail, you are hoping yours will be different. This ignores the serious damage that a failed initiative can do to your organization's morale and effectiveness and, perhaps even more importantly, to you and your career. Would you go on a jungle safari without a guide or map? Those crocodiles that look so indolent – how could they be a risk? Because they are swifter than a horse over a short distance. This chapter will prepare you for your great organizational adventure so that your career does not disappear down the jaws of fate.

This book is about teams and teamworking and the advantages to be gained from structuring the work of your organization in this way. However, in this chapter we first take you back to some basic considerations to ensure that you reap the benefits while avoiding the pitfalls. It is essential to realize what is different in the business environment now that makes teamworking so effective. Without this level of understanding you may not recognize the main drivers that have brought about this change and so will not adapt your teams if these drivers change over time. No way of working can be regarded as the Holy Grail – everyone needs to change and adapt with the business environment. One of the strengths of teams is that they are inherently more evolutionary than traditional structured organizations. Having raised your awareness to the business environment issues, we then revisit some of the previous 'one best approaches' to organizational change, that is, TQM, re-engineering and empowerment, to demonstrate that there are lessons to be learnt from the application of these techniques and that these should not be discarded because 'teamwork' is now the way forward.

In case your organization has tried all of these initiatives one after another, we spend some time on overcoming initiative fatigue before looking at your organization and why you want to establish teams. We then lead you through a series of checklists to ascertain whether your organizational change will support teams, the types of teams you already have and how far you want to go with the introduction of teams against these reality checks. We finally introduce a few new paradoxes that arise from teamworking, and then leave it to our colleagues in the rest of the book to illustrate the true effectiveness of teams and teamworking and how to introduce them.

ORGANIZATIONAL CONSIDERATIONS

Organizations operate in a business environment that is very much more hostile than even ten years ago. They are confronted by stakeholders whose competing interests they somehow have to reconcile. There are the customers who take quality as given. Their incessant search for the latest fashion means that they lack customer loyalty to any given brand and are continually seduced away by more creative competitors. Even if your organization stays at the creative forefront, with similar products readily available customers can desert it for those who provide a superior service. Availability is paramount for everything except the most exclusive products. It does not matter how wonderful your products are because, if they are not instantly accessible at the right place, customers will go elsewhere. For example it is no longer considered acceptable to customers to have banks working such limited hours. The take-up of 24-hour banking and financial services has been phenomenal.

Speed is very important to the market to capture the footloose customer and to maximize the ever shorter product life. This is true for services as well as products, when a too long development phase can lead to market share being lost to a more nimble competitor. Banks and insurance companies have found that erstwhile loyal customers have been won over by their rivals by attractive, once-only packages.

Another formidable set of stakeholders are the shareholders. Very few buy shares for the long-term gain in Britain and America because of the current investment patterns of individuals and institutions. Their main interest is the annual dividend payable and the share price, both of which impact on their return on investment. They are therefore less interested in changes that the organization may wish to make for its longer-term advantage that do not produce immediate returns. Shareholders are also extremely risk-averse, particularly the institutional investors who are likely to view with extreme cynicism the devolution of important decisions and financial accountability. It continues to be a formidable challenge for CEOs to carry the financial markets with them when they propose to restructure their organization radically, unless of course they are downsizing! The good thing is that there are now some shining examples where adopting more innovative ways of working have added significantly to company profitability. The West has been slow to learn from the most successful eastern organizations that

8

dominate world markets by taking a longer-term view of both strategy and investment.

The one asset that does not feature on the balance sheet, yet is fundamental to the organization's ability to survive, is its staff. Firms around the world are facing increasing employee-related problems such as falling productivity, faltering product quality, persistent absenteeism, work dissatisfaction, poor morale and high levels of turnover. These have exacerbated the inappropriate handling of change in response to the worldwide recession, increasing global competition and the uncertainties in both local and international markets. The need to respond effectively to these problems is of paramount importance for organizations. They must enlist the hearts and minds of staff rather than just their hands.

Suppliers form a group of stakeholders who are needed more and more as close allies. If an organization is to be flexible and ready to act it must have both vertical and horizontal alliances with suppliers. A vertical alliance means it has to ensure that its suppliers of basic materials understand and respond to the basic aims of the business; a horizontal alliance is where non-core activities have been contracted out so that these suppliers feel in partnership with the organization in delivering the product or service. These alliances need to cover not only supply but also involvement and appreciation of design and development of any new products or services.

The wider community should not be forgotten as a legitimate stakeholder that can make demands on organizations to be ignored at their peril. A good example of this is the boycott of Shell products by consumers in continental Europe, who were opposed to the Brent Spar oilfield platform being dumped in the North Sea. However, there are a number of examples of organizations working with their local community for the benefit of both sides. Both Sainsbury's and Marks and Spencer sponsor community projects in some disadvantaged areas where they operate. In spite of the anti-nuclear lobby, British Nuclear Fuel's communication campaign convinced the community of Sellafield to support the continued development of the site for nuclear disposal as being safe as well as a source of much needed local employment.

This shows that organizations must respond to a rapid pace of change, shortened product cycles, stringent customer demands, high financial expectations, the need to involve a potentially demoralized workforce – in order to balance the requirements of this diverse range of stakeholders. This leads to the conclusion that, in organizations today, the only certainty is that there will be change, which can be swift and savage or insidiously incremental. In either case the organization's survival depends on its ability to manage change. The days when advancement was based on managing the status quo within carefully prescribed parameters are long gone. Innovation, positive reaction, flexibility and the ability to learn are now the main sources of competitive advantage. Companies that cling to hierarchical structures and bureaucratic procedures that stifle individual initiative and cross-fertilization of ideas are greatly at risk. Top managers who continue to monopolize the strategic level of decisions and fail to make use of front-line knowledge and expertise are a danger to company growth. In other words, the climate for companies managed and structured traditionally is extremely hostile. How can they structure themselves to become the creative, innovative customer-driven organization of the twenty-first century? One successful way of lessening resistance to change is to involve staff at all levels within the organization. The formation of teams is certainly one important step forward to achieving this. Rosabeth Moss Kanter wrote in *The Change Masters* that teams are a good way of 'energising the grass roots', but this is not as easy as it sounds.

You will now be aware of the main changes that have occurred in the latter part of the twentieth century and that teams are one way of dealing with these, but do not forget the evidence of both success and failure illustrated by the management gurus of total quality management, re-engineering and empowerment. It is dangerous to assume that, in your progress towards establishing teams, nothing can be learnt from these approaches to change.

LESSONS LEARNT FROM IMPLEMENTING TOTAL QUALITY MANAGEMENT, RE-ENGINEERING AND EMPOWERMENT

Important lessons can be learnt from the implementation of both Total Quality Management (TQM) and re-engineering. Teams and teamwork play a central role in total quality management. This was not always fully appreciated in its early days in Britain and America. Many quality circles were set up without thought as to their impact on the power structure. Their innovative ideas disappeared into managers' pending trays, who felt threatened because they saw their role as the 'brains' of the organization undermined. Staff became despondent and top managers did not see enough results to justify the investment in time. Many quality circles were disbanded as ineffective. However, western firms fell further behind in performance, losing out both in export markets and in their home patch.

Later, attempts to introduce TQM were more successful when the role of the line manager, or supervisor, was looked at carefully. Fewer managers were needed as they acted as coaches and helped solve problems that their staff were unable to resolve themselves. Some organizations went a step further and introduced self-managed teams, dispensing with even more of the management function.

Teams are frequently taught to use the tools and techniques to monitor quality themselves. They become entirely responsible for their own work and are often given the authority to stop a production line on their own say-so if they suspect the existence of a quality problem. Another feature is that staff whose work affects others' work significantly come together to use group problem solving methodologies to identify problems and to generate solutions.

One of the attractions for TQM of creating teams was improvement in
10 quality. It meant that jobs could be enriched, as staff were no longer

restricted to short-cycle, repetitive jobs where they never saw the end product. Instead, a team was given the task of making the whole product by enhancing their roles and skills. Even where this resulted in lower output, it could be often justified in terms of lower total production costs, as there was less reworking, waste and staff absence. Levi Strauss & Co. has introduced teamworking in its American plants so that they can compete against overseas plants with lower per capita labour costs.

However, there were many cases of TQM failing to achieve the desired objectives. This was frequently due to making a large number of small, unfocused improvements that were not sufficiently related to customer needs or business objectives. Other reasons for failure were underestimating the resources required to implement significant change and adopting too short a time horizon. Often the sources of error or poor quality were not the result of bad workmanship; rather they were the fault of dysfunctional policies, processes and work systems. Another drawback was that TQM left functional boundaries unchanged resulting in a lack of effective teams covering whole processes. This meant coordination was difficult as each department had different priorities and objectives. Pay and reward strategies were sometimes inconsistent with the objectives of TQM and rewarded individual performance rather than group achievements or learning.

Many of the reasons why quality programmes failed can be explained by looking at the UK/European model below (Figure 1.1). It is geared to producing business results while dealing with the needs of the key stakeholders, that is, customers, staff and the wider community. It also deals with the issue of improving processes, taking quality improvement closer to re-engineering. Research by Keith Ruddle and David Feeny of Templeton College, Oxford shows that organizations that implement broad measures of change are more successful than those that concentrate on narrowly targeted financial ones. The model can be applied to evaluate the outcomes of any change initiative as its nine factors have been shown by extensive experience to be central to success. It could therefore be very helpful in assessing the outcome of introducing teams and teambuilding. You can also employ the model for external benchmarking purposes as it is widely used. The percentages shown next to each factor indicate the importance attached to it in the assessment process.

The appeal of re-engineering is its ability to 'achieve dramatic improvements in critical, contemporary measures of performance, such as cost, quality, service, and speed', in the words of Hammer and Champy. Incremental improvements in quality were not enough for many organizations that looked to dramatic improvements for their survival or, for the more fortunate, their supremacy. There were many converts inspired by Hammer and Champy's *Reengineering The Corporation: A Manifesto for Business Revolution* when it was first published in 1993. Re-engineering seeks to cut out the error and delay that results from staff 'passing off' tasks to each other so that the next step of the process can be completed. This is done *11*

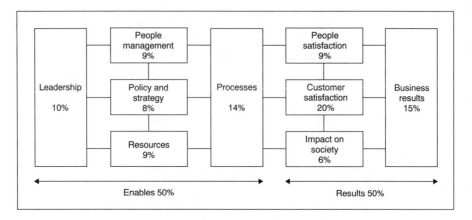

Figure 1.1   The UK/European quality assessment model
Source: Towards Organisational Excellence (1994), The British Quality Foundation, p.8

by redesigning the process to simplify it as far as possible without compromising the service to customers.

The redesigning can involve sophisticated computer systems, as in the case of insurance where one person, a caseworker, can handle all aspects of a transaction. Previously, many people in different departments were required, often resulting in delays and poor service to customers. With re-engineering one employee can answer customer questions about the merits of different policies and tell them how much the premium would cost. If the customer wanted to purchase the policy that same employee would complete the transaction by taking payment by credit card and then sending the documentation to the customer. These re-engineered processes can replace functional departments and, occasionally, teams. However, there are products and services that are too complicated for one person to deal with, so it is then necessary to create a case team. This takes staff out of functional departments in different locations to work together, thus speeding up the process by easier and quicker communication.

Re-engineering encourages organizations to look outside their own walls. Large improvements in cost and performance can be achieved by including suppliers in research and development, acknowledging that they should be a formal part of the R&D process and thus also should be part of the team.

After the excitement of the early days 're-engineering is in trouble', according to the first sentence of James Champy's sequel on the subject (1995). The main reason he gives is that re-engineering programmes often produce disappointing results because of the failings of managers; some of them relate directly to teamwork. Champy quotes from Robert Hall's *The Soul of the Enterprise* to make just that point: 'The future belongs to those [managers] who can frequently reorganise high-morale teams
12   around the needs of changing processes.' The emphasis in re-engineering is

increasingly on giving greater attention to the skills of cultural and behavioural change.

Empowerment can make an important contribution to teamworking by giving staff the authority and the responsibility themselves, so that teams can be more self-sufficient and respond to customer needs more rapidly. Cost reductions can then be supported through having fewer managerial and supervisory staff, and staff are often required to have self-management skills and be effective problem solvers.

Of course, you may not only have learnt the lesson from these techniques first-hand, but bear the scars. It is tempting to assume that teamworking may succeed where other initiatives have failed, but to give it the best chance of success you need to consider whether or not your organization is suffering from initiative fatigue.

OVERCOMING INITIATIVE FATIGUE

It is easy to be swept away by a belief that teams and teamworking are self-evidently good. However, your staff may not share this belief as they may be suffering from initiative fatigue. They might have heard senior managers extolling earlier miracle cures that have since been abandoned. Staff are not taken in by the frequent, cosmetic name changes such as business process re-engineering becoming re-engineering, only to be succeeded by organizational transformation and by managers quoting from books entitled *Beyond Re-engineering*. TQM has similarly been repackaged as continuous quality improvement. Has your organization dallied with empowerment, total quality management or re-engineering? If you have experienced downsizing, it will have left the survivors feeling battered and bruised.

If you think we are exaggerating how many staff may feel, cast your eye over the following piece of organizational change character assassination (Box 1.1). It shows that bad news and cynicism travel fast, as this was carelessly left in the photocopying machine some 40 miles from its original source. However, do not let it put you off implementing change. It is better to learn from the bitter experience of others rather than your own.

So how can you avoid your initiative being seen in the same light? The most important way to counter staff cynicism is to involve them as fully as possible in planning and implementing the change initiative. While it will take longer to get the project off the ground, the later stages will move forward much more quickly as there should be far less staff resistance. This is vastly preferable to having wonderful plans and excellent documentation that are undermined at every turn, because the staff do not feel any sense of ownership. This is even more important when it comes to implementing teams and teamworking. While you can teach staff how to problem solve jointly and communicate effectively, you cannot force them to do so!

Part of signing staff up to the necessity and importance of teams and teamworking is to have clearly defined objectives. If staff perceive teams as *13*

Box 1.1 How your staff might see your initiative

Source: Found in a photocopier of a nameless West London organization
Thanks to Kent Social Services' magazine: *The Ferret*

Strategic management = Clutching at straws.
Maintaining an overview = Finding someone else to do it.
Consider it a challenge = I can't find anyone else to do it.
I haven't seen you for a while = Weren't you made redundant?
Medium-term plan = Tomorrow's schedule.
Service provisions group = Direct services without direction.
Service development team = Which home should we close this week?
Restructure = A repeat of yesterday's mistakes.
Hidden agenda = Everyone knows what's going on.
Networking = Looking for a new job.
Global overview = Not having a clue what's happening.
Over-arching = Something to do with the Dartford Bridge.
Service policy options = Consider if we'll answer the phone.
Devolution of functions = Creating total havoc.
Grapevine = The only way to find out what's going on!

ends in themselves, as opposed to a means to an end, they are far more likely to believe that management has been carried away yet again by the latest fad. They will react by carrying on regardless while paying only lip service to the latest idea.

WHY DO YOU WANT TO ESTABLISH TEAMS?

A basic requirement is to develop clearly defined success criteria for each of your stakeholders. That way you will be very clear about what needs to be achieved, and how you can monitor your progress effectively so that any shortfalls can be more readily rectified. The key question for you to answer is: if your teams and teamworking were entirely successful how would your customers, staff, shareholders and suppliers know? Would it result in more sales due to better customer retention, as they will be no longer shunted from department to department? Or could it be that your sales and profit margins will be higher because your products or services will be first to the market as your product development process will be faster? Will your costs be lower because of the increased productivity of multi-skilled teamworkers? Will it improve staff morale and commitment as they have more control of duty rosters? To assist you in defining your own success criteria, complete Table 1.1.

Table 1.1
Success criteria checklist for your organization

Topic	Success criteria
Product development	
Customer retention	
Gaining new customers	
Total sales	
Operating costs	
Profits	
Staff	
Suppliers	

DOES YOUR ORGANIZATIONAL CULTURE SUPPORT TEAMS?

Before you even consider whether or not you should move to teamworking, you should look at your organizational culture. Would it support the attributes of a successful team, namely:

- Specific, interdependent roles
- Common objectives
- Shared values
- Mutual trust, bonding
- Frequent interaction
- Honest communication
- Definable membership
- Ability to act in a unitary manner.

Do you recognize any of these behaviours and beliefs in your organizational culture? If the prevailing culture is individualistic with fragmented fiefdoms where conferring with the enemy is considered the ultimate treachery, then multifunctional teamworking is not going to be easily achieved. In addition, if managers have grown up in a blame culture where large amounts of energy are expended on ensuring that the blame always lies elsewhere, then it is unlikely that there will be extensive mutual trust and bonding between individuals. There is more likely to be collusion to avoid blame. Traditional, hierarchical structures rarely produce high levels of creativity and initiative. Many managers have prospered by maximizing control and minimizing risk taking, while pandering to the omnipotence of the most senior manager. This has not encouraged discussion around shared values which might be perceived as to be a little 'touchy feely' for such environments. However, in a successful team there must have been a debate and a distillation of a set of shared values so that there is empathy and understanding between team *15*

Table 1.2
Where are you starting from?

Factor	Points scored		
	1	2	3
Levels in the organization	8 or more	6 to 7	5 or fewer
Number of departments	10 or more	6 to 9	5 or fewer
Use of part-time teams	Rare	Moderate	Extensive
Discretion of junior staff	Little	Moderate	Extensive
Training at all levels	Little	Moderate	Extensive
Total			

members and the capacity to interpret or act for one another in given situations. As well as cultural factors, management style and work process issues can militate against teamworking; for example, performance systems that reward the achievement of individual rather than common achievements. We will explore this in greater detail later in this chapter. If you recognize any of these issues as being part of the climate of your own organization, then it is necessary to deal with them. Only then should you put in hand any processes for forming and developing teams; otherwise those troublesome issues will come back to haunt you.

A further question before you can establish your starting point is: how extensively do you use teams and teamworking at the moment? What types of teams are they? Are they permanent teams, or part-time roles occupied by staff who primarily operate within a departmental structure? How successful are they? To help explore these issues we have produced a scorecard (Table 1.2). It has been designed for a large organization, so if yours is small to medium-sized, do not get too complacent if you get a high score!

If you score mainly 'ones' and a few 'twos', you have far to go. On the other hand, scoring mainly 'twos' and 'threes' means that you have the beginnings of a firm foundation on which you can build. Do not feel disheartened if you have a low score, just realize that it will take longer to implement change, and will require more resources. It also means that you have more to gain from introducing teams and teamworking!

At this stage those of you who currently use teams should look at the type of teams you have, their strengths and weaknesses, their purpose and how easily they could be changed or developed to evolve as teams to lead and facilitate change. The main types of team we have identified are listed here with a brief explanation of their purpose. We have then set out these teams with boxes (Table 1.3) to note their strengths and weaknesses and the changes and developments needed to get these teams up and *16* running.

Table 1.3
Development plan for your current teams

Type of team	Strengths	Weaknesses	Action required

1   *Project team*: part-time membership to achieve a given task within a specified time period. Runs alongside the existing management structure. Could be multi or unifunctional.

2   *Process or case team*: not time limited; set up to achieve outcomes or outputs prescribed by internal or external customers. It is usually multifunctional. It cuts across functional management lines but is normally at a fairly low level of the organization.

3   *Quality circle*: periodic meeting of staff, whose working roles impact on each other, to improve their outcomes from a customer viewpoint or to reduce waste and costs. Ideally, they should cut across functional lines.

4   *Briefing team*: a group brought together on a regular basis to give or receive information, normally organized on a functional basis.

5   *Steering group*: a high-level group to give strategic leadership to a project or a group of projects, normally crossfunctional.

6   *Natural work group*: people who work together closely on related tasks or in the same work area.

7   *Informal*: people who come together under their own volition to confront a particular issue, or to take part in a particular activity, easily crossing the business/social divide.

8   *Ad hoc groups*: these include negotiation/staff-side representation.

Most of these teams or groups could be self-managed but the most extreme examples of these types of groups will be empowered to take all decisions required for their successful functioning. They radically change the management structure and crossfunctional working of the organization.

HOW FAR DO YOU WANT TO GO?

There is no such thing as a perfect blueprint to fit all organizations – only management consultants wanting to sell you inflexible products will try to convince you otherwise. You need to design your initiative to suit your own organization. The issues to consider are: *17*

Recruitment – will this be delegated to teams? If so, this provides a real incentive for staff to build a close working relationship with a new entrant, as they would find it difficult to complain about one of their own recruits not quite fitting in. Another advantage is that it can release the time that managers and personnel spend in this role. Care needs to be taken not to recruit teams in their own image and personality profile, especially where creativity or exercising initiative is important. Such inbreeding can be as fatal for organizations as it was for the French aristocracy. Equal opportunity problems can arise such as an over-preponderance of white, working-class males aged 20 to 30 on the shop floor.

Training – will the team take complete responsibility for induction and training to full competence? This course of action has the benefit of building stronger bonds within the team. Members will be under greater incentive to keep their own skills well-honed if they are going to have to pass them on to others. They will, of course, need to be trained in training techniques and mentoring skills as appropriate.

Managing output, quality and improving customer satisfaction – what will be the role of the team? What information does the team need to carry out its tasks? Who records the information? Who analyses it? Who presents it to the group? Who is in a good position to assess the performance of teams? Should it be team members themselves? What scope is there to include customer feedback?

Shift rostering and annual leave – will teams be given this responsibility? Rostering and leave are important issues where services or production takes place around the clock. Any difficult decisions made about allocating unpopular shifts are usually more acceptable when these decisions are left to the staff themselves. Annual leave has similar problems with the usual battle for August holidays.

Absence management – will this be delegated along with the line management function of providing cover for annual leave? This problem arises in some production teams where staff are required to cover for each other's absences. From a management point of view, this can be an advantage, as absence tends to be lower as staff do not want to let their teammates down. However, staff may feel that they are being morally blackmailed to turn up to work when they are unwell.

New product development – while management and staff are gaining from the benefits of teamwork, it is important for them not to lose all of the strengths of the functional organization that is being discarded. One such strength is the expertise of those in specialist roles that can prove invaluable when change is required. Such staff may well have professional knowledge that extends outside existing practices. Where team members have wider roles this pool of knowledge and experience can be lost. The issue is how to have access to this capability when it is required. It could be bought in from outside the organization, or team members could also be assigned a specialist role. However, they would need the time and supporting structure to make this a reality which will cost time.

Decision making/discretion – what decisions can be made without reference upwards? How large should the devolved budget be? What expenditure limits should be set? Will staff be able to stop production when defects or problems occur? Weighing up the benefits against the risks will influence these answers. For instance, giving customer-facing staff the authority to give rebates to dissatisfied customers may make your accountants feel uneasy. How much would it cost if they were overgenerous to 'professional' complainers? However, your marketing staff will point out that dealing effectively with dissatisfied customers means you can secure their custom for the future. How far should you devolve involvement in marketing? In a very fast-moving organization, probably quite far, as speed of action is all. In other settings this benefit needs to be weighed against a possible lack of consistency from a customer viewpoint, with different parts of the organization possibly being in competition with each other.

Reward strategy – how consistent is this with teamworking? While the responsibility for deciding on reward strategy will remain at the centre your reward system will need to support staff working in teams. If you use individual performance pay, this will need to be replaced as it undermines teamworking, with each member seeking to shine at others' expense. Competency-based pay where staff are paid for acquiring and effectively deploying key skills would be an option. Gainsharing, where staff are given a team bonus for achieving specific objectives with defined time limits, is another approach. This has the advantage of rewarding improvements in productivity. However, its fairness can be called into question, as it is the least efficient teams that have more scope to improve their productivity! Your best-performing teams will feel hard done by; they could even argue that they deserve a bonus for their past achievements.

How will human resource function be carried out? – depending on how many of its responsibilities you intend to delegate to teams, what will this mean to the HR department? It will probably require fewer staff.

The following hypothetical example will give you a feel of some of the options (Table 1.4).

Complete the following chart for your organization (Table 1.5). If you have in mind a series of rather different types of teams, you may wish to complete the table for each type.

If you are uncertain about some of your answers, no matter. These topics are explored in much greater detail in subsequent chapters. The purpose of *19*

Table 1.4
Powers and responsibilities to devolve to teams: example

Now			Future		
What	Who?	How?	Who?	How	Implement when?
Recruitment	HR	Open advertisement	The team	Interview and informal assessment by all team members	After training in recruitment and selection
Training from induction to full competence	Supervisor	Formal induction and on-the-job training	Experienced team members	Induction and on-the-job training	When confident of competence levels after appraisal
Managing absence	HR and supervisor	Supervisor send returns to HR	Self-monitoring by peers in team	Absence chart on wall	System in place for designated team member to record absence for everyone
Shift rostering	Supervisor	On seniority	Team	Mutual negotiation	When ground rules on cover agreed
Discretionary expenditure	Manager	Proposed then supported by director	Team	Via budget statements	When financial responsibility and accountability line agreed
Managing output and outcomes	Supervisor and production manager		Team	Through self-monitoring techniques adapted from TQM	After appropriate training
New product development	Marketing; design; production managers	Functionally managed	Multi-team membership	Project team	In response to marketing strategy
Managing change	Senior management	Through various new initiatives	Team	Constantly reviewing processes and performance and learning from others	Continuously evolving
Reward strategy and performance	Individual	Assessed by boss	Team-based	Competence or gainsharing?	When reward strategy is in place

Table 1.5
Powers and responsibilities to devolve to teams: to fill in

What	Now			Future		
	Who?	How?	Who?	How?	When?	
Recruitment						
Training from induction to full competence						
Managing absence						
Shift rostering						
Discretionary expenditure						
Managing output and outcomes						
New product development						
Managing change						
Reward strategy and performance						

presenting them now is to provide an overview of the wide range of options available to you.

HAVING THE BEST OF BOTH WORLDS

While there are some undoubted benefits of teamworking, it is easy to ignore that some of the benefits of your existing organization could be lost in the changes. If you are about to remove most of your departmental structures, you could well also be losing specialist groupings of staff who mutually reinforce each other's expertise. Replacing all your specialists with multi-skilled staff could seriously compromise your capacity to know where and how to innovate in the future. Specialists often belong to professional networks that provide insights into other organizations. If you guard against this risk by retaining a specialist in each key area, they could easily become isolated and feel their career prospects could be better in a more traditional organization. In order to counter this, ask these valued staff to present interesting developments from other organizations to the rest of the team. They could also have an overview of training and development, without undermining the role of experienced team members.

Undoubtedly teams and teamworking have a number of benefits, but, as *21* we have cited on a number of occasions in this chapter, they are not the ultimate answer to all our dreams. Research is beginning to reveal that they do introduce some paradoxes of their own that need to be addressed.

NEW PARADOXES

Tom Peters, in his book *Liberation Management* (1992), observes that while we are trying to move beyond traditional hierarchies and to involve everyone via membership of teams with shared values, communication, and so on, staff are having to cope with some new emerging paradoxes:

- Organizing/focusing and disorganizing/de-integrating: on the one hand we are putting together tightly tied networks of largely self-contained units that take responsibility with accountability, but on the other we are selling off pieces of non-core business or subcontracting out whole services or processes.
- Smaller and bigger: here the company is breaking down into smaller, self-contained units, but still needs to be 'best in class' at a key task or process to survive.
- Accountability and teamwork: the need to develop products and bring them to market more quickly are all signs pointing towards more accountability for the work team. Yet that accountability is also imbedded within a necessity to support other network partners.
- Autonomy and partnership: individuals are being encouraged to become more autonomous, with responsibility for creativity, innovation and managing their own careers, but at the same time they are engaged in more partnering activities, increasingly dependent on each other as team mates and on other members of an expansive network.
- More speciality/expertise/development and less specialist/expert staff: developing value-added skills becomes more important than ever and each team member and each team/business unit becomes more responsible for specialist knowledge. On the other hand, old-fashioned centres of expertise or specialist functional enclaves are going.

Now is the time for you to embark on your safari. We have drawn your attention to snake pits, the snoozing crocodiles and the mosquito-infested swamps along the way. With the detailed map provided in the rest of the book you should now be able to continue your exploration towards teams and teamworking with a much greater chance of success.

REFERENCES

Champy, J., *Reengineering Management*, HarperCollins, London, 1995
Hall, R., *The Soul of The Enterprise: Creating a Dynamic Vision for American Manufacturing*, quoted in Champy, J. *Reengineering Management*, p. 77

Hammer, M. and Champy, J., *Reengineering The Corporation: A manifesto for business revolution*, Nicholas Brealey, London, 1993

Kanter R.M., *The Change Masters*, George Allen and Unwin, London, 1984

Peters, T., *Liberation Management*, Alfred A Knopf Inc., New York, 1992

Ruddle, K. and Feeney, D., *Transforming the organisation: New Approaches to Management, Measurement, Measurement and Leadership*, Templeton College, Oxford, 1997

The British Quality Foundation, *Towards Organisational Excellence*, London, 1994, p. 8

RECOMMENDED READING

Belasco, J.A., *Teaching the Elephant to Dance*, Century, London, 1990

Blair, G. and Meadows, S., *A Real Life Guide to Organizational Change*, Gower, Aldershot, 1996

Oakland, J., *Total Quality Management*, Butterworth Heinemann, Oxford, 1993

RSA, *Tomorrow's Company: the Role of Business in a Changing World*, London, 1994

USEFUL ORGANIZATION

British Quality Foundation, 215 Vauxhall Bridge Road, London SW1V 1EN, telephone: 0171 963 8000.

2 The flexible organization

Valerie Garrow and Linda Holbeche

The last few years have seen considerable changes in the world of work as organizations have struggled to survive and thrive in an increasingly competitive market place. The most frequent response to these competitive challenges has involved various forms of restructuring to drive down costs and increase efficiency. A dominant form of restructuring has been the slimming down of the number of management levels, or delayering, to produce a 'flat' structure.

The business rationale for this is clear. Conventional hierarchical and functional structures have long been criticized for inherent inefficiencies and duplication. Such structures often encourage employees to look inwards, rather than out towards customers, and the very complex levels of accountability often slow up decision making. Such criticisms may be exaggerated, but the phenomenon of 'checkers checking checkers' will be familiar to many.

Of course in relatively stable times, when organizations could reasonably predict and plan for business growth, hierarchical structures served them well, since everyone knew where they fitted in the hierarchy and maintaining existing processes was relatively straightforward. However, many organizations have realized that predictability, eager customers and easy profits can no longer be relied on. What seems to be called for instead are the kinds of structures which facilitate horizontal working, where business processes flow seamlessly across the organization in order to satisfy customer needs in a way which both pleases the customer and makes a profit.

For many people, the horizontal working implicit in flat structures is something of a novelty. In particular, horizontal working lends itself to teamworking, which should enable a greater output to be achieved by fewer people if the team is functioning appropriately. Research carried out by

Roffey Park Management Institute (Holbeche, 1995), suggests that teamworking is on the increase in organizations in all sectors of the UK economy. Indeed, the practice of teamworking appears to have become a new commercial doctrine, with many organizations producing value statements extolling the virtues of teamworking and where employees are appraised on the way they have demonstrated teamworking, even if they are individual contributors. Arguably, there are instances when teamworking may not be the most appropriate approach for certain types of activity.

In one organization, for instance, which specializes in sorting fine gems, the craftspeople sit at individual booths sorting gems according to size and value. To carry out their tasks effectively they need concentration and quiet. When a craftsperson is in doubt about a particular stone he or she consults a more experienced colleague. The system has worked well for years. A new managing director introduced teamworking, involving production meetings and peer coaching. Productivity actually slumped in the first few months of operation and 'teamworking' was quietly dropped once the new MD had really settled in.

However, the reasons behind the introduction of teamworking are easy to understand. Teamwork should enable individuals to achieve a collective output which is greater than the sum of its parts. Team 'synergy' should lead to cost savings, by the elimination of duplication and effort. It should lead to greater innovation and customer satisfaction. Working in teams should increase people's skills, job satisfaction and motivation. That is the theory.

RHETORIC VERSUS REALITY

Sometimes the theory holds true. Effective teamwork can result from simply identifying the right individuals to achieve a clear set of objectives that they could not accomplish on their own. In one government department, multi-disciplinary teams were introduced without any specific support in the form of training and are now operating successfully across previous functional boundaries. It should be noted that a characteristic of many of the individuals in these teams is that they share a military background and are familiar with the concept and practice of teamworking. As long as there is clear leadership, taking on a more flexible way of working has not phased these employees. In another part of the same government department, a move towards self-directed teamworking came to grief as employees found it impossible to relate to the idea of a team without a leader.

In general, teamworking does not happen automatically just by putting together a group of employees with a common goal. Often there are political rivalries or a resistance to giving up individual spheres of influence, which may make it hard for people to really share in making the team project a success. Sometimes teams develop a common approach to the extent that they develop the insidious 'groupthink' which can cause them to reject new ideas and outsiders. The Roffey Park research found that while teamworking was reported to be on the increase, so too were the difficulties.

25

The challenges of teamworking

Some of the challenges in making teams work effectively are linked to the kinds of teams and the way they are expected to operate. The commonest version of a team is the work group with a manager. Whatever the nature of the operation in which the team is involved, when teamworking is deliberately introduced it usually requires people to make some decisions which were formerly the responsibility of the manager. Flat structures can result in greater flexibility when decisions are made at the level which is most appropriate. With the proper training, this should usually be at the point of contact with the customer, where employees are 'empowered' to use their initiative and business sense to deal with customer issues. There are often problems when managers are reluctant to relinquish power and are unwilling to trust team members enough to be able to delegate tasks and decisions to them. For such managers, teamworking can represent a real threat and they may undermine teamworking by interfering with or countermanding team decisions.

Similarly, not every employee is happy to take on the added responsibility of decision making in spheres with which they may be relatively unfamiliar. A common complaint about the way empowerment works in practice can be summarized in the words of an associate working in the financial services who said: 'In this organization you are expected to be responsible and accountable for just about everything, but you don't necessarily have the authority. The directors have passed the buck to us. When things go well they take the glory; when they go wrong, guess who takes the blame?' While this may be an example of hierarchical attitudes prevailing even in a flat structure, the remark highlights some of the potentially contradictory messages within team structures. It also points to the importance of clarifying lines of authority and levels of responsibility, together with the appropriate levels of training, if empowerment is to become a reality in the team context.

TYPES OF TEAM

In some organizations, process teams have become commonplace, with different departments handling parts of a business process. Usually the biggest difficulty in managing processes is the 'handover' point at which the work of one department is dependent on the work of another. Ironically, teams which may well operate very successfully as a workgroup often see other departments as rivals and pay lip service to the need to collaborate beyond the immediate team. In such cases, it is important that team members develop a cross-functional mindset through an increased understanding of how each part of the process contributes to customer satisfaction. The role of leaders in demonstrating cross-functional teamworking in practice should not be underestimated.

Other types of team include project teams which are brought together for specific business purposes. Often such teams operate in a matrix structure with team members continuing to report through their regular (functional) reporting lines as well as to the project sponsor. The challenge for team members is that these different reporting lines can result in real conflicts of interest and, in some cases, members of project teams become 'cut off' from their own manager. The joke 'if my boss rings, ask him who he is' may become a reality for some employees, which can cause difficulties if the manager is a key gateway to career opportunities.

Some of the biggest challenges relate to so-called 'virtual' teams. There are many variations on a theme. In some cases, independent consultants work together on an *ad hoc* basis under a common banner. In others, operations have been outsourced and teleworking results in people working on a common activity who may never meet except via electronic mail. Increasingly, as organizations operate globally, the need to offer worldwide customer service to common standards results in virtual teams being established. In the case of one software supplier, the move towards teamworking was made more complicated by a shift in the nature of work carried out by different parts of the team. Instead of all country operations being able to sell software and provide customer service independent of one another, business thinking dictated that selling operations should be concentrated in the UK and that all other locations should merely provide customer service. Since the reward system clearly favoured sales, it is hardly surprising that employees outside the UK were unenthusiastic about the new team system. The fact that they never met with their UK counterparts added to the problem.

More and more there is a move towards self-directed teams which are typically groups of up to a dozen people who work without direct supervision. Relatively common in manufacturing organizations, such teams make decisions on the tasks of the day, take responsibility for quality control, set their own goals and learn all the jobs which fall within their team's area of responsibility. In some cases, teams also make decisions relating to recruiting, disciplining and rewarding team members. While self-directed teams appear to make manager roles redundant, problems can arise if the manager's role is phased out too quickly. Often the reality is that the team becomes 'semi-autonomous' with a manager role being retained, but the manager being much less involved in day-to-day supervision of work processes. Research suggests that teams do not automatically take to being self-directed without some help. Later in this chapter we have outlined some of the helpful initiatives we have found in use in different organizations.

Teamworking puts pressure on hierarchical relationships in organizations. In particular the philosophy of self-directed teams is a revolutionary concept and challenges the traditional management structure, posing a potential threat to the role and status of senior people. Authority from formal position will be challenged by authority from technical knowledge with a new generation of highly-qualified technical experts seeking decision making powers to work more effectively. Even where the organization has *27* assumed a flat and flexible appearance, however, old hierarchical policies may still be supporting barriers to effective teamwork.

POWER-DISTANCE

Power-distance, both inside and outside the team, can threaten the development of creativity and mutual responsibility. From within the team it may mean that members with lower power status are constrained and feel that their contributions are not valued. Brooks (1994) suggests that the rational hierarchy is historically and culturally ingrained, leading to the belief that knowledge is brought to the workplace by technicians and scientists, while managers and engineers solve the problems using semi-skilled and unskilled workers to enact this knowledge. The customer-driven approach to change now suggests that those who are closest to the customers' needs might provide the stimulus for new knowledge, products and development.

Outside the team, knowledge is often a political issue, reflecting power and factional interests. Higgs and Roland (1992) in an appropriately titled article 'All Pigs are Equal', describe the difficulties involved in imposing an egalitarian culture on 'status-ridden, hierarchical bureaucracies'. The unwillingness of some managers to share power has been described as 'Management Luddism'. Nevertheless, if teams are to succeed in their own function, they must be aware of the wider picture and of how their own work fits in. Knowledge should no longer be the property of a privileged few. Hackman (1990) identifies six key areas in which teams need organizational support: targets; resources; information; education; feedback; technical/process assistance. To some extent all of these involve the sharing of knowledge, particularly in supplying information and feedback on performance.

ENABLING TEAMWORKING

Whatever the form of teamworking being introduced, team members need to be clear about what the team is set up to achieve and understand their role within the team. Obviously, if people lack the skill or the will to contribute to the team their performance is likely to suffer. Consequently, care must be taken in selecting the right people, providing appropriate training and eliminating where possible the conflicts of loyalty which being a member of a team can entail.

LEADERSHIP

Leadership can be a fundamental issue in negotiating the team's relationship with the organization and beyond the organizational boundaries. Leadership is often a fluid concept within a team. In general, although teams may organize themselves according to the requirements of their work, direction still ultimately comes from outside the team, whether in the form of organizational targets or a strategic overview which defines the team's goals. One of the dangers of having highly cohesive teams is that they forget the wider context in which they operate.

Leadership theories have traditionally concentrated on the qualities, behavioural characteristics and style of the leader. The *substitute leadership* school of thought, popular about ten years ago, attempted to identify the conditions under which the need for leadership would decrease, such as in situations where employees are experienced, trained and knowledgeable and where the organization is cohesive and formal. Since then, however, several theories of *distributed leadership* have begun to emerge, which allow for the multiple roles of leadership to be allocated within the group and to coexist at any one time. These might include task, administrative, social and intra-organizational functions which can be shared or rotated, enabling all group members to develop leadership skills in several areas. The various leadership styles and functions will have different emphases at different phases of a project.

NEW MANAGER ROLES

Where the development of teamworking is linked to organizational restructuring and, in particular, to the delayering of management levels, many former managers may take on new roles such as *team coach* to encourage and give feedback on effective performance and *facilitate* group processes. They may act as *role models* in demonstrating required behaviour or as *advocates* in gaining access to top level support. They may also take on the *boundary roles*, liaising with suppliers and ensuring the team has adequate resources. These roles might rotate around the group or may remain constant. It is unlikely to be a controlling and directing role normally associated with leadership in the past. Some former managers may simply become team members working alongside former subordinates and pooling expertise. Others, who find it difficult to relinquish the 'command and control' management style, may find they are unable to adapt to the team environment and leave the organization. Former supervisors and managers may certainly find themselves in an ambiguous and uncertain role during the transition period and will need support and guidance to demonstrate new paradigms and offer support to others.

Nevertheless, clear leadership seems to be an element contributing to the success of the Japanese production teams which, although flexible, are highly structured in terms of procedure. Smith et al. (1994) link high work quality in Japan with the seeking of the superior's advice in unfamiliar circumstances, while Western supervisors favour more contingent responses and are more likely to adopt self-managed styles.

SUPPORTING STRUCTURES

Recruitment

A consequence of teamworking should be the forging of a new relationship with human resources functions. Recruitment, formerly a stronghold of the HR/Personnel department, may now involve team members using HR specialists purely as consultants or support. Traditional recruitment, with its emphasis on the job description, may no longer be appropriate and roles may in some cases be so fluid that they cannot be classified. The ability of applicants to work in a team will be a prime competency, as will the ability to learn and adapt flexibly to organizational needs. Dangers, however, might befall inexperienced teams where too much responsibility in the area of selection is handed over too quickly. The tendency to recruit similar people who might be thought to 'fit in' can lead to highly homogeneous groups which may be overly cohesive, falling prey to 'groupthink' and lacking the diversity to engender creative ideas and solutions. Organizations must also meet legal requirements with regard to equal opportunities and fair selection practice. A close partnership with HR professionals therefore is certainly to be recommended in the early stages of self-directed teams.

Teams may also need to tackle dismissal where individuals are unwilling or unable to make the transition to new working practices. Interpersonal difficulties may be an obvious cause and training might offer a solution. A certain degree of positive conflict can be healthy and stimulating, but where an individual continually sabotages all attempts to create an open and efficient team they may need to move back into a more traditional environment in order to allow the team to function properly.

Training

Appropriate training is that which allows the team to achieve its objectives. This can involve training for the specific business activity on which the team is focused as well as in teambuilding, team leadership and team membership skills. At a basic level, people find it useful to understand something about team dynamics and the stages of teambuilding. It is also helpful for people to have insights into different team roles and types, so that they can understand and maximize the benefits of diversity. Facilitation skills are useful, as is training in how to handle conflict constructively. Most importantly, since managers are often a key barrier to teams working effectively, training managers in developing more participative styles of management can result in the team being better able to achieve its objectives.

Team members who are taking on self-managed roles will need training in both management and administration skills as well as interpersonal and teamworking skills. It is appropriate for some teams to become multi-skilled and able to do any job within the team. With other cross-functional teams this is not possible and team members will concentrate on working interdependently rather than interchangeably. It is inevitable that teams will also need a broader grasp of business strategy as they receive more information with which to manage themselves. They may need to deal with production figures and measure their own performance against the organization as a whole. They will need to budget and forecast as well as be prepared to defend the team's strategy with substantiating data. This will require skills in formal presentation and negotiation. Many teams, introduced in times of change, will experience the additional problems of making sense of changing systems.

If the team takes on responsibility for its own selection process, then training in assessment and appraisal will be needed. An understanding of the nature of team roles might also be an advantage. Other personnel skills might include health and safety as well as discipline and conflict resolution. As the team begins to identify its own training needs over time, this will become another of its functions and 'train the trainer' programmes may be more suitable to meet these needs.

Team learning

Looking beyond formal training for individual members, the team must also concentrate on learning as a team if it is to rise to the challenge of increasing complexity in work processes. Senge (1990) warns that, 'A group of talented individual learners will not necessarily produce a *learning team*, any more than a group of talented athletes will produce a great sports team.' To achieve synergy, members must practice learning together so that the sum of their learning is greater than its individual parts. Teams that are able to build up this sort of experience, learning from mistakes and identifying causes of success, are able to work with increasing confidence in themselves and their colleagues. An interesting piece of research into the building up of trust within the Red Arrows Display Team (Owen, 1996) demonstrates how this confidence grows. Owen identifies the stages required, starting with self-awareness and building up self-esteem in others, to developing openness by giving and receiving feedback in order to learn from mistakes.

The appraisal system

Where teams work interdependently the individual appraisal system has difficulty in disentangling individual contribution. Where teams are self-managed they may be held responsible for their own appraisal, and a more appropriate method might be peer or 360 degree appraisal, which could include other stakeholders such as internal and external customers. Most feedback research has been aimed at individual behaviour but, as organizations move to teamworking performance, measurement is increasingly seen in terms of group productivity. Pritchard et al. (1988) conducted research in a military setting on a group performance measurement system (ProMES), *31* which involved giving feedback at group level. Results showed an increase in productivity after five months of 50 per cent. During the following five months goal setting was added, which increased productivity to 75 per cent over baseline. Such experiments show important progress in developing feedback practices which capture interdependencies and complexities of groups and teamwork.

Here again the context should be carefully considered. Teams who are competing for rewards, bonuses and resources – or even prestige – may find it in their self-interest to present their team in the best light to the rest of the organization. This may go under the well-intentioned guise of supporting weaker team members, or it may encourage them to ostracize poor performers rather than give them necessary support. Peer feedback is particularly susceptible to modification, due to fears of damaging colleague relationships and often fails because individuals have not been trained to give it in a constructive and acceptable way. Current writing on peer and 360 degree feedback seems to indicate that it works best when used for self- or team development, rather than in the context of formal appraisal that may be linked to pay and reward.

The reward system

One of the difficulties of introducing self-directed teams is how to reflect the new ways of working in the reward system. Pay and reward can be a powerful reinforcer or inhibitor of teams as the basic work unit. Rewards will probably be distributed on a team performance or on a skill or knowledge basis rather than on seniority. Attention must also be paid to the management aspects of the roles because, if reward is solely based on production targets, there may be a temptation to bypass essential processes related to safety and 'housekeeping tasks' in favour of outputs which produce direct rewards. Bonus schemes will similarly need to reflect total team performance, although individual incentive may be a deterrent to 'social loafing'.

However, the balance between recognizing individual effort and team-working is a precarious one. Wall et al. (1986) cited as a possible contributor to lack of increased motivation in autonomous groups the fact that rewards had been distributed on an individual basis while feedback had been mixed between individual and group levels. Nevertheless, recent research by Roffey Park Management Institute found that 91 per cent of respondents felt that reward systems should take into account personal achievement and development, while only 9 per cent were in favour of team reward (Holbeche, 1997).

Some advanced teams may be able to decide how to divide a bonus themselves between members. In whatever way the reward scheme operates, it must be considered fair by each member of the team. Perceived lack of equity is known to be a key demotivating factor. Both Equity Theory (Vroom, 1964) and Social Comparison Theory (Festinger, 1954) are relevant to team situations where individuals will compare their own effort and reward against that of other team members and, where it is not perceived to be fair, will adjust the amount of effort expended to compensate for lack of reward. Time spent on achieving an acceptable and open reward system is therefore time well spent.

Career development

Another aspect of the reward system related closely to the concept of the *psychological contract* is that of career development. Individuals need to have a sense of how being part of a non-hierarchical team will affect their career prospects. In terms of broadening their range of skills, including management experience and cross-training, it is possible that increased job satisfaction may cloud the issue for some time. However, ultimately high flyers will begin to ask 'What next?'. In flatter organizations, where teams are the basic unit throughout the organization, the psychological contract may need to be more explicit in terms of what can realistically be offered. It may be that individual goals such as qualification programmes, flexible working arrangements or the opportunity for secondments can be met within the existing team arrangement so that motivation is maintained (Holbeche, 1997).

CONCLUSION

The seemingly irreversible trend towards teamworking may indicate a general change in business culture and organizational structure, although the underlying concept of power sharing is still a bitter pill to swallow for some traditional managers who have previously competed as individuals. Nevertheless, the increasing demand to achieve more from less, or at the very least to create synergy, suggests that teamworking is likely to become more prevalent as time goes on.

Where failure occurs it is frequently blamed on lack of vision, lack of resources, lack of preparation, too little time spent on training and developing team processes and lack of support. Unrealistic expectations may have arisen regarding roles and responsibilities which ultimately cannot be realized, and this may lead to demotivation. Leaderless teams may find it difficult to concentrate on priorities amid the new management functions they are expected to undertake. Boundaries that are clearly defined are necessary to provide structure in the life of a team. They help define relations with other working groups and with the organization as a whole.

Finally, it may be necessary to consider whether teams are an appropriate solution for the organization. The following points provide a useful checklist of what to take into account:

- Is a high degree of interdependence necessary so that every member's contribution is valued, or would a cooperative group work as well?
- What form of leadership will be most appropriate? Should management

functions remain with a team leader, could a facilitator help the team become semi-autonomous or should the whole team share the management functions?

- Does the team need to be permanent and formal?
- Is the organizational context, and especially the HR function, ready to provide support for a self-managed team?
- How will a team work with the rest of the organization?
- Are there resources and sufficient time to ensure a high level of training with attention paid to processes as well as to tasks?

In organizations which have dealt with these issues the rewards of team-working have reportedly been high, although few report that the transition has been easy. It seems that, as structures change and new technology directs the future of work, teams and possibly self-directed teams will become the standard work unit of the future.

REFERENCES

Brooks, A.K., 'Power and the Production of Knowledge: Collective Team Learning in Work Organizations', *Human Resource Development Quarterly*, 1994, **5** (3), Autumn, 213–235

Festinger, L., 'A Theory of Social Comparison Processes', *Human Relations*, 1954, **40**, 427–48

Hackman, J., *Groups that Work (and Those that Don't): Conditions for Effective Teamwork*, Jossey-Bass, California, 1990

Higgs, M. and Rowland, D., 'All Pigs are Equal', *Management Education and Development (UK)*, 1992, **23** (4), Winter, 349–62

Holbeche, L.S., *Career Development in Flatter Structures: Organisational Practices*, Roffey Park Research Report, 1995

Holbeche, L.S., *Motivating People in Lean Organisations*, Butterworth-Heinemann, Oxford, 1997

Owen, H., *Creating Top Flight Teams*, Kogan Page, London, 1996

Pritchard, R.D., Jones, S.D., Roth, P.L., Stuebing, K.K., and Ekeberg, S.E., 'Effect of Group Feedback, Goal Setting, and Incentives on Organisational Productivity', *Journal of Applied Psychology*, **73**, 1988, 337–58

Senge, P., *The Fifth Discipline: The Art and Practice of the Learning Organization*, Doubleday, New York, 1990

Smith, P.B., Peterson, M.F. and Misumi, J.M., 'Event Management and Work Team Effectiveness in Japan, Britain and USA', *Journal of Occupational and Organisational Psychology*, 1994, **67**, 33–43

Vroom, V., *Work and Motivation*, Wiley, New York, 1964

Wall, T.D., Kemp, N.J., Jackson, P.R. and Clegg, C.W., 'Outcomes of Autonomous Workgroups: A Long-term Field Experiment', *Academy of Management Journal*, 1986, **29**, 280–304

3 Corporate alignment and cultural realignment

Nigel MacLennan

Why do some team cultures produce enviable results and others in the same industry providing the same products hover on the edge of bankruptcy? Why are some cultures so well aligned they take your breath away, and others so hopelessly fractious that working in them induces nausea? Answering those questions is the objective of this chapter.

We shall first discuss the general principles behind corporate alignment and realignment, then present the components of a Corporate Alignment Model, and finally examine the 9 Rs of change or alignment.

UNDERSTANDING ALIGNMENT

If you had visited NASA in 1965 and asked any of the staff there, 'What is your organization's vision?', what do you think they would have told you? 'To increase return on capital?' 'To optimize shareholder return?' 'To produce tax returns on time?' I think not.

When John Kennedy announced to America and the world that the country would put a man on the moon and return him safely to earth he gave the world the most powerful vision in history. When Winston Churchill announced that Britain was defending democracy and would free Europe, what happened? When Steve Jobs announced that Apple was going to make computers useable by all, what happened? When Henry Ford announced that he was going to make cars accessible to all, what happened? What do these examples and countless others have in common? They created an AWESOME PURPOSE!

Examine in detail any high-achieving team or company, and behind the success you will find an awesome purpose. An exciting vision with which all the staff can identify and behind which all the staff are aligned. If you want alignment create an awesome purpose.

How do you create an awesome purpose? That, I'm afraid, is the tough part. Aligning a company or team behind anything is notoriously hard, but the rewards when you can do it are very worthwhile, way out of proportion to the apparently simple act of alignment. Why? Because in such companies people are all pointing in the same direction, trying to achieve the same end (see Figure 3.1).

Compare that with the situation in most companies. Political infighting (Figure 3.2), one department trying to achieve one thing while another is trying to do something else (Figure 3.3), staff having no clear picture of where the organization is going, and worse . . .

How much of such a company's resources are wasted on internal conflicts and lack of shared vision? Ten per cent? Fifty per cent? Eighty per cent? On the basis of the widely quoted figure – 80 per cent of most companies' problems are caused by poor or a lack of communication – how much advantage do you think shared AWESOME PURPOSE can give to a company able to align its staff behind one?

An awesome purpose does not just materialize out of thin air. It is the supreme output of a much deeper and involved process. Those organizations which have one seem to share many other characteristics. Rather than run through a list of those characteristics and then show you the model which pulls them together, let's do it the other way round. Let's look at the Corporate Alignment Model (CAM) (Figure 3.4) and discuss the characteristics in the context of that model.

THE CORPORATE ALIGNMENT MODEL

Why is a model needed to help align team cultures? Because one of the biggest difficulties in aligning a team culture is that so few people actually understand culture (although most people claim to) and most of them use different terms to mean different things. In short, there is no shared understanding of culture, no shared framework with which to describe and explain culture, no mechanism with which to guide culture. And, thus, no means by which to align a team or organization culture.

Test those assumptions. Go round your company and ask the first twenty people you see to define culture. Then ask another twenty to define strategy. Ask another twenty to define a vision. If people don't have a common language about the factors that determine whether a culture is aligned, how can they possibly have an aligned culture? There is a clear need for shared terms.

Here is another assumption. Most people in your company will not know what your culture is, or is supposed to be, do not know what your organization's vision is, and do not know what your strategy is. Fine, the same routine as before will be useful now. Go out and test those assumptions. Ask another twenty to define your culture, your strategy, your vision.

If your company is like 99 per cent of those I work with, you found that the senior staff were able to provide answers to your questions, but the answers varied between one senior staff member and another. The middle

ALIGNED CULTURE

Figure 3.1   Aligned culture   © 1997 N.T.R. MacLennan

Figure 3.2   Non-aligned culture – lack of direction   © 1997 N.T.R. MacLennan

Figure 3.3   Non-aligned culture – infighting   © 1997 N.T.R. MacLennan

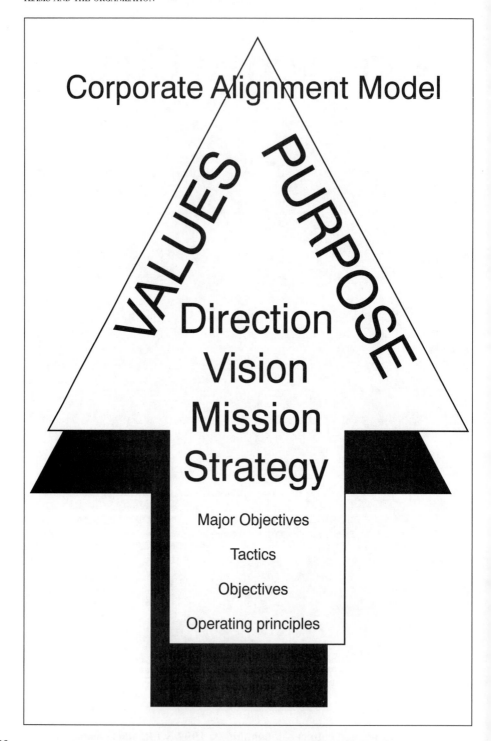

Figure 3.4   Corporate Alignment Model   © 1997 N.T.R. MacLennan

level staff provided even more disparate answers, when they were able to answer the questions at all, and the junior staff were unable to answer the questions at all. Given that most of the people in any organization are junior staff, that is, the ones who produce most of the organization's output, wouldn't you think that they were most in need of the clear guidance that knowledge of those elements of culture would provide? Of course they are!

The above assumption (most people in your team/company don't know what your culture is or what the team/company is trying to achieve, or how) is based on another; that is, that your company has defined its culture, has articulated its vision and specified its strategy. Is that true? Probably not. If it were true you would have a well-aligned culture and you would not need to read this chapter.

In an aligned culture every member is provided with guidance; it is the means by which people make their decisions. It tells them what they are trying to achieve and how they are trying to achieve it. If people don't have that guidance how can they fill in the inevitable gaps in the instructions of their superiors?

Some people answer that question by saying, 'ask their superiors to fill in the gaps'. That's fine, so your company takes that approach but your competitors have such an aligned culture that their staff don't have to stop work, stop their superior working on something else and ask for a gap to be filled in. Who is going to be more productive, you or your competitor? It is obvious, and that's why companies aligned behind a strong culture and clear vision are always (all other things being equal) more effective than those who are not.

Having established why we need a coherent culture management framework, let's examine each of the elements of the CAM.

Purpose

Purpose is what the organization will always be doing.

The standing of purpose in relation to the other elements of the CAM is that purpose, along with values, is 'who you are'. Purpose gives an organization a common aim to focus on at the highest level. Even if all other guidelines have failed to provide you with a goal, this one should not. Purpose is expressed using the infinitive form of a verb, as in 'To improve mental effectiveness'.

A few examples (some actual, others inferred from commercial behaviour):

3M: 'To solve unsolved problems.'
Disney: 'To make people happy.'
MacLennan: 'To improve mental effectiveness.'

Purpose must motivate people. It should give the company and your team a lifetime and never-ending pursuit; it is that which you will always be doing. A purpose is something that never stops, as distinct from a vision or mission *41* which have discernible end points and as distinct from strategy, tactics and operating principles, which are 'how to' guides.

In companies where the purpose is not known you'll hear many platitudes instead. 'To optimize return on capital.' Can you imagine inspiring a country to fight for itself 'to protect the cash of those who have invested in our stock market'? Blatantly not. Yet tens of thousands of company 'leaders' think exactly that notion expressed in different words will impassion their staff. I think not. What do you think?

What is your organization's purpose? Is it articulated or assumed? If it is assumed, test the assumption. Go out of your office and ask the first twenty people you meet, 'What is the purpose of our company?' Don't prompt them, just ask the question repeatedly until it is clear that they either don't understand the question or don't know the answer.

Many of the most creative brains in the world queue up to work at Disney. Can you imagine Disney recruiting the kind of men and women that currently make up the company on the basis of the purpose 'to make consistent profits'? Can you imagine the kind of quality of movies that would produce? Can you imagine what kind of unenterprising people would be applying to work at Disney in those circumstances?

A purpose once identified requires no justification; others either commit to it or they get out. If you find yourself or others justifying the purpose, you probably have not identified your purpose.

Values

Values are the core beliefs the organization or team holds or wishes to hold (and is not prepared to compromise under any circumstances).

The standing of values in relation to the other elements of the CAM is that this, along with purpose, is 'who' you are. Values are the guiding philosophy of any organization, and are usually put in place by the founder. If not, 'The leader's role is to distil and to instil them' (Sir Adrian Cadbury).

Shared values are enormous time-savers. Have you ever sat on a board (or any other committee) which has no clearly articulated and shared values? It is a nightmare! Proposals are presented, the debate starts. One person objects to it for one reason and someone else supports it for exactly the same reason. A third party suggests it should be held over for further consideration for the same reason the other two had who wanted to block or support it. Then someone introduces another value and the same let's agree, let's disagree, let's have some neutral posturing, starts all over again.

Obviously I am exaggerating the degree of chaos for the purpose of conveying the point, but you've been there, you've seen it, you know it goes on and on and on, and nothing is decided. Why? Because there are no agreed values, and there is rarely a clearly spelled-out vision. Of course you hear plenty of seemingly well-intentioned platitudes, but nothing people can use for guidance. And what happens in the absence of a clear and agreed set of
42 values to use for guidance? People supply their own personal values. When

Figure 3.5 The relationship between the elements of the CAM © 1997 N.T.R. MacLennan

you have a group of individuals with their own personal values for guidance what happens? Debate, chaos – and not a lot else.

Values are distinct from purpose in that . . . values express who you are and what you stand for. Purpose expresses why you are, and what you exist to do. Here are some examples of values used by extremely successful organizations and people. So that their values make sense out of context, some have been paraphrased for a general readership, but the central meaning remains intact. Anyone who knows the organizations will know that they live by these values, and make all their decisions with reference to these values. As Sir Adrian Cadbury put it: 'The glue which holds a company together is its beliefs and values rather than its structures and systems.'

IBM
- Respect for the individual

- Careful attention to service
- Superiority in all things.

W.L. Gore (Goretex)

- Fairness
- Mutual development
- Self-responsibility
- Information sharing.

Nelson Mandela, South Africa
Most people know that all Mandela had to do to be released from prison many years before that eventually happened was to renounce violence as a means of struggle. Why is he held is such high esteem throughout the world? Because he held, and holds, justice for all as a value above all other values, even that of his own freedom. How can we help but follow such an example?

China
The ideas which have governed Chinese society for 2 500 years are based on the teachings of Confucius. I'm not sure how Confucius would have turned his principles of government into a values list, but here is my attempt.

- Meritocracy
- Economic control
- Utilization of surplus
- Information control.

Whether you approve or disapprove (as I do) of these values, there can be no denying they have held together the largest population in the world for over 2 500 years. They are by far the longest surviving mass civilization in the world today.

Winston Churchill, Britain, World War II

- Liberty
- Justice
- Freedom.

Winston Churchill in, 1940, spelled out the most important of our values when he first took office: 'I speak to you for the first time as Prime Minister in this solemn hour for the life of our country, of our empire, of our allies, and above all, of the cause of *freedom*.' Merely holding a set of values is not enough. They have to be perpetually to the fore; they have to be reinforced.

Churchill gave, perhaps, the most famous of all value reinforcement speeches, although at no point does he need to state to what values he is referring. From all his previous speeches, everyone listening knew that he was referring to freedom, and that the young men who fought and died were protecting something much, much more important than a small island: 'Never in the field of human conflict has so much been owed by so many to so few' (House of Commons, 1940).

Hundreds of times I have read those words and they still bring tears to my eyes. Why? Because I, too, passionately believe in democratic freedom, and I can imagine the mix of passion and fear that drove those youngsters to stand up for what is just and be prepared to take the consequences.

That is the kind of spirit that achieves awesome things. That is the kind of spirit that all wise business leaders would like to harness. And wouldn't you? Wouldn't you like to have your staff achieving awesome results because your awesome purpose reflected values they deeply held? Wouldn't you expect superior performance in those circumstances? Yet, sadly, many business 'leaders' set goals more likely to take all the 'fire' out of people. 'Increase shareholder value.' 'Double our return on capital.' 'Make more profit.' They fail to draw on the values of the people who are expected to achieve the goals.

When, oh, when will they realize the mistake they are making? People do not jump out of bed blazing with passion to put more money in shareholders' pockets. People do not spend their weekends dreaming up ways to double return on capital. All of those kinds of behaviour are the result of achieving something awesome. Give people exciting values to stand up for and they will give you all the boring but necessary things on their way to what really matters to them.

What are the values of your organization? Are they clearly articulated and documented? If they are not, how can you expect people to use them for guidance?

Direction

Direction is the road along which you choose to travel in pursuit of your purpose.

The standing of direction in relation to the other elements of the CAM is that this is the first level 'what to'.

What does setting a direction do? It makes the purpose more specific, while at the same time separating purpose from the direction in which you choose to pursue it. It clarifies thinking on the subject; it distinguishes key elements of a previously muddled concept usually expressed in the question 'what business are we in?' The answer to that combines purpose and direction. Some people think that is one of the best questions a company can ask and answer. It is. It asks 'what is our purpose?' It also asks 'in what direction do we pursue that purpose?' Now we can make an even more acute distinction when thinking about the company's future. In collective decision making it concentrates the minds of the participants more acutely on the key issues. Anyone who has ever been involved with collective decision making will know how desperately tools of that kind are needed.

A few examples take the place of a thousand explanations:

| *3M*: | To solve unsolved problems |
| Direction: | Technology problems (technological as opposed to methodo-logical problems) |

| *MacLennan*: | To improve mental effectiveness |
| Direction: | Business thinking effectiveness (methodological as opposed to technological effectiveness) |

| *Disney*: | To make people happy |
| Direction: | Entertainment (as opposed to many other possible directions) |

In which direction is your organization pursuing its purpose? Is it articulated, is it shared, is it documented?

Vision

Vision is an 8–25 year end point or target, the most future distant and (possibly) achievable manifestation of your purpose you can see along the direction you have chosen.

The standing of vision in relation to the other elements of the CAM is that this is the second level or long-term 'what to'.

What does a vision do? It gives teams and all staff:

- The means to interpret day-to-day activities in terms of a higher level goal
- A focus for their activity
- A means by which to make decisions
- A clear picture of what the organization will look like
- A sense of being involved in something worthwhile.

Having such a long-term target provides a distant benchmark against which everyone in the company can make decisions. Combine that with a well-defined purpose, a clear set of values to provide guidelines not obvious from the vision and an articulated direction, and you are well on the way to having an aligned team and company: 'A vision is only seen if everyone is looking in the same direction' (N.T.R. MacLennan). The stronger the vision the more each of the above benefits will apply.

Without a vision people become activity-focused; agenda rather than objectives-driven. Without a vision people have no means by which to judge their contribution, and managers have no means by which to set outcome measures. Without clear vision people have no means by which to resolve the dilemmas presented to them on a daily basis. The weaker the vision the more these problems will be evident. Sir Adrian Cadbury said: 'Vision is central to ensuring that everyone in an organization knows what the goals of an enterprise are and how their particular job contributed to them.'

46   Here is an example of one of the best presented visions in history – Martin

Luther King spelling out a vision for all America and the world on racial equality at the Lincoln Memorial in Washington, in 1963:

> I have a dream that one day even the State of Mississippi,
> a desert sweltering with the heat of injustice and oppression . . .
> will be transformed into an oasis of freedom and justice.
>
> I have a dream that my four little children . . .
> will one day live in a nation
> where they will not be judged by the colour of their skin
> but by the content of their character . . .
>
> I have a dream today.
> I have a dream . . .

If that has not persuaded you that visions must be inspiring, perhaps this will – Martin Luther King, 1968, restating the vision in the face of multiple barriers and even threats to his life, a few hours before his assassination:

> I just want to do God's will.
> And he has allowed me to go up to the mountain top.
> And I have looked over.
> And I have seen the promised land.
> I may not get there with you
> But I want you to know tonight
> That we as a people will get to the promised land.

Within a very short period segregation in the USA was outlawed and some years after that 'Martin Luther King Day' was created in memory of the man and as a symbol aimed at further promoting racial harmony. Just over 25 years later apartheid fell in South Africa. The vision created by that man lives on today, long after his death.

'Vision must be communicable, coherent, comprehensible, communicated and captivating' (N.T.R. MacLennan). Martin Luther King's vision certainly is. What is your organization's great vision? What point have your CEO and board stated that you are trying to reach in the long-term future? Does it send shivers down your spine?

Mission

Mission is a three to eight-year end point. Having a mid-term target provides a more immediate benchmark against which everyone in the company can make decisions.

The standing of mission in relation to the other elements of the CAM is that this is a mid-term or third level 'what to'.

Most managers cannot quote their company mission. Go for a wander around your business and ask the first 50 managers you meet; I guarantee that if your mission statement is more than nine words long less than 20 per cent of the people you meet will be able to recite it. As the number of   *47* words increases to over 30 or more I will bet that you can find no one other than its author(s) who can quote it. If 50 managers cannot quote it, what chance is there that lower level managers or staff can? If people cannot remember a mission how do you expect them to achieve it?

Examples of great – and memorable – missions are:

John F. Kennedy, 1962:	'We will put a man on the moon by the end of this decade.' (Mission setting)
Neil Armstrong, 1969:	'One small step for a man, one giant leap for mankind.' (Mission completing, as it was intended to have been said)
Winston Churchill, 1942:	'We will defend our island, whatever the cost may be' (Spoken from Mansion House) 'This is not the end. It is not even the beginning of the end. But it is the end of the beginning.' (Reinforcing the mission after the Allies' victory in Egypt)
Komatsu:	'To encircle Caterpillar' (their biggest competitor).
British Airways:	'To be the world's favourite airline.'
TSB (Bank):	'To be the UK's leading financial retailer.'

Some mission statements are actually purpose statements, for example: 'We are in the business of preserving human life' (Merck, USA, health care).

Why is that a purpose statement? Because it can be engaged in perpetually. It is a perfect example of a purpose statement, but it is not a mission statement. Why not? Because it has no manifestable end point; it lacks the 'we know when we have achieved that' indicator required for a good mission statement.

You may say, 'they are a successful organization, and confusing a purpose statement with a mission statement can't be that serious'. You would be right. Having a mission statement, no matter how bad, may be better than the vast majority of organizations in the world, but presumably you are not reading this chapter or this book to be a little better than dismal. You are, I hope, reading this to be the best. Think how much better that organization could be if their mission statement actually told their staff what their mid-term target was in the same perfect way, as well as stating the purpose?

Think about your current mission statement, if you have one. Does it state a clear mid-term target?

Strategy

We are going to approach this element of the CAM from a different angle to make an important point.

One of the many reasons that the terms used in business cause regular confusion is that the same word is used to mean many things. For instance, 'strategy' is used to mean different things in at least four different levels in organizational life. At the highest level it is often used to mean 'purpose'. At the competitive level it is used to mean the 'method of attack in the market place'. At the middle management level it is often used to mean 'tactic'. At the operational level it is used to mean 'operating principles'. For that reason, this term and all others central to the CAM have to be clearly defined.

So in what ways could we define 'strategy'? Here are a few:

- Strategy is individual or group behaviour aimed at securing some competitive advantage
- Strategy is the means of delivering your core competence to your chosen market place
- Strategy is the way an organization harnesses its resources to deliver something its customers find attractive
- Strategy is the management of mission.

All of the above have some truth in them; most have something lacking. The one that comes closest is: 'Strategy is the way an organization harnesses its resources to deliver something its customers find attractive.'

The following is the best and most understandable definition I've been able to come up with while accepting that there is always a conflict between academically rigorous definitions and those that are useable in the real world: *Strategy* is the means by which the organization's resources are brought to bear on, and found to be attractive by, the target market* to achieve the mission.

What do strategies do, in terms of team alignment? Knowing the means by which resources are being brought to bear gives everyone a high level guide on making decisions about 'how to'. Strategy is the first level 'how to', illustrated by the following examples:

Virgin (pensions):	Provide pensions with the lowest possible overhead charges.
Nike:	Provide sportswear with the strongest association with sports achievement.
Boeing:	Provide the fastest delivery at the lowest cost.

For a strategy to be effective it must be understood by all those contributing to it. If your people don't know the means by which you are seeking to deliver what the customer wants, how can they help you do so?

Even if everyone knows it and applies it, it must be in tune with your values and purpose to be delivered effectively. A theoretically-right strategy works only when conduct is the consequence of belief. In other words, the strategy must be drawn from your values and purpose. The values, purpose

* Target market also means 'customer's desires', whoever the customer may be.

and vision of an organization can be seen or inferred from a good strategy. In fact, in some instances, a purpose, vision and strategy can be crystallized in one phrase. In one awesome purpose.

What is your organization's current strategy? Where is it documented? Ask twenty managers to 'state our organization's strategy'. No prompting. If you have an aligned culture you will receive twenty identical answers. The fewer identical answers you receive, the more alignment is required.

Major objectives

Major objectives are the key targets which will have to be achieved using the strategy if the mission is to be successful.

Setting the major objectives gives people an even more immediate benchmark than the mission against which to make decisions. On the occasions on which the major objectives prove inconclusive as a decision making guide, reference can be made to the higher level 'what tos': mission and vision.

The standing of vision in relation to the other elements of the CAM is that this is the fourth level 'what to'. For example, Boeing's major objectives are to reduce the time to manufacture a plane (747s, 767s, and so on) from 18 months to eight months in four years, and reduce costs by 25 per cent in six years. One of 3M's major objectives is to generate 30 per cent of revenues from products which did not exist four years ago.

Can you list your organization's major objectives, those that are dictated by the strategy to achieve the mission? Probably. For that reason I will be providing less detail at the lower levels of the CAM. Objective setting was well covered by Drucker over 50 years ago and is now well-taught at most business schools and on professional courses.

Tactics

Tactics are another 'how to' guide. They are the micro methods used to achieve the key objectives drawn from the strategy.

Strategy is often too blunt an instrument to make day-to-day micro-level decisions. Strategy has different manifestations for the various functional groupings within any organization. Spelling out the tactics as they apply to each grouping gives them a means to focus their efforts and a means by which to make decisions about 'how to' (second level) on a local scale. Tactics are the short-term components of strategy (the methods by which the major objectives, derived from the strategy, are achieved). Tactics are the interpretations of strategy at functional levels.

If speed of service is your strategy, then the methods your marketing team use to convey that to your potential customers is a tactic. The methods your operations people use to deliver quickly are tactics. The means your order processing people use to clear the order and put it in the hands of your operations people are tactics.

Nintendo allegedly restricted the supply of its computer games to keep up demand, maintain prices and keep the balance of power between themselves and retailers tilted in their favour. When people are queuing outside your retail store for a supplier's game, you don't force them to drop their prices, do you?

List the tactics your department uses to deliver your major objectives.

Objectives

Objectives are the necessary component targets to achieve the major objectives using the tactics chosen. This is the fifth level 'what to'.

Well-run companies are objectives- and outcomes-driven, and both are derived from major objectives. They, in turn, are derived from the strategy, which is derived from what the customer wants and your awesome purpose. All are derived from, and are in line with, your values and purpose. Poorly-run companies are agenda-driven. Meetings are dominated by going through the sequence on the agenda. There is no overarching framework to guide behaviour.

Poorly-run teams and companies are budget-driven. Activities are centred around fulfilling the budget commitments. Managers are more interested in making sure their budget forecasts are met than in delivering benefit to customers. The decisions made in the last budget round nearly a year ago are used to make decisions, in preference to the customer-provided information of today. Little wonder their customers look out for better suppliers until they find them.

Poorly-run teams and companies are process-driven. They allow the process to be more important than that for which the process was created, which is to say an outcome, a deliverable. Academics are notorious for this. Each year they produce millions of perfectly written papers in thousands of journals, and less than one in ten thousand actually achieves any kind of outcome.

Take the major objective that applies to your function or department and list the objectives that have been set to achieve that major objective.

Operating principles

Operating principles are those guidelines (in addition to values) which are used to make day-to-day decisions about how to achieve your objectives. In the same way that tactics are the localized interpretation of the strategy, operating principles are the very localized interpretation of tactics. This is the third level 'how to'.

You may have the same tactics and operating principles being used throughout the company. That is one reason most people confuse values with operating principles. Each department does not need to have its own unique operating principles, although each will have some. They can be shared, but that does not make them values.

How do you distinguish between values and operating principles? The highest possible quality in a particular customer deliverable may be an operating principle. It may be driven by a current demand by customers, but if one of your values is 'giving the customer what they want', and customers start demanding lower prices for lower quality goods, you'll drop quality as an operating principle instantly.

What are your operating principles? In the department you have most contact with, list the operating principles that are used to guide staff activities.

USING THE CAM

Does your company currently have some values (articulated or not)? Does you company have a purpose (articulated or not)? Does your company have a strategy (articulated or not)? Does your company have a mission and maybe even a vision (articulated or not)? Does your company have major objectives, tactics and operating principles (articulated or not)? Of course it does. They are there in the minds of your team. What is not are the same values, the same vision, the same strategy in the minds of all of your team. That is what the CAM illustrates. It gives you a framework or structure with which you can align your culture. It shows you how to ensure that the same values, purpose, vision, and so on, are in the heads of the members of your team.

Once you have distilled all the elements of the CAM and worked towards a common version of each element, you are well on the way to an aligned culture. But there is one further stage. You need one symbol, one image, one slogan which encapsulates everything you are striving towards. You need something that is going to inspire every member of staff. You need an awesome purpose.

Completing the CAM, arriving at an awesome purpose.

How do I arrive at the completed CAM? How do I generate an awesome purpose? In a short chapter we just do not have the space to cover the tools you need to distil values, generate a vision, and so on, and make one coherent whole of these to generate an awesome purpose. But we can show you 'the 9Rs' you need if you want to create any lasting change or alignment in a team or company.

'THE 9RS' OF CHANGE OR ALIGNMENT

- Realization
- Rallying
- Recognition
- Reframing
- Re-visioning
- Redesigning
- Realigning

- Revising
- Retaining.

Let's take each of these in turn.

Realization

No organization changes or starts to become aligned unless and until someone in that organization realizes there is a need to do so. Realization is useful only if the need for change or alignment can be precisely identified and articulated.

Rallying

Support for the realization of the need for change or alignment is required before the organization or team can even begin to contemplate change. The realizers must have sufficient influence to be taken seriously, and have sufficiently powerful communication skills to convey the message properly. The 'realizer' must rally the initial support for alignment or change.

Recognition

The recognition phase is about reaching the point of critical mass of people who are aware of the need for alignment or realignment and who also acknowledge something needs to be done about it.

Reframing

Companies and teams rarely define their problems in terms of their own behaviour. Until they do, until they redefine the problem in self-aware and self-responsible ways, there is no hope of successful alignment or realignment. To reframe successfully you must know what you are dealing with and that requires an expert understanding of team and company cultures.

Re-visioning

Re-visioning involves completing the CAM and identifying an awesome purpose which will unite and align the team or organization. No awesome purpose, no alignment. If you can't encapsulate the awesome purpose in one memorable phrase, forget it. Pack up, go home, forget about any alignment – you are wasting your time.

Redesigning

Redesigning means that the team or company structures are set up in such a way that they deliver and are perfectly in tune with the awesome purpose   *53* and the CAM. For any redesign to be successful it must be perfectly in tune with the culture, the vision and the market.

Realigning

This is the phase of alignment that tests whether all the previous stages have been successfully completed, and when you actually work out the serious business of implementation.

Revising

No completed CAM is ever perfect, and no redesign is ever perfect either. All your plans will have to be altered in the light of the real world. So, set up mechanisms to collect feedback on how well the implementation of the plan is going and what problems there are. The entire process from realization to realignment should be examined if the team or organization is to learn how to make realignment easier in the future.

Retaining

Cultural alignment is not something you can do once and walk away from. It is an ongoing process, albeit not as intense in the retaining stage as in the other '8Rs'. Set up systems to make the team aware of the changes in the market and commercial environment that will make them aware that perpetual realignment is essential.

You must also set up systems to ensure that the team culture as it now exists is being practised consistently by the members of that team. In other words you need systems to ensure that people's behaviour is consistent with the culture. If you don't have that, you don't have an aligned culture.

SUMMARY

The 9Rs' model offers you a sequence with which to conduct your team alignment, realignment or change. The CAM provides a framework with which to align your culture or team, and it gives you a common language to share an understanding of culture and the importance of its alignment.

Much more important than 'the 9Rs' and the CAM put together is awesome purpose. If you have an awesome purpose you can expect to see truly remarkable levels of performance from your team. If you do not . . .

RECOMMENDED READING

Crainer, S. (ed.), *Leaders on leadership*, Institute of Management Foundation, Corby, 1996

MacLennan, N.T.R., *Awesome purpose*, Gower, Albershot, 1998

4 Creating a team-based organization

Colin Hastings

A consistent theme running through most recent studies of effective organizations is the importance of teamworking. The word has historically been used to describe permanent functional teams such as production and sales. However, in its recent resurgence it is cross-functional and multidisciplinary teamworking that is seen as an important ingredient of success. This form of collaboration is vital to solving complex problems fast, gaining commitment to change, and tapping the full reservoir of latent energy and ideas possessed by most organizations.

As a result, much of the work in organizations is now carried out by temporary project groups or task forces. Their briefs are often complex and frequently difficult to define. They range from organizing an office move to launching a new product, from testing a new drug to making a bid for a new advertising account, and from implementing a new process to managing a merger. Whatever the objective, and even where multiple project teams are used, a wide range of skills and experience now exists to make teamworking successful. It does not always come naturally, especially in organizations that think mainly in terms of hierarchy and functions. Learning how to assemble and develop teams to full advantage and how to create the organizational culture in which they survive is a challenge to which senior management, line management, team leaders, human relations specialists and external consultants can all contribute. This chapter summarizes the key conclusions from the author's research and consultancy on how to make teamworking work in your organization.

THE ROLE OF SENIOR MANAGEMENT

Senior management must create the conditions within the organization that help both functional and cross-functional teams to perform. Teams without   55 senior management sponsorship are like plants without water. Some of the most important 'do's' and 'don'ts' for this sponsorship role are:

1 *Divest responsibility and authority to teams* If senior management provide an exciting vision, ask much of the teams, train them and then trust them, they will achieve significant results.
2 *Ensure that you are open to the teams' ideas* The teams will become very authoritative. If management respect them and learn from them, they and the organization will benefit hugely.
3 *Do not delegate responsibility for the project elsewhere* A common pattern is that senior management are much in evidence only at the interesting time when a team project is launched. Managers should ensure their continuing commitment and visibility.
4 *Demonstrate commitment by removing obstacles* Find out about and act against organization blockages facing teams. This is another test of commitment.
5 *Allocate a budget to develop teams and their leaders* Just as in capital investment, under-investment in human resources is often wasted investment. Outstanding teams do not materialize out of thin air.
6 *Ensure that teams are clear about what is expected of them* This often takes time and a lot of discussion. Do not assume that the objectives are clearly understood.

CREATING HIGH-PERFORMANCE TEAMS

Planning the 'how'

Many teams seriously underperform. Even those whose performance is acceptable often look poor when compared with outstanding teams. Successful teams spend time developing ground rules about how they need to operate in order to be successful. Some of the general ground rules or values that characterize high-performing teams include:

- A shared belief in, and excitement about, what they are trying to achieve
- A persistent and obsessive pursuit of their goals while maintaining flexibility in their strategies for reaching them
- A realization that no team is self-sufficient: it needs resources from the organization and elsewhere
- An attitude which is always looking to find a better way to do things
- An action orientation; high-performing teams do not wait for things to happen, they go out and make things happen
- A realization that the team exists to produce something for someone, a client or user, allied to a deep-seated commitment to understand and deliver what they want.

In practical terms, however, there are a number of qualities common to all outstanding teams. There are seven key aspects to a team's functioning, which are covered in the following sections.

Negotiating success criteria

Teams seldom specify their own success criteria. These usually come from a number of external sources, both inside and outside the organization. They need to map out who expects results from them and what it is that they would want.

Who is the client?

A systems development team in a life assurance company had a number of customers to satisfy. The board as sponsors of the project had definite expectations about cost and timing. The sales forces wanted the system to be able to provide specific information within certain time-frames to their customers. The head of systems wanted compatibility and uniformity with other systems. What they all forgot was the users, that is, those clerks who were going to make the system work for the company! It is very important to ensure that a team considers all the different people they need to satisfy their differing requirements and expectations.

What are they looking for?

Many people find it difficult to express what they need, and many teams find it equally difficult to be precise about what they are trying to achieve. However, the greater the clarity and understanding the greater the chances of success. Some of the ways in which this clarity of purpose can be achieved are as follows:

1 Help the team to use good open questions to draw information out of clients. Some useful ones include:
   a) What *must* we do?
   b) What must we not do?
   c) If we were to satisfy your most outrageous hopes, what would we be doing?
2 Ask the team to suggest a range of alternative approaches from the conservative to the way out. Then suggest that they ask clients to list systematically what they like and dislike about these. This helps both client and team to be much more specific.
3 Distinguish hard (tangible, quantitative) criteria and soft (intangible, qualitative) criteria. Most teams concentrate on the former because they are easier to specify, but clients and sponsors make their judgements on both.

TEAMS AND THE ORGANIZATION

Keeping success criteria in sight

Once teams are involved in their tasks it is very easy for them to lose sight of what they are really trying to achieve. First, make sure that all the team fully understand all the subtleties of what is expected of the team. Second, make sure that they constantly remind themselves of the key question: what are we trying to achieve and for whom?

Managing the outside

A design team in an engineering consultancy was bemoaning the fact that it could never get prints of drawings done when they were needed and that the woman in charge of the print room was always uncooperative. Eventually they realized that they always made demands on her at the last moment, and had never thought about the conflicting priorities that she faced.

They cannot go it alone

Teams never have all the resources that they need. They are frequently dependent on other departments, external specialists, subcontractors, consultants and even their clients for help and information. Some teams may need help to locate and make contact with external resources (known as the invisible team).

Tangible and intangible resources

Most teams will seek the tangible resources such as money, people, materials and information that they require. What they may ignore are the intangible resources of support, commitment, protection and clout that they need, as well as resistance or ignorance in others.

In particular, a team should be coached to anticipate the opportunities and problems presented by the invisible team. These key outsiders should be involved at an early stage. The team should prepare the ground, cultivating positive relationships, and above all motivating them to want to help the team achieve its purpose.

Planning the 'what'

It is surprising how many teams launch themselves into a task without defining the problems adequately, evaluating alternatives or developing a coherent plan to guide their efforts.

Make sure they do some planning together

We have found that it is not so much a team's plan that is fundamental to success, but rather how they go about the process of planning. Above all, it is essential that all team members develop a clear and shared understanding of the 'big picture', that is, the broad plan to be taken by the team with key time, role and cost milestones. These factors provide important and frequent targets for achievement. If it is a small team, the best way to do this is to have everyone involved in developing the plan, thus ensuring that it is both realistic and believed in. In a larger team, beware of the leader or planner who wants to prepare a plan for the team in isolation. Each level should plan their own work in detail within the big picture.

In predictable situations, where the team has considerable experience, the plan can be prepared at the beginning and the team can reasonably expect to keep to it. However, in more ambiguous situations where there are many unknowns, you should encourage a different approach. Do not let the team spend too much time trying to plan detail. Encourage them instead to go and find out by doing, and aim to bring the information back quickly to use in more informed planning. In short, do not let a team waste time on trying to plan the unplannable. Equally, do not allow a plan to become a straitjacket when the situation has clearly changed. The outstanding team is one that does plan, but can also adapt and improve a plan as it learns and discovers better ways of doing things.

Leading a team

A big food firm promoted one of their best scientists to lead an important new research team. He rapidly discovered that he was out of his depth, as the work and the team disintegrated about him. An alert personnel manager understood his predicament and realized where the company, not the scientist, had gone wrong.

Choosing team leaders

Effective team leaders will have a record of success in their own specialism, combined with a broader technical view of how different specialisms integrate. Equally, they should be known and respected within the organization. Leaders like this have a head start when it comes to negotiating success criteria and resources with the team's sponsor, resource providers or users. However, specialist achievement and credibility is insufficient in the leader role; for this role contenders should also have demonstrated ability to inspire and motivate others towards a goal. They must be able to plan and prioritize their own and other people's work, being able to stand back from detail, monitor progress and anticipate problems before they become serious.

The role of the personnel function is to help identify and then train *59* suitable candidates for these roles and to influence those who make the selection to apply not just technical, but managerial criteria to the process. See Briner, Geddes and Hastings (1990) for a comprehensive guide to selecting and developing such team leaders.

Preparing leaders

The ideal leader is seldom available and any appointment is a compromise. Additionally, more and more organizations are using their more talented specialists to lead teams as an important personal and career development opportunity. Senior management should ensure that team leaders are fully prepared for, and supported in, their new and demanding roles. There is a range of options available:

1   Ensure that each team leader has a sponsor at senior level who is prepared to spend time coaching that leader.
2   Ensure that leaders have regular feedback from senior management, users, service departments and even the outside client about their own and their team's performance.
3   Provide training and development opportunities in skills and knowledge areas that are lacking (having previously helped leaders assess their strengths and weaknesses). Programmes are particularly relevant that look at the human aspects of managing teams and projects, for these are the skills most specialists lack.
4   If feasible, bring a number of team leaders together as a regular support group. Get each to bring a success and a problem to each meeting. Share and analyse the successes, and motivate them to help sort out each other's problems.
5   Suggest to leaders that they run team development workshops with their teams, using either internal or external consultants to help them improve performance.

Team members

A team's members are its life-blood. Senior managers and personnel specialists should be giving thought to how the organization plans its resources to ensure that the team gets the right people for its job.

Getting the right mix

The range of specialist technical knowledge required by team members is dictated by the task. Care should be taken not to define this too narrowly. One new product development team consisted purely of marketing and technical specialists. Their progress was slow and they met tacit resistance from other departments when they made demands of them. Their solution was to diversify the team so that it had representatives of all those parties who had a key role to play at any stage in the process. Therefore they acquired an accountant and a production engineer. They also asked the account executive from their advertising agency to join them regularly. The result was a relatively conventional new product, but one that was manufactured and packaged in a revolutionary new way, and to which the whole company became involved and committed.

Membership qualities

In addition to their technical skills, however, members should be good teamworkers. Ideally, they are people who can accept leadership and direc-tion – which does not mean that they should be passive and compliant individuals. On the contrary, personnel specialists should be looking out for individuals who have the confidence to contribute actively and take a share of the responsibility within a team. They need to be active followers. They should also be people who are not so blinkered in their own specialism that they cannot appreciate the contributions of other specialists. But, perhaps most important of all, team members should have a fundamental commitment to quality of performance not only in technical terms but also in terms of being sensitive to the needs of clients, the leader, fellow members and the rest of the organization. They should also be reliable in meeting targets and deadlines and be honest when facing problems.

The team together

Everyone has their ultimate story about boredom, wasted time and lack of results from badly planned and badly run meetings. For those experienced in meetings it is easy to forget that it is a skill that requires learning, and one that many specialists have little experience of until they suddenly find themselves in a team. Nor should it be just the leader who develops the skills; no team can function fully unless all members share the basic disci-pline needed to work effectively together. The organization should ensure that teams receive this basic training, and that they actually do use the knowledge. A few informal questions to team members after a meeting will soon establish whether they practise what they preach.

Another simple technique is to ask a team to end each meeting with a simple review of how effectively they have worked. Team leaders or per-sonnel specialists can give them the following checklist for discussion:

- Are agenda, discussion notes, and information circulated in advance for people to digest?
- What are we trying to achieve as a result of this meeting?
- Given what we have on the agenda, how much time do we need for each item and which is the most important?
- Do people listen, summarize, clarify and demonstrate interest and attentiveness to others?

- Do people get sidetracked away from the particular agenda item without realizing?
- Does the team use the full skills and diversity present, or do just a few people dominate?
- Do they search for better alternatives or just grab the first idea at face value?
- Is conflict ignored, smoothed over or used positively as a source of ideas and energy? Do they have ways of resolving conflicts? Can they compromise?
- Do members ever make observations about how the meeting is going or ask to stop the discussion momentarily to discover how best to proceed on a problem?
- At the end of the meeting, do the team members ask for commitment from each person to produce specific actions by particular times?

The team apart

A group of companies formed a purchasing team from buyers in its five divisions spread round the country. The team met for a day every three months. Little seemed to happen in between meetings and each meeting appeared to go over the same ground as before. In the end the team was disbanded on the grounds that no area for significant cost saving had been identified.

This is an extreme example. But it is true that all teams spend relatively little time actually working *together*. It is also true that most of the problems occur when the team disperses between meetings. The problems are exacerbated when team members work on different floors, in different buildings, on different sites or even in different countries.

Keeping it together

The paradox of the team apart is that it merely highlights the importance of the team coming together. If you survey teams in your organization that seldom get together, you may find that they lack identity, the 'we-feeling' that is so important to a good team. The organization should be encouraging these dispersed teams to meet regularly, not just to work but to spend social and leisure time together to build the bonds. One highly dispersed team we know found they have had to come together at least every six weeks just to keep all their efforts on track. They used to rotate their meetings round the different sites and always met the evening prior to their meeting with a social event organized by the local host. The personnel or human relations department can influence members to come together through its ability to organize company conferences, briefing sessions and training courses.

Out of sight – but not out of mind

It is a frequent complaint of people in distant sites that they are ignored and forgotten by the centre. This is a direct challenge to the leader. The leader often has great difficulty in visiting and staying in touch regularly. Human relations or personnel department members can help by visiting, staying in regular contact and ensuring that all housekeeping issues (which often assume greater importance at a distance) get speedily sorted. Personnel can, in fact, become an extra pair of eyes and ears for the team apart, being aware of what is happening and, in particular, looking out for any early warning signals that things might be going wrong in the human system.

Communication, communication and more communication

Outstanding teams think hard about how they are going to preserve their sense of urgency and identity when they are working apart. They will develop formal methods such as regular reports, meetings and circulation lists. Subgroups within the team that are perhaps not too far from each other will agree to meet in between formal meetings. Members will talk frequently on the telephone and the leader in particular will act as central communications for disseminating up-to-date information to those who need it.

The growing power of information technology to link distant sites has important implications for a company's communications policies. It can make a dramatic difference to helping the 'team apart' to stay in touch.

DEALING WITH CONSULTANTS

In many cases the organization will lack the experience of high-performing teams, their development and the multiple ways in which teams can be used to help transform the organization. In these circumstances an internal or external consultant, with the necessary experience and skills, has an important role to play. Consultants will work directly with senior management, personnel department, service departments and teams.

The consultants' first role is to take the broader view, reviewing team-working within the organization and agreeing action as necessary to improve it. Their second role is to work on the ground in a training, development or consultancy role with senior management sponsors, leaders and members of their teams to help them improve their performance. Senior management and personnel departments have a leading role in assessing and selecting consultants for projects of this nature. Here are some of the considerations to test out:

1 *Find out if they are results-oriented* Sometimes consultants in this area are only interested in group process and relationships as an end in 63

themselves and are neither sufficiently performance-oriented, nor interested in the real work issues facing teams and organizations.

2 *Test them out on senior management to assess their credibility* Senior management must feel comfortable with them because much of the consultants' role is to influence them in their role as sponsors.

3 *Check that they can work on the team's external relationships and not only on its internal workings* If they only work on the team's internal functioning they are missing important factors that affect a team's performance.

4 *Assess their flexibility and realism* Do they just offer a standard package, questionnaire or workshop? This is unlikely to have a real impact in helping teams with actual performance issues or create the conditions for teamworking success within your organization.

5 *Can they also work with leaders and members on an individual basis?* Do they have good counselling skills and sensitivity to help individuals improve their personal contribution?

6 *Would they be prepared to call a halt?* Consultants are employed to use their professional experience and judgement in order to help their clients' teamworking projects to succeed. If the consultants find that some of the ground has not been properly prepared, or if insufficient support or investment is forthcoming to make it work, then they must confront those issues with their client and sponsors. The motivation is twofold. First, they do not want their client and all the others in the organization to waste time, energy and money only to fail or at best achieve mediocre results. Second, they themselves like to be associated with success not failure.

CONCLUSION

Creating the teamworking organization that is able to mobilize the talents of all its people in order to adapt fast and solve complex problems is one of the basic management challenges. When successful, the results are spectacular, but no organization should be under any illusion about the investment of time and money needed to make it work.

RECOMMENDED READING

Belbin, R.M., *Management Teams – Why they Succeed or Fail*, Heinemann, London, 1981. A very useful look at the different roles that an effective team needs.

Briner, W., Geddes, M., and Hastings, C., *Project Leadership*, Gower, Aldershot, 1990. A practical book on the neglected role of project leaders in organizations. It also gives more insight into the nature of the teamworking organization.

64 Francis, D. and Young, D., *Improving Work Groups: A Practical Manual for*

Team Building, University Associates Inc., San Diego, 1979. Just what it says – a practical manual of 'do it yourself' team building exercises.

Hastings, C., Bixby, P. and Chaudhry-Lawton, R., *The Superteam Solution: Successful Teamworking in Organisations*, Gower, Aldershot, 1986. A more extended treatment of the ideas described in this chapter, with many examples and suggestions for performance improvement. Also has case studies of the different ways that improved teamworking can contribute to organizational performance. Readable.

Moss Kanter, R., *The Change Masters*, George Allen & Unwin, London, 1984. A heavyweight study of corporate entrepreneurs at work. Especially good on how to 'manage the outside'. Good insights, but needs patience.

Peters, T.J. and Waterman, R.H., *In Search of Excellence*, Harper & Row, New York, 1982. A modern management classic that is very readable. In particular, demonstrates the crucial contribution of multi-disciplinary teams in successful USA companies.

5   Organizing for project work

Dennis Lock

There are many definitions of 'project' but for the purpose of this chapter I will assume that a project is any venture which requires strategic and tactical planning, and which needs resources to fulfil objectives that the organization has agreed with a customer. Usually the customer is an external buyer but, in internal management projects, the customer is the corporate body itself.

Projects do not always have the benefit of the best possible organization. Many project managers are given little or no authority to set up or change the organization structure in which they are expected to work. Yet the organization of people and the communications between them are recognized as key factors in the success of any project.

BACKGROUND

Projects and their organizations are as old as human civilizations. When the principal work effort of our ancestors was concentrated on peasant farming, local crafts and fighting, formally structured organizations were obviously not widespread. One area in which they might have been found was in military fighting units, where discipline and a clear command structure were essential. Military organizations were not always directed at fighting, however. Young (1993) gives an example of a Chinese army bridge-building battalion which seems unremarkable today as a project organization until we notice its date (Ming dynasty, 1368–1644).

This chapter is concerned with team structures for modern industrial and management projects. Modern projects differ in many ways from those of olden times. One of the greatest of these differences is our concern for making the best use of people who, far from being considered cheap and expendable, are now expensive to employ and expect proper consideration for their welfare and safety.

Modern projects demand a far greater proportion of people with technical and professional skills – people who are able to think for themselves and will be expected to do so. The authoritarian military style of 'command and obey without question' has become inappropriate, and we have to look elsewhere for motivators that will inspire people to work hard and creatively for project success. Some of these motivators are bound to be dependent on the particular organization structure.

ORGANIZATION CHARTS

Much of the argument that follows is made with reference to various organization charts (sometimes called organigrams). Organigrams cannot show every organizational intricacy or nuance. They are nonetheless very useful devices. The charts used to illustrate this chapter obey the usual conventions, which are as follows:

1　Each rectangle on a chart represents a job title or departmental grouping in the organization.
2　Job titles or function names are used rather than individuals' actual names. This approach is considered sensible because of the following factors:
  • Stability and long-term usefulness of the chart. In a stable and successful organization, job titles tend to remain fairly constant, but the names of people filling those jobs are more likely to change through promotions, staff transfers and people joining or resigning.
  • The use of job titles better explains the organization and allows easier analysis of the functions and their relationships.
3　Unbroken lines drawn between different job holders indicate the following:
  • Direct lines of command from top to bottom
  • Communication feedback in the reverse direction.
4　Broken lines show principal lines of communication where no lines of direct command exist.

Status

In general those with the highest status or authority are placed at the top of the chart with the most junior members at the lowest level. The charts illustrating this chapter follow this rule approximately.

This arrangement can lead to resentment in those individuals who find that the levels to which their jobs are assigned on the chart do not accord with their perceived idea of their own status. It is often prudent to avoid such disagreements by printing a disclaimer on the chart to the effect that 'levels do not necessarily denote status'. At least one company tries to circumvent this problem by using circular charts, drawn so that there is no top position.

LINE AND FUNCTION MANUFACTURING ORGANIZATION

The principle of the line and function organization structure is shown in Figure 5.1, which some readers will recognize as the management structure typical in many medium- and larger-sized conventional manufacturing companies. I am using 'conventional' here to describe organizations that were common around the middle of the twentieth-century, just before the explosion of electronic technology and the introduction of total quality management.

The organization has some departments directly in the line of command for carrying out actual manufacture, while other departments (such as the accounting groups under the financial director) provide essential functional support.

No doubt there are still many factories organized along the general pattern of the illustration, although a few features of our example might now be considered out of date or inappropriate. These anachronisms have been introduced into Figure 5.1 deliberately as discussion points. In particular:

- The personnel manager would now more likely be known as the human resources manager, emphasizing today's greater appreciation of the value of people.
- The inspection function would probably be headed by a quality manager reporting directly to senior management, independently of the manufacturing or engineering managers. Reliance on achieving quality is now placed more on the skill and commitment of individual workpeople instead of on attempts by inspectors to search for and 'inspect out' nonconformances.
- An information technology or computing group might be added, under its own manager.

Line and function organizations operate strictly within departmental boundaries. Thus the engineering director is responsible for the design and development of new products, leaving the works director to concentrate on the production aspects of the business.

The organization might work very well for routine production, in which manufacturing takes place continuously or in large batches on products of relatively stable design. The manufacturing group might, for example, develop successfully as a stable self-contained team, taking pride in both the quality and quantity of its output.

Projects in line and function organizations

A project conducted in a line and function organization is less likely to fare well than routine operations. It is certain to be handicapped from the start by the formal compartmentation caused by the top-down lines of command. Departmental managers generally have no direct responsibility (and perhaps

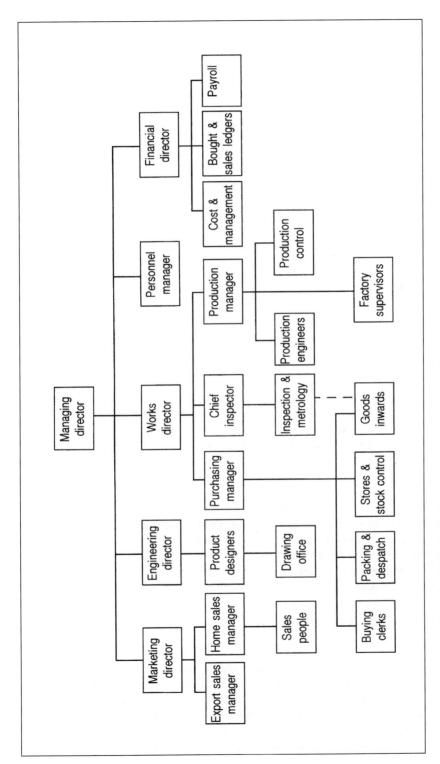

Figure 5.1 Typical organization of a manufacturing company, mid-20th century

little concern) for activities lying outside their own departments. There is no specific provision for cross-boundary communication, other than on a formal basis (such as the exchange of drawings, specifications or memoranda).

Although each function might individually be expertly managed and staffed with competent people, there is no one specifically given responsibility for planning and coordinating the project itself; no one to see that the project flows smoothly through all stages of its cycle; no one to ensure that the demands of routine production will not be allowed to take priority over critical project tasks. No one is charged specifically with ensuring that the project is a success. In other words, there is no holistic management approach to the project. Any idea of promoting a team spirit in which the project objectives are uppermost is difficult, if not impossible to fulfil.

PROJECT TEAMS

The pure project team is the extreme alternative to the functional matrix. In the pure project team organization (an example of which is shown in Figure 5.2) the project manager is given supreme authority. Those working on the project are assigned to the team until all their tasks have been completed. They are collectively responsible only to the project manner.

Advantages

A well-defined project team is a good motivator, at least while the project is in its most active phase. People identify with the project as their main work purpose rather than with their specialist function. Communications between the different skills or functional groups should be excellent. Rigid compartmentalization is actively discouraged in favour of complete cross-functional communication and working together. There is unity of command (no one has more than one boss).

A project team is the easiest type of organization for the project manager to lead. If competently staffed, it is excellent for getting results in the short term. The team can be given a project 'war room', which is an office or conference room where plans, progress charts and the like can be permanently displayed and where *ad hoc* discussions or more formal meetings can easily be organized.

Disadvantages of project teams

In a pure project team, every specialist function has to be represented by at least one full-time member, even where the amount of work is not sufficient to keep that function fully employed throughout the active life of the project. A team can, therefore, be extravagant in its demands for staff and lead to inefficient and inflexible use of manpower resources.

A project team is an unstable organization, in the sense that its life can be only as long as that of the active phase of the project. When the end of

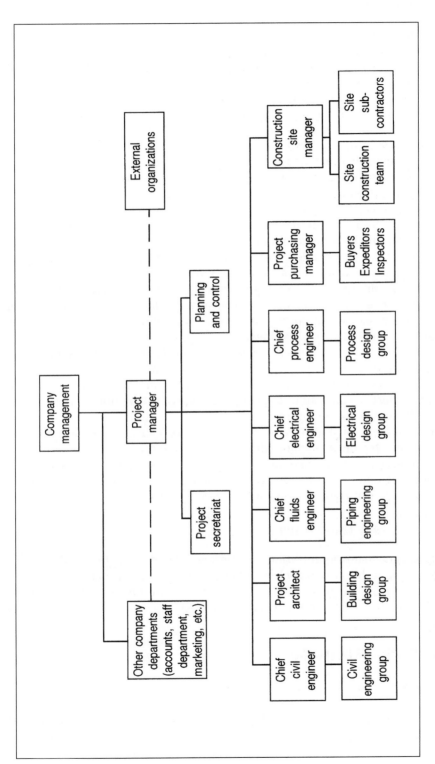

Figure 5.2 Team for a large project

the project is in sight, members of the team might become unsettled when they start to contemplate their unknown fate after the project has ended.

When considering any option within an organization structure it is always good practice to imagine yourself as a person working within it. In the project team you will have a firm sense of purpose as far as the project goes, you will feel part of the team and you will have easy access to everyone else in the team. All work is connected directly with the project and there are no distractions. If, however, you are a specialist in your technological field you might feel isolated when you need a second opinion or a source of expert information – all things that would have been available to you when working in a group of your own speciality within a functional organization.

Now, still imagining yourself as a member of the organization, consider your longer-term career development as a technology specialist. In the project team there is no continuity for your development. When the project ends, the team is disbanded. That, coupled with the fact that your manager is unlikely to understand your own technology specialization, is not likely to lead to fair appraisals of your work performance. Further, the team structure does not create promotional advancement status levels within your chosen specialization: if you are (for example) an electrical engineer there is no chief electrical engineer's position to aspire to.

If the project is for an external customer, long-term customer service can suffer if the original project was built using a team organization. Once the team has been disbanded, there is no natural home in which the focused project expertise can reside should operational or other support be required by the customer in the future.

This problem of finite team life has a more acute aspect for projects that require technical support during construction at a remote site or for commissioning on a customer's premises. These activities take place towards the end of the average project's active life, when the team is likely to have been run right down or actually disbanded.

Indications for using a team

Pure project team organization can be considered as a good solution for large projects that are expected to have long duration. It can also be used very effectively in 'rescue operations' where, for one of many possible reasons, high priority and activity are needed to get an ailing project back on course.

MATRIX ORGANIZATIONS

The matrix concept

The matrix is an attempt to combine the best features of a line and function organization with those of the project team. The matrix can take many
forms.

All matrix organizations have the advantage of relative organizational stability (so far as any organization can be considered stable). The same management structure and the same people can remain in place to carry out one project after another and (in most cases) with the capability of dealing with several projects at the same time. The staff report to their relative functional managers, and the stable organization allows them to have some idea of their longer-term career prospects.

Functional matrix

The functional matrix is seen in companies that, accustomed only to routine production activities, attempt their first or second complex multifunction project. Recognizing the shortcomings of their line and function organization (possibly from bitter experience with an unsuccessful first project) they appoint a coordinator to plan and progress the new project through the original organization. A functional matrix is shown in Figure 5.3.

Although the appointment of a project coordinator is a big step in the right direction, the functional matrix is not usually the best way to ensure effective project management. Project coordinators (they might be called project managers or project leaders) working in such conditions are usually given very little or no line authority. They have to work principally as coordinators and must use their persuasive powers to gain the necessary cooperation from managers in the line.

The project coordinator's task in a functional matrix is difficult and not always successful. Managers and workpeople in the line might see project tasks as an unwelcome complication and interference with their day to day production activities and their attempts to meet production targets. The coordinator's role is dependent on the goodwill of line managers, which is essential for several reasons:

1 To provide information needed for planning and estimating.
2 To accept commitment to those plans and estimates.
3 To work according to the project specifications and plans, and to give priority where necessary to critical project tasks at the expense of meeting routine production targets or other work which is considered more attractive.

In the absence of such cooperation the coordinator can always attempt to call down the wrath of more senior management on the erring line managers, but this is likely to breed resentment and is hardly a recipe for long-term cooperation and teamwork.

Project services matrix

Figure 5.4 depicts an organization structure which I call a project services matrix. It is very similar in concept and operation to the functional matrix,   *73*

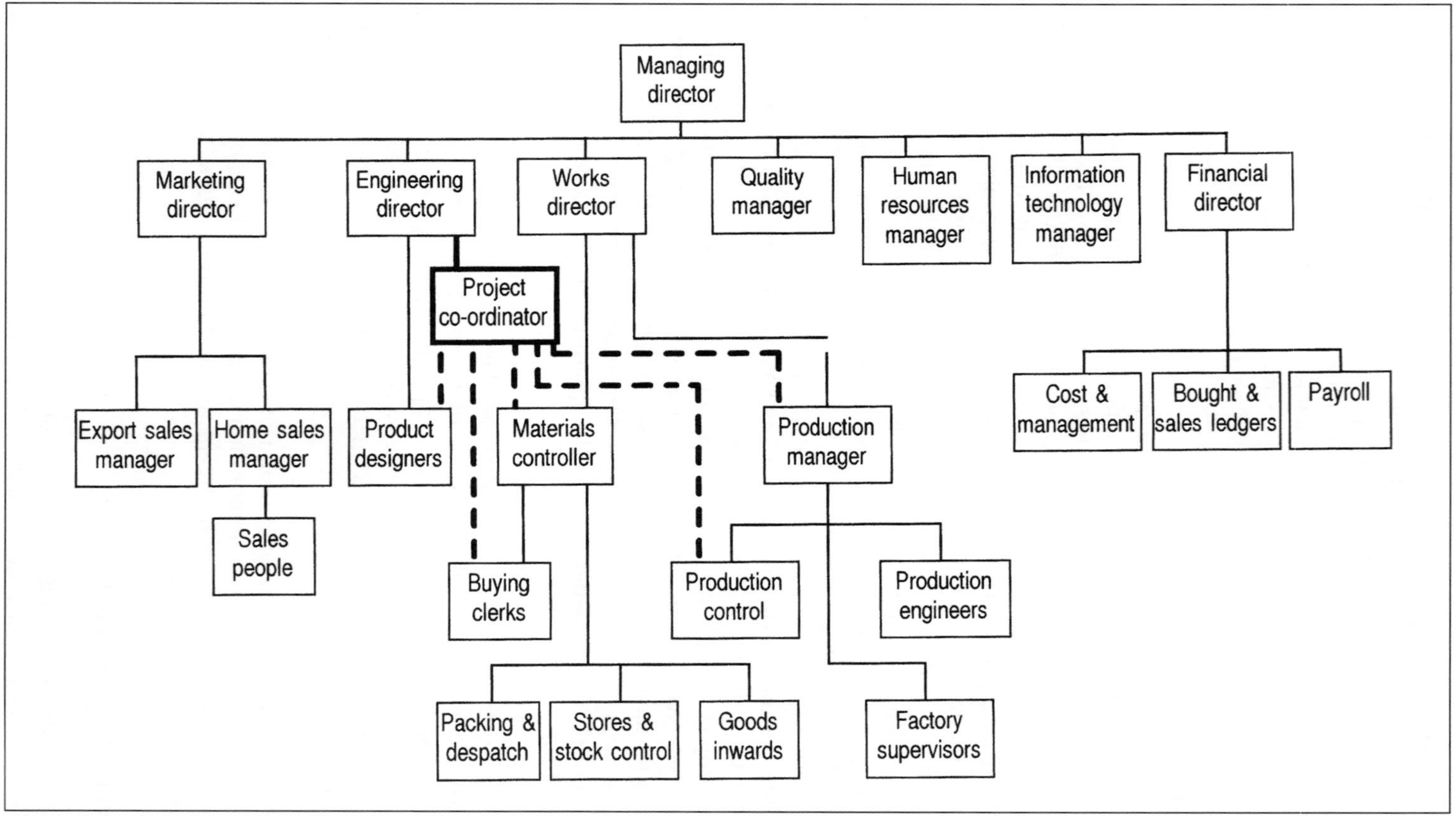

Figure 5.3 Functional matrix

just described, except that it is set up to cope with several simultaneous projects rather than with a single project. The project coordinator's role has been taken over in the example illustrated by a project services group, whose duties include estimating, planning and progressing all projects handled by the company.

In the example shown in Figure 5.4 the project services manager is shown reporting to the engineering director. It is quite usual for the engineering department to assume responsibility for projects where no independent project manager has been appointed. The engineering function is, perhaps, the logical choice under such circumstances for industrial projects: it is within that function that the overall project concept must be understood and developed through all its stages from the creation of working drawings and specifications into actual project fulfilment.

Project services groups can exist also in many other forms of the matrix, where they can perform a supporting role in estimating, planning, cost control and progressing to separately appointed project managers.

Balanced matrix

In the balanced matrix, power is shared equally between an appointed project manager and the functional managers. This means that staff report not only to their departmental function manager, but also to the current project manager. This arrangement can obviously result in conflict if the functional and project managers disagree on any work aspect, and can be confusing or upsetting for individual members of the staff.

An example of a balanced matrix is shown in Figure 5.5. This example shows an organization for handling several projects at the same time, but the arrangement can be adapted for any number of projects from one upwards.

A mistake often made by writers and students is to draw the lines of the matrix across all company functions. This, however, rarely takes place in practice. In Figure 5.5 note that the matrix does not include functions that should more rightly be regarded as departments supplying a general or common service, that is, departments that are purely administrative and in which no direct project activity takes place. The role of the purchasing department is debatable in this context and might be included within the matrix in some organizations where a high degree of specialist project purchasing is involved.

The organigram of Figure 5.5 attempts, within the limitations of the conventional notation, to illustrate the power-sharing partnership between the project managers and the departmental (functional) managers. Typically, all the functional managers and the project managers would report directly to higher management.

Some authorities would emphasize the principle of equally shared management in the balanced matrix by rotating the whole of the organigram through 45 degrees, so that neither the project managers nor the functional managers are in the superior position at the top. Figure 5.6 demonstrates this idea.   *75*

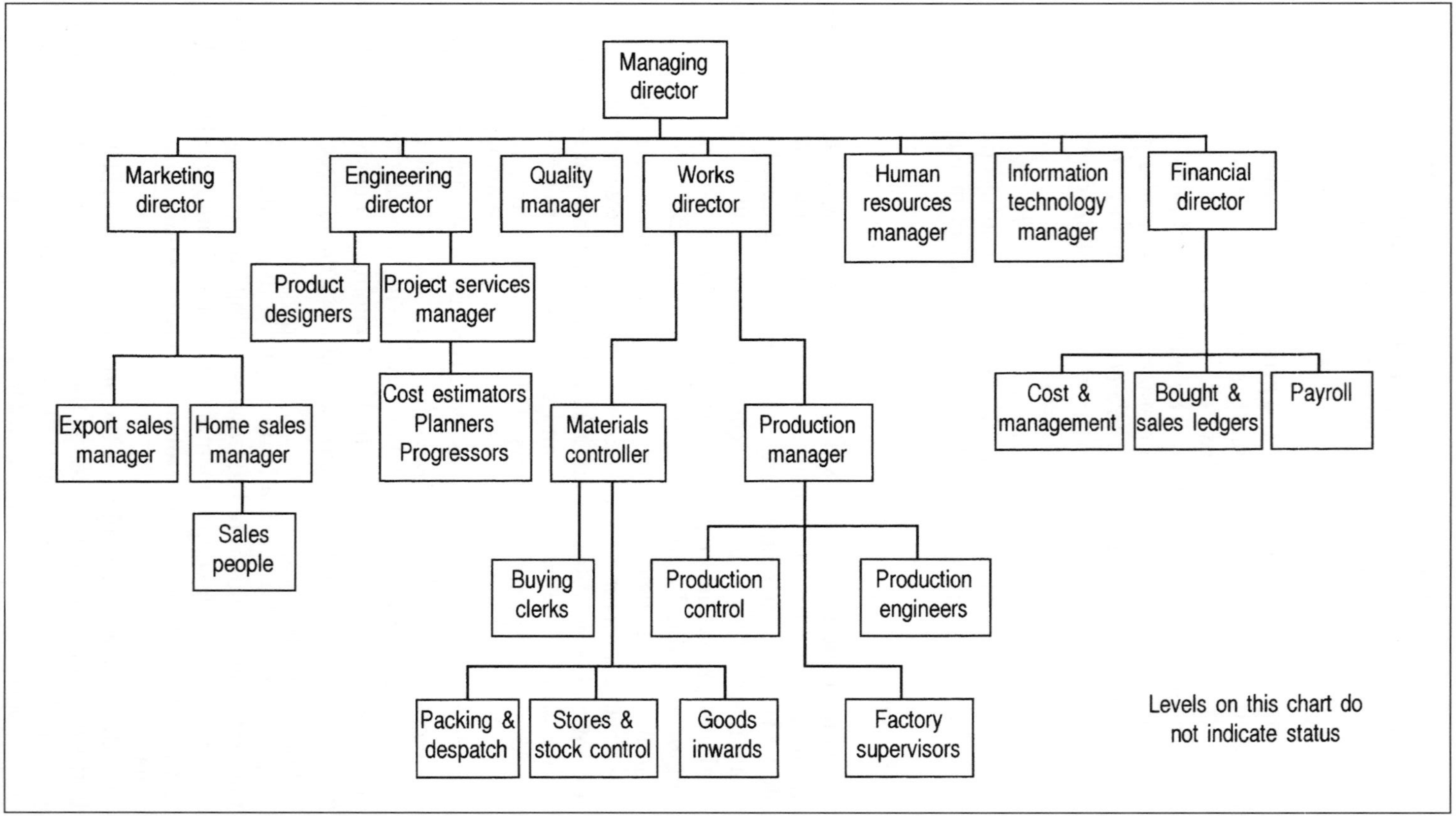

Figure 5.4 Project services matrix

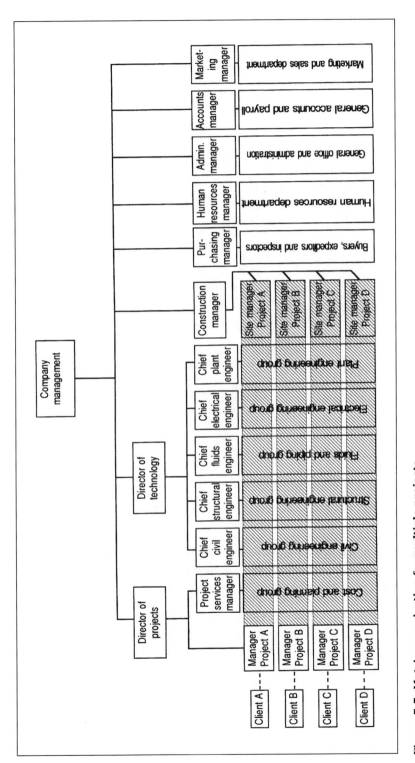

Figure 5.5 Matrix organization for multiple projects
Note: This organigram could represent a balanced, strong or project matrix.

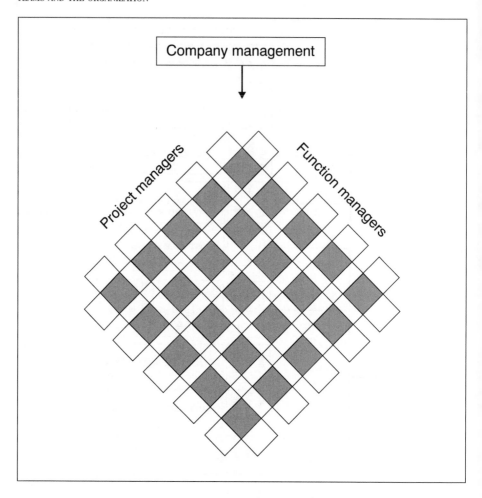

Figure 5.6 Organigram for a perfectly balanced matrix

People talk about creating a project team spirit across the matrix, but this is difficult to achieve in a balanced matrix, where the functions themselves are more likely to operate as introspective specialist teams.

Try, once again, using your imagination to picture yourself working as a specialist within one of the functional groups in a balanced matrix. You might well experience the well-being of feeling to be part of a team, but that team would be the specialist team of your function and not a team dedicated to the needs of the project. Technically, however, you would be well served, working for a group or departmental manager who is qualified and experienced in your own special discipline and to whom you can turn for professional advice. Your working environment is with others of your own specialization, so that you will have ready access to a common bank of knowledge, catalogues, standards and other specialist information.

78   You can expect to have your performance reviewed at the appropriate intervals by your regular boss, who witnesses your progress over several years in the stable organization and speaks your own specialist technical language. There is one potentially serious problem, however, which is that you can face interference on an almost daily basis from one or more project managers, who are empowered by their status to follow up your work and criticize your progress. On some occasions you might receive conflicting instructions from your group head and from a project manager.

Comparison of the balanced matrix organization with the project team alternative

Figure 5.7 is a concise comparison of the attributes that can be expected from using either a project team or a balanced matrix organization.

Variations of the balanced matrix

In a *strong matrix* the same organizational pattern applies as that given in Figure 5.5, but the balance of power is shifted in favour of the project manager. This gives the project manager the power and right to overrule any functional group manager in terms of work allocation, priority and progress. It would be a very unwise project manager, however, who attempted to use such power to countermand functional group managers in quality or reliability aspects of work that require expertise in the particular specialization.

When this shift of power is taken to its limit, the *project matrix* is reached, in which functional managers are required to assign designated members of their departments to the project manager's command for as long as necessary. The individuals concerned will probably remain physically within their specialist group office but will be responsible primarily to the project manager. This type of organization has many of the advantages usually associated with the pure project team (such as high team motivation and close communications) but allows more flexibility in deploying staff. It is also more likely to preserve quality of engineering design because, although assigned to the project, individual engineering staff still have direct access for professional guidance within their specialist disciplines to their functional managers.

Limitations of conventional organigram notation mean that charts cannot easily be made to show subtle gradations in power between project and functional managers. The organigram in Figure 5.5 is, therefore, valid for the strong and project matrix as well as for the balanced matrix.

Contract matrix

Large projects are often carried out on behalf of companies that have no expertise at all in the work needed to plan and carry the project through to *79*

Characteristic	Organization indicated	
	Team	Matrix
Maximum authority and freedom of action for the project manager	✓	
Clear lines of command. No person answering to two or more managers	✓	
Maximum motivation of staff and commitment to meet project targets	✓	
Best internal project communications	✓	
Highest degree of information and physical security:		
● by enclosing project work in a secure area	✓	
● by restricting the total number of staff who need to know details of the projects	✓	
Best sharing and deployment of rare professional skills throughout several projects		✓
Suitable for large project of long duration	✓	
Suitable for crisis or rescue action for a project that is in serious trouble (task force approach)	✓	
Organization with several simultaneous projects		✓
One-off project in remote or self-contained area	✓	
Design excellence through concentration of expertise in each specialist discipline		✓
Best long-term career prospect and motivation for individuals:		
● by creating a hierarchy of senior job positions to which people can aspire within their specialist discipline		✓
● through relative organizational stability, offering continuous improvement, learning and progression		✓
● through a stable command structure that allows time for fair appraisals of individual performance		✓
● performance appraisals conducted by managers from the individual's own specialist discipline		✓
Best post-design technical support to commissioning and construction team		✓
Post-project support to customers		✓
Long-term accumulation of expertise and retained information for each specialist discipline, of benefit to future projects		✓

Figure 5.7   Project team compared with balanced matrix organization

completion. A common example is for construction projects, where a company (the project owner) with no construction experience whatever decides that it needs new, specially built accommodation for its normal operations.

Such companies will obviously seek professional advice. They might start by consulting an architect but, for the full construction project, many com-
80   panies will engage a managing contractor. The managing contractor is likely

to be a specialist organization which is very experienced in construction projects and which can carry out all the main tasks from planning and design through to the execution of construction and building commissioning.

Organizations for construction projects can take a very wide variety of forms but Figure 5.8 shows a possible organization for a construction project of the type just described. Some people would call this organization a 'contract matrix'. In the version shown, the managing contractor acts as project manager as well as employing all building workers (in this case using subcontractors) and other participants on behalf of the project owner.

The contract matrix shown in Figure 5.8 illustrates a number of interesting points. Note that several sub-organizations within the overall project have their own project managers. This is logical and necessary because, in a large project, portions of work allocated to subcontractors and the suppliers of substantial items of equipment constitute sizeable projects in their own right. Each, therefore, is a sub-project of the main project and each needs proper management to satisfy its own objectives. All the sub-project managers must, of course, be responsible to and be coordinated by the managing contractor's project manager.

The project owner (the managing contractor's client) has funded the project with bank help. A bank will usually only advance substantial sums against some guarantee that the project will be a success, and that monies paid out to subcontractors and others are in respect of work properly executed. In Figure 5.8, the bank has insisted on the project owner finding a guarantor who will offset any risk to the bank.

The guarantor, in turn, has sought protection in the form of an independent professional consulting engineer, who is able and suitably qualified to verify that design work satisfies the terms of contract in respect of quality and the amount of work claimed for by the managing contractor when each stage payment becomes due. When the project design has advanced to the point where the project enters its construction phase, this verification role will be underpinned by quantity surveyors who can measure the work actually done on the project site.

HYBRID ORGANIZATIONS

Sometimes companies adopt the solution of a hybrid organization, operating a matrix organization in general, but with teams set up for certain projects when the need arises. It might typically be arranged principally as a matrix, such as that shown in Figure 5.5, with specialist groups under their respective highly-qualified and experienced chief engineers. The project management group contains project managers and project engineers who draw on the resources of the specialist groups for the skilled engineering and expert advice needed for most projects in typical matrix fashion.

If, however, a project should arise which is predominantly within one of the specialist skills, the company might decide to appoint a project manager   *81*

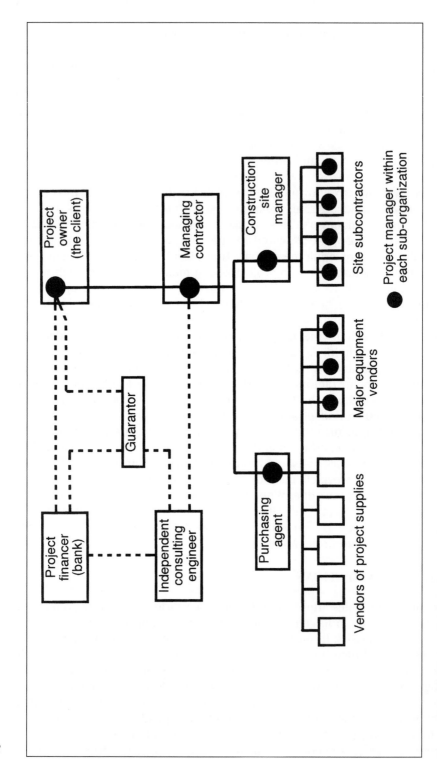

Figure 5.8 One form of a contract matrix

Project owner (the client)

Managing contractor

Construction site manager

Site subcontractors

● Project manager within each sub-organization

●

Guarantor

Major equipment vendors

Purchasing agent

Vendors of project supplies

Project financer (bank)

Independent consulting engineer

from within the relevant specialist group, managing a team contained within the group.

For example, a project to install a new electrical generator in an existing plant might be regarded as a project that could be handled entirely by a team within the electrical department. Similarly, a land reclamation project might be assigned wholly to the civil engineering group, who would appoint a project manager and form their own small team.

MORE COMPLEX VARIATIONS

Most of the organizations described in this chapter are simple, pure examples of their various types. In real life, however, every company has its own ideas about how to organize itself and its work. It is highly probable that if three companies doing similar work could be compared, three different organization structures would be found. Further, all three companies might be equally successful, implying that it is not always possible to say with determination or accuracy that there is one best organization solution.

For very large projects several companies might agree to share the technical problems, expense and risk by forming a consortium or joint venture company. This obviously adds complication to the organization. For example, each significant sub-organization within the main structure would appoint a project manager to manage its own activities. The project organization, therefore, contains more than one project manager. Although important in simple organizations, when complexity reaches these levels it is even more necessary to define responsibilities without ambiguity and to see that the lines of communication between all the parties are efficiently established and clearly defined.

RESPONSIBILITY MATRIX CHART

The responsibility matrix chart is a notational device for assisting in making decisions about the allocation of project responsibilities to key people. When the decisions have been made and agreed, the chart becomes the tool for communicating those decisions throughout the organization. The principle is illustrated in Figure 5.9.

Some textbooks advise that all project tasks should first be listed in the left-hand column. Then, the argument goes, the primary and secondary responsibility for each task can be indicated in the body of the chart, using appropriate symbols.

Even in quite a small project, however, there might be hundreds, if not thousands, of tasks. Moreover, this list of tasks can be expected to change as the project progresses. Compiling a responsibility chart along those lines must require considerable effort from the senior people who are needed to assign the responsibilities. Yet more effort will be needed to keep the large and complicated chart up to date with changes.

A responsibility matrix should, therefore, be compiled using common- *83*

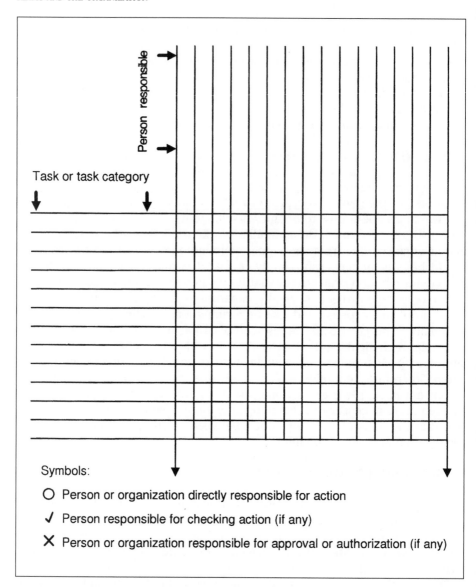

Figure 5.9   Responsibility matrix

sense and discretion. It should be as concise and simple as possible. It is not necessary to list every task. The better course is to list categories or groups of tasks. Consider, for example, the preparation and approval of drawings. It would be unwise to list every drawing. Rather, the compiler should list only each main category of drawing. The drawing tasks for a project requiring thousands of drawings can usually be represented adequately by just a few rows on the matrix, using task description labels similar to the following:

- Design concept schematics and process flowsheets
- Layout drawings
- Wiring drawings
- Piping drawings
- Detail drawings.

The most important symbol used on the matrix will denote the person required to take primary action. Ideally, no task should have more than one primary action symbol: identifying two or more people as being responsible for primary action is a recipe for achieving no action at all.

Other symbols can be chosen to indicate those who need to check or approve the primary action or those who simply need to be informed in reports. Try not to complicate the chart by having too many different types of symbol. In the case of the drawings, the primary symbol would mean the act of making the drawing, and there would be a secondary symbol for checking, plus probably a third symbol to be placed in the column of the manager or customer responsible for drawing approval.

A similar matrix chart is often used to determine how documented information should be distributed throughout an organization. There is no reason why the document distribution matrix and responsibility matrix should not be fused into one chart.

THE PROJECT MANAGER

It would be wrong to leave the subject of project teams and matrixes with no mention of the key figure in such organizations, namely the project manager.

Power, management level and status

The amount of power given to the project manager will depend on whether or not the organization is a team or a matrix and, if a matrix, on the type of matrix. However, all project managers should be given sufficient status in the organization which, in an industrial or commercial company, means a management level at least equivalent to the company's departmental managers. This is important not only for internal communication purposes, but also where the project manager has to deal with external authorities and customers and must, therefore, represent a significant part of the corporate image which the company presents to the outside world.

Personality

The key personal characteristic of the project manager is the ability to motivate people, by whatever means. The typical project participant will appreciate being led by a manager who displays competence, makes clear decisions, gives precise, achievable instructions, delegates well, listens to   *85* and accepts sound advice, is enthusiastic and confident, and thus generally commands respect by example and qualities of leadership. Personality will play a very important part in resolving conflicts, especially those which are likely to arise as a result of conflicting priorities or from the duality of command in most matrixes.

Perception

Other essential characteristics of the project manager can be grouped under the heading of perceptiveness. The project manager must be able to select the salient facts from a set of data or a particular arrangement of circumstances. Most project managers are often presented with information that is incomplete, unduly optimistic, inaccurate or deliberately misleading. The perceptive project manager will spot-check received information and will know what questions to ask to probe its validity.

All project managers of any merit will know the frustration caused not simply by receiving inaccurate information, but also through receiving no information at all. On international projects, in particular, it can be very difficult to obtain reliable and regular reports of cost and progress from distant locations.

The ability to gather and assess relevant data is, therefore, another necessary skill. The project manager must take (and be seen to take) an active interest by visiting those parts of the organization on which project success is dependent. It might be necessary to visit vendors, subcontractors, the customer and a remote construction site at suitable intervals to resolve local disputes, generate enthusiasm, or simply to witness progress at first hand, a process sometimes known as 'management by walkabout'.

Techniques and training

Whatever the project manager's professional background and qualifications, he or she will certainly need to be trained in one or more of the current special project management techniques. In addition to purely technical knowledge, the project manager also needs a general understanding of administrative procedures as they will be applied throughout the project organization.

There is little doubt that the evolution process will continue for project planning and control techniques. The project manager must keep abreast of this development, undergoing training or retraining whenever necessary, and passing this training on to other members of the organization where appropriate.

The project manager must be able to choose and use appropriate techniques, either directly or adapted to suit the project's particular purposes, whenever they are needed. On the other hand, the temptation to impose unsuitable methods on an organization for the sole reason that they represent the height of current fashion must be resisted.

Senior management support

Even the most experienced, competent, enthusiastic and intelligent project manager cannot operate effectively without adequate support and cooperation. This obviously includes the willing cooperation of all staff engaged on the project, but it also includes support from higher management in the organization. The senior executive management must take an active interest in the project, yet delegate authority to the project manager rather than interfere in the management process. Senior management should at least ensure the provision of essential finance, accommodation, facilities, equipment, training, manpower and other resources when they are needed.

CONCLUSION

Some of the more common types of project organization have been described in this chapter. The organization actually chosen should depend on the characteristics of the particular project. In recent years there has been a tendency among some authorities to consider the matrix solution as the universal option, although that view is now less widely held (it has never been held by me). There are occasions when a dedicated team or task force is clearly the appropriate choice. It is not always possible to declare with certainty exactly which is the best organization to suit a given situation. Even where that is possible, it is far from certain that senior management will choose correctly or will be willing to change the structure that already exists.

Under all these conditions, the true project manager is the person who can create and motivate a team for project success, whatever the organization structure imposed.

RECOMMENDED READING

Belbin, R.M., *Management Teams: Why They Succeed or Fail*, Butterworth-Heinemann, Oxford, 1996

Belbin, R.M., *Team Roles at Work*, Butterworth-Heinemann, Oxford, 1996

Harrison, F.L., *Advanced Project Management*, 3rd edn, Gower, Aldershot, 1992

Kliem, R.L. and Ludin, I.S., *The People Side of Project Management*, Gower, Aldershot, 1992

Young, E., 'Organization', in Lock, D. (ed.), *Handbook of Engineering Management*, 2nd edn, Butterworth-Heinemann, Oxford, 1993, pp. 27–52

6 Developing strategic team leaders

Hugh Brawley

The global market place is rapidly changing. New technologies, markets and competition are revolutionizing business relationships. In an attempt to survive, organizations are blurring traditional boundaries in response to a more fluid business environment. Therefore the roles of individuals, teams and leaders have become more and more blurred and ambiguous. Increasingly, organizations will depend on the knowledge worker more than the physical worker for survival. Required are self-reliant, adaptable people who can communicate, cooperate and develop new skills, knowledge and coalitions or partnerships as the market place evolves.

Today, because of the long-term emphasis on the short-term goals of productivity and profit, many organizations have decided to rationalize to remain competitive. This rationalization obliges fewer people to produce more and adapt quickly, though the negative effects of rationalization on people is to move them more deeply into behaviours and limiting beliefs that create shells or compartments which feel safe, unconsciously endangering themselves and the whole organization.

Paradoxically, the pressures which cause rationalization also underline the importance of the contribution people make to an organization; at a time when economic pressures are greatest, to survive organizations need teams to be at their most creative. Therefore, when organizations introduce change programmes, development of team values and beliefs is critical to future success and, more specifically, to the values and beliefs of the people at the top who are leading the change. In order to create sustainable change, the leaders need to understand the complexity of belief change. Change at the level of environment and behaviour is only sustainable if the leaders concerned have also challenged and adapted or confirmed these beliefs. Behaviour is driven by beliefs, so if management say one thing but are seen to do another there can be only incongruence and dissatisfaction as a result.

Senior management's lack of self-awareness and their 'belief' that change can succeed at the level of environment and behaviour only can undermine any organizational change programme.

PEOPLE: THE MISSING ELEMENT

Recent research by Roffey Park (IPD, 1996) found that many organizations are failing to take account of the strains flatter structures impose on people and their motivation.

For a change initiative to succeed, it has to have the buy-in of the people concerned. Their feelings, emotions, beliefs and values have to be part of the change initiative itself; otherwise there will be hindrances, unforeseen problems, and issues not accounted for in the initial plan. The ensuing delays and difficulties cost time and money, and they increase the pressures on managers and individual employees.

Voices of experience are beginning to demand a fresh look at change. My own experience in large manufacturing companies supports the demand for a new and creative leadership model for today's reality. Such a model needs to be designed to 'loosen up' organizations, to enable free and flexible thinking which can be put into practice as part of a wider framework, to move away from the blame culture prevalent in most organizations today.

At the 1997 European Association for Personnel Management conference in Lisbon Thomas Sattelberger, Lufthansa's personnel chief, noted three approaches managers tend to take to change:

- The 'engineering' model – treating people as computer programs that can simply be rewritten
- The 'medicine man' model – force-feeding employees painful medicine
- The 'evangelist' model – urging employees to change by appealing to their better nature.

Arguing that pain is inevitable, Sattelberger noted that Lufthansa was emerging from a period of heavy losses, characterized by bureaucracy, political interference and restrictive work practices. The company's recipe for change included: excluding management consultants, working with the unions, and using middle managers as the 'samurai of change'. At the other end of their change process, two-thirds of the old board members are gone, and all managers are now subjected to 360 degree appraisals.

Norsk-Hydro is trying to ease pressure on employees by helping solve the 'work–family puzzle', according to vice-president Ragnhild Sohlberg. She is looking at teleworking, and ways to focus on results, rather than how hard people appear to work, or how many hours they work.

By the time the penny drops with the boards of many organizations, their people have 'initiative fatigue' and believe they have failed, or are only being pushed from fad to fad, with little understanding. This creates serious levels *89* of stress and illness, not only in employees and their managers, but actually in their organizations as a whole.

For the last 50 years organizations have consistently asked only for intellect and skills from their individual employees and teams. Now they need people's hearts, but don't know how to ask, or how to gain that commitment.

THE NEED FOR A NEW MODEL

If you always do what you've always done, you always get what you always got.

(Alex Barr)

Gary Hamel, in a recent interview, commented:

> The centralised, top-down strategic planning of the sixties and seventies focused on competitive position and winning market share. The new strategy must emphasise transformation, imagination, breaking the rules, and democratising the strategic process.

Hamel quoted Nobel laureate, economist Friedrich Hayek, who argued that practically every individual possesses unique information that can be put to use only with his or her active cooperation. Getting that active cooperation may well turn out to be one of the key managerial issues of the next few decades.

My own experience of developing change leadership in large manufacturing organizations supports these views. The new model needs to be more holistic – linking together thinking and feeling with acting and believing. If the top leaders are not sufficiently involved, it is virtually impossible to impose effective change from below, particularly in a team environment. Real success comes when a critical mass of senior managers begin to understand and trust each other to a greater extent – and hence to understand and trust their people more.

We need to create a process of helping individuals to resolve the personal and organizational issues that have been embedded over time. These issues reduce people's effectiveness and clamp down on their creativity. As a result, people are limited in the contribution they can make to the organization.

To meet the demands of the future, we need to create a questioning attitude towards what we don't know, and may need to know, focusing on how to gain this knowledge, skill or experience. Davies, as cited by Foy (1994), gives a recent example:

> Many years ago I asked an executive responsible for the future development of a very large corporation: 'What do you worry about most in your job?' His answer was startling: 'I worry about what my people don't know they don't know. What they know they don't know, they're able to work on and find an answer to. But they can't do that if they don't know they don't know.' During the past few years many people have come to feel like this executive.

Concern with the human element has to start from the top. The people at the top of most large organizations grow increasingly remote from themselves, as well as from their people, as they are caught up in achieving the results by which top management is measured. They communicate in terms of profit and productivity, and thus don't discern obstacles. Claims that are too optimistic are seen from below as hypocrisy, and hence create cynicism. People at the top need to unblock their own feelings and values. Compliance is not enough. If nothing changes with the top people, by trying to implement change, particularly in a team environment, they actually widen the gap between their perceived and actual values. The hypocrisy gap may be unconscious, but that makes it no less devastating.

Before an organization can change its processes, it needs to change its own beliefs and values. Dilts (1996) offers a model that helps focus on the importance of an individual's perceptions at various levels. These rise, like Maslow's, from a baseline – Dilts calls this the 'environment' level. Progressively, the levels are 'behaviour', 'capability', 'beliefs/values' and 'identity' – with a 'spiritual' level at the very top of the structure. The first five levels are shown in Figure 6.1.

The first triangle shows the amount of system influenced by a change in beliefs and values. The second shows much less system influenced by a change in behaviour. In this scheme of things, for example, issues may arise at any one of these levels, for example:

- *Identity* 'I am not a project manager'
- *Beliefs/values* 'Managing a new project is difficult and time-consuming'
- *Capability* 'I don't know how to manage a project effectively'
- *Behaviour* 'I don't know what to do in this situation'
- *Environment* 'There weren't enough resources to complete the project'

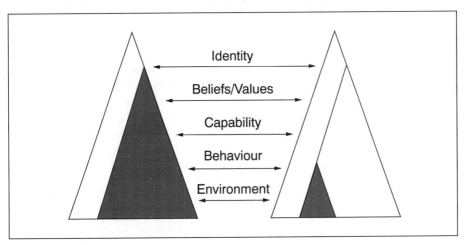

Figure 6.1   Dilts' Logical Levels (1996)

I found this model extremely useful to support practical change pro-grammes in a real company. It gives you a checkpoint, a reminder that all these levels have to be addressed. A change in a person's perceived identity involves a much more pervasive and difficult change (and consequently more risk) than a change at a lower level. It is much easier to change something in the environment, or a specific behaviour, than to change values or beliefs – which are actually necessary to sustain and maximize new behaviours.

Changes in values and beliefs have to be rooted in individual development. This, in turn, needs to be linked to team development – but the team can't develop fully until it has a leader who has gained some team development skills. From the point of view of the team leader, the first step is to under-stand yourself, so you can understand others, so you can build a better team. What are your limiting factors? Organizations are made up of people like you. What stops you walking your talk, believing it, living it? What stops your people?

Warren Bennis (Bennis and Townsend, 1995) once defined leadership as: 'the capacity to create a compelling and plausible vision and to translate that vision into organisational realities'.

A PROGRAMME TO DEVELOP STRATEGIC LEADERSHIP

Personal experience supports this definition. Change has to start with vision, and leaders have to translate the vision into organizational realities. It is not an easy task.

Several years of major change initiatives were not sufficient to bring success to a manufacturing subsidiary of a major aerospace company, employing several thousand people. Supported by leading consultancy organizations, the company tried Kanban, KPS, TQM, MRPII, JIT, lean manu-facturing, and full-scale BPR. It trained all the front-line team leaders, put facilitators into every department, implemented integrated production teams, and manufacturing cells.

Though limited benefits were achieved in most areas, the change initiat-ives were not viewed as a success, either by corporate headquarters or by the local organization and its members. Training had been carried out on the 'hard' systems operational skills. This approach worked well throughout functional layers of the organization, where award-winning training and per-sonal development initiatives had already led to a flexible, well-trained, highly motivated workforce used to the challenges of continuous improvement.

However, this development had largely passed by the very people respons-ible for leading change and making it happen. Far from encompassing the kind of culture essential for continuous improvement on such a scale, they were still operating in a task-oriented fashion, focusing on problems, mis-takes and blame, using a paternalistic, macho-management style. This led to frustration, disillusionment and disinterest, and to front-line leaders asking questions about their 'right' to manage in this new environment.

Furthermore, the macho senior managers were agreeing to market-driven timescales that were aggressive and caused conflict, since there was perceived to be little consultation between management and unions at various stages in the process.

What the site needed was a means of developing leadership skills within its most senior management population to meet these challenges. I developed a long-term modular programme called the 'Business Leaders Programme' (BLP), in partnership with Alex Barr of Addition, a Glasgow-based consultancy that applies business and psychotherapy principles to the people side of business.

Team leaders have to learn for themselves

The programme had to differ from any previous management course the individuals had experienced. It had to impact each person on a personal level, to enable lasting change. The leaders had to learn for themselves that successful change depended on people. They had to learn about themselves, how they thought, and the impact of their own beliefs, attitudes and behaviour on the issues they faced. At the same time, the programme had to provide concrete practical skills and techniques to address the problems they wanted to resolve.

Imagine a leader trying to encourage a team to question what they do, and why they do it, without acknowledging any benefits from the present system. Most change programmes take this tack. The demand for 'radical change', out with anything old, and so on, devalues the present system – and is usually taken as devaluing the individuals who have dutifully been making the present system work, with all its flaws. This is especially pernicious if the people doing the job had any part in designing or initiating the present system.

Leaders are just as human as their team members. They have their own beliefs and values to defend. By what magic are they expected to gain the ability to discover and question their own beliefs, while simultaneously acquiring the skills, language, thinking and insight to implement organizational change with flair? In real life, the leaders are just as threatened by change as their subordinates. It takes away their directing role; it demands that they become coaches instead of bosses; it questions their specialisms and expertise.

We select careers that we believe will match our skills and ambitions. We have a variety of beliefs about unnameable aspects of reality. The trouble with beliefs is that they are not necessarily true.

There is no instinct in *Homo sapiens* about what is and is not real. We build our models of the world based upon our unique experiences of it – both sensory and imaginary. The fact is, we can imagine things that are *not*   93 real. Furthermore, we cannot perceive reality directly; we can only be aware of what comes through the filters of our senses, which can be quite limiting.

Getting to know yourself thus has a value for strategic leaders. This comes about through valuable stimulus, combined with specific coaching and mentoring. Only then does the leader really have choice, about how to behave to be most effective, and ultimately which beliefs and values are most appropriate.

Norman Lear (Bennis and Townsend, 1995) once said:

> To be an effective leader, you not only have to get the group of followers on the right path, but you must be able to convince them that whatever obstacle stands in the way ahead, whether it's a tree or a building that blocks your view, you're going to get around it.

Levels of commitment

The objective for any strategic leader is getting teams committed to the organization and its goals. They have to be helped to find the path towards a new cultural vision. This 'co-alignment' process, instantly seen as dangerous by any red-blooded survivor in corporate warfare, involves identifying, defining and clarifying the areas of overlap between various members of the present system – especially those related to beliefs, values, identity, mission, and vision. The basic steps to co-alignment, similar to those for creating and aligning beliefs within an individual, are shown in Table 6.1.

Individuals go through these levels of process, changing their perceptions at each level, as each level of the process takes in more of the system.

Influencing beliefs and values

Change comes about from

- a *person* changing his or her *behaviour* in order to achieve an *outcome* in the environment.

In this 'grammar of change' the person is the subject, the behaviour is the verb, and the outcome is the object (see Figure 6.2).

The motivational issues relating to change involve people

- wanting to achieve a different result; gaining the capabilities to achieve the new outcome; and having a chance to apply the new capabilities to attain the new result.

Another aspect of motivation is the degree to which a person values the consequences or results of change (see Figure 6.3). Are they desirable? Another is credibility – does the person expect that the new skills or behaviours being learned will actually produce the desired benefits within

Table 6.1
Seven steps to co-alignment for strategic leaders

Step 1	Identify the environment surrounding the project or goals
Step 2	Define the behaviours to be enacted in that environment
Step 3	Identify the capabilities needed to generate those behaviours
Step 4	Establish the beliefs and values needed to support those capabilities and behaviours
Step 5	Form a description (or metaphor) for the role identity expressed by those beliefs, values, capabilities and behaviours
Step 6	Identify the vision and mission that identity is 'servicing'
Step 7	Make sure all the different levels are connected together, and are supporting each other

the environment? One might express this as a 'perceived self-efficiency' – one's degree of confidence in one's own personal effectiveness or capability to learn the skills or enact the behaviour necessary to reach the desired outcome.

DEVELOPING THE LEADERSHIP SKILLS

Sheep-dip training is not the solution. There is a perceptible gap between the knowledge taught by the academic world and the knowledge actually being put into practice in the light of the fires people are fighting in the 'real world'. Instead, we need to encourage change by consistently creating new experiences from which leaders could derive new beliefs, or at least challenge the more unhelpful old ones.

BLP was launched with 20 participants. The managing director, at short notice, decided to postpone the start because he wanted some of the participants to take part in the visit of a high-level delegation. The group discussed the proposed postponement and then approached the MD, who reversed his decision. This established the high priority of the programme from the start.

The workshops took place one day a month (except the first, which was two days with an overnight), in casual dress. Exercises and other work were based on experiential learning concepts. During many of the meetings real issues were the focus, with content and style adjusted to deal with them. In one meeting a major IT issue was resolved. The programme coach spent considerable time between meetings in one-to-one sessions to deal with difficult or pressing issues, to make sure people were learning and reflecting on their experience. The workshops included, for example, the following content:

Workshop 1 covered the way people think, why they think that way, and the

Figure 6.2 The grammar of change

effects this has on behaviours and how they deal with situations. This session worked as a teambuilding exercise, with participants developing networks that exist to this day.

Workshops 2 and 3 covered managing, motivating and understanding other people, especially those who are 'difficult'.

Workshop 4 was designed to help leaders communicate clearly, especially through a period of change.

Workshop 5 dealt with creative time management and delegation.

Workshop 6 dealt with coaching skills.

Workshop 7 was on the finer elements of leading teams through change, handling a real issue and incorporating all skills learned to date.

Workshop 8 was an evaluation and integration day.

Programme content is shown in Table 6.2

PROGRAMME RESULTS

The evaluation commenced with an occupational stress indicator (OSI) questionnaire and 360-degree appraisals, with end-of-programme discussion. Six months after the programme a questionnaire was sent out to all participants, which provided significant evidence of personal and organizational benefits, and helped persuade the directors of the merits of running another programme.

One of the main benefits to participants, difficult to quantify, was the ongoing support they received from other participants as well as the tutor. One-to-one work meant support with difficult personal issues, as well as putting new concepts into practice.

As a result of the programme the team of strategic leaders moved from a problem-based to a solution-based approach. Everyday attitudes were seen as growing gentler. One leader said, in fun, 'I now apologize before putting

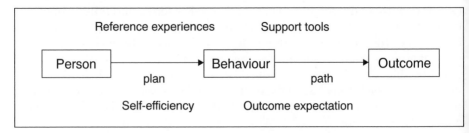

Figure 6.3   Personal expectations influence change

the boot in!' One director observed that his team now talks a different language. A number of other benefits to the company emerged:

- Overall, the participants became extremely good at communicating at an appropriate level. They became much more aware of group interactions, and tended to be more open and honest.
- Many participants had previously *understood* concepts such as ownership, teamwork, or empowerment, but they became much more comfortable about allowing effective delegation of entire processes. They learned that their delegation and leadership skills could minimize difficulties.
- They became more adept at using practical problem solving techniques. They also used creative thinking, within their teams and outside, to help solve problems.
- Participants grew more positive in their approach to issues, even issues where they had previously been edgy.
- Team spirit grew. Participants met outside work. They spoke as a team, and developed a team language.
- Management of their own teams improved significantly.
- Participants say they are now able to influence their teams, peers and directors more effectively.
- The focus on achievement within the team has been reflected in business results.
- Participants are much more confident in their own abilities and belief systems, and have a much clearer sense of purpose.
- Individuals report they are much more health conscious, for themselves and their team members. This, together with higher levels of competence and self-awareness, has helped bring about a significant reduction in the stress levels they perceive, both on-site and at home.

BENEFITS FOR THE ORGANIZATION

The organization measures benefits against five values: customers, people, innovation and technology, partnerships and performance. Significant gains were recorded on all five.

1 *Customers* An internal Customer Satisfaction survey showed a rise from 70 per cent satisfaction to 80 per cent, against a range of criteria. These included meeting the demands of customers (up 32 per cent), and the belief that the company is oriented to customers (up 23 per cent). A major contract was lost just before the contract began, but through a process learned in BPL, management saved the contract and gained a new five-year contract to the value of £20 million.

2 *People* People are now buying into continuous improvement because their leaders are more encouraging, and everyone can see that new ideas will receive positive responses. Formalized communication pro-   *97*

Table 6.2
Workshop programme content

Workshop 1	Workshops 2 and 3	Workshop 4
Self-awareness Stress awareness Recognizing workplace stress Power and logic of positive thinking Self-esteem Moving from problem to desired outcome Personal motivation, values and goals Understanding that others think differently and why Taking control and reducing blame True assertiveness Understanding difficult people Applying the techniques in the workplace	The art of pacing and gaining rapport Hearing the language people speak Body language Handling criticism Coping with compliments Moving to win/win Protecting your energy Empowering others by thought Learning from experience Applying the techniques to a real issue	Pacing someone through speech Minimizing rumour 'Cleaning up' language for clarity Moving towards a common goal Facilitating a group towards what they want Learning to hear and see understanding Communicating effectively with groups Applying the skills to the workplace
Workshop 5	**Workshop 6**	**Workshop 7**
Motivating yourself through values Ability of all to work 'uptime' Using personal 'downtime' to solve issues Discovering your priorities through behaviours Applying knowledge from Workshop 1 Delegation and devolvement Using delegation to empower Changing beliefs about time Changing language Moving towards the 'liveline' Applying the techniques to the workplace	Manager as a coach Role of coaching within delegation Role of personal development plan A coaching model to follow Applying skills from previous workshops Deciding who to coach and when Using coaching to facilitate attitude change Using coaching to raise confidence Using coaching to reduce blame Using coaching to reduce stress	Research into how leaders think Models for emulating critical factors Revisiting true assertiveness Aligning oneself with company vision Knowing when to lead and when not to Taking decisive action Learning to use 'gut' instinct Communicating energy, excitement and enthusiasm Aligning individual motivation to end goal
Workshop 8		
Evaluation		

cesses are working effectively, with information cascaded from the managing director to operators. People talk and listen more effectively, within a culture where leaders are seen as more approachable and people feel they can play a part in improvements. This is illustrated in the site (compared to all others in the corporation) gaining the highest participation level from the shopfloor in a new involvement scheme. Personal Development Plans are being implemented, and by the end of 1997 everyone on site will have one. Fear has diminished regarding mistakes, and the focus has shifted from 'Who caused the problem?' to 'How can we solve it?'

3 *Innovation and technology* Innovations in financial systems led to a 35 per cent drop in invoice mismatching. MRPII, previously failed, was reintroduced successfully, with a massive effort to clean up many years of 'dirty data'. As a result, a new 'inclusive' pricing system was developed, a major development for the industry.

4 *Partnerships* The corporate opinion survey showed positive trends since 1995. These included a 31 per cent improvement in perceptions of teamworking, 31 per cent up for communications, and 21 per cent for delegating skills. Partnerships with suppliers have resulted in major cost and risk reductions. Comments from internal partners have been increasingly positive.

5 *Performance* The main measure for success within the corporation is the EFQM 'business model'. This showed a 150 point improvement in enabling (where 100 is exceptional). Work in progress dropped from £26 million to £17 million. Lead times were reduced by 30 per cent. The improvement in late orders was 50–60 per cent. Productivity was up 20 per cent, and the site also had a 30 per cent reduction in assembly jigging.

CONCLUSION

Organizations wishing to remain competitive in today's increasingly challenging and changing environment will need to continually review their business improvement strategies – a core element of which must be how to effectively address the continued commitment of their people. I suggest it commences with people's beliefs and values, an area neglected by most organizational change initiatives to date. Also noteworthy, today 60 per cent of the strategic team leaders who had taken part in the Business Leaders Programme (BLP) are contributing to the organization nationally in support of corporate initiatives, in more senior roles, and this may have a message for us all.

REFERENCES

Books

Bennis, W. and Townsend, R., *Re-inventing Leadership*, Judy Piatkus, London, 1995

Dilts, R., *Visionary Leadership Skills*, Meta Publications, USA, 1996

Foy, N., *Empowering People at Work*, Gower, Aldershot, 1994

IPD, 'Lean Organisations', 1996

Articles

Baron, A., 'The Lean Organisation, Managing the People Dimension', *IPD Consultative Document*, 1996, September, 1–5

European Association for Personnel Management Conference (EAPM) *People Management*, 1997, July, 19

Taylor, J.A., 'Don't Obliterate, Informate, BPR for the Information Age', *New Technology Work and Employment*, Institute of BPR, Blackwell Pables, 1995, 83–88

RECOMMENDED READING

Cunningham, I., *The Wisdom of Strategic Learning*, McGraw-Hill, London, 1994

Hammer M. and Champy J., *Re-engineering the Corporations*, Nicholas Brealey Publishing, London, 1992

Hawkley, J., *Reawakening the Spirit of Work*, Berrett Koehler Publishers, San Francisco, 1993

Lessem, R., *Business as a Learning Community*, McGraw-Hill, London, 1993

Wheatley, M., *Leadership and the New Science*, Berrett Koehler Publishers, San Francisco, 1992

Wrycza, P., *Living Awareness*, Gateway Books, Bath, UK, 1997

7 Teams and the learning organization

Julia Pokora and Wendy Briner

We read regularly that the world is changing and that survival in the future depends upon both individuals' and organizations' abilities to learn and change more rapidly and effectively than previously. If we accept such assertions a number of questions follow. How is individual and organizational learning linked? What is a learning organization? Are some types of organization more effective at learning? Do teams help learning? What learning processes can be created? This chapter will discuss these issues from various perspectives and make some proposals regarding the nature of learning and teams.

LEARNING: INDIVIDUAL AND ORGANIZATIONAL

Individual learning – what is it?

The dictionary defines learning in the following ways:

- To gain knowledge or skill
- To commit to memory
- To gain by experience
- To become informed.

These definitions are easy enough to understand when we think about how we learn. We know that we each have preferences in the ways we learn. Some like the classroom, some like books, others learn best through dialogue, others only from direct experience. Some need challenge and competition to learn best, others security and nurturing. Some place a premium on knowledge and intellectual pursuit; for them learning is the acquisition of information. Others regard 'real life' as the vehicle of learning. *101*

Naturally our preferred approach to learning will be part of our personal world view, or as Peter Senge (1993) calls it, our 'mental map'. As the philosopher Kant said, 'We see things according to how we are, not how they are'. The dictionary definition, though strong on methods of learning, does not tell us what to do with a 'mental model' that fails to help us interpret the world successfully, both because it is too narrow and because it leads us to actions that are ineffective, counterproductive or destructive.

How do we apply our learning to specific situations, particularly if the situations are new and we need to be innovative? Or how do we combine our learning, know-how, skills and experience with other people to respond to old situations in new ways or to create new opportunities?

If we reflect on our own experience of learning, we notice that it is an unpredictable thing. Sometimes we learn when we are supposed to: an opportunity to learn is offered and we want to learn. Sometimes, in contrast, it happens 'spontaneously'. We seem intuitively to grasp an idea or skill, or can just do something new without thinking. For these reasons, in considering the relationship between teams, individuals and organizations, an important question is: how in organizations can we provide opportunities which are conducive to all kinds of learning, the programmed and the spontaneous?

Organizational learning – the same as individual learning?

Organizations learn in some ways like individuals. Learning is part of a company's culture and traditions. Each organization will have preferred ways of learning, preferred topics that are listened to and given importance. It will be blind to, or not competent at, some other aspects of learning. This selectivity will be dependent on the organization's 'mental model' of itself and the environment in which it sees itself operating. The mental model will determine the kind of questions asked and the kinds of information sought or paid attention to. In turn this will contribute to an organization's core competency.

Organizations are naturally better at some aspects of their business than others. For example, Hewlett-Packard has a good track record at being early in the market with new technologies, but is less innovative in its ability to organize and run logistics. The company's founders were research engineers, who wanted to develop new technologies that would make a contribution to industry and commerce. Their mental model, given their research background, may have affected Hewlett Packard's ability to learn how to develop new products.

Why, then, if organizations do learn naturally, albeit along the lines of their preferences, is there so much discussion about learning organizations?

We think that these natural ways of learning do not meet the multiplicity of demands that are currently driving and shaping organizations, exhorted to pay close attention to customers, competitors, employees, potential markets, regulators, politics, ecological and social trends and the like – as

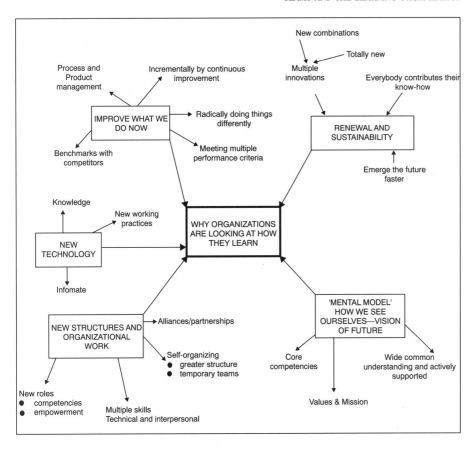

Figure 7.1   Pressures on organizations

Hydra they should have heads and eyes everywhere. In order to 'ride the waves of change' (Hawkins) the ability to learn and apply learning is of fundamental importance.

Figure 7.1 illustrates some of the underlying pressures on organizations.

Mike Pedler et al. (1991) suggest that a learning company is 'an organisation that facilitates the learning of all its members and continuously transforms itself'. The implication is that learning companies have the following characteristics.

SOME CHARACTERISTICS OF LEARNING ORGANIZATIONS

1   Organization design and development of learning processes

Conscious attention is paid to learning – learning is seen as a process which the organization is aware of and is seen to be actively enhancing. Learning is regarded as tangible, a valuable product and process, a component of organizational life like inventory level, service standards or customer com-   *103* plaints. An example is the Centres of Learning created by consultancy firms, which are devoted to codifying and disseminating the information and learning gained by consultants in the course of their assignments.

Other organizations are searching the world for best practice that could enhance their own. A South African chemical manufacturer took its top managers around the world to study in depth 40 companies' experience with approaches to becoming a learning company.

Anita Roddick of The Body Shop develops new products through combining ingredients that are being used in different parts of the world. She seeks to enable the people who become part of her business to benefit by becoming economically self-sustaining.

Organizations are looking at the business processes that cut across organizational and functional boundaries. Through either re-engineering or total quality, they are seeking to improve the way in which they deliver to the customer so that their loyalty is maintained.

Progressive organizations are concentrating as much on developing their future as they are on delivering even better today. The processes of innovation in all its guises are being opened up. At 3M they target that 25 per cent of each unit's sales come from products introduced within the past five years. Ghoshal and Bartlett (1995) suggest that innovation *per se* is a value and a goal.

Innovations may be quantitative, that is the many and small improvements, or qualitative, that is the fewer radically different discoveries that become new products or services. Often the source of both is a combination of an individual's ideas and perspectives, which can be the seed of new products and services. They need nurturing to create a future and the ways of nurturing are at the heart of a learning organization.

2 Commitment to engage everybody in continuous learning

In learning organizations attention is paid to everyone in the organization, not just a few. Traditionally, organizations vested wisdom only in those at the top; what they learned in meetings and through experience was attended to and acted upon. The learning of others in more junior positions was assumed to be of lesser or no value. This idea is increasingly being challenged. Today organizations know that they disregard at their peril what the truck driver delivering product learns about the customer on his drop-off. Companies are creating channels to enable ideas, complaints, know-how, imagination and energy from all parts of the organization to be heard and acted upon. This goes against some of the commonly held views of how organizations should operate.

3 Acting on what is learnt

In a learning organization there is not just concern for the acquisition of information, there is action, individual and collective. The organization does something differently as a result of learning. It values action, and change is not necessarily seen as threatening. Learning organizations are constantly asking the question, 'so what?' They are open to the possibilities of change on three dimensions: what they do, why and how they do it. They review constructively what they do internally, listening to the individual and collective voices of all participants. They are also in contact with customers, suppliers and external influencers to be in tune with what is going on outside the organization. They then try to balance these forces, learning as they go what to do differently and how to put these initiatives into operation. A learning organization is organic and interactive, which is a long way from being a rational, logical machine.

Traditional organizations, in contrast, may knowingly or unconsciously suppress or distort learning that does not concur with their corporate fixed views of how things ought to be. Acknowledging such learning might lead to pressure for action. Traditional organizations place value on maintaining unity and stability. History and precedent are powerful forces, so traditional organizations are slow to adapt, and are given to repeating the same mistakes or missing opportunities.

4 Creation of links between individual and organization learning

In a recent lecture to a group of UK Health Service Managers, Mike Pedler asked the question, 'How can it be that every individual in an organisation can know something is wrong or could be better and yet the organisation itself does not know it?' The challenge of the learning company is to create *organizational* knowledge (Pedler et al., 1991). An organization is more than the individuals who make it up. If one person leaves, then the organization will continue, even if it momentarily notices or regrets their absence. No one individual can know what the organization knows. Nor can an individual single-handedly change an organization. Organizations are complex interactions of relationships between people, the organization's structure and systems, both formal and informal, the ways things are done, the myths and history. Teams and teamworking are an important part of the process by which individual learning can become collectively known, understood and translated into organizational action. Teamworking refers mainly to functional work teams, or temporary teams put together to deliver a project. These easily recognizable teams can be effective in generating some individual and organizational learning about current activities.

Having considered these four characteristics of a learning organization, we will now move on to look at two very different types of organization, to examine to what extent they demonstrate these characteristics, and what sort of learning seems to occur in teams.

HOW DO TRADITIONAL ORGANIZATIONS LEARN?

The role culture

The predominant organization type is the bureaucracy or role culture. Roger Harrison (1972) describes the characteristics of this kind of organization. In a role culture, jobs are clearly defined, systems and procedures delineate authorities, responsibilities and define standard practice. People work separately to deliver their part of the work. Bureaucracies see learning as the acquisition by an individual of skill and knowledge to enable him or her to perform the job to the required prescribed standard. Learning is codified in procedures. At best, these describe best practice, saving wasted energy and effort in reinventing the wheel. At worst they rigidify – 'the way we've always done things round here'. For learning to become part of a bureaucracy it is codified and made visible in the approved format – a new standard operating procedure. Because bureaucracies are rigid and formal, learning and change are often restricted to improving ways of getting the current job done. It is difficult to question whether the job is needed at all or if it could be done in radically different ways.

How information flows

Information, and frequently decisions, flow from the top down, often in the form of written material – briefs, memos or directives. Communication across different parts of the organization, except at the top, is restricted by lack of legitimate channels, and factors such as physical separation of departments. The organization disapproves of and punishes non-standard communication. A symbolic example was found in the corridor of a role-culture organization. The staff notice board was headed by a large sign saying, 'This board is for approved official communications only. Any other material, which has not been authorized by X, will be removed.' Such an example demonstrates how non-standard information flow was filtered and checked. In such organizations, it is difficult for an individual to communicate through the organization and across departmental or functional boundaries.

Rewards and punishments

In a role culture, power comes from position and from rules and regulations. Reward comes from doing your job in the approved way. Punishment may result from deviating from or challenging the rules and norms, or from attempting to work outside your job boundaries. It is more important to 'do things right' than to 'do the right thing'. The norm is to 'play by the rules' – not to take risks.

Focus of organization learning

In such an organization there is, of course, learning, but it is restricted in ways that are part of the culture. Such organizations are often very resistant to hearing information from staff or from their environment (be it customers, competitors or other external stakeholders) which would cause them to change. They believe that their way is the best, right and only way. They are often introverted or inward-looking, which means that they do not naturally pay attention to and learn from their environment and the changes in it. They function well when the environment is static or slow moving.

Teams and learning

The kinds of teams most often found in bureaucracies are functional teams. The lateral flow of information between departments is restricted, and teams focus on learning within their department. It is hard for ideas and information to cross boundaries. Just as the whole organization may be introverted, so teams often look inwards. Information is shared and learning contained within the team and not spread outside. Teams are stable units, and team learning may be restricted in nature to 'first-order' learning (Watzlawick et al., 1974). This means that they only look at how to do things better; they do not question purpose or scope or look beyond their functional boundary, nor do they consider how the actions impact on other departments' effectiveness, never mind the external customer.

Case study 1: learning in a role culture – a central government department

We were recently asked to consider a team development activity in a department within a central government department which is a traditional role culture. The client described their situation in the following way:

1 Most employees and management believed they were under-utilized, their skills and abilities not being employed to the full.
2 Their team was under increasing pressure from a heavy workload, staff reductions and reorganization.
3 A strong norm within the department was that there must never be a mistake. The team's outputs included papers for government ministers and answers to parliamentary questions. Since some outputs were highly sensitive, a system operated where all work was checked and re-checked by each level in the hierarchy.
4 Work practices and job definitions were clearly understood and well-established, and an individual's authority was linked to published job grade and salary levels.
5 The aim of the team development activity was to help the team to look *107*

within itself to review the way it operated, and devise more efficient ways of working.

The constraints

When we began to explore how to proceed, it became clear that there were rules and principles that the department was not willing to have questioned, or even explored, which included:

1 The team development activity must not involve or impinge on anyone outside the team. We had suggested that some key stakeholders, such as internal customers or a senior manager, should be involved. The view was held that the input from anyone outside was irrelevant and it was suggested that such an approach was too dramatic and might 'create waves'.
2 The outcome of the team development activity must not pre-empt the results of a job grading review currently underway, so the definition of responsibilities between jobs was assumed to be stable.
3 The team's role and purpose within the organization, and how it related to other departments and teams, was not open to question and could not be changed.
4 The team development activity must be contained within the team. If it were 'successful' it might then be communicated to other departments and teams.

The learning potential

In our view, the organizational context limited the learning potential to what at best would only marginally improve the existing situation. At worst it might raise people's expectations and hopes of what they could achieve, while making it clear that there would be very little hope of realizing these possibilities. This disappointment might lead the people to become more frustrated or cynical, and disengage with the organization that they now see as thwarting their positive energies.

It is worth saying that there might have been a strong justification for embarking on team development if the team had defined acute performance or relationship difficulties. However, in this instance, we were unable to identify this as an important issue. The organization described above typifies the traditional model. Its characteristics constrain the ways in which it was prepared to engage in learning and use that learning, even though the approach was team development.

HOW DO TEAMWORKING ORGANIZATIONS LEARN?

The nature of a teamworking culture

In the newer, high-tech organizations there are an increasing number of teamworking cultures, where there is emphasis on the task being carried out by a team of people. This arrangement may take the form of semi-permanent teams, matrix management or project teams. Teamworking cultures usually have flat hierarchies – people work together because their contribution is necessary to the task, not because they represent an organizational level or have the longest service record. Performance is defined in terms of output and what has to be achieved. Individuals decide themselves with other team members the most appropriate way of getting to the end points. Individuals manage the development of their own technical skills, taking advantage of internal or external opportunities to keep on top of their technical know-how. Teams are usually composed of people with different functional or professional backgrounds. To be effective and respond to changing demands, they need to learn to work together, which means that the team leader has an orchestrating role to generate an effective spirit of collaboration that focuses on enabling the individuals to deliver as a team.

Teamworking cultures tend to be informal, with few rules or rigid working practices. What holds the teams together is their collective sense of achieving a task that is consistent with the organization's sense of purpose and values. There are usually a range of different success criteria that have to be dynamically balanced to meet the customer's and organization's interests. There is considerable scope for the individual and the team to ask 'how can we do this most effectively?' or 'does this make any sense?' If not, 'what do we need to do?' The teams then engage in redefining their deliverables with customers. A team can look at its own management practices and effectiveness, and alter what it does and how it does it in order to become more effective. In contrast to a bureaucratic organization there will be short planning cycles, an emphasis on action and – in the best circumstances – review to find out what happened and why. The cycle of activity and learning can be tracked in movements illustrated in Figure 7.2.

Learning from direct experience feeds forward to create modified plans and consciously build what is now known into further action.

Unfortunately, in our experience, one of the drawbacks of an action-minded teamworking organization is that it forgets to plan and review, leading to an exciting whirlwind of activities that becomes exhausting and unproductive. Having the right amount of planning and review is a key part of the art of leading a team that learns, otherwise the learning is not fed back into the next round of action.

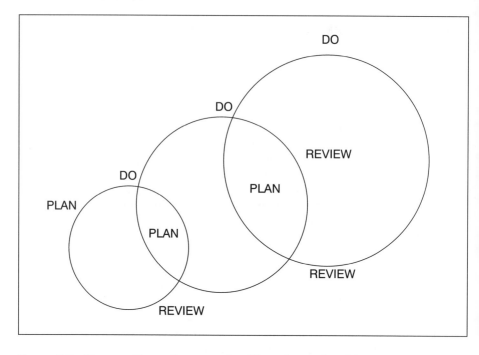

Figure 7.2 Teamworking cultures: cycle of learning and activity

How information flows

Information flows in all directions. The 'need to know' is what enables people to find out. The information culture is open, where people ask and expect to be told. Reciprocal information exchange is also anticipated, and is demonstrated formally and informally. Formally there will be regular communication meetings. In one computer company, for instance, everybody on site meets for 15 minutes on a Friday morning once a month. Any visiting senior manager will take the opportunity to talk to the whole body of employees, which perpetuates the feeling that individuals are part of the organization. They are kept up to date with corporate wide initiatives, external trends, new products and local successes.

Informally people are encouraged to go out and find out, contacting colleagues in other parts of the company or outside the organization. In this way they learn not only that they can cross organizational boundaries but that they should do so, bringing back what they have learnt to the team and helping the other team members to understand and make use of the information. Electronic communication, particularly E-mail and groupware can underpin rapid exchanges of ideas at a distance. Requests for information, or best practice tips, are sent through corporate worldwide networks and the Internet. Software developers can find out if anybody else has discovered the same bug as they have and can build on the solution found elsewhere. To be useful under-pinnings of team learning, these electronic media need to be built into the teamworking practices. Simple rules of etiquette and convention must be agreed, so that people know how to use the systems. Electronic systems are an extension of the teamworking culture, not a substitute for it.

Rewards and punishments

Formal rewards, such as pay, are based on performance, as well as comparative contribution and market value. Some teamworking cultures are moving towards team rewards rather than individual rewards. Likewise performance appraisal is moving towards frequent project reviews by the team members, project leader, customer and other stakeholders. The line manager becomes much less significant. There may be upward review, from team member to team or project leader looking at how they have enabled the team to perform. Hence the inputs to an individual in terms of the demands on them and the criteria against which they will be measured come from different directions.

In teamworking organizations the following kinds of behaviour are considered poor performance:

- Inability to communicate
- Inability to build effective working relationships across boundaries
- Inability to organize and manage own work in a self-directed way – waiting to be told what to do and how to do it.

Teams, individuals and team leaders have much more information on which to base their decisions on how to improve their individual and collective performance. Dynamic learning within the context of the team is formally rewarded.

Focus of organizational learning

The formal learning processes concentrate on socializing the employee into the organization's purpose and culture. On training programmes there is emphasis on the teamworking culture, the importance of the individual's contribution and ability to take initiative in order to further the organization's purpose. Often senior managers, who are role models or custodians of the culture, take an active part in these occasions. Training programmes will consist both of formal presentations and informal interactions, so that the culture can be experienced first-hand. Heroic stories are exchanged about what happened in the past, and these are used to discuss 'what we are trying to do today'. There is a great deal of dialogue, comment, suggestions and feedback. Everybody is encouraged and expected to be listened to: the distance between manager and non-manager is minimized.

Teamworking organizations have been among the first to formally recognize that individuals should take responsibility for their own careers and *111* not be dependent on the organization to provide life-long careers with accompanying training, development and promotion. Self-managed learning or personal development are approaches to an individual's continued development that is consistent with a teamworking organization.

Teams and learning

Teams in a teamworking organization are often good at discovering 'on the hoof' what needs to be done and how to improve their performance, which means that 'on the spot' individual and team learning can be significant. Teams receive inputs from other people and learn to live, within the dynamics of organizational politics, by managing their environment. What teams are less effective at is learning from their collective experience, so that this learning can be passed on to other similar teams. The transmission, dissemination and utilization of know-how about what works and does not work is rare. So, for example, we have discovered that in an inter-governmental high-tech agency there is a repeated pattern of not defining research projects clearly enough with the stakeholders in the project start-up phase. Consequently many projects do not meet expectations, much frustration is experienced and money is wasted. Everybody who had been a project team member knows that this is always a problem, ascribed repeatedly to the particular features of the specific project. The review process has not looked at the patterns of project management itself so this experience does not go into the organizational memory and become organizational learning, typical in teamworking cultures where people rush from team to team believing from their experience that 'this is how things are and how they have to be'. This assumption, of course, is not true. Teamworking cultures do not value looking at how we get to where we are, partly because people fear that their independence and flexibility will be undermined by analysis and standardization. As mentioned previously, from an organizational point of view, great value is given to looking forward and to action. Therefore, analysis and reflection as ways of learning tend to be seen as counter-productive because they slow things down and restrict freedom of action.

Case study 2: learning in a teamworking culture – an environmental planning and economic development consultancy

One client described his organization in the following way:

1 We are small, only about 35 professional town planners, economists and business developers, with five administrative staff. We are all highly motivated professionals. We want to give everybody plenty of scope to use their capabilities.
2 We have difficulty in simultaneously marketing, managing the tendering process to win business and actually delivering. As a business we just

manage to make ends meet, but we do not seem to make that all-important step forward that we all want to consolidate our future.

3   We work on a project basis but there always seem to be problems when we are producing final reports to the customer. Coordinating the inputs and producing the reports puts pressure on people at the end of the chain. As a result we are late, and the quality of the work is not as good as it should be.

4   We seem to live in a panic, the adrenaline certainly flows. We end up doing everything within a hair's breadth of a crisis, if we are lucky. While this is fun, we are becoming exhausted and bad-tempered.

The constraints

During our interviews with people they reported that:

1   The organization gave individuals plenty of scope to learn – sometimes too much. They feared that there was no safety net and their inexperience might lead them inadvertently into serious difficulties.

2   Panics meant that any project management process that was supposed to exist, was overridden, in turn meaning that individual team members did not understand how they could contribute effectively. Their contribution was a hit and miss affair. People with scarce skills faced unlimited and apparently unscheduled demands.

3   At times the chaos seemed unbounded with energy being dissipated and tempers rising. People felt stressed but could see no end to it; their growth seemed self-limited by too much flexibility.

The learning potential

Looking at it objectively, this small teamworking organization is also trapped by its own culture and ability to learn, despite much discussion about the introduction of 'simple systems to make life easier'. There is limited evidence of people collectively and consistently being able to establish and use a project management process, or a scheduling process, or indeed financial procedures. In order to institute these anchors the clock would have to stop and the panics abate. Everybody would need to find time within overstressed diaries to pay attention to working out what to do and how to do it. Unfortunately this does not seem to happen because there is never the space. In addition, it would take more than the efforts of a few individuals. In fact there are several employees who have successful experience of similar anchoring systems, but so far they have not been able to pass on the working practices that they know are needed. Without more emphasis and value being placed on these anchoring systems, it is unlikely that significant organizational learning will take place.

It would seem that an organization that gives scope to individuals and teams to learn from varied experience finds it hard to learn as an organiz-   *113* ation. It wants to survive and prosper, and believes that professionally it has a valuable contribution to offer its customers and society, but despite its teamworking nature it is having difficulty learning what does not come naturally.

INDIVIDUAL AND ORGANIZATIONAL LEARNING IN TEAMS

In summary we conclude that individuals can and do learn in teams, but what they learn is likely to be constrained by their organization's culture and values about learning. Teams and teamworking training events give people the opportunity to improve their current performance and to understand and build better relationships between team members.

Organizations with a teamworking culture do seem to provide individuals with greater personal scope and responsibility for their own performance and learning. The range of contacts, sources of information and the ability of a team to take decisions about how they do things, give more opportunity to be flexible and pilot innovative approaches. If we review our experience against the characteristics of learning organizations we could say that teamworking cultures are moving towards engaging everybody in learning opportunities and encouraging teams to act on what they learn.

However, the main limitation seems to be that both bureaucratic and teamworking organizations are constrained by their 'mental models' and cultures that favour certain ways of operating and learning but undervalue and ignore others. A particular difficulty seems to be in creating links between the individual's learning and the organization's learning to enable the organization to balance its current performance by learning in those areas that it naturally overlooks. In the next section we will consider how this aspect of organizational learning might be enhanced.

However, there is another related difficulty: how do organizations transform themselves and what contribution can teams make? The most important and most difficult organizational learning that needs to take place is how to continuously regenerate a future that provides new products and services through different organizational structures with different delivery mechanisms. For this to happen, you need to know what your organization is good at, and also constantly seek new opportunities to expand or extend those strengths into new areas, thereby learning how to create areas of sustainable growth. You must give attention to doing better what you currently do. Simultaneously let viable opportunities emerge that need nurturing and shaping to provide an organizational future. We shall consider this challenge in the final section.

LINKING INDIVIDUAL AND ORGANIZATIONAL LEARNING: BECOMING AWARE OF THE EXISTING MENTAL MODEL AND DEVELOPING IT

Both individuals and organizations need to start with understanding themselves, becoming aware of their view of the world and particularly their learning habits. Much of this self-awareness will be confirming and will help them to understand their own energies and distinctive strengths. If this understanding is compared to the changing demands of the outside world, then sometimes the dissonance or blind spots can be made visible. Once they are visible you can decide how important they are to current and future individual or organizational health, which may lead to a search for alternative ways of learning.

Becoming aware of how the collective mental model operates, and may block organizational learning, is an activity that needs to be acknowledged and discussed throughout the company. One oil company has incorporated trend management and organization dynamics into its senior management workshops. As the company believes it needs to be more flexible internally and externally, a change in the collective mental map is seen by top management to be necessary. Senior managers are asked to look at external events, not in isolation but in terms of their impact on each other, so that underlying knock-on effects can be traced. They are also encouraged to become aware of their company's 'mental model' – what it sees and how it reacts, plotting the typical patterns of interaction and the consequences. They become aware of the 'organization dynamic' that is underlying the company's efforts to learn and change, and are invited to consider how they and others in the organization would have to think and act differently, if they wanted to change the organization dynamic to allow new learning to take place. They consider what they would need to do if they were to see a new business opportunity. How would this activity need to be organized? What sort of different structures, system, values and ways of working would need to be put into place? They are asked to engage in metaphors, to imagine what would need to be different in order to bring out something unique – creating a new mental model out of combining the existing with different perspectives and ways of being.

SHARING LEARNING

Once the organization is aware of its mental model, it can widen its ideas about what learning is and what are considered to be learning events. One legitimate and very valuable type of learning that is often under-recognized is sharing existing learning or know-how and generalizing it so that others can learn from it. As we have previously mentioned, many organizations find it difficult to recognize that the same things happen time and again but are never noticed. For example, one police force embarked on its fourth *115* programme of reorganization, and was surprised to notice that it was running aground because of opposition from local units in much the same way as its three predecessors. Feedback about what was working and what would need to be different, and how the initiative could be run, was neither encouraged nor heard when it erupted as resistance. This organization could have, in a planned way, investigated the shared experience of best practice, and sought suggestions which could have then been built into its next teamworking event. Instead they trod a very similar path without apparently learning.

Sharing learning is a valuable activity that needs planning, structuring, facilitating and capturing. It is an interactive process where individuals need to be provided with a form in which to exchange their ideas and know-how. To make this process useful to the organization as well as the individuals, the events need to be designed to focus, generalize and disseminate the know-how that emerges. Creating networks, both through groups of individuals and electronically, is an important way of making learning circulate and become widely available.

The European Healthy Cities Movement of the World Health Organization has created an environment where this kind of know-how sharing is designed into the way it operates. Cities joining the movement have to be prepared to come to a number of conferences and meetings to exchange their experience. The project leader for the city, politicians and leaders of initiatives are all expected to take part regularly. Evaluation studies of a particular city's initiatives are agreed. They are reviewed to assess the extent to which the Health For All objectives have been enhanced by the initiative. Evaluation looks particularly at what can be learnt, for the next stage of this initiative, and at how other cities might constructively take it further. Cities who joined the movement early offer training and advice to new cities, spreading the know-how and combining learning as they go. One of the main vehicles for sharing information is a regular conference, where through interactive workshops best practice is examined and traded. Unsolved issues or problems are raised and ideas about possible ways forward are generated.

For teams to contribute to their organization's learning, there needs to be more sharing of learning between individuals and teams to capitalize on this hidden know-how. This sharing also helps to discover the aspects of the 'mental model' that are currently holding organizational learning back, and to identify new ways of doing things differently.

USING TEAMS TO DEVELOP A LEARNING ORGANIZATION

We mentioned earlier in this chapter that many organizations are trying to transform themselves to ensure a sustainable future. We have observed that this requires a number of different aspects of organizational learning that in turn require teams to work with distinct learning purposes. These reasons for learning are to build a critical mass of individuals who have similar understanding of the strategic options, dilemmas and possibilities, who can learn to initiate, nurture and evolve a viable future. Teams can be used to enable transformation, but this needs to be not only a designed and managed process, but interactive and evolving.

In order to innovate both in what products or services can be offered and in how they might be delivered, we have identified in Figure 7.3 six organizational learning processes, which we then go on to discuss in detail:

Organizational learning processes

Directional feel

This establishes the broad parameters of the current organizational strengths, competitive challenges, operational weaknesses and the dilemmas and constraints that have to be balanced. Usually the organizational sense of mission or fundamental underlying purpose is restated or reviewed, along with the core values that are evident from history and current practice.

Teams are usually set up with mixed hierarchies, functions and operating sites, to gain optimum mix. The purpose is to understand and explore the challenges and options, and to build a widespread critical mass of people who appreciate the external and internal positions and have started to think seriously about future directions.

Teams at this stage are usually asked to clarify their concerns and foreseeable difficulties and to make suggestions about new directions that they would support, but which require further work.

Parallel exploration

Following on from the suggestions regarding new directions put forward above, small teams are set up. These teams are often formed from a range of people, including outside experts, suppliers or other organizations with useful experience. The aims are to rapidly explore the possibilities, understand the options, appreciate what has to be done, find out how difficult it will be and what risks are involved.

Parallel exploration teams enhance the depth and breadth of organizational learning because team members know that they are part of the organization's investigation into options. With their appreciation of the directional focus, they can help to generate wide understanding about innovations and what these would mean for the organization's learning. Because people are spread around the organization a wide range of perspectives is engaged.

In a typical organization, parallel exploration is undertaken by many teams, with a strict brief about what they should explore, and a short timescale so that the divergence, although great, can be certain. They are often encouraged to be inventive about how they explore, to look outside   *117*

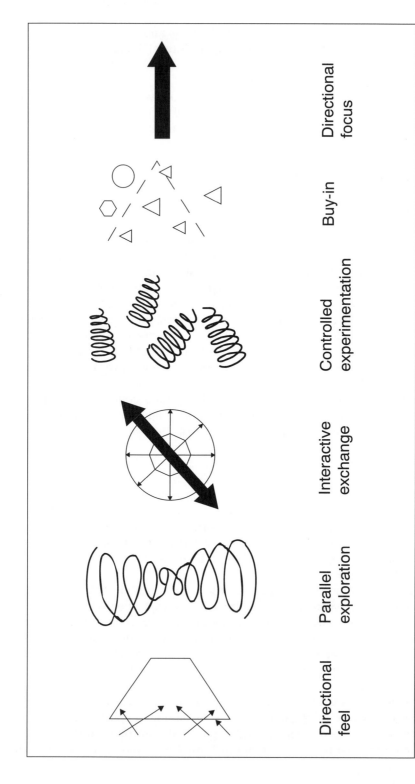

Figure 7.3 The key learning processes

the prevailing 'mental model' and to challenge existing assumptions. Small teams work on their own linked to a sponsor who is a senior manager.

Interactive exchange

To capture the learning that is coming out of the exploration and to exchange it interactively, the teams of volunteer members meet as a big team, thus connecting to the directional feel events and reviews, strategic themes and sense of mission. The purpose of interactive exchange events is not only to concentrate on the viable options and to close off the impossible, knowing *why* they are impossible, but also to highlight possibilities that seem to have potential, and combine opportunities that are emerging through exploration. The interactive exchange meetings also provide a large forum where people from different parts of the organization can understand better the organization's culture and how the organizational dynamic might be changed. Champions supporting particular ways forward normally emerge from groups of informed volunteer supporters. Decisions need to be made by sponsors about which initiatives to take forward and over what timescales.

Controlled experimentation

Small project groups are set up, sponsored by senior management to take the most supported initiatives forward. A portfolio of strategic change projects is set up to take these forward in an agreed way and to pioneer the next phase on behalf of the organization. The controlled experimentation teams are usually a mixture of champions, volunteers and people who need to be there because of their expertise. Their task is not just to launch a new service, or to explore further, but they are also asked to look at what they are learning about their own abilities, the new ways of working they evolve, the difficulties they encounter and how they are regarded by the rest of the organization.

These teams test feasibility and build organization consensus about the realigning necessary to be able to become integrated with the organization's adapting culture.

Buy-in

The small project groups make their experiences available to wider groups in the organization, spreading best practice and making clear what, why and how things have to change in order to successfully take on the new initiative. The learning – both good and bad – has to be realistically understood and new deals have to be struck. Relationships will need resetting, expectations clarifying and trade-offs made. New activities have to be set up, but some practices have to be stopped. Coaching, mentoring and support become important activities for those who have taken part in the controlled experimentation teams, with the result that their learning is formally and *119* informally extended through experience into the organization's ways of working.

Directional focus

Teams, both new experimental and operational, are functional teams, learning from the buy-in activities, sharing the collected experience and beginning to find their own way forward.

These organizational learning processes use functional teams, mixed teams, project teams and big team events to combine the opportunities for different types of individual and organizational learning to take place.

We have come to understand that, without continuously incorporating these sorts of learning events into organizational life, it is unlikely that much organizational learning will occur.

For each learning process, the teams, their managers, and sponsors, and the rest of the organization need to understand their purpose and how each process will be taking the organization's learning forward. Sometimes these teams are set up to achieve particular tasks – such as investigating new market opportunities. They achieve their task, but little is learnt about the market or, most importantly, the organization's capability. To capitalize on this valuable learning, processes such as those outlined above are needed to capture, combine and create viable innovations collectively.

We find that many organizations run *ad hoc* events that start to foster individual and team learning, but few are considering seriously what could be called their 'architecture of organizational learning'.

SUMMARY

This chapter has examined individual, team and organizational learning. We suggested that individuals learn in their own way, and that organizations influence what and how individuals learn. Organizations themselves are strengthened and limited in their ability to learn by their culture and 'mental model' of the world. Teams within different cultures will tend to have differently limited learning patterns, but teamworking organizations offer more scope and opportunities to both individuals and teams to learn.

However, the learning that may take place in a particular team does not seem to extend organizational learning unless the organization itself is aware of its existing 'mental model' and is prepared to modify it. Becoming a learning organization seems to be at least partly dependent on generating organizational learning processes using different constellations of teams, interacting with each other to combine, codify and create learning.

REFERENCES

Ghoshal, S. and Bartlett, C., *Changing the Role of Top Management: Beyond Structure to Process*, H.B.R., Jan–Feb, 86–97, 1995

Harrison, R., *How to Describe your Organisation*, H.B.R., Sept–Oct, 1972

Hawkins, P., Lecture – NHS Management Course, 1996

Pedler, M., Burgoyne, J. and Boydell, T., *The Learning Company*, McGraw-Hill, London, 1991

Senge, P., *The Fifth Discipline*, Century Business, London, 1993

Watzlawick, P., Weakland, J. and Fish, R., *Change: Principles of Problem Formation and Problem Resolution*, William Norton, New York, 1974

RECOMMENDED READING

Briner, W. and Hastings, C., 'The Role of Projects in the Strategy Process', Chapter 15, in Cleland, D. and Gareis, R. (eds), *Global Project Management Handbook*, McGraw-Hill, New York, 1994

Handy, C., *Understanding Organisations*, Penguin, London, 1976

Katzenbach, J.R. and Smith, D.K., *The Wisdom of Teams*, Harvard Business School Press, Boston, Mass., 1993

Nevis, E., Di Bella, A. and Gould, J., 'Understanding Organisations as Learning Systems', *Management Review*, Winter, 1995

8 Transient teams and organizational structure

Tony Molony

Teams don't exist by in splendid isolation, but operate and interact within the structure of an organization. Earlier chapters have examined, from various perspectives, the effect of the business environment in causing organizations to adopt structures in which teams play an important part. In addition to structural changes, the modes of operating, for example, project-oriented organizations with self-directed teams or virtual teams, have also produced changes and realignments of the culture of the organization.

Not surprisingly there are stresses and strains involved in these changes, and companies that can manage these and learn how to operate teams effectively in this environment are more likely to survive and prosper.

There will obviously be problems that are specific to each organization, whether it is in the public or private sector, and the type of operation, such as manufacturing, marketing, finance or service. However, there are many that are common to all organizations. They include: clear strategic goaling; people management; task performance monitoring; relationships to other teams and structural issues. To take this last example, within an existing organizational structure and culture new teams may develop their own structures, hierarchies and control mechanisms, in order to achieve their goals. These may be congruent with the organization or in conflict with it.

This chapter looks at a particular environment, that of the Army, and shows how structural conflict can arise and ways in which it can be resolved. Conclusions are then drawn from these case studies which apply to most organizations in both the private and public sectors.

THE WORK ENVIRONMENT

Working underwater can be a stressful business, especially in a military context. Most of the time divers find themselves alone, in completely black water, carrying out tasks that may involve placing explosives, searching for bodies, cutting away steel structures or pouring concrete. This harsh environment which demands teamwork, is the one studied here, one where teams work in a hostile environment and where the demands of the task conflict with the accepted models of the society in which the teams must exist.

The rationale for the Army having divers at all is worth explaining. They exist because the Army must be able to deploy anywhere in the world to meet the demands put upon it by Her Majesty's Government. Ports, harbours, docks, rivers and canals may all require engineering work to make access possible. The Army therefore concentrates most of its diving effort in the Engineering service, but recognizes that this task is a minor role not often required, and keeps diving as a secondary qualification, employing the divers on other trade tasks for the majority of the time. Thus, although most large engineering units have a diving team, it is not permanently formed and comes together for tasks – it is a transient team; the leader cannot rely on having the same personnel each time, which has important implications for team building.

This chapter examines the team structures that develop in the Army to cope with these demands, and the conflicts that can occur within the Army structure. The chapter starts with a short explanation of the military hierarchical system and then examines three case studies to see how well this model works in practice. Some general conclusions are drawn from the case studies.

THE HIERARCHICAL MODEL

The Army is run as a hierarchical society, based on the POMC model (Planning, Organizing, Motivation and Control). The ownership of the task, process and tools lies firmly with the management. Planning is centralized and kept at as high a level within the organization as is possible. The organization is fixed and structured to reinforce the top-down social and command model. Information and orders flow down from the top to the workers to carry out, and there is not expected to be any debate about them. Information upwards is in the form of progress reports and statements of completion, not discussion. The formation of *ad hoc* project teams is discouraged as they disrupt the command and control structure.

In most circumstances that the Army is designed to meet, that is, when fighting a battle, this rigid command structure, where everyone knows their place, is a great strength. It is resilient to the shock of battle, the loss of people, and has been proven to work in countless wars, skirmishes and peace-keeping operations. In the context of the battlefield this works extremely well and British forces are renowned throughout the world.

The weakness of the rigid structure lies in its inability to adapt where circumstances dictate a flexible approach. The sort of tasks that require improvisation, brainstorming, quick reactions and decisiveness are not   *123*

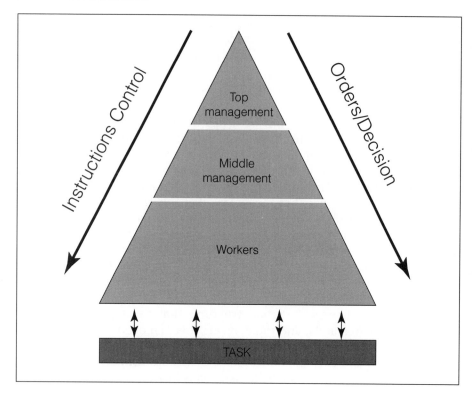

Figure 8.1 Traditional management structure

easily carried out by a rigid adherence to this top-down structure, but require cooperation and teamwork.

The bedrock of this model is respect for ability, but this is often masked by the more overt presence of the visible rank structure. The system depends on the lower ranks obeying the orders of the senior ranks, and this works very well when all concerned have the skills to carry out their part of the task. Most of the training in the Army is geared to equipping people to carry out these tasks, appropriate to the rank they have attained. Indeed, promotion is conditional on proving competence at one level and having the ability to work at the next highest level. This reinforces the hierarchical model.

This POMC model needs information: information is power. Depending on the skill of the individuals in disseminating or hiding information, the pyramid they command will succeed in its task or fail. In war the dissemination of information is vital. In peace the manipulation of information may be more important to preserve the structure – normally found to be the main function of a bureaucracy.

Army diving teams are products of the hierarchical structure. They only occur at low levels in the large structure of the Army; they are few in number

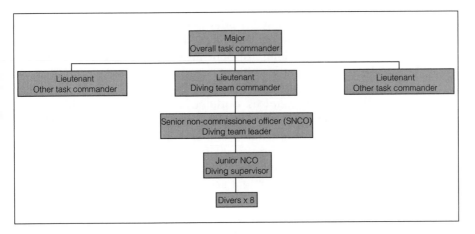

Figure 8.2 Expected management strucure of a diving team

Note: task orders flow down the chain; results are reported up the chain

and are regarded as unimportant even in the very regiments that support them. In a diving team the expected structure looks like the one above.

In the context of the traditional management model (Figure 8.1), the overall task commander equates to top management, the diving team commander and the SNCO equate to middle management, while the workers are found from the diving supervisor and the divers. Orders are devised by the overall task commander and passed down through the chain to divers. Results are passed up the chain, normally originating with the diving supervisor.

In the military context this management structure appears to work quite well. However, the model above (Figure 8.2) does present some difficulties:

- Hierarchical lines of control and communication
- Status-ridden teams
- Inflexible approach to work
- Slow response to changes
- Competition between workers
- Motivation problems.

Rigid lines of control and communication are not normally associated with efficient teamworking. The constraints imposed by the hierarchy hinder the free flow of ideas and the exchange of views that create an atmosphere of cooperation. In a system that brooks little or no argument, free communication is at best difficult.

The same hierarchy imposes a very visible rank structure that enforces status. The sharp distinction between workers and managers is based on the rank structure and status. The rewards for hard work and ability are there but take a long time to be delivered and only appear in a rise-up-the-rank structure. Thus status is important to the hierarchical system.

The inability of the hierarchy to adapt to different work situations is almost guaranteed by the application of the first two factors in the above list. Acceptable ways of working are built into the thinking and training of everyone involved in the system; although a knowledge base of what works is very valuable, rigid application of it stifles creativity.

A system built on the premises outlined above will have difficulty in adapting quickly to change. It could be argued that it is incapable of change, but this judgement may be a little harsh. Certainly there is little incentive to change, because change involves challenging the *status quo* and, in a hierarchy where reward is based on promotion, that is not wise.

Competition between workers might seem almost impossible to engender and, given the nature of the hierarchy, undesirable. It is generally assumed that some competition is necessary to obtain the best out of workers. With no measurable productivity targets and no reward system capable of providing short term incentives, it would seem to be impossible to forge any competition between workers. In these circumstances motivation problems could be expected.

Examples of some of these problems, and ways they can be overcome, are provided in the case studies that follow.

CASE STUDY: THE TEAM IN TRAINING

This study looks at one training course, based on the author's own experience. Twelve students started the course. They had similar levels of experience in diving, a minimum of 35 hours working underwater, but came from a widely varied background of trade experience. Ten of the 11 starters were soldiers or junior non-commissioned officers, aged between 19 and 23. The author was an officer and aged 28. These factors are significant, as rank status is important in a hierarchy and the age difference made physical fitness a serious problem.

The course is designed to teach qualified divers to use a wide variety of tools for underwater engineering. It is very similar to that taught by civilian diving schools to produce air range divers for the commercial diving market. The equipment used is heavy, bulky and dangerous; chainsaws used underwater in nil visibility, use of explosives for cutting and 'thermic lances' all have their obvious hazards.

The course ran for nine weeks, starting in September. It was clear from the very first day that the staff had decided that there were too many people on the course and that this was not a course that an officer should do – despite the fact that the officer had been posted to the training establishment, his position dependent upon successful completion of the course. This pressure to reduce numbers manifested itself largely in a very hard physical regime, under the guise of physical training (PT). Certainly by the end of the second week PT and diving had reduced the student numbers by two, who left the course through injury.

This regime had led to some interesting developments among the

126

students. The hierarchical structure based on rank had completely broken down – quite simply it was inappropriate. In its place a task-based leadership structure had evolved. Set a task for the day, some were better at organizing the stores and equipment and some better at the trade skills required. All, however, pulled together in the PT, which was becoming harder and more plentiful all the time. Why was this? It appears that the staff were still determined to reduce the numbers and PT seemed to offer the best way to break the students. If an eight-mile 'jog' carrying a length of steel pipe, dressed in diving suits, did not affect student morale, there were other ways.

In the face of this the students banded together into a very strong team, willing and able to help each other in every situation. It had become clear that nothing less than everyone passing the course was good enough. The group started to enjoy socializing together in the evenings and firm friendships developed, based on mutual respect of each other's strengths and tolerance of individual failings.

A significant hurdle was the mid-course exam; revision of the theory was led by those with a strength in the written word and the practical session by those with trade skill. All but one passed at the first attempt, which led to some frantic revision; everyone was involved coaching the individual before his second attempt the next day. It failed to get him through, by three marks. The effect on the team was marked – there was no celebration of the successful students, just a muted send-off for the man departing.

The second half of the course opened with a distinct change of atmosphere; this was a fight and all the students knew it. A record of the equipment failures, which were far too common, was maintained, as was a training diary. The students began 'beating the system' by keeping equipment that worked in the team's possession and maintaining it without recourse to the official repair system. It had become obvious that the control system for the training was concerned that the diving was not proceeding according to plan, as the level of equipment failure was preventing certain training taking place. The reaction was to make the students work longer hours. At the six-week point the existence of the students' diary was discovered. As the suspected instigator of this diary, the officer was summoned to school authorities and ordered to stop making entries. There were assurances given that grievances noted would be investigated; the student team was not impressed and agreed to keep the diary going, despite the realization that this course of action was a direct challenge to the hierarchy.

Despite the continued pressure and the added spice of deeper and inherently more dangerous diving, it became obvious that the student team was going to finish the course. Final exam revision was planned completely outside the official course programme, and indeed no one failed any part of the final exams.

From the six-week point the students had sensed that all would be well, and the mood shifted from survival to ensuring that the system was changed to prevent so much valuable training time being lost to future courses. The resentment at the treatment being meted out changed focus, away from the   *127* instructors individually towards the more distant and abstract 'training system'. This was epitomized by the students' decision, made before the last day of the course, to delay all travel plans away from the course for a full day, to allow time for a protracted debrief on the Friday afternoon. The allotted 40-minute period overran by three hours as, aided by the diary, the students were able to graphically illustrate the systems failures of the last nine weeks. Of course the hierarchy won; the officer, having passed the course, was now officially on the staff and was promptly tasked with reforming the support to all training.

What of the team that had formed? Its *raison d'être* gone, it dispersed; firm friends made, and kept, and a sense of great satisfaction at achieving such change is still apparent at reunions. What had happened was extraordinary, however. A highly unlikely social grouping, given the nature of rank and background, had banded together to overcome extreme physical challenges, in face of overt organizational opposition. Certainly the nature of the individuals on the course made this easier as friendships soon formed and, more importantly, no outright hostility to any course member was ever apparent. To a certain extent this is an example of a strongly bonded team resenting outside interference and reacting against the established Army hierarchy. This could be an explanation for the reaction of the team when we failed to ensure everyone's success at the mid-term exams. The strength of the team at the end of the course seemed to lead it to believe that it could run the organization more effectively than the established authority. Complete arrogance, or perhaps there is a grain of truth there – the reader can probably judge.

Consider also the reaction of the hierarchy. By its very nature it was almost completely unable to react to problems in a timely manner. Upwards communication was almost entirely absent and, in the absence of any negative feedback, those in command failed to appreciate that was a problem. This is a critical failure, often found in rigid command hierarchies. Without a mechanism to provide feedback, the command system will either receive no information at all (and therefore assume all is well) or it will only hear what those below think will be acceptable, which is even more dangerous.

The solution adopted after the course, for all future courses, was to hold a debrief session at the end of every week led by a senior member of the command staff, and without the instructional staff being present. This allows the students to raise any matters necessary, without fear or favour. Of course it cuts across the defined hierarchy structure, but it works.

CASE STUDY: THE TEAM UNDER TEST

Diving in the UK is governed by rules laid down by the Health and Safety at Work executive and backed by law (Diving at Work regulations). The Army took a decision that, despite crown immunity, it would adhere to the rules and indeed be represented on the H&SE committee that formulated the rules. One of the effects of this regulation is that divers and diving equipment must be inspected for fitness to work annually. Certain types of diving equipment have differing operational tests requiring a complex range of inspection and testing.

A team was formed at the diving school to carry out these inspections. It included an officer, to give the inspection sufficient status to matter in the wider hierarchy of the Army. A senior non-commissioned officer was assigned to the task to provide the technical experience. He was backed up by a very experienced junior non-commissioned officer, who provided additional technical experience. The author was privileged to set up the team and carry out the first two years of inspections. The team was required to travel to every diving team in units based anywhere outside Germany. Inside Germany a similar inspection role was carried out by the extension of the diving school based in Kiel.

This study examines the hierarchical structures actually found or developed in operational diving teams. It is drawn from an inspection of one team, but reflects the inspection of many others. The team was based in an operational unit, assembled for diving operations as required, but supported by a full-time diving storeman responsible for the upkeep of the diving equipment.

The team was in a unit famed for its high degree of motivation, reflected in the selection procedure. All were trained divers, some with considerable experience. They were led by an experienced and highly capable young officer. Additional motivation came from the knowledge that the inspection resulted in an individual who passed the tests being given a licence to dive for the next year, with consequent financial rewards, and for the team to be given a report based on their collective performance. The inspection covered all aspects of the team's performance. Each individual had to pass a written test, the store was inspected for equipment serviceability and the team was tasked to perform certain diving tasks.

The conventional team structure, as shown in Figure 8.2 above, was employed to make sure the team was ready for the tests. The officer did the planning and gave the orders, the soldiers went ahead with the tasks. This model also served to bring the team together for the individual written tests and for the inspection of the store.

At the task stage matters became interesting. The inspection team expected to give the task instructions to an officer as normal, and it would be natural to assume that he would lead the team through the tasks. In fact the junior non-commissioned officer (JNCO), who was in fact the most highly trained diving supervisor, took over at the briefing. He, despite his relatively lowly position in the hierarchy, was actually in charge of the diving operations. The officer and the senior NCOs worked alongside the other divers and did exactly what they were told. Why was this?

Diving is a specialist business, one where training and experience really do matter. Although the officer and SNCOs were trained to undertake simple diving tasks, the more complex ones demanded in the test conditions were beyond their training. The JNCO, by contrast, had been specifically trained

129

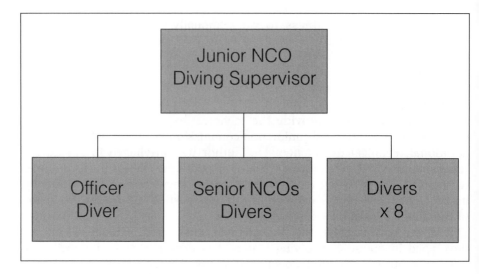

Figure 8.3   Diving site organization

to undertake complex diving tasks and had the skill and experience to do it. Figure 8.3 shows an example of a successful team that developed its own hierarchical structure appropriate to its defined needs. Thus on the diving site the command structure looked like the one above.

At the successful conclusion of the diving tasks, command reverted to the normal model. There is potential for difficulty at this point, since releasing power is often more difficult than acquiring it. That this conflict very seldom arises is due to the mutual respect built up within the team for each other's skills. Thus the officer feels no resentment being 'ordered around' by someone who is far below him in the strict hierarchy, as he realizes that his own skill is inadequate for the task. He is prepared to submerge his own status for the common good. The Junior NCO, on the other hand, realizes that he is not yet prepared to take on the broader range of responsibility that is expected of the officer, and thus has little difficulty in handing back control at the task's conclusion.

It is important for this case study to consider the problems that might have been expected, confirm that they did occur and then explain how they were dealt with.

The problems of hierarchical lines of communication and control were thought to be a hindrance to effective teamworking, as was a status-ridden team. As can be seen, by abandoning the established hierarchy and working with their own team structure the team members had completely eliminated any problems of communication and status.

In this way the team had developed a culture where blame and guilt for failure had no room to flourish. Ideas were freely discussed and everyone 'owned' the solutions to the problem. The absence of blame prevents the
establishment of guilt and allows everyone to concentrate on success. In

the normal hierarchy it is easy to hide behind the structure and avoid becoming involved – easy to say 'not my problem' and thus avoid any responsibility for failure. In the flexible team this is not possible as everyone is fully engaged in the solution to the task; weaknesses are worked around, blame is absent and thus there is no guilt. In this culture team building and mutual support flourish and success, while not guaranteed, is very much more likely.

Inflexibility and slow speed responses are also noted as properties of rigid hierarchies. In the team we have examined it is clear that these dangers were avoided by communication based on mutual trust and respect. Roles were established, filled at the appropriate time by the right individual, and then changed to reflect the stage of the task. Thus changes in the task could be quickly made, and flexible and imaginative approaches to problem solving are possible. A willingness to try new ways of working was apparent and used to good effect.

Motivation was provided, on the surface, by the promise of money if the inspection result was satisfactory. In fact money has never been a significant motivator in any diving team I have inspected; the real motivator is the team spirit. The service culture of helping your 'mates' is what makes the teams work – based on mutual respect – and the ability to change the hierarchy to suit the team is what distinguishes a good team from the less good. The only competition needed is that of doing the job before someone else in the team has to do it.

CASE STUDY: THE MIXED RACE AND CULTURE TEAM

One of the more arduous inspections was the requirement to travel to Hong Kong to visit the Gurkha diving team. This case study examines the way in which two races and cultures work in the extreme conditions of a diving team. Diving is an unusual activity for a hill people to take up; most Gurkhas have never seen the sea before they are given their initial training, yet it is quite remarkable how quickly they adapt to the totally unfamiliar.

In principle the same hierarchical model found in the rest of the Army applies in Gurkha units. There are two important differences; one overt, the other covert. The overt one is that there exists a parallel chain of command, in that there is Gurkha representation at all levels, to act as an interface between the British and Gurkha peoples. This is illustrated in Figure 8.4.

At first glance this structure seems impossibly top-heavy and riddled with potential problems of communication. In fact this communication is eased by the requirement that all British officers serving with Gurkha units must reach a basic proficiency in Gurkhali. Some obtain higher levels of skill in the language, to their great advantage. It is however difficult to fully absorb all the cultural nuances, particularly those relating to the social standing of the individual Gurkha in his home environment in Nepal. This is significant and is the covert factor mentioned above. It is significant because there can be a difference between a Gurkha's social standing at home and his status   *131*

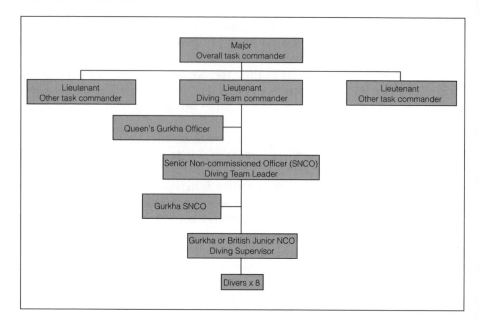

Figure 8.4   Hierarchical model: Gurkha unit

in the Army hierarchy. It is entirely possible for a Gurkha to be a senior figure at home but a junior one in the Army system.

The logistics of setting up a diving test in Hong Kong were not straightforward and required close cooperation between the British, the Gurkhas and the Hong Kong Chinese crew members on the support ship. The tasks were simple enough – underwater cutting, some search patterns and a diver rescue. The first part of the testing was designed to put the British officer and his SNCO under pressure. This went extremely well, aided by the officer's superior knowledge of Gurkhali. The whole team performed excellently and the tasks were successfully concluded in the shortest time the tester had ever seen.

The next task, the search patterns, were designed to be led by the Gurkha Diving Supervisor. It became noticeable that, although he was highly competent, he took more time to become organized. At first I put this down to the need to confirm actions with the British officer, which necessitated some complex language translation. After a couple of tasks I began to notice that the Gurkha Diving Supervisor was seeking an opinion from one particular individual more often than not. As the task was underwater cutting, using a mixture of hydrogen and oxygen – highly explosive – and the man being consulted was a welder, I thought no more about it. Only after the tasks were finished did I have the opportunity to ask him what the exchanges were all about. His answer was, as ever, extremely polite, but evasive. It turned out after a lot of digging that the man being consulted came from the same village in Nepal and was closely related to the headman. It seemed that, out of politeness, the Diving Supervisor was asking permission before giving orders, thus recognizing the tribal influence in juxtaposition with the military hierarchy.

This team suffered from all the potential problems identified earlier. The hierarchy was almost impossibly top-heavy, with the added complication of status, both apparent and hidden. Despite this the team worked well and proved to be a very effective diving team. A large part of this is probably due to the enormous pride the Gurkha soldier exhibits in everything he does. Failure is not a concept that comes easily and team spirit is a very important part of the make-up of a Gurkha unit. Given the additional bonding that happens when facing a physically dangerous task together, the team developed a strong team loyalty. It seems as if team spirit overcame the obstacles of the hierarchy and status. Communication, despite the language barrier, can be maintained, although it did seem a little ponderous at times. I also suspect that, as an outsider, I saw only what I was supposed to see; however what I did see convinced me that I could trust my life to this team, and did so on the underwater demolitions dives we undertook.

One other likely problem identified earlier was a slow response to changes. In fact, there was a very fast response to changes in that the team came up with solutions very quickly. Longer-term changes, such as changes to techniques that required training, did take longer to achieve due to the inability to beat the language barrier. It is after all very difficult to teach technical subjects in a second language, especially when the second language contains no words to cover the concepts that are being taught. There is little in Gurkhali to cover the concept of a shaped demolition charge being deployed to cut into rock in 50 metres of water. Despite this, communication was effective as the will to get the message was present, and there was always someone willing to spend the time translating or explaining.

As for competition between workers, and motivation problems, the only problem was how to make them stop working. With perfection the only acceptable standard and loss of face, caused by failure, a cultural disaster, being motivated was never a problem. To understand the motivation it is perhaps necessary to remember that joining the British Army is the highest ambition a young Gurkha can have. Selection is extremely competitive, starting with the three-week walk from home to the recruiting point. With only one in a hundred being selected, getting in was tough enough. Volunteering to become a diver, where historically no knowledge of the sea exists, is a brave step. Actually surviving the training is a serious challenge. Having overcome that much, it is unlikely that anyone is going to give up when asked to do a fairly simple task, such as attaching a demolition charge to a live land mine in 25 metres of water, at night.

CONCLUSIONS

It is possible to derive some conclusions from the case studies. From the first study it became clear that, when threatened by external forces, a team can bond to accomplish some common aim. Provided that the aim or goal is clearly understood, seen to be achievable and is 'owned' by the team, it becomes very difficult to stop the team achieving it. It is also apparent that if the goal is removed, or once it has been achieved, the team will disband quite quickly, although residual loyalties may remain.

The first case study, 'The team in training', also illustrates that hierarchies are good at downward passage of orders but not good at upward flow of information, particularly bad news. Unless a determined effort is made, there is only one channel of information, downwards, and no method of obtaining feedback. This leads to the second point, that hierarchies are slow to change. This is understandable, because if they have no feedback they do not know there is anything to change. Given the layered model of the hierarchy, it takes considerable time to establish change, made more difficult by each layer having to invent a communication channel with which to address the next layer above.

In the second case study, 'The team under test', we discovered that even in this rigid hierarchy there is room for task-based teams to emerge and work effectively, based on the mutual respect of each person's skill set, not his position in the hierarchical model. The real skill of the established leader is getting the old structure back working at the end of the tasks. These teams are highly effective, because they make the best use of everyone's skill at the most appropriate place in the task cycle. Their coexistence in the hierarchy is more difficult to manage and requires a high degree of commitment from all parties. That they work so well in diving teams is explained by the extraordinary motivation and commitment shown by service divers.

The third case study, 'The mixed race and culture team', shows that even with very mixed cultures and races effective teams can be formed. Work is required to explain the common aim, and this will be assisted by a knowledge of each other's language and culture. Understanding breaks down any lingering racial differences, and a respect for each other's ability makes any race issue completely irrelevant. Of interest was the demonstration of stronger forces at work than the established hierarchy. The deep-seated cultural model seemed to be stronger than the expected hierarchical bonds, yet at no time did they threaten the task or the team's cohesion.

This chapter has looked at an extreme environment in an already unusual organizational structure. Diving is by nature a team effort, and engineering diving is more demanding in that respect than diving for sport. In the Army it has to take place in the knowledge that completion of the task is the only priority, even at the cost of lives. For this reason service divers tend to be more highly motivated to succeed than most 'ordinary' people. The conclusions that may be drawn from this study should take account of this unusual environment.

GENERAL CONCLUSIONS

Despite the peculiarities of the environment there are some general conclusions that can be drawn, and common themes that run through the case studies, which are applicable to a wider range of situations and organizations.

The first is that *communication* has the power to break down hierarchical barriers. Communication based on mutual respect of the other's ability means that the message is not distorted by mistrust of motivation. Talking and an ability to listen to, and act on, the other's point of view is not a trait normally associated with a rigid hierarchy, but in all the examples above it is clearly the key to communication. Once this is established, problems of status, competition and motivation disappear. In any fundamental structural change to an organization, particularly where new teams are being established and others disbanded on a continuous basis, the reason for the team being formed must be clearly communicated, together with its organization goals and the boundary of its power to establish its own goals. Similarly, in operation, the organization must be kept informed of decisions within the team which may affect the organization's strategic direction. Communication between teams must also be effective so that complementary activities and possible conflicts may be dealt with and organizational learning encouraged.

The second point is that *hierarchies* are inflexible and slow to change. A changing environment demands a flexible team that adapts to its role, changing to meet the prevailing context. Thus each member is able to contribute his skill at the time it is required, at the appropriate level. As we see in the diving teams, the lead changes at different stages of the task; but if mutual respect in ability has been established this does not cause a problem of status. Any organization that is changing from many levels of formal status to a flat flexible team-based organization structure must allow time for the whole organization to adapt to changing work practices such as transient leaders.

The third point is that there is no need to blame anyone in *team cultures*. Solutions are derived from joint efforts and every team member contributes; the task is to work together to produce the required solution. There is also no need for guilt as the responsibility for success is everyone's. In the case of diving teams the spice of danger helps to ensure that this is the case, but does not guarantee it. In teams in other environments there has to be a conscious effort to develop this collective responsibility, and good application of leadership skills and a good understanding of the role of communication help this team culture to work. The emphasis is on the success of the team, while not forgetting each individual's role in that success.

It seems that good communication, the ability of the individual to con- *135* tribute his or her whole skill at the right time and place, an emphasis on success and the absence of blame all combine to make teamwork a method of working that is very hard to better.

Part II
UNDERSTANDING TEAMS

Introduction to Part II

Whereas Part I was concerned with the team environment, the structures adopted by organizations and change management, the chapters in Part II take a closer look at what goes on inside teams. A group of individuals is not necessarily a team, and an understanding of the processes involved in teams and how to make them work in the organization is the theme of this Part. There are two main themes: teams in general, and team processes.

TEAMS IN GENERAL

The chapter by Leslie Rae on team needs analysis deals with the necessary definition of what are the needs both of a new team and of an existing team. It explains how to ascertain the present state of a group or embryonic team. Two further aspects are covered: the usefulness of a variety of models of effective teams and effective team leaders, and a model of individual and team development.

The effectiveness of teams depends, of course, largely on the mix of people within the team. While the formal structure within a team is important, the informal way in which people work together can have an important impact on the team performance. Even if the team environment has been fully recognized, the organization culturally aligned and appropriate structures put in place, the business re-engineered and the team needs identified, the success of the team still depends on how well the people work together. Nancy Foy, in her chapter on using team roles, describes how the roles people adopt in the team can be identified and provides a Team Role Inventory that can be used to balance the team.

In addition to balancing teams there is a need to monitor and control the progress of a team. The chapter by Alan Mumford concentrates on the learning process that, if controlled properly, enables groups and teams to *139* develop. Starting with the characteristics of effective teams, the author goes on to discuss the types of learning that occur – for example, knowledge, skills and insights. The learning that can arise from success as well as failure is examined, followed by a consideration of the task and learning cycle and the role of the manager. Exercises and case studies are used to illustrate the points made.

A successful team learns from its mistakes and anticipates the problems that may arise in the future. In her chapter Joyce Fortune uses systems thinking to explore what a team needs in order to be successful. She then puts forward a way of predicting what might cause a team to fail and of investigating failures after they have occurred. A model of a robust system that is capable of purposeful action without failure is provided, together with a method of looking back at past failures to establish their causes and of assessing a situation in order to predict failures that might occur and so point the way to their prevention.

TEAM PROCESSES

This section covers some of the common processes that go on within a team, for example, communication, creativity and negotiation. Understanding and improving these processes will enhance the performance of any team.

Chris Moore focuses on communication within the team, the concept of quality communication and why it is important. An observational approach, based on social theory, to the capturing and analysis of communication patterns in teams is used. These patterns enable the one-to-one relationships that exert a high level of influence on the quality of team communications to be identified. There are examples of the team tasks that provide the basis for observation, together with instructions on how to run them.

Teams are formed, people choose – or are allocated – join and leave them. In all these cases individual expectations are involved. Chris Elgood examines the concepts relating to a team and the expectations of an individual within a team. An understanding of these factors is valuable to the team leader, who may not share the same view or the same motivation. The author proposes a series of questions (and answers) that team leaders might ask of themselves about the teams that they have joined and left, as a means of identifying the feelings that some of their own team members may be currently experiencing.

Most, if not all, teams need a degree of creativity or innovation. In his chapter Tudor Rickards explains how to help a team to be creative in discovering new and unexpected ways of doing things, and in developing creative behaviours. The MPIA approach, used by the Manchester Business School for supporting project teams seeking new ideas on behalf of industrial sponsors or clients, is described in detail together with its associated activities.

Stress is common in many teams, whether caused by the processes in teamworking or by the striving to achieve goals. It is not necessarily bad, but it does need to be managed. Jane Cranwell-Ward puts forward a five-stage approach to the understanding and management of stress with the aim of optimizing team performance. It encompasses the following areas: understanding the nature of stress and its possible consequences; individual differences and stress issues; recognizing stress in individuals and teams; identifying the sources of stress for individuals and teams; managing stress to optimize performance.

All teams experience conflict. Teams that are set up to deal specifically with inter-team conflict resolution and dispute handling are an interesting case in that they must handle their own intra-team conflict to arrive at a uniform agreed position before entering the inter-team conflict. Maggie Dunn and Chris Wills examine a trade union negotiating team and draw conclusions about the actual behaviour of team members compared with their self-identified Belbin Team Roles (see Nancy Foy). The results of this case study enable valuable general conclusions to be drawn about the process of teams involved in a negotiation.

9 Team needs analysis

Leslie Rae

Training and development practitioners are familiar with the process of training needs identification and analysis as part of the earliest stages in developing a training programme. The time spent on analyses of this kind is amply rewarded when the programme runs effectively. In a similar way, in order for the team to develop into a mature, highly effective team, the earlier stages of team development require a detailed analysis of the team's current position. For example, what type of team and team roles are required to attain the objectives; where do the individuals and the team stand at this initial stage in terms of skills and behaviours; and the future developmental needs of the individuals and team.

This chapter:

- Introduces the model underlying team needs analysis
- Describes the stages of team needs analysis
- Describes how the existing state of a group or embryonic team may be ascertained
- Examines models for the effective team and the effective team leader
- Considers a model of individual and team development.

ACTION-CENTRED LEADERSHIP

Team needs analysis is based on the action-centred leadership model of John Adair (1983) – Task, Individual, Group (or, in this case, Team).

Within each division, teams as groups do not evolve independently, but are linked with each other through each need or requirement – otherwise an imbalance occurs. If too much emphasis is placed on the requirements of the task, the individual and team dynamics suffer from being ignored to some extent. Similarly, if too much emphasis is placed on the needs of the   *143*

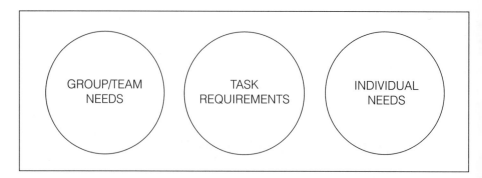

Figure 9.1   The divisions of the action-centred leadership model

individuals, team cohesion is slow to develop and there is a danger of losing sight of the task objectives. If there is too high a concentration on the group as a whole, awareness of the needs of the individual members is lessened, perhaps with dangerous consequences. However, if the appropriate attention (which may vary with time and other situational aspects) is paid to each need, and the interests of the circles overlap, as shown in Figure 9.2, more effective development is possible and the much sought-after synergy should be achieved.

THE STAGES OF TEAM NEEDS ANALYSIS

Although it is not always possible in practice, the logical sequencing of analysis action can smooth the process and ensure that all stages are covered effectively. The stages are shown in Figure 9.3 and explained here in more detail.

Stages 1 and 2

Although the details of these stages are out of the hands of the team needs analyst, the maximum amount of information is very important. Before any approach to the team building process can be attempted, the analyst must be aware of:

1 The reasons for the team development
2 The support of the organization's senior management in the development of the teams and the extent of the support that will be available
3 The team's specific objectives
4 The time scale for a) initial development and b) the team effectiveness
   process
5 Any barriers imposed by the organization and/or senior management
   on the development
6 The timescale and facilities (including barriers) for the analysis
7 The analysis report timing, extent and destination.

The analyst must establish in as much detail as possible, and preferably directly with the team sponsors (for example, the senior management group) what support can be expected, in what form, and their recommendations. Will this support be overt in the organization; will it be practical or purely verbal support; how will it be expressed or conveyed to the analyst; to what extent will the analysis be considered, and so on. Obviously these factors will depend on the extent and nature of the recommendations, but a vague 'You carry on and we'll look at what you have to say' is not enough to support an effective analysis operation.

The list above leads to the specific questions that must be asked of the sponsoring group by the analyst, either directly or through a responsible third party and, although showing the most significant information required, omits supplementary questions that will need to be posed. These can include (as either direct or indirect questioning):

- To what extent do the sponsors believe that the group in question needs to be a team in the full definition of that term? If so, what are the reasons for saying this?
- What problems, if any, do the sponsors know of or envisage in the development of the group as a team? This may seem to give the analyst a bias before the analysis starts, but any responses to this question must be accepted as views only of the sponsors, who may or may not be in effective touch with the group and its attitudes. The information can be stored until the end of the analysis and then taken into account in the final deliberations.
- How has the development of the team been broached with the group? Has the group been won over to the concept of group development,

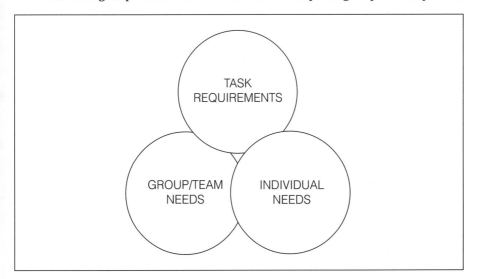

Figure 9.2 The essential overlapping of the action-centred leadership model   *145*

or, as is the case in so many instances, has it been told that it is to develop into a team? If the latter, every attempt should be made by the analyst to encourage the sponsors to participate more in setting up the group, or be given the authority to do this.

- To what extent do the sponsors expect the group to be developed into a team in the allocated time period? Will the sponsors be willing to change their opinions if many substantial recommendations are made in the final analysis report? The responses to these questions will have a significant effect on the content and extent of the recommendations made by the analyst and the manner in which they might be made.
- To what extent have the sponsors notified others in the organization who might be involved in or affected by the team development, and with what reaction – overt or covert – has this advice been received. This information will be of particular interest to whoever will be responsible for putting the team development process into action, but forewarning could save the analyst time, resource and energy during the analysis.
- Although not really part of the analysis, loss of time and problems will be avoided at a later stage if the sponsors are reminded of the need to decide at this early stage about the evaluation steps that will be necessary when the team has developed and is operating fully.

Following responses to the analyst's questions to the sponsors, the role responsibilities of the analyst, and the nature and role of the proposed team will have been agreed. For example, the proposed team might be:

- A temporary project group
- A 'permanent' project group that will be responsible for a sequential series of projects
- A temporary team that will work together on a normal operation basis, but with a finite life
- A permanent, operational team such as a group of middle managers as the middle management team; a set of supervisors responsible for a three-shift, continuous system; an integrated team, under a leader or manager/supervisor responsible for a specific part of the organization's practice.

Stages 3 and 4

Armed with the sponsor's brief, the analyst can now start to determine the existing situation of the team, as a group of individuals and as an embryonic or developing team. Stages 3 and 4 will return us to the three circles: task, individual and group.

The nature of the team identified at the end of Stages 1 and 2 will influence the analytical approach, although, in general, a common approach can be

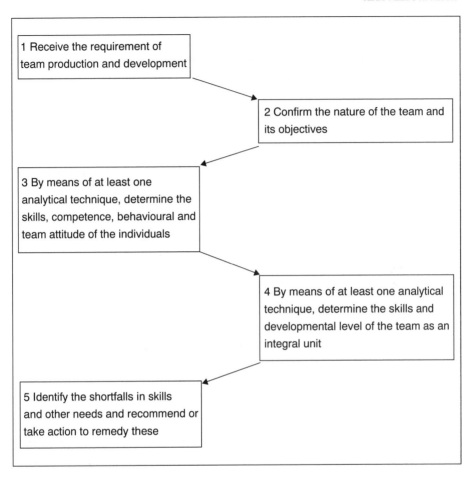

Figure 9.3 Stages of team needs analysis

applied. For example, if a temporary project team is involved, there will be a greater emphasis on the nature and requirements of the task, than in the case of the permanent group of the organization's middle management, where the greater emphasis will usually be on the group and its internally interactive nature.

Methods of collecting information about the task, individual and group will vary according to the nature and availability of the team, but two approaches will be of great importance in this collecting, that of asking questions and observing the people in action. Task information should be available from job specifications and competences statements, and the degree of success of the team in completing the task can be weighed against these. The analyst will need, however, to note whether the team expends too much time and energy on the task at the expense of the other areas.

Assessment of the individual and group abilities and behaviours will be based principally on observation of the team performing the task, their   *147* skills being 'measured' against accepted models of individual and group behaviour needed for the effective operation of the team.

The common features and the approaches available to identify and analyse their levels will be described later in diagnosis of teams.

Stage 5

In a training needs analysis, the identification of the needs of the training project will be compared with the existing skills, and so on, of the people concerned. Any lack or failing determined by this comparison is described as the 'training gap', the elements of training needed to bring what exists in line with what is required. In a similar way, the team development analysis will result in the identification of a similar gap – what does the existing 'group' need to develop, on an individual and/or a team basis, to make it an effective team. The analyst can then make recommendations, in a general or detailed form, to the sponsors for whoever will be responsible for taking developmental action with the group. Of course, the analyst will often be the one, or one of a group of people, responsible for taking action on the needs identified by the analysis.

DIAGNOSING THE EXISTING GROUP OR EMBRYONIC TEAM

It is important for the analyst to consider the following areas.

Analysis – events and techniques

To analyse the needs of the existing group or embryonic team, the analyst must meet the individuals. The most effective action will be to attend a pre-development event during which the potential members can be brought together – perhaps for the first time – and their present attributes identified. Again, this should be undertaken by the practitioner who will be responsible for the actual team development, since, although the principal reason is analysis, the analysis activity itself is part of the team development. Experience shows that every effort will be made by the sponsor group to combine this event with the initial team development event itself, but this event is usually so restricted in time, with so many aspects to be covered, that the analyst argues strongly for a separate event.

The pre-development analytical meeting

One of the most effective ways of performing an analysis of existing and desired abilities, is to hold a pre-development event at which *all* the existing group members, or those who will develop into the team, must be present. Some of the detailed activities, particularly those not directly related to the analysis, will depend on the circumstances. For example, the reasons for the team development; a temporary project; or the development into a team of an existing grouping; and so on. Other more personally interactive activities might be performed on this occasion in which the 'group' is encouraged to increase its mutual openness – an integral part of team development. Never try to force this process or take too many steps too quickly.

Three principal analysis approaches will be rewarding to the analyst during an event of this nature:

1 Observation of the group for indications of level and development
2 Feedback from the group on attitudes to team development (for eventual sharing with the intention of increasing openness and trust)
3 Clarification of the team's and team leader's mutual perceptions and concerns about the role of each.

Observation of the group

Ideally, this observation should be made while the group is performing some task or activity that is part of its normal, at-work pattern – for example, a group meeting, a group problem solving session – and an assessment made of its skills, and so on, using the list of team characteristics described previously. However, if the group is a new team in the making, such an active observation is not possible. Instead, a pre-development event might be the start of the development process. In such situations, training activities (albeit engineered to be as realistic as possible) can be performed by the group and the assessment made from the learning objectives included in the activity. Such activities could include meetings and meetings management; creative problem solving sessions; decision making using an in-tray exercise; and so on. Although the latter approach is artificial, it gives the analyst the opportunity, denied elsewhere, to observe directly the individuals and the group in action.

Feedback from the group

It is too frequently assumed at the start of the development of a group that everyone involved – organization, team members, supporters – is enthusiastic and committed to the team and its development. Such assumptions are dangerous and a clarification of the real feelings supports the analysis of the team's starting point.

The views can be obtained by individual interviews or even group discussions, but this, although it gives the analyst the opportunity to question and challenge the statements of the interviewees, could be an extensive and expensive exercise. A less 'expensive' method, although perhaps not producing complete and fully honest information, is to use questionnaires. How accurate these are will depend on the culture of the organization and the willingness of all concerned to complete the questionnaires honestly (perhaps some degree of anonymity might help to ensure this). On a recent   *149* team development programme, in which I was involved, questionnaires, seeking views on attitudes and expectations were completed by the embryonic team members, the team leader and the sponsors (senior management group).

The first questionnaire was to the sponsors, and sought the organization's attitude to internal teams and its expectations of the team to be developed. The second questionnaire was to the team, and sought their views on their assumptions of the organization's expectations, hopes and concerns about their team. A third questionnaire, again to the team, sought their views on their attitudes to teamworking and their expectations, hopes and concerns about the team development end result. (As this was part of a complete programme, questions were also asked about their expectations, hopes and concerns about the team development programme itself.) A fourth questionnaire to the team sought their expectations and concerns about the team leader's role. Finally, the team leader was asked for his views on teamworking and his expectations, hopes and concerns about the team development.

When all the questionnaires had been completed, summarized copies of each set were circulated among the three groups and subsequently discussions were held to analyse these views, clarify any misunderstandings and seek to produce as much common agreement as possible. In this way the existing state and attitudes of the team were identified and a start made to rectify any dysfunctions. As a result, a realistic training and development programme could be produced in the knowledge that this would go a long way to satisfying the real, identified needs of the team and the organization.

Team leader/team perception clarification

One of the problems that can arise at the start of a team development process, and information about which provides substantial views for the analyst about the existing state of the 'team', is the interrelationship between the perceived role of the team leader by the leader and the team. A similar approach can be used in the case of an existing team, perhaps where it is starting to develop into an effective team or where there are problems in its development. Simple questionnaires, one completed by the leader, the other by the members, can give a good 'picture' of the current situations. The leader-specific questionnaires can also be supplemented by similar questionnaires – usefully based on the model of team development covered later – seeking the views of the leader and members about their perceptions of the stage of their team.

THE EFFECTIVE TEAM MODEL

Many definitions exist of an effective team and the analyst must be quite clear which model has to be taken into account in analysing the existing situation and the developing needs.

The following list of positive factors, drawn from experience of real and effective teams, serves as a practical working model for defining effective teams and team leadership.

1   Appropriate leadership
2   Enthusiasm and member commitment
3   Effective problem solving and decision making techniques
4   A creative atmosphere
5   Balanced planning and action
6   Acceptance of task achievement
7   Appropriate mix of relevant skills
8   Good interactive behavioural skills
9   Total information sharing within the team and, where appropriate, with other groups or teams
10 An atmosphere that encourages and supports risk taking and flexibility
11 Role clarity and inter-role knowledge
12 Total involvement and participation
13 Optimum and relevant membership
14 Clear objectives
15 An environment in which, although the emphasis is on task and team development, the process is enjoyable and fun.

Although this seems to be a formal list of requirements and the description of a model, it in fact suggests the questions that the analyst will need to ask to determine the existing extent of the group's attitudes and abilities, and what will be needed to develop the group.

In any teamworking model three aspects must be taken into account:

The team members

Questions can be asked of the team members to establish the following:

- Their attitudes towards team development and working
- Their expectations and views of the team leader's role
- Their expectations, hopes and concerns of the organization's attitude to team development and their team in particular
- Their concerns about their own abilities and the ability of the group to develop into an effective team.

The team leader

The team leader, where appointed, will be approaching the development with similar concerns, and can be asked:

- To what extent will the development be supported actively by the sponsor group?
- To what extent have I the abilities necessary to be a member of the team in addition to being the leader?
- What expectations have the individuals of the team of me as leader?
- How will the other members of the team accept me as the leader?
- How will my failure or success in this development affect my career?

The organization, or sponsoring group

The concerns of the organization/sponsor group will include:

- Will the group develop into an effective team in the timescale allotted?
- Are the people who have been selected the most appropriate ones for this particular development?
- Is the selected leader the most appropriate one for this role?
- How much time can we afford to take an active interest in this development?
- How will we assess the ultimate success or failure of this development in terms of human achievement and cost/value benefit?

THE EFFECTIVE TEAM LEADER MODEL

The analyst also needs to know the types of question that will need to be posed to determine the abilities – existing and potential – of the team leader, and a model similar to the effective team model can be applied. Obviously the leader, in addition to that specific role, is also a member of the team and many of the previously listed aspects will be relevant. But there are also specific ones relevant to the leader:

1 The ability to manage and lead the team in the most appropriate manner
2 The ability to develop a flexible approach to leader roles and methods
3 Awareness of, understanding, and preferably with skill in a range of problem solving and decision making techniques, including creative approaches
4 Ability to encourage and support risk taking among the team members even when mistakes are made
5 Ability to focus the team on achievement of the task at the same time as generating team development
6 Willingness to be the link between the team and the sponsors and to be prepared to fight the corner of the team
7 Openness in sharing information within the team when obtained from, for example, the sponsors and where absolute confidentiality has not been imposed
8 Skill in reviewing individuals and tasks and giving effective feedback

9   Encouragement of a sense of direction, enthusiasm and commitment, particularly when the team is at a low ebb
10 In addition to being the team leader, being able also to fulfil effectively a team member role.

Model considerations

Some of the items stated in both models need some detailed explanation (the prefix 'L' refers to the team leader's model and 'T' to the team model).

L1   *Appropriate leadership* – Although much of the onus of providing effective team leadership will fall on the leader, the members must be aware of the skills, concerns and needs of the leader who, in fact, is additionally a team member. In working teams, the leadership is not always vested in the appointed leader. When there is a need for specific skills or knowledge, the appointed leader is frequently not the person most appropriate to give a lead in completion of this part of the task. The 'expert' member then takes on the leadership role for that period. The appointed leader must be prepared to accept this and revert to a membership role.

T3   *Problem solving and decision making* – As usual, there is rarely only one way of solving a problem, and team members who frequently encounter problems need to have a ready toolkit of problem solving and decision making techniques from which to select the most appropriate. Members must have the flexibility of thought to be able to include creative problem solving in these situations and in many organizations and disciplines. If this creative ability is low or missing, it needs to become part of the process of the team development.

T5/6   *Balanced planning and action* – One of the problems encountered by developing teams is achieving the balance given to planning what has to be done and actually doing it. It is very easy, particularly if the task is not popular or is particularly difficult, to use more time than is actually necessary on planning what has to be done. The abilities of the team members in achieving as close to the ideal balance as possible can be identified at the analytical stage.

Linked with this balance is the acceptance by the team that, although in the early stages team development is very important, the purpose of a team is to achieve a task. This must be kept in mind all the time, in spite of the attractiveness of the process and the interactivity within the team that can delay the end of the task.

7/11/13   *Appropriate mix of relevant skills and team roles, and role clarity* – There are a number of models of team role and membership identity, and these can be used in the analytical process to determine the status of the team and the need to develop other roles and skills. The required mix of team roles and strengths will vary according to the demands of the team   *153* objectives. Ideal teams will result from the deliberate selection of members who fulfil the various roles, but unfortunately this is rarely a practical situation. More commonly the team leader is told 'You will have a team to work with you on this project. These are the people!' However, an effective team will include members with labels and roles such as:

Innovators – puts forward ideas for consideration
Investigator – researches previous instances of the ideas proposed
Developer – relates as necessary the various ideas to the task in mind
Evaluator – assesses the pros and cons and values of the various ideas proposed
Decision maker – from guidance, makes a decision on the task approach
Implementer – the practical, pragmatic role whose strength lies in action
Controller – if the task is to be achieved, a role holder is required to see that implementation is carried forward
Reviewer – when the task is complete, its success or failure has to be evaluated; the reasons for this identified and presented for discussion
Maintainer – if the task result is a continuing one for which the team is responsible, its continuance in an effective manner must be ensured
Coordinator – a valuable member or role in any team who ensures that everyone is performing to their optimum ability and is behaving as an effective team member in addition to a task achiever. In many cases coordinating will be a function of the leader, but another member might be allocated to this role when the leader is otherwise involved.

Many of these roles will be performed by members who have multi-skills, and many by all or most of the members of the team, but the analyst, in considering the abilities and needs of a team, must identify that the role requirements can be fulfilled, either from existing abilities or with training and development.

Other than the model team roles described above, it may sound obvious that team members of a particular team should be relevant as members of that team. However, only too frequently people are allocated to a team without that criterion in mind, and at best contribute nothing to the team, and at worst are a danger to the effective operation of the team. They may need to receive training and development so that they can be effective members of the team – this, however, is not always possible or opportune. The ideal, of course, is for the team leader to be able to select the team, but again this is not always possible and some aspects of irrelevant membership occur and have to be accepted.

The question of how many people should be involved in a team is equivalent to the enigma of 'How long is a piece of string'! The string should be as long as is necessary and, similarly, the team membership should be as small or as large as necessary, bearing in mind certain numerical aspects. The minimum for a team is generally considered to be three: one produces egocentrism, two can take opposing attitudes with only a painful compromise as a possibility, but three not only introduces a balancing role, but also extends the scope when creativity is demanded. However, with three there is always the danger that the third member will side with one of the original pair and produce conflict. At the other end of the spectrum, too large a group introduces different problems – those of leader control, overlap of role positions and resulting conflict, exclusion of quieter members, and so on – although, where creative ideas are sought, the more the merrier. A compromise, usually found to be satisfactory, is to have a working team of about eight people, preferably those with a variety of team roles between them, creative and flexible attitudes and a willingness to take an active team part.

TEAM DEVELOPMENT

The team development analyst has a dual role interest in assessing existing situations in order to recommend development action – the individuals and the team. Analysis of the individual will identify the individual skills, the intrinsic roles and the necessary ability to develop. Role identification linked to team requirement will demonstrate the extent to which the team or group possesses the role skills that will (or will eventually) enable optimum team performance. But teams as entities within themselves have aspects that can change with time and assistance, and the initial analysis can aid the development practitioner by identifying the existing stage of the team in this developmental process.

Most groups and teams develop with practice and over time in a reasonably predictable manner. A number of models have been developed to describe this process, one of which is suggested by Tuckman (1965). In this type of model the development of a team is described as four stages, demonstrated in Figure 9.4.

Forming

This model suggests that when a new team or group comes together for the first time, they enter a forming mode that is characterized by:

Politeness	Non-controversial discussion
General quietness	Limited personal disclosure
Acceptable comments	Avoidance of over-serious topics
The forming of cliques as a result of apparent mutual attraction	
Strong leader dependence	Frustration through little movement

As the stage progresses and forms, the behaviour of the members starts to open out, although the cliques can continue to exist and can occasionally cause problems. More personal statements are made and challenges begin to appear. Towards the end of the stage, the members are starting to become unsettled because they realize that there should be movement, but may be uncertain about their personal roles in this.

155

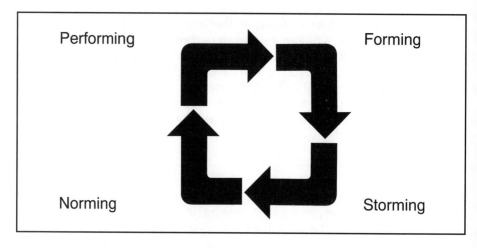

Figure 9.4 Team development model

Storming

The second stage is probably the most difficult one for the members, although it is relatively easy for the analyst to identify. Its characteristics include:

The (over-)strong expression of views
Reduced listening to others
Withdrawal by some members for a variety of reasons
Competition for control
The negative use of cliques
Tendency for the team to withdraw from active performance

Challenging the views of others
Challenging the leadership
Greater expression of emotions
Reduced collaboration
Defensive attitudes
Enforced voting for majority decision

Norming

By the end of the storming stage, if the team has realized the futility of continuing in this way but is determined to progress, an atmosphere of normality starts to appear and the development of this stage produces:

Real listening to others
Development of more systematic ways of working
Receptivity to ideas of others
Active participation by all and reference to the quieter ones for their views
Open exchange of ideas
Greater tolerance

Shared and flexible leadership
Willingness to change ideas and behaviour
Recognition of conflicts with attempts made to resolve them

Increased self-disclosure
Increased interdependence

Performing

By this stage the group is starting to work together as an integrated team in which there is the realization that cooperation is more likely to produce synergy. The characteristics include the following, and an analyst who identifies a group with these will have the much easier task of concentrating on the development aspects of individuals within the team:

High-level but balanced contributions

High degree of openness

Leadership is accepted but sharing is commonplace when expertise demands

Strong support for individuals trying to change

Conflict resolved in a cooperative manner

Appropriate behaviours or strong movement to develop more appropriate behaviours

Easy acceptance of others' points of view, but still with open challenges

Creativity

Members trust each other

The members have developed strong relationships

A warm and friendly atmosphere

Less dependence on structure and sequencing

Wide use of team roles and interchangeability

The principal problem by this stage is that the team might close in on itself, to the exclusion of other teams or groups and with a resultant lack of cooperation with them. True maturity recognizes this and accepts that other groups are as effective as they are. In effect this is a return to the forming stage, but with a multi-team situation.

A recognition of the stage a group is at will enable the analyst to determine what the needs are in order to assist the group to develop into a team.

CONCLUSIONS

Full and open use of the completed questionnaires mentioned earlier in the chapter will not only provide substantial information for the analyst, but will also allow the team to establish the reasons for building a team. The questionnaires can, in addition, give a diagnosis of existing states and clarify what makes an effective team and team leader. Questionnaires have been suggested not only to provide substantial information for the analyst, but also to give the team the opportunity to develop its openness, trust and ability to clarify and resolve possible disagreement and conflict. The use of a team development model gives a structure to understanding how near the team is to achieving its most effective performance and what may be addressed to assist the team.

In conclusion, the key to analysing a team's needs is to ask questions.

REFERENCES AND RECOMMENDED READING

Adair, J., *Effective Leadership*, Gower, Aldershot, 1983

Eales-White, R., *Building Your Team*, Kogan Page, London, 1995

Moxon, P., *Building a Better Team*, Gower, Aldershot, 1993

Parker, G.M., Kropp, R.P., *Team Building: A sourcebook of activities for trainers*, Kogan Page, London, 1992

Tuckman, B.W., 'Development Sequence in Small Groups', *Psychological Bulletin*, 1965, **63**, 284–499

10 Using team roles

Nancy Foy

Anyone who has ever explored family history will have discovered Rule One: *be a lover, not a fighter.* The fighters had their moments of glory, but it is the lovers who managed to leave enough descendants to bother with family history. So it is in organizations; despite all the blether about 'competition', it is the ability to *cooperate* that makes the difference between extinction and survival.

The trouble is that human beings prefer a bit of fun, including glory, including competition, including winning. Competition seems strongest when it is closest to home. Measure any element of performance and lo and behold! Managers scrap with each other to climb the slippery league table, within a department, or across the geography. Little teams compete to improve performance when they can see other little teams pulling ahead. Individuals vie with each other – it's a natural thing, competition. It starts in the cradle with sibling rivalry, and we all take part in it too often.

It takes wit and wisdom to convince people that the winning – and often the fun – are greater when you can win as a team. There are sneaky ways to begin this process (red/black, or prisoner games – the tools of traditional team building, which appear elsewhere in this handbook). I prefer the honest approach, where you start by opening up, even just a little bit, to people you are beginning to trust.

A person can be a winner in one setting and a loser in another. Why? Whatever the leadership situation, when the mix is right people work better. The sum *can* be greater than the parts.

Dr R. Meredith Belbin worked for many years under the aegis of Cambridge's Industrial Training Research Unit to develop a profile of the membership of an effective team (see his 1981 book *Management Teams*). He studied syndicates working (and competing – so their success could be measured) in the Henley College management programme, and tracked them over weeks or months. He found that the teams which were most effective had a number of different roles covered. Those teams with many similar roles were less successful.

Belbin's first work along these lines was in the 1970s. Since then other experts have suggested slightly different roles. Many Belbin-type instruments now include a single-minded, self-starting 'specialist' role. When in the early 1980s I started using this version of Belbin's profiles with K. John Burns, then at the Oxford Centre for Management Studies (now Templeton College), we incurred the disapproval of several colleagues by changing some of the role names to make them seem less academic. But Belbin's roles they were, and are, and will remain, and a new verb – to Belbinize – has entered the management language. Homage to Belbin!

Belbin's approach differs from navel-scrutinizing psychology because it is aimed at using individual strengths to strengthen the team. It takes extra energy to force the people choosing team members to scan the mix of people already there and fill the gaps, instead of selecting more of the same so 'everyone will get on well together'.

WHY 'BELBINIZE'?

The first step towards building a team is to encourage members to be open with each other. One of the more effective tools for opening up is Belbin's team-role analysis. I can think of several reasons for using it, not only at the birth of a team, but also as membership or tasks change, and whenever the team wants to revisit its own internal processes:

- To clarify who is doing what, and why
- To reinforce respect for people unlike onself
- To absolve people from guilt for not being perfect at everything.

It is always helpful to understand how different members of a team may fit together, but this tool can specifically be used to help members or potential members of a team begin opening up to each other, and revealing personal preferences, in an uncontrived setting, with no 'touchy-feely' psychological claptrap to put them off.

The side effects of 'Belbinizing' a team can include reduction in what Warren Bennis, around the time of Richard Nixon's impeachment, called 'the doppelgänger effect'. A doppelgänger, or 'ghostly double' is, in Bennis's terms, a sidekick like Haldeman or Erlichman who uses the same expletives, smokes the same cigarettes, or otherwise behaves much too like his boss. Doppelgängers are not good for organizations, or countries, as Nixon and company learned too late. People *do* subconsciously or consciously try to select others who share their values, prejudices, habits. It's reassuring, and it speeds the process of becoming 'us'. But to build a great team, you need

a way to recognize and appreciate those characteristics that are *not* like your own, otherwise the sum cannot be greater than the array of nearly identical parts.

Another positive side effect of the Belbin instrument is guilt reduction. The first time it was tried on me the proverbial lightbulb flashed over my head. In a forced-choice questionnaire, there was no way that I could be the contacts and ideas person I am and still do the i-dotting and t-crossing of the finisher. You can't have a high score on every possible answer. I had to *choose*, and what I choose to do or be carries with it another choice – what I choose *not* to do or be. In this day of downsizing and superwomen (or superpersons) there is an expectation (of ourselves more than our colleagues) that we will go on achieving more and more, into the glorious sunset. What really happens is that we go on trying to achieve everything, to be all things to all persons, until the stress catches up, the bottom falls out, or our sense of achievement goes off the top of a cliff. For people motivated by achievement, overload reduces the chance to do a good job. Superman is a modern myth, and has no place in an effective team. Recognizing such inflated self-expectations can be the first step towards adjusting them in directions that will be helpful to the person as well as the organization.

The following Belbin inventory is taken from my book *Empowering People at Work* (Gower, 1994). If I ever wrote another I would probably use it again, because I am so convinced that this approach really does help teams – and that effective teams are the unacknowledged bedrock on which organizations rest. The self-scoring test takes about ten minutes. The important thing is for team members to share their scores, and negotiate among themselves to fill the missing roles. Like Dr Belbin, neither Gower nor I wish to keep people from xeroxing or otherwise copying these pages – if you can use them, be our guest! Every 'instrument' carries invisible shreds of its progenitor's prejudices. After using this one for 20 years, I think its results are generally consistent with other Belbinizing instruments, with perhaps a slight prejudice against the critic (or planner) and finisher. (My i-dotting is rather eccentric and long-range planning in our house seldom extends further than what's-for-dinner, and these preferences taint the results slightly.) To eliminate the prejudice factor, simply review your scores when you finish and ask yourself or your team: 'What score would you like to make higher?' Three points more here? Fine. Which role or roles are you going to take them away from? The results, like management credibility, belong to the team member, not a trainer or team leader. You can change them any way that fits your self-image, so long as they add up to 70.

Every team needs every one of the roles Belbin identified. Someone needs to take an interest in crossing the t's, or moving the team from discussion to action. If you don't have a natural finisher or implementer, someone will have to consciously take on the role. Even three people have to perform all eight roles among themselves if they are to succeed at doing a task together. Most people are fairly happy with at least two or three of the roles – and most of us can quickly identify ourselves with one role in particular, once *161* we've taken in the descriptions. By the same token, most people would be quite uncomfortable in one or two of the roles.

There can be no wrong answers. Nobody can score any higher than anybody else. Each section contains ten points, for a grand total of 70. Everyone achieves that 70 (if not, find a numerate finisher to find the error). But the way you apportion the points shows who can fill each role in the team.

DIY TEAM ROLE INVENTORY

Below are sets of statements describing attitudes and personal preferences. Each statement includes eight choices. You have ten points to apportion among them. The more you feel a particular response fits you, the higher the number of points you give it. As long as they add up to ten per statement and thus 70 in total, all scores here are 'good'.

1 When involved in a project with other people . . .

f ——I can be relied on to see that the work we need to do is organized.

h ——I detect slips and omissions that others fail to notice.

b ——I react strongly when meetings look like losing track of the main objective.

d ——I produce original suggestions.

e ——I analyse other people's ideas objectively for their merits and their flaws.

c ——I am keen to find out the latest ideas and developments.

a ——I have an aptitude for organizing people.

g ——I am always ready to support good suggestions that help to resolve a problem.

2 In seeking satisfaction through my work . . .

b —— I like to have a strong influence on decisions.

h ——I work best where work requires a high degree of concentration and attention.

g ——I am concerned to help colleagues with their problems.

e ——I like to make critical discriminations between alternatives.

d ——I tend to have a creative approach to problem solving.

a ——I enjoy reconciling different points of view.

f ——I am more interested in practicalities than in new ideas.

c ——I particularly enjoy exploring different views and techniques.

3 When the team is trying to solve a particularly complex problem . . .

h ——I keep a watching eye on areas where difficulties may arise.

c ——I explore ideas that may have a wider application than to the immediate task.

e ——I like to weigh up and thoroughly evaluate a range of suggestions before choosing.

a ——I can coordinate and productively use other people's abilities and talents.

f ——I maintain a steady, systematic approach, whatever the pressures.

d ——I often produce a new approach to a long-continuing problem.

b ——I am ready to make my personal views known, in a forceful way if necessary.

g ——I am ready to help wherever I can.

4 In carrying out my day-to-day work . . .

f ——I am keen to see that there is nothing vague about my task and objectives.

b ——I am not reluctant to emphasize my own point of view at meetings.

a ——I can work with all sorts of people, provided they have something worthwhile to contribute.

c ——I make a point of following up interesting ideas and people.

e ——I can usually find the argument to refute unsound propositions.

d ——I tend to see patterns where others would see items as unconnected.

h ——Being busy gives me real satisfaction.

g ——I have a quiet interest in getting to know people better.

5 If I am suddenly given a difficult task with limited time and unfamiliar people . . .

d ——I often find my imagination frustrated by working in a group.

a ——My personal skills are particularly appropriate in achieving agreement in the group.

e ——My feelings seldom interfere with my judgement.

f ——I strive to build up an effective structure.

g ——I can work with people who vary widely in their personal qualities and outlook.

b ——I feel it is sometimes worth incurring some temporary unpopularity to succeed in getting my views across in a group.

c ——I usually know the person whose specialist knowledge is particularly apt.

h ——I seem to develop a natural sense of urgency.

6 When suddenly asked to consider a new project . . .

c ——I start to look around for possible ideas and openings.

h ——I am concerned to finish and perfect current work before I start.

e ——I approach the problem in a carefully analytical way.

b ——I am able to assert myself to involve other people if necessary. *163* d ——I am able to take an independent and innovative look at most situations.

a ——I am happy to take the lead when action is required.

g ——I can respond positively to my colleagues and their initiatives.

f ——I find it hard to give of my best in a job where the goals are not clearly defined.

7   In contributing to group projects, in general . . .

f ——I think I have a talent for sorting out the concrete steps that need to be taken, given a broad brief.

e ——My considered judgement may take time, but it is usually near the mark.

c ——A broad range of personal contacts is important to my style of working.

h ——I have an eye for making sure the details are right.

b ——I try to make my mark in group meetings.

d ——I can see how ideas and techniques can be used in new relationships and situations.

a ——I can see both sides of a problem and take a decision acceptable to all.

g ——I get on well with others and work hard for the team.

Now add the scores for each letter, and put the totals in the boxes below (Table 10.1):

Table 10.1   Scoring grid for team role inventory

a	b	c	d	e	f	g	h

The highest score indicates your preferred role style in a team, but you are probably comfortable in any of your 'top three' roles. Here are the descriptions that go with the letters above. See if they fit your own perceptions:

a   **The Chair** ('chairman' in olden times, but we are politically correct now). This is the coordinator (not the boss). He or she likes organizing people, mapping their strengths, using them productively. This is the person who engineers consent and consensus, developing agreement among different interests. The chair commands respect and inspires enthusiasm, talks and listens well, and has a sense of discipline, focus, timing and balance. The chair may not necessarily be the smartest or most creative member of the team.

b   **The Shaper** This is the outgoing, forceful task-leader type who likes to make a mark in meetings, to influence group decisions. He or she will risk being unpopular to put ideas across. The shaper concentrates on setting objectives and priorities, and making sure the discussion and action take on the right shape or pattern. The shaper's drive and self-confidence may carry a hint of intolerance or impatience with vague or fuzzy people or ideas. This is the one exception to Belbin's rule that you need all roles in a team. A team does *not* need both a chair and a shaper – they often work against each other.

c **The Contacts Man** (or woman – Belbin calls this role 'The Resource Investigator') This is the sociable, relaxed 'butterfly', flitting around the boundaries, looking farther afield than the immediate task, bringing in outside ideas, developments and phone numbers. The butterfly works by personal networks and contacts, likes new ideas and techniques, and can usually find the right specialist to help at a moment's notice. He or she works well on the phone, probably has an outgoing personality, is willing to see possibilities in anything new. The curiosity asset may be paired with over-enthusiasm, or a lack of follow-up.

d **The Ideas Man** (or woman – Belbin calls this role 'The Plant') This is the innovator, the most original, independent, intelligent, imaginative (and sometimes introverted) member, who often feels frustrated at the pace of group work. The ideas person is a source of new approaches to old problems, new ideas and strategies. The innovator likes puzzles, patterns and problem solving. The team values its innovator for independent outlook, as well as intelligence and imagination. An innovator's weaknesses are quite tolerable: a tendency to be impractical, a carelessness with details, or weakness at communicating ideas to members with different outlooks and attitudes.

e **The Critic** (Belbin's 'Monitor–Evaluator') This is the analyst, the careful, critical member, often slow but right. The critic's judgement wins over feelings, and his or her contributions are analysing problems and evaluating other people's ideas and suggestions. It's useful to have someone who can poke holes in unsound proposals before they have cost a lot. The critic is a necessary part of quality checking. The critic also wants to be sure all the information is on hand before a decision is made. This member is long on evaluation and objectivity, but probably over-serious, unexciting, and occasionally *too* critical. It's best to send him (or her) away to do something useful elsewhere when the team is at the creative stage of problem solving.

f **The Implementer** (Belbin's 'Company Worker') This is the practical type who turns ideas into manageable tasks, meeting targets and deadlines. The implementer wants clear objectives and procedures – and is sometimes uncomfortable with new ideas. This is the solid, systematic, trustworthy member who can make a practical plan to achieve the objective when the others have finished arguing about it. The team needs its implementer to turn concepts and plans into practical *165* working procedures, and for carrying them out methodically. Implementer strengths include self-control and self-discipline, realism and common sense. This member may be a little inflexible or unexciting, perhaps unresponsive to new ideas that aren't yet proven – but the Implementer is probably the best at administration.

g **The Team Builder** (Belbin's 'Team Worker') This is the nurturer, the one who likes people and works easily with them, even when their ideas differ. The team builder will hold the team together, supporting the others in their strengths and filling in for their weaknesses, while oiling their communication machinery. The team builder is more concerned with the process than the precise result (where the Shaper concentrates on the task itself and is less concerned with the process). Strengths include listening, encouraging, harmonizing. The team builder is characterized by flexibility, humility – and popularity. These may be balanced by a lack of decisiveness or toughness, and a dislike for competition and friction among team members. (My mother, a fine Team Builder, used to caution her children: 'Birds, in their little nests, agree!')

h **The Finisher** This is one of the most important, and often least appreciated, members of the team. While the ideas person or the innovator starts things, the finisher completes them. This member's fine eye for detail is most likely to notice omissions or mistakes. The finisher checks details and schedules, makes sure the team makes few errors, and keeps track of the parts of the task that need extra attention. This member also maintains a sense of urgency, and acts as the team's conscience. Failing enough current problems, the finisher will worry about future problems. Strengths include a sense of order, a well-focused purpose, self-control and strength of character. Foibles include impatience, intolerance to more casual members, and an inability to suffer fools or foolishness gladly.

ADJUSTING TEAM BALANCE

There are more elaborate (and expensive) ways to obtain accurate team role profiles. Some have computerized scoring systems; others have longer, more sophisticated 'instruments'. But there are also cheaper ways: Review the descriptions above and decide for yourself what you are – and guess about your fellow team members. Then check up and discuss your roles. This instrument may help the process by putting numbers on it, but most people know themselves well enough to choose the appropriate categories.

Sharing the team role information, and using it to sharpen the team's performance is the real breakthrough.

Most people are able to fill more than one of these roles. (The finest restaurateurs I ever knew were Creative Finishers.) In any group from five to ten or 15, the roles can be shared out if balance is maintained.

Problems may occur when a strong manager chooses too many doppelgängers. A team of ideas people doesn't want a finisher throwing cold water on their constructions. A practical team of implementers doesn't appreciate the butterfly contacts man or woman.

The first step to balancing a team is appreciating and respecting the natural styles of the other members. If everyone fills out the inventory, and then each person puts the scores on to a single flip chart, the overlaps and gaps will show up immediately. That's fine. You can fill gaps by finding the members whose second or third choices were highest in those categories – but there will have to be explicit discussion of ways to help them fill the under-represented roles.

Except for the potential power problems between the chairman and shaper, it's acceptable if more than one member prefers a role – perhaps taking turns to be the chief critic, or monitoring and evaluating different aspects of a project. As with marriage, it's the process of discussing and negotiating, surfacing the differences, that makes them manageable. (Indeed, the team role approach can be useful in families, too.)

Whenever the project changes, or the team feels a bit frustrated, it's useful to haul out the team role flip chart and see whether all the roles are still being covered effectively. It can also be useful when a new member joins, or when two teams share a project.

'COUNTER-BELBIN' TEAM WRECKERS

People who can't have fun doing good things will still find ways to have fun – like wrecking other people's good things.

One day, after a particularly hair-raising day among a bunch of down-at-the-mouth purchasing clients, Alison Waugh, a Scottish creativity consultant, and I whiled away the two-hour drive homeward generating a list of counter-Belbin characters. These were people who shared the basic characteristics of the Belbin team-role examples, but had seen their bright hopes go sour, or never nurtured anything bright to begin with. Here they are (Table 10.2), related to their more wholesome alter egos:

The Hijacker   The hijacker will dive into the team process as if he (or she) had Semtex strapped around his or her middle, grabbing the magic marker and wielding it as if it were a Kalashnikov, diverting a meeting or project for his (or her) own ends, usually to fill personal psychological needs. I recall a woman dressed in magenta and gold, know-it-all chips on her shoulders, and an obvious axe to grind. Sometimes, especially in teams which are able to take turns at the leadership role, a power-hog becomes a hijacker.

A hijack can occasionally illuminate some forgotten corner of a topic, but usually antagonizes other team members, and stops the process. 'It's just Reg again!' If the hijacker isn't stopped, the project sits on the ground while its members steam, starve, and don't get anywhere, like an aircraft stuck in a dangerous middle-eastern airport.

You can try diverting a mild hijacker into harmless and possibly useful activity, but it takes time and energy, and you have to keep an eye on them all the time – you can't trust a hijacker. The only way we know to deal with a hijacker is for the entire team (usually alerted by eyebrow signals) to pounce all at once, and sit on the hijacker while the chair applies a gag and stores the Semtex for another foray.

The Tight Cannon   The tight cannon is carefully aimed at a particular target or issue. All it can do is point and shoot, which can be dangerous if you're in the way. The tight cannon may aim himself (also herself), or be wound up and aimed by others. Like the shaper, the TC has an objective, and intends to achieve it by fair means or foul. The analogy is more to a steamroller than a hijack. The hijacker is wielding power, but the tight cannon is pursuing an *idée fixe* with all the concentrated firepower at his or her command.

Cannon-conversion is difficult. He or she isn't really suited to being a member of a workable team. Nor is it practical to melt down your cannons and turn them into ploughshares. The TC may be passive when outside his or her own context, and might be usefully deployed for some occasional missionary work. Underneath that unmanageable exterior is a nearly unmanageable shaper.

The Loose Cannon   Here's the bright one who blurts out the team's plan before they've had a chance to bulletproof them, or energetically springs an alternative from a different source just as implementation of the agreed approach is beginning. The loose cannon is as dangerous for himself or herself as others. It can be particularly interesting if a loose cannon accidentally finds his way (or hers) into management. Loose cannons can create untold (and sometimes unattributed) wreckage at higher levels, often in the name of openness. When they get to the very top, with subordinates chasing down data about every trend or possibility they've encountered at august meetings of colleagues, whole organizations can creak to a halt. If your old

Table 10.2   Belbin and counter-Belbin team roles

Belbin Team Role	Counter-Belbin Role
Chair	Hijacker
Shaper	Tight cannon
Contacts	Loose cannon
Ideas	Sponge
Critic	Yebbut
Implementer	Passenger
Team Builder	Helper
Finisher	Hausfrau

contacts person is turning into a loose cannon, export to the competition ASAP!

The Sponge   Where the ideas person sparks off ideas in all directions, the sponge absorbs all, often very genially, but gives nowt. I remember a ski trip organized by a company club, where the organizers worried all weekend about Marshall. He sat on the sidelines, saying nothing, talking to nobody, blank. The leaders took turns sitting by Marshall, chatting to him, looking for ways to include him in activities. No response. The following Tuesday in the staff canteen, one of the leaders overheard a conversation – Marshall describing to a mate in glowing terms all the wonderful events of the ski weekend, as if he'd taken part in them! For Marshall, watching other people do things was sufficient.

The sponge absorbs energy from the leader and the team, and gives back very little – unless asked. Find ways to ask effectively.

The Yebbut   An active resister is not expressing the doubt of the critic, who sees problems at the planning stage, or the finisher who can envisage perfection, but the Yebbut's deep, dyed-in-the-wool 'We tried it before and it won't work'. There's every reason to learn from experience, but Yebbuts take energy out of the group process, simply as a matter of knee-jerk no-no reflex, or the joy of breaking other kids' toys. Yebbuts are often attracted to large bureaucracies, where their mastery of what can't be done can push them up the ladder. At least they can be identified early and tagged.

'Fire hose' is Tom Peters' (1982) term for a weapon against negativity. At one meeting the fire hose turned into a water pistol, with instructions to shoot anyone who said 'yes, but . . .' One member reached into the middle, picked up the water pistol, and shot his mate square in the centre of his forehead. The Scots version of the Yebbut is the 'Cannae-do'.

One thing the team can do with a Yebbut member is turn the problem on its head. Build a script that has other queries:
  'Why not . . .?'
  'How to . . .?'
  'Yes, and . . .?'

The Passenger   A passive resister. Passengers are made, not born. They tend to sit with arms crossed, negative vibes emanating gently. The passenger may be a know-all, but he (or she) is not talking while the flavour lasts. If something flops, the passenger will very likely point out how it could have been predicted. This kind of behaviour demotivates others if it's allowed to flourish, though passengers can sometimes be enticed into partial participation. A team can't afford to carry passengers unless they pay their fare. Once a member has taken on a Belbin team role, force him (or her) to take responsibility for it or depart.

The Helper   This cheery soul reinforces other counter-Belbin characters.   *169*

He or she supplies Semtex for the hijacker, polishes cannon balls, gives sponges someone to talk to, and encourages the passenger's 'I told them so'. The helper tends to push a wayward project into 'fast forward' instead of getting back on the rails (to mix a metaphor).

The Hausfrau Beyond finishing is the finicky hausfrau, who can't let go of a project, always adding a little more spit and polish, demanding one more inspection, looking for procedures that will absolve her (or him) of blame, and generally inducing delays the others would rather do without. Clarity about priorities and deadlines can help keep hausfrau tendencies under control, but the real cause here is anxiety, and as organizations downsize this phenomenon may be worsening because symptoms of anxiety are rising.

One generalized solution to counter-Belbinism is to have a whistle-blower, licensed by the group, to call a halt if behaviour destructive to team processes is getting out of hand. Another is to respect individual differences (especially as revealed in Belbinizing) and make use of special characteristics. A potential Yebbut can be sent out with a young project to have it 'fire-proofed' by potential critics or customers. A potential passenger can be consulted at the beginning: 'Where are the pitfalls we're going to have to watch out for?' A potential tight cannon can be asked: 'Super idea. Could you take a couple of minutes to show us?'

CONCLUSION

Characteristics are what make up character. They only go sour when they're not used properly. If every member of a team has a clear idea of what's expected, the tools (including time) to do the task, and some recognition from other members for his or her contribution, counter-Belbin behaviour will dwindle, and team members can enjoy achieving tasks together.

RECOMMENDED READING

Belbin, C.M., *Management Teams*, Oxford, Butterworth-Heinemann, 1981. The best source for information about Belbin's work is Belbin himself. Many others have interpreted Belbin, or re-cast his characters, but the original taxonomy stands up under fire. There are many different ways to use Belbin's model, but I don't think the computerized approach is necessary. The purpose is for individuals and teams to understand each other a little better, and to give them a language to express their preferences and personalities without threatening them with imminent shrinkage. For me, the best use of Belbin is a group exercise, with the results flip-charted for the benefit of all.

Berg, P.-O., *The Emotional Structures of Organisations*, Lund University, Sweden, 1978. This is an increasingly useful tool in my kit. Berg studied a Scandinavian glass company by identifying 63 dramatic events – 'Was that before or after the HR director left?' He found there was an important difference between 'key actors', who did everything, and 'key observers', who saw everything. This helps explain so many disappointed expectations in organizations: 'If he saw that coming, why didn't he do anything about it?' Or 'How could he have missed seeing the changes coming? He was right in the middle of the action.' If one expects *good observation* from the observers, and *rapid action* from the actors, one is less disappointed. I think Berg caught the nature of both, and it is we who demand inappropriate responses from them who must change our expectations.

Ewing, D.W., *Inside the Harvard Business School*, New York, Times Books/ Random House, 1990. Ewing is another person who taught me about teams in various ways. His career as Managing Editor of the *Harvard Business Review* gave him unique access to ideas that are important today, like informal groups, participative management, and power sharing. His work on whistleblowers deserves more attention today as corporate ethics finally comes into the limelight.

Gyllenhammar, P., *People at Work*, Reading, Mass., Addison-Wesley, 1977. I helped Pehr Gyllenhammar give birth to this book, which describes the ideas behind his achievements at Volvo, including the pioneering autonomous groupworking, and the importance of bringing the stores to the team instead of dispersing the team to go get the stores. The book also raised such questions as why we should be trapped in an eight-hour working day, and how job sharing might be organized by the sharers.

Hofstede, G., *The Game of Budget Control*, New York, Van Nostrand, 1967. Geert Hofstede first noted that a 'negotiated' budget, where a manager or team has a chance to influence the process, has a better chance of being met than an 'imposed' budget, where the subject has little voice. This work is probably at the root of my own later work on management credibility and how to manage the hypocrisy gap in large organizations.

Mintzberg, H., *The Nature of Managerial Work*, New York, Harper & Row, 1973. In this book, Mintzberg first revealed that, for most managers, the interruptions are actually the heart of the job. He went on to explore power and structure in some depth. His 1979 book *The Structuring of Organizations* (Englewood Cliffs, NJ, Prentice-Hall) configures organizations on the basis of five basic parts (operating core, strategic apex, middle line, technostructure and support staff). These are fed by five flows (formal authority, regulated information, informal communication, work constellations and *ad hoc* decision making). Coordination comes from another fivesome (direct supervision, mutual adjustment, standardization, output and skills). The resulting 5 × 5 cube can be used to describe or prescribe for any organization.

Peters, T. and Waterman, R., *In Search of Excellence*, New York, Harper & Row, 1982.

Revans, R., *Action Learning*, Harlow, Longman, 1975. Reg Revans, the founder of action learning, has influenced organization and team development far beyond his personal magic. This is the 'bible' but Revans' work underlies much of today's emphasis on the learning organization as well as project work, cell manufacture and shared problem solving. At its heart is a group of individuals, tackling together or separately problems with some unfamiliar elements, and 'co-consulting' as they do so. If they are helped to reflect together as they progress, problems are solved, and people develop, in quite remarkable ways.

Wickens, P., *The Road to Nissan: Flexibility, Quality, Teamwork*, Basingstoke, Macmillan, 1987. In Peter Wickens' Nissan experience we find such treasures as the five-minute morning meeting, the well-chosen supervisor, the well-developed team with a clear target and the right tools to achieve it.

11 How groups and teams learn

Alan Mumford

A great deal of attention has been paid in the 1990s to the concept of, and sometimes the practices in, a learning organization. Powerful though the metaphor of a learning organization is, and important though the actual issues addressed through the metaphor are, a great deal of the discussion seems to have been based on flimsy foundations (Mumford, 1996). Not many people have yet tackled in depth the issue of how to develop effective learners. Nor have the issues involved in developmental relationships between one person and another been properly discussed. My picture of the learning organization expresses these issues through the following Figure 11.1

Powerful though the organization as a whole is in its impact on the individual, the most potent expression of influence comes from the particular actions of other individuals. The organization is a convenient expression for the perceived totality of powerful influences. This chapter concentrates on the influence of something larger than the individual, and smaller than the organization – the group

How line managers can help their subordinates or colleagues to learn in groups is considered here, since they are the people with the clearest responsibility and accountability for helping others. The role of colleagues in the group is also important, particularly the effect of their activities on whether and how colleagues learn within the group.

THE MANAGER AS A SOCIALIZED WORKER

Among the defining characteristics of managers, as compared with senior researchers or professionals, is that they achieve their goals in part through their direct responsibility for the work of others. Another aspect of that characteristic is that managers work in and through a variety of groups,

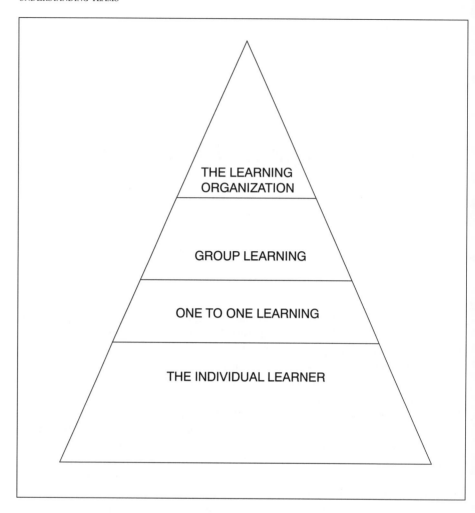

Figure 11.1   The learning pyramid

some temporary and some relatively permanent. Managers do not spend much time on their own; but mainly in a variety of social interactions. The effectiveness of those interactions is itself a subject for learning by individuals and, of course, by the group as a whole. This is usually described as the 'process' aspect of a working group – the extent to which it facilitates achievement of its objectives and goals through the management of the group dynamic.

Most managers see the prime purpose of a working group as being the carrying out of managerial tasks – the facilitation of achievement by either individuals or the group as a whole of larger-scale or intertwined objectives.

Generally groups spend very little time on process issues unless they have been introduced to some discipline for doing so by attending a course, or by interventions through a process consultant at work. It is even more rare for groups to consider their effectiveness as vehicles for learning. Whereas there is material on how direct managers, mentors and coaches can assist individual development, there is much less evidence on how groups can be made into more effective learning vehicles at work.

Watkins and Marsick (1993) present one of the few processes for identifying and developing team learning processes. This chapter concentrates very much on learning 'at work'. There is a great deal more available on how effective learning groups can be created off the job through courses, workshops, and so on. However, these are designed, constructed and facilitated by trainers and specialist developers, not usually by line managers. For that reason the learning groups constructed in courses are referred to only in passing in this chapter – just to illustrate areas of knowledge and awareness that a manager might take to a course, or bring back from it. This chapter deals with how the line manager helps directly, which predominantly means through real teams at work.

TEAMS OR GROUPS

It is not our intention to summarize all the available knowledge about teams. The aim is just to provide sufficient comment on some of the characteristics of a team at work to highlight some of the issues likely to affect the willingness or ability of individuals to learn from the working of the team or group. Once that has been established we can move on to the more specific attributes of the learning group or team.

From a managerial point of view there is a significant difference between a collection of individuals brought together in a group, and a collection of individuals brought together as a team. The former is more likely to be temporary, to have no agreed managerial objectives, to have no clear accountability for its performance and often no clear leader. A team, by contrast, is usually more permanent in nature, is accountable for the achievement of defined areas of performance and has a defined leader. A group may have no internal cohesiveness, and may have no real requirement at any level of significance for such cohesiveness. A team may also have no internal cohesiveness in practice, but usually knows that it ought to have this in order to achieve its purposes.

This distinction is not always vital because the issues discussed here largely apply whether the collection of people is a group or a team. The significant difference is that because there is a leader of the team – the manager or other person designated to be accountable for its performance – the responsibility for encouraging learning is more obviously centred. The team leader can take the initiative in, for example, describing learning opportunities, encouraging learning reviews and rewarding effective learning behaviours within the team. Within a group, there may be no clear leader and therefore no individual with strong feelings of managerial accountability for encouraging attention to learning. There may, of course, be a particular individual who wants to concentrate on learning issues, but *175* such an individual will have a harder time than will the leader/manager within a team.

In the rest of this chapter no distinction will be made between a team and a group unless it is central to the point being made.

CHARACTERISTICS OF EFFECTIVE TEAMS

Precisely because teams can provide ideal situations for the encouragement of effective learning, it is helpful to start with a review of what goes into making an effective team. Not only will the participants recognize those characteristics which enable them to achieve their managerial objectives, they will also begin to see correlations between those behaviours necessary to managerial achievement and those appropriate to learning. Chart 11.1 is reproduced with permission from Peter Honey.

Some aspects of teams are very familiar to us. They consist of people with all their individual personalities and ways of behaving, but also with managerial functions (for example, finance, production). People bring with them their individual personalities and ways of behaving; they bring with them experience, skills and insights into effective management. The team will use disciplines and methods of structuring its work. Group dynamics will involve attitudes and emotions of one person for another, or one sub-set of people for another, which will help or hinder the effective work of the team. It will develop for itself a culture and norms of behaviour.

There are two important learning characteristics. The group or team is both a method of learning and an object of learning. It is a way of providing for cross-fertilization of ideas, techniques, problems and solutions. It is also an object of study – 'How does this team achieve its results and what can I learn from that?'

One of the differences between groups and teams identified earlier is that teams tend to be relatively permanent and groups are often temporary. Within the team the opportunities for learning tend to arise from two different kinds of situation. A departmental management team, for example, will work as a team on fairly regular and routine occasions. Most obviously it will meet from time to time under the chairmanship of the departmental manager. My research shows that managers learn relatively less from the stable and routine situations and events than they do from the second kind of situation, in which the normal managerial team takes on special responsibilities or a special task. Situations of this kind range from the annual production of the business plan or budget, to the investigation of a problem or special decision about some activity, such as: 'In view of the decline in sales shall we close down the following three branches?'

In addition, of course, special teams can be created – task groups, working parties, think-tanks, quality circles. These again have the characteristics of teams – an identified purpose, accountability and usually a chairperson/ leader.

Since we know how powerful teams can be in pursuing shared objectives,

---

Chart 11.1   Characteristics of a good team

- A good team has a high success rate, i.e. more often than not they achieve what they set out to
- A good team agrees clear, challenging objectives, i.e. everyone in the team contributes to, shares understanding of, and is committed to the objectives
- A good team has a leader (it may not always be the same person) who adjusts the leadership style along a spectrum from participative to autocratic in the light of circumstances
- A good team has a mix of people who contribute in different but complementary ways thus achieving synergy, i.e. the team produces more than the sum of its individual parts
- A good team operates in such a way that a balance is struck between concern for the task (the 'what') and concern for the process (the 'how')
- A good team creates a supportive atmosphere where people are happy to go at risk, say what they really think, develop one another's ideas, and commit to an agreed course of action even though there may have been differences of opinion
- A good team learns from experience, both successes and failures, by reviewing its processes and thus constantly improving its own performance
- A good team works hard and plays hard, i.e. members not only achieve challenging objectives but enjoy themselves as they do so.

---

the potential for teams to be effective learning vehicles, if they choose to pursue learning objectives as well as task objectives, is considerable. This exercise will help to reinforce some of the points made so far:

Exercise – review of effective teams

1 Consider groups or teams in which you are currently the leader/manager/chairperson/participant.
2 Which do you regard as most effective in achieving its task purpose?
3 Which do you believe is best in terms of managing interrelationships – the process of working?
4 Which do you think is most effective at providing conscious opportunities for learning?

Note that we have started with real teams at work with managerial performance objectives. It is within these real teams involved in real managerial work that learning within a group starts.

WHAT SORT OF LEARNING?

For a long time one of the familiar ways of describing training was to say that its outputs were knowledge, skills and attitudes. In research work with my colleagues, Peter Honey and Graham Robinson, we concluded that a more helpful concept than 'attitudes' was 'insights'. Definitions of these three words are given here:

Knowledge   is the acquisition of data or information. Sometimes it is not new knowledge but confirmation of past information.

Skills   are the means used to carry out managerial work effectively. The most obvious examples include making decisions, running meetings and negotiating.

Insight   or perceptiveness – some people would call it developing wisdom. You can acquire knowledge and skills, but lack the extra dimension provided through insight. Insight is often expressed as conclusions; it helps you generalize from particular experiences.

Examples of Knowledge, Skills and Insight through learning in the group include:

Knowledge   Acquiring information from others in the groups, tapping into the expertise of others.
Awareness of skills and techniques used by others in the group.
Awareness of own skills and techniques.
Awareness of interaction between self and others, and between others.

Skills   Personal use of skills of communicating, influencing and listening.
Team use of team skills (see Chart 11.1).

Insight   Awareness of why individuals interact together in the way they do.
Awareness of why the group or team achieves or does not achieve its objectives.

Case study – the new manager

A senior manager newly arrived in an organization made a presentation to a management meeting on one of the issues in his department. His arrival in the organization had been greeted with at least polite acceptance and in some cases warmth by his new colleagues. He was surprised to find that a number of participants in the meeting fell on his proposal like hungry wolves. In reflecting afterwards on what had happened at the meeting and what he had learned from it he identified the following:

Knowledge   He had acquired information during the meeting which had not been available to him in the files he had studied and from people he had spoken to previously. Indeed he had a feeling that some individuals had previously held back information that would have been helpful to him in preparing his proposal. He noted which of his colleagues seemed to him possibly to have been guilty of that, and thought about how he would handle them next time.

Skills   His boss had seen and approved his proposal before it was submitted to the meeting. He admired the way in which she identified a number of positive conclusions arising from the discussion, emphasized the areas in which there was agreement and clarified further action. He admired the way in which she had demonstrated skills in influencing the climate towards a more positive conclusion, while at the same time not appearing to attack the criticisms directed at his proposal.

Insights   He concluded that he had not done a good enough political job before the meeting. In his previous organization senior managers were expected to operate through their own initiative and to secure only *concurrence* for any proposal. His insight from this meeting was that there would be *consensus* about any proposal from any of the participants, that is, 'We agree that is what you should do', rather than 'We accept that is what you will do.'

As the example shows, learning within a group consists of:

- Learning about yourself
- Learning about others
- Learning from others
- Learning about the group.

Case study – the project review

A team of managers worked for an organization with a single main product. The main product had variations in which individual managers were expert, and which they were keen to sell. As part of the business plan for the year it had been agreed to make a major sales push with prospective and existing clients. This push was intended to form the main priority for all managers, and was called 'Project Multiply'.

Project Multiply appeared as an agenda item for one of the normal team management meetings. Discussions at the meeting revealed that:

- Of the five managers, only two were able to register additional new sales as a result of the project
- There was nonetheless argument about whether the new sales could be attributed to the project. This argument was caused by those who had achieved nothing and who apparently wished to denigrate the achievement of their colleagues

179

- There was no analysis available of reasons for success or failure
- There had been no specific targets set for individuals or for the team as a whole
- Individual members of the team had pursued in some cases the same clients, to offer slightly different products.

The Project Review resulted in a number of decisions, including the identification of targets for individuals, the selection of a prime contact for each client in order to reduce competition between managers, and a commitment to sell the organization's services rather than just those preferred by the individual manager. In addition, the team decided that it would in future require that analytical papers should be prepared and circulated a week before any discussion of items of similar significance. It had learned from its experience that it needed to manage itself better (Experience – Review), had made decisions (Conclude) and agreed what to do in future (Plan Actions). This is an example of Honey and Mumford's Learning Cycle in operation (Figure 11.3, p. 183).

This case demonstrates not only learning *within* a group, but learning *by* a group.

LEARNING FROM SUCCESS AS WELL AS FAILURE

Many of the missed opportunities for individuals and for groups to learn occur because there is a greater emphasis on the need to review failure than success. Understandably, in view of the pressures and workload for most managers, the tendency is to accept success, sometimes because it is 'normal', sometimes with relief. Failures or partial successes are most likely to be reviewed because it is recognized that something different will need to be done next time. Unfortunately one of the consequences of not spending enough time on reviewing success is that because the causes are insufficiently understood, the superficial reasons for success are applied inappropriately in some subsequent situation – which, of course, leads to failure!

Exercise – reviewing success and failure

Look back over the last six months. Consider the following questions:

1 Has your team reviewed, during that time, a significant area of problem, difficulty or failure?
2 What did it learn from this review?
3 Was the learning specific to the particular event, 'This is what we should do if faced with this situation again'? Was the learning more generalized, 'This experience has told us something general about the way in which we operate'?
4 Has your team reviewed a significant success over this time?

5   What did it learn from this review?

Exercise – looking at new manager case study

Read again The New Manager case study. This manager was reviewing a failure in his own performance within a group.

1   When you review what he drew from the experience, do you think he learned something specific to presenting a proposal, or something more general?
2   Can you think of similar experiences within your team?
3   What do you believe you learned and what do you believe others may have learned from the experience?
4   What, if anything, have you learned from reading the case study and completing these two exercises?

BALANCING ATTENTION TO TASK AND LEARNING

The last section shows that careful and conscious review of what happens within a team gives the basis for, although it does not guarantee, improved performance in the future. The learning and improvement may, as in the case of the new manager, be primarily individual. Or the learning may, as in the case of the 'Project Review', be very much learning for the team as a whole.

BALANCING TASK AND LEARNING

In the cases given above, individual and group performance requirements have provided both the occasion and the need for learning. In fact neither the individual nor the group was really aware that they were learning as well as managing until the question was put to them afterwards. They saw themselves as going round a version of the Task Cycle (Figure 11.2). Only after the event were they helped to see that in fact they were also going round the Learning Cycle (Figure 11.3).

It is true that achieving the task itself requires that each stage of the Task Cycle be undertaken. Unless the individual manager and the group in the cases mentioned carried out the Reviewing stage, any conclusions about what needs to be done, and any plans about what to do next time, would be likely to be flawed. Effort to take a balanced view of this kind around the Task Cycle in effect also ensures that the Learning Cycle is completed as well. However, the interaction of the two apparently different types of question 'What do we need to do to improve task performance?', and 'What have we learned from undertaking this task?', deepens and enhances the quality of the answers for both. The group, asking itself questions about the specifics on the project, was also asking itself questions about what it had learned from the fact that information was missing.

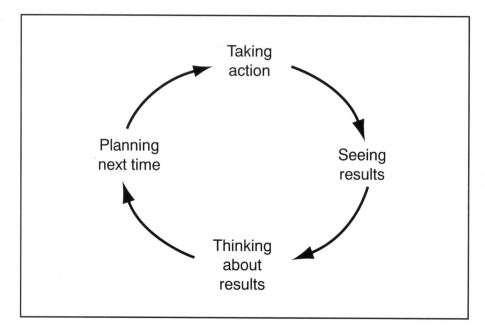

Figure 11.2   Task cycle   © Honey & Mumford 1989

The case for paying close attention to learning is, however, not only that by doing so performance on the task will be improved. Explicit attention to discussion of each stage of the Learning Cycle improves the likelihood of individuals or teams generalizing effectively and appropriately from the particular experience. Note the emphasis on 'effectively and appropriately'.

The issue is not whether managers generalize from particular experiences. This they certainly do. The issue is whether they generalize appropriately and relevantly. My research with managers, both as individuals and groups, shows that consistently they have learned from experiences at work, but their learning has been inefficient, insufficient and sometimes misdirected. It is only when they have sat down with me after the event – perhaps months or years after the event – that they have fully realized what was involved in an experience, what they learned from it, and sometimes what else they might have learned.

ASSISTING WITH LEARNING IN THE GROUP

One of the differences between teams and groups is the presence of a manager accountable for the output of the team. In team situations the responsible manager can provide the most direct help. The absence of such a manager in less structured groups means that other people, also often present in teams, will be more evident as helpers. So colleagues, subordinates and clients for services or projects come into play, and in wider

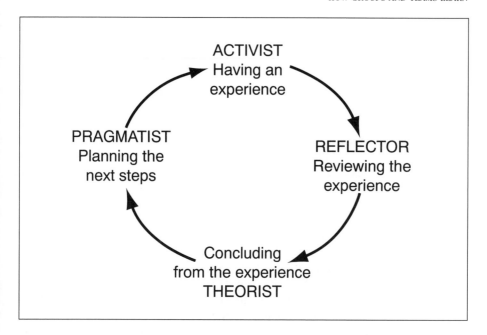

ACTIVIST
Having an
experience

REFLECTOR
Reviewing the
experience

Concluding
from the experience
THEORIST

PRAGMATIST
Planning the
next steps

Figure 11.3   Learning cycle   © Honey & Mumford 1986

groups the senior manager may appear. Sometimes the mentor may make an appearance. Indeed one of the ways in which individuals become mentors informally is through meeting someone in a working group.

The most significant helpers in the team situation are the direct manager and colleagues.

The direct manager has to cope with one difficulty which can be inhibiting for learning. While any management discussion can be constrained by the degree to which participants respond to 'what my manager thinks', or 'how my manager behaves', this general issue of expectations and style affects the potential for learning quite specifically. Since learning usually involves asking questions, responding honestly to issues, and taking some personal risks, if these behaviours are inhibited in work situations they will similarly be inhibited when people are asked to discuss openly what they have learned, how they have learned and what they propose to do about their learning.

The effective learning environment is primarily created by the direct manager. Individual leadership is demonstrated through that person's behaviour as illustrated by the following:

- I communicate a clear vision of the ideal learning environment I believe it is important to create
- I actively encourage people to adopt 'learning' behaviours such as asking questions, experimenting, reviewing and assessing mistakes   *183*

- I set up meetings where my people swap experiences and share learning
- At regular meetings it is normal procedure to have a learning review as an agenda item
- I give help and encouragement for others to learn when things go wrong.

These behaviours form part of a Learning Environment Questionnaire, produced by Honey and Mumford (1996). This questionnaire enables individual managers to assess their own contribution in these (and other) respects. The full resource goes on to indicate how managers displeased with the rating they give themselves on these questions may set out to improve.

One of the most useful things a manager can do is to ensure that in the construction of temporary groups or teams attention is given first to the learning process in general. This means establishing for most of them that, in addition to their managerial task endeavours, they should adopt some learning objectives. 'I want a report on how we should restructure our branch organization. And I also want some comments on what you have learned from working together and generally from the experience of producing the report.' This has been expressed in very brisk, relatively vague, but recognizably managerial terms, and will give readers the general idea of what could be attempted more often with groups.

Of course, it is possible to be much more sophisticated in setting out learning objectives and including a more substantial learning review. Chart 11.2 shows this.

The last point on Chart 11.2 is worth emphasizing. One of the potential characteristics of groups, and certainly of teams, is that the totality of their analysis and thinking is greater than even brilliant individuals working alone. Synergy rules OK! Recognizing and sharing learning adds to the learning achieved by each individual.

Exercise – the direct manager as encourager of learning in a team

1. Consider each item on Chart 11.2 and score yourself on a scale 0 = I rarely do this, 10 = I always do this.
2. Think of a recent team meeting which you managed; how might you have improved your contribution to encouraging learning from it?
3. Which of the characteristics in the chart do you believe are closest to the way you feel comfortable in operating?
4. Which are most foreign to you?
5. Can you select one or more which you might experiment with at a future meeting? Which?
6. Which meeting?

Chart 11.2   Role of the direct manager in learning in teams

- Puts learning explicitly on the agenda for the team
- Identifies learning opportunities arising from managerial work
- Sets objectives for learning
- Rewards discussion of learning
- Suggests criteria for evaluating success of learning
- Offers personal statement about own learning
- Demonstrates skills of learning
- Uses the Task and Learning Cycles as a means of checking the learning process
- Identifies and uses individual Learning Styles
- Encourages the use of skills of learning
- Reviews learning process and achieved learning
- Encourages collaborative learning rather than competitive learning behaviour.

Case study – learning from experience

A director decided that it would be useful to extend his personal review of learning from experience to his management team. He arranged that each of his regular management meetings should finish with two items:

- 'What have we learned that is important about our business since our last meeting?'
- 'What have we learned today?'

At the first two meetings he gave his own responses first to show he was serious about the process. Subsequently he stood back and let others lead.

SETTING UP TEMPORARY LEARNING TEAMS

Another important role for the manager is the selection of individuals to work on particular tasks or projects. Normally this will be done on the basis of the personal contribution likely to be made by individuals – from their functional knowledge, their experience and their style of contribution. Selection may also be on the basis of 'it would be a good development experience for you'.

A more complex approach can be used by looking at not only the particular learning needs of individuals, but also at their learning styles in Figure 11.3 (Honey and Mumford, 1992). It is possible to create more effective groups by ensuring that a group has a mix of learning styles.

Case study – constructing project teams

In South Africa Mohale Mahanyele, Chief Executive of National Sorghum Breweries, used the diagnostic results of Margerison and McCann's Team Management Roles, and the Honey/Mumford Learning Styles information as part of the process for constructing project teams. He ensured that there was a distribution of preferred learning styles, so that no group comprised wholly Theorists or Activists, for example. Chart 11.3 gives ideas on how to use temporary teams for learning.

LEARNING SKILLS IN A GROUP

The general proposition on the similarity between the Task Cycle and the Learning Cycle, and specifically on the stages involved, can be extended to the similarity between skills usually identified as being managerial, and skills particularly appropriate to learning. With a few exceptions the skills required for learning are those which managers require for other managerial activities anyway. This is indicated in Chart 11.4, which suggests the kind of skills necessary for effective learning in a group or team. The skills are not only required by individuals, but for effective development and understanding of learning within the group. For synergy to be achieved, these skills have to be employed. To be employed they need to be encouraged. Chart 11.5 spells out some ways of achieving this.

As shown earlier, while it is certainly the role of the manager to provide encouragement, it is also the responsibility of other members of the team. In looking at skills of learning in the group, we are also looking at how colleagues help the development of others. The importance of collaboration rather than competition has already been pointed out in The Project Review case study earlier in the chapter. One of the reasons why temporary groups on training courses can be more effective as learning groups than similar groups at work is that competition is reduced, although never entirely elimi-

---

Chart 11.3 Actions to improve learning in temporary teams

1 Review the information you have on the members. What skills, experience and knowledge do they bring?
2 What do you know about them as learners? Is there a development purpose in their participation? Do you know their Learning Styles/ Team Role preferences?
3 What sort of opportunities for learning do you anticipate:
   • from the team's work
   • about the way the team worked?
4 Can you agree a process for discussing learning?
5 Which members are most likely to help in what way?

nated. If a team sets itself an objective to be an effective learning team, it needs each individual to take a collaborative stance with each colleague in the team, at least as far as learning experiences are concerned. It needs to encourage the constructive use of differences instead of the destructive acceptance of conflict. Most of us have had experience of good and bad teams, and will probably agree that one of the distinguishing characteristics is precisely the greater emphasis on collaboration – even though individual members may be competitive from time to time on particular issues. Outside management we see the power of collaborative support in endeavours such as Alcoholics Anonymous and Weight Watchers. The support offered through such groups and its effectiveness is a powerful indicator to us of what can be achieved on similarly difficult and often very personal issues in management.

The Action Learning process is, of course, one of the most powerful of group learning opportunities, in which participants ('fellows in adversity' (Revans, 1982), or as I prefer, 'fellows in opportunity') help each other learn by sharing discussions on real work problems. A detailed description of this is provided in Chapter 22 of his handbook, 'Effective Learners in Action Learning Sets'. The demonstration of the power of articulated shared learning objectives and processes is one that should be passed on more often to 'normal' management teams.

Exercise – learning skills in groups

1 Think about the teams of which you are a member.
2 Identify the one which you believe contains most opportunities for the team to learn with and from each other.

Chart 11.4 Individual behaviours in effective learning groups

- Enabling fellow-members to share air time appropriately
- Non-defensive about own actions and learning
- Supportive about issues/concerns of others
- Open in initiating and responding to issues
- Analytical
- Questioning in style, eliciting information not defensiveness
- Listening effectively
- Accepts help
- Creative in response to problems
- Innovative in recognizing learning from task
- Risk taking
- Uses Task and Learning Cycles
- Understands and uses Learning Styles
- Uses strengths of others as learners
- Helps motivate others as learners.

Chart 11.5   Assessing learning skills in a group or team

1   The members review the strengths and weaknesses of the team or group as a learning unit.
2   Members decide the actions necessary
   • to make effective use of strengths
   • to reduce any weaknesses.
3   Members decide which individuals will have particular responsibilities for their actions.
4   Members decide on a process for monitoring effectiveness in carrying out the actions.

---

3   Think back to the most recent relevant meeting. How far in general do you think the group as a whole exhibited appropriate learning skills?
4   Assess the group on each of the skills in Chart 11.4. Which of the skills were most frequently evident in the meeting you have reviewed?
5   Which of the skills were most evidently not present?

GROUP LEARNING REVIEW

Clearly a significant feature of group learning is the review process. In principle this is established through the Task Cycle and Learning Cycle. The questions that could be put to a group in conducting a learning review are essentially those which are asked of individuals (Chart 11.6).

It will be noted that yet again essential to achieved learning is the collection of relevant information – the review stage. one of the main contributing factors to this will be learning logs kept by individuals. Not all individuals will be equally good at this, so one of the roles of the team or group leader is to identify and make use of those individuals who will have kept learning logs or their equivalent, and may therefore have an extra contribution to make (Strong Reflectors are likely candidates).

Chart 11.6   Group learning review

1   What task, process, project or activity are we looking at?
2   What are its main characteristics?
3   What information do we have on problems, opportunities, successes and failures around the activity?
4   What conclusions do we draw about what we have learned from reviewing the activity?
5   What actions need to be taken by whom and by when to make our learning productive?

HELPERS AS LEARNERS IN GROUPS

The experience of helping is something which can be shared with other helpers. A direct manager or mentor might choose either to share experiences with another individual, or in a larger group.

Exercise – sharing experiences of helping others

1 Are there currently occasions on which I can share experiences with others on the issues discussed in this chapter?
2 Can I take an initiative myself to establish a process for exchange?
3 Do I need help from someone else (for example, my direct manager, personnel) in order to do so?
4 What benefits would I expect for myself?
5 What benefits would I be able to suggest for others?

OTHER ISSUES

Emotions

The emphasis so far has been substantially on conscious, rational processes for helping learning. However, there are significant factors which are mainly emotional in character. While this chapter has concentrated on how the process of learning in groups can be managed, because it is seen as simply another example of the management process, this is not the sole issue. Around the more careful, conscious, reflective and analytical processes, emotional responses are present. They can be motivating, releasing and energizing – seen in managers whose attitude to life in general, and to learning opportunities in particular, is positive. Perhaps more often there are managers, whose emotions are engaged positively in some situations or on some issues, who react in a more negative emotional way in other circumstances. These issues, of course, are well beyond the impact of emotions on learning, for which help and discussion is available in other books. Peter Honey and I have spelled out in our workbook *The Opportunist Learner* how some of the attitudes and emotions issues can be tackled by individuals.

Group learning as a method

This chapter has shown the variety of opportunities available to learn within groups, and to learn about groups. It can be a very effective method of development in a variety of situations. Unfortunately, as is the case with many other methods, the particular contribution it may make to learning has not been properly identified. What group learning is particularly suitable for is discussed in Mumford (1997). Also discussed there are issues not raised elsewhere in this chapter about the possibly different reactions of individuals related to either gender or national culture. Sadly these latter points can be discussed briefly because there is too little information available on which to make sound judgements. Such information as there is, is sometimes confusing. Looking at the gender issue, for example, it is not clear whether it is more or less effective to place women in women-only groups.

Note

This is a revised version of a chapter first published in *How Managers Can Develop Managers*, Gower, 1993.

REFERENCES

Honey, P. and Mumford, A., *The Manual of Learning Styles*, Honey, Maidenhead, 1992

Honey, P. and Mumford, A., *The Opportunist Learner*, Honey, Maidenhead, 1995

Honey, P. and Mumford, A., *How to Manage Your Learning Environment*, Honey, Maidenhead, 1996

Mumford, A., 'Creating a Learning Environment', *Journal of Professional HRM*, **4**, 1996

Mumford, A., *How to Choose the Right Development Method*, Honey, Maidenhead, 1997

Revans, R.W., *The Origins and Growth of Action Learning*, Chartwell Bratt, Bromley, 1982

Watkins, K. and Marsick, V., *Sculpting the Learning Organization*, Jossey Bass, 1993

12 A systems approach to team effectiveness

Joyce Fortune

A great deal of work has been done to try to find what makes teams successful. Most of that work looks at one or another of the various aspects of managing teams such as the selection of members, training, motivation, process design and the like. This chapter takes a different approach; it uses systems thinking to explore what a team needs in order to be successful. It then provides a way of predicting what might cause a team to fail and of investigating failures after they have occurred.

The main advantage of a systemic approach is that it enables the inner workings of a team and the context in which it operates, including its relationships with other teams, with the unit or organization as a whole and with the outside world, to be considered at the same time. This is achieved by regarding a team as an 'organized whole', or 'human activity system' and looking at the features that whole must possess if it is to be capable of carrying out its transformations successfully while at the same time considering the design and behaviour of the system in relation to a wider system and an environment. In systems terminology 'wider system' is the name given to the system that is hierarchically above the one being considered, and so for a team the wider system would probably be the unit or the organization in which the team operates. The term environment refers to the collection of entities outside the system which affect the system and are affected by it, but which cannot be controlled by it. For a commercial organization the environment would be likely to include existing and potential customers, suppliers, competitors, the financial institutions, legislation, and so on and the environment of a particular team would comprise that subset of the organization's environment with which it interacts. A team's environment is also likely to include other teams, or functional groupings from within its own organization, especially those at the same or a lower hierarchical level.

THE FORMAL SYSTEM MODEL

The core of this chapter is a model of a robust system that is capable of purposeful action without failure. It is called the Formal System Model (FSM) and is represented diagrammatically in Figure 12.1.

Capacity for purposeful action, that is action that involves choices, is very important in relation to the sorts of teams that are operating in matrix and network organizations. Teams have always been used in the world of work; indeed, before the introduction of mechanical power they were indispensable. However, until recently the strategies, tactics and methods of operation of most teams were defined externally and so the teams were only required to act in a purposive manner. Now many teams are autonomous or semi-autonomous and are thus required to be self-managing. Although they usually work towards given objectives and are required to stay within certain constraints, usually of a budgetary or cultural nature, they are largely free to devise their own means of reaching their targets in terms of allocating work within the team, selecting processes and so on.

So what does the FSM imply for the design and operation of successful teams?

The FSM is a hierarchical systems model which combines all the features needed in order for purposeful action to be carried out without failure. These are:

- A continuous purpose or mission
- A decision making capacity
- Ability to monitor performance
- The resources needed to carry out transformations
- A degree of connectivity between the components
- An environment with which the system interacts
- Boundaries separating the system from its wider system and the wider system from the environment
- Some guarantee of continuity.

This chapter will now consider each of these features in the context of a team.

Continuous purpose or mission

The purpose or mission of the team should have been set by the management of the unit or organization in which the team operates. The extent to which it needs to be 'continuous' depends to some degree on the way the word team is used. There is no single universally accepted definition of a team and longevity is one of the properties that varies according to the different usages, especially when people are trying to draw distinctions between work groups and teams. For example, some would regard the permanent group of officers who run an organization as 'the management

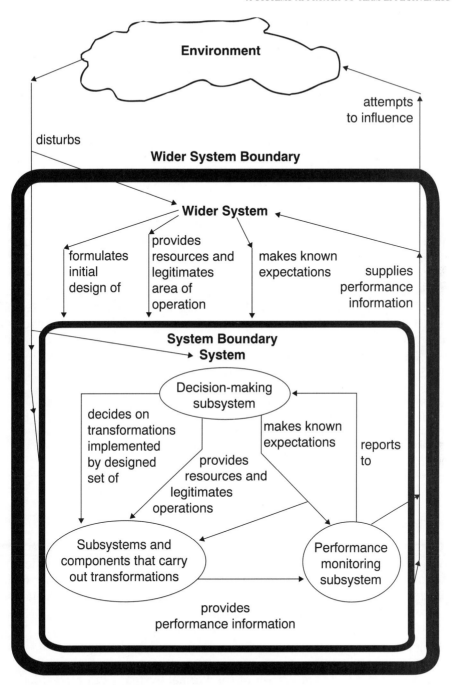

Figure 12.1   The Formal System Model
Source: Fortune, 1993: adapted from Checkland, 1979

team', whereas others restrict use of the word team to a temporary grouping of individuals who have come together to accomplish a specific task such as undertaking a quality improvement project or designing a new product. However, the important point here is that the purpose or mission must endure for the life of the team regardless of the time span that occupies. Purposeful action without failure requires the wider system to make its expectations known to the system; specifying the purpose or mission of the team is the way this is achieved. Within this requirement factors such as appropriateness, clarity and the amount of contradiction will have consequences for the degree to which the team will be able to be regarded as successful.

The importance of making expectations known has been borne out by a number of studies. For instance, a study by Fortune and Peters (1995) was able to establish a link between failure to make expectations known and the failure of electronic patient record systems in hospitals providing care to acutely ill patients. In the area of product design and development a benchmarking study carried out in the electronics industry (Oliver et al., 1995) found that one of the most important factors which discriminated between relatively high and relatively low performing projects was 'the existence of a common picture of the project's requirements amongst the team members'. Successful organizations are recognizing this importance, as the following description of Microsoft's approach to software development shows:

> Microsoft teams begin a project by creating a 'vision statement' that defines the goals for a new product and prioritizes the user activities that need to be supported by the product features. Product managers (marketing specialists) take charge of this task, which they do while consulting program managers, who specialize in writing up functional specifications of the product. Next, the program managers in consultation with developers, write a functional specification that outlines the product features in sufficient depth to organize schedules and staffing allocations.
>
> (Cusumano, 1997, pp. 8–9)

Because the distinction between purposive action and purposeful action is the degree of choice involved, the two forms of action have very different decision making requirements in terms of both the number and the complexity of the decisions that have to be made. Capacity for decision making is thus another important feature of the FSM.

Decision making

The decision making subsystem of the Formal System can be regarded as responsible for the decisions about the transformations to be carried out. Because the subsystem decides how the purposes of the system are to be achieved, it is the area that exhibits most choice and which enjoys the highest degree of autonomy. It makes its expectations for the performance

194

of each component known to the components themselves and to the performance monitoring subsystem and it allocates resources.

The way decision making is accomplished will vary from team to team but it must be a feature that is actively considered when the team is put together. For some teams, unitary decision making, in the form of a clear leader who is responsible for all the decisions made within that team, will be appropriate. (In such cases the decision making subsystem should more properly be regarded as an element than a subsystem.) However, in most cases, even within organizations like the military that have traditionally operated as strict hierarchies, a more pluralist style is appropriate, in which case decision making is very properly regarded as a function to be undertaken by a subsystem. In some teams the subsystem may be made up of people who share a single world view and are strongly united in their common purpose, in which case their decisions are likely to appear unitarist for much of the time. In other cases the decision making subsytem may appear to contain a changing balance of forces representing different stakeholders or different perspectives in a state of dynamic equilibrium, in which case the team will tend towards a consensus style of decision making. In a large team the decision making subsystem could comprise disparate groups of people who are constantly forming and reforming and making temporary alliances, sometimes gaining and sometimes losing dominance as they jockey for position. Because particular individuals may be seen as participants in the activities of more than one subsystem, and by personal contact appear able to influence the activities of subsystems of which they are not members, all the members of a team may, in effect, be part of the decision making subsystem. This highly democratic form of decision making is becoming more prevalent as teams, like organizations, move away from hierarchical structures, but it does not lessen the need to ensure that capacity for making timely and appropriate decisions that will enable the team to carry out its transformations and make judgements about its own performance is built into the design of the team.

The behaviour of the decision making subsystem is also likely to vary according to the cognitive styles of its members. Some individuals tend to be analytic decision makers who look at quantitative information whereas others tend to be heuristic decision makers who are more intuitive and more interested in general concepts. Distinctions such as these may be important when selecting the members of the team.

Performance monitoring

The performance monitoring subsystem serves to check whether the performance of the system is consistent with the expectations of the decision making subsystem. It observes behaviour and outputs and reports any deviations from the expectations to the decision making subsystem so that informed remedial actions can be taken. The form this takes may range between an individual monitoring the performance of all the team to each *195* member being responsible for monitoring his or her own performance. Just as there is an increasing tendency for more people to be involved in decision making, so performance monitoring is increasingly being devolved to individual team members. This is particularly the case where quality performance is concerned. In manufacturing various forms of operator control of quality have been credited with bringing about significant improvements and paving the way for major shop-floor reorganizations such as the introduction of lean and just-in-time production. Similar initiatives are now being taken up in the commercial and public service sectors.

Resources to carry out transformations

The set of sub-systems and elements which carry out the tasks of the system and thus effect its transformations by converting inputs into outputs are there to achieve the purpose of the system. The question of resources is particularly important in relation to the activities of this sub-system. These will include not only people and physical resources, such as materials and equipment, but also skills, knowledge and access to information.

Connectivity

Without a degree of connectivity between the members it would not be realistic to regard a team as a system or 'organized whole'. The connectivity will be a product of the structure and processes of the team. In some cases, such as cellular manufacture, it may be physically visible but often it will manifest itself mainly in the form of communication links, not all of which will involve face-to-face communication.

The importance of good communications within and across teams has been widely recognized, but the communication models which have been used to explore and explain the networks have not kept pace with the complexity of real-life interactions. This is illustrated in Figure 12.2. Figures 12.2a and 12.2b show the standard models for centralized and decentralized networks within teams, while the outer circle of (c) shows the actual patterns within a team and the inner circle of (c) shows the actual patterns between teams. (These 'actual' connections were revealed by a mapping method based on sociometry and use of a software package called 'Netmap'.) Clearly, in designing teams allowances must be made for the complexity of pathways and the consequent requirement for multiple processing points.

Opportunities for communication breakdowns and misunderstandings can arise from the different ways in which individuals interpret the same information and the distortions that can arise when information is passed between team members. It is very unlikely that all team members will have direct access from primary sources to all the information they rely on. Indeed March and Simon's words have almost certainly grown in relevance with the increased use of purposeful teams:

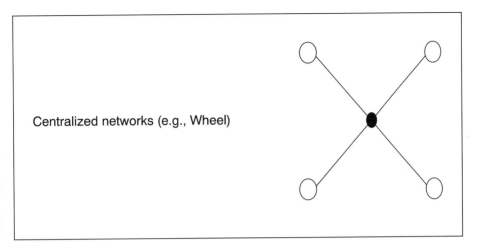

Centralized networks (e.g., Wheel)

Figure 12.2a   A centralized network within a team

The vast bulk of our knowledge of fact is not gained through direct perception but through the second-hand, third-hand, and nth-hand reports of the perceptions of others, transmitted through the channels of social communication. Since these perceptions have already been filtered by one or more communicators, most of whom have frames of reference similar to our own, the reports are generally consonant with the filtered reports of our own perceptions, and serve to reinforce the latter . . . perceptions of the environment are biased even before they experience the filtering action of the frame of reference of the perceiver. Salesmen live in an environment of customers; company treasurers in an environment of bankers; each sees a quite distinct part of the world.

(March and Simon, 1958, p. 152–3)

Environment

Powerful environmental influences are frequently, but not always, disadvantageous to a system, but although a system can be constrained by environmental influences from which it derives no benefits, environments do sometimes provide opportunities as well as threats and can thus play a supportive role in the performance of a system. For example, a powerful customer may force a supplier to adopt certain quality procedures or to invest in information technology so as to be able to process transactions electronically. However, it may also offer training and other support and commit to a longer-term trading relationship that will be advantageous to both parties. Many examples of this can be seen in manufacturing and the retail industry. For instance, Marks & Spencer is well known for its relational contracting, and though the Ford Motor Company will only enter into contracts with suppliers that meet the QS-9000 standard (which now forms part of its Q1 quality award) it does provide assistance in meeting this requirement.

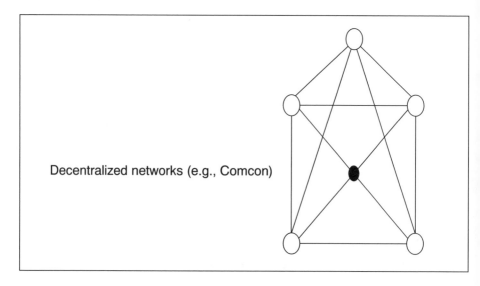

Decentralized networks (e.g., Comcon)

Figure 12.2b   A decentralized network within a team

Boundaries

Even though a Formal System would, by definition, have requirements of its subsystems, such relationships would not preclude each subsystem having a certain amount of autonomy in deciding how those expectations were met. An equivalent relationship could be said to exist between the Formal System and its wider system. When a system is seen as having a wider system sitting above it, the wider system sets the objectives or defines the purpose of the system, strongly influences the decision making subsystem, monitors, or measures the performance of, the system and provides the resources to allow the system to function. The boundaries separating a system from its wider system and the wider system from the environment are purely notional, but conceptually they are very important in understanding the behaviour of a system.

If a team is deemed to be successful, its members are much more likely to place a high value on their membership and to feel more autonomous from the team's surroundings. Indeed, they may feel that there really is a boundary surrounding the team, making it clear who is inside the team and who is outside. Although this strong sense of coherence brings many advantages it can also have drawbacks. A strong team tends to display behaviour which encourages members of the team to conform to the team's own view of the world and this can lead to members developing a view of outsiders which is stereotypical. This in turn can then cause members to put internal pressure on those members who do not share the rest of the team's view of a situation. The ultimate result of this is that the team becomes less successful because it ceases to look outwards and becomes unable to deal with environmental changes.

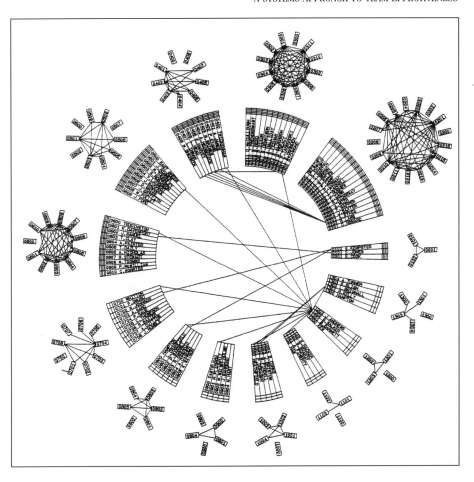

Figure 12.2c **Netmap showing actual communication links within a team and between teams © 1991 Active Analysis Ltd.**

Janis (1972 and 1982) has given the name 'Groupthink' to the phenomenon described above. He describes it as 'a mode of thinking that people engage in when they are deeply involved in a cohesive in-group, when members' strivings for unanimity override their motivation to realistically appraise alternative courses of action'. He goes on to say that Groupthink 'refers to a deterioration of mental efficiency, reality testing, and moral judgement that results from in-group pressures' (Janis, 1972, p. 9).

From an examination of a series of American policy 'fiascos' Janis has discovered strong evidence that Groupthink has led to very cohesive groups making defective decisions. The examples he cites include the Kennedy administration's unsuccessful orchestration of the Bay of Pigs invasion of Cuba, and the attack on the US Navy at Pearl Harbour by the Japanese. It could be argued that a more recent and closer to home demonstration of Groupthink led to the introduction of the Poll Tax (Community Charge), the   *199* hasty withdrawal of which played a large part in the downfall of the then Prime Minister, Margaret Thatcher:

> 'Is he one of us?' was asked by Mrs Thatcher of colleagues about other colleagues . . . The criteria were political or economic rather than social. 'Wet' was used by her to rebuke colleagues who lacked her singleness of purpose or disagreed with her economic or social policy.
>
> (Watkins, 1991)

One of the benefits of a powerful wider system is that it can inhibit the opportunity for Groupthink to develop. The organization in which a team will be embedded should therefore consider how best to achieve a balance between commitment to the team and commitment to the organization.

Some guarantee of continuity

The distinction that was drawn earlier between teams as permanent and temporary groupings is equally relevant here. Suffice it to say that the guarantee of continuity should hold for the life of the team. It may not be possible, or even desirable, for the membership to stay exactly the same, but the team as a whole should retain its sense of continuity.

FAILING TEAMS

Failure is a subjective term that is coloured by personal perception, by expectations and by the circumstances under which the judgement is made. Invariably, though, it will be related to objectives which are not met, or to undesirable side effects, or to objectives which are met but which turn out to have been inappropriate in the first place.

One thing that is common to most, if not all, failures is that they involve people, be they the original designers and decision makers who shaped the situation, the current actors and managers working within it or the victims and rescuers. Although it can be important when investigating failure to consider the part played by people as individuals, it is also very important to look at the way they act together as members of teams and of even larger groupings. It is sometimes tempting to just concentrate on the individual but this invariably leads to major institutional problems being neglected. For example, following the 1988 Clapham rail crash in which 35 people died and over 60 were injured, a senior British Rail technician accepted responsibility for a wiring error in some signalling work carried out in a relay room which led directly to the failure. However, the official inquiry into the disaster found a wider network of causes. These included the following team- and organization-related problems:

• Over the 13 weeks prior to the accident the senior British Rail technician (referred to above) had worked every day except one; furthermore he had had no training in electrical or mechanical engineering.

- On the day the wiring was installed five teams were needed to carry out the required work, but only five people of senior technician or supervisor status were available and the signals supervisor who should have inspected the wiring worked for over 13 hours with only a five-minute break.
- Despite his requests to be based with his team of seven staff, the signals supervisor was based at Wimbledon while most of his team were located at Waterloo.
- The project engineer for the resignalling scheme as a whole described his design teams as having 'their backs to the wall' to try to meet deadlines, with the result that wiring drawings often had to be changed on site.
- The testing requirements contained in a resignalling safety manual issued over a year before the crash had not been implemented; some senior officers said they did not know the manual represented official policy, others claimed not to have received it, and the man who was the testing and commissioning engineer for the South West Region until seven months before the Clapham disaster said he had never had time to read it.

The form an organization takes can make it more robust; indeed, one of the arguments in favour of the network form of organization is that it is less prone to failure. However, working in teams is no guarantee of success. Indeed, because it involves a continuous process of adaptation by individuals to one another and to their mutual needs and problems, it may of itself make failures more likely in certain situations, especially those where speed of intervention or reaction are important. Furthermore, because some failures will always occur, the increasing pervasiveness of team working will mean that the role of a team or teams will inevitably be important in some of those failures.

Valuable lessons can be learnt from failures but many organizations do not take advantage of this important learning opportunity, partly because of the traditional culture of blame and partly because they are not sure what the lessons should be. By putting a mechanism in place that will allow failures at a relatively mundane level to be investigated it is possible to generate insights that can provide this knowledge and thus facilitate learning. (Interestingly, Senge (1990) points out that the team rather than the individual is the key learning unit in most views of a learning organization, primarily because a team can be regarded as a microcosm of a whole organization. This may be another reason why it is particularly appropriate to consider success and failure at team level.)

One tried and tested mechanism for investigating failures will now be outlined. It relies on use of a method which has the FSM at its heart. It is   *201* called the Systems Failures Method and, as well as being used to look back at past failures, it can also be used to assess the strengths and weaknesses of actual or proposed situations with a view to predicting the failures that might occur and so pointing the way to their prevention.

THE SYSTEMS FAILURES METHOD

The Systems Failures Method has two key features. The first is conceptualization and modelling of the failure situation as a system(s). The failure is regarded as an output or lack of outputs, of the transformation processes carried out by that system. Therefore, because failure is itself a subjective judgement the decision as to which aspects of the situation are to be regarded as constituting the system can vary depending upon the purpose of the study and the perspectives from which it is being carried out. Although a study of a failing team would probably begin by regarding the team as the system, the hierarchical nature of the FSM does mean that each of the subsystems could also be perceived as a Formal System with its own decision making, performance monitoring and transformation-effecting components, and so on, if necessary. Similarly the analysis can be extended to the next hierarchical level upwards with what was the wider system being regarded as the system. Therefore the same situation can be examined at a variety of levels from the micro to the macro. The second feature of the Method is comparison of the system(s), first with the FSM, and then with other models based on typical failures. A representation of the Method is shown in Figure 12.3.

In the brief description of the stages that follows here, illustrative examples are taken from a study by Pearce and Fortune (1995). It used the method in forward-looking mode to assess the strengths and weaknesses of the Gold, Silver and Bronze command and control structure that is now used by some Forces to police major incidents/operations. This structure, which is loosely based on the command spans employed by the military, was developed to cope with the growing number of incidents such as urban riots and demonstrations requiring mass deployments of police officers in atmospheres of high uncertainty. The 'Gold' part of the structure is responsible for strategy, 'Silver' is responsible for tactics, and 'Bronze' implements the tactics on the ground.

Stage 1 – Pre-analysis

In Stage 1 of the method the purpose of the analysis, and the perspectives from which it is being carried out are defined. The situation is examined from the various viewpoints that have been identified as important, and the information is organized into forms such as spray diagrams, relationship diagrams, multiple cause diagrams and rich pictures.

In the Gold, Silver, Bronze example the purpose of the analysis was to

identify the strengths and weaknesses of the structure, with a view to con-

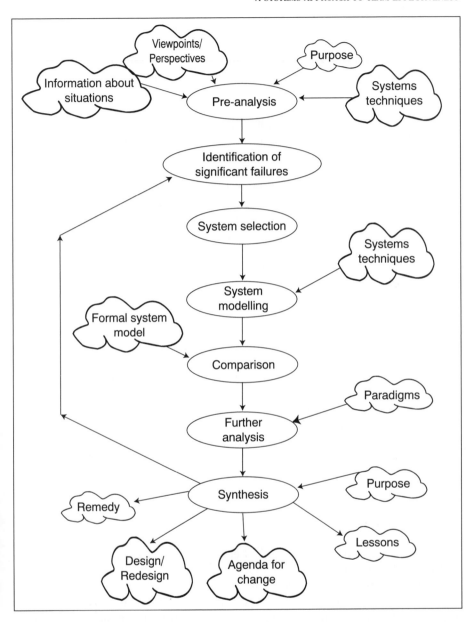

Figure 12.3 The systems failures method

tributing to the debate as to which areas of police activity it is most suited and under what circumstances, if any, its use would be inappropriate or sub-optimal.

Stage 2 – Identification of significant failure(s)

At Stage 2 the actual or potential failure(s) is specified more precisely in accordance with the outcomes of the pre-analysis. Trial boundaries are used to structure relevant aspects of the situation into a range of possible systems.

Gold, Silver, Bronze is now applied in a wide variety of situations including peaceful events requiring large police officer deployments, such as festivals and carnivals, and operations where firearms are involved. One potential failure is that its successful application in certain classes of situations may lead to its use being extended beyond its area of optimum capability. One possible system would regard 'Gold', 'Silver' and 'Bronze' as three sub-systems in a command system; another would envisage a hierarchy with 'Bronze' as a subsystem of 'Silver', which in turn would be a subsystem of 'Gold'. A third option would regard 'Silver' and 'Bronze' as a system with 'Gold' at the next hierarchical level upwards.

Stage 3 – System selection

At Stage 3 the system(s) to be carried forward in the remainder of the analysis is selected from the range identified in the previous stage. In the example being discussed here the third option identified in Stage 2 was selected and was named the command and control system.

Stage 4 – System modelling

At this stage the nature of the selected system(s) is clarified and diagrammatic models of structure and process are built. As an example, Figure 12.4 shows a systems map of the command and control system as selected above.

Stage 5 – comparison

At Stage 5 a comparison is made between the system and the FSM. The output of the stage is a set of discrepancies between the model and the systems representation of the situation.

Wide experience (see Peters and Fortune, 1992) of comparing systems representations of failures with the Formal System Model has shown there to be recurring themes which emerge from comparisons with the FSM. The following are typical points of difference:

1   Deficiencies in the apparent organizational structure of the system, such as a lack of a performance monitoring subsystem or a control/ decision making subsystem.
2   No clear statements of purpose supplied in a comprehensible form to the system from the wider system.

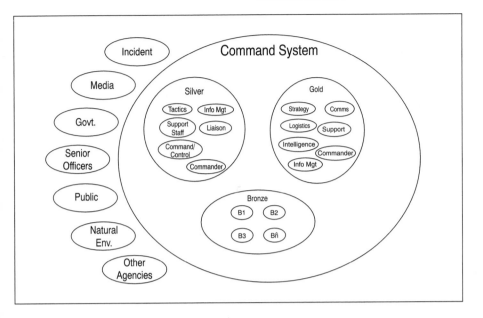

Figure 12.4 Systems map of the command and control system
Source: Pearce and Fortune, 1995

3 Deficiencies in the performance of one or more subsystems – for example, the performance monitoring subsystem may not have performed its task adequately.
4 Lack of an effective means of communication between the various subsystems.
5 Inadequate design of one or more subsystems.
6 Not enough consideration given to the influence of the environment, and insufficient resources to cope with those environmental disturbances that were foreseen.
7 An imbalance between the resources applied to the basic transformation processes and those allocated to the related monitoring and control processes, perhaps leading at one extreme to quality problems and at the other to cost or output quantity problems.

Figure 12.5 shows the command and control system in the appropriate format for comparison with the FSM. 'Gold' is seen as the wider system. It makes its expectations known to 'Silver' through the strategy it sets out, which is communicated downwards as policy. 'Gold' also provides resources and by setting strategic parameters for the command and control of an incident or event gives 'Silver' authority and hence legitimates its activities. 'Bronze' is perceived as the subsystem which carries out the transformations in this example, but the teams that make up 'Bronze' could equally well be regarded as a single system or as a series of systems.

This comparison reveals some discrepancies. For example, where the   *205*

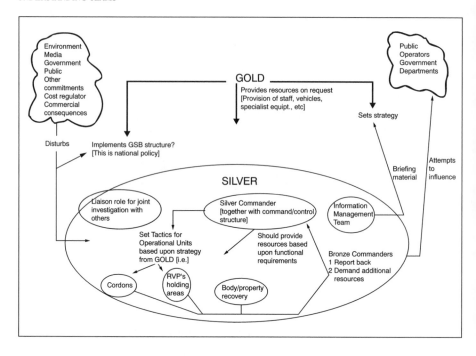

Figure 12.5   The command and control system in the form of the FSM
Source: Pearce and Fortune, 1995

provision of performance information is concerned it could have been expected that information in respect of the state of activity and operations would be passed from 'Bronze' to 'Silver', either on demand or voluntarily as part of the management of the incident or event. Although it was recognized that some form of performance monitoring must take place within 'Silver' as part of its decision making process, no performance monitoring subsystem that would enable comparisons to be made between the expectations of the decision making subsystem and the performance of 'Bronze' could be perceived.

In this particular example the nature of the system was such that its environment could be regarded as largely hostile, generating high levels of disturbance. (When considering the environment in this case there is a conflict between everyday language and systems terminology. In the former the purpose of using Gold, Silver, Bronze is to gain control over a situation, but in systems terminology a system cannot, by definition, control its environment. Influence over the environment is the closest to control that can be achieved.) Looked at in systems terms, environmental disturbances were very much in evidence but neither the system nor the wider system appeared to be making significant efforts to influence the environment.

Table 12.1
Symptoms of Groupthink (after Janis, 1982)

Type I Overestimates of the group: its power and morality
1   An illusion of invulnerability, which creates excessive optimism and encourages taking extreme risks.
2   An unquestioned belief in the group's inherent morality, inclining the members to ignore the ethical or moral consequences of their decisions.

Type II Closed-mindedness
1   Collective efforts to rationalize an order to discount warnings or other information that might lead the members to reconsider their assumptions before they recommit themselves to their past policy decisions.
2   Stereotyped views of enemy leaders as too evil, weak or stupid to counter the risky attempts to defeat their purposes.

Type III Pressures toward uniformity
1   Self-censorship of deviation from apparent group consensus, thereby minimizing the importance of any self-doubt.
2   Shared illusion of unanimity partially resulting from self-censorship and partially from the false assumption that silence meant consent.
3   Direct pressure for loyalty on members expressing arguments counter to the prevailing view.
4   The emergence of 'mindguards' who protect the group from adverse information.

Stage 6 – Further analysis

The discrepancies between the systems representation of the situation and the Formal System Model are investigated further at Stage 6. The primary tools are other models, often system-related models, concerned with control, communication and the human aspects of the analysis. For instance, Janis (1982) has specified eight symptoms of Groupthink which could be used to identify the Groupthink syndrome by observation. These are summarized in Table 12.1.

In the Gold, Silver, Bronze example performance monitoring was one of the aspects that was seen to require further investigation. Comparison with a control model of the type shown in Figure 12.6 was indicated, but the interaction between communication and performance monitoring was also likely to be important. Comparison with the FSM showed that communication channels were available and being used to transmit expectations. However, without performance monitoring there was no feedback to check that communication had been effective.

Stage 7 – Synthesis

At Stage 7 the findings of Stages 5 and 6 are used to re-model the system at various key levels. The output may be a report to a client which may in turn be fed into the preparation of a training programme or the drafting of a policy document. For a situation that has not experienced irretrievable   *207*

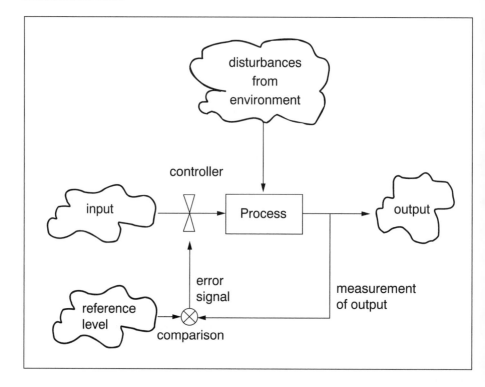

Figure 12.6 Feedback control

failure the findings may suggest a possible remedy. (This is more likely to be the case if the consequences of the failure were systemic but its causes were simple.) In situations where the causes and the consequences were systemic, redesign may be indicated and the findings can be fed into a process for generating an agenda for change.

In the Gold, Silver, Bronze study the output was a series of advantages and drawbacks of the command structure. It was also a suggestion that some of the structural and behavioural weaknesses identified by use of the Systems Failures Method be investigated in relation to specific classes of application such as major incidents, public disorder, precise and imprecise firearms situations and event management.

SUMMARY

This chapter has presented a model based on the notion of system that can be used to design and organize teams that will be capable of purposeful action without failure. It has also provided a brief introduction to a method of investigating and predicting failure in complex situations. As part of their search for greater effectiveness and greater responsiveness, organizations *208* are shifting to team-based working. The mere existence of teams is, however, unlikely to deliver success. Only well-directed successful teams capable of influencing their environments can do that.

REFERENCES

Checkland, P.B., 'The Shape of the Systems Movement', *Journal of Applied Systems Analysis*, 1979, **6** (1), 129–35

Cusumano, M.A., 'Making large teams work like small teams: software product development at Microsoft', paper presented to the International Conference on New Product Development and Production Networks – Learning from Experiences in Different Industries and Countries, Wissenschaftszentrum Berlin Fur Sozialforschung, Berlin, 20–22 March, 1997

Fortune, J., *Systems Paradigms*, Open University Press, Milton Keynes, 1993

Janis, I., *Victims of Groupthink*, Houghton Mifflin, Boston, 1972

Janis, I., *Groupthink: Psychological Studies of Policy Decisions and Fiascos*, Houghton Mifflin, Boston, 1982

March, J.G. and Simon, H.A., *Organizations*, Wiley, New York, 1958

Oliver, N., Gardiner, G., Mills, J. and Frankenberg, M., 'Design and Development Benchmarking', Judge Institute of Management Studies, University of Cambridge, 1995

Pearce, T. and Fortune, J., 'Command and Control in Policing: A Systems Assessment of the Gold, Silver and Bronze Structure, *Journal of Contingencies and Crisis Management*, 1995, **3** (3), 181–187

Peters, G. and Fortune, J., 'Systemic Methods For the Analysis of Failure', *Systems Practice*, 1992, **5**, 529–42

Senge, P.M., 'The Leader's New Work: Building Learning Organizations', *Sloan Management Review*, 1990, Fall, 7–23

Watkins, A., *A Conservative Coup, the Fall of Margaret Thatcher*, Duckworth, London, 1991

RECOMMENDED READING

Fortune, J. and Peters, G., *Learning from Failure*, Wiley, Chichester, 1995

13 Intra-team communication

Christopher Moore

This chapter represents a personal view of group and teamworking based on many years observing the behaviour and interactions of individuals and teams, both within their normal working environment and team development programmes.

Since starting my career in management development in 1980 I have been very fortunate, in two main respects, as to the type of client I have been able to work with. The first is that I have been able to work in many organizations of differing size from different sections of manufacturing, commerce, education and service sectors. No two companies have ever been the same, each has had its own peculiarities and has provided me with a wealth of experience and anecdotal evidence to support the work that I now do. Paradoxically the second fortunate aspect has derived from the similarity between all these organizations, and that is their commitment and enthusiasm for staff development and an understanding that people are not only the most influential element in any change process but also the most important. People are not only the means of change but also the reason for change. Anyone working in the field of HR development knows that without this understanding, commitment and support from high levels in the organization any attempt at significant change is futile.

THE DIFFERENCE BETWEEN A TEAM AND A GROUP

I see the quality of inter-personal communication with its many facets as one of the products of the complexity of teamworking and, although, for the purposes of this chapter, one-to-one relationships are taken as the basic component, a holistic view of team/groupworking must also be taken.

A group is not a team simply because the managers say it is. Many
organizations purport to be a team and expound the philosophy of team-

working as an important part of their mission statement. They often use the concept as a feature of their marketing, attempting to convince themselves, customers and others, such as the bodies that award Investors in People status, that they are a 'people-centred' organization. The sad fact is that although many organizations genuinely want to encourage teamworking, the nearest employees come to working as a team is through some non-work-related, 'after-hours' activity or through employee association. This chapter will examine one of the basic building blocks of teamworking – that of quality communication. If this is understood and managed appropriately, it will help companies to establish effective teams.

A comprehensive definition of the concept of 'team' will have been given elsewhere in this book. However, in order to set the scene for the rest of this chapter I offer my own working definition.

> A group of people can be described as a team if they all have commitment to a set of shared values and objectives, together with an acceptance of how those objectives are to be met. In other words, they are not only in agreement as to where they are going but also on how they are to get there.

There are, of course, many more characteristics that can be ascribed to a team, but it is this sharing of values, objectives and processes that I see as fundamental and which must be in place before attempting to develop or install other characteristics.

A team is a group of people who are brought together in an *organized* way and, not withstanding their own personal aims and agenda are, at least initially, *committed* to *work together* in order to achieve worthwhile and challenging *objectives*. Team membership means that each individual *affects* and *is affected by* the team, and that both the team and each individual is *changed* by membership. Other differences are that teams, unlike simple working groups, seem to *communicate* more efficiently both within and outside the team; *leadership* tends to be of high quality; *support for the individual* seems also to be greater with a team than can be found in mere groups of co-workers. Teams also tend to see themselves, and are seen by others, as quite *distinct* from other groups and they will often take deliberate action to increase any difference. Of all these characteristics, however, it is the *quality of communication* that sets teams apart from other groups: communication is in itself not enough.

QUALITY COMMUNICATION

Organizations often make the mistake of thinking that their communication problems can be resolved by increasing the amount of information that is available. On the contrary an excess of information can overload and confuse, to the point where individuals become inactive, metaphorically 'swallowed up' by an avalanche of data. Under this condition people can experience a sense of helplessness, which, in turn, can cause fear, frustration and even panic – all of which are counter-productive to good teamworking. For most companies with communication problems the issue is not quantity but quality. Much time and money can be wasted on installing communication systems that fail to be used simply because the quality of information they carry is poor. To be effective a company's communication system must have a means of monitoring and controlling the level of quality of information that it carries. Without effective communication, the organization of work, the commitment, motivation, cooperation of staff and the achievement of objectives are significantly limited and often impossible. To be effective, communication must be of the right quality.

A definition of quality communication

Of all the questions that can be asked of managers one of the most difficult is to define the characteristics of quality communication. These five characteristics, identified as central to the quality of communication, add up to a good working definition, based on *Grice's Maxims* (Grice, 1975).

- *Quantity* Provide a quantity of information that is appropriate to the current purpose
- *Quality* As far as possible only the truth should be communicated
- *Relevance* Avoid providing irrelevant information
- *Method* Adopt a method that is appropriate to the purpose
- *Timely* Ensure that information is delivered within an appropriate timescale.

We should also ensure that our non-verbal communication is congruent to all this – a task that is not always an easy one, as our non-verbal signals are not always within our control and, even when they are, are open to misinterpretation.

Key concepts in quality communication

Control and communication

The concept of a collective objective, mentioned earlier as a primary characteristic of an effective team, promotes the idea of control. For the team to be effective this control must be exercised, albeit to varying degrees, at all levels within the team. Consequently teams have a control or leadership function that is not exclusively sited in one person: even though it may well be a single person who makes the final decisions, all members must be party to the exercise of control. The multifaceted role of leadership may be shared by the whole team or, possibly, a small cadre. Whoever controls must have an understanding of what internal and external influences may be affecting the team's performance.

Effective control requires an appropriate quality of communication, and for communication to be of the right quality it must be controlled. In using the concept of controlling communication I do not wish to imply suppression. In this sense control means to manage communication to ensure that it is of a quality that is appropriate for the needs of the team. Leaders, managers and other team members must understand what is going on before taking action to change the situation. This knowledge of how the team is operating is not restricted to hard and/or measurable data. The subjective assessment of the quality of interpersonal relationships is just as important as understanding the range of practical and conceptual skill and knowledge held by the team as a whole.

All this may seem obvious and yet, if it is, why do many employees, when asked to identify the one most important issue that is preventing the organization from reaching its full potential, often speak of 'a failure in communication'? There may well be a number of reasons for this apparent inability to deal successfully with a problem that has so often and clearly been identified. However, I think that there are three reasons, equally important factors, which will have a greater influence than any other. I have dealt with, or at least highlighted, the first two, that is to say the need to ensure an appropriate level of quality in communication and the crucial reciprocal relationship of communication and control. The third is the level at which team communication is analysed, and I intend to deal with this in the rest of this chapter.

Taking an appropriate viewpoint

Teams are viewed and analysed from different angles: as a whole, as a set of individuals or, as in this chapter, collections of bilateral or dyadic relationships. One of the primary assertions of this chapter is that the quality of inter- and intra-team communication is affected, *at a fundamental level*, by the quality of interpersonal relationships.

Interpersonal relationships

Think of all the people you have contact with and consider the qualities of each relationship. You may get on equally well, or badly, with most. Or, on the other hand, you may find that there are only a few with whom you relate to well or badly. There may be predominant characteristics that can be found in each relationship; however, the qualities that characterize any one relationship will not be *exactly* the same as any other. Like Citizen Kane we, consciously or unconsciously, present different 'personas' to different people. My next-door neighbour will think of me and describe me in terms quite different to those of say, the Managing Director of a client company who will, in turn, present a different view from that of a fellow tutor in the Open University.

The relationship with *each* of the other people in our lives is unique. Each *213* relationship is the outcome of the interaction of two *developing* personalities, together with all the other factors which make up the social context within which the relationship exists. These factors will include culture, the structure and processes within our organizational environment, and the quality of face-to-face verbal and non-verbal communications.

In a working team the culture, climate, effectiveness and/or efficiency in meeting its objectives, the quality of communication and the quality of relationships can be seen as emergent properties of this complex system of dyadic interactions. Accepting this concept will enable us to see that manipulating relationships by changing the quality of communication can change a group into a team and vice-versa, and thereby affect these emergent properties.

Misunderstanding or ignoring this point results in managers often being surprised at the results of adding or subtracting people from a team or group. If there are six people in a team there are fifteen dyads. Managers often fail to see that removing or adding one person affects the whole team. By subtracting one person the manager has effectively removed one half of each relationship and affected all the others. By adding one person the manager not only changes the balance of all existing relationships but also adds a further six dyads. Sadly many managers still recruit on the basis of whether an individual is technically capable. Little, if any, consideration is given to how they will fit into and affect the existing team.

The egocentric viewpoint and the apparent need to apportion blame

Many people work and live in a blame culture. When things go wrong we look for the thing, or more often, the person who will 'carry the can'. When the rains failed our primitive ancestors would look for the person within the tribe who had offended the gods, then sacrifice them. By identifying and punishing this 'guilty party' the tribe would make itself blameless and therefore be spared their deities' wrath. In modern companies we see a similar arrangement. Consider the true example of the sales department which failed to win a particularly important order. To placate and deflect the MD's displeasure the sales manager instigates an immediate search for the culprit. Once found the hapless victim is disciplined and the other members of the office can 'sleep', not too soundly, at their desks, in the uneasy knowledge that, although they escaped punishment on this occasion, they may not be so fortunate next time. This blame culture is so strong that, if no one else is available, we are even willing to blame ourselves. Fear of blame will stifle clear and open communication. Above all, fear of blame will often prevent people from owning the problem, and with the absence of ownership comes the inability to change the situation.

When a bilateral relationship is seen as inappropriate and/or counterproductive to the wants and needs of the individuals involved, there is a natural, yet wholly wasteful, temptation to apportion blame, either to oneself or the other person. A more appropriate response is to analyse the situation and identify how things can be improved.

The rest of this chapter is concerned with presenting a method of analysing and changing the qualities of relationships, discussing these key concepts and thereby affecting the quality of communication.

SOCIAL CONSTRUCTIONISM[1]

Although the approach used may appear to draw on concepts of traditional psychology the main influence comes from social constructionism. It is appropriate, therefore, to provide some brief explanation of this, relatively, new approach to understanding human experience.

One of the biggest dangers to the advancement of knowledge of people that psychologists, and the rest of us wishing to understand the human experience, have to contend with is the assumption, derived from natural science, that for every question regarding social interaction there is a single answer and that it is out there somewhere waiting to be discovered. The second biggest danger is the apparent desire in many to have psychology and its methods accepted by scientists as a genuine science. These two issues influence many researchers and analysts to treat the human experience as if it were just like any other natural phenomenon, and apply reductionist thinking to something that requires a much more creative and holistic approach. For many years there has been a tendency to use techniques, more appropriate to biological reductionism, to try to explain social phenomena such as aggression, criminality, drug addiction, homosexuality, altruism, and so on. In recent years this approach has been given increased impetus with the early success and progress of the worldwide project to identify and catalogue the entire human genetic make-up. There is an assumption among many that 'the cause' of these conditions will be found in our genes. There may be a genetic disposition to these behaviours, but, without the additional influence of the social environment, they will not necessarily manifest themselves.

Although social constructionism rejects the *emphasis* of the internal states and processes as the sole or primary influence of behaviour of the individual it does not reject the possibility that they may exert an *influence*. With apologies to social constructionists for squeezing their subject into a very small nutshell, I think that a reasonable summary of social constructionism would be that our view of that which is outside of ourselves, our environment, and the way in which we interact with it is constantly being constructed and re-constructed through the verbal and non-verbal linguistic

---

[1] A more comprehensive explanation of the comparison between social constructionism and psychology is give by Vivien Burr in the 1997 edition of *The New Psychologist*, the annual journal of the Open University Psychological Society.

		Observed characteristics		
1	Helpful	« or »	1	Unhelpful
2	Cooperative	« or »	2	Uncooperative
3	Friendly	« or »	3	Unfriendly
4	Sympathetic	« or »	4	Unsympathetic
5	Trusting	« or »	5	Suspicious
6	Involved	« or »	6	Indifferent
7	Attracted	« or »	7	Repelled
8	Conciliatory	« or »	8	Argumentative
	Plus (+)			Minus (–)

Figure 13.1 Bipolar constructs

interaction that we each have with others. It is this one-to-one verbal and non-verbal interaction which forms the basis of study for the methodology presented in the rest of this chapter.

RESEARCH AND ANALYSIS

As with any process of managed change we develop an understanding, through observation, of the *apparent* situation. I have emphasized the word 'apparent' because what we see is not reality but our own interpretation of it. The observation is made during an artificial team activity, such as those commonly found on team building courses. To comply with the principles of ethical research, participants are told that they will be observed and that notes regarding their interactions with others will be taken. This knowledge will, no doubt, affect their behaviour. However, my experience suggests that any uncharacteristic behaviour gives way to 'normal' interaction once participants become absorbed in the task. To this end it is imperative to choose tasks that stimulate interest and enthusiasm. Because of the need to keep all participants within an observable distance, outside activities are less appropriate than indoor ones. Two team tasks, much used by myself to good effect, are suggested at the end of this chapter. You may want to familiarize yourself with these before reading on.

During the early part of the team task the observer makes a note of the prevailing relational characteristics. For reasons of simplicity and as a means of clarifying the process, the example used here requires the observer to decide whether the observed characteristic is either plus (+) or minus (–). No *degree* of helpfulness is identified, only if the individual *is or is not* helpful. These assessments may change and as they do so the record should be changed. The relationships are expressed in terms of bipolar constructs such as those in Figure 13.1.

The numbers are only used as means of notation, and signs simply indicate the ends of each construct. Instead of using 'plus' and 'minus' you could, for example, use 'L' and 'R' to indicate left and right or 'U' and 'D' for up and down. Numbers and signs are noted on a matrix such as the example given in Figure 13.2.

The characteristics used should be those observed, as each team will have its own set of characteristics, the combination and intensity of which will be unique to it. The above list of relational characteristics may be useful, but they should not be taken as a model for every group.

Analysis matrix

For ease of recording a *paired factors analysis* matrix is used, see Figure 13.2. In this context the factors are the team members, as indicated by the letters A to J. The numbers indicate the characteristics, as in the examples shown in Table 13.1 above. The signs show which end of the bipolar construct is the most appropriate general description.

The process is as follows: each pair, AB, AC, AD and so on, then BC, BD, BE and so on through to J are considered, but not necessarily in alphabetical order. The facilitator/observer makes a subjective and qualitative assessment of their relationship, placing the appropriate numbers and signs in the intersecting square. Remember that it is the relationship that is being assessed and not the behaviour of individuals. Of course interaction will occur randomly and not in alphabetical order – therefore, they are recorded as they occur.

The partly completed example, given in Figure 13.2, indicates that, of the four individuals *thus far* assessed, 'H' seems to be party to relationships of a poorer quality than the others. Do not jump to conclusions as to the causes for the apparent quality, or lack of it, in any observed relationships, nor decide which individual is to blame. As emphasized earlier, a relationship is the outcome of the contributions made by two people. The relationship and its degree of quality is, therefore, the responsibility of both parties.

Within any working group or team there will be key relationships that have a high level of influence on the overall quality of group communications. In the example given in Figure 13.1 it can be seen that there are, apparently, some strong negative characteristics associated with the relationships that 'H' has with each of her colleagues. Again I must emphasize that apportioning blame is counterproductive. Blaming one side of a bilateral relationship for its apparent poor quality will serve to cause one side to be antagonized and the other to relinquish all responsibility for the situation. This analytical tool helps to identify the qualities of the *relationship* shared by two people at any one time, **not** the *personal attributes* of any one individual. Like many diagnostic tools it is simply a convenient way of presenting data. Information is obtained through the interpretation of that data. The strengths and weaknesses of the method used must be considered when making these interpretations.

On completion of the matrix the team is invited to comment, without recrimination or blame, on the results and asked to suggest means by which *each* of them can affect *each* of the relationships, to either maintain or   *217*

	B	C	D	E	F	G	H	I	J	Most significant characteristic for each individual
A	1+, 2+ 5+, 7+ 8+		1+, 2+ 4+, 5+ 7+, 8+				2+, 3+ 4-, 5- 6-, 8-			
B			3+, 5+ 6+, 7+ 8+				2+, 5- 8-			
C										
D							1+, 3+ 5-, 8-			
E										
F										
G										
H										
I										
J										

Figure 13.2   A partly completed matrix showing the dyadic relationships between four team members

change them. Although the two individuals who share a particular relationship are perhaps the most influential in its quality and development, others are also encouraged to see how their behaviour and actions will affect them. It should not be forgotten that the primary purpose of this technique is to stimulate constructive discussion leading to appropriate plans for change.

THE TEAM TASKS

These team tasks, developed, used and modified by the author many times since August 1989, are a mechanism by which the observer may assess bilateral interaction. In addition they also allow a great deal of freedom and creativity and encourage the disclosure of hidden agenda, bringing into the open issues about which individuals would otherwise find it impossible to speak. The first team task is very much a means of stimulating a high level of cooperation. On the other hand the second does provide the opportunity for competition. Each in its own way will provide the observer with plenty of opportunity for gathering some very useful information. These team tasks also serve as metaphorical bridges between the past, present and future, providing the means by which a contract for change can be made between individuals and the team of the present and the individuals and team in the future.

Duration of observation

Each of the team tasks is conducted over approximately half a day. Any shorter period might not provide enough data of sufficient quality, and any longer may cause the participants to become frustrated with the task and thereby provide an unintended variable with a disproportional influence.

Team task – 'The corporate news'

Although this task could, with considerable modification, be used with a group made up of members from different organizations, it is primarily intended for management teams from the same company.

The task is for the team to produce one copy of a company newspaper which reports all the news and current issues affecting the company. One important feature is that the newspaper is *dated one year ahead* of the time in which the task has been set. This gives the participants the opportunity of predicting how they believe the company will, or how they want it to, perform over the coming year and beyond. This pre-dating also locates the publication in the realm of fantasy, where all things are possible, an as yet, unreal place in which anything can be said without fear of retribution. Another feature is that once the publication is completed it is not easy to attribute any one particular piece of material to any particular individual. These two features allow a significant degree of freedom, which has a profound effect on the individual's degree of willingness to *print* what they really want to say. I encourage the team to keep the finished newspaper and to review it on the date of its publication in one year's time.

The process is quite simple insofar as the group organizes itself into a production team and manufactures a newspaper. This is done by means of cutting and pasting from existing publications. The newspaper contains all the usual sections that you would expect to see in a national publication.

Rules

There are few rules given to the participants other than they are to have fun, allow their imaginations complete freedom, to inject as much humour as possible into the finished product, to ensure that all material has some direct or indirect link with the organization for which they work, and to organize themselves into a production team in which every member plays *219* an equal part. They are also told that the paper should contain all the usual elements found in a national newspaper. After this briefing they decide among themselves who is to be editor in chief and how long they will need. Generally groups underestimate the time required so encourage them to decide on at least three hours. When this has been decided it becomes the deadline. As with a real newspaper the deadline has a profound effect on the activity of the group. As the deadline approaches, the enthusiasm, commitment and creativity increase at almost an exponential rate. Generally speaking far more work is done in the last half hour than in the preceding two.

Materials

The materials required are simple and cheap and consequently do not detract from the true meaning of the task. They consist of a quantity of old newspapers, magazines and corporate publicity materials, together with scissors, fine felt-tip pens and glue. Flip-chart paper is used as a backing on which to stick the various bits and pieces, photographs, and so on that are cut from the papers and magazines. Groups are also given access to photocopiers, Polaroid cameras, computers and any other appropriate materials and equipment that can be made available.

Participants

This task has been used, with considerable success, in a wide variety of teams including: a sales team which was finding great difficulty in developing 'honest' internal lines of communication, the management team from shop-floor supervision to managing director that was having considerable difficulty in accepting the validity of the CEO's mission statement, and the group of university academics, consultants and lecturers who wanted to develop a clear picture of where their institution was heading.

In all these cases, and many others, the team task did not give the answer or solution. What it did do was to set the team members off in an agreed direction, armed with a set of common concepts and language with which to discuss the problem or issue. Perhaps most importantly it established a quality of communication more appropriate to the needs of the team and the company.

Team task – 'May the force be with you'[2]

As with the first task this is primarily intended for a group of managers and other key staff all from the same organization.

The objective of the task is to identify which factors within a situation or problem will inhibit a desired change and those that will facilitate it. These

[2] Adapted from Lewin's ideas on force field analysis (Lewin, 1951).

factors, referred to as forces, will include not only those derived from people (their attitudes, feelings and values), economic (including the activities of competitors and customers), but cultural, societal (legislation, environment, community expectation, and so on) and technological factors.

Preparation

The group is divided into two sides. One side plays the role of those who want to prevent the change, and the others play the role of those who wish it to succeed. Each group spends some time in separate rooms brainstorming to arrive at a list of factors. One group develops a list of facilitating or driving factors, the other a list of preventative or resisting factors. Each separate factor is written on to a stick-on note, then stuck to the end of a drinking straw in the manner of a flag on a flag pole. The other end of the straw is then stuck into a piece of reusable adhesive which in turn is pushed on to a small piece of card. This assembly forms one 'playing' piece similar to a pawn in a chess game. Once each group has assembled their playing pieces they all return to the main room which, while the groups were brainstorming, has been set up by the facilitator as follows.

A board table, ideally about two metres long, is arranged so that all-round access is possible. A length of soft, thin rope is laid down the length and in the centre of the table. A length of masking tape is placed along the length of the table and approximately 15 centimetres in from each edge. The rope signifies the starting point or equilibrium point, and the two lengths of tape are the starting points for each opposing side. Each group then sets up their playing pieces behind their respective lines of tape. The force for change side moves first by placing one of their playing pieces on the table and pushing the rope towards the other side to a point commensurate to that piece's strength. The strength of the piece is decided through rational and logical negotiation between the two sides. This first move is then directly countered by the force for resisting change moving one of their pieces to oppose the first move. As before, the final position of these two opposing forces is arrived at through rational and logical discussion. The forces for change then either add more weight to their first move by bringing up another related force, or they can attack another part of the line. This process continues until all the pieces are used or until sufficient work has been done to give a clear picture of the areas of most concern. Once this has been achieved a plan of campaign is formulated to increase the effectiveness of the forces for change and decrease the effectiveness of those that are resisting. This is done by identifying what new forces need to be created on the side for change, how existing forces for change can be strengthened, which forces resisting change can be illuminated and how the remaining resistance can be weakened.

Rules

Again, despite the potential for confrontation, the emphasis should be on enjoyment. Any inability, on the part of the two opposing forces, to come to an agreement is resolved by the facilitator. Each group must argue their case, bearing in mind that the objective of the task is to arrive at a clear picture of the relative position of the forces for and against change and not simply to 'win the game'. During the game each side is allowed to add to their forces with the agreement of the other. The important thing to remember about providing a set of rules is that they should help to stimulate the process and achieve the objective.

Materials

- Large table. Alternatively this game can be played on the floor
- Thin, soft, flexible rope long enough to run one and a half times the length of the table
- Stick-on notes, one pack green, the other red – or any other dissimilar colours
- Two packs of drinking straws
- Reusable adhesive
- Card for the bases of the flags
- Masking tape

Participants

Because of the nature of this task, participants should be those who have some power and authority to influence the required changes.

Each of these team tasks provides the opportunity for observing and reflecting on the way in which individuals relate one to another, which will lead to constructive and informed debate as to how the situation can be changed. Subsequent rerunning of these tasks with the same group will also give the opportunity for experimentation, based on the previous abstract conceptualization, in which team members can try techniques and methods within a safe environment.

CONCLUSION

Effective teamworking requires good quality communication, and this is determined by the quality of the basic building blocks of group activity, that is the bilateral relationships that exist within each dyad. Through careful observation these relationships can be identified sufficiently to allow useful discussion.

The relationships that we, as observers, see are in a state of dynamic equilibrium, which changes in response to the influence of factors that are both within and outside each individual. All bilateral relationships are, therefore, in a constant state of change, and this will often bring about uncertainty which can lead to tensions and/or conflict within or between each individual. Understanding the inevitability of change in bilateral relationships and how these changes may be managed will allow individuals the opportunity of developing their relationships so that they are more appropriate to their needs and those of the organization for which they work. The team development tasks identified in this chapter, when *skilfully* facilitated, provide individuals with the opportunity of developing this invaluable understanding.

Blaming any one individual for the state of a relationship, of which they are only one part, is a waste of valuable time which would be better used trying to understand the social influences that affect them.

RECOMMENDED READING

Kelly G.A., *The Psychology of Personal Constructs*, W.W. Norton, New York, 1955

Lewin K., *Field Theory in Social Science*, Harper & Row, London, 1951

The New Psychologist, the annual journal of the Open University Psychological Society, 1997

14 Choosing, joining and leaving teams

Chris Elgood

A group of people described as a team normally has a purpose: the team is intended to achieve something. Consequently, many examinations of teams and teamwork concentrate on their effectiveness in reaching an objective. The questions asked are, 'Does it succeed? If not, then why not? What can be done to make it succeed better?' Those concerned to ask and answer such questions are likely to be leaders of teams or people interested in the concepts of teams and leadership. They look at the subject from one particular viewpoint. They probably set up teambuilding activities with hopes and intentions like these:

- That all team members should understand the team objectives, and how they are to be achieved
- That team members should know each other as human beings and not just as office-holders. That they should understand each other's skills and qualities and strengths and weaknesses
- That team members should have the skill and the inclination to communicate fully with each other
- That there should be no subject about which team members feel unable to express their feelings
- That team members should watch out for any opportunity to support and assist each other, and act accordingly
- That team members should have an awareness of all aspects of the work, and abhor the attitude that says 'That is not my responsibility.'

Not all members will necessarily accept these concepts. One reaction may be 'What do you mean by a team?' Another might be 'Who said that this

was a team anyway?' A third might be 'My needs are adequately met, even if the level of team success is quite ordinary. All this "getting to know each other" is pointless.' Let's examine each of these reactions.

WHAT DO YOU MEAN BY A TEAM?

A good many traditional ideas about teams remain influential. The most powerful one is the idea of defining separate areas of skill, then training staff to perform tightly defined skills at a high level, and organizing the work so that the right people perform the right task at the right time and leave their work in order, to pass on to the next team. The observer who looks at a warship of the Napoleonic wars – like HMS Victory with its masses of masts and spars and sails – might well think 'How on earth could you organize this ship for fighting except by rigid training and discipline?' Could the collections of human beings organized in this way be called 'teams' at all? They often sank or survived as single groups (certainly one team characteristic), but membership might have been compulsory, through the press gang or conscription. Can something that one is compelled to join be called a team?

The traditional concept also operates when building a house. Different groups of professionals build the walls, install the plumbing, wire the house for electricity and plaster the walls. Each group knows what to do, and keeps to its own task. Working to this concept, the idea of taking any great interest in the work of another specialist is actually counter-productive. It represents interference and can cause resentment. If each specialist does the specialist job to a high standard, and the planning/scheduling process is correct, then all will be well. It is not necessary that the plumber should be friendly with the electrician, or the plasterer should know that the architect has diabetes.

To illustrate how previous and present concepts conflict, consider the extreme case of a team-building workshop that included the cleaners. It could be justified on the grounds that the phone often rings just before 9.00 a.m. or just after 5.30 p.m. and that callers might be impressed with an intelligent response rather than no answer or just 'There's nobody here!' Perhaps a better impression would be created if the phone was answered and the caller was told, for example, 'I think the person you need is Mr X. I will make sure he telephones you.' But if the idea for such a workshop was put forward, one can imagine how some of the cleaners might respond: 'I get paid to clean the office. I do it and go home. If you want a low grade clerk, advertise for one. Don't try and fool me into doing the job!'

It is important to note in this connection that the traditional view of team organization offers a degree of security. One only has *limited* obligations – just those associated with doing the job one is paid for. If a member of some other department fouls up, one is not involved. Competence in a well-defined task is an achievable objective and one can leave at the end of the day knowing 'I have done what was required of me.' The modern idea of a team, which suggests that all members have a legitimate interest in all aspects of   *225* team operations, is extremely demanding. A conscientious person might find the demands intolerable, inducing constant worries like 'Should I say or do anything about *that* situation?'

The reality is that we can't define the word 'team'. It exists only as an ideal, the 'team state' being one in which all members understand and approve of the goal and constantly adopt the behaviour that is best for the team rather than the behaviour that is best for the self. This seldom happens, and even in organizations that are universally referred to as 'teams' – such as national sporting teams – we see instances in which individual glory appears to be put before the good of the team. The response should be to face up to the facts and acknowledge that people commit themselves to teams according to the benefits they expect to receive by doing so. It is a psychological contract. Some people seek forms of satisfaction that appear more high-minded than others, but the element of selfishness is always present. Footballers have been known to go for transfers because they want prestige rewards – such as a cup-winner's medal – which are seen as impossible while remaining with the present club. Others find intense satisfaction in comradeship, and will stay with a team that appears to be losing. In both cases the individuals are seeking personal satisfaction. It just happens to take different forms.

The point to remember is that people have different ideas about what constitutes a team, about what the obligations of membership are, and about how a team member should behave. No leader can assume that the team members share all his or her concepts. One particular danger arises from differences in personality type, such as are demonstrated by question-naires like the Strength Deployment Inventory of Personal Strengths Publishing. These show that some of us are motivated by a desire for action and results, while others gain satisfaction from helping and supporting others and from creating a good working climate. The latter group some-times appear to the former as time-wasters with no concern for practical outcomes. The former group may appear to the latter as impatient, insensi-tive slave-drivers doomed to destroy their own teams! It is not easy for a person of one orientation to place the right value upon the orientation of another.

WHO SAID THIS WAS A TEAM ANYWAY?

It may be that some members don't consider the group of people they have joined to be a team at all. Each of them will have joined in pursuit of different goals and will be judging the group by whether it delivers. What were those goals? One can start hypothesizing by asking oneself: 'Why should I (personally) join a group in the first place?'

The obvious answer is 'To receive some benefit which (a) I currently desire and (b) I believe to be more readily obtainable through belonging to this group than through individual action.' Both elements in this response are personal judgements reflecting personal values. What I desire is peculiar to me and may change. Likewise the ease with which I can obtain them for myself may change: I may, perhaps, learn skills while working in a team that later enable me to set up as an independent consultant! Since there is always a cost to being a team member, the balance of cost against benefit may switch from positive to negative. If I find that the cost of belonging has come to exceed the benefits membership brings, then I reduce my commitment to the team, or leave altogether. In fact, we spend all our lives joining and leaving teams because our motives are largely selfish. 'Is this a team?' 'It may be a team to you (the leader) because if it functions effectively as a team then that will be specially rewarding for you. That does not make it a team to me!' Sometimes the treatment an individual receives falls below an acceptable standard. The response then is: 'You call this a team? A real team would never treat its members the way you have treated me!'

MY NEEDS ARE ADEQUATELY MET EVEN IF THE LEVEL OF SUCCESS IS ORDINARY

The objectives of the team – what the leader defines as success – may not be the same objectives as those which motivate all the members. For those who merely sought *a job*, the only requirement is that the team should do well enough to continue in existence and be able to pay wages. Or there might be a football player who did not want his team to be promoted because of the additional responsibilities promotion would bring. He might enjoy his football, and the comradeship of the team, on the basis of one game a week and one training session! More than this he would find distasteful. 'You, the leader of this team, want team success. I just want a congenial pastime!'

LESSONS FOR LEADERS

Among the ideas that team leaders need to grasp are these:

1 That their definition of a team may not be shared. If they want it to be shared, they must structure a debate about the matter within the team.
2 That the motivations of those they think of as team members may differ widely.
3 That different motivations can contribute to the same goal. For a member to be useful and valuable it is not absolutely necessary that he should be driven by the same desires as other members, or as the leader. The only condition necessary is that the individual contract is currently advantageous, so that by putting in more (which the leader can define) the individual gets more out (which he or she defines).

What the leader thinks of as his team may (at one extreme) be a mixture of people held together only by the short-term satisfaction of diverse motivations, none of whom think of what they belong to as a team at all. At the *227*

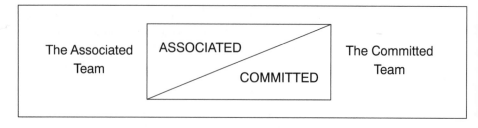

Figure 14.1 The committed team and the associated team

other extreme the group may have the common motivation of achieving team success, with all members in no doubt about being a team. Successful sporting teams like the All Blacks are the obvious example. Yet even here the unity may conceal the fact that different benefits are being sought. One player may value success for reasons purely of personal pride. Another may value it because it will lead to a second career as a sports commentator. A third may value it because of the financial benefits he can gain by endorsing products. In France, during the German occupation, groups which might have been united by their desire to free the nation were divided by their ideals for post-war society.

The idea can be shown by the diagram above, in which (on the left) motivation within the team is totally diverse and (on the right) it is common – at least in the sense that it is linked to team success. It may be helpful to use the words 'associated' and 'committed', to indicate that one extreme implies a variety of separate 'psychological contracts' and the other implies one contract to which all members subscribe. It is to the committed team that present day team-building activities really make sense, for their objective is greater team success and the members have equated that with the satisfaction of their own needs.

Can an *associated* team be transformed into a *committed* team? Can a team at the left-hand side of the rectangle be dragged along the scale towards the right? In theory, yes. It can be done by arranging that the rewards offered to each member are those that he or she values, and in such a way that their quantity increases as team success increases. To achieve this piece of engineering the leader must do two things:

1 He must find out what motivates his people, what they value, and will strive to achieve.
2 He must present team success as a clear, attainable objective (almost a totem) which can be relied on to bring the desired benefits. It must become a common, maxi-objective which will represent all the others.

THE REALITIES OF PERSONAL MOTIVATION

What are these personal benefits that people value, and which they will give more to obtain? The short answer is that they are exactly the benefits – the satisfactions of human needs – that writers have been discussing for decades. They start with satisfying physiological needs and move gradually upwards towards self-actualization needs. What is sometimes not apparent from the textbooks is the huge number of different needs that can be identified within the accepted categories, the way these categories overlap, and the manner in which some motivations operate at the micro rather than the macro level. The textbooks do not always make clear another significant point, which is that a motivator can 'pull' – using the hope of getting a benefit in the future – or 'push' – using the fact that what is happening at this moment is enjoyable.

Identifying feelings within teams

Here are some questions (and possible answers) that team leaders might ask about themselves about groups they have joined and left. It is offered as a means of identifying the feelings that some of their own team members may be currently experiencing. It can be related to any identifiable group – irrespective of whether it was called a team, a club or anything else.

Question – Why did I join?

Possible answers:

- I wanted a job
- I wanted to be with my friends. ('I joined the Natural History group because I had a crush on the teacher')
- I wanted to take part in an activity, to learn about it, practice it and improve my skills
- Joining this team seemed the most promising way to reach another goal. (I wanted to join Manchester United as it was the best way to get a cup-winner's medal)
- I saw an opportunity. ('Their wicket-keeper was retiring and I wanted to become one')
- It was fashionable to join and I did not want to look odd
- It was the only way to avoid doing something I hated. ('The school said I had to play games and I joined the Badminton team to avoid playing Rugby')
- I wanted the privileges that the members enjoyed
- I wanted power, and I thought I could work my way up this particular hierarchy
- They needed new members if they were to be effective, and I always like feeling needed
- I was pushed into joining it by people who said I had a talent, and must use it. ('I joined the choir because my mother liked music')

When answering, remember that any 'I joined because . . .' statement is a statement about motivation. Remember also that many motivators are psychological in nature and not immediately visible to the observer. Our thinking about motivation is still limited by the old concept of working just for money, and we don't always realize how many satisfactions are achieved, almost without realizing it, from the activity we call 'work'. A specially important fact is that people really like using and displaying and improving their skills. It is a form of self-expression, increasing the feeling of identity.

Question – What commitment did I give to it?

Possible answers:

- The absolute minimum
- Quite a lot during the 'official' hours for which I had contracted. Outside those, none
- A great deal. Far beyond what I had officially contracted for, or was rewarded for.

Question – Were there others who viewed the group more as 'a team' than I did?

Possible answers:

- The 'leading light' was absolutely fanatical. He got very angry with 'casual' members
- Everybody was pretty relaxed
- There was an inner circle who continually wanted us to do better, while the rest of us were enjoying ourselves at an amateur level
- There was a ruling clique that operated as a team within a team.

Question – Why did I leave?

Possible answers:

- A change in personal circumstances made it unavoidable
- I lost sympathy with the objectives
- The work became far more serious and demanding than I cared for
- Most of my friends had left and I did not like the new people
- There was nothing more I could learn. I moved on to a higher level
- There was a personality clash
- I failed to win sufficient influence to make the group do what I wanted it to do
- The group developed in ways to which I was opposed

- The behaviour of the group became stereotyped and repetitive. I got bored
- Standards were rising, and my skills did not keep pace with the changes
- There was a cultural shift within the group that was unwelcome to me
- I was head-hunted away.

Such questions reveal the variety of motivations that influence people. A further necessary step is to recognize that the words used can conceal significant differences of interpretation. Consider the idea that 'I want a job'. The traditional interpretation of this is 'I want a job in order to provide materially for myself and my family' – which implies that the money is what matters. That does not have to be true. What sort of job, and under what conditions? Having *a job* promises benefits to the person who is currently without one, but as the concept of working 9.00 a.m. to 5.00 p.m. for forty years passes into history, great variety becomes apparent in possible contracts. There are casual workers who positively enjoy the sort of life in which the phone rings and a voice says 'Can you come in for eight hours tonight?' They like being able to say 'yes' or 'no', and if the money falls too low then they just register with a few more casual employers. Their motivation contains elements of 'being wanted', 'not wasting time' and 'being free to choose'. These are motivations linked to self-image. Among casual workers there are also skilled people who get satisfaction from the job itself – like a bar person who won't do anything else except tend the bar. By contrast there are other job-seekers who are desperate to turn casual or part-time employment into 'a real job' with holiday benefits and redundancy entitlement and a considerable degree of security.

ONE MEMBER – MANY TEAMS

When thinking back to the days of being an ordinary team member, the leader will recognize that he or she probably belonged to many different groups, at least some of which were seeking to operate as teams. Personal choices had to be made about the level of commitment to give to each. Those teams were not inter-conscious. The leader of one might seek to arouse greater motivation in his people by increasing the rewards attainable through membership. This might make the one group more attractive, but would be of no avail if another group did the same or better. Groups, or teams, were competing for loyalty when this notional leader was young, and they still are.

In one sense the problem is worse because of the present-day flexible lifestyle. There was a time when work finished at 5.30 p.m., the Stamp Club met every Monday evening, Wednesday evening was the Sewing Guild and Friday evening was the Bowls Club. It was possible to work out which commitments might conflict, and avoid double-booking. Today even employment commitments are flexible and it is quite common to be told 'The person you need to speak to is not in today.' We have thrown away many of the constraints that regulated our lives, and a consequence is that we have to make more choices.

Financial pressures have also slimmed down organizations to the point where a team member may have no effective backup. We are told at railway stations that a train cancellation is 'due to staff shortage', and we sometimes hear of hospital operations being postponed because 'there is no anaesthetist (or whoever) available'. As a result, some team member has made, or been forced to make, a choice that leaves the team unable to function.

A third modern problem is our habit of forming Project Teams made up of different specialists. The head of a group of specialists may be required to provide one of his staff for attachment to a project. He or she assigns someone who notionally becomes part of that project team. The person may not want the assignment, may already be part of other project teams and may have to make choices about which should be given loyalty at a particular moment. This attitude will be significantly different from that of the Project Leader to whom the person has been assigned.

A WAY FORWARD

So how does the ambitious team leader cope? One answer is to accept that total loyalty is impossible but to maximize individual commitment by exploring with each team member the balance of commitment versus reward. It then becomes possible to strike an agreement about priorities so that both parties know what is expected and can deliver. Exploring attitudes with team members is not in itself difficult. What sometimes proves almost impossible is ignoring three traditional concepts. These are:

> That one can treat human beings on a group basis and formulate a single motivational strategy that will work for all of them.

> That a motivational strategy that works for one person today will also work for that person tomorrow.

> That considering the individual motivation of team members is an inappropriate way for a leader to use valuable time: time which should properly be spent making mind-boggling decisions or boosting the leader's own image.

A word not often found in the literature of motivation, but mentioned once before in this chapter, is *identity* – the recognition of each person as in some small way different from all the other millions of human beings, and deserving of personal attention. In our crowded world a feeling of identity is hard to achieve. Leaders who can impart it will be well repaid.

RECOMMENDED READING

Belbin, R.M., *Management Teams*, Heinemann, London, 1981

Elgood, C., *Using Management Games*, Gower, Aldershot, 1996

Porter, E., *Relationship Awareness Theory, Manual of Administration and Interpretation*, Personal Strengths Publishing Inc., California, 1996

15 Creativity in teams

Tudor Rickards

This chapter describes the principles and practice of a system for supporting project teams seeking new ideas on behalf of an industrial sponsor or client. It takes as given the importance of general principles of team selection, building, and development. The approach, MPIA, has been applied in over 30 countries, with thousands of project teams. Clients have been from large and small companies, from many different kinds of industry, with a wide range of task requirements. The teams have been professional, technical, educational, cross-cultural, and social. The projects have one main characteristic – they deal with real needs, and call for creative ideas rather than routine application of existing knowledge.

The basic system has been applied within the Manchester Business School's MBA programmes, and specifically as part of the Manchester Method of learning through doing. It has recently been adapted by the ESRC as the standard approach for supporting innovation projects within UK Business Schools.

The approach avoids the trap of providing an over-rigid and prescriptive set of rules and procedures. In use, the variety of differing tasks and situations requires some general framework for operating, with means of making adjustments before and even within the project teamwork. For this to happen the team needs:

1 A theory-based template or general structure
2 A range of simple techniques that can be applied in one or more components in the general structure
3 Some way of selecting among the technique options, in light of specific circumstances.

There are various models purporting to help individuals and teams become more creative in their work. In general these approaches take the form of stages through which the team arrives at better, more valued, and more imaginative outcomes. They have become known as structured creative problem-solving approaches. The rationale and evidence of real-world success remain topics of some theoretical and practical controversy. Advocates point to extensive trials and commercially rated outputs. Critics remain unimpressed by the anecdotal nature of reports, and the possibilities of deliberate or unconscious bias on the part of the users of such techniques.

Among practitioners of the creative problem-solving approaches, there is a recognition that the models are related, even if the labels and numbers of the stages differ from version to version. The Manchester approach offers <M><P><I><A> as a framework for creative teamwork:

> *M-activities* stand for efforts directing towards Mapping the (Messy) situation.
> *P-activities* stand for activities directed towards Perspective seeking (although sometimes terms like *Problem*, *Project focus*, or even *Paradigm* may be substituted, according to the overall situation).
> *I-activities* refer to activities directed towards Ideas and, by implication, ideas not yet connected with actions. In unreflective routines, ideas may actually be a mixture of abstracted knowledge unconnected with the specific circumstance, and ideas directly linked to actions (more strictly I/As).
> *A-activities* refer to actions, and by implication therefore connectable to I, P and M activities.

MPIA can be introduced as a flow chart of well-defined stages (Figure 15.1). This representation is effective as a training tool. However, an interesting alternative representation is to consider the components as no more than descriptions of highly interrelated processes (Figure 15.2), serving to remind users that in practice teams 'weave in and out' of conceptual activities and action activities. When the system is first introduced in training, the linear model is more appropriate, and only one technique need be offered for each stage.

After introductory training sessions with one technique per component of the MPIA structure, more technique options are needed for the team to experiment and find its own preferred 'tool kit' for specific needs. Team members may also find ways of importing other techniques based on knowledge gained in other organizational initiatives. For example, idea generation plays a part in Re-engineering approaches, Risk Evaluation systems, and various proprietary methods advocated by quality consultants. The creativity training can 'bolt on' if the team can translate aspects of the system to fit into the other one.

When an experienced practitioner decides on a combination of techniques within a specific project he or she draws on understanding and experience of the scope/limitations of techniques in related contexts, and of the characteristics of the situation. A sample of such possibilities is shown in Table 15.1.

The structural features of MPIA and other approaches for stimulating 235

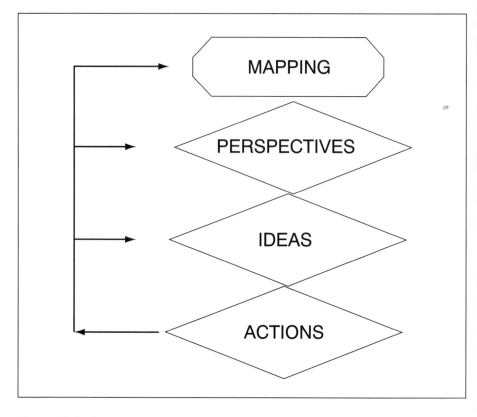

Figure 15.1 The MPIA model represented as a linear structure with iterations between stages

The version here has application in introducing the model, and in comparing its components with those of models that are normally represented as a sequence of linear stages.

creativity in teams are shown in Table 15.2. Note the emphasis on interactive methods in some cultures, and non-interactive methods in other cultures.

MIND MAPS AND PLATFORMS OF UNDERSTANDING

The best mind-mapping tool has been found to be a spider diagram. In practical applications the spider diagrams can be a good way of building a powerful 'platform of understanding' within a project team. For example, a challenge to speed up a production line can be mapped by the team. This is likely to lead to a spider with 100–200 components and may take several hours. The construction of the spider can pinpoint assumptions held by team members and clarify differences. Once produced it can help in the targeting of areas for brainstorming.

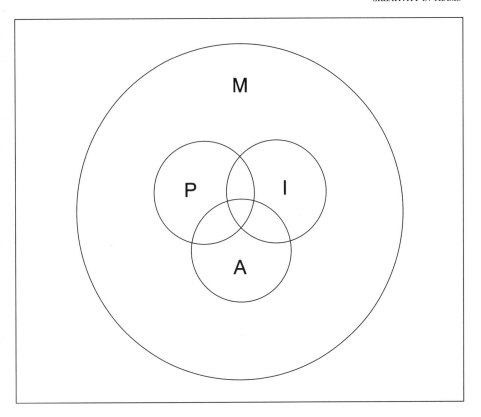

Figure 15.2 The MPIA model represented as interrelated groupings of activities

Note: M = Mapping; P = Perspectives; I = Ideas; A = Actions. The version here reframes the more common linear-type model shown in Figure 15.1. It reminds teams that their processes are a complex mix of activities which may be simplified into four components for purposes of study. The non-linear model also supports experience and reflection on the use of creativity techniques, permitting 'creative analysis' (a form of experiential learning directed to creative behaviours).

To produce a spider diagram

1 Turn the page lengthwise (you will then use more of the page).
2 Start writing in the centre of the page, with the topic in the body of the spider.
3 Put descriptions of six to eight key themes – one for each 'leg' of the spider.
4 Build out sub-themes ('fingers and toes') from each leg.
5 Look for links and connections between themes.
6 Enhance by using different colours for differing kinds of themes.
7 Redraw if needed after reviewing – you may have a quite different view of things at that time.

PERSPECTIVES AND PROBLEMS

Goal orientation

Goal orientation is first an attitude of mind which regards problems in terms of personal objectives to be obtained through creative problem solving. It is also a technique to encourage such an attitude. The goal-oriented solver is constantly seeking to find goals ('what I really want to do'). The simple-to-use technique translates goals into 'How To' statements. With practice it becomes possible to find a whole range of 'How To' statements which reveal differing ways of looking at any problem. The technique is an important one to develop because it makes us more aware of mind-sets influencing our initial perception of a problem.

The more imaginative you are in redefining problems, the more chances you give yourself of finding unusual yet practical new ('breakthrough') perspectives. Within the MPIA approach, the generation of a wide set of definitional possibilities or 'How Tos' helps the client to an awareness of the restrictive or dominant mind-set that is driving assumptions about the nature of the situation. This reality testing is part of the encounter at the heart of change processes triggered in creativity sessions. Lateral thinking seems particularly helpful in generating new How Tos. The team becomes open to wishful thoughts, and to the prospects of turning dreams into realities.

IDEAS AND ACTION IDEAS

Generating and building ideas

The divergent or search stage of all P-activities and I-activites operate with the postpone judgement principle common to brainstorming. The 'Yes And' technique is perhaps one of the most powerful for teams to develop leads to ideas being built upon, rather than being simply generated without attention, or with too rapid negative attention. 'Yes And' implies 'There is something that can be improved about this idea. I am willing to work at it to improve it as best I can.'

To take a simple example:

> 'I have just thought of the idea of a flypaper to go in cars to stop insects distracting you when you are driving.'
> 'Yes But . . . wherever you put it, it would stick to someone sooner or later.'
> 'Yes And . . . if you could design it so that it would not stick to passengers, it would be even better . . .'
> 'How about an insecticide block . . . or putting the paper inside a mesh with fly attractant? Or how about combining it with the air freshener?'

Table 15.1

The MPIA model, preferred introductory techniques, and additional techniques for testing as experience is gained

Activity	Technique	Additional techniques	Notes
M-activities	Mind-mapping as Spider Diagrams	Stick-on notes; Hexagons; Graphic representations	Graphic representations for lower-information content situations
P-activities (divergent)	Mind-map re-examined, and Single focus goals suggested without evaluation, using the 'How To . . .' format	Unexpected How Tos through Lateral Thinking invitations; Hitchhiking 'How Tos' through 'Yes And'	Mindmap is explored in a search for dominating perspective(s); divergent techniques help client to go beyond habitual perspectives
P-activities (convergent)	Client indicates a few 'How Tos' which have potential for changing his or her previous belief or dominant perspective	Multiple clients may commit to personal, or to shared 'How Tos'	The 'emergent' process is one in which chances of perspective occur in supportive climates. The 'best' 'How To' is one which produces greatest willingness to commit
I-Activities (divergent)	Brainstorming principles for uninhibited idea generation	Lateral Thinking and 'Yes And' approaches may be included for greater richness of ideas Metaphoric 'excursion' often overcomes over-technical and professionalized responses	Interventions help break the set if brainstorming appears to be similar to ideas from a conventional meeting; pre-training increases proportion of I-A activities (Ideas associated with envisioned actions)
I-Activities (convergent)	Simple shortlisting removes bulk of 'no action impact' ideas; Criteria Matrix method provides structured discussion on merits of ideas; Client expertise may identify high-promise ideas	Voting may have a place for issues where values and personal beliefs override more quantifiable criteria	People from technical and commercial cultures place their confidence in quantification in evaluation methods. The more action-oriented team may prefer more intuitive methods
A-activities	Each promising idea can be developed to reveal a clear action story	More complex action criteria may be built in to the treatment of each idea (e.g., according to principles of Lewin's Force Field theory)	If no idea is rated as acceptable, a non-judgemental review may lead to reflective insights and perspectives on which to build further creative activities

Table 15.2
Cultural variations in creativity enhancing systems

Interactive group systems	Nominal (non-interactive) group systems
MPIA System (UK) <M> <P> <I> <A>	**KJ Technique** (Japan) Ideas written by individuals on cards, then these are shared and patterns sought using intuitive powers of participant(s).
Parnes-Osborn CPS system (N. America) Sequences of divergent and convergent stages. Interactive group principles hold for the divergent stages. A typical version comprised the stages <O> <F> <P> <I> <S> <A> (Objectives, facts, problem defining, ideation, solution seeking and acceptance seeking).	**Metaplan** (Germany; Scandinavia) Ideas are written by individuals on cards, one idea per card. Facilitators help structure the material generated. The cards are assembled on large sheets of paper for classification and exploration purposes.
Synectics (N. America) Training and facilitation help shape constructive team dynamics. Novel ideas are sought through special processes, especially involving metaphors.	**Round Robin Brainstorming** (Germany) Ideas are written by individuals on sheets of paper or card; the sheets are exchanged sequentially ('round robin' process) which stimulates fresh ideas, and improvements to existing ideas.
Braincalming (India) Facilitated process to produce a meditative state prior to developing shared images and ideas. The minds of participants are focused on a visual image and emptied of intrusive thoughts.	**NM Technique** (Japan) A kind of visual brainstorming in which images rather than words are developed.

Action ideas

In the introductory representation of MPIA, I-activities are followed by A-activities. The intention is to develop increased skills in teams so that fewer non-action ideas are produced. That is to say, the I-A stages become increasingly blurred.

Any abstract idea can be converted into an action idea by a process in which participants try to visualize activities in the execution of the idea. For example, in a brainstorming, the client may choose as a preferred idea 'to improve communications between manufacturing and end-users'. Through the invitation (intervention) by the facilitator the team members attempt to visualize what this idea is about. A word picture might be built up collec-

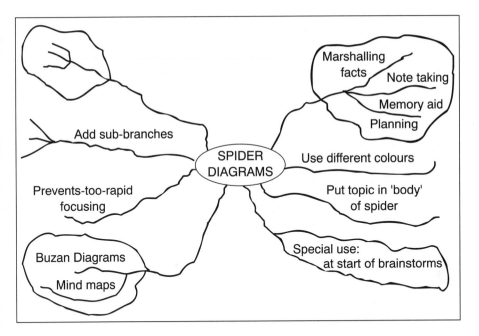

Figure 15.3 Spider diagrams

tively, at the request of the facilitator, who (as sometimes happens) resorts to more 'How To' vocabulary.

> Facilitator: 'Can we build up a picture of how this communication might work? How to improve that?'
> First team member: 'The manufacturing team could talk more often with the customers.'
> Second team member: 'They could get on an intranet . . . and check out each day.'
> Client: 'I could talk with IT; see the best way to do that' [visualizing herself as part of the action].

CONVERGENCE PROCESSES (RATIONALITY AND JUDGEMENT)

The priority of client acceptance during convergence

The effectiveness of teamwork may be limited if the search process is followed by inefficient selection or decision processes. A useful aphorism here is *search widely, choose wisely*. Often the assumption is that a good decision can be reached through a rational evaluation of options using success criteria. However, new viewpoints (for that is what new perspectives amount to) may actually require the client to adjust his or her pre-set criteria in order to discover previously obscured possibilities. What is sometimes believed to be a rational approach may be an over-mechanistic application of pre-set criteria which reduces chances of shifts in self-awareness. The   *241* client plus supportive team is likely to be trapped by those very assumptions that the approach is designed to expose and challenge.

In unclear conditions (most innovation-seeking project work) decisions should be those that support intuitive judgements under uncertainty. The creative support team is trained and able to provide the client with suggestions (the generated sets of perspectives). Evaluating these is like searching for a clue that would solve a scientific puzzle or even a detective mystery, or perhaps a hunt as in the party game of blind-man's buff or 'getting warmer . . . getting colder'. The creative experience here is at odds with the rational model of comprehensive evaluation of possibilities. It is also at odds with the behaviours of some clients who would rather invite a fresh view from other team members as a means of avoiding previous beliefs or assumptions. The purpose of the process is to kick-start the client into action through accepting a new possibility as 'worth thinking about'. At the How To stage, moving towards a new goal, and getting away from directions shaped through habitual actions are more important than seeking rational justification for the shift.

The frustrations of group members with the client acceptance maxim

For client and team members alike, there is a heightened experience or encounter with 'Idea'. More often than not, however, those previously less involved in the project take different perspectives from the ones favoured by the client. Inexperienced members of project teams find themselves being involved and attracted to a particular 'How To' or 'Idea' during client work. To such team members, the client often appears blinkered, and unable to abandon prior assumptions. These tensions appear to highlight the pitfalls of leaving the choice of new perspective to the client.

Under such circumstances the facilitator and team are well advised to be aware of their own biases. The essential feature of the creative problem solving approach is to enable discovery change through ideas into action. The principle is that of empowering someone with responsibility to take fresh actions. Like other situations of empowerment, the process also requires some acceptance of the legitimacy of the actor to take charge of the actions. The consolation is this. With experience, facilitators as well as team members learn to trust to outcomes of letting go, and encouraging clients to follow their intuitions.

The legitimate role of rational decision processes

There are many situations, including those found in team projects, when more traditional rational approaches are valuable in reaching decisions. Even in these circumstances, the more abstract kind of ideas identified as

242

objectively superior benefit from further creative efforts to connect them to visualized actions.

One common situation arises if the client has a brief to provide a shortlist of ideas to some other stakeholders – in effect, clients of the client. While the process is likely to be more creative and successful if the stakeholders can be brought together for the idea generation and evaluation, this may not be feasible in practice. Such chains complicate the processes of enacting change, and are increasingly the reality in networked organizations. In these situations, various methods of evaluation may be introduced. Voting helps to discover preferences within the team (although this may not even lead to the most rational analysis of available information). The construction of a criterion matrix of ideas and success factors described next helps develop a credible shortlist because the process can be explained without any reference to intuitive client preference.

Criterion matrix

There are times when more conventional modes of decision making during convergence are valued. For example, a comprehensive evaluation of ideas might lead to the setting up of a criteria matrix and a weighted coding of ideas by criteria. These quantitative approaches have been known for many years, and play a part in various Quality and Business Re-engineering methods.

When you have a set of ideas it is generally possible to examine them in terms of a criterion matrix. This technique requires the ideas to be as unambiguous as possible. It is less effective if the ideas are of very differing characteristics. For example, very loosely defined and new ideas are difficult to compare with ideas that are variants of ideas well-known to the evaluators. This means that a pre-screen helps to eliminate the well-worn and trivial ideas, so that you evaluate six to eight ideas in your criterion matrix that do not present themselves in an obvious order of quality. The following rules for developing a criterion matrix can be adapted to many practical circumstances:

1 Generate your ideas before setting your criteria. They should be as action-oriented as possible (I/A-activities).
2 Generate criteria (again taking care that these are unambiguous). A set of five to eight criteria is most convenient and effective. Typically these will contain a criterion of cost or cost/benefit; one of technical feasibility; one of time-constraints; one of acceptability; one of 'potential for knock-on adverse effects'; one of novelty. The set may have some criteria specific to the project itself.
3 Evaluate each idea across all the criteria. Use a preliminary non-quantitative assessment to test the matrix. We recommend a plus or minus sign for acceptable/non-acceptable; with a question mark for items that are difficult to assess. This approach quickly reveals the most *243*

promising ideas. You are left with the possibility of improving any of the front runners, within the time-constraints you are facing.

4   The team always has the option of re-constructing the matrix by mod-ifying the criteria if the result seems counter-intuitive.

MPIA STEP-BY-STEP

Teams are advised to follow the steps closely while becoming used to the system. Later it is valuable to experiment and introduce versions that have been found to be more satisfactory.

M1 Getting ready (examining the mess)

Agree on the purpose of the meeting; share information you have available using a spider diagram; set time limits for the meeting; check that all group members understand the process (the following stages of the problem solving system).

P1 Searching for new perspectives (listing How Tos)

Keeping evaluation to a minimum, list all possible ways of looking at the problem the group can suggest. Use the How To format. Avoid complex How Tos (split them into ones with a simple central objective). Include wishful How Tos.

P2 Selecting a new perspective (to escape 'stuckness')

Select one How To which offers the promise of new and useful ideas. If possible invite the client (the person who has to act on the results) to select the How To. The selection is a first trial. Other How Tos can be chosen at a later time.

I1 Idea exploring stage (searching for idea possibilities)

Using the rules of brainstorming, generate as many ideas as possible without evaluation in any way. The group tries to help the leader avoid 'translation', or idea omissions. Include all way-out ideas as one of these may become a trigger to a winning idea.

I2 Idea exploring stage (producing an ideas shortlist)

Produce a criteria checklist of key aspects of a 'good' idea, according to the information available. Pay particular attention to the needs of the problem-owner(s). Use the checklist to agree as a group on a quick intuitive culling of ideas, removing those that fail on two or more key criteria. Work towards a quick rejection of at least half of the ideas. Keep culling until you have a good shortlist. Note: in the absence of a client it is valuable to set up a Criterion Matrix to collect views of the relative merits of the ideas generated.

A Ideas into action

Select a highly promising idea from the shortlist (criteria: novelty and 'face-value potential' for impact on the problem). Concentrate on the aspects of the idea believed to give it its strengths. Then list the most troublesome shortcomings. In each of these processes, it is the client that is encouraged to confront enthusiasms as well as worries and concerns. The process and the team can help the client to identify with the idea, visualizing him/herself as the main person in action. A discursive word picture, or graphical representation may be used. Repeat for as many key ideas as requested by the client.

Any important concern can be examined as a How To. This visit to P-activities is generally much faster than the time spent previously on P-activities. The How To should be less complex than the first selected in stage P2 – that is, fewer uncertainties, more focus, more under the control of the client. If the 'new How To' appears to make movement to I/A-activities less promising, something is going wrong with the process, and a stage of reflection may be appropriate.

Time structuring for a two-hour session (guidelines only, for inexperienced groups

Getting ready (preparation)	15% available time 30 min
Problem exploring (opening up)	15% available time 30 min
Problem exploring (selection)	10% available time 20 min
Idea exploration (opening up)	20% available time 40 min
Idea selection (closing down)	15% available time 30 min
Idea(s) into action	10% available time 20 min
Slack (provision for lost time)	15% available time 30 min

THE PROJECT TEAM: BASIC PRINCIPLES

Composition

The basic ingredients for a project team are clients with a project task, and other team members. Facilitators from outside the team are favoured by many large organizations concerned about the process skills of their project teams and project managers. Wherever possible, the use of outside facilitators should be seen as a necessary yet temporary phase, while team members develop their own facilitation skills.

When there is discretion over the team numbers (for example, in training projects) teams with five or six members have proved particularly effective. *245*

In larger teams, quieter members are marginalized, to the detriment of team and individuals. Smaller teams of three to four members are vulnerable to role overloads, and to an inadequate variety of views and mindsets.

A general principle: members in a team with similar outlooks and experiences are likely to get on, but may not learn from one another. Members that have wide differences in outlooks and experiences are in principle more likely to have valuable learning opportunities, yet may prefer to avoid the hard work required to accommodate to the possible differences. Awareness of these vulnerabilities will help a team transcend the potential weaknesses in its composition.

Attempts within a team to exclude members mostly arise if teams are not working at team development. Multi-cultural teams, for example, have great potential, but also require careful self-management to avoid domination by the most articulate members.

Client involvement

As far as practicalities permit, the team members and client will benefit from experiencing the MPIA approach in a low-risk (training) mode before addressing the issues of real concern for the client.

Under consulting conditions, the scope for training, and interaction between team and client may be limited. Experienced facilitators may take up the challenge and work to such imposed constraints. One line should not be crossed. It is of key importance that the client and team encounter the core challenge together as a creative problem solving unit. Two-stage processes of team ideation followed by presentation to the client should be avoided. The dynamics of creative teamwork have much in common with those achieved through trust-building activities. If the client is reluctant to accept the benefits of this, the omens are unfavourable and the likely outcome is denial of any benefits in the proposed ideas. Reluctance (often expressed as 'being too busy') can be overcome if the client is involved in some aspect of the team training or briefing. We will see later why the client has to be drawn into a direct encounter with the team as new ideas are generated.

Training

We have found team training most successful when strongly connected with the required skills of working creatively within a project team with a client. Thus a two-day introductory programme (as shown in Table 15.3) is geared to teams applying the MPIA system to a realistic or actual commercial project supplied by a volunteer client. As trainers are too aware, suitable projects are not easy to come by. The committed trainer has to work at building up contacts willing to give up some time to the process. Some ingenuity may be called for to widen the range of clients. Relevant projects can be unearthed from local charitable, educational and social organizations.

Team members can also help in this process, by bringing 'owned' projects to the training sessions.

Trial runs

A two-day training programme is adequate for team-members who will be able to work well within the MPIA approach on more challenging projects. However, the internal facilitator may require a few more trial runs before the process loses some of its unfamiliarity.

During this period of skill development, the temptation among inexperienced facilitators is to seek out high-profile projects and offer help. The experience may be both a powerful accelerated learning one – and a cruel disappointment. For example, our records include an account of members of an enthusiastic team of relatively junior officers in a police force who found themselves mediating an important strategy session for very high-ranking officers in their own force. The two-day training had cushioned them from the more habitual behaviours outside their creativity sessions. The meeting never broke the dominance of the high status members and the resistance of these to being 'ordered around' by low status facilitators. Remarkably, the facilitators regrouped, reflected on the experience, and over time rebuilt their confidence until they were able to facilitate important events involving senior colleagues and lay-participants.

Briefing (prior to a team meeting a project client)

The project team working for an external client will reach a stage that calls for a briefing. The external client may be a senior figure from within the same organization, or a volunteer described above. Both team and client are briefed prior to the actual shared encounter.

The client who has never experienced the MPIA approach as a participant/ observer will almost certainly have misconceptions about what is going to happen. The person carrying out the briefing (course trainer, or team representative) has to accept that no amount of pre-briefing will substitute for direct experience. The briefing can, however, explain how earlier sessions were conducted. An invitation 'to see what might happen if you spare a couple of hours' is better than rash promises of what the session will achieve. Perhaps the most important point is to convey the importance of coming with a willingness to explore ideas that challenge conventional thinking. This is probably worth reiterating even for more experienced clients.

The team briefing (which may serve as reinforcement for the client, if present) emphasizes that the process helps everyone to break out of old perspectives and find new ones. Client and team members alike can become trapped by premature commitment to an idea – either an old one or a new one. Such behaviours are strongly conditioned by mind-sets.

Table 15.3
A two-day training programme to introduce a team to the MPIA system

DAY ONE	DAY TWO
Session 1 Warm-up exercises, objectives, background to creativity and its enhancement	**Session 1** Review of Day one: Introduction by MPIA client of his/her project
Session 2 Overview of MPIA system Behavioural and role considerations for effective teams M-activities (Mind Maps) P-activities (Goal finding and selecting) Building (Yes And); and Stretching (Lateral Thinking) techniques	**Session 2** Teams M-activities and P-activities. Client indicates most promising perspectives
Session 3 I-A activities (brainstorming variants) Teams practice MPIA on a case exercise (business improvement) with trainer(s) as client/business owner(s) Exploration of ideas for envisioned actions	**Session 3** Teams I-A activities. Client selects most promising action idea(s)
Session 4 Task/process review of case Preparation for MPIA project	**Session 4** Discussion of overall learning and refinements (for example, metaphoric techniques) for future projects Behavioural feedback to individual participants

Platform of understanding

Any group of individuals requires ways of sharing their individual caches of knowledge. This lies at the heart of various approaches to knowledge engineering. The Manchester method emphasizes knowledge sharing as a creative act in experience. A powerful metaphor is that of building a platform of understanding. The facilitator encourages an environment in which individual information is experienced with a minimum of internal evaluation and processing. The key principle is supported by techniques for developing ideas to mutual satisfaction (Yes And), rather than confronting all differences as battles to be won (Yes But).

The encounter

The stages of MPIA determine the structure or shape of the meeting. If the session proceeds mechanistically the behaviours will remain close to those found in a typical business meeting. With a more open and trained group, the experience becomes less habit-bound. Participants behave more supportively towards new ideas, and there is a sense of common purpose. This has a particular impact on the client, who has had the greatest prior conditioning regarding the possibilities and impossibilities within the project.

One MBA group had visited a senior executive who had appeared less than enthusiastic in getting involved. His ambivalence arose from a wish to do something in his new role as finance director, and concern that the project team would take too long to understand his problems. At the start of the MPIA session the client again indicated his views along these lines. Yet as the session proceeded he became more open to new possibilities. He subsequently gave full support to the team in their efforts to find ideas for his company. One team member found the shift of belief by the client through the direct encounter the most important learning for himself during the project. The importance of this direct involvement by the client can not be overestimated.

'Going solo'

The opportunities for going solo are increasing, as company-wide change programmes become more common. For example, the MBA participants who experienced the MPIA approach subsequently often find themselves taking up a job within project-based organizations. The most successful efforts at going solo have come from those participants who 'work with the grain'. This requires understanding of existing project activities and a merging of the MPIA know-how into these processes and even into the existing vocabulary. This prudent strategy is consistent with learning through doing, and the need for the new clients to experience and encounter the benefits of creative problem solving. For the newly-solo facilitator, studying the sessions afterwards is an important part of the developmental learning.

CONSTRUCTIVE TEAM DEVELOPMENT

A successfully developing team reveals itself in a sense of well-being about the contributions of all its members. There is some evidence that highly diverse teams such as multi-cultural ones have the most potential for achieving creative outputs, yet may underperform more than less heterogenous teams. The conditions for underperforming include tasks that are too routine and capable of being dominated by a few members of the team to the exclusion of others. A team striving to improve its performance can help itself by setting challenging goals. Mini-collaboration on tasks can also help make the situation one in which there is more interdependence, which helps build trust and respect.

When things go wrong: a creative approach

There are no quick fixes. It helps if the team can agree to take time off from the task to refocus on issues of a personal kind. The availability of an experienced team facilitator may speed up processes that always have to be owned by the team itself. Established approaches to team building have their own techniques for helping teams over the commonly encountered problems of rejection and stereotyping of members. One frequent need is for the team to bring into the open the most important personal goals and needs of members in search of common, shared goals.

There is a quite specific link here with creativity training. The creative analysis approach can be reapplied to exploring and developing improvements in team behaviours.

RECOMMENDED READING

Adler, N., *International Dimensions of Organizational Behavior*, 2nd edn., PWS-Kent, Boston, Mass, 1991

de Bono, E., *Serious Creativity: Using the Power of Lateral Thinking to Create New Ideas*, Harper Collins, London, 1992

Goodman, M., *Creative Management*, Prentice-Hall, London, 1995

Isaksen, S. (ed.), *Frontiers in Creativity Research: Beyond the Basics*, Bearly Publishers Inc., New York, 1987

Morgan, G., *Imaginization: The Art of Creative Management*, Sage, Newbury Park, 1993

Parnes, S. (ed.), *Sourcebook for creative problem-solving*, Creative Education Foundation Press, Buffalo, NY, 1993

Rickards, T., *Creativity and Problem-solving at Work*, Gower, Aldershot, 1990 (reprinted 1997)

Rickards, T. and De Cock, C., 'Creativity in MS/OR: Training for Creativity – Findings in a European Context, *Interfaces*, 1994, **24** (6), Nov, 59–73

16 Managing stress for optimum performance

Jane Cranwell-Ward

Stress management can make the difference between a high performance team and a poor performance team. Managing stress to optimize performance first of all requires an understanding of stress and its impact on individuals and teams. Team members also need to be able to recognize when stress levels are becoming excessive and how the team may react as a whole.

These days there is a tendency to treat symptoms of stress rather than the root cause. Effective teams spend time identifying causes of stress and take appropriate action to solve the problems.

Stress management requires teams to use the appropriate strategy for a given situation. The emphasis may be on stress management itself, or the team may need to deal with process or task- and job-related issues to alleviate negative effects of stress.

The chapter will adopt a five-stage approach to understand and manage stress and to optimize performance. Stress will be viewed both from an individual and a team point of view.

UNDERSTANDING THE NATURE OF STRESS

Growing importance is being attached to stress in organizations. Is this because it has been much talked about in recent years, or are people more prepared to recognize and acknowledge its existence? The latter is probably the case, but still it is a concept that is not clearly understood.

To understand stress better, defining the term is a way forward. It can be defined as:

The physiological and psychological reaction which occurs when people perceive an imbalance between the level of demand placed upon them and their capacity to meet those demands

This definition can be broken down into a number of components to deepen understanding of the relationship between stress, individuals and teams.

Stress as a physiological and psychological reaction

Many use the words 'stress' and 'pressure' synonymously. Stress is the reaction which occurs as a result of pressure, or signs that there are increasing demands being placed on the person. The physiological changes which occur are the fight/flight reactions. People also experience psychological reactions such as fear, anxiety or instability. Details of the stress reaction will be described later as an aid to recognizing stress.

Stress can be positive as well as negative

Most people concentrate on the debilitating aspects of stress. Certainly when stress is excessive the experience is negative but, when pressure is maintained at an appropriate level, stress can be stimulating, energizing and enabling people to perform in a well-directed way.

Stress can be internally generated

Almost as much stress is self-generated as it is generated from external sources. Important individual differences explain why some people are less likely to experience the negative effects of stress than others. Fear of failure, or of appearing foolish, or needing the approval of others can all result in increased stress levels. Satisfaction of needs, motives, shared values and beliefs are also important determinants of stress levels.

Perception of the individual is very important

Stress levels result from a complex interaction between the individual and his or her own situation and environment. The person makes an assessment either consciously or subconsciously as to the extent to which they are able to deal with the situation. The greater the gap between perceived capacity and the demands of the situation, the more stressful the situation is perceived.

Feeling in control or out of control

At optimum levels of stress individuals report they feel in control of the situation. When stress levels rise to unacceptable levels people describe themselves as being out of control, in a panic and unable to cope.

Stress as a result of insufficient pressure and excessive pressure

Most people would associate stress with excessive pressure. There is however a high level of stress resulting from people operating in situations with lack of stimulation and boredom, resulting in frustration or apathy.

The experience of stress varies from individual to individual

Everyone has their own threshold for stress levels becoming excessive. Some people can thrive on stress levels which others would find intolerable.

Personal acknowledgement of stress as an issue

Individuals vary in the extent to which they are prepared to acknowledge levels of stress. Some are unaware of its existence and others deny it.

Relationship between individuals, teams and performance

The relationship between pressure and performance is best explained with the aid of Figure 16.1.

Performance increases with pressure until the level of pressure becomes too great and the individual experiences exhaustion and ultimately burnout. The stress relationship moves from a situation of higher stress with low pressure, to lower levels at optimum pressure followed by high levels of stress and a condition referred to as 'burnout'.

Burnout usually includes signs of withdrawal and decreasing involvement in the job, especially by people who have been highly involved in their work. People also experience mental, physical and emotional exhaustion. Research by Sonnentag et al. (1994) reported that teamwork can influence the impact of stress. Within software professional teams social support and high-quality social interaction reduced burnout. The paper also reported further research which found the cohesiveness of work groups reduced emotional exhaustion in high-stress organizations. Keeping pressure at optimum levels to ensure maximum performance will be discussed later.

In recent years teamwork has been seen as a mechanism for increased involvement and autonomy, devolved responsibility and shared decision making. Project teams and self-managed work groups are regularly encountered in today's organization. While success stories such as that of Ford Motor Company and its Mustang project team give rise to improved quality and performance, there are also many failures.

Stuart Klein (1995) outlined some of the problems experienced by self-managed autonomous teams. Increased tension to achieve performance may well lead to individuality rather than collaborative teamwork. Winning teams, for example, sports teams, experience solidarity. Losing teams appear to disintegrate with the pressure to perform.

Opinions vary as to the relationship between work pressure, group *253*

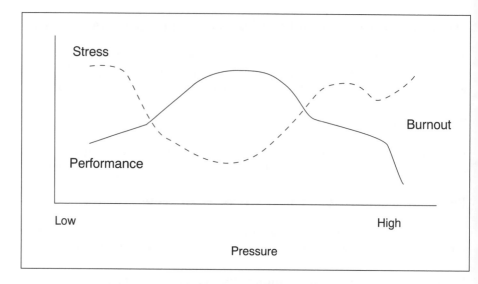

Figure 16.1 Relationship between performance, pressure and stress levels

dynamics and performance. One view is that put under common pressure, groups will respond by becoming more cohesive with a shared goal of reducing pressure. In the Ford example the Mustang team pulled together in this way.

The alternative view is that as pressure increases, group solidarity is a short-term phenomenon that applies only when groups can see an end in sight to the pressure. When pressure continues long-term, pulling together is replaced by the attitude of everyone taking care of themselves.

INDIVIDUAL DIFFERENCES AND STRESS

What causes stress varies from individual to individual. Teams are usually made up of individuals who come from a range of backgrounds, experiences, cultures and who possess different personalities, skills and capabilities. These differences will affect the extent to which a team successfully manage stress. The various differences which influence stress are outlined here:

Preferred stress levels

Some individuals are comfortable operating at quite high stress levels while others, particularly those who have a high need for control over their life, are likely to feel much more comfortable when stress levels are much lower. Mismatch of stress and comfort levels will have an effect on team performance.

Values, beliefs and attitudes

Individuals possess a range of values, beliefs and attitudes which govern behaviour. Some effective teams and organizations go to great lengths to ensure these are shared. Often organizational values are implicit and, as they are historically based, they may be outmoded today, giving rise to added stress. From the time a team is formed a particular set of values and expectations will develop. The most powerful of these will be informal and relate to the way the team operates together. Others may be less significant and allow for individual variations. Where there is a clash of values, stress levels will increase.

Personality characteristics and work style

Earlier in the book reference was made to Belbin team roles in the context of the definition of roles of team members. Ideally, individuals in a team should possess a range of different personalities all making a contribution to team effectiveness. In effective teams individuals have developed mutual understanding and respect for differences. When a team is new or ineffective its individual members may experience conflict because of the different ways of working exhibited by team members. For example, important differences in work style which provide a potential for conflict drawn from the Myers Briggs Type Indicator include:

- Thinking orientation versus action orientation
- Past orientation versus future orientation
- Attention to detail versus big picture
- Emphasis on rationality and logic versus emphasis on values and harmony
- Controlled versus spontaneous and flexible.

As Cartwright and Cooper (1994) reported, a particular personality, that of the abrasive hard-driving individual, creates stress for their colleagues. Harry Levinson of Harvard suggested that the reason the abrasive hard-driving people cause stress to others is because they require interpersonal aspects of feelings and the sensitivities of interacting with others. Highly technical, achievement-oriented hard-driving individuals devote insufficient time to build working relationships and as such may be a source of interpersonal stress for others.

Individual differences and resilience

Individuals vary in the extent to which they can withstand stress. Research indicates that a person's resilience is determined by three factors: commitment, control and challenge.

Commitment – People both accept challenge and sustain a balance of commitment to home and work. They are able to prioritize, set goals and achieve them.
Control – People believe in their capability to control work and home environments. They make positive choices to manage stress.
Challenge – People see change as an opportunity to move forward and once one set of problems have been resolved they move on to a new situation.

Basic needs which individuals seek to satisfy

Individuals have certain basic needs which need to be met if they are to feel satisfied. Failure to meet these needs and expectations will increase stress levels and result in feelings of frustration.

Need for recognition and contact

Teams provide individuals with the opportunity to satisfy these needs. The extent to which individuals have a high need for recognition is dependent on early upbringing. Team leaders need to understand each individual to ensure varying needs are met. Too much or too little contact with others are potential sources of stress depending on personality make-up.

The need for structure and stability

Everyone needs a degree of predictability in the way time is spent and with whom it is spent. The threat of change can affect what you do and the quality of relationships. The level of stability and structure needed by individuals is variable, but teams are important sources of stability.

The need for interest and stimulation

When people experience a high degree of routine, stress levels are raised as a result of boredom. Teamwork can help to increase variety and stimulation. Alternatively individuals may seek to satisfy this need outside work by pursuing a demanding or dangerous pastime.

RECOGNITION OF STRESS IN INDIVIDUALS AND TEAMS

To manage stress within teams, people need to be able to identify both individual reactions and the way stress might manifest itself collectively by the teams. Much as the concept of stress contains different meanings for different people, so their reaction to stress will be different also.

When individuals experience a stressful situation, reflect on a stressful event or even anticipate the future, they react both physiologically and psychologically.

The physiological and psychological reaction

When the body is faced with a stressful event, a chain of physical reactions is triggered, known as the 'flight/fight' response. This response is a natural reaction to enable the body to sustain balance. However, over a prolonged period of time the reaction can result in a range of physical manifestations of stress. The reaction can be broken down into three key stages for more stressful situations.

- The alarm phase
- The resistance phase
- The exhaustion phase.

The alarm phase

When a stressful situation such as a near miss in the car or a confrontation at work occurs, a chain of physical reactions is triggered which prepares the body for immediate action. What are the signs at this stage?

- Speeding up of activity
- The heart beats faster
- Muscles tense up
- Breathing becomes faster.

When the stressful situation is over the body returns to its normal state, provided there is time to relax before the next stressful situation. Often stressful situations can continually occur without giving the body a chance to recover, which leads into the next stage.

The resistance phase

During this phase the body has to adjust for longer-term protection, with the result that energy stores get run down and the body becomes weaker as the pressure increases. What are the signs at this stage?

- Irritability
- Indigestion
- Muscle tension in the neck and back
- Fatigue
- Sleeplessness
- Headaches
- Allergies
- Difficulty concentrating
- Anxiety
- Loss of emotional control.

These signs are all the warnings to take life easier; when people ignore the signs and pressure continues, the person moves to the exhaustion phase.

The exhaustion phase

When stressful situations continue the body gets no time to rebalance, people become exhausted and feel really ill. At this stage errors and accidents can occur. What are the signs?

- Recurring headaches
- Inability to concentrate
- Absence from work
- Withdrawal from people
- Frequently feeling unable to cope
- Emotional shutdown except for anger and frustration.

Once people have reached the exhaustion stage steps need to be taken to restore the balance.

Recognizing stress in others

People who work in teams need to be vigilant for signs of stress in others. Sometimes other people are quicker to identify stress in another person than in themselves. Some people go to great lengths to conceal stress, particularly in organizations with a macho culture, where stress is viewed as a sign of weakness. There are a number of indications including:

- Irritability
- Making mistakes
- Behaving differently from usual
- Loss in productivity
- Absenteeism
- Withdrawing from others.

Once team members recognize the signs they can help to reduce stress levels by providing support and reducing work pressure.

Recognizing stress in teams

When external pressures are high, such as the pressure to increase productivity, change and uncertainty or tight deadlines, whole teams may become excessively stressed. Teams manifest stress in a number of different ways:

Team climate – trust is low, atmosphere is cold and hostile and people put one another down.

Relationships within the team – backbiting, gossip, in and out groups, power struggles, lack of cooperation and little acknowledgement of one another.
Work-related signs – tasks not achieved, errors made, work below acceptable standards and missed deadlines.

In general, short-term project teams are more likely to operate at optimum pressure when stimulated by clearly stated goals. By contrast a healthily stressed team will:

- Have effective team relations and build on the strengths within the team
- Rise to the challenges which face them
- Sustain a high level of productivity
- Make the best use of the resources available.

Understanding and recognizing levels of stress is a necessary step to managing stress. Recognition of the sources of stress is equally important when seeking to optimize performance.

SOURCES OF STRESS FOR INDIVIDUALS AND TEAMS

Pressure is both internally and externally generated. Whether operating individually or as a team, understanding what triggers stress is the first stage in gaining control. A model of stress triggers is proposed (see Figure 16.2).

Triggers of stress can be subdivided into four categories, which are not mutually exclusive:

- External triggers – work-related/non-work-related
- Internal triggers – self-generated
- Non-work-related triggers
- Triggers within the team.

The first three categories are individually experienced while the fourth category focuses on stress generated specifically within the team.

Both Cooper and Marshall (1976) and Cox (1993) have extensively researched sources of stress. The model in Figure 16.2 summarizes their findings and extends them further to include team-related stress.

External triggers – work-related

Triggers operate at the macro level such as organization culture and climate, or specifically relate to an individual situation within the workplace. In recent times many organizations have been changing their culture so as to move from one where individuals feel the pressure of autocratic leadership styles, the experience of a blame culture and fear of making mistakes, to a   *259*

EXTERNAL TRIGGERS WORK-RELATED
Organizational
Job itself
Working conditions
Work overload
Relationship
Career development
Uncertainty and insecurity

INTERNAL TRIGGERS
Unrealistic expectations
Lack of confidence
Lack of assertiveness
Poor self-management
Unsatisfied needs
Poor health
Drive for perfectionism
Fear of failure, incompetence
Looking foolish

IMPACT OF THE INDIVIDUAL / TEAM

STRESS RESPONSES

NON-WORK-RELATED TRIGGERS
Work—home balance
Commuting
Major life change
Lack of finance
Family commitments
The environment

TRIGGERS WITHIN THE TEAM
No clear objectives
Poor communication
Poor working relationships
Conflict of values
Team leader/member relationships
Poor decision making
Poor team performance
Team meetings
New team member

Figure 16.2 Model of sources of stress
Source: After Cooper and Marshall (1976); Cox (1993)

more involving culture. Autocratic management stifles innovative approaches and creates increased stress.

Organizations have restructured to remove bureaucracy, increase flexibility and enable employees to respond to changes more quickly, thus enhancing competitiveness. While these changes have resulted in a leaner, more efficient structure, it has been at human cost. It has created uncertainty and insecurity as individuals have struggled to deal with redundancy of colleagues and new ways of working.

One trend which is emerging is flexible working. This includes becoming home-based, 'hot desking', having no designated work space, and working flexible hours. This trend can work either as a stressor or, in some cases, alleviate stress. Most of the stresses applicable to job-related stress will affect both the individual and teams.

Stresses range from the volume of work, to achieving tight deadlines, to the nature and level of interest of the work itself. Many individuals complain of work overload as organizations have downsized and at the same time require employees to improve the quality of their work. In Japan *karoshi*, death through overwork, is widely recognized, and each year employees work until they literally die. Working long hours in the UK applies particularly to doctors during their final training in hospitals.

Conditions of work can also make individuals and teams feel more or less stressed. Many organizations have either moved to new office space or renovated existing office space to improve working conditions of teams and individuals. A well-air-conditioned office can greatly alleviate stress. Organizations have also tended to move towards open plan office space to help teams work more effectively together. When this is well-designed this can alleviate stress. However, it becomes stressful when conditions are cramped and people are regularly interrupted by their colleagues.

In general, working relationships can be a very great source of stress. They are equally applicable at team and individual level. The problem is obviously exacerbated when individuals are located close together.

In recent years employees have become increasingly dependent on IT. When the technology works well tasks are completed much more quickly, but when systems crash stress levels are greatly increased. People also need appropriate training to ensure they have the skills and capabilities to benefit from the IT.

Training in the broader sense and career development have also become more problematic in the 1990s. As organizations have become flatter, with fewer people, career opportunities have greatly diminished, resulting in stagnant workforces in many organizations with only limited scope for promotion, and frustration for those less fortunate. Organizations are therefore searching for ways to continuously develop their employees.

Non-work-related triggers

Stress tends to pervade the lives of people; stress generated at work will go home with individuals, while home-based stress will be taken into work. As the number of women in the workforce increases, one source of stress is managing the balance between home and work. This is equally applicable to men and women, although women still often have to cope with the pressure of managing the home and bringing up children.

Studies such as Holmes and Rahe (1967) have identified a range of life event changes which greatly contribute to stress levels and, in turn, ill health. These changes range from death of spouse to moving home to getting married. All have an element of change, which necessitates new ways of operating and the changes create stress.

Internal triggers of stress

Most people are prepared to admit that quite a high proportion of stress is self-generated. This may be due to lack of development of key skills such as assertiveness or self-management, or may be attributed to a lack of confidence. Fear was mentioned earlier as a source of stress in organizations, and this can range from fear of making mistakes to fear of appearing incompetent or of failure to achieve set objectives. Other factors internally *261* generated can range from unsatisfied needs to having unrealistic expectations for oneself.

Triggers within the team

Stress is likely to be generated on a team basis, either because of the impact of process issues or because of interrelationships within the team. High performance teams have shared clearly stated objectives. By contrast a lack of clear shared objectives is likely to generate stress. Communication within the team is an indispensable part of effective teamwork. Poor communication will not only affect performance but will also raise stress levels. In some organizations a move to team-based working has caused increased stress among employees. The particular reason for the increased stress is attendance at meetings.

Why do teams find meetings stressful? There are a number of specific issues including participants' inability to concentrate during the meetings, difficulty in reaching consensus, too much time spent in meetings, time spent 'catching up' after meetings and a lack of skilled chairmanship of meetings (*Training and Development*, October 1995).

Relationships within the team can either give rise to support and reduction of stress levels or greatly add to stress. Personality conflict, conflict of styles and clashes of values all contribute to increased levels of stress. These differences may well become evident when there is a change of members within the team which alters the team dynamics. New team members often challenge shared norms and values and may disrupt team cohesiveness.

At different stages in the development of a team different factors will be a source of stress. Tuckman (1965) identified four key stages of development:

- *Forming* – at this stage team members are getting to know one another and establishing ways of working together. Little vent is given to feelings and the stress of unfamiliarity or any conflict is likely to be kept suppressed.
- *Storming* – at this stage team members display their feelings towards one another and stress is likely to be released. Stress at this stage is likely to be generated as a result of being a part of an immature team that lacks clear direction and ways of working together.
- *Norming* – as shared values and ways of working become established, negative stress is likely to give way to the positive stress in being a part of a team which is becoming more open.
- *Performing* – at this stage the team is able to operate effectively and intuitively. Positive stress will be generated from the knowledge that team members are in tune with one another and using the strengths of the team to the best effect.

MANAGING STRESS TO OPTIMIZE PERFORMANCE

Teams which can manage stress are more likely to be able to perform effectively together. Warren and Toll (1993) identified a number of key attributes of a healthy stressed team:

- Creates and rises to challenges
- Shares the pressure and team members support one another
- Monitors performance and achievement learning from success and mistakes
- Members work well together harmoniously, building on the strength of the team and using conflict to generate synergy
- Performs to high standards and seeks to improve continuously
- Maximizes the use of the resources.

Strategies to help teams manage stress fall into three broad categories:

1 Those related specifically to the management of stress
2 Those related to process issues within the team
3 Those related to the job, task and the organization.

Twelve categories are proposed and summarized in Table 16.1.

Strategies for managing stress

1 *Keeping pressure at an appropriate level* – As was noted earlier keep stress at an appropriate level and the team can achieve objectives, keep focused, calm and in control. When stress becomes excessive, work performance deteriorates, relationships are impaired and morale within the team suffers. Members of teams need to take collective responsibility for individual stress levels of one another.

If the triggers of stress are team-based then all the members are likely to experience excessive stress. Under these circumstances the team will need to take steps as a team to lower its stress levels. There are a number of different alternatives:

- Take time out to discuss the situation
- Renegotiate work load/seek outside help
- Ensure team members take adequate rest and relaxation to lower stress levels
- Identify reasons for the situation and address the causes
- Take steps to gain perspective.

Sometimes pressure levels will vary within the team. Individual members will need to help others reduce stress levels possibly by a reallocation of   *263*

Table 16.1
Strategies for managing stress in the team

Strategies for managing stress
1 Keeping pressure at an appropriate level 2 Stress monitoring 3 Appropriate mechanisms for dealing with stress 4 Seeking outside help when necessary
Strategies for dealing with process issues in the team
5 Team building to create an appropriate climate 6 Effective communication 7 Encouraging the supportive nature of teams 8 Building stress-free relationships
Strategies for achieving the task and job-related issues
9 Ensuring the team is equipped to deal with the task 10 Visioning for the future and objective setting 11 Having realistic expectations of one another 12 Using effective approaches to change management

workload, or giving certain individuals the chance to alleviate excessive stress by rest and relaxation.

2 *Stress monitoring* – Effective teams are vigilant for signs of stress reaching unacceptable levels and are better equipped to deal with stress before it becomes an issue. When team members know one another well they are better able to detect early warning signs – usually by change in the behaviour of others. Project teams and teams brought together for a short term find stress monitoring more difficult. Without knowing people well a typical behaviour or changes in people are more difficult to pick up. These teams need to be able to create a climate and way of working which encourages people to disclose feelings of excessive stress.

3 *Appropriate mechanisms for dealing with stress* – Teams need to be equipped with ways of dealing with stress, either to prevent it from becoming excessive or to be able to deal with it.

The approach used extensively in the United States (as reported by Training and Development, November 1995), and also gaining in popularity in the UK, is playing 'paint ball'. This is an excellent way of helping teams raise morale and decrease stress. Wearing protective gear, participants are supplied with paint guns to shoot small balls of paint at one another. This is also a successful way of releasing pent-up harmful stress.

Laughter is another very effective way to counteract the negative effects of stress. Laughter can reduce the size of a problem and it has beneficial physiological effects. It speeds up breathing, increases heart rate and body temperature and triggers the release of hormones – endorphins which kill pain and lift mood. Laughter also helps the face muscles relax.

Crew Resource Management is widely used in the aviation industry, and its application has been extended to other industries where teams may need to operate in an emergency. It involves improving team effectiveness by increased understanding of human performance, particularly good decision making. It is designed to reduce operational errors and give teams additional skills to deal with problems when faced with an emergency (Flin, 1995).

As part of the training a module was included on stress, designed to improve understanding of the causes and effects of stress, recognition of stress and ability to cope with its effects. This type of module would be helpful for any team needing to increase its coping strategies. During times of excessive pressure teams must also ensure they allow adequate time for rest and relaxation. Team members need to support one another in taking adequate breaks, not working excessive hours and taking holidays.

4 *Seeking outside help when necessary* – If any of the team members become particularly stressed, professional help may become necessary. Counselling can sometimes be arranged through welfare departments. Alternatively, GPs may be able to give advice. There are also specialized stress counsellors who can provide help if necessary. People can solve their problems more effectively and thus reduce their stress levels more quickly using a counsellor than if they try to manage without professional help.

Strategies for dealing with process issues in the team

5 *Team building to create an appropriate climate* – Successful teams develop a climate of openness and trust. Teams may be able to handle an away day themselves to help build the team. However, if the team considers it is undergoing difficulties, an external facilitator would greatly add value to the benefits derived from a team-building experience.

6 *Effective communication* – Successful teams are able to communicate effectively. Failure to communicate is an important source of stress in organizations. To manage stress teams need to audit their communication effectiveness. This involves looking at both formal and informal communication. Effective mechanisms need to be in place to enable teams to communicate, especially on a face to face basis. The quality of communication will also affect morale and decision making within the team. Individual communication skills are an important element of team communication and stress management. How well do team members listen to one another verbally and non verbally? Are they sensitive to underlying issues? Do they handle interpersonal difficulties effectively?

7 *Encouraging the supportive nature of teams* – Support is a key need which can be provided by the team for its members. This becomes particularly important in times of change and uncertainty. The stress related to managing change, an idealistic view of helping others and fulfilling an influencing rather than a controlling role. The stress generated can be managed effectively with a well-developed team able to support one another through bonding, openness and trust, and sharing innovative ideas and learning from each other's mistakes.

8 *Building stress-free relationships* – People trigger stress in others, but by interacting positively the team can become a support mechanism rather than a source of stress. Active listening, consulting, informing and giving constructive feedback will all help to build stress-free relationships. In contrast, aggressive behaviour, negative feedback and ignoring certain members of the team will all increase stress levels. Successful teams find interpersonal relationships much easier than those teams that are failing to achieve their targets. Time spent building positive relationships will contribute to positive team performance.

Strategies for achieving the task and job-related issues

9 *Ensuring the team is equipped to deal with the task* – Teams will only be able to work at optimum performance if team members have the necessary skills and capabilities to perform their jobs. Too many demands, in a team where the members lack the necessary skills and capabilities to perform their jobs will lead to excessive stress, which in turn will harm team relationships and team performance.

Excessive stress will also occur if the right procedures are not in place. Teams need to clarify roles and responsibilities to help ensure goals are achieved. Teams also need to develop mechanisms to ensure effective integration of activities.

10 *Vision for the future and objective setting* – Research by Katzenbach and Smith (1993) has emphasized that effective teams and high-performance teams have commitment to shared goals and clarity of vision for the future. Without this clarity excessive stress is likely to develop. Teams need to meet regularly to ensure team members have a shared vision. The vision can then be translated into team objectives and sub-objectives for members of the team.

11 *Having realistic expectations of one another* – As part of the process of working effectively together, teams need to build up realistic expectations of one another if they are to optimize performance. This requires members of the team to have a clear understanding of the capabilities of one another, current demands, priorities and deadlines to be met. Team members also need an accurate assessment of preferred stress levels to ensure that pressure is kept at acceptable levels for individual team members.

12 *Using effective approaches to change management* – Change and uncertainty is a common feature of the modern world of work. Many people still find change disruptive and stressful. If teams approach change in the right way they can provide team members with stability and support which helps to alleviate some of the stress associated with change. Regular communication is necessary to develop a direction for the future. Once the vision is clear teams are then in a position to identify new ways of working, and new skills and capabilities to meet the changing situation. These days teams are

likely to need to pay attention to managing interfaces, which helps integrate the efforts of others and achieve the goals of the organization.

CONCLUSION

Stress influences performance. Individuals need a certain level of stress to perform effectively, and within the team context individuals can support one another to keep stress at acceptable levels. However, at high pressure levels there is a risk of the whole team becoming excessively stressed unless team members are supportive of one another.

Team members need to be highly vigilant to spot signs of excessive stress in one another and as a team. The team itself may be the cause of stress, or individual team members may have personal situations which trigger excessive stress.

Strategies for dealing with stress range from those that address stress levels specifically, to those that emphasize team dynamics or task- and job-related strategies. Effective stress management within the team will greatly help team performance and help individuals keep stress at acceptable levels.

REFERENCES

Cartwright, S. and Cooper, C., *No Hassle! Take the Stress out of Work*, Century, London, 1994

Cooper, C. and Marshall, J., 'Occupational Sources of Stress: A Review of the Literature Relating to Coronary Heart Disease and Mental Ill Health', *Journal of Occupational Psychology*, 1976, **49**, 11–28

Cox, T., 'Stress Research and Stress Management: Putting Theory to Work', *Health and Safety Executive Contract Research Report*, 1993

Flin, R., 'Crew Resource Management for Teams in the Offshore Oil Industry', *Journal of European Industrial Training*, 1995, **19**, 23–27

Holmes, T.H. and Rahe, 'The Social Readjustment Rating Scale', *Journal of Psychosomatic Research*, 1967, **11**, 213–18

In Practice: 'Meetings, Stressful Meetings', *Training and Development*, 1995, Oct, 11

In Practice: 'A Brighter Shade of Team Building,' *Training and Development*, 1995, Nov, 9

Katzenbach, J. and Smith, D., *The Wisdom of Teams Creating the High-Performance Organization*, Harvard Business School Press, Boston, 1993

Klein, S., 'Teams under Stress, the Effects of Work Pressures and Management Action', *IIE Solutions*, 1995, May, 34–8

Sonnentag, S., Bradbeck, F.C., Heinbokel, T. and Stolte, W., 'Stressor – Burnout Relationships in Software Development Teams', *Journal of Occupational and Organisational Psychology*, 1994, **67**, 327–341

'Teams Help H.R. Unstress – With Success,' *Personnel Journal*, 1995, June, 118

Tuckman, B., 'Development sequences in small groups', *Psychological Bulletin*, 1965, **63**, 384–99

Warren, E. and Toll, C., *The Stress Work Book*, Nicholas Brealey, London, 1993

RECOMMENDED READING

Arroba, T. and James, K., *Pressure at Work: A Survival Guide for Managers*, 2nd edn., McGraw Hill, Maidenhead, 1992

Cartwright, S. and Cooper, C., *No Hassle! Take the Stress out of Work*, Century, London, 1994

Cooper, C., Cooper, R. and Eaker, L., *Living with Stress*, Penguin, London, 1988

Cranwell-Ward, J., *Thriving on Stress*, Routledge, London, 1990

Rick, J. et al., *Stress: Big Issue, but What are the Problems?*, The Institute for Employment Studies, Brighton, 1997

Stress at Work – A Guide for Employers, HSE Books, 1995

Warren, E. and Toll, C., *The Stress Work Book*, Nicholas Brealey, London, 1993

17 Negotiating teams in industrial relations

Maggie Dunn and Chris Wills

Disagreement and conflict are endemic to all organizations. Without these the organization does not benefit from sharing different ideas, different perspectives are not examined and new avenues for the organization may not be explored. In addition, where the expectations of parts of the organization are not the same and a conflict exists, the resolution of differences is a necessary process, which will prevent the organization from fragmenting, expending its time and energies in internal strife and losing sight of its goals. Examples of disagreement include: the effects of the introduction of new technology in manufacturing – efficiency versus job satisfaction and lower levels of employment; adoption by marketing departments of long-term strategies versus that by sales departments of short-term goals; training versus time out from the job; project teams and available resources. The main question is, therefore, not whether conflict exists or should exist, but how well it is resolved and how effective is the negotiating process.

Many organizations are changing structures to cope with rapidly changing markets and, as has been mentioned in previous chapters, one of the commonest strategies is to create flattened or horizontal organizations in which teams are an important element. Not only will there be conflict and its resolution by negotiation within the teams, but in addition conflict between the teams, also resolved by negotiation. Figure 17.1 represents this latter type of situation.

Each term debates and resolves its internal differences, arriving at an agreed position. The negotiation is then undertaken between the teams and eventually an agreed solution is arrived at. Each team tries to be as effective as possible, and one of the techniques adopted is to balance the team in terms of the roles people prefer. This chapter examines one such technique in a specific type of negotiating setting, and draws some general conclusions for teams.

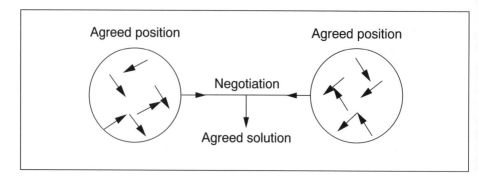

Figure 17.1   Inter-team negotiation process

INTRODUCTION TO THE CASE STUDY

Unlike the members of many other team settings, most members of a staff-side negotiating team are there as a result of a democratic procedure. Individuals become members of a staff-side negotiating team because being a member of the team is one of a range of trade union roles they have been elected, or delegated, to fulfil.

In such a setting, there is no potential to engineer a balanced mix of personalities or individual attributes. In view of this, it is interesting that many staff-side teams operate as effectively as they do. To illustrate this, we have used the example of the Ambulance Council Trade Union Side Meeting. This chapter describes an attempt to explain this phenomenon through Belbin testing, and close observation of the twenty-member staff-side negotiating team responsible for negotiating agreements with the employer's side at a national level.

An excellent outline of the Belbin[1] approach is contained in Chapter 10, *Using Team Roles*, by Nancy Foy, therefore the detail of the method will not be repeated here.

Methodology

In advance of the meeting each of the twenty members of the team completed a Belbin self-perception profile. Each respondent's form was allocated a number between one and 20. Out of the 20 people who attended the staff-side meeting, 11 participants (numbers 1, 4, 5, 7, 10, 11, 12, 16, 18, 19, 20) made active verbal contributions to the meeting. Only self-perception inventories (SPIs) from these active participants were analysed.

Table 17.1 sets out the primary team role of each participant that emerged as a result of their Belbin Self-Perception Inventory. Six of the eleven participants had shaper as, or among, their predominant role.

The context in which the 'active participants' made their verbal contri-

[1] Belbin, R.M., *Management Teams, Why They Succeed or Fail*, Heinemann, 1981

Table 17.1
Participants' primary team roles

Active participant number	Primary role
1	SH
4	SH
5	SH
7	SH
10	CW
11	RI
12	SH
16	RI
18	SH
19	CH
20	RI

butions is set out in the account of the meeting that appears in the Appendix at the end of this chapter. The frequency of *proactive*[2] verbal contributions made by active participants is illustrated in Table 17.2.

Proactive contributions have been analysed by reference to the type of verbal contribution made. We have attempted to match the proactive verbal contributions made by active participants with the eight different types of role identified by Belbin.

Despite the fact that the process of ascribing individual verbal contributions into those Belbin types that seem most to reflect the nature of the contribution made is necessarily a somewhat subjective exercise, it is nonetheless useful for examining the relationship between the participants' Belbin profiles and their behaviour in a team setting.

Table 17.3 sets out in tabular form the types and frequency of proactive contribution made by each participant. Table 17.3 is intended to give an indication of the behaviour in terms of role-type displayed by each participant during the course of the team's meeting.

A comparison of the results of analysis of Tables 17.1 and 17.3 seems to suggest that the behaviour of the members of the negotiating team bore little similarity to their SPI role type. The authors decided then to explore the relationship between the predominant Belbin role type that emerged as a consequence of the SPIs and the behaviour displayed by team members during the course of the meeting. A richer and more detailed method of

---

[2] *Proactive* in the sense that the contribution made was primarily declarative, as distinct from being reactive, to a comment made by another team member.

Table 17.2
Frequency of proactive verbal contributions

Active participant number	Number of verbal contributions
1	6
4	9
5	6
7	2
10	3
11	13
12	6
16	8
18	6
19	6
20	18

analysing the contributions made by participants was developed. This was done by categorizing both proactive and reactive members' contributions, as follows in Table 17.4.

Using the categories of contribution from Table 17.4, Table 17.5 sets out the authors' expectation of the type of communications they would expect to be displayed by each Belbin role type. A comparison between Tables 17.4 and 17.5 strongly suggests that the members of the negotiating team did not behave in the manner one would have expected from their SPIs. Many of the team members who had shaper as their predominant role displayed behaviours wholly uncharacteristic of what one would expect of a shaper.

Table 17.3
Behaviour in terms of role type

Frequency and type of contribution	Active Participant Number										
	1	4	5	7	10	11	12	16	18	19	20
Chairman (CH)			1						1		4
Shaper (SH)											
Plant (PL)		1						1			1
Monitor Evaluator (ME)		2			1			2			1
Company Worker (CW)						2	1			1	
Resource Investigator (RI)	2	1			1						
Team Worker (TW)			1		1	4	1	1	2	2	
Completer Finisher (CF)					1	1					

Table 17.4
Categorizing proactive and reactive members' contributions

Member number	Categories	Controlling	Proposing ideas	Soliciting ideas	Supporting ideas	Regulating	Conflict handling	Disagreement
1	(SH)		1	4	6			1
4	(SH)		1	1	2	1		5
5	(SH)		3	1	4			
7	(SH)		1		3			
10	(CW)		2		4			2
11	(RI)	3	4	4	5		1	1
12	(SH)		1	1	5			4
16	(RI)		2	1	5			4
18	(SH)		2		5	1		
19	(CH)		3		4			
20	(RI)	1	18	1	2		1	

For example, of the 12 contributions (both proactive and reactive) made by team member number 1, whose SPI profile was predominantly shaper, only two of the contributions – those of proposing and disagreeing – were typical of the shaper role type. Similarly, of the 12 contributions made by team member 16, whose SPI profile was predominantly resource investigator, only one contribution was to type.

Further comparison between each of the team member's SPIs, and the behaviours they displayed during the course of the meeting, suggests that, at best, there was a very weak relationship between behaviour and Belbin Role type; indeed in some cases there appears to be no relationship at all.

CONCLUSION

Clearly, the behaviour of the members of the team could not be explained by reference to the Belbin SPIs. The authors interviewed a selection of the members of the team to discover if the members themselves felt that they had moderated their behaviour during the course of the meeting. Significantly, those interviewed spoke of being very aware of the need to obtain consensus among the members of the team. This appeared to them to be almost as important as representing and arguing in favour of their particular interests.

We conclude from this finding that expediency affected the behaviour of the members of the team. The team comprised lay trade unionists with considerable experience. The authors surmise that the pronounced experience of the team was central to explaining the team's behaviour. The clear perception of individual team members of the importance of obtaining consensus among the members of the team governed their behaviour to a significant extent.

Table 17.5
Belbin roles and communication categories

Roles	Controlling	Proposing ideas	Soliciting ideas	Supporting ideas	Regulating	Conflict handling	Disagree-ing
Chairperson	✓		✓		✓	✓	
Shaper		✓					✓
Plant		✓	✓				
Resource Investigator			✓				
Monitor Evaluator					✓		✓
Company Worker				✓			
Team Worker				✓		✓	
Completer Finisher					✓		

In the future, the authors hope to explore further the apparent relation-ship, and causal links in team settings, between experience, perception and behaviour.

GENERAL CONCLUSIONS

The case study was set in a particular environment, that of a trade union in a preparatory meeting before negotiating with their employer. A technique was used for examining the actual behaviour of the trade union council and this was compared with their preferred team roles established by a self-perception profile. In relation to the inter-team negotiation process shown previously in Figure 17.1, this meeting was to establish an agreed position in one team prior to the negotiating meeting involving both sides. A tran-script of the meeting is included as an appendix to this chapter.

It was apparent that the need to have an agreed position to bring to the negotiating meeting took precedence over the members' individual interests and modified their behaviour accordingly. Their preferred team roles appeared to be put aside in the interests of reaching a consensus within a restricted time-frame.

There are important lessons here for teamworking in general.

1 Formal roles, such as chairperson and secretary, are by and large adhered to, in order to retain a structure capable of taking a decision.
2 If the task in hand is particularly important and there is an unalterable time-frame, then the team behaviour may not be the same as on other occasions.
3 The effect of the environment of the team must be considered when any aspect of teamworking is examined.
4 Informal roles, such as preferred teamworking styles, that people adopt in one situation can be different from those adopted in another.
5 Where there are different perceptions of the situation and different

personal objectives, disagreement and conflict arise. In some circumstances the manner of conflict resolution will change, and the normal defending of individual positions and the resulting debate will be subsumed by the overriding need to achieve a team position.

APPENDIX

Background

This was the first meeting of the Trade Union Side since the General Election. The main item on the agenda was pay and, following the Trade Union Side meeting, there was to be a joint meeting with managers from the Department of Health and Ambulance Services to settle pay for 1997/98.

The one million people employed in the Health Service have their pay and terms and conditions of employment determined either through one of seven functional councils based on occupational groups, or one of two pay review bodies. The Ambulance Council covers all staff working in the Ambulance Service, and is one of the seven functional councils.

At the time of our meeting, in June 1997, pay had been settled and agreed by the pay review bodies covering nurses, midwives, health visitors and professions allied to medicine, for example doctors and dentists, and two of the functional councils, which covered administrative and clerical staff, and professional and technical staff. In addition, the three trade unions represented on the Ambulance Council, that is, UNISON, GMB and the TGWU, had all agreed, through their own democratic structures, to accept the 'going rate' for this year.

The settlements were arrived at through a complicated formula which ensured that offers made to the functional councils were not less favourable than those made to the pay review body groups. It was clear, based on the two offers and settlements referred to above, that the remaining functional councils were to receive the same offer as the pay review bodies. In addition, the Secretary to the Trade Union Committee had taken the precaution of arranging a pre-meeting discussion with the management side's Secretary, and had been assured that the offer to be made to the staff side of the Ambulance Council would not deviate from other offers and settlements to date. It was also custom and practice for the two Secretaries to discuss the Joint Agenda and go into detail about the objectives and aspirations of each side on each of the agenda items.

The Ambulance Council Trade Union Committee is a 20-member committee, ten of whom are from UNISON, five from GMB and five from TGWU. The gender balance is two women and eight men from UNISON, five men from GMB and five men from TGWU. UNISON hold the secretariat positions on the Committee and these are the lead negotiator positions.

The Chair of the Committee alternates on an annual basis between GMB and TGWU, the GMB being the present occupant. The format for the Committee is that the Trade Union Side meets on the morning before the   *275* afternoon joint meeting. They deal with their own agenda and then proceed to address and determine an agreed trade union response to, or position on, items on the Joint Agenda for the afternoon meeting. Staff-side meetings are usually between two and three hours in length, depending on length of agenda. It is usual practice for the Secretary to discuss the agenda with the lead officer from GMB and TGWU prior to the meeting, in order that any difficulties, for example, unions having opposing policies on an item to be discussed, can be identified, also in order to allow for 'feedback' where policies are not public.

On this occasion, a brief discussion took place between the lead negotiators of the three unions in order to ascertain whether each of their democratic structures had agreed a position on pay for 1997/98. The Secretary was able to receive confirmation from her colleagues that on this occasion all three trade unions had the same policy, which was to accept the anticipated pay offer and settle pay for 1997/98. There was, therefore, some considerable preparation before the meeting to ensure that possible areas of conflict or difficulty were identified, and that the Joint Secretaries of both the Trade Union Side and Management Side were aware in broad terms of each side's position. This did not, however, negate the need for either Staff Side meeting or Management Side meeting to go ahead as, despite union policies, it had been the case in the past that the elected members on the Council took a contrary view to their organization's policies and, given the semi-autonomous nature of the Committee, they could reject an offer that had been accepted by others. In the case of the Ambulance Council in 1989, when all other groups in the Health Service settled their pay claims and offers, ambulance staff rejected and during the course of 1989 and 1990 were involved in national industrial action seeking to improve their offer.

It was, therefore, by no means clear that on 25 June the Trade Union Side would accept Management Side's offer.

The typical arrangement of meeting rooms is, except where absolutely unavoidable, boardroom style. This is in order to avoid having a 'top table'. There is also an attempt to integrate members of the Committee from different staff-side organizations, and avoid the potential for opposing groups to be seated separately.

As the main item of business for the day was settlement of pay 1997/98, the remainder of the agenda was very light, and only items requiring decision/ agreement or matters of information were scheduled on the agenda in addition to pay, in order that the major agenda item could have sufficient time for discussion and decision. Similarly, on the Joint Agenda of the meeting with the management side in the afternoon, the main item was pay, with three additional matters arising and no new agenda items.

Meeting

Throughout the following description of the meeting, with the exception of the Secretary and the Chair, we have used respondents' numbers to identify the individuals who made contributions, and have endeavoured to give an indication of the nature of the contribution made, that is, whether they had prepared prior to the meeting and made strong statements, whether they made tentative statements, whether they were thinking and speaking reactively.

The Chair (No. 11) opened the meeting and received from constituent organizations apologies for one member and their named substitute, the retirement of one member and their replacement. It was agreed that the retiring member should receive best wishes from the Committee and be invited along to a future meeting of the Trade Union Side for an appropriate presentation. This suggestion was made by the Secretary (No. 20) and was enthusiastically received. Numbers 1 and 12 suggested that we should, rather than invite the retired member to a meeting, hold a social event in a hotel, that is, dinner and overnight accommodation. This suggestion received overwhelming support.

The minutes of the previous meeting were received and approved as a correct record. Number 4 complained that the minutes had taken too long to be circulated and that he relied on the minutes in order to report back on meetings. The Secretary (No. 20) advised No. 4 that the Committee had agreed that minutes should be distributed either with agendas for meetings or, within a week or two, prior to meetings, as Committee members were invariably unable to locate their minutes before meetings, thus necessitating reprinting.

Number 12 asked that we should circulate minutes within two weeks of the meeting, circulate minutes with agendas for future meetings and provide spare copies of minutes at meetings. Number 10 said this was a nonsense, that we were likely to lose rain forests as a result of Committee members' inability to keep track of paperwork. Number 11 said that he could see both sides of the story and asked No. 20 for their view. Number 20 responded that minutes were a record of decision rather than discussion, and that Committee members should take their own contemporaneous notes in order that they were able to report back. She also said that some considerable time had been spent in this discussion, only at a meeting at the beginning of the year a decision had been reached at that time, and advised that the decision reached should be endorsed. After brief discussion involving No. 5 supporting Secretary, No. 18 supporting Secretary, No. 19 supporting Secretary, No. 16 against, No. 4 against, No. 12 against, it was eventually agreed that the decision made at the beginning of the year should be endorsed.

Secretary's report

The Secretary reported on a number of issues on which the Staff Side view was being sought. These issues were primarily equal opportunities issues, for example, proposals to introduce changes for part-time staff, proposal to improve maternity agreement (which fell short of Trade Union Side claims). The Chair (No. 11) asked the Staff Side Secretary (No. 20) for their advice   *277* on how the Trade Union Side might respond. The Secretary (No. 20) expressed her view. The body language of Committee members, that is, nods of head, led the Chair (No. 11) to suggest that the Secretary respond on behalf of the Trade Union Side in line with her suggestion.

An additional item within the Secretary's (No. 20) report was to advise the Committee of a meeting which she had had with the employers on their behalf. This meeting was to pursue a number of items which had not, in the view of the Committee, made as much progress as was hoped through the Joint Committee structure. The Secretary reported on the individuals present at the meeting, the content of their discussion and a proposed way forward. A number of questions were asked, primarily by No. 5, No. 16, No. 1, No. 12 and No. 4. Of these, No. 16 was critical that we had failed to make as much progress as we would have hoped. Number 4 was critical that the Secretary had not made more progress. The remainder of people identified were generally supportive of the Secretary. Towards the end of the discussion, No. 19 quietly, but firmly, moved a motion of thanks and congratulation to the Secretary (No. 20) on the basis that she had used her initiative and taken forward Staff Side concerns outside the formal Committee structure. Numbers 10 and 11 supported the motion, and again body language indicated that there was general support. Number 20, the Secretary, suggested that no formal vote needed to be recorded, rather they should proceed to the next item on the agenda. This was agreed.

The next item on the agenda was a report on the work of a sub-committee of the Trade Union Side. Secretary (No. 20) at the invitation of Chair (No. 11) gave a brief report and then invited No. 19 and No. 5 to supplement her report, given that the three individuals, 20, 5 and 19, had worked closely on the sub-committee work. Number 19 gave a report from his written notes giving some detail of the work of the committee. Number 5 supplemented this report without notes. Number 11 then spoke in some detail about the work of the committee, following which there was an additional contribution, albeit very brief, from No. 7, who was also on the sub-committee. Number 1 asked two or three detailed questions, which were answered by the Secretary (No. 20). Number 18 thanked the sub-committee for their work.

The Committee now considered the Joint Agenda for the meeting, the first item of which was pay. The Secretary (No. 20) reported on the expected pay offer which was likely to reflect the pay review body awards made earlier in the year and the recent settlement in the Administrative and Clerical Council and Professional and Technical Council. She reported that the unions represented in today's committee had accepted that this was the 'going rate', and had agreed that we should settle this year's pay and work towards significant improvement for the following year, given the new Government's commitment to a return to national pay bargaining.

A general discussion ensued, during which No. 16 made a very long and detailed contribution about the fact that ambulance staff had consistently fallen behind and taken pay cuts in real terms, and stating that the members he represented would be prepared to take industrial action. Number 4 similarly made a contribution which was briefer, but saying again that members would be prepared to take industrial action. Number 1 said that the offer was totally unsatisfactory and that we ought to explore other ways of gaining an improvement without industrial action as, in his view, members would not be prepared to take industrial action in order to improve the offer. Number 19 said that although it was disappointing we had to be realistic and recognize that there would be no improvements this year, and he thought we should settle. Number 12 again expressed disappointment but said he did not believe that we would be able to secure industrial action to improve the offer. Number 5 reminded the Committee that each of their organizations had agreed to settle on this year's pay offer, and said that it would not be to the benefit of our members to enter a fight with the new government so soon after a general election, given that the decisions on pay awards for this year were made by the previous government.

Number 18 reminded the Committee that in 1989/90 ambulance staff were the only group who failed to settle, that they took industrial action over a period of six months and that at the end of that time there were very few improvements to staff wages, terms and conditions. He expressed the view that the 1989/90 dispute was still fresh in people's memories, and that they would not be prepared to take industrial action and that we should settle in line with the trade unions' policies and decisions. Number 11 gave a long contribution in which he said that he would be happy to lead the troops over the barricades, but that he was not going to go over the barricades on his own. He asked for the Secretary's view on whether we could delay and pick up the offer from the table today but not settle it.

The Secretary (No. 20) responded that the situation in 1997 was different to the situation in 1989; then the majority of staff were on national contracts, now they were on local contracts, thus even if it was possible to have a hundred per cent industrial action from those affected, it would still be the minority of staff. We had recently had a general election with a new government committed to a different method of settling pay. We did have the trade union agreement that we should settle this year on what was an offer coming from the previous government, but that we should put significant work into the claim for the following year, do intensive research, lobby both Health and Treasury Ministers, as appropriate, and that we could use job evaluation principles to show that the pay and conditions of ambulance staff had slipped significantly against their comparators. Numbers 1, 16 and 4 were still unhappy. However, No. 18 proposed that if the offer we received on meeting management was not less favourable than the offer settled to date, that we should settle at our joint meeting. This was seconded by No. 5 and No. 11 (the Chair), without putting the matter to the vote, said that he was content that there was a consensus within the Committee and that this should be our way forward.

Training

At previous meetings the Trade Union Side had presented Management with a paper on training, expressing their concerns that the traditional training schools were being closed, methods of training altered and the universality of the qualification and transferability of qualification between services was being prejudiced. The Side had also raised a number of other concerns.

Management had agreed to take the paper and circulate it among managers of ambulance services and trainers within the service and within the Department of Health, and give the Trade Union Side a response at the meeting in the afternoon. The Secretary (No. 20) advised the Committee that given that they were in a position now agreed to receive and accept the pay offer, this did leave the time within the agenda to discuss training in detail, and she advised that we should push very hard for a response from Management.

Number 16 had worked closely with the Secretary on this item and it was a matter that he was very keen to pursue. He made a detailed contribution in which he reminded the Committee of the problems that were being encountered in the service and the reason for putting forward the paper. He also expressed the view that he was pessimistic about Management Side wanting to 'stop the rot'.

The Chair (No. 11) made a contribution in which he repeated the contribution of No. 16 agreeing with him. Numbers 5, 18 and 19 all made contributions that said that although this agenda item was slipping, the ball was now firmly in Management Side's court and it was their view that we should push positively, seeking to work with managers who shared the same concerns as the Trade Union Side, given that a successful outcome was to the benefit of our members and to the Service.

The Secretary (No. 20) outlined a proposal for the way in which this agenda item could be handled that in her view would satisfy the concerns of No. 16 in particular, but which would take their work forward. The suggestion was that we form a joint working group with a very short timetable to report back to full Council by the end of the calendar year. The Chair (No. 11) asked if this was agreed. It was agreed.

European directive on working time

This health and safety legislation, formulated in Europe, but effective for all member states, when implemented in the UK would result in maximum numbers of working hours, maximum lengths of working days and minimum rest periods. There was significant implications for the Ambulance Service where many staff worked 12-hour shifts, there was a history of overtime, on call and rest-day working. Without variegations these methods of working would be outside the Directive and would result in significant changes to working practices. This was an item that the Side had discussed on a number of occasions, it was not necessary, therefore, to go into detail on the Directive itself rather to discuss the strategy for both recognizing that the Working Hours Directive was a positive health and safety initiative and at the same time seek to protect the earnings of our members and defend working practices which they found beneficial.

The Secretary (No. 20) reported on a meeting which she had held with the Management Side Joint Secretary, and was able to confirm that managers of the Service had similar concerns to the Trade Union Sides and that this was again an area on which we could work positively with management to seek mutually beneficial solutions.

Number 5 stated that in his service, which was the London Ambulance Service, the shift patterns being worked by staff would fall within the Directive, but that rest-day working and overtime could potentially put them outside the Directive. In his view it was not a major problem. Number 12 said the opposite was true of his service, which was a rural service, where 12-hour shift working was the routine shift pattern, but because staff had rest breaks while on duty they did not find this onerous. Number 7 reported that they had a mixture of urban and rural, but generally 12-hour shift patterns were popular. This was echoed by No. 1 and No. 18. Number 16 supported the contribution made by No. 5, he came from the same ambulance service. Number 4 said that we should be seeking to reduce the working week, but we had to lobby the government to do this without loss of pay.

The Chair (No. 11) expressed the view that the Directive was a two-edged sword and that we should look for advantage while safeguarding practices which our members enjoyed.

No. 10 made a careful contribution in which he reminded the Committee that historically much progress that had been made by workers had been opposed initially as it was considered to be detrimental but, given the passage of time, was recognized as being very beneficial and universally accepted. His view was this was a matter of health and safety rather than the organization of working hours, and that we should embrace the concept of a reduced working life and a reduced working week.

The Secretary (No. 20) proposed a way forward on the item for the Joint Agenda and arrangements to work with appropriate employers between meetings. She suggested that should the government make any announcements on the implementation of the Directive, then an urgent meeting of the Staff Side should be convened. This was agreed.

There remained two items on the agenda. The final item was to agree a schedule for future meeting dates.

The penultimate item was, once again, the Secretary (No. 20) giving a report, this time on meetings that had taken place between herself and the Management Side Secretary. One of the duties of the Joint Secretaries was to discuss and seek to resolve problems referred to them by ambulance services on interpretation of terms and conditions of service. Also to deal with any universal implications concerning national terms and conditions. There were two major items currently being pursued by the Joint Secretaries. *281*

The first was a dispute with the Inland Revenue over taxation of meal allowances. The Joint Secretaries agreed that the allowances should not be taxed, Inland Revenue insisted that they should. The Secretary (No. 20) reported on meetings that had taken place and exchanges of correspondence and the programme of future meetings.

The second item was from a number of services where, because of changes to shift patterns, the National Handbook, which identified annual leave in days, was no longer appropriate.

The Joint Secretaries had agreed to give advice based on annual leave being expressed in hours and, although this had been accepted by the Service and resolved satisfactorily, there was now a dispute over public holidays and extra statutory days. The Joint Secretaries did not agree on this point and the Secretary (No. 20) wanted to bring this disagreement to the attention of the Committee.

Other cases with Joint Secretaries were discussed in brief but, given that they concerned individuals, they were considered to be confidential and the individuals and the services were not identified.

There was further discussion of some of the principles of the items under joint secretarial discussion, and this discussion was taking place when the Management Side Secretary knocked on the meeting room door and asked to speak to the Trade Union Side Secretary (No. 20). The purpose of this intervention was to seek information on when the Trade Union Side might be ready for the joint meeting.

Number 20 advised him that we should be ready in approximately ten minutes. The Secretary (No. 20) returned to the Trade Union Side meeting and told them that she had advised Management that we should be ready to meet them in approximately ten minutes.

Number 4 expressed the view that we should not be rushed into meeting Management. This was endorsed by No. 16. Number 11 said he agreed that if they had not finished their agenda, Management could wait. Number 10 said that we had, in fact, finished our agenda, with the exception of agreeing the date of the next meeting, and that he thought the Secretary (No. 20) had been correct in advising Management that we would meet them in ten minutes.

The Secretary (No. 20) suggested that they should agree the date of the next meeting. This was agreed. Number 11 closed the meeting, advising the Committee that they should proceed to the joint meeting room after a ten-minute rest break.

The meeting closed at this point.

Part III
MANAGING TEAMS

Introduction to Part III

The previous two Parts have covered the context of teams and understanding the processes involved in teamworking. Part III concentrates on the operational aspects of building and managing teams.

Julia Pokora and Wendy Briner offer an alternative to the traditional models of teamworking which concentrate on team building and team development. The characteristics of a 'superteam' in negotiating its success criteria, managing its environment, planning and leadership roles, are examined and a model developed. An example of how one organization successfully applied the superteam model is used to show its key features.

It is important for team meetings to be well-organized, as anyone who has suffered from badly run meetings knows. Poorly managed meetings can occur at any stage of teamworking, but are particularly common when a team is being set up. In his chapter on leading team meetings, Quentin de la Bedoyere discusses the running factors involved, such as size, membership, frequency and agendas. He also analyses the softer aspects of leadership style, influence and the skills involved in the meeting dynamics.

Malcolm Crockford examines the myths and constraints of team selection when trying to form the ideal team and deals with how to make existing teams work better. He discusses the project team, a particular type of team increasingly being used. Psychometric instruments are being more widely used and a range of these is outlined. The author also comments on the use of feedback processes for improving team performance.

Leading teams is an essential part of managing teams. In his chapter Terry Gillen looks at the changing world of work and shows that an assertive management style is more effective in dealing with the problems faced in modern-day teams. He compares contrasting management styles and provides techniques for the development of an assertive management style.

Any manager of a team will from time to time face problems within the team that can only be handled one-to-one. The assertive management style covered in the preceding chapter may be one method for dealing with this situation. An alternative, described by Quentin de la Bedoyere, is the LEGUP method. LEGUP, with its iterative cycle of listening, exploring, goal-setting, underpinning and pursuit, provides a structure to deal with the interpersonal problems that occur within teams. Examples are given with each stage.

An earlier chapter by Julia Pokora and Wendy Briner discussed the concept of a superteam, and in this chapter by Gisela Hagemann the concept is extended, showing how successful the development of the superteam can be as long as four basic conditions exist within the organization: a motivating corporate culture that balances hard and soft values, a clear and convincing purpose, a shared vision, and focus and consistency. The author explains how to determine the current organization status.

Teams need assistance to continue to thrive and Nigel MacLennan discusses the benefits that arise from the coaching and mentoring of teams. Coaching can be regarded as the means of inspiring team members to 'want to do', and mentoring is the process by which team members can be helped to work out 'how to do'. The MacLennan Seven-Stage model is presented as an approach to helping: the formation of the team; individuals to fit into the team; the team to analyse itself; individuals and the team to support each other; the adoption of high achievement characteristics; individuals to perform as effectively as possible.

Many organizations use specific events, usually run by an outside facilitator at a place away from the normal workplace, to develop individuals and the team. Such events need careful planning. In his chapter Malcolm Crockford provides a practical guide to the process by which team development events are designed, facilitated and evaluated.

Many of the team members have specialist skills relating to the tasks required, but the skills involved in working in a particular team need to be practised. Often this practice takes the form of management games. In this chapter Chris Elgood discusses the relevant concepts, such as understanding and commitment to objectives, communication, leadership, climate, maintenance and morale, which can be incorporated into 'games'.

Another approach to developing teamwork, over and above individual performance and the managing of cultural change, is described by Ronnie Lessem in his chapter on turning teamwork into knowledge creation. The basis is an organizational change programme in which a developmental trajectory, using three projects, enables a team to progress from 'ordinary' to 'extraordinary' to 'masterly'. This approach has been developed by City University Business School in conjunction with industrial partners.

18 The superteam approach

Julia Pokora and Wendy Briner

Recent developments in the world of work have imposed huge demands on the personnel of most organizations, forcing them to rethink what they do and how they do it. For many, the main strategy for survival has been the search for increased efficiency and attention to competitive pressures. In its most visible form this has meant slimming down the labour force, tightening up financial controls, trimming costs and investing in new technology. This strategy is attractive, based as it is on analysis, rationality and objectivity; and, of course, it can be a successful one. Its limitation is that it is often based on an acceptance of the traditional model of organizational life: it aims to 'do better' without questioning *what* is done, *why* it is done, or *how* it is accomplished.

The questions of what, why, and how are complex. They involve values and beliefs, and they challenge the traditional model and thinking. However, these questions are being asked most often by organizations whose members believe that they are in the business not of reacting to the future, but of creating it. Many organizations have developed new models of organizational life in response to these questions and in order to meet their new purposes. Such organizations have created non-traditional methods of combining the way in which individuals work together to produce more efficient results and greater flexibility.

The key challenges faced by most organizations today are:

- Developing innovative products
- Managing a number of small, independent, decentralized divisions
- Responding to increased customer demands without generating radical increases in costs.

The response is often to set up some activity or set of activities that enable   *287* individuals working in the organization to form a team, so that ideas and energies from different parts of the organization are used to investigate and experiment with new ways of operating. The resulting experiments are not universally successful, but a significant number produce real benefits in terms of developing the business or improving effectiveness. This form of teamworking is an important tool for many successful organizations; however, not all ventures into teamwork are as useful as they might be.

DEVELOPING A SUPERTEAM

Traditional models of teamworking have emphasized team building and team development. With these models the team is usually seen as an intact, ongoing group trying to achieve a defined task. The organizational reality is that a team is often temporary, and its membership changes; the members spend a large part of their time apart, may have unclear or changing demands that have an impact on what they are supposed to be doing, often have conflicting pressures placed on them by other parts of the organization, and operate within a complex organizational network of contacts.

The Teamworking model has sought to identify what 'superteams' – outstanding ones – do to achieve excellent performance despite difficult conditions, and what differentiates them from ordinary or below-par teams. Although there is no magic formula for developing a superteam, observation and analysis suggest that there are some significant common characteristics and themes:

- A superteam persistently pursues its goals, but uses very flexible and unorthodox means.
- A superteam is motivated to achieve high standards; its members drive themselves and others, and they enjoy success.
- A superteam actively cultivates a network of contacts at all levels in its own organization as well as in the customers' or clients' organizations. Its members use the network to influence in order to achieve more effectively. They are 'streetwise' and understand how things really happen in organizational life. They know that visibility is important.
- A superteam is action-oriented. Its members try new approaches to find out how to move forward, and they use planning and analysis to take them to the next phase of action. They are optimistic even when life is hard.
- A superteam's members retain a sense of unity while they are apart by communicating frequently via all available methods.

Superteams can be used in organizations for several different purposes. Some of these uses are as follows:

• To develop and implement strategy

- To solve problems
- To determine ways in which to restructure or reorganize units or activities
- To develop the skills of team leaders.

Figure 18.1 illustrates the superteam approach, and the following paragraphs describe it in greater detail.

Negotiating success criteria

Superteam members believe that it is important to spend time and energy making the criteria explicit against which they will be judged – the standards of success. These criteria are of two types: *tangible* criteria (for example, timeliness and adherence to budget) and *intangible* criteria, which are just as important but often more difficult to specify (for example, the degree to which a new product is 'exciting'). Superteam members understand who will influence their success; they can easily differentiate between the sponsor, the senior person in the organization championing the team, the client, the person or group commissioning the team's output, and the user (that is, the person or group who will ultimately use or work with the team's output). Armed with this understanding, they are in a good position to plan their ventures in such a way that they meet their own criteria of success.

Managing the outside

Superteam members spend time building networks and relationships with the key people who will influence their success, and they pay attention to how the team is seen and 'marketed' by these people. They acknowledge and look for friends and champions, but they also acknowledge and work with (or around) those who may try to block their progress.

Planning the what

Superteam members possess standards of excellence in what they achieve. They challenge notions of 'just good enough', and often negotiate their success criteria upwards so that they must work harder to achieve higher standards than are expected of them. They do not fall into the linear-logic trap of adhering to one master plan; instead, they plan for the known and then try to anticipate the unknown by frequently checking to see how their plans need to be modified in light of new information.

Planning the how

Superteam members not only talk about *what* they will do, but also *how* they will do it. They develop explicit ground rules for the way in which they   *289*

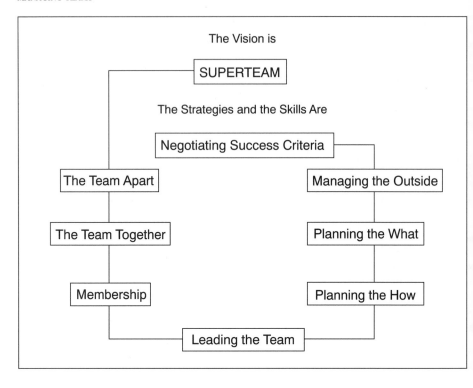

Figure 18.1 The superteam approach

will operate, and – as is the case when they plan *what* they will do – they frequently review how they are working as a team and whether the ground rules need changing.

Leading the team

The *superteam* leader plays a fundamental role in sustaining the team's energy and in articulating the team's vision of success. He or she must monitor forces that are external to the team as well as those that are internal, and must keep the planning process on track by reviewing past activities and altering future ones if necessary. The leader is an information gatherer, ensuring the team is in touch with the outside environment, and an information disseminator, 'marketing' the team's progress to the outside.

Membership (the team together)

Superteam members have a sense of individual responsibility for the team; they are active followers rather than passive ones. They acknowledge individual differences, plan ways in which they can integrate specialists, and see diversity as a help rather than a hindrance. They also acknowledge conflict as inevitable and recognize that results can be improved by confronting differences rather than avoiding them. In addition, they develop a common language, and they articulate rules for managing themselves productively. Superteams celebrate their successes and enjoy themselves.

The team apart

Superteam members understand that they will spend much of their time apart and that the 'real work' is accomplished when they are apart. They pay attention to how they will work when apart – how they will stay in touch, keep up energy and commitment, spot problems early and communicate successes quickly. They manage the balance between holding in and letting go – keeping team objectives to the fore while managing their individual priorities.

APPLYING THE SUPERTEAM MODEL

The following example comes from the experience of one organization in applying the superteam model. As the history of a particular superteam is related, the reader will notice phrases in brackets set in italics; each phrase represents the superteam characteristic being illustrated by the example at that point.

Every year the company's employees complete an organizational-survey audit to pinpoint achievements as well as opportunities for growth. Achievements, once identified, are celebrated and further encouraged. After opportunities for growth have been identified, they are separated into two types: (1) those that pertain exclusively to a particular work unit and (2) those that have relevance for the entire organization.

Using the superteam concept, top management assigns the organization-wide opportunities (issues or problems) to a task force, whose responsibility is to examine the company-wide scores on each issue and to come up with a viable response or solution. This task force is composed of representatives from each work unit in the organization. Its life is short and clearly defined at inception – generally about two months. Because this task force always functions so successfully and has not yet failed to become a 'superteam' – despite the fact that its membership changes every year – it is worth examining the way in which it strives to achieve and then manifests the superteam characteristics.

The task force that was assembled to work from December of 1986 through mid-February of 1987, met for the first time on 18 December 1986. Also in attendance was the manager who had been chosen as the liaison between the task force and the management group; this person's responsibility was to present the task force's recommendations to the managers for approval, explaining the rationale and intentions as necessary. The first subject the members considered was the establishment of guidelines about how they would proceed (*planning the what*) and what norms would govern their   *291* meetings (*planning the how*). The following guidelines were determined at that meeting:

1 The members of the task force will share with one another all facts (data from the organization-wide survey as well as from other sources) related to each problem or issue addressed. The members will not try solving any problem until all members have agreed on the definition of that problem.

2 The members will analyse the negative results of each problem by determining whose work is negatively affected and in what ways the problem keeps the organization from realizing its objectives.

3 The members will identify the desired end result of solving each problem by clearly stating the target situation and what will be, look, or feel different after the problem has been solved.

4 The members will formulate action steps to be taken in order to actualize the target situation (the desired end result) for each problem. The following will be specified:
   • Who will take each action step
   • Who outside the task force will need to be involved and in what capacity
   • Whether management's approval will be needed for the proposed solution
   • What organizational procedures and/or behaviours will need to be changed and in what ways
   • What deadlines and time-frames will be set.

5 The members will determine a follow-up procedure for each problem to ensure that action is taken as planned. Those responsible for follow-up will be identified, and dates will be set up to review progress.

The members decided that their meeting times would be from 9.00 a.m. until 12.00 noon each Wednesday, that they would spend one meeting period addressing each issue or problem, and that they would not meet if any member could not be present, because each person's participation and contributions were critical (*membership/the team together*). Another important decision involved choosing a leader. After considerable discussion, they decided to share the leadership of the group, with a different member chairing each meeting. Each week's leader would be responsible for facilitating, keeping the members on target, and ensuring that the objectives of the meeting were met (*leading the team*).

Subsequently, they established a sample agenda to be used by the chairperson as a guideline for conducting each meeting. This agenda is shown in Table 18.2. Note that the members decided to rate their satisfaction with their meetings on a regular basis as part of their agenda.

Also included as part of the process of each meeting was the assignment of pre-work to specific members, who would gather additional data, make necessary phone calls, and investigate and work the issue on their own between meetings (*the team apart*). The members agreed to check with one another between meetings when additional help was needed or when particularly important data came to light. They also agreed to enlist one another's help when writing reports of what they had discovered and when writing memoranda about their activities as progress reports for all personnel.

The task force members also discussed how to determine whether they had succeeded in their work (*negotiating success criteria*). They realized that the most important criterion of their success would be improved scores the next year on the survey issues that they were about to address. After discussion, however, they decided to set two additional criteria: (1) the satisfaction of the other members of the organization who were not serving on the task force and (2) their own overall satisfaction with how they worked together. Consequently, they selected one task force member to develop an evaluation questionnaire to be distributed to all employees at the conclusion of the task force's work (see Table 18.1).

This individual agreed to devise the questionnaire in the next week and to present it to the task force at the next meeting. They also decided to ask management for a follow-up all-personnel meeting the following June to review progress on the issues addressed by the task force. In addition, they agreed to assemble twice after their work was finished: once to evaluate and discuss their overall satisfaction with their own work, and once after the next year's survey data was available to determine whether there had been improvement in the issues they addressed. They further agreed to write recommendations for the next task force, based on their experience.

During the next week, the liaison member met with the managers and presented the task force's guidelines, sample agenda, evaluation questionnaire, success criteria, and recommendation for a follow-up all-personnel meeting. At this time the managers formally approved all that was presented so that the task force could continue its work as planned; they also asked the liaison member to convey their congratulations to the task force for their thorough, careful work.

In subsequent weeks the task force members continued working in accordance with their intentions. As each issue was discussed, recommendations were determined and presented to the managers by the liaison member. One recommendation was disapproved; at this point the task force readdressed the issue, and the liaison submitted new recommendations, which were approved. With each new issue, approved recommendations were acted on, and progress was always reviewed during the weekly meetings. Employees were consulted at intervals about the various issues being addressed, and several who were not members of the task force were asked to help with special projects or tasks. The employees were always thanked for their assistance, and the special helpers were both privately and publicly acknowledged in memoranda and in companywide meetings (*managing the outside*). In addition, several outside experts were contacted for help with

293

Table 18.1
Sample agenda for task force meeting

9.00 a.m.	Decision on next topic and next chairperson
9.05 a.m.	Department feedback on topic; of previous meeting*
9.15 a.m.	Review of survey data for current topic
9.30 a.m.	• Where we are • Where we want to be • Restraining/driving forces • Key factors: Is the issue significant enough to warrant addressing? Is it changeable? • Decisions, recommendations • Evaluation.
10.30 a.m.	Ten-minute break
10.40 a.m.	Progress report
10.45 a.m.	Continuation of process
11.30 a.m.	Summary
11.40 a.m.	Pre-work for next meeting
11.55 a.m.	Rating at this meeting by participants
Noon	Adjournment

* Information gathered from individual departments about reactions to what the task force did the previous week.

particularly difficult issues, such as that of regulating temperature within the building to ensure the employees' comfort.

By the middle of February, the task force had dealt with all of the identified company-wide issues. An all-personnel meeting was scheduled, and at this meeting the members of the task force presented a progress report on each issue. At the conclusion of the meeting, each employee was asked to fill out an evaluation questionnaire about the task force's work. After all questionnaires had been completed, the members of the task force and the liaison member were formally congratulated for their accomplishments, and all employees were thanked for their willingness to help. Arrangements were made for the task-force members, the liaison member and the company president to celebrate at a lunch that same week.

After the meeting two of the task force members met to review the evaluations and to tally the results. One of these two prepared a report, which was distributed to all of the task force members as well as the liaison member at a meeting the following week. The members discussed the results and identified ways in which they functioned well in addition to ways in which they could have improved their functioning. One member typed a formal report on the results of the discussion in the form of recommendations for the next task force, and the liaison member submitted it together with the questionnaire results to the managers. Then the task force stopped meeting formally, although some of its members continued to work on ongoing issues, such as temperature control.

In June the task force members met again to discuss the current status of the issues and to plan their follow-up report. Only one issue was thought to be unresolved (the temperature issue, because the solution had not yet been tested during the warm summer months); plans were made to monitor temperatures throughout September and to act on the results. Two weeks later the follow-up all-personnel meeting was held, and the task force members presented this report. At the end of the meeting, the task force was disbanded, and its members were again congratulated. They, in turn, again expressed their thanks to all employees for their help and support. After the meeting the members of the task force agreed to reconvene after the data from the next year's survey were available, so that they could check scores on the issues they had looked at.

CONCLUSION

Although superteams are the stars – the best performers in the organization – any team can raise its performance to this level. In an organization that encourages flexibility, creativity and experimentation, the proper climate for fostering superteams already exists. With training and guidance in how to function in accordance with the superteam characteristics, group members can actualize their potential, thereby benefiting both their organizations and themselves.

RECOMMENDED READING

Dyer, W.G., *Team Building: Issues and Alternatives*, Addison Wesley, Reading, Mass., 1977

Francis, D. and Young, O., *Improving Work Groups: A Practical Manual for Team Building*, University Associates, San Diego, Ca., 1979

Katzenbach, J.R. and Smith, D.K., *The Wisdom of Teams*, Harvard Business School Press, Boston, Mass., 1993

19 Leading team meetings

Quentin de la Bedoyere

The leadership of meetings is only one part of the armoury of skills which the manager needs to gain the most effective performance from his team. Yet it is such a characteristic forum for these skills that it can largely stand as a microcosm of the whole.

The communication needed for an effective team is vertical and horizontal. Vertical communication is required because the leader has a mandate to achieve stated or unstated objectives. He or she has the responsibility for forming and maintaining the team and for directing it towards its objectives in a way which makes best use of its individual and collective characteristics.

Horizontal communication occurs between the members of the team precisely because they are a team working in concert. It will cover work-related information such as task coordination and sharing, and collective problem solving. It will also provide morale, support and shared team commitment. While horizontal communication is carried out by the members (which may include the leader for this purpose), it is a part of the leader's responsibilities to create the conditions for horizontal communication and to foster it.

Because team meetings are by definition the only occasions when the team is physically together, they are the forum in which the skills of vertical and horizontal communication are most clearly seen – notwithstanding the other occasions and media for communication which occur formally and informally elsewhere.

MEETINGS AS AN INVESTMENT

Meetings are an investment. If you calculate the cost merely taking into account salary and benefits for a modest meeting you will usually be talking about a four-figure sum; multiply that by the potential productivity of the members and you have to conclude that a large expense is always involved.

This is not an argument against meetings but an argument for having only necessary meetings, running them well, and controlling the use of time. If this enables you to maintain a committed team whose skills, both technical and personal, are brought to bear effectively on worthwhile objectives, then you will have a good return on the investment.

Like many other investments the value of team meetings can go down as well as up. The potential of a meeting is greater than the sum of the individuals because of the added strength and commitment arising from the stimulus of being part of a group. You are hoping that this enhanced potential will be constructive, but handled badly it can become destructive. So, if you are going to have meetings it's worth doing it right.

NUMBERS

The numbers at a team meeting naturally depend on the size of the team and the way it is organized for work. The ideal number is between five and seven. Less than five may make for quicker decisions but narrows the input; as numbers increase over seven so it becomes increasingly likely that a virtual 'inner' meeting of those with the real influence will form, leaving the remainder as bystanders. The effective maximum is about 15. However, in certain kinds of meeting – perhaps where the purpose is restricted to reporting on progress with little dialogue between the members being required – numbers are more likely to be decided by who needs to be present and the time allowed for the meeting.

The leader may pre-empt the formation of inner groups by opting for sub-meetings, whose representatives will report to a smaller senior meeting.

MEMBERSHIP

Leaders rarely have an entirely free hand in picking membership; nevertheless they must do what they can. Occam's razor is a useful principle: 'Entities should not be multiplied without necessity.' So every member should have a clear and necessary contribution to give, there should be no makeweights, and the temptation to include people because they might be hurt by their omission should be resisted.

Meetings work best when there is no great disparity of rank, although leaders can overcome this to some extent by demonstrating the equal value of contributions. If there are two people present in the same reporting line it will be hard for the junior to contribute candidly, so this should be avoided. However each member must carry an adequate mandate; otherwise the boss concerned should be there instead.

On the other hand, homogeneity of personality is not desirable. A team of like-minded people will not produce the depth or interrogation of ideas required for good work. Every team needs its producer of creative ideas, its realist, its sceptic and even its barrack-room lawyer. A mix of sexes and experience is usually fruitful. Making a team out of disparate personalities *297* without losing their specific characteristics is a challenge, but the results are worthwhile.

You should have a policy about substitutes to cover unavoidable absences. You will need to weigh up the disruption caused by a new face against delays in the work caused by an absence. Possible loss of confidentiality may also be a consideration. Do not let it become easy for your members to field a substitute; if this occurs too often it at the very least suggests a lack of commitment or interest – and this may be your fault.

Remember that meetings work best when they are enjoyed by the members. Stress and boredom are the enemies of creative and constructive thought. If your members look forward to your meetings you must be running them well.

FREQUENCY AND REGULARITY

The intervals between meetings will be dictated by the nature of the work. Unless there are sufficient matters of substance for discussion, members will soon regard them as a bore, and an obstruction to their more useful work. On the other hand, the actual process of meeting allows the team to recognize itself as a team and to draw strength from membership. Intervals of more than a month are likely to require the team to re-form itself psychologically on each occasion before they can work as a team, and the accrual of team bonding from meeting to meeting may be lost.

It may seem more practical to hold meetings on an *ad hoc* basis, because this will ensure that they occur when needed and when there is work to do. And there are certainly kinds of team function which lend themselves to this. But generally regularity is desirable. *Ad hoc* meetings all too often never get called and – when they are – it is difficult to bring the team together without sufficient notice. Their infrequency makes it hard to maintain team identity, while regularity becomes in itself part of the team's structure and identity. Careful choice of intervals, good agenda planning, and having a maximum but no minimum length of meeting will help to make sure that the meetings have enough substance and are not seen as wasting time.

MEETING VENUE

Choice of venue and seating arrangements go a long way towards defining the nature of a meeting:

- Comfortable armchairs suggest a conversational swopping of ideas rather than specific work; upright chairs with writing facilities suggest the opposite. Which do you want?
- A boardroom table meeting restricts lateral discussion and focuses communication through the chair. A circular shape helps free discussion but diminishes the executive role of the leader. A horseshoe giving the leader a degree of prominence is a compromise.

- A meeting away from the office or in another part of the building gives importance to the meeting – which its conduct must live up to.

None of these possibilities is right or wrong. But they do require the leader to choose how he wishes to influence the character of the meeting by conveying a powerful non-verbal message to the members.

AGENDAS AND SO FORTH

Perhaps the most valuable period of time relating to a meeting is that which the leader spends in preparation. He or she needs to consider in a very practical and concrete way what the meeting is expected to achieve, and how it is going to do this. It is useful to write this down for reference at later stages – and of course as a reminder during the meeting itself. Here is an example:

- To agree the average percentage rise for salaries for Grades F and below
- To split this into cost-of-living and merit rises
- To agree criteria for merit rises and indicative percentages
- To ask Damien to discuss recommendations in detail with senior managers outside the meeting, and to present a recommended schedule at the following meeting.

A good test of your objectives is to ask yourself whether they will enable you to judge after the meeting whether they were achieved.

This clarity of objectives suggests other factors which will be important. Who is empowered to make final decisions here? The meeting? The leader? Senior management? Clearly deciding salaries is a businesslike task, and the venue must be suited to it. What will the leadership style be? Will the leader be producing a definite proposal and confining discussion to details, or asking for a discussion from scratch – and, if so, within what constraints? What stages will be needed to guide the meeting through to ensure that all issues are considered? What papers will be needed for study beforehand? How long is the item likely to take?

This preparatory thinking takes effort and sadly it is often omitted. But it is the only way to give the meeting the best chance of arriving at good decisions, with the right level of participation in the shortest space of time. From this planning comes the agenda. Think of this important document as a briefing for the meeting to be studied beforehand. Agenda items should be sufficiently descriptive to enable members to do necessary preparation work. Contrast an item listed as 'Staff salaries' with an item listed as 'To consider our salary policy for next year with particular attention to Grades F and below'.

Any papers for consideration by the meeting should be available beforehand. Reading time at the meeting itself is uneconomic.

Thought should be given to the ordering of items, and the leader, at least, should have a rough notion of the time each item is likely to take. You may, for instance, want to inhibit lengthy discussion on a particular issue, and so place it immediately before coffee. You will make sure that items requiring deep consideration are placed so that members are feeling fresh (perhaps after a break), and not distracted by a forthcoming item which causes them concern. You will encourage prompt attendance by starting (always to time, of course) with an item on which everyone wants to have a say, and finishing similarly.

You may well be inviting members to submit agenda items. If so, this must be in sufficient time to consider including them in your programme for the meeting. There should be no item for 'any other business', since this will have been properly notified, described and timed.

Your agenda should show the latest finish time, which should be adhered to out of respect for the members. Aim to keep your meetings to no more than an hour and a half – members will find it hard to concentrate on good work for longer periods. And avoid the temptation to extend a meeting to its full scheduled time. Members rarely complain if a meeting finishes early.

It will usually be necessary to keep some record of the meeting, and it is best to have a non-member secretary (who need not, of course, be secretarial) for this purpose. It is the leader's responsibility to train the secretary in the level of record required – which may vary from full description to a simple list of agreed action and follow-up points. The briefest record consistent with need is desirable. A short record produced within twenty-four hours will be far more useful than a full record several days later.

The agenda will indicate the venue, in itself an influential decision (see above); it will also remind you of such details as what equipment may be required, and what refreshments, if any, will be provided.

LEADERSHIP STYLE

A review of the points above may convey the impression that a highly disciplined meeting is envisaged, perhaps inhibiting the free discussion necessary to maximize the value of the team for many of its functions. It would be more correct to describe it as a highly disciplined framework into which different leadership styles may be imported as required. A good framework in which both leader and members understand their tasks is a necessary background for focused creative work. Let's look at some possible leadership styles:

Authoritarian

This style would be appropriate when the leader, acting in a hierarchical capacity, is announcing decisions which he or she has made – or is conveying from senior management. If members participate at all, it is likely to be restricted to questions of clarification. Horizontal communication is not an issue.

Guided structure

In this mode the leader is presenting provisional decisions which may well be modified by discussion or, occasionally, be radically altered. Having a clear idea of what needs to be discussed or refined, the meeting has been structured so that this will be done. The leaders aim is to improve his or her decisions and also to get commitment from the team through at least some degree of participation in them. Normally the leader retains the power of final decision.

Guided democracy

The leader wishes the objectives to be achieved through active participation by the members, making use of their creative contributions for the benefit of the work. They may even share in the setting of objectives. In order to focus thinking he or she will be guiding the, meeting through various stages, but is ready to do so flexibly as it progresses. The aim is to obtain group consensus and commitment to decisions and, even if the final decision rests with the leader, a good measure of executive authority is traded for the benefits of team participation.

There are, of course, other forms, such as the autonomous committee in which decisions are made by voting, or specialist meetings such as brainstorming sessions. And the ones that I have listed are never as clearcut in practice as they are in theory, but they indicate the main options which may be needed to match your objectives.

Choosing a leadership style

There are two difficulties about choosing a style. The first lies in the leader's personality. Some people find the idea of ceding authority very difficult; they feel insecure when they are not in full control. Others are so reluctant to control that they do not run meetings with sufficient firmness, and may well allow the objectives of the meeting to be lost, or conclude with decisions which are ultimately unacceptable. All of us have temperaments somewhere between these two extremes, so it is as well to know where we are so that we have the chance of modifying our natural approach when the task requires it.

The second difficulty lies in the fact that different objectives, even within the same meeting, may call for a different leadership style. For example, it can be difficult to move from an authoritarian style to a democratic style, given that the members are being asked to switch hats from humble servitor to valued participant. It is sometimes better to have two different meetings, *301* perhaps in different venues; alternatively, a natural break can be used (coffee again?) to allow the meeting to re-form itself in a different atmosphere.

Members need to know what is expected of them. Over a period of time they will learn the nuances from their observation of the leader but, particularly at the early stages, they need explicit indications. For instance:

> You will have seen in the papers I circulated what I am proposing by way of increases for Grades F and below. I'd appreciate your views on this before I make my final decision. Do you see any anomalies, or points I've omitted? I've retained £10 000 in the budget for modifications, but that's all there is. Fred, what are your reactions?

or

> I think we're all concerned about the level of absenteeism among the younger staff. You've seen the statistics in the meeting papers. There could be many reasons for this and I think we ought to pin these down and make an action plan. It's really up to us as senior managers to decide. Let's start by pooling some possible reasons. Mr Secretary, would you stand by the flip chart and note the ideas down.

You will notice that the leader not only indicates the character of the discussion but clarifies who makes the final decision and what constraints may operate. Meetings and committees need to know whether they are influencing another's decision or are themselves making the decision. They can live with restricted authority, but removal of ostensible authority after decisions have been made is frustrating.

While different tasks call for different styles, it can be argued that the bias should always be towards the democratic style to a degree consistent with the objectives. In this way maximum value is obtained from the team's horizontal communication, and the sense of active and powerful participation boosts commitment among the members.

CONDUCTING THE MEETING

There is a sense in which leading a meeting is like conducting an orchestra. The conductor has stipulated the piece to be played and the pace of the different passages. It is essential to be aware of each section of the orchestra continually and bring them into action as required, also to be immediately aware of the player who is out of step, so that the necessary discipline is maintained. Nevertheless the actual playing is done by the musicians; the conductor's function is to enable them to contribute most effectively to the piece as a whole.

Just as the conductor must be aware of the characteristics of the orchestra, and their strengths and weaknesses, so the leader of the meeting must be versed in the characteristics of the group. Here are some aspects that will need watching:

The hidden agenda

There is nothing mysterious about this. Think of the last occasion you attended a meeting as a member. Externally you presented your viewpoint as constructive contribution to the task of the meeting, but internally there may have been other considerations weighing with you. You may have wanted to make a good showing to impress your boss. You may have been concerned that the decisions of the meeting should benefit your own area of work. You may have been inclined to reject any ideas coming from old Fred whom you dislike. You may have been keen to side with Jo on certain issues – she's a useful ally.

Dodging the issue

In the normal course of events meetings will often diverge from the task and be absorbed in unprofitable discussion. But from time to time the leader will suspect that the group is avoiding some awkward issue; and it will not be discussed unless they are encouraged to deal with it.

Scapegoating

A group may decide that one of their number should accept responsibility for some problem; and so they join forces against that person. Similarly they may fail to support a member who is expressing a dangerous view with which they agree but with which they do not want to be too closely identified.

Sometimes the group may collude in blaming some outside agency, perhaps another department, for a difficulty – thus avoiding the need to take responsibility for action themselves.

Easy consensus

A group may arrive at a consensus very quickly – either for or against an idea. The leader must consider whether all the issues have been properly discussed, including those which the meeting may have ignored, and may suspect that some hidden agenda is operating. The leader will also be aware that groups are naturally conformist, and can bring strong psychological pressure to bear on those who might want to disagree.

Anticipating the leader

A group, or individuals, may develop the habit of trying to guess the leader's view (or the view of someone who will have a strong influence) and then promote it. If this occurs often, the leader should ask the question: In which ways may I have contributed to this?

303

Personalities

A leader who is fortunate enough to have diverse personalities at the meeting will, to return to the simile of the orchestra conductor, be able to bring in the different instruments in order to ensure good discussion and, when the moment is judged right, to lead the meeting to a constructive consensus.

The leader will be aware of the shyer personalities and, while not obliging them to contribute unduly, know how to bring them into the discussion at the best point. He or she will also be aware of the over-assertive, the endlessly repetitive, the domineering, the moaner – and all the other instruments who can make good music or destroy the symphony depending on how they are handled.

PURPOSE – AGENDA – DOCUMENTS

Having prepared the agenda some days before, the leader may well feel enough preparation has been done. But there is one more important stage which should take place just before the meeting itself. Ideally an uninterrupted 15 minutes should be written into the diary.

The leader will use this time for PAD – *P*urpose, *A*genda, *D*ocuments – to act as a reminder of the purpose, or purposes, of the meeting, and the route to follow to get there. The agenda must be checked, as must be the planned discussion stages, and the timing; finally the leader must check that all the required documentation is to hand.

HANDLING THE DISCUSSION

It may seem premature to visualize at this pre-meeting check how the discussion may go. After all, if the discussion is to be free it can scarcely be planned for – the leader must react to what actually happens. In practice such a visualization of important and sensitive agenda items can prove very useful. The leader who knows what to expect is able to plan the necessary actions in advance. Of course the discussion may take a different turn; in which case the divergence will at least be easily recognizable. But surprisingly often the discussion runs to pattern, and so the leader will be well prepared to handle it in the most constructive way. Let's imagine that the item on salary policy for grades F and below appears. The leader's thinking might run along these lines:

> We might have some difficulty with Fred and Mary – they have large staff departments, and Fred has already been complaining that he can't hire the right quality with our salary scales. Fred will probably choose to sit right opposite me, which normally means trouble. I expect Jo will be happy to agree with modest increases, which will help our bottom line. But she'll be nervous of standing up to Fred, so I'll need to make sure she has a hearing.

William's an unknown quantity. He's a bit of a barrack-room lawyer so he may make his usual attack on the company for being too mean. Ordinarily that wouldn't worry me, but there's a danger that the whole meeting will take up that discussion rather than watch Fred trying to spill blood. I'm going to have to be firm here.

I asked Damien, because of his personnel responsibilities, to do some comparisons with local firms. Perhaps I'll just keep that in hand – and launch Damien when things get sticky. Looking at those will quieten them down. He and Mary are as thick as thieves, so she'll be inclined to go along with what he thinks.

And so on. Having finished thinking the leader will be well prepared for most of the likely eventualities.

THE LEADER'S INFLUENCE

We may like to think that the discussions we lead are, within the limits we have set, entirely free. Unfortunately it is virtually impossible for the leader to be without influence, and so it is as well to be aware of how it is exercised, if only to make sure that it is exercised constructively.

Signalling the right answer

More often than one might expect, a leader will open an agenda item with the words: 'Before we get down to discussing this let me tell you my views on the question.' And useful discussion has ceased before it has begun. But there are other, subtler, ways of signalling the right answer. The leader can invite a heavyweight to express his views at an early stage; if he is strong enough it will prove the definitive view. The democratic leader will inhibit statements which carry too much power until the meeting has had the opportunity to express itself. For example: 'I'd just like to hear some general views on this before asking Fred for his opinion.' A leader can attempt to disguise his or her views: 'Just for the sake of playing devil's advocate, what would happen if we kept the rises down to two per cent?' But if the meeting has learnt that the 'devil's advocate' view is always the leader's view, this might just as well have been said.

Bringing in the instruments

As the preceding paragraph suggests, the leader can do much to control the discussion by bringing in the instruments in a chosen order – and by avoiding the eyes he or she prefers not to see. The utopian leader will do this from the pure motives of encouraging free discussion; the rest of us will be tempted at least to some degree to use it as a steering device. A leader will of course be skilled in noticing the non-verbal signals of those about to come in, or would like to participate, but may miss their opportunity.

Encouraging a view

There are many ways in which a leader can support a view without even being aware of doing it. Facial expression, the stance or direction of the body, the intentness of listening are all messages which the group will receive and understand. Repeating or returning to a favoured view will keep it high in the consciousness of the meeting.

A leader may use a view as a stepping stone: 'Mary's point about keeping up with the big employers in the town is an interesting one. Damien, how do we stand?' This can be a useful way of moving the discussion to the next stage without appearing to be doing so. Mary may have intended no more than an incidental remark, but the leader has grabbed an opportunity.

Asking the questions

It is the duty of the leader to see that the group addresses all the relevant questions. But the relevant questions may only be those which steer the meeting in the direction of the leader's view: 'Given the limitations on our budget, what redundancies will we need if we choose the high option?'

This is not always conscious manipulation. After all, the leader has identified these questions as the key ones in taking this view in the first place, but should be aware that the questions he or she chooses will affect the answers that come back. It might be better to include questions which lead away from his or her view; the discussion will be more thorough and the leader will have avoided signalling his or her own conclusions.

Challenging the group

Once a leader has the group's confidence, it may be possible to challenge it from time to time. For instance: 'I wonder why we're all avoiding the question. Perhaps it's a bit uncomfortable to look at,' or 'We've spent the last ten minutes telling ourselves why the problem lies with Central Purchasing, but aren't we part of the problem too?' Challenging can be a threatening move, so use it with discrimination.

The summary

Summaries are an important tool for the leader. They serve as reminders to the group of the point they have reached, so that they can go forward without rehearsing old ground. And they can check that the leader has read the consensus aright. They may serve as a guide for the minutes secretary.

Summaries can also be used to alter the consensus. Because they are necessarily an edited version of the proceedings, the possibility of editorial bias can enter. A skilled editor will not be challenged; the less skilled will get another opportunity when the minutes are being prepared.

Promoting discussion

A group has a natural tendency to communicate through its leader, who is employed as a telephone exchange through which all messages pass. For some kinds of discussion – particularly the more formal – this is appropriate. But usually the leader will want to promote a horizontal discussion, being able to intervene as he or she sees fit.

We have seen that the seating arrangements can influence this; eye contact between all members is important. But discussion can also be actively promoted. A phrase like 'Let's all discuss this among ourselves' will help. And so will a deliberate direction of the conversation: 'Damien, it looks to me as if you don't agree with Fred's point. Tell him where you think the difficulty lies.'

It will be necessary for the leader to be ready to promote horizontal discussion in these ways throughout the life of the meetings because the tendency to avoid it will always be there. Nevertheless a group meeting regularly will gradually develop good discussion habits as the leader gently indicates the skills. But this puts an emphasis on the part that early meetings play in setting patterns for the group.

TRAINING THE GROUP

A group which has not met before has by definition not learnt to work together or to feel any sense of loyalty to the group. Consequently there is likely to be an unsettled period while the group is forming. People have to discover their roles, and recognize the roles of others. Time may be spent in this adjustment before real work can be done. Members need to establish where each of them stands and whether they share common views and values. They will also carry the baggage of past experience: if the marketing department has often felt frustration from the IT department, for instance, this feeling will be carried into the initial meetings.

The leader will be ready to assist this forming process, knowing that real work will be difficult until it is completed, and that the patterns established in the early meetings, bad or good, will tend to persist. He or she may well choose initial subjects for the first meeting which will interest all the members but have few traps likely to cause difficulties. A leader will not want complete agreement, of course, for the members have to learn how to disagree in constructive ways. Individuals who would not naturally relate to each other may be encouraged to do some project work together outside the meeting, in the hope that this will enable them to discover each other's value.

A leader will encourage discussion in the ways I have suggested, and also model the preferred ways of behaving. One example is demonstrating in the natural course of the meeting how to disagree without being obstructive, another is how to ask questions that elicit useful information without carrying an overtone of interrogation or challenge. And a leader will teach them how to listen by example: 'So what you're saying, Mary, is that rises lower than the cost of living may cause a morale crisis in your department, and you're worried that it will lead to resignations from some of your key people. Is that it?'

Of course the group will be learning at the same time about their leader as a leader, who will want to be sure to be in control of the messages he or she sends.

NON-VERBAL COMMUNICATION

In describing these techniques I have often referred implicitly to non-verbal communication. For example, the seating arrangements, the angle of people's bodies, the tone of their voices are all versions of NVC. You will have noticed that it is two-way: the leader communicates by NVC and picks up the feeling of the group or its individual members by NVC. Some people are naturally good at this, but it is such an important skill for leaders that they have to work constantly to improve.

The subject is too large to deal with here, but some useful suggested reading is provided at the end. A tip which many leaders have found helpful is to write the letters NVC on their own copy of the agenda. Their eye will catch this private reminder from time to time, and keep them up to the mark.

POSTMORTEM

You may remember that the leader records his or her objectives in a way that makes it obvious whether they have been achieved. And it is important to review the meeting against objectives in order to identify how to do even better next time.

SUMMARY

This chapter has indicated that the skills demanded of the team leader in running meetings are varied and demanding. No one achieves them to the fullest degree and so the leader must constantly work to improve them. But when a good standard has been reached the leader will be aware that his or her meetings make a central contribution to the working of the whole team. Here are some reminder points:

- Meetings are an expensive investment – the leader's skills make them value for money.

- Meetings are the occasion when your team is most conscious of its membership, and when horizontal and vertical communication can most easily take place.

- Every member of the meeting should be important to its work; keep your numbers small enough to involve everyone; try to avoid gross rank differences but welcome different personalities.
- Regular meetings help the group to work together; choose the frequency with an eye to this, but give them substance.
- Pick the venue of the meeting to give it the right level of importance; your seating arrangements will indicate the kind of communication you want.
- Express the purpose of your meeting in written objectives; plan your agendas carefully in good time; make them descriptive so that members can prepare; include documents; plan the stages for the discussion when major or complex items are included.
- Be aware of typical leadership styles and decide which is likely to work best for different meetings or items; the group should know the constraints within which they are working.
- Review the ways in which groups or their members tend to react, considering how they may impact on the work of the meeting: hidden agendas, scapegoating, easy consensus, second guessing the leader, the response of different personalities are among the phenomena which typically occur.
- Review Purpose, Agenda, Documents – PAD – before each meeting; this is the time to visualize the course of the discussion and what actions may be needed to help it go well.
- The leader will always influence the meeting so make that influence constructive; signalling the desired decision, deciding whom to bring in and whom to inhibit, asking questions, challenging, using summaries and promoting discussion are ways in which influence is brought to bear.
- Early meetings require careful handling to settle them down and to establish good patterns; the leader has a training role here.
- Develop your skills in two-way non-verbal communication, and keep yourself up to the mark.
- Review your meetings against objectives; remember that you will always need to improve.

RECOMMENDED READING

Argyle, M., *Bodily Communication*, Methuen, London, 1975. This is a comprehensive text for the serious student of NVC, but very accessible.

Handy, C.B., *Understanding Organizations*, Penguin Books, 1981. A comprehensive text on many aspects of business organizations, with a good section on leadership of meetings.

Nierenberg, G.I. and Calero, H.H., *How to Read a Person Like a Book*, Heinrich Hanau, London, 1973. The best practical book I know for anyone starting *309* to look at non-verbal communication for the first time. Good line drawings.

Sidney, E., Brown M. and Argyle, M., *Skills with People*, Hutchinson, London, 1973. Subtitled *A Guide for Managers*, this covers a wide range of skills including leading meetings.

20 Team selection, psychometrics and feedback

Malcolm Crockford

One challenge that has faced organizations over many years is how to put to good use the vast body of research about group dynamics and team-working in order to form teams most likely to produce the best short- and long-term results for the enterprise. This chapter discusses the constraints that organizations face in attempting to achieve this aim, the psychometric tools that exist to facilitate the process of team selection and development, and processes for allowing teams to monitor their performance by giving and receiving feedback.

TEAM SELECTION

If there is one question that those involved in team building and team development are regularly asked, it must relate to the formation of 'ideal' or 'perfect' teams. Why is it, they ask, that considering all the research, models and instruments available to organizations with which to select the membership of perfectly performing teams, such teams are rare? Why don't organizations practise what they preach in their management development programmes, and form teams according to the requirements for complementary team roles and a balance of personality types?

Organizational teams

The cruel reality is that organizations rarely have the flexibility to create new teams from scratch, or to provide their management with complete freedom to choose their team members. This is particularly true of 'organizational' teams which have a continuous role within functional or specialist boundaries, and may have to conform to hierarchical conventions consistent with the corporate culture. For example, where an organization has   *311* developed and institutionalized functional 'stove-pipes', and cross-functional career moves are discouraged, the stagnancy this creates limits the possibilities in the creation of new teams. Similarly, where organizations allow such specialization to occur, team formation can be confined to meeting the needs of skills, knowledge or experience, without any regard to personality, attitude or motivation. Moreover, following the waves of downsizing that have been a feature of organizational life in the past decade, specialists are less likely to cross functional boundaries for fear of failure in an alien culture.

In the past, risks were minimized by providing supportive HR policies which allowed for a dignified return to the original function. Such nurturing strategies become less possible in an environment of reduced headcounts, tight manpower accounting and flatter structures. Organizations can no longer afford to offer temporary 'parking bays' where displaced staff can work on projects, research or personal study. Those organizations that have encouraged cross-functional moves, job rotation, and national (or even international) assignments have probably fared better through recessionary periods. They have developed a culture of functional or corporate generalists who can move more readily and can provide flexibility in the face of ongoing change. These may also be the people who are groomed or have been conditioned to accept joining and leaving teams as second nature.

Another constraint on the formation of ideal organizational teams, (that is, those conforming to the precepts of psychological balance or predetermined diversity) has been the need to adhere to legal or company policy considerations. The proliferation of employment laws in the last 20 years has made internal selection more precarious for employers. Mandatory moves have been difficult to implement legally to suit business needs or meet the requirements of a perfect team formation, except on a short-term basis. Fear of accusation of discrimination, constructive dismissal or even harassment make enforced people moves more difficult for management to achieve.

Moreover, changes in the 'psychological contract' that employees have with their organizations (Herriot and Pemberton, 1995) have made employees less willing to uproot, take unnecessary career risks, or work under unreasonable conditions for the sake of the company. Employees no longer wish to be manipulated or treated like pawns on a chessboard. Companies themselves are more aware of the changing values of the working society; for example, the growth of the two-career family, the number of lone-parent families and the increasing need at all levels in the organization to maintain a healthy balance between work and home. Additionally, during the last few years staff movement in organizations with a national or international spread has been affected by the slump in the housing market.

Organizations that allowed themselves to become rule-bound and bureaucratic during more stable business periods, usually involving the development of complex grading and remuneration systems, found themselves increasingly burdened by the challenge of moving people to jobs and teams required by the needs of the business. Moves could not be achieved without occasionally fudging the issues of equity and consistency. Individual anomalies grew in number to accommodate the need to meet ever changing business circumstances. As a result, when the need for large-scale downsizing and redundancy became insurmountable, organizations opted for flatter and more flexible structures, wider bands of job/skill families, and more adaptable HR policies.

Project teams

Various circumstances, both external and internal, have combined to make project or short-term teams more practicable and indeed of great importance in today's organizations. The pace of change in business life, the intensity of competition, the restructuring and rationalization of whole industries through mergers or takeovers, and the introduction of powerful new technology have transformed the way that people are organized in the workplace and the nature of the workforce. It is estimated that only 57 per cent of the UK workforce have permanent, full-time jobs. There has been a massive growth of part-time, fixed-contract and freelance workers. Departmental outsourcing, the use of consultants and the widespread use of fixed-term contracts have taken us further towards Charles Handy's concept of the 'core worker' (Handy, 1989). Jobs have less permanence, and are overtaken by the concept of skills groupings or families. Lateral moves are encouraged for skill development, as formal career ladders or paths are less in evidence, or non-existent. Generalists are encouraged and cross-functional movement is often a business necessity.

Organizations are creating cultures that can cope with unplanned or unexpected change. Teams are formed for projects, not for life. Teams are more likely to be balanced functionally to ensure all essential units are represented, are in sympathy with and are committed to the goals of the project. Territorial skirmishes are frowned upon, and traditional areas of conflict (for example, between HR and Finance) are overtaken by the 'one company' concept. A former Chief Executive of the Prudential described this as all employees being 'in the same canoe', paddling in the same direction and avoiding splashing each other (that is, engaging in organizational politics). Other organizations have incorporated teamwork in their corporate values statements (for example, BT's 'We work as a Team', IBM's 'Commitment to Teamwork' and the 'X-Teams' initiative at Rank Xerox).

Project teams present more opportunities for the use of personality balancing techniques. Given that a representative mix of function, specialism or geography is required, the team can be created from new, and account taken of team role or working preferences. As the working life of the team may be very limited and the goals may be more specific, it is easier to release people from their current roles, and less risk is presented to team members about their re-entry to 'home territory'. IBM has a tradition of using such teams, sometimes called 'task forces', to address specific strategic issues and offer recommendations to senior management. As functional representatives, team members have access to the data and support of their functional *313* colleagues, and can gain from collaboration with other parts of the business. Team members can be selected for their potential contribution, for their personal development or for the particular personality they bring to the team's work. Even in short term or *ad hoc* project groups there is scope for the use of internal or external consultants as facilitators. They can support the team, getting a fast start on the project by helping the team to recognize its strengths and potential deficiencies, to appreciate the diversity or homogeneity of its personality types, and to gain an understanding of team members' working preferences and motivation. It can also serve to avoid role ambiguity, clarify goals and establish effective working norms.

SELECTION CRITERIA AND PROCESSES

Traditionally selection criteria were established in organizations to achieve the best fit between the person and the job. This usually entailed using a structure for the assessment of the candidate, focusing on general education, professional qualifications, general and specialist experience and perhaps language facility. Personal characteristics and qualities were identified to fit the individual most successfully into the job, the function or the corporate culture. Often recruitment, or at least the advertising of vacancies and initial interviewing, was carried out by the personnel department and the line manager made the final choice.

Bearing in mind the changes mentioned above that have taken place both in the public and private sectors, there is a greater tendency for line managers to play a greater role in internal and external recruiting, and to place a greater emphasis on the personality and motivation of the candidates for all jobs. A greater emphasis is placed on energy, self-motivation, communication and interpersonal skills and being a 'team player'. Assessment Centre approaches, multiple interviews and the use of psychometrics, previously used for graduates and managerial candidates, are more widely used. These approaches allow the candidate to be viewed as a team member and not solely as an isolated individual. Their ability to join and interact with a team is assessed, as are the roles they are most likely to play in teams. Some selection processes include work simulations or team exercises to identify team behaviour, and are supported by interaction or behaviour analysis techniques (Rackham et al., 1971).

For internal recruitment or placement the recruiting manager may have more evidence, through personal acquaintance, performance reviews, or 'track record' on which to base a judgement. Many share the selection process with their staff, so that the team may form a view about how the candidate may work in the team environment. Some allow a period of secondment on a trial basis, although this tends to be a luxury few organizations can now afford. Some truly empowered organizations even allow the team to make the recruitment decision, particularly where the degree of interdependence and shared reward is high, although examples of this in British organizations are still rare.

One dilemma that all organizations face is the degree to which they select for homogeneity or diversity, whether consciously or unconsciously. This can range from personal appearance (the white shirts and dark suits for the 'old' IBM or the relaxed dress code at Virgin) to personality profiles. IBM has abandoned its rigid dress code and now recruits from outside the company to a very senior level (including the Chairman of the Board!). This allows for more variety of experience and creativity to be imported into the company, and less possibility of complacency or strategic tunnel vision. The 'old' IBM allowed for 'wild ducks' only so long as they were prepared to fly in formation! Such policies can create closely bonded corporate families who work well together, share common feelings about team processes, have similar aspirations and beliefs. They can also become cosy, inward-looking and slow to challenge accepted corporate wisdom and ideas. Sacred cows are protected in the face of reality until a mass cull is desperately needed, and then it may be too late. 'Not invented here' attitudes prevail and many wheels are reinvented!

Organizations that recruit for diversity can expect some team and company processes to be difficult and not without challenge or conflict. Decision making may be slower and noisier, but the decisions may be sounder and more creative. There is therefore a great temptation for managers seeking a more stable and harmonious existence to recruit team members who will conform to existing team norms and preferences. This may give them more control and allow them to achieve more in quantity or quality of work outputs. Some managers will be more adept at picking team members with variety of experience and personality, and are able to harness the energy created by the diversity of the team. Others may 'poach' team members they have worked with in previous managerial roles in other divisions or in other companies: the recruits are known quantities and balance can be achieved reasonably quickly. For this reason, executives recruited at top level may not only negotiate their pay and benefits, but also the flexibility to select their own teams from outside their new employer.

THE USE OF PSYCHOMETRICS IN TEAMWORK

Ethical considerations

Most of the tests and instruments described later in this chapter require substantial training and certification before users are allowed to use them in their organizations. They are usually also accompanied by specific ethical and professional conventions which may apply in their use. This may relate to conditions of testing, confidentiality and the uses to which they are put. For example, some instruments should not be used in isolation and without feedback and discussion. Some should not be used primarily for selection, as they may not provide the precision and validity that the inexperienced user may hope for. There are also generic ethical considerations in the use 315

of psychometrics which are published by professional bodies (such as IPD's *Guide on Psychological Testing*, 1997) and test suppliers themselves.

Such tests should always be kept in the hands of trained users and not allowed to be photocopied or distributed to untrained staff for (usually) inappropriate use. There are also many other tests and instruments available for team selection that may not meet stringent requirements of validity and reliability. Beware the use of these without professional support and advice!

How and where to use tests and instruments in teamwork

Most of the instruments listed in this chapter were not primarily designed to be used in selection, except maybe to generate a discussion with the candidate to learn more about their motivation and work preferences. This would be in addition to the normal selection process of interviews, analysis of c.v., group discussion, and so on, and would require feedback to the candidate. Within organizations which may make wide use of personality instruments for development and counselling, it may be legitimate to link their results with placement decisions, provided it is with the agreement of the candidate and involves feedback.

What would be inappropriate and demonstrate a lack of understanding of the purpose and scope of psychological testing would be for a recruiter to seek out, for example, an ESTJ (a Myers-Briggs type) or a Completer (a Belbin Team Role) in order to complete what is felt to be an unbalanced team. Apart from the stereotyping or pigeonholing involved, the instruments do not offer the precision that makes such predictions viable. Nor do humans work in such predictable ways! Teams are dynamic, and the 'chemistry' of team relationships may be affected by circumstances totally outside the scope of psychological testing. The sudden departure of a team member, or a serious change in work content can have a significant effect on the relationships between team members.

The tests mentioned in this chapter are ideal for use in team development, at any stage in the team's life. At the time of forming, or significant re-forming, they can help team members explore and articulate their work and personal preferences, their motivation and needs. This can be combined with other personal disclosure exercises to increase people's awareness of each other and to develop trust and openness. Such activities can 'jump-start' the new team, and build a 'background of relatedness' as a foundation for effective teamwork. To prevent a feeling that the activity is too introspec-tive or 'touchy-feely', it is usually prudent to balance the event with essential business goal setting and planning (see Chapter 25 on the design of team development events).

A review of psychometric instruments for teams

The Myers-Briggs Type Indicator® (MBTI™)

The MBTI is widely used in a variety of applications for career development, team building, management development and individual counselling. Based on the work of Carl Jung, the questionnaire was developed over many years of research by the mother and daughter team, Katharine Briggs and Isabel Myers. It is now regarded as the world's leading indicator of personal styles, and it is estimated that several million people take it every year.

The questionnaire, which (in its shortest, self-scoring form) takes about 20–30 minutes to complete, provides an initial classification into one of 16 personality types, based on four bi-polar scales. Subsequent counselling, using appropriate elements of extensive support material, allows the client to arrive at a 'best fit' type, so that the client does not feel pigeonholed by the 'reported' type. The four bi-polar scales cover extroversion and introversion, sensing and intuition, thinking and feeling and judging and perceiving.

The MBTI contains valuable insights into preferred styles of working and interacting with other people. Because it is based on a comprehensive model of personality, it provides a logical framework for understanding people's behaviour. It is widely used to help people understand their own preferred style and to appreciate the value of others, which is ideal for team development.

An excellent overview of the underlying theory and development of MBTI is available in a book written by Isabel Briggs Myers (Myers, 1980). There is also a comprehensive manual covering applications in organizations and containing much reference material (Hirsh, 1991).

The Perception and Preference Inventory (PAPI)

PAPI was developed by Dr Max Kostik, Professor of Industrial Psychology at the State College of Boston, in the early 1960s, and is now available under licence from the PA Consulting Group. It consists of 90 pairs of statements from which the participant is required to choose the one statement in each pair that most represents them (mostly in a work situation). The statements, some of which are repeated several times in different combinations, allow a picture to emerge of the participant's needs and preferred roles. The Inventory is quick (10–20 minutes), user-friendly and has high face validity. It is widely used in selection, placement, counselling and team building as a means of generating discussions of work style and motivation.

The results of the scores against 20 different factors (ten needs and ten roles) are plotted on a simple chart profile like a wheel, into seven key areas covering Work Direction, Leadership, Activity, Social Nature, Workstyle, Temperament and Followership. In team development, following individual   *317* feedback, the charts of team members can be displayed and comparisons made. Potential conflicts between team members can be identified and the combined strengths and preferences of the team discussed and addressed.

PAPI is currently being updated by PA and this is to be accompanied by more stringent requirements for competence in administration and interpretation.

The Team Management Index

For this process of identifying individual work preferences, participants complete a questionnaire (the Team Management Index) from which a personal computer-scored Team Management Profile of 4 000 words is derived. The process was developed by Dr Charles Margerison, formerly Professor of Management Development at the Cranfield School of Management and at the University of Queensland, and Dr Dick McCann, an international management development consultant.

The Team Management Index consists of 60 pairs of statements, and participants allocate points to indicate which is preferred in a work situation. It is quick to complete (10–15 minutes) and user-friendly. It has been used with over 400 000 managers in large organizations around the world and is well-researched and validated. It is also based on the work of Carl Jung and concentrates on four key issues in work situations: how people prefer to relate to others; how people prefer to gather and use information; how people prefer to make decisions; how people prefer to organize themselves and others.

The questionnaire translates this into scores against four scales: Introvert/Extrovert, Practical/Creative, Analytical/Beliefs and Structured/Flexible. As part of the personalized report, participants receive a Team Management Wheel which identifies their major and related role preferences. There are eight major roles: Explorer-Promoter, Assessor-Developer, Thruster-Organizer, Concluder-Producer, Controller-Inspector, Upholder-Maintainer, Reporter-Adviser and Creator-Innovator. These are arranged in four sectors (Explorers, Organizers, Controllers and Advisers).

Team Management Profiles are widely used as a vehicle for bringing team members together to discuss how they can work more effectively. This is usually achieved by a voluntary sharing of Profiles between team members so that each person begins to understand the work preferences of their colleagues. The team can discuss how the different styles can work together and what adjustments in behaviour may be required.

The authors of the Team Management System have written a book which covers detailed studies of the Index (Margerison and McCann, 1990).

The Learning Style Questionnaire

This questionnaire is based on the work of Peter Honey, a consultant Psychologist and Peter Mumford, past Professor of Management Development at

International Management Centres and a specialist in director development (Honey and Mumford, 1992). It consists of a questionnaire with 80 statements, which participants score according to whether they agree or disagree with the statement as it applies to them. Based on the original work of David Kolb on the learning cycle (Kolb, 1984), the questionnaire presents self-scored data on the participant's preferred learning style(s). There are four basic styles: Activist, Reflector, Theorist and Pragmatist. The questionnaire indicates the extent to which each style is preferred in learning situations.

The instrument is used both in the design of training events according to the results produced by potential trainees, and in team development where the role of the team may involve a high degree of learning or tackling new ground. This has proved particularly valuable in the start-up stage of self-managed learning groups. It is also especially helpful in supporting individual development and the establishment of personal learning contracts.

The INSIGHT Inventory

Dr Patrick Handley of the University of Missouri and Thomas Krieshok of the University of Kansas developed this self-report personality inventory. It is based on the work of three noted psychologists: Kurt Lewin (1890–1947), who was the originator of Field theory and proposed that behaviour is a product of the interaction of personality and environment (B=f(P, E); Gordon Allport (1897–1967), who used adjectives as test items for measuring personality traits; and Raymond Cattell (born 1905), who worked on factor analysis and originated the widely used 16PF (Personality Factor) inventory.

The INSIGHT Inventory questionnaire contains two sets of the same 32 descriptive adjectives. Participants rate themselves on a four-point scale on how well the adjectives describe them, both in their work style and in their personal style. It is important for participants to refer to the expanded item descriptions on the reverse of the form to ensure consistency when discussing their personal results in a team setting. They are encouraged to self-score the results and plot them in an interpretation booklet which describes the implications of the scores, and provides development input on style flexibility and stress management. The interpretation booklet is useful in preparing participants for team development events, as it allows a great deal of personal preparation, and saves time in explanation at the event.

The instrument provides a measurement in four key areas of behaviour:

Getting Your Way	(Indirect–Direct)
Responding to People	(Reserved–Outgoing)
Pacing Activity	(Urgent–Steady)
Dealing with Details	(Unstructured–Precise)

The scores are plotted on a profile chart so they can be compared and discussed with other team members on a voluntary basis.

The Inventory provides for discussion of differences in behaviour between work and home. This enriches and deepens the level of disclosure within the team, and allows for a discussion about the shifts in behaviour participants have to make to ensure they achieve balance in their life. In some cases this balance is not being achieved, and team members can share the frustrations this creates. They can also discuss the stress they experience in their working lives when applying themselves to less preferred situations or dealing with people with different preferences. Individuals and teams can use the data to improve working relationships, particularly within the team, and understand the sources of stress they experience.

The Belbin Team Roles Inventory

In its various formats this inventory allows participants to discover which team roles they tend to use in team situations. These are based on the long-term research by Meredith Belbin that started with his study of management teams working on development courses at Henley Management College (Belbin, 1981 and 1993). Belbin's nine team roles are: Plant, Resource investigator, Coordinator, Shaper, Monitor evaluator, Teamworker, Implementer, Completer and Specialist. These roles and their implications in organizations today are described in more detail in Chapter 10.

TEAM FEEDBACK PROCESSES

Successful teams regularly spend time reviewing their performance (even if only for a few minutes at the end of each meeting). In a mature team this should lead to actions for improvement for the team, rather than blaming other team members or the leader. Various forms of feedback have been developed to allow teams to monitor their performance, including the current trend towards upward and 360 degree feedback.

Upward or 360 degree feedback processes were virtually unknown in British organizations until the 1990s, apart from multi-nationals who had imported this process from their more enlightened US colleagues. IBM, who have a tradition of surveying employee opinion and attitudes on a regular basis, developed a method of providing focused feedback from direct reports to their manager about the effectiveness of their management activities. The company researched those competencies critical to the success of the IBM manager within the accepted culture of the organization. This was achieved internationally so that corporate norms could be established against which to measure national and functional variations.

The process that was adopted was known as MAP (Management Activities Profile), and allowed staff to give anonymous feedback to their manager (assuming a minimum number of respondents) in ten key areas of management activity (five people-related – Development, Motivation, Recognition,

Consideration and Communication, and five related to task performance – Decision Making, Planning, Organization and Control, Delegation and Work Facilitation). Managers were encouraged to discuss the feedback as part of a team development event. This meant that the feedback could be used to improve the performance of the team as well as the effectiveness of the manager. This served to spread the responsibility for improvement and avoid scapegoating the manager. The events were facilitated by an internal consultant to ensure the consistency of approach and sensitivity in handling difficult feedback situations.

The upward feedback process was accepted by an increasing number of UK companies, usually with an extremely high level of facilitation. This fostered the development of numerous generic formats commercially available to organizations to provide upward and team feedback. These are advertised in professional HR journals and take advantage of advanced technology now more widely available to organizations with distributed PC networks. Some organizations that have adopted the competency approach to management development, have developed their company-specific set of competencies, and use these as a format for upward and peer feedback. The concept of peer feedback, or 'collegiate review', has grown to the extent that it now forms an essential part of individual development plans and team development events.

Of the generic feedback mechanisms available, the INSIGHT inventory described in the previous section offers the possibility of providing standardized 360 degree feedback to team members as part of their team development. The INSIGHT Style Feedback Set can be completed by the participant's manager, peers and direct reports, and the data synthesized to compare with the participant's own self-perception. This provides a high level of data to a management team addressing its performance as perceived from many directions.

Ever since the early days of the Organization Development movement in the 1960s, team effectiveness questionnaires have been developed and published, for example in Edgar Schein's seminal work on process consultation (Schein, 1988). They are widely available through publishers such as Pfeiffer and Management Learning Resources Limited, and versions are published in numerous books on team development and team building (for example, Moxon, 1993 and Harshman and Phillips, 1995). These usually relate to the traditional criteria for measuring the effectiveness of teams, for example, goal orientation, involvement and participation, openness in expression of feelings, decision making, trust between members, leadership, problem solving, handling of conflict and communication. These can be handled anonymously by a facilitator or expressed openly, depending on the stage of development of the team.

A highly creative approach to team feedback has been developed in the form of a board game named Team Talk®. Team participants play with dice and counters to move around a board and land on squares that prompt them to specific actions. They may be asked to express an opinion about *321* their experience of the team, to give feedback to other members of the team, to give a two-minute presentation or run a brief brainstorming exercise about some aspect of the team's work. Several versions of the game are available, which take account of new and established teams and sales teams. Activities can also be customized to fit company or functional cultures.

The objectives of Team Talk are to: review past success and difficulties for the team; consolidate elements of successful teamworking; consider what team members want from each other; uncover obstacles to effective teamworking; and provide feedback to each other. The game can be used on its own (it takes about two to three hours) or as part of a longer team development event. At the end of the game participants review the activity and agree the allocation of improvement tasks and activities collected on a flip chart. As the process is largely driven by the words on the cards, the level of facilitation needed for most teams in normal circumstances is not high, and experienced teams should be able to run it for themselves.

SUMMARY

Few organizations have the flexibility to create totally new organizational teams, so the emphasis is on making existing teams work better.

There is an increased use of teamworking in organizations, especially across functional barriers, to ensure harmonious working. Project teams are increasingly being used to ensure organizations can respond quickly to changing business circumstances and represent all functional views. Project status allows more scope for creating balanced teams paying attention to team roles and preferences.

A variety of psychological tests is available to help organizations understand how people will interact in teams. A number are described, and the point is made that most require in-depth training to interpret. There are also professional and ethical conventions surrounding their use.

There is a trend towards more open feedback in organizations to colleagues and management about their use of skills. These techniques can be used to give feedback in teams, as well as generic or customized questionnaires and team exercises.

REFERENCES

Belbin, R.M., *Management Teams: Why they Succeed or Fail*, Heinemann, 1981
Belbin, R.M., *Team Roles at Work*, Butterworth-Heinemann, Oxford, 1993
Handy, C., *The Age of Unreason*, Hutchinson, 1989
Harshman, C. and Phillips, S., *Team Training: From Startup to High Performance*, McGraw-Hill, New York, 1995
Herriot, P. and Pemberton, C., *New Deals: The Revolution in Managerial Careers*, Wiley, Chichester, 1995
Hirsh, S.K., *Using the Myers-Briggs Type Indicator in Organisations*, Consulting Psychologists Press, Palo Alto, CA, 1991

Honey, P. and Mumford, A., *The Manual of Learning Styles*, 3rd edn., Honey, Maidenhead, 1992

Institute of Personnel and Development, *The IPD Guide on Psychological Testing*, IPD, London, 1997

Kolb, D., *Experiential Learning*, Prentice Hall, Englewood Cliffs, NJ, 1984

Margerison, C. and McCann, D., *Team Management: Practical New Approaches*, Management Books 2000 Ltd, Chalford, 1995

Moxon, P., *Building a Better Team: A Handbook for Managers and Facilitators*, Gower, Aldershot, 1993

Myers, I. Briggs with Myers, P.M., *Gifts Differing*, Consulting Psychologists Press, Palo Alto, CA, 1980

Rackham, N., Honey, P., and Colbert, M., *Developing Interactive Skills*, Wellens, Northampton, 1971

Schein, E.H., *Process Consultation, Volume 1*, Addison-Wesley, Massachusetts, 1988

RECOMMENDED READING

Adair, J., *Effective Teambuilding*, Gower, Aldershot, 1986

Herriot, P. and Pemberton, C., 'A New Deal for Middle Managers', *People Management*, June 1995

Hirsh, S. and Kummerow, J., *Life Types*, Warner Books, New York, 1989

Isachsen, O. and Berens, L.V. *Working Together: A Personality Centered Approach to Management*, New World Management Press, Coronado, CA, 1988

Jones, S., *Psychological Testing for Managers*, Piaktus, London, 1993

Myers, I. Briggs, and McCaulley, M.H., Manual: *A Guide to the Development and Use of the Myers-Briggs Type Indicator®*, Consulting Psychologists Press, Palo Alto, CA, 1989

Board game Team Talk®, TMS Development International Ltd, York, YO24 4FL

21 Managing teams assertively

Terry Gillen

Team leaders learn about assertiveness for a variety of reasons. Some have been promoted and find that their confidence has not kept pace with their new responsibilities; some have problems with specific people or situations; some want to improve their interpersonal skills; some find that the traditional command and control approach to management does not help them in situations where they have no authority over the people with whom they have to achieve results; and some, having heard of assertiveness, are inquisitive to see if there is anything in it that will help their further development. Whatever their starting point, assertiveness will help a wide range of people manage better, and the need for an assertive style of management was never greater than now as we learn to cope with, and capitalize on, the huge changes we have experienced at work in the past decade.

What will you learn from this chapter and how is it organized? I am a great believer in the benefit of context when learning anything, so the first topic we are going to discuss is what is happening in the world of work and what that means for us as managers and team leaders. Next, we will deal with the relevance of assertiveness to leading a team in contemporary organizations. This will be an important part of the chapter because in it we will have to compare assertiveness with aggressive and passive styles of behaviour. That way you will understand how the three styles of behaviour differ and what those differences mean to your team. We will also discuss what, for many of us, are two fundamental questions: 'What makes us behave the way we do?' and 'What can I do to change my behaviour?' Next, to help you relate this information to your own situations, we will examine some of the typical problems that team leaders encounter and show you how to handle them assertively. But first that all-important context.

THE CHANGING WORLD OF WORK

In the not too distant past, the most important wealth producers were manufacturing companies who competed on cost, and who strove to become as big as possible so as to capitalize on economies of scale. These organizations needed multi-layered management to command and control the workforce.

These days, however, the large wealth producers include many service companies which compete on the skill, knowledge and responsiveness of their staff. This approach to competition has permeated a substantial number of manufacturing organizations, where tasks have become much more cerebral than they used to be, and even affect public sector services to give us organizations characterized by an increased importance of people at every level. Quite simply, in the past we needed people who were good with their hands and who were happy to do as they were told. Now we need people who are good with their brains and who can use their initiative to implement corporate policies and achieve what we want.

How has this affected management? In the past we needed managers who, as well as understanding the technicalities of their tasks, were good at directing and controlling their staff. Now we need team leaders who, as well as understanding the technicalities of their tasks, can facilitate *synergy* by providing *leadership*. These two words are so important as to warrant explanation.

SYNERGY AND LEADERSHIP

Most leadership takes place in teams. A team is a group of people working in an interdependent manner to achieve a commonly understood goal. The most effective teams have synergy. Synergy means that the team members interact in such a way that they achieve more than they could possibly achieve individually. In the same way that lead plates and hydrochloric acid interact to produce electricity, the people in a team interact to achieve results that would be impossible on their own. Turning a group of people into a synergistic team requires good leadership.

Leadership is the process of motivating people to achieve a goal and directing their efforts so that they achieve it. It translates into practice in a variety of ways. If the team members are already motivated, all the leader has to do is point them in the right direction and monitor their performance so that he or she can offer help when needed. If the team members are not motivated, the leader will have to use closer monitoring, more frequent interventions and more directive behaviours to get the task done.

In modern organizations, team leaders face more ambiguity than they used to face. Many of them feel that if they empower their staff too much, they run the risk of losing control. Yet if they control their staff too closely, they run the risk of stifling initiative and eroding motivation. Furthermore, they may increasingly find themselves leading a team of specialists *325* over which they have no direct authority, but through whom they have to achieve results. Therefore, modern organizations need team leaders who can work within this ambiguity and who know when to be tolerant, when to stand their ground and who are skilled at managing situations involving confrontation. To appreciate how assertiveness will help you to understand and manage this ambiguity, you need to know how assertiveness differs from aggressive and passive behaviours.

THE THREE STYLES OF BEHAVIOUR

Aggressive behaviour

When people behave aggressively, they are keen to win an interaction, often at someone else's expense, even in situations where a win/lose outcome is inappropriate. They do so by body language and actions characterized by excessive eye contact, a loud, obtrusive voice, by intimidating gestures such as finger wagging, by invading the other person's space and by tactics such as personal criticism, sarcasm, not listening, bullying, and so on. At one extreme, aggressive behaviour is simple to recognize. At the other extreme, it can be very subtle, seen in, for example, a belittling phrase, a 'put-down', disguised as humour or just persistent interruption.

Passive behaviour

Passive behaviour is the opposite of aggressive behaviour. When people behave passively, they are keen to avoid confrontation even if that disadvantages them in some way. They do so by body language and actions characterized by avoiding eye contact, by speaking quietly and hesitatingly, by beating about the bush to avoid getting to the point, by 'protecting' themselves with their hands and by excessive fidgeting. They are also quick to blame themselves, to ask permission for even little things and to seek sympathy. At one extreme, it is characterized by extreme shyness, while at the other it is characterized by a reluctance to state one's own preferences or to ask for something, and a tendency to beat about the bush and drop hints instead of speaking plainly.

Assertive behaviour

Assertive behaviour is not a compromise between the two extremes of aggressive and passive behaviour; it is a third style of behaviour. When people behave assertively they are standing up for their own rights, while (and this is an important point) recognizing that other people have rights that they want to uphold. This means that they combine the ability to be very resilient with the tendency to be very tolerant. Assertive behaviour is characterized by enough eye contact to show confidence, a moderate, neutral tone of voice and body language which is congruent with the words that are being spoken. You will also notice getting straight to the point and being prepared to stand one's ground on certain issues, combined with a great deal of listening and probing to understand other people, demonstration of respect for others and a willingness to reach a workable compromise that is satisfactory to everyone.

How do these styles of behaviour manifest themselves in practice? Here are three examples. In each case, a team leader has delegated a report to a member of staff with the clear and accepted request that it should be ready at 4 p.m. It is now 4.15 p.m. and the report has not appeared.

The *aggressive* team leader might approach the member of staff with excessive eye contact, lean over their desk invading their space and say, 'So where's that **!!** report? I suppose you'll try and tell me that you've been too busy. Well one or two of us around here have to stick to deadlines so where the **!!** is it?'

The *passive* team leader might approach the member of staff and, fidgeting excessively while avoiding eye contact, say, 'Hello. That . . . er . . . little report I mentioned this morning . . . I know you're very busy but I was just . . . er . . . wondering if you . . . er . . . have had a chance to look at it yet. I sort of promised the boss that it would be ready tonight. If that's all right.'

The *assertive* team leader might approach the member of staff calmly and with good eye contact and a neutral tone of voice ask, 'John, we agreed that report would be ready by four o'clock and it's now four fifteen. I need it quickly. Is there a problem?'

The aggressive team leader has ignored the staff member's right to be treated with respect and the possibility that there might have been a problem outside the staff member's control. The effect of the conversation will be to cause resentment or even fear in the staff member's mind and to have a detrimental effect on their relationship. The passive team leader has ignored their own right to delegate work to their staff and to have deadlines adhered to. The effect of the conversation will be to undermine the manager's authority and the staff member's respect for the manager, and to reduce the likelihood of future deadlines being met. The assertive team leader has recognized their own right to have agreements honoured and the staff member's right to be treated with respect. The effect of the conversation will be to clarify the reason for the delay and reinforce the relationship.

The three behaviour styles are summarized in Table 21.1. As you read it, you may like to tick off the behaviours you recognize in yourself.

To clarify your understanding of the three behaviours further, it is worth understanding their advantages and disadvantages.

With *aggressive* behaviour, you tend to get what you want in the short term. It is a hollow victory, however. You tend to lose in the long term because other people learn to avoid you, to resent you and even to retaliate against you. It can be acceptable in a crisis where people need to obey without hesitation but in every other situation its results are counterproductive.

Table 21.1
The three behaviour styles

Behaviour	Recognized by	Advantages/ Disadvantages
Aggressive Keen to win, even at others' expense; more concerned with own needs than with needs of others	Excessive eye contact; loud obtrusive voice; blunt; intimidating gestures; personal criticism; sarcasm; bullying; not listening	Short-term victory; long-term loss; causes resentment; stifles initiative
Passive Keen to avoid confrontation even at own expense; more concerned with others' needs than with own	Avoidance of eye contact; quiet, hesitant voice; protective gestures; beating about the bush; self-blame; seeking permission for everything; sympathy seeking; reluctance to state own preferences	Avoids confrontation; diminished self-respect; diminished respect from others
Assertive Keen to stand up for own rights while accepting that others have rights too	Good, comfortable eye contact; tone of voice and body language congruent with words; open; honest; prepared to stand ground; listens; respect for others	No disadvantages; the kind of behaviour/ characteristics we like to see in other people; respect for oneself and from other people

With *passive* behaviour, you avoid confrontation but at a great and damaging cost. People lose respect for you and you lose respect for yourself, people ignore your views and your effectiveness is diminished. It can be acceptable in situations where the outcome is unimportant but in every other situation it is counterproductive.

With *assertive* behaviour, you achieve a great deal. Because you have treated your colleagues with respect, they tend to respect you. They are open and honest with you, making it easier for you to suggest satisfactory solutions to problems. Your effectiveness increases and, with it, your own self-esteem improves. While you may choose not to assert yourself if the timing is wrong or emotions are running high, it is a style of behaviour that is appreciated in almost every situation.

This last point is worth emphasizing. On assertiveness courses, I have asked delegates to list the characteristics they have appreciated in their favourite boss. We have then compared that list against a list of assertive behaviours. They are usually identical. It seems that we like our team leaders to be assertive because we appreciate the way they show their respect for us, listen to us, suggest compromises, yet are prepared to be straight with us and to take decisions or insist on actions that we would shy away from. Assertive behaviour makes it easier for team leaders to lead well and to stimulate synergy. All of which has maybe started you thinking, 'What do I have to do to be more assertive?' To answer that question, you need to understand what underlies assertive behaviour.

What underlies assertive behaviour

Our behaviour in conflicts tends to be a product of two things: our dominant feelings and what we believe we are entitled to.

Dominant feelings

Most of us like to think that we use our behaviour to help us achieve what we want. In reality, in situations of potential conflict, our behaviour is more likely to be geared up to our dominant feelings. This increases the likelihood that we will behave aggressively or passively and get the outcome we do not want. Let us go back to the example of the late report.

One team leader might have feelings of resentment towards the member of staff because all he or she can visualize are the problems that the late report will cause. These emotions make it easier for the team leader to behave aggressively. A second team leader might have feelings of insecurity at the prospect of confronting the staff member about the overdue report. That feeling causes the team leader, when 'confronting' the member of staff, to minimize the problem and to beat about the bush to defer, even if only by a few seconds, the moment of confrontation. A third team leader might have more control over their own emotions. They might know that negative thoughts lead to negative behaviour which leads to negative results, and so holds the thoughts in check long enough to confront the member of staff rationally and directly.

You can apply this concept to yourself by thinking of situations where you feel your behaviour was aggressive or passive, and where assertive behaviour would have enabled you to achieve more. Ask yourself what your thinking might have been. Was it positive or negative? How would you change it to increase the chances of your behaving assertively?

This concept poses another question. What can you do about it if your thoughts tend to lead more readily to aggressive or passive behaviour rather than to assertive behaviour? The answer lies in the concept of rights.

Rights

A right is something to which you are entitled. You need do nothing to earn it. It is yours by right. The concept of rights is relevant to assertive behaviour because of the relationship between our rights and our feelings. And here I need to make it plain that I am not talking about your legal rights, or your rights according to company policy, but the rights your emotional make-up assumes are yours. Some people will assume they have a right:

- To be treated with respect
- To state how they feel
- To ask for what they want
- To express their opinion
- To be listened to
- To make the same mistakes as every other human being
- To put themselves first on occasions
- To stand up for themselves, and so on

Where you assume that you have many rights but the other person does not, your feelings tend to lead to aggressive behaviour. Where you assume that you have no rights but the other person has many, your feelings tend to lead to passive behaviour. Where you assume that both you and the other person have rights, your feelings tend to lead to assertive behaviour. Table 21.2 shows how rights lead to thoughts and then to behaviour in the example about the overdue report.

The way rights, emotions and behaviour interact can be summarized in Figure 21.1.

You might want to ask yourself the following questions to see which part of your assertive model needs attention – your rights, your thoughts or your behaviour.

- Do you feel that it is 'not your place' to take the kind of action that other team leaders might take? (*If so, think through your rights.*)
- Do you feel 'powerless' to address issues that other team leaders seem comfortable addressing? (*If so, think through your rights.*)
- Do you find that you easily visualize situations going wrong? (*If so, think through your thoughts.*)
- Do you find yourself saying negative things to yourself, such as 'That will be too difficult for me' (*If so, think through your thoughts.*)
- Do you feel quite positive but find that it all goes wrong as you begin interacting with someone else? (*If so, think through your behaviour.*)
- Do you find that some people trigger off aggressive or passive behaviour in you? (*If so, think through your behaviour.*)

By now you will have a good understanding of the differences between the three behaviour styles, and which style you tend towards in confrontational situations. You will also be aware of the disadvantages of aggressive and passive styles and of the advantages of an assertive style. To help you further, you need to know how to use the main *assertive techniques*.

Table 21.2
Rights, thoughts and behaviour

Rights	Thoughts	Behaviour
Team leader – to be obeyed *Team member* – none	When people do not do as I tell them, they are at fault	Aggressive
Team leader – none *Team member* – to make mistakes, to misunderstand, to have difficulty handling work volume	I probably didn't make myself clearly understood; if I chase the report now they'll think I'm being too pushy; I feel uncomfortable having to ask for the report	Passive
Team leader – to delegate work, to have deadlines met, to be told in advance if there is a problem, to be treated with respect *Team member* – to discuss deadlines, to admit to work problems, to be treated with respect	I expect team members to tell me if there is a problem so, as the report has not been brought to me at the agreed time, I had better find out if there is a problem	Assertive

Assertive techniques

In this section, I am going to describe the main assertive techniques and show how they combine naturally to give you an assertive style.

Techniques to help you stay in control of your feelings

Too often we allow our feelings to dictate our behaviour, rather than using our behaviour as a tool to reach the outcome we want. It follows, therefore, that the more we can stay in control of our feelings, the easier it will be to behave assertively. Here are two techniques to help you.

Acknowledging is a response from you which lets the other person know that you have heard what they said without it affecting your emotions. All you do is acknowledge what they have said. If they were attempting to be sarcastic, your acknowledgement can be rather blunt. That signals to them that, if they want to influence you, sarcasm will not help them very much, so they might as well be assertive with you. If they were attempting to communicate with you genuinely but lack the emotional control to do so, your acknowledgement will help them communicate assertively. Here are some examples:

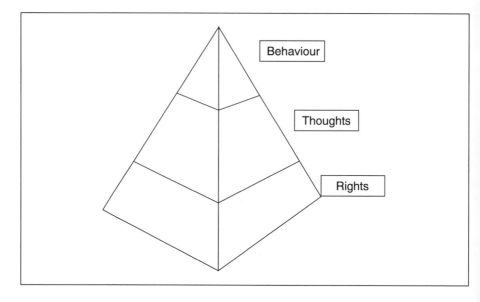

Figure 21.1 The assertiveness pyramid

Attempted sarcasm	**Your acknowledgement**
I suppose this is another marvellous idea of yours.	I suppose it is.
That's just typical of people from your department.	It can seem that way.

Attempted communication	**Your acknowledgement**
I'm fed up with the way you're always asking me to do this rotten job. It's not fair.	You feel I ask you to do this job too often.
Is this it? Is that all your team can manage despite your best efforts?	You expected more than we produced.

Notice how, in the last two examples, you would have encouraged the other person to continue the dialogue. They might still be emotional as they speak, but at least now the content of what they say will be factual. It will not be long before the conversation will be assertive.

Probing is a response from you in which you ask a question about what the other person has just said. It prevents you from becoming emotionally involved and, if they were trying to be sarcastic, they quickly learn that sarcasm does not work with you. If they were trying to communicate but could only do so emotionally, again, you help them behave assertively. Here are some examples:

Attempted sarcasm	**Your probe**
I suppose this is another marvellous idea of yours.	In what way do you feel it's marvellous?
That's just typical of people from your department.	Really? In what way?

Attempted communication	**Your probe**
I'm fed up with the way you're always asking me to do this rotten job. It's not fair.	What is it about this job that you dislike?
Is this it? Is that all your team can manage despite your best efforts?	How does it compare with what other teams have produced?

Techniques that help you stand your ground

If, by nature, you tend towards passive behaviour, these techniques help you stand your ground. They are also useful for people who tend towards aggressive behaviour because they help those people stay assertive.

The three-part sentence, as the name suggests, is a sentence in three parts. You use the three parts to show that you have first, heard what the other person has said, second, to communicate how you feel and, finally, to state what you want. For example:

Is this it? Is that all your team can manage despite your best efforts?

I appreciate you'd have liked better results, however I feel that that as they are new to the task they worked well, so I'd like you to accept the figures this time.

The three-part sentence enables you to show empathy, which is important because people listen to us more readily if they feel we have first listened to them. It also makes your case stronger because people find it difficult to disagree with your feelings in the same way that they might disagree with facts or opinions. Finally, it paves the way for what you want to say which, if said on its own, may appear too one-sided.

The broken record is a statement that you keep repeating and repeating. It enables you to stand your ground in the face of bullying, manipulation and sympathy seeking and, as such, it is of most use to people whose behaviour can be too passive, causing them to give up too soon. It can, however, also be of use to people whose behaviour can be too aggressive, because it helps them stay assertive. Here is an example:

Is this it? Is that all your team can manage despite your best efforts?
They're new to the task so I'd like you to accept the figures this time.
But how can I when they're worse than every other team's?
Because they're new to the task I'd like you to accept the figures this time.
I'm just not sure.

I know it may not be easy but I'd like you to accept the figures this time.

I don't want this to become a precedent.

I'm sure it won't because it's only now that they're new to the task. That's why I'd like you to accept the figures this time.

Techniques to help you confront an issue

These techniques help you initiate a conversation and, as such, they are more useful when you have to confront an issue with another person.

Pointing out a discrepancy means that you compare two things, such as what was agreed to what actually happened, or what has happened to what usually happens, and ask the other person for an explanation. It makes it easy for you to raise an issue without being judgemental or appearing as if you are making an accusation – as long as you keep your body language and tone of voice neutral. For example:

> We agreed that this report would be ready by four o'clock and it's now four thirty. Why isn't it ready?

or

> Your timekeeping is normally fine, but this last week you've been arriving up to half an hour late. Why is that?

Pointing out a consequence means that you inform the other person of what will happen if the situation persists. It is almost a threat. The difference is that there is no malice in your voice, the responsibility for avoiding the consequence rests with the other person and the consequences will follow naturally for anyone in their position. Here is an example:

> We've spoken twice now about your coming in late and your punctuality hasn't improved. If it isn't back to normal by the end of the week I'll have to begin the formal disciplinary procedure.

or

> I understand your department would prefer not to have new procedures. However, this is a matter of company policy so if you won't agree then I'll have to see your boss instead.

Combining the techniques

Here is an example of how these techniques string together to form a natural conversation. A member of your staff wants to take some leave when other members of staff have cancelled their leave to cope with an unprecedented workload. The assertive technique appears in brackets alongside.

334   Boss, I was wondering if I could take next week off.

Other people in the team have cancelled their leave to cope with the current workload. Why do you want to take your leave now? (*Pointing out a discrepancy*)

A mate of mine has invited me to go rock climbing and I haven't been for a long time so I'd like to go.

Why next week? (*Probing*)

That's just when it's suits him to take time off.

John, I understand how much you'd like to go. However, I would feel very awkward granting your leave when I've asked other members of the team to cancel theirs so I'm going to say no. (*Three-part sentence*)

That's not fair. I haven't taken any leave yet this year.

That's true, you haven't. However, I still can't approve this request. (*Acknowledging* and *Broken Record*)

This really puts me in a spot. I've already promised him I'd be able to go.

I know it isn't easy having to break a promise. However, I still can't approve this request. (*Acknowledging* and *Broken Record*)

I could just go sick, you know. Then you'd have to manage without me.

We would have to manage if you were sick. However, after what you've told me, if you were absent next week I'd have to phone you at home, and if you weren't there I'd have to get you examined by the company doctor on your return. (*Acknowledging* and *Pointing out a Consequence*)

It's not fair.

I know it may seem that way and if I could let you take next week off I would. Perhaps I can be more flexible in a couple of weeks. However, with the current workload I can't. (*Acknowledging* and *Broken Record*)

Problem situations and how to handle them assertively

Understanding assertiveness, and how assertive behaviour differs from the two other styles of behaviour is undoubtedly useful. To help you be assertive in practice, however, you may need some detailed guidance. Here are four typical confrontational situations in which team leaders can find themselves, with suggestions on how to handle them. For each one, we will examine the situation, describe what can go wrong in it and give you an assertive dialogue you can use as an example.

Handling resentment

Several factors can combine to cause resentment against team leaders. First, team leaders are often promoted from within the team, which can mean, as far as staff are concerned, they are no longer 'one of us'. Second, younger people with energy and ideas can be promoted more quickly than people who have been there longer, causing bad feeling. Third, team leaders are often the ones who have to ask the team members to do unpleasant things, such as work late, accept tough targets or agree new practices imposed from above.

Team leaders can make two mistakes. They can attempt to assert their authority by being autocratic, they can misinterpret differences of opinion as insubordination, and they can be deliberately critical in their comments on performance. They come across as aggressive. Alternatively, perhaps *335* through fear of losing the support of the team members on whom they rely, they can be far too easy going, accepting performance and behaviour far below standard, or even apologizing for having been promoted, or putting their promotion down to luck – none of which reassures the team members as to the team leader's ability. Both these aggressive and passive approaches harm the team leader's credibility. Here is an example of an assertive dialogue between a new team leader and a resentful team member. They have just finished a discussion about targets and are seated in a private meeting room.

> Bill, now that we've finished the discussion about targets there's another matter I want to raise.
>
> Yes, what's that?
>
> I've been team leader now for just over a month and in that time I've had the feeling that you're not happy with my appointment. Is that so?
>
> Who told you that?
>
> No one has needed to tell me. I've just listened to the comments you've made about me and observed your general manner towards me. Do we have a problem?
>
> Not as far as I'm concerned we don't.
>
> Good, because we have some targets to achieve and that means we need to function well together, so if there was a problem I'd need to know.
>
> Well, I had thought I might have got the job. After all, I have been here seven years to your two.
>
> Sometimes they look at length of service when they make these appointments. However, the appointment has been made and we need to ensure that we can work well together.
>
> Well, we'll just have to see, won't we?
>
> I'm sure our working relationship will develop as we get to know each other and I want you to know that I value your experience. However, I place a high priority on team relations so, from now on, if you have a problem with anything I do, I'd like you to see me about it rather than make negative remarks to other team members. Can I have your commitment to that please?
>
> Yes, OK.

Dealing with a performance or behaviour problem

When faced with a performance or a behaviour problem it is very easy for an aggressive team leader to see it as the start of more serious matters and deal with it heavy-handedly without considering the cause. Aggressive team leaders add to the problem by supplementing their comments with personal criticism and liberal amounts of sarcasm. All this does is leave the offending team member with strong feelings of resentment at the unfair way they have just been treated. Passive team leaders, on the other hand, go to the opposite extreme. They convince themselves that there is not really a problem to address, that the problem will right itself, or that to highlight it would only make matters worse.

Please convince yourself of one thing. Performance and behaviour problems *are* the thin end of a wedge because they indicate a lower standard for other team members to follow. They need to be dealt with. Here is an

336

example where a team leader is talking to a team member in private about a performance problem.

John, I've asked you to come in to talk about performance standards. I've been looking at the figures and for the third month in succession your figures are lower than everyone else's. Were you aware of that?

Well, I knew they were a bit lower than other people's.

They started out at ten per cent lower then everyone else's, and last month they were 25 per cent lower. Your performance used to be consistently within the acceptable range. Now it isn't. Why is that?

I don't know.

Let me check a few things. Are you aware of what you are supposed to be achieving?

Yes.

And has anything changed in the last three months to cause your performance to change, or is the job substantially the same?

More or less the same.

Is there anything outside work which is causing difficulties for your performance in work?

No, everything's fine. It's just that ... well ... I'm getting bored with the job. I see some of the people I joined with getting promoted and I'm still doing the same job, and I think I'll still be doing it in ten years time. It makes me fed up.

Let me make sure I understand you. You've always been able to perform well in this job, and nothing has changed to affect your performance. It is just that you now feel frustrated when you see your contemporaries being promoted and you see yourself doing the same job. That frustration has affected your performance.

Yes, that's it.

OK, it seems to me that there are two issues here. How you feel about your job and your performance in it. The first we can look at in more detail later, the second we need to deal with immediately because to change your job in some way, or to transfer you into another job, can only happen when your performance in this job is back up to former standards.

Can't we look at a transfer now?

I understand you feel frustrated in your current job, however, I feel that moving you from your present job because your performance has deteriorated would look bad on your record. I'd prefer you to work at your performance until it's back to where it was before we look at transfers.

How long for?

Three months.

Three months? That's a long time.

I understand it may seem like a long time now. However, I need reassurance that your performance is back up to its former standards before I can consider a transfer.

OK.

So that I can help you we'll have weekly reviews for the first month. Do I have your commitment?

Yes, all right.

Delegating an unpleasant task

Anybody can delegate a pleasant task. It makes us feel good. Delegating an unpleasant task is quite another matter. How you do it says a lot about you. Team leaders who see themselves as 'top dog' delegate in one way, while team leaders who feel a need to 'buy' the goodwill of their staff delegate in another. Aggressive team leaders delegate the task abruptly, leaving the team member feeling unhappy with the way they have just been treated. Passive team leaders either do the task themselves (and doing so persistently may not be the best way of establishing credibility) or delegate it in an ingratiating and apologetic way, minimizing the size or unpleasantness of the task, which serves to make the team member resent the team leader. How might a team leader assertively delegate an unpleasant task? Here is an example:

> Sally, thanks for coming in.
> That's OK. What can I do for you?
> I want you to handle this month's statistical analysis for the Board.
> But that's John's job.
> Normally it is. However, John's on a course next week and I want him to finish all outstanding jobs before he goes and, as you are familiar with this analysis from before you were promoted, I want you to do it this month.
> I already have enough on my plate. I'll never be able to do it by Friday.
> You are very busy and I know this analysis will involve some extra hours. However, I'd still like you to do it by Friday.
> But it's so boring.
> I feel the same myself when boring jobs come along – which they do from time to time. Will you do it by Friday please?
> Yes, it'll be ready by Friday.
> Thanks. I want you to know that I appreciate it.

Telling the team about tough targets

Tough targets seem to be a fact of life these days. As organizations have 'downsized' and the workload spread among fewer people, we have more to do. As budgets become tighter and competition more intense, demands for increased productivity are on the increase.

I have noticed several styles used by team leaders to tell their teams about tough targets. Some adopt an aggressive approach, stamp on those who raise doubts or who highlight problems and tell their staff to get on with it come what may. Team members resent this approach. Some adopt a 'cheer leader' approach, presumably thinking that the more they talk up the capacity of their team to cope, the more likely they are to accept the targets enthusiastically. Team members see through this approach. Some team leaders adopt an apologetic approach, seeking to minimize the size of the targets, to allocate the blame for them elsewhere or to wallow in communal pity at the impossibility of the task. Team members hate this approach.

When telling your team about tough targets it is vital that you treat them with respect as intelligent human beings. They know the targets are tough. There is no point in pretending otherwise. They are likely to react negatively to begin with. That is where you have to persevere and not see their reaction as adversarial. They are looking to you for leadership. Here is an example:

> All right, everyone, I promised that as soon as I had our fourth quarter targets I'd share them with you. They were given to me at this morning's meeting and I now want to pass them on to you. Does anybody want to say anything first? . . . No? . . . OK, here they are.
> Good grief/Phew/They're crazy/We'll never achieve those figures.
> Does anybody want to say anything specific?
> Boss, they're the toughest figures we've ever had. We'll never do it.
> They are tough figures and it'll be hard work but they are our fourth quarter targets, so that's what we have to work to.
> But it's crazy. Didn't you tell them that they're too tough?
> I pointed out that with current headcount and budget restrictions I considered the figures too optimistic. However, the Board wasn't going to change them, so these are our new targets.
> I don't think we'll do it.
> It's possible we won't, but we'll aim to be as close to them as we can so I'd like to suggest that we discuss how we tackle them. Let's start by examining what we have left over from last month.'

CONCLUSION

Whatever your reasons are for learning about assertiveness, you can be sure that this fits perfectly with what we know about effectiveness in team leaders. It gives you the skills with which to be firm when you need to, and the attitudes to be tolerant when that is more appropriate. By definition, the more assertive you are, the less aggressive or passive you will be. Hence you will be displaying the characteristics we value in team leaders. And if people value them in other team leaders, your team members will value them in you.

Remember that our behaviour is preceded by our feelings and they, in turn, reflect what we believe our rights to be. Therefore, to fine-tune your assertive skills, you may want to look carefully at how you think about yourself and other people in the kinds of team situations in which you want to improve your performance.

RECOMMENDED READING

Gillen, T., *Assertiveness for Managers*, Gower, Aldershot, 1992
Gillen, T., *Assertiveness*, IPD, London, 1997
Gillen, T., *Positive Influencing Skills*, IPD, London, 1995
Honey, P., *Problem People and How to Manage Them*, IPD, London, 1992
Knight, S., *NLP at Work*, Nicholas Brealey, London, 1995

22 Solving problems face-to-face

Quentin de la Bedoyere

At successive progress meetings Cassandra's project team manager became concerned at her tendency to miss deadlines. The draft texts she was preparing never seemed to be completed to timetable; there was always some good reason – waiting for information, usually – but he suspected there was more to it than that. It wasn't as yet a big problem because of the slippage time allowed, but it could become one. Moreover there was a danger that her lateness would begin to affect the others, slackening the prompt tone of the whole group.

Was it because she lacked commitment to the project? Perhaps she had difficulties at home? Maybe her normal line boss was putting pressure on her? Perhaps she was finding some aspect of the work particularly difficult? He didn't know. All he did know was that there was a problem that needed to be solved.

The sensitive team leader will usually become conscious of the underperformance of individuals at quite an early stage. He may choose to overlook this for a period, hoping – as often happens – that it will correct itself. Occasionally he will try to tap the influence or the information of a third party to rectify matters. But he may be reluctant to confront the poor performer and deal with the difficulty face-to-face. Past experience may have taught him that direct action leads to trouble, and the last state is worse than the first. Besides, what exactly is he going to say?

Even if Cassandra initiates the meeting because she has recognized her poor performance, he knows that the rest of the discussion will not be easy to handle. He is good at coping with difficulties himself, that's why he's team leader, but he has never found it easy to communicate his neat solutions so that others can employ them effectively.

He is not alone. Even among the professions who are directly concerned with problem solving – the clergy, the social worker, the doctor – problem solving skills are not high. Most of us find it difficult to be genuinely helpful to people, much as we should like to be. Prominent among the reasons for this failure is the lack of a good methodology! In other words we are not trained in the necessary stages and methods we need to use in order to be effective in helping people to solve their problems.

For such a methodology to be of practical use it must satisfy certain conditions:

- It must be a natural and logical way to proceed from the discovery of the problem to its solution
- It must readily adapt to minor or more serious problems of varying types
- It must deal with the emotional as well as the practical elements of the problem
- It must respect the individual and build on the ability and willingness of the presenter to take responsibility for the problem, and to internalize the solution.

The first two conditions are practical requirements from the leader's point of view. First, no one is likely to make use of a methodology which does not appear to correspond with common sense; moreover, in the stress of problem solving a logical progression keeps both parties naturally on track. Second, it is valuable to have a methodology which has become habitual because it has been used effectively in many different circumstances.

The next two conditions need a little more discussion. Occasionally one encounters problems which arise from purely practical causes. An individual who is lacking specific skills or required knowledge will have difficulties which can be tackled by equally practical means. But, as Cassandra's manager suspected, most problems have a deeper, and often emotional, content. For example, do we assume that someone who has unusual difficulty in passing a driving test suffers merely from unpractised hand and eye coordination or lack of knowledge, or do we suspect that emotional elements – perhaps relating to nervousness – are playing a part? So good problem solving must take into account the emotional factors involved.

Since some degree of emotional change is likely to be an important factor it follows, first, that solutions are not easy to find; each solution is unique (although it may share common elements) in the sense that it works for that individual alone. It is not *the* solution but *that individual's* solution. It follows that the methodology must be directed towards assisting the presenter to find a personal solution – with the added advantage that the sense of ownership will be a strong motivation to continued success. To illustrate this in another context, people often wish to become marriage counsellors because their experiences, bad or good, indicate to them that they know the answers. The first lesson they have to learn is that the answers are not transferable, and that their urge to impart information is an obstacle to be overcome.

A methodology which fulfils these conditions is named after the mnemonic *341*

'LEGUP'. The letters stand for **L**istening, **E**xploring, **G**oal setting, **U**nderpinning and **P**ursuit.

LEGUP – AN OVERVIEW

Listening, the initial stage, is devoted to helping the presenter to express the problem and its accompanying feelings as freely as possible. While not contributing new material, the manager is active in promoting this expression through acceptance and reflective responses.

In the *Exploring stage* the manager is helping the presenter to disentangle some of the often confused material which has emerged, and to discover the real cause or causes of the problem.

The *Goal setting* stage is where the goals (they are usually plural) are agreed; normally goals are expressed in concrete terms of changed behaviour.

Underpinning is the opportunity to provide any help which may be needed. For example: additional training, increased resources.

Pursuit is the agreed programme of follow-ups to review the achievement of goals, or to modify them as experience dictates.

LEGUP is an iterative process: returns to earlier stages are used as new problems or concerns are raised, and the cycle is repeated wherever necessary.

The listening stage

The key to good listening is to hear what is being communicated from the viewpoint of the speaker. Contrast this with the way we ordinarily listen: we hear what is being said but we instantaneously process it. Like a verbal tennis match we assess the message coming across the net and quickly reposition ourselves to make an effective return. The good listener does not think about the next stroke, but is intent on understanding how the world, or the particular circumstances, looks and feels to the speaker. The listener does not necessarily agree with what the speaker is saying, and may have feelings about the situation which are different or contrary; but at this moment the only relevant need is to understand the message which is being communicated – and to show that it has been understood.

Most of us have little experience of this kind of listening – whether as speaker or listener. Imagine what it would be like to try to explain something which is important to you to someone who is really listening. They are deeply interested in what you are saying, you sense they understand how it is for you, they do not judge. If you have had that fortunate experience you will know how it becomes possible for you to peel off your defensive skins, to express – however many awkward attempts it takes – what you really feel. Your confidence in the listener grows, and you become more and more willing to trust that person at greater and greater depths. You find that you are saying things you have never said to anyone before, and which often you have never even articulated to yourself. Perhaps the act of expressing your feeling in words enables you to understand it for the first time. When, eventually, you have expressed yourself fully, you are more than open to explore the situation constructively with your listener, who has earned the right to help you through showing understanding of just how the world looks to you.

Learning to be a good listener is hard, and it continues to be hard. We are so ego-based that to be more interested in someone else than we are in ourselves goes against the grain. Even when the skill has been mastered it is only too easy to slip back into our old egocentric ways. Fortunately it is a rewarding experience and we are surrounded by opportunities for practice.

The most common response of the good listener is the reflective, or mirror, response which shows the speaker that the listener has understood what has been said. Here is an example:

Speaker   Maybe I shouldn't be as good as I am at doing my job. People keep being promoted over my head, but I am left where I am because they've no one to replace me.

Listener   So you're wondering whether the problem is that no one dares promote you because they haven't anyone else to do the job.

That response is reflective because it is confined to confirming what has been said, but in the listener's words. It leaves the speaker encouraged to go on to the next point, or perhaps to modify the first point:

Speaker   Well, perhaps that's not the whole story, but it's certainly part of it. It seems so unfair.

Listener   So it's one element – and you feel it's unjust.

We might contrast the first response with the tennis return:

Listener   You seem to assume that it is somebody else's fault. But perhaps it's something *you* do wrong.

That may be a sensible suggestion but it's not helpful at this stage. The speaker is blocked, goes on the defensive, the tennis rally continues, and problem solving becomes a confrontation rather than a mutual activity.

A more subtle temptation is the interpretive response:

Listener   You're beginning to think that if only you did worse in your present position you might be kicked upstairs.

There's nothing wrong with that response in itself; at the Exploring stage it might well be appropriate. But, since it entails an interpretation going beyond what has been expressed, it is premature. Again, the speaker is blocked and the listener is trapped into steering the conversation.

From time to time the listener will want to ask a question to make sure   *343* nothing has been understood. And that can be helpful because a confused expression can often be elucidated in the speaker's second attempt. But there will be occasions when the listener will merely note the point for subsequent exploration rather than break the flow. And care must be taken to avoid the Socratic question that is really designed as a concealed tennis return – with a heavy spin on it – :

Listener   Do you have any evidence that that's what management thinks?

This apparently innocent question is in effect already challenging the presenter's interpretation of events. Socrates used to annoy his students by asking a series of such questions which gradually forced them into accepting the view which he held. It's a good technique for debate but not helpful at the Listening stage of problem solving. Socrates was eventually offered a cup of hemlock.

Listeners who are learning their trade are often thrown by silences. Instinctively they rush to fill the pauses. But those pauses may be necessary to the speaker, who is wondering how to express the next point, or is sorting out a whole range of personal feelings. The listener must regard silences as fruitful, and bear with them.

There is no need to respond to every statement which is made. But the listener should recognize the key points where reflection will reassure the speaker that he or she has understood. And reflective responses are complemented by summaries. These are used periodically to draw together a number of points, to remind the participants where they are, and to check that the listener is receiving the picture which the speaker is seeing. The listener will be aware that it is possible, perhaps unconsciously, to skew the summary and thereby force the speaker unintentionally into a false position.

Where the material is lengthy or complex the listener may choose to summarize by marking down the important points on paper so that both people can look at this together. This is likely to be most useful as the Listening stage draws to an end, since it can be a basis for the Exploring stage. But you should not be surprised if the summary itself triggers further considerations in the speaker's mind, which must be added to the picture.

You may like to experiment with the techniques for good listening. The next time someone – perhaps a colleague, a spouse, a child – starts to tell you about something which is important to them apply what you have learnt about good listening. You may be surprised at the gratifying and gratified reaction you get.

Moving to the next stage

Because the LEGUP methodology is an intelligent procedure, the principles always take precedence over the formula. It can often happen, for instance, that the very process of being listened to enables the presenter to explore the problem personally, to arrive at a clear view of its nature and to see the solution – at least in general terms. Consequently no specific Exploring stage is required. Similarly no Underpinning (see below) may be required. The manager need only (but it is important to remember this) check that the function of each stage has been fulfilled.

The movement from one stage to another is a matter of judgement. The manager will judge that the presenter has expressed the problem as fully as possible at that point (and this may be confirmed with a summary of the listener's understanding), and will move naturally into the Exploring stage. If this move is premature the presenter will return to the earlier material, and no harm will have been done.

However, the manager should be wary of the rambling presenter who may continually bring in irrelevant points, or who may frequently return to an earlier point which has already been heard out exhaustively, and will tactfully but firmly shepherd the presenter into returning to the problem solving process. The manager may find that sharing a written note of the points made with the presenter (see above) is a useful device to get the discussion back on track, or to demonstrate that a point has been taken into account. If it is suspected that the wandering habits of the speaker may themselves be part of the problem, this may need to be raised, at the Exploring stage, as a possible issue:

Listener   I notice that you frequently return to that argument you had with Bill in the canteen. It really seems to bother you. Let's talk about that for a moment, and see if we can clear it out of the way.

or

Listener   I've noticed while we've been talking that you frequently wander off the point. Is that a habit of yours? If so, do you think it's possible that it may lead to people seeing you as a rather vague and unfocused person?

The exploring stage

The purpose of the Exploring stage is to clarify the nature of the problem so that possible solutions begin to suggest themselves. The manager is helping the presenter to review and explore what has been said so that what may have started as a tangle begins to resolve itself into a clearer picture.

It is common for the presenter initially to misrepresent the problem. This may be through a lack of insight, or it may be because the problem presented is a respectable Trojan Horse which contains a less flattering difficulty. For example, the presenter might genuinely feel overlooked for promotion when the real problem is jealousy of a particular rival who has just been promoted. Alternatively the presenter may acknowledge resentment directed at one   *345* individual, but is more comfortable about presenting the problem in impersonal terms.

Notice that, although the manager may have identified the real problem at an early stage (or believes this to be the case), the approach is still tentative. It will be preferable to help the exploration along so that the presenter is allowed to discover the truth rather than being influenced towards accepting the manager's answer. Once again we observe the principle that owning an idea through personal discovery has a higher motivating power than when it has been wished on us. It also leaves the responsibility for finding the solution clearly with the presenter rather than the manager.

The most frequent intervention by the manager at this stage is the interpretive response. We met one of these above.

> *Listener*   You're beginning to think that if only you did worse in your present position you might be kicked upstairs.

It would be important here to use a tone of voice which makes it clear that this is only a suggestion to be considered – and not a conclusion which the manager has reached. It might be better to recast it as an interpretive question:

> *Listener*   Do you ever think that if you did worse in your present position you might be kicked upstairs?

In fact the manager will make good use of questions, for instance to query an apparent pattern of behaviour:

> *Listener*   I remember you told me that you didn't mention any of this at your annual assessment. And just now you were talking about how rarely you intervened at project meetings. Now that could suggest that you're the sort of person who is nervous about speaking out. Do you recognize that, or was this just a coincidence?

Which, of course, it may have been. Another clue can come from apparent contradictions or inconsistencies:

> *Listener*   You've been describing how you feel management has ignored your qualities, but just now you mentioned how Bill made sure that the work you did on those new measurements was featured in the company newsletter. That doesn't seem quite to hang together. Does it to you?

We don't like having our inconsistencies pointed out so the manager here has been particularly careful not to make this seem like a challenge. There may be a good explanation, or it may lead the presenter towards a deeper insight.

This does not mean that challenges are excluded – but they should only be used when necessary, and when the manager feels they will have a positive rather than a negative outcome:

> *Listener*   So you've said that you realize that a lack of qualifications is a
> big factor holding you back, yet you haven't taken any steps
> to investigate how you could get qualifications. You seem to
> have painted yourself into a corner.

During this stage the manager is continuing to use his listening skills, and may, for instance, have noticed what seems a significant remark or a significant omission from the earlier material; querying this may well uncover elements which clarify the problem.

> *Listener*   You mentioned last year's Christmas party in passing. Was that
> just a chance remark or did you have something particular in
> mind?

Throughout, the manager will seek to make the expression concrete.

> *Listener*   You say that you think you need a higher profile in the company.
> Tell me just what you mean by having a higher profile – it
> sounds a bit vague to me.

This search for clarity is an important element in turning a vague, amorphous cluster of difficulties into a well-defined problem, in which the incidentals have been put to the back of the stage and the real nature of the problem has been seen and understood.

As the stage continues and the picture begins to clarify these interpretive responses take on more substance:

> *Listener*   It sounds as though you think it possible that your lack of formal
> qualifications may be holding you back. Is that how you see it?
> Or do you think it's something else?

or

> *Listener*   So you're beginning to feel that the real problem lies in the fact
> that you tend to keep very quiet about your opinions, and
> management doesn't get a chance to see what you could do.
> Have I heard that right?

Later, as the stage draws to a close the listener will be exploring potential solutions:

> *Listener*   So you think it might be a good idea to volunteer to chair the
> publications committee; that would put you more in the public
> eye. Will that be sufficient on its own or will you need to reinforce
> that with other steps?

The process of exploration is guided by the manager helping the presenter to probe the situation and any thoughts and feelings about it, in order to end up with a clear picture of the real problem, which will in turn set the scene for the Goal setting stage. Of course multiple problems may be established, but experience generally shows the basic problem to be in the singular though usually accompanied by ramifications. The moment the heart of the problem has been grasped the real possibility of a solution becomes apparent.

The goal setting stage

It is tempting, once the problem has been clearly seen, to heave a sigh of relief and to conclude the discussion with generalized intentions for putting the matter right. It is likely, however, that all the previous work will be wasted because few of us are good at general reform. What we need for progress is the well-defined objective – one which is expressed in terms of different behaviour, and whose results can be judged.

For example, the objective: 'I am going to try to be more assertive at meetings', is very different from: 'At each meeting I attend I will make at least one contribution in which I express my own opinion.'

A good objective can be tested by the 'CROW' criteria:

Concrete	– it is expressed in definite and recognizable terms
Realistic	– it is within my power
Observable	– I will know when it is accomplished
Worthwhile	– it will make a worthwhile difference

An objective must be under the control of the presenter. For instance, 'making your work group accept you as assertive' cannot be a goal for *you*; only *they* can do that. What you can do is to take the action which you calculate will lead to that result.

In practice there will often be plural objectives; this is not only because one may want to tackle different aspects of the problem, but because the distance from the current situation to the desired future may be too long. We cannot leap from the ground floor to the first floor, but we can go up easily by each step of the stairs. Presenters may well be keen to solve the problem at one swoop, and the manager must be ready to advise caution and discuss a way of splitting the complete objective into sub-objectives of manageable size.

The use of sub-objectives will also help to focus the presenter's mind – concentrating his action on one front at a time. Usually the manager will suggest that they are tackled with the easiest objectives first. This enables the presenter, who may well have had a loss of confidence from the problem itself, to gain early experience of success and to realize that he actually does have control over what is happening. This becomes a strong motivation for more difficult sub-objectives yet to be tackled.

Except in very simple cases it is helpful to ask the presenter actually to write down the programme of objectives with possible timescales, checking with the CROW criteria. This deliberate act gives the intentions an additional firmness. The manager should not do the writing; these are the presenter's objectives, not his. We will return to this programme at the Pursuit stage.

The underpinning stage

The exploration of many problems reveals a need for help of some kind. It may be coaching, or training, or additional resources. Sometimes action which only the manager has the powers to perform is required. While the manager's instinct should always be to leave the responsibility with the presenter he or she must, of course, be ready to act when this is not a practical possibility.

The pursuit stage

Human beings are motivated by rewards of various kinds. And we may think that the presenter receives adequate reward from personally accomplishing his or her objectives. Once the problem is understood and a programme of goals provided – that should be sufficient; we can bow out.

This view does not take into account three considerations. First, some of the sub-objectives are not necessarily strongly rewarding since they are only steps on the way to the final reward – solving the whole problem. It is only too easy to lose heart and let good intentions dissolve. We may need some stiffening to keep our courage going.

Second, we tend to be more motivated by short-term rewards, even when they are small, than by long-term rewards, even when they are large. The cigarette smoker and the dieter both know this to be true.

Third, we made a judgement about the sub-objectives which may not have been correct. They may prove more difficult to achieve than we thought or, achieved, they may not lead to the outcomes we planned. It may be desirable to modify these with experience. It may be important to do so if the presenter is not to be cast down by early failures.

The Pursuit, or follow-up, stage is needed to complete the job. It involves one or more meetings, or contacts, to report on success with objectives. In a difficult and complex case a number of contacts may be required – perhaps as each objective is due to have been accomplished. In other cases a single telephone conversation may be sufficient.

We should not underestimate the reward which is provided by the simple act of demonstrating to our manager that an objective or sub-objective has been accomplished. Nor indeed the negative reward of failure. In children parental approval is a strong and continuing source of reward and motivation – superior in many ways to the more tangible rewards of, say, a new bicycle or a trip to a football match. This response seems to continue into adult life where the approval of a respected third party fulfils the same function.   *349*

Approval rewards are of course relatively immediate, but the manager should schedule Pursuit meetings to make sure they are not long delayed. As the Latins say, he gives twice who gives quickly. Similarly the modification of objectives should be made promptly so that the presenter is moved quickly again into positive action.

Interpersonal problems

So far in this chapter we have been looking primarily at the individual problem – though this will often involve other people. However, problems within a team may well arise from personality clashes within the team itself. How is LEGUP employed here?

The Listening stage is key, as always. The manager would, ideally, listen to all the involved parties separately – understanding the problem from each presenter's point of view but not, of course, taking sides.

The manager would then preside over a meeting, the first objective of which is to encourage the parties to listen to each other. This means, in fact, coaching them in listening skills, checking continually that the different perspectives have been properly understood, for instance, checking the tennis rally of argument and allowing each presenter separate time while getting the others to reflect their understanding of how it looks to the speaker. The manager will use the information obtained at the separate meetings, provided this is not confidential, with discretion and delicacy to secure the level of frankness which may be necessary. Having provided a safe atmosphere, the manager supplies the occasion and the stimulus for really honest discussion.

Sometimes this kind of listening dialogue (which may be spread over more than one meeting) is sufficient to resolve the problem. There is now understanding, and an increase in the level of trust arising from the depth of discussion. But the manager will be wary of taking for granted that general good intentions will be robust enough to survive future points of difference. The Exploring and further stages will be needed to formulate concrete goals, provide the Underpinning, and supply the Pursuit. Interpersonal problems will often recur until the habits of a new relationship are well established.

Exploration will sometimes reveal that part of the difficulty actually lies with the manager – an element which can be corrected at the Underpinning stage. Conflict often arises from demarcation disputes that come about because responsibilities and expectations have been confused through imprecise delegation. The manager may be reluctant to use executive power, a tendency which may have been the original cause and, in a virtuous endeavour to act as liberal coach, may forget that authority is a service to the team when used to settle questions which are his or her responsibility.

Naturally, interpersonal, and interfactional, problems are not confined to the team. The same methodology can be used, for instance, when two areas of the company are in dispute or in trade union negotiations. The LEGUP

process provides an orderly and non-confrontational way of sharing a real understanding of the problem, its potential solution, and the steps to be taken to achieve this.

Team planning and problem solving

This chapter has been concerned with the problems at the level of the individual, but LEGUP has a group application, too. Faced with solving a team problem or the planning of work, the Listening stage takes place when broadly based suggestions are made, either informally or through a process of brainstorming. The task of the group at this stage is not to inhibit the flow of ideas or to get bogged down in their discussion, but to listen to them, suspending judgement. In the Exploring stage joint examination takes place in order to concentrate on the nature of the problem and its most promising solutions. At Goal setting the concrete tasks to achieve the solution are identified, timed and allocated. Underpinning and Pursuit fulfil their roles equivalently.

LEGUP – A ROBUST AND VERSATILE METHODOLOGY

Seeing the uses of LEGUP in a variety of situations may lead to the reaction: 'It's obvious, isn't it? It's really just commonsense – all those stages are needed to solve problems. I knew that.'

No more is claimed for LEGUP. Its virtue lies in the fact that it makes explicit the stages which we recognize but so often forget – which in turn lead to problems being half-solved or not solved at all. And it obliges us to concentrate on developing the skills of each stage as we realize what part they need to play in the process.

Because it is commonsense, because it corresponds to the way the human mind works, its application to problems is very broad. Any manager who has mastered the methodology will find this is a ready tool which will substantially increase his or her effectiveness in a number of circumstances.

RECOMMENDED READING

Berne, E., *Games People Play*, Penguin, Harmondsworth, 1964. The original analysis of psychological games playing that originated a whole movement in the understanding of relationships.

de la Bedoyere, Q.M., *How to Get Your Own Way in Business*, Gower, Aldershot, 1990. A leading communications consultant described this as ' . . . the most educationally rewarding book on human skills I have ever seen'. I am much too modest to agree with him.

de la Bedoyere, Q.M., *Managing People and Problems*, Gower, Aldershot, 1988. Available in paperback, this book is about practical ways to help people change their behaviour.

Egan, G., *The Skilled Helper*, Wadsworth Publishing, Belmont, California,

1975. Egan first introduced me to skilled problem solving, though he bears no responsibility for the ways I have adapted his basic methods.

Nierenberg, G.I. and Calero, H.H., *How to Read a Person Like a Book*, Heinrich Hanau, London, 1973. The best practical book I know for anyone starting to look at non-verbal communication for the first time. Good line drawings.

Sutherland, S., *Irrationality, The Enemy Within*, Constable, London, 1992. A scientific but highly readable account of the strange ways the normal human mind works.

23 Motivating teams

Gisela Hagemann

A superteam consists of people of varying professional competence, experience and personality who, together, achieve better results than would be possible for a more homogeneous group or single person (synergy effect 2+2=4++++). Why should the company have superteams? A manager can be highly motivated, intelligent and hard-working, working all the hours of the day before dropping from exhaustion; however, the chances of success without help from others diminish with the increasing complexity of technical processes, management decisions and changes in the environment of the company.

In a knowledge industry, especially, management and staff can be assumed to be highly qualified in their respective fields of expertise. The challenge is, however, to integrate the individual experts into a superteam that will consistently produce products and services better than competitors and will optimize the knowledge and skills of the individuals – the company's most important resource.

The concept of the superteam helps the company to achieve success through motivation, shared vision, development of trust and involvement in the decision process.

Companies which develop strategy, organization and human resources in teamwork will harvest many benefits:

- Holistic thinking results in better quality of decision making: you see not just part of the picture, but the whole picture.
- Balancing logical reasoning and intuitive imaging releases and channels creativity in a customer-oriented direction.
- Clarification, communication and implementation of the company's vision, goals, and values increases efficiency and effectiveness.
- When the management team develops a spirit of cooperation and

strategic cohesion, the employees benefit from consistent signals from the top. In particular, the salesforce will benefit from continuing dialogue between production and marketing. Products will reach the market quicker and sales will increase.

- Increased self-esteem helps the individual to be and stay successful.

Imagination is the most important asset of a company. Thus the key to becoming the best organization is a flexible, creative and well-trained workforce who work together as a team – not only in projects, but also across the boundaries of departments or other business units. Optimizing the human potential (this might mean obtaining more from less) will open new avenues for success. In particular, teams need to be used and developed in a more creative and focused way. A company can recover its competitive edge by channelling its human resources behind a driving corporate vision based on shared values and a clear company purpose. When the company as a whole functions as a superteam, sales will increase automatically. A precondition is however that top management is motivated, embraces change and understands the value of teamwork.

In order to make teams thrive four important conditions have to be met:

1 A motivating corporate culture
2 A clear and convincing purpose
3 A shared vision
4 Focus and persistency.

A MOTIVATING CORPORATE CULTURE

We tended to react to any new situation by reorganizing, and a wonderful method it can be for creating the illusion of progress, while producing confusion, inefficiency and demoralization.

Petronius, AD 66

Corporate culture is the way we treat each other. It reflects our values, norms, underlying beliefs, social and emotional competence. Corporate culture can either amount to putting a spanner in the works or giving them a good greasing. Corporate culture itself cannot be measured, but its characteristics can certainly be observed: are team members bursting with ideas and taking the initiative, or do they only act on specific orders from above? Are they proud of their company or do they give vent to their frustration with jokes at management expense?

Balance between hard and soft values

When it comes to setting goals, most companies have done their research. Do the following ring any bells: 'profit', 'productivity', 'competence', 'quality'? This is the standard jargon of action plans and strategy. The difference between private companies and public service is that the former tend to print their guidelines on glossy, luxury paper, adorned with photos and prints, while the latter compensate for their lack of artistry by the sheer volume of documentation. In both cases they usually lie around in drawers, unread, gradually curling up at the edges.

If I ask employees about their company's goals and the ways in which their own work contributes to achieving them, the answers I usually receive are looks of amazement, indicating a thought process along the lines of: 'Goals? What goals? I seem to remember hearing something about a goal system somewhere along the line, but what's that got to do with me? I'm just a minor cog in the works. What on earth has achieving goals got to do with me?'

A very good question! Why should an employee do more than is necessary to help the firm achieve better results? Surely only if he or she feels part of the company and can identify with its goals. This assumes it is possible to participate, have one's contribution recognized and realize oneself. Every day we make important and not so important decisions. Only when our inner convictions concur with external demands can we intuit what will lead us to our goal.

Thus it is essential that the team concentrates on both the 'what?' (goals and putting them to practice) and the 'how?' (inter-human relationships and the working atmosphere). Balance is the key word: balance between achieving targets ('hard values') and a motivating corporate culture ('soft values'); balance between optimism and realism in formulating goals and balance between sympathetic understanding and the need to achieve.

Productivity and high returns on turnover are directly linked to identification with goals, while a decline in identification leads the company into the red. Cost control, rational working procedures and production methods ('hard values') can only be fully effective when employees are allowed to develop their resources and receive recognition for their achievements ('soft values').

In a nutshell, this means that those who are supposed to realize the targets set should participate in formulating and implementing these goals in their own jobs. Problems should be solved on the level at which they occur – not by means of a suggestion box, emptied once a month, but in a permanent dialogue with immediate superiors and colleagues.

Just as there are close ties between productivity and a sense of belonging, these also exist between knowledge and motivation. Why should an older employee refresh specialized knowledge? Surely only if he or she is motivated to do so. Motivation thrives in a free and open working atmosphere, with interesting tasks and a boss who takes notice of staff and trusts them.

The quality of products and that of inter-human relationships is closely linked. Why should a worker on the production line feel personally responsible for the product leaving the section being absolutely perfect, and not rely on the engineers in quality control discovering and rectifying the faults? Surely only if the contact between the staff and their superiors is so good   *355* that the superior feels able to discuss awkward points with the staff in an amicable fashion.

Norms, values and underlying beliefs

The corporate culture of a company permeates the walls of the building. You can see it, hear it, feel it when you enter the entrance door. Do people smile? How is their body posture? How do they dress? How do they interact with each other? How do they talk to each other?

The corporate culture is based on norms, values and internalized rules that everyone knows and follows, although they don't exist in written form. Examples of negative norms are as follows:

- It is best to keep a low profile, because suggestions for improvement are interpreted as criticizing one's superior
- We sit silent and nod our heads in meetings. Afterwards we rebel and spread rumours in the corridor
- It is acceptable to take sick leave when I am not in the right mood for working.

It is very difficult, if not impossible, for one person alone to change a culture. This has to be a joint effort. Let's imagine that the staff of a company represents the B-type of performers (demotivated, 'inner immigration'). Now a creative newcomer (an A-person) is appointed, sees everything with fresh eyes and makes proposals for change. Guess what happens after a short while? The A-person is constantly beating his or her head against the wall, frustration is setting in and there are two choices: either to quit the company and find another job (which might be difficult in these times of high unemployment) or slowly become resigned, gradually turning into another B-person. In this way the corporate culture perpetuates itself. It is like syrup covering the floor, which sticks to everybody walking across it.

That's why it is necessary to bring norms and underlying beliefs to the surface and to work together in order to change the negative into the positive:

- We trust and support each other
- It is acceptable to show one's disagreement openly
- We welcome suggestions for improvement.

Underlying beliefs are unconscious thought patterns which inhibit the full realization of the individual's potential. Management might underestimate the knowledge, skills and commitment of the employees and therefore hesitate to delegate and instead insert detailed control. Instead of releasing creativity the flow of ideas is thus stopped. The employee might have a negative self-image with self-destructive commentaries such as:

- I am a failure
- I am unworthy
- I am powerless
- I am incapable
- My opinion counts for nothing in this company.

No matter if the demotivation is coming from above or from within, the result is that human potential remains untapped for the company. Therefore organizational change should be supported by increased self-knowledge and self-esteem. Team development should deal both with improving individual performance and inter-personal communication skills.

A motivating corporate culture is based on clearly defined, accepted and practised values (Box 23.1).

A CLEAR AND CONVINCING PURPOSE

This is the true joy in life, the being used for a purpose recognized by yourself as a mighty one ... the being a force of nature instead of a feverish, selfish little clod of ailments and grievances complaining that the world will not devote itself to making you happy.

George Bernard Shaw

Before building a shared vision, the team's purpose and contribution to its internal and external customers should be clarified.

Just as a person needs a strong backbone to prevent being blown over by the first gust of wind, a team needs a common basis of conviction if it is to create internal cohesion in spite of external upheavals. The greater the extent to which the individual values of the team members concur with

---

Box 23.1 Values of a motivating corporate culture

Developing a set of shared values means:

- An open discussion about spoken and unspoken values in the company: which values do we want to take care of, introduce, strengthen, weaken, take leave of and get rid of?
- Changing *norms* from the negative into the positive. For example: 'Rumours spread like wildfire' into 'We trust each other'.
- Bringing to the surface *underlying beliefs* which might stand in the way of success.
- Fundamental change of *attitudes* by developing social and emotional competence.
- Developing an inspiring *working climate* and motivating teams.
- Restating the company's standards of *ethics* and clarifying possible goal conflicts such as profit and credibility, team spirit and internal competition, personal well-being and demands on productivity.

the leadership principles of the team leader and the general manager of the company, the greater the degree of energy which can be released.

The challenge is to combine personal goals and values with the company's self-image in order to create a common basis of values. Participation leads to motivation. Let the team as a whole participate in formulating its purpose and objectives (Box 23.2).

A collective self-image is the foundation for developing a shared team or company vision. Management guidelines are a declaration of intent. But only the vision can turn the goal into something concrete and release the energy necessary to turn thought into action.

A SHARED VISION

There is no more powerful engine driving an organization toward excellence and long-range success than an attractive, worthwhile, and achievable vision of the future, widely shared.

Burt Nanus

Visionary thinking is holistic thinking, that is, strategies relating to markets, the alignment of internal organizational structures and the development of human potential unite to form an indivisible whole. Attention is directed outwards and inwards simultaneously. Visionary thinking goes beyond the necessary adjustment to changes in market structures and consciously tries to create something new. The greater the extent to which the vision is supported by values to which everyone subscribes, the greater the chance of realizing it in practice.

You start at the end. Begin with the result desired. Act as though you have already reached your goal. Imagine putting on your seven-league boots and travelling three to five years into the future. All the doors in the world are open to you. You simply have to walk in and look at what there is to be found in the various rooms.

The sequential order of visionary- and result-oriented thinking is:

1 *The vision*
   A vision is an optimistic, but realistic, image of the future. You can describe it in present time just as though it were already reality:
   - What is the company looking like in three- to five-year's time?
   - What can we achieve if we give free rein to our imagination and simply push all obstacles aside for the time being?

2 *Analysing current reality*
   - When you are clear about your vision, make an analysis of current reality in relation to the desired outcome.
   - What information do we have about the current situation?
   - How does current reality differ from our vision?

Box 23.2   Common basis of values

The following questions might help in this process:

- What are our basic convictions? How do they express themselves?
- Why do we do what we do? Do we really do what we want?
- What is our internal motivation?
- What is the heart of our work?
- What truly binds us together?
- What is the deeper meaning of our work?
- Why does the team/company exist? In which direction is it developing? In which direction should it be developing?
- What makes the team/company unique? What differentiates the team/company from others in the field?
- What social responsibility does the company take? What are the consequences of our decisions for state and society?
- What does the company mean to its staff, share-holders, the town or community, our country, the world?
- What is our public image? What image would we like to have?

- What are our personal and team strengths?
- Who or what is preventing us from making our dreams come true?
- Are we, perhaps, getting in our own way?
- How can we strengthen our trust in ourselves and one another?

3   *A plan of action and strategy*
- Visionary thinking is more than just wishful thinking. In order to reach your goal you have to do something.
- How can we overcome real or assumed obstacles?
- What are we going to do?
- Who is doing what and when?

Be prepared for the path from the vision to reality to be strewn with stones. Your inner identification with your vision will give you the strength and endurance required to reach your goal.

When I recommend my clients to learn visionary thinking I'm often told: 'We don't need that. We already have a strategy document.' And this is the reason why I want to emphasize that visionary thinking is not only a method for determining long-term goals, but also helps decision making on an ordinary everyday basis. It is a creative way of thinking which gradually enters your bloodstream and becomes integral to your way of life (Box 23.3).

Optimistic but realistic

Don't restrict your imagination to what you have already done or think you can do, but discover what you really want. Many people never reach their goal because they impose mental censorship on themselves: 'I can't', 'I don't deserve it', 'others maybe, but not me'. Or perhaps they fool themselves into denying their dreams. Suppressing forbidden thoughts and feelings is enervating. You can spare yourself a good deal of muscular strain and stress by being honest with yourself about your desires: being straight with yourself is preventive medical care.

When you think you have found what you really want, consider whether you can imagine something even better. Have the courage to go beyond your previous limits and do not indulge in self-censorship, such as 'It doesn't work!' Draw a clear dividing line between the formulation of your goal and speculations about whether or not it is 'possible' to reach it. Whether you can or not will only become plain when you actually have. If you don't manage to reach your goal you will never be able to prove conclusively whether it was due to your lack of persistency, the difficulty of the task or external circumstances. You will only prove once and for all whether something is do-able at the moment you accomplish your goal: 'There! I've done it!' All previous speculation is a waste of time.

Of course there is no guarantee that you will end up at your destination. Perhaps the journey will lead somewhere totally different. Nonetheless, it is important to have a clear picture of the desired future. Faith in the vision provides the strength to bear the exertions of the journey and to rediscover the original path which we lost. It is a signpost to the summit. The higher we climb, the better the view. The nearer we get to our goal, the more clearly we are able to see whether it is really the place of our dreams. There is no shame in turning back; we are free to choose another mountain to climb.

Identification through information and involvement

When all team members know the vision, goals and strategy they will be able to set the right priorities (even under time pressure or in difficult situations). Information and participation creates identification and increases motivation and performance.

People are only willing to work hard if they have the feeling that it is all worthwhile. Employees who do not realize themselves in their jobs transfer their motivation to achieve to their leisure activities. After work they reveal a degree of enthusiasm and tenacity which would halt their bosses in their tracks with amazement.

A vision is a driving force giving us direction. It is the light, illuminating a path in the dark. In order to ensure that even the canteen worker understands his or her contribution in reaching the goal, the vision has to be broken down into manageable lumps and communicated to all levels of the organization. This restates the need for developing interpersonal communi-

23.3 Developing a vision

The following questions can help you to develop your vision:

Looking inside: In which business are we?

- Who are we? What are we particularly good at?
- What do we want? Why do we want it?
- Assuming we have reached our goal: what is different by comparison with current reality?
- What do we see/hear/feel/taste/smell when we reach our goal?
- Are we using our potential to the full? Can we imagine something even better?
- What kind of corporate culture do we need in order to reach our vision?
- What is the atmosphere like in the company? What is teamwork like?
- What attitudes and behaviour do we expect from our managers and staff?
- What incentives do we offer to encourage the relevant behaviour?
- Do we have an overview of what knowledge we need? What knowledge our staff actually has and how we can fill the gap?
- Are we using the existing resources to the full?
- What are our training needs in order to make our vision become reality?
- When we are re-filling positions do we consider the applicant's human profile of qualification or do we only recruit professional competence?
- Can we extend the bounds of possibility even further?
- Can we imagine breaking out of all previous boundaries?

Looking outside: Customer focus

- Who are our customers?
- Why do our customers buy from us?
- What use are our products and services to our customers?
- How can we provide our customers over and above the pure utility aspect with added value they would not get from competitors?
- What changes do we see in the market place?
- How are we affected by globalization?
- How do we turn satisfied customers into loyal customers?

cation skills such as creating a common perception of reality, giving and receiving information, positive and negative feedback, listening and asking smart questions. Developing creative thinking skills will help the sales force sell more profitably in the more challenging environment. When the vision is clear, every single staff or team member has to formulate concrete individual goals and draw up a plan of action for how he or she wants to contribute personally to realize the company or team vision.

The best is no longer good enough. It's not just a case of trying to see into the future but to form it according to one's own ideas. When the people affected are able to participate in formulating the vision, they have the feeling of controlling their own lives. They themselves are active creatively and not just at the mercy of fate. They do everything within their power. When the vision is internalized a great deal of external control will be unnecessary. With less hierarchy decision making will speed up.

Visionary thinking is a mental procedure aimed at creating the future according to one's own ideals. However, talking is not walking. Formulating a motivating vision–statement with which the team as a whole can identify is, however, only the first step. In order to implement the vision team members have to learn to think constructively by focusing on the desired outcome instead of on problems.

Goal-orientation instead of problem-orientation

Many companies start organizational development with a *problem-oriented* analysis of the situation without being clear what goals they are pursuing. The result is an overwhelming mass of problems. Those involved try to put the blame on everyone else. Corporate culture is poisoned by conflict. Motivation suffers and apathy reigns.

When you develop a vision with which everyone can identify, you build up mental reserves of strength. The assessment of current reality is then given in relation to the desired end result. Irrelevant problems can be put to one side, which alone reduces the mass of problems to be dealt with.

The same is true on a personal level. Therefore practise thinking and acting in a goal-oriented rather than a problem-oriented fashion, because constant thinking about problems culminates in a feeling of helplessness leading to apathy. Direct your energies to what you want and not to what you don't want. If you concentrate on reaching your goal you release positive energy. If, on the other hand, all you can think of are problems you are in danger of becoming apathetic and demotivating others, too.

People without clear objectives have a tendency to be dissatisfied with the world in general and themselves in particular. Everything looks black to them and they dwell on their problems rather than think about what they want instead. Hell is other people. From here it is only a small step to rumour and gossip. Once in a while allow yourself just to take a back seat and listen when you are sitting together with others. How often are disparaging remarks made about people who are not present? How often do people complain about the government, taxes, laws, society, colleagues, bosses and so on, and so on, and so on? As a rule of thumb you can assume that those who complain the most are the least able to realize themselves in their work. The greater one's own frustration, the more negative one's view of external circumstances.

First comes the 'what?' and then the 'how?'

Differentiate between the goal ('what?') and the means ('how?'). Consider initially what result you want to achieve, independently of 'how' you want to go about it. You can decide on the method when you are absolutely clear about the goal (Box 23.4).

A vision is a goal which you want to achieve for its own sake. It is the fulfilment of all your wishes and not the springboard to a yet greater goal.

Is a big salary a goal or a means to an end? What do you want to do with the money? Which needs will you satisfy by buying things? Are there other ways of satisfying these needs?

Is fame a goal or a means to an end? What does it mean to you to be 'famous'? Would it help your career? What direct steps can you take to bring you nearer to your goal? If you become obsessed with becoming famous you run the risk of doing anything just to get your name in print and neglecting what you should actually be doing. Many politicians and managers have realized that the media can give you a career boost, but they can also destroy you at a stroke.

Is maximum profit a goal or a means to ensure the continued existence of the company? Companies which are completely fixated on quarterly statements often fail to invest in training, research and development which would only bear fruit in the long-term.

Analysing current reality

A clear vision is the pre-condition for a *goal-oriented* analysis of the current situation (Box 23.5).

To implement the vision, management has to understand the predictable psychological reactions in a change process, assist with conflict management and create a pro-active, flexible learning organization.

Only when these fundamental questions have been answered is the time right for drawing up a plan of action and developing a strategy.

Box 23.4 Clarifying the goal

If you are not sure whether you are trying to achieve a result for its own sake or only as a stepping stone towards an even greater goal, ask yourself:

- What does goal accomplishment mean to me?
- What purpose will be served by the result?
- If I were to reach the goal would I really be satisfied?
- What would be different by comparison with the present?
- Would I really want it if I got it?

Box 23.5 Analysing the current situation

The following questions may help you along the way:

- Which organizational structure would facilitate goal accomplishment?
- Which information systems do we need in order to turn our vision into reality?
- Do our information systems fulfil their purpose?
- Which internal attitudes and behaviour determine success or defeat?
- To what extent does current reality deviate from the vision? How do we fill the gap?
- Do we have an appropriate organizational structure?
- Do our managers and staff have the right attitude to change?
- Which attitudes and modes of behaviour do we value?
- What do we do in order to encourage the right attitudes?
- What do we do in order to ensure motivated colleagues stay with the company?
- Do we have the necessary know-how?
- What kind of competence do we require now and in the future?
- Do we really know who knows what?
- Do we have an overview of our own human resources?
- Who profits from the competence?
- Are competent colleagues able to pass on their knowledge to others?
- Which other ways are there of acquiring know-how?

Planning and action

Planning means being task-oriented, clarifying goals, setting clear priorities and sticking to deadlines.

Measurement means a continuous evaluation of performance and results. The company will have well-developed systems for this task in the context of commercial results but new measurements may be needed for the development and application of creative management and the quality of teamwork.

Action is the most difficult part of any vision, goal or plan (Box 23.6).

FOCUS AND PERSISTENCY

A mistake is an event, the full benefit of which has not yet been turned to your advantage.

Ed Land

To reach its goal the team has to direct all its actions with perseverance

---

Box 23.6 Starting the action

- What steps are necessary in order to proceed from current reality to realizing the vision?
- What do we have to change?
- How should we go about it?
- When do we expect the vision to turn into reality?

---

and a strong will to succeed. Therefore it is important to develop the attitudes and skills which will turn any setback into an opportunity to learn (Box 23.7).

When you know precisely what you want it is easier to set your priorities and grasp opportunities. In the absence of clear goals you are always in danger of doing too many things at once, so that you end up totally burnt-out without having achieved anything important. Concentrate on essentials. Even if it is sometimes flattering to say 'yes' when you are asked to take on a position of trust, give a lecture or join the board of a charity organization, you are in danger of dissipating your energies. In the end everything you do will be superficial. You probably don't even have time to look through the documentation before a meeting. How do you imagine you can make a useful contribution in these circumstances? Remember that there are other people who would welcome the chance of a new challenge.

Start every day with the question: 'What will take me nearer my goal?' Use your most effective working time (for example, from 10 a.m to 12) for doing the things which move you closer to your most important goal.

One course of action brings you closer to your goal, the other does not. The art of creating something new is the ability to correct your course when necessary.

Your goal should be crystal clear, but the paths leading to this goal must be flexible (Box 23.8).

No one gives you something for nothing. To turn your personal vision into reality you have to do something about it. It is better to take small steps in the right direction on an everyday basis rather than huge sporadic leaps. If you want to learn a foreign language you will do better if you spend half an hour a day learning in a relaxed atmosphere rather than a single weekend cramming. You can improve your figure much faster by doing half an hour of exercises a day than by pushing yourself to the very limits of your physical ability once a month.

The same can be said of realizing corporate or team visions. If everyone is going in the same direction, products and services are constantly being renewed and the staff are able to pursue specialized in-service training and refresh their minds on a regular basis, which is more effective than turning all the organizational structures and working procedures on their heads every two years.

Managers who make constant change into an everyday process tend to   *365*

23.7 Suggestions for promoting focus and persistency

- Be enthusiastic. The intensity of your feeling will determine how quickly you reach your goal. A lukewarm attitude produces mediocrity. Overwhelming conviction leads to first-class achievements. Your positive aura invites trust. A good mood is contagious.
- Give your undivided attention to everything you do.
- Every so often put aside all the things you *have* to do in favour of doing what you really *want to do*. The things you really enjoy doing are probably those you also do best. If you enjoy getting down to work your chances of success are enhanced.
- Increase your ability to concentrate (for example, by doing relaxation exercises). When you are working on something go at it heart and soul. Put all other thoughts to one side for the time being. In this context Zen Buddhism preaches a simple rule: When you are sitting, sit. When you are drinking a cup of tea, drink a cup of tea.
- Be flexible enough to swap from one task to another, but when you start on something new, mentally switch off the former one completely.
- Be entirely convinced about everything you do. The greater your interest in something, the easier you will find it to concentrate on this task.
- Before making a decision consider the interests of those affected by it. Seek out allies before making suggestions for change. Take into account from the word go what consequences your decisions will have for whom.
- Be patient and persistent. Don't give up at the first sign of black clouds on the horizon.
- Be honest with yourself. If you notice that your energies are waning don't try to push your body further than it is able to go. Let others take the tiller. Job rotation is one way of enlivening an entrenched situation. Create a working atmosphere in which constant change is the norm so that no one loses face when taking on new tasks or passing on old ones.
- When you have learned to think and act in a goal-oriented way you can start excluding acitivities which do not lead you to your goal.

understand their role as one of service. However, a quiet evolution is less sensational than a complete turnaround. These managers don't attract as much interest in the media. Journalists want heroes who roll up their sleeves and haul the carriage out of the mud with their bare hands, while the rest of the world stands round applauding. Thus a manager or team leader needs a good deal of courage and self-confidence when defining his or her role as

that of the coach and coordinator rather than the commander-in-chief.

Box 23.8   Flexibility in approaching the goal

- Try out various possibilities leading to the goal.
- Follow up your thoughts with deeds.
- Cultivate contacts with anybody who might be important in accomplishing your goal. Don't only think of your superiors but also of your staff and customers.
- Be alert and well-informed about what is going on around you.
- Make sure that everyone is pulling in the same direction.
- Take an interest in new social trends and international developments and ask yourself early on how they might influence your working situation.
- Try to think and act proactively.

Even when the vision is clearly defined and everyone is motivated to turn it into reality, there will always be moments when everything seems to grind to a halt. When one suddenly becomes conscious of the immense disparity between the actual situation and the vision, one often feels hopeless, impatient, doubtful or disappointed and strongly inclined to throw in the towel. Instead of simply dismissing these unpleasant feelings as negative, or denying their existence, you can use your frustration as a source of energy. It's a setback to make you get a move on. If you were living in paradise on caviar and champagne would you feel the need to create a new world?

Creative tension

Creative tension is the feeling of wanting but not being able, or rather: not being able to quickly enough. You are impatient and want to see results straight away but it doesn't happen as quickly as you had imagined.

You are under time pressure and the little grey cells in your brain are refusing to do their job. Your mind is a blank. When you do eventually have a brainwave, the computer goes on strike. In the middle of a massive distribution campaign the photocopier breaks down and the mechanic is on holiday. You desperately need some information and can't get hold of anyone at all. You are waiting for a phone call which doesn't come. There is a complete hiatus. Everybody else is doing all right. There's a conspiracy against you. It's totally unfair and quite pointless. You feel like giving up. The company doesn't deserve a genius like you. They might just as well see how they can get on without you. You might as well emigrate – no one in this provincial backwater understands you anyway. You toss and turn in bed and don't get a wink of sleep although you need to be fresh in the morning.

The gap between the vision and reality can be reduced in two ways:

- Reality approaches the vision, that is, you do something in order to reach your goal

367

- The vision approaches reality, that is, you reduce your level of ambition and lower the bar.

Choosing the easier alternative often means deceiving yourself. Even the reduced level of ambition is difficult to achieve. The bar is lowered even further. Your childhood dreams fade away. Service suffers. Delivery dates are not met. Quality is reduced. Slowly but surely a first-class company sinks into the mire.

This is the reason why it is so important to take time working out the vision and to make sure that those affected have a chance to identify with it by participating in the process. The vision must be so convincing that it releases the energy for change.

How you deal with difficulties along the way is a question of attitude: a personal defeat or an opportunity to learn something. When self-pity comes knocking at your door, don't let it in. When things don't work out as you had hoped, look on obstacles as welcome feedback. Perhaps your picture of reality is not accurate – so broaden your perspectives. Maybe your strategy is not functioning as expected – so alter your strategy.

The difference between success and defeat is often only a question of perseverance. Success is evolutionary, a steady process of continuous learning rather than a sudden breakthrough.

SUMMARY

For the superteams to thrive in an organization the environment must be right. The four conditions are:

1   A motivating corporate culture
2   A clear and convincing purpose
3   A shared vision
4   Focus and persistency.

All these have to be present. This chapter has identified the areas that affect each of these four conditions and provided sets of questions and actions that can help to create an effective teamworking environment.

RECOMMENDED READING

Hagemann, Gisela, *The Motivation Manual*, Gower, Aldershot, 1992

24 Coaching and mentoring teams

Nigel MacLennan

What are coaching and mentoring? What can they do? They are the means of inspiring people 'to want to do'. They are the means of encouraging people to work out for themselves 'how to do'. If you want your people to think for themselves, to solve problems for themselves, to develop themselves, you must show them not just that it is all right to do these things, but also how to do them. Coaching particularly will achieve those objectives, and much more besides. How are 'coaches' and 'mentors' defined? A coach is someone the team can learn *with*. A mentor is someone the team can learn *from*. Note that the distinction implies more control from the team in coaching.

The same principles that apply to individual coaching, apply to team coaching and mentoring – with one difference: the whole group must be involved in the team coaching. Is there a systematic coaching process? Yes, the MacLennan seven-stage coaching model, illustrated in Figure 24.1.

MACLENNAN SEVEN-STAGE MODEL

Rapport creation

As must be obvious, if the coach/mentor and team have a poor relationship not very much is going to be achieved. On the other hand, if they enjoy mutual trust, respect and a genuine interest in each other's lives, the outcome will be highly positive. Some of the skills involved in this stage are: Active and reflective listening, what you should be listening for and how to convey to your coachees that you really are listening; Pick up and carry on questioning and other coaching

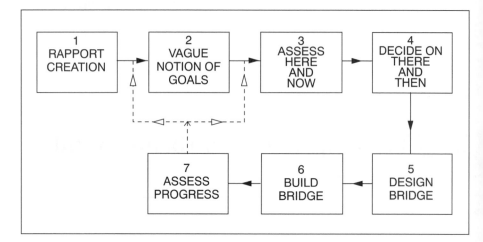

Figure 24.1 The seven-stage coaching model

questioning methods; Matching and pacing; Listening switch ons and switch offs.*

Vague notion of goals

At the start of the process there will probably be a vague sense of the objectives by all parties, and that is how it should be. The objective setting can only become precise when all parties have a clear picture of the point of departure. At this stage coach and team should also agree how to structure the coaching/mentoring sessions.

Assessing the here and now

The team's current achievement levels – the departure point – must be objectively assessed (using a range of tools*) and agreed against the appropriate dimensions for that team's role.

Deciding on the there and then

All parties discuss and agree on an arrival point, in terms of both actual performance and the time by which that level will be reached. When I say 'discuss', I mean the coach/mentor helps the team to decide. Middle and junior teams are usually charged with achieving specified goals, in which case the 'there and then' is already set. Despite that, the team members should take as much responsibility as possible for deciding how to get to the there and then. A large part of this stage is dedicated to aligning the

* Throughout this chapter an asterisk means there is a more detailed explanation in my book
Coaching and Mentoring.

missions of the individual team members with that of the organization and or department. The closer to an 'awesome purpose' (see Chapter 3) an organization's main objective is, the less alignment will be required; people are more inclined to identify with awesome purposes.

Designing a bridge

The team will examine the gap between the current and the desired situation and decide what options are available for crossing it. The most appropriate options are then chosen and turned into an agreed formal achievement plan.* You should be aware there are many factors to consider and methods to help you: Ingredients analysis/situational analysis; Barrier analysis; Paradigm analysis; Success style analysis; Choosing between bridge design options; Drawing up the achievement plan.

Building the bridge

The team sets about implementing the achievement plan. Coaching or mentoring input at this stage should be minimal. If the team requests input, the most effective assistance is usually to ask questions aimed at bringing more attention to and improving observation of, the relevant factors.

Assessing progress to the other side

The coach is there: To help the team confront and overcome the inevitable obstacles to success; To help decide whether the goals should be fine-tuned or whether the methods of achieving them should be improved or altered; To enhance ownership and focus (more on this later); To encourage perseverance and resilience.

ASKING QUESTIONS: THE MASTER TOOL

The most important coaching skill is the asking of questions. Questions are immensely powerful; they serve a multitude of different purposes. Coaching at its best is a never-ending chain of team-centred questions. Let's examine them in more detail. Questions can be:

- Thought directors
- Empowering mechanisms
- Catalysts for change.

Thought directors

If I asked you to tell me the time, what would come into your head? If you were asked what you did for a living, what would you be thinking about? If you asked whether or not questions asked by yourself or others dictated   *371* what you thought, what would come into your mind? Questions are the steering system of our thinking ship, intellectual rudders. With the astute use of questions you can steer your team into lucrative ports, or leave them in pieces on the rocks.

Empowering mechanisms

Questions empower the high performers. They use questions to find ways of achieving. Successful people and teams habitually ask themselves empowering questions: 'All right, so conventional sources of finance won't respond to this project. What are the unconventional sources? Where can I find them? How do I go about persuading them? How can I make the case irresistible?'

Catalysts for change

Questions can be the factor that changes your behaviour. Salespeople have known this for centuries. The persuasion method of the top salespeople worldwide is asking catalytic questions: 'Do you know anywhere you can get the widget you need better or cheaper than at Bloggs and Co.?' 'No,' you reply, 'two please.' Every coaching question aims to be a catalyst for change.

Pulling out – Putting in

Questions are used by the coach/mentor to bring the desire to achieve out of the team. Questions are used by the coach to inspire the team to put in whatever is necessary to help their performance, to encourage the team to decide what they have to add to their performance to improve it.

OBJECTIVES, OWNERSHIP AND FOCUS

Objectives: The unifying thread

In coaching or mentoring objectives are achieved by using questions, which work by enhancing the ownership and focus of the team and its individual members. The whole purpose of coaching and mentoring should be to increase the ownership and awareness of the team.

Ownership

How can the world's top business performers work 14–18 hours a day every day for years and still enjoy it? Simply because they have ownership. Not necessarily ownership of the company but ownership of their efforts. They take total and unconditional responsibility for their beliefs, thoughts, feelings, skills, behaviours and results. The Wright brothers were out there fine-tuning their flying machine while the world's academics were arguing over why mechanical flight was impossible. They owned the problem of flight. They were totally committed to solving the problem. Edison owned the problem of creating the electric light bulb. The NASA team responsible for putting the first humans on the moon owned the problems standing in the way of their dream.

A sense of ownership is central to commitment and persistence. If you own a problem, if that problem is inside you, if it has become part of your soul, finding the energy, commitment and persistence to solve it is easy. So how is ownership acquired? It can be sought or it can be given. If it is given it must be willingly accepted to be of any value. Ownership is increased by asking the team how they propose to . . . how they will . . . what they might do to . . .?

Focus

Focus is what we do when we concentrate on something we are trying to achieve. Focus is the single-minded application to one goal. Focus is enhanced by asking questions that require the team to pay even more attention to the task to be able to answer sensibly. If a team were trying to improve their cash flow projection or management skills, you would ask questions like, 'How regularly does ABC plc pay us?' 'When do Accounts write payment cheques?' Note that the questions, while being open, require only a short or one word answer. The idea is to increase observation and awareness, but not to engage in analysis.

DECIDING WHAT TO ASK: AN OPERATIONAL MODEL

The greatest worry in coaching for those who can see the value of empowering the team is 'How can I decide when to ask what?' There are five main stages in generating the appropriate question.

1 Purpose or objective – Checking the desired direction of the questions
2 Sub-objective – Setting the purpose of the question
3 Method decision – Deciding what type of question to use
4 Question formation – Structuring the sentence for the individual
5 Assessing the answer – Assessing the new level of understanding/ focus/ownership
5a Loop back to Stage 1 to modify objective and repeat.

1 Purpose or objective – Checking the desired direction of the questions

Stage 1, the objective analysis stage, is largely dictated by whatever stage of the coaching process you are currently engaged in.

2 Sub-objective – Setting the purpose of the question

The decision to be made at this stage: Is a question aimed at enhancing ownership or awareness/focus most appropriate? All questions are aimed at either increasing focus or ownership. There must always be some trade-off between focus and ownership, at least on a temporary basis. Asking the team to concentrate on some aspect of performance takes away some ownership. Enhancing ownership necessarily dulls focus for a short while. 'To make an omelette you have to break some eggs'.

3 Method decision – Deciding what type of question to use*

Having set the objective and sub-objective, you now have to decide what questions are most likely to achieve them. There are two main types of question, open and closed. Within these two categories there are numerous types of useful questions between the two extremes:

Open questions All questions, except confirmation reflections, should be open focus-enhancement questions and should require short predictable answers.
Very open questions Ownership enhancement questions should require free-ranging answers.
Assertion questions Used when you want to express an opinion or fact, an issue on which the team's opinion is sought.
Leading questions Naughty little beasties, used to reinforce shared assumptions and encourage ownership.
Probing questions Ideal in helping teams clarify pre-articulate thinking.
Hypothetical questions Best used to persuade teams to contingency plan.
Justifying questions Used to invite the team to justify an unsound position.
Open self-persuasion questions Used to help the team persuade themselves of a desired belief/action.
Prefix/suffix questions Most often used when digging yourself out of the statement-making hole.
Socratic questions Used when you have decided on a conclusion the team should come to.
Stage jump questions Used to establish whether the team has understanding ahead of the current position.
Empathetic questions Designed to encourage team members to think of other parties' feelings.
Discrepancy questions Used to take issue with the team.
Negative feelings questions Used to air, seek explanation, and resolve negative feelings.
Consequence analysis questions Used to have the team think about the likely consequences of their thoughts or plans.
Silence Often the most powerful question you can ask is no question at all.

4 Question formation – Structuring the sentence for the individual

In this stage you plan how to communicate with the listener in the language of the listener. That involves considering their thinking/communication style, educational level, experience, and a whole host of other factors. Don't worry too much about this stage – you already have a lifetime's experience of relating to others, and most of us do this automatically. After you have tuned in to someone's thinking and communication characteristics once, the mind seems to take over automatically.

5 Assessing the answer – Assessing the new level of understanding/awareness/ownership

This process, like the last, is virtually automatic. During communication we are continually checking whether or not the respondents have understood our message as we intended. We also check whether the question has been answered, and to a lesser extent (than we should) to see if we have understood the response. If our listener has not understood the question – made obvious by the answer, our responsibility is to clarify our communication. If the question has not been answered, the team may have deliberately chosen to do so by giving priority to what they see as a more important issue. In which case the coach has to decide whether to re-phrase the question, or adopt the newly identified successor to the sub-goal behind the question. Strictly speaking the team should be asked if they have identified a more important point, and if that ought to become the new priority.

5a Loop back to Stage 1 to modify objective or sub-objective and repeat

When the question has been answered, or the team has satisfied the purpose of the question in some other way, the coach/mentor will make a decision as to how far along the road to closing the gap – defined by the sub-goal – the answer has gone. That decision will then lead to the next decision, which is, if the gap has been closed what is the next sub-goal or, if the gap has not yet been closed, what has still to be achieved?

There will be many occasions when discussing the relevant issues will be more productive, appropriate or simply easier than asking questions. If you must discuss rather than ask, put the emphasis on issues that facilitate self-responsibility in the team, issues such as their mental models of the task or objective they are addressing, or the processes/methods they plan to use, or . . . any of the issues that you would normally ask questions about.

WHAT AFFECTS TEAM PERFORMANCE?

There are numerous factors. Assuming the obvious has been attended to (we all know how dangerous assumptions can be), the most important factors are the level of genuine cooperation and honesty between all the members of the team, and the effects that individual performances of team members have had on achieving the goals of the team. But most of all, the factor which determines high team achievement is purpose. Teams that have a clear, shared and powerful vision (an awesome purpose) are enormously effective.

Coaching a team therefore, is most productively aimed at achieving: A powerful sense of purpose; True team cooperation and mutual support; And improvement of individuals' team-orientated achievement behaviour. We will cover team coaching under the following three headings, providing suggestions for effective coaching at the appropriate point: Understanding teams/organization formation; Team analysis; Applying the MacLennan seven-stage coaching model to teams.

UNDERSTANDING TEAM/ORGANIZATION FORMATION

Although in practice the formation of a group may seem to be a seamless, gradual process, for the purposes of understanding what is going on, it is best to consider this process in seven distinct stages:

1 Decision to create group
2 Inclusion
3 Influence establishment
4 Norm formation
5 Performing
6 Evolving and self-regeneration
7 Termination.

1 Decision to create group

The decision to create the group may be made by one or two people in an organization who may – or may not – be involved. If they are, it is likely they will go on to lead the group. The group may be newly founded, or formed by giving new purpose or powers to a long established group, or have evolved from some previous organizational entity.

Coach/mentor input – If the group is to be newly formed the coach's main responsibility is to ask questions aimed at helping those establishing the group to provide a clear statement of purpose and remit, if that has not been provided by some higher authority.

2   Inclusion

Inclusion is primarily a self-selection and fitting-in phase. Each individual decides whether or not they want to be, or are willing to strive to be, a team member. This is an apparently non-productive phase when individuals are too insecure, anxious and introverted to think of much beyond their own inclusion needs (see below). Those passing this stage quickly are in a better position to adopt early leadership roles.

Coach/mentor input – Conventional training methods to ease the inclusion phase are regarded as 'petty and inappropriate little games' by some. The coach can best help during this phase by asking the members of the group how they would like to get to know each other. Be wary of following the first suggestion by the most forward member of the group – they will definitely not be speaking for the others. Asking how they wish to conduct the induction process sets the precedent for later levels of group involvement and cooperation.

3   Influence

During the influence phase there is an intense, but subtle, struggle for position in the group hierarchy. There is much boundary marking and power play. This phase can be highly destructive: potentially good working relationships can be destroyed and much distrust can be created, by even a mild level of over-enthusiasm for dominance.

Coach/mentor input – Damage limitation. Training methodology has much to offer here. Team development exercises can allow the dominance struggle to take place in a relatively safe emotional environment. The exercises provide a referee in the form of the exercise leader or coach. A referee's presence will enable the formation of a hierarchy without the destruction of potential working relationships before they start.

4   Norm formation

The norm formation stage involves the laying down of ground rules. Very often they are built up during the last two stages. There is an ongoing process of norm establishment and norm maintenance throughout the life of the team. Group norm formation, if left to its own devices, occurs by a process of gradual accumulation of unspoken rules. The most effective teams develop norms to a level of absolute cooperation, mutual support and total trust, even when there is disagreement.

There is often a period of dissatisfaction in the norm formation stage. The initial level of enthusiasm fades as the size of the task becomes apparent.

Coach/mentor input – There are many team exercises and games available in books aimed at helping groups develop and establish their norms. Groups   *377* can establish their norms fastest by deliberately setting out to do so. That is, the coach will ask the group how they wish to organize their norms. This is a question that assumes the group should make such a deliberate attempt. Another appealing advantage, is that structured norm formation prevents or minimizes the likelihood of inappropriate, unfair, divisive and demotivating norms emerging.

The coach can also harness the sense of emptiness created by the period of dissatisfaction by encouraging the team to 'fill the gap' by making the development of an inspiring shared purpose their interim goal.

5 Performing

The group carries out its work in the form of a repetitive cycle consisting of four stages: Preparing; Energizing; Activity; Rest and Recovery.

Preparing

Preparing involves mutual support, nurturing and sharing. This is the stage when group identity is reinforced and bonds are strengthened.

Coach/mentor input – Ask questions that will help the group give priority to these issues.

Energizing

Energizing involves proposing, debating, challenging, constructive argumentation, planning, decision making, enthusing, and group self-motivation building. Infact the energizing process is a clone of Stages 3 to 6 of the coaching process, or vice versa. Most of what has been said about Stages 3 to 6 applies to the process of energizing. The group applies the sequence in an abbreviated way:

3   Assessing the here and now
4   Deciding on the there and then
5   Choosing a bridge between here and now and there and then
6   Building a bridge.

Coach/mentor input – Ask questions which will help the group consider how to conduct these processes more effectively, and questions aimed at increasing their collective ownership of the processes and their efficiency.

Activity

Activity involves activating plans, implementing decisions and providing mutual support and assistance to progress the objectives.

Coach/mentor input – Help individuals increase their ownership of and concentrate on their part of the objectives, and to be responsive to the support needs of other members of the team.

Rest and recovery

Rest and recovery involves recognizing the end point, finishing the odd bits and pieces, celebration of the achievement, expressions of gratitude and thanks, or, expressing gratitude for the efforts each contributed and taking a break before deciding how to learn from a non-achievement. Like the preparing phase, rest and recovery is important for group bonding.

Coach/mentor input – Ask questions which help the group appreciate the need for, and take action towards, a distinct period of rest and recovery. That is especially important in a group of high achievers who may wish to start planning their next achievement on completion of the last.

6 Evolving and self-regeneration

The group must continually move with the times to survive, and it must also be able to continue uninterrupted should any one member need to be replaced for any reason. It usually plans for the succession of its own members in some way.

Coach/mentor input – Ask questions aimed at encouraging the group in considering and taking ownership of longevity issues.

7 Termination

Every group eventually breaks down, even at a societal level. Few society structures survive more than ten generations. Most companies do not survive one. If a group was set up to achieve a specific objective and terminates on completion, there should be provision for the members to celebrate their existence and mourn their loss.

Coach/mentor input – The provision of coaching in the termination of a group is unlikely, unless it is a project team or some other deliberately short-term team. The most likely situations are commercial reorganization and liquidation. It may come as a surprise to some readers that receivers are not particularly interested in team coaching. Whatever the situation, the involved coach can ask questions aimed at facilitating emotional expression.

TEAM ANALYSIS

Group performance will now be examined in more detail by discussing: group dynamics – the means by which a coach can analyse what is happening; and the means by which a coach or mentor can facilitate group performance based on the information obtained.

The power of purpose

In many ineffective groups, purpose is not defined, not understood, not shared, and not achievable because there are no clear targets. For example, a group may be set up to make decisions about a particular task, but on closer inspection it may turn out that one, or a small number of, the group make the decisions prior to the meeting and the remainder of the group rubber stamps them. The role of the coach in this situation is to alert the group to the long-term consequences of such a situation and, more importantly, to help them adopt the elements of purpose contained in Chapter 3 of this book. The sad reality is that most employees in most companies worldwide have little idea of their company vision or strategy. Lack of shared purpose is one reason a single entrepreneur can regularly achieve more than the combined resources of huge multinational organizations: No individual is more effective than a team working well; most individuals are more effective than all teams working badly. The numbers of successful entrepreneurs testifies convincingly to the validity to the following: A shared awesome purpose creates simply awesome power.

Coach/mentor input – Help the team to create a shared vision.

Individual needs

For successful group participation, each individual member has three needs which must be satisfied: Inclusion; Influence; Affection. The precise nature of the needs and the route to their satisfaction is:

Inclusion

The individual: determines whether they have a sense of similarity to the others; makes the choice to self-include or not; is included by the others or not; is included by the leader individual or not; engages in self-including behaviour or not.

Coach/mentor input – Team inclusion is a process and decision that individuals conduct mainly without support. There are at least two ways that the processes can be conducted with minimal threat to the participants. First, the coach can ensure everyone present knows what is going on. Second, some ice-breaker games can get the process started.

Influence

The individual has a desire to: influence others and needs the leader to respond to their influence attempts; be supported in those attempts by at least some of the others; avoid feeling that their inclusion is dependent on the outcome of the influence attempts. Each member of the group should feel they are empowered by the group and within the group. They should feel that resources are available for the pursuit of their part of the common purpose. They should feel that the organizational or team procedures do not block their attempts to achieve on behalf of the team or organization.

Coach/mentor input – Ask questions of individuals designed to help them increase their influence abilities and skills, and on how the group can empower each member of the team.

Affection

The individual needs to: feel liked; delight in the achievements of the others in the group; have others delight in their achievements; be willing to express their affection to others; be liked by the leader; like the others in the group; feel a variance of views is valued; feel that openness and honesty are the norm.

Coach/mentor input – Asking questions of individuals that will emphasize the positive aspects of other group members. Ask questions emphasizing the achievements of others. In fact the asking of any question that will facilitate the above affection elements will help.

Norm analysis

Every group forms a set of shared and agreed values. In the same way that an organization's recruitment policies are best assessed by the profiles of existing staff, a group's norms are best assessed by what is actually done, not by what is said to be done. The norms can be inferred by observing and seeking answers to the following questions:

- What is the apparent priority given to facts, statistics, emotional expression, vision, political issues, and so on?
- What is the decision making style? Is it autocratic? Democratic? *Laissez-faire*? Or something in between? That is, does the leader appear to conduct a democratic process, but overrules the outcome if it is not as he or she had expected?
- Is the decision making process consistent? Or does it vary depending on . . . depending on what?
- How are conflicts handled?
- What is the reaction to lateness, non-achievement, failure to carry out an agreed action, challenging the head of the hierarchy . . .

Coach/mentor input – Ask questions designed to have the group think about its norms,* to identify those which are empowering and disempowering. Ask the group to consciously choose, to adopt and enact empowering achievement-oriented values.

Group participation patterns

There is considerable overlap between norm analysis and group participation analysis. In fact the actual group participation patterns reveal a great
deal about the norms active in any team; they are separate but linked. The
participation patterns are to norms what symptoms are to disease; they
are the manifestation not the mechanism, the consequence not the cause.
Analysing group participation patterns will give the coach a rapid way of
understanding the functioning of the group.

Coach/mentor input – Ask questions designed to direct the attention of the
group towards the group participation patterns, and then learn from those
observations. Ask questions that enable the group to make inferences about
and then improvements on: the underlying norms; the decision making
methods; the communication patterns; the conflict resolution methods;
the . . . whatever problems need to be addressed. The coaching input for
norms applies from then on.

Leadership analysis

Leadership is a funny business. The nominal leader of a group may not be
the actual leader. In some countries, the President or Head of State actually
functions in that capacity, in others they are figureheads obliged to stay out
of management affairs. The same applies in groups of a smaller nature. All
types of leaders can be official or unofficial, that is, functioning as recognized
by some higher authority, or not recognized, but operating in that capacity.
There are three leadership roles in any group. Some leaders combine the
roles and fulfil them, others delegate them by design or default. The roles
are: The accountable leader; The effective leader; The emotional leader.
Determine who fills what role by asking appropriate questions.*

Leadership can also be analysed in terms of the three functions required
of it. Namely, to fulfil the purpose of the group, to maintain group cohesion
and address team development needs, and to satisfy individual needs of
team members. A skilled leader blends in and continues working to find the
common ground in the three needs. He or she may place different emphasis
on one of the three areas for a period to ensure that the total mix remains
in a functional balance.

Coach/mentor input – To ask questions aimed at focusing the group's attention on the way it leads itself. To ask questions aimed at raising awareness
of the assignment of the three leadership roles. Asking questions aimed at
having the group decide how best to lead itself. To ask questions of the
leader(s) aimed at bringing their attention to how they can satisfy the three
needs of the team, the individual and the objective more effectively.

Role analysis

There are a huge number of roles that could be played in any team other than the constructive, supportive, dedicated team member, or one of the three leadership roles. Some of the more common are: The Scapegoat, The Rebel, The Abominable No Person, The Yes Person, The Bully, The Pedant, The Critic, The Time Keeper, The Referee/Umpire, The Saint.

The roles, and there may be more than one per person, are best analysed by examining the actual behaviour, as opposed to the claimed behaviour of team members. The most common empowering and disempowering behaviours in meetings are: Bringing in; Building on; Stimulating; Proposing; Accepting person, not idea; Inclusion; Clarifying; Simplifying; Enlivening; Initiating; Understanding testing; Consensus testing; Information seeking; Information provision; Summarizing; Unifying; Expressing motions; Harmonizing; Compromising; Gate keeping; Supporting; Habitual supporting; Blocking out; Shutting out; Picking; Hurrying; Disagreeing; Habitual disagreeing; Attacking; Habitual attacking; Defending; Scapegoating; Kneejerk objecting; Burden sharing; Burden shifting. If you want to give these behaviours role labels, just turn them into nouns.

Coach/mentor input – Ask questions of those team members who engage in disempowering or destructive behaviours. Questions which are aimed at first helping them to become aware of the behaviours and second, aware of the consequences of those behaviours. It is better to help the maladaptive team see the consequences of their behaviour, and to develop their own motivation for change, than to point them out. The coach should also ask questions aimed at encouraging others to resist the impact of inappropriate or destructive team behaviours in others. Further questions can be asked of the group to encourage them to ask questions aimed at helping the maladaptive team member become aware, and take responsibility for, their behaviour.

Health checklist

The atmosphere during a team's operations is a very accurate predictor of the health of its functioning. Below is a list of healthy team behaviours. To compile one for terminal team behaviours just substitute the opposite for each entry.*

- Common purpose
- Established organizational structure
- Membership criteria agreed
- Continuity of group
- Growth and adaptability
- Free from cliques
- Individual freedom and acceptance

- Willingness to accept discontentment
- Willingness to resolve conflict internally
- Decision making methods agreed and flexible
- Absolute cooperation with, and faith in, the team
- Mutual support, acceptance and recognition
- Group support individuals, individuals support group
- Group is mostly self-leading.

APPLYING THE COACHING MODEL

Assessing the team here and now

The toughest part of assessing teams is persuading the members to be honest. Just as 98 per cent of drivers think they are good drivers, 99 per cent of team members think their team is the best and they're just waiting for the chance to prove it. Ho, hum! Asking the team if it functions well is like asking the fox if it guards the hen house well. It will say yes because it won't let a single chicken escape! So, how can you obtain a clear assessment? By asking the team to compare its results against quantitative measures, and by self-assessment aimed at detached analysis.

Team assessment

Compare the team's performance to that of other teams, departments or industries. This sounds easy, and it is for the top team, the board of directors; financial and other performance factors like labour cost, return per employee and so on, are readily available. For non-top teams the objective performance figures are a little harder to obtain. They can be deduced by breaking down the elements of the company's overall performance into departmental contributions. For instance, the performance of the finance department can be assessed by comparing the ratio of finance labour costs to total expenditure, or to total labour costs against another company's performance on the same ratio.

If the group decides that they will assess themselves on objective measures, they should decide what measures and how to compile them. The performance of every group can be measured, despite what some will try to tell you. For some, like public sector employees, it may be harder to measure performance, but 'harder' is no excuse not to. To the contrary, 'harder' is even more reason performance should be measured. If it is difficult to quantify then there is more scope for poor performance to go undetected, and the universal experience of human nature is: what is inspected is to be expected – and what is ignored will be neglected. Excellent performance will also go undetected, with the consequence that there can be no rational basis for deciding who is performing well enough to justify promotion or a bonus. This begs the question, how do public sector bodies which resist performance assessment make promotion decisions? It can't be on the basis of performance because they tell us that can't be measured!

If the team resists quantitative performance assessment it is the coach's responsibility to diplomatically raise awareness and seek team ownership of the notion that the only way to improve is to know how well they are doing, what their starting point is and what their weaknesses are. The only way to have that accuracy of information about a group is to use impartial assessment measures.

Team self-assessment

On what bases should a team assess its own effectiveness? The two most frequent subjects for assessment are process and outcome.* Outcome self-assessment involves examining the perceived achievements of the group in numerical terms along various, not quite objective, dimensions. 'Not quite objective' because the means of measuring the performances are entirely within the team's control, or within an individual member's control. There may be the occasional group or group member who will try to pass off self-assessment measures as quantitative assessment data. Of course this is very rare, and in your entire coaching career you will be most unlikely to witness this in business or in politics.

Coaching team cohesion

Some trite phrases sum up the best courses of action in team coaching, and one in particular that works well is 'People who play together, stay together.' They stay together not just physically but mentally, too. Suggest and discuss the possibility of the team members having some kind of social time together. The bonding process would also be helped if they engage in a group learning experience, or in some kind of charity event during which they could work together for the benefit of others.

At some stage in team coaching, the group should have a chance to learn about group functioning, particularly about healthy and unhealthy group behaviours. If the whole team knows the most effective team process behaviours, they will subtly expect each other to behave in those ways. Since we know people tend to rise to fulfil high expectations, the whole team performance can be enhanced by virtue of mere common knowledge and shared expectation.

Coaching the organization

The most effective way to achieve any change in an organization is from the top down. To set up a coaching culture in the whole organization the top team should set an example; set the precedent. Even if there is no systematic attempt to introduce or push coaching company-wide, there will probably be a natural spreading of coaching. There will be an active 'pull' by staff as a result of the 'trickle down' and 'boss mimicking' effects. Corporate culture reflects the culture displayed by the top team. What the team above or the top team has, everybody wants. Resistance to coaching is likely to be minimal under those circumstances.

Coaching individual team members

We have mentioned in passing, but not stated explicitly, the goals of coaching teams as they apply to the individual. There are two distinct purposes in coaching individual team members:

1 To improve their team-orientated achievement behaviour. Which might include:
    • Team participation skills – influence skills, presentation, argumentation, negotiation, assertiveness, and so on.
    • Personal paradigm analysis,* in relation to the team, an analysis of the members' empowering and disempowering beliefs *vis-à-vis* the team.
    • An analysis of individuals' motivations towards the team. People at different stages in the personal motivational needs hierarchy will be differently motivated towards the group.
2 To improve individuals' role performances so that their contribution to the team is greater.
    • Improving the performance of individual team members is achieved by coaching their individual contribution to the team effort as if it were an individual effort.

Coaching the team to coach the individual members of the team

The ultimate level of team functioning is total cooperation. Having reached this ideal, the teams coach themselves and their individual members. One of the devices that can be used to reach this level is to ask each member of the team to rate themselves on how they think they have performed in terms of their role, and to specify where they can improve. The team then offers honest, constructive feedback, support, and advice on the self-rating and the proposed improvement methods. The beauty of this system is that everyone can help everyone else. A genuine air of mutual support develops quickly because of the trust necessary to conduct the exercise without injuring the feelings of others. One will, after all, be next on the chopping block if one has not been helpful and supportive!

The coach has at least two choices with such self-coaching devices. He or she can introduce self-coaching methods when the team is functioning well and is ready for self-coaching, or coach them towards self-coaching as a rapid way of bringing the team to the highest levels of cooperation.

Coaching logistics

If you remember our earlier discussion on the coaching process, we emphatically stated that concentrating on performing and analysis ought to be two separate processes. There should be separate meetings for the purposes of coaching (analysing) and group performance, that is not to say the coach should not be present at performance meetings. He or she can obtain the most accurate observational information about team functioning from meetings where performance is the purpose. Meetings where coaching is the purpose are likely to encourage members to be on their best team behaviour, thereby making analysis of the process by the coach more difficult.

CONCLUDING COMMENTS AND SUMMARY

Coaches and mentors can help team performance in several ways: a) by helping the formation of the team be as beneficial as possible for future working relationships; b) by helping individuals fit in to the team; c) by helping the team to analyse, understand and improve its own functioning; d) by helping individuals to support the team and the team to support its members; e) by helping the team to adopt the characteristics and sense of direction necessary for high achievement; f) by helping individual members perform as effectively as possible in their individual contributions to the team effort.

In principle the coaching or mentoring of teams follows the same sequence of events as coaching an individual person. The main difference is in the number of voices with which the team speaks.

REFERENCE

MacLennan, N., *Coaching and Mentoring*, Gower, Aldershot, 1995

25 Designing and facilitating team development

Malcolm Crockford

This chapter provides a practical guide to designing, facilitating and evaluating team development events. It makes several assumptions.

First, it assumes that, although there are some managers who are highly capable of facilitating their own events, in most cases facilitators or trainers, either internal or external to the organization, are used. This is because the experienced facilitator will have access to a variety of design ideas and techniques, and will be able to support the event with resources and materials not so readily available to the line manager. Most modern managers also recognize the need to fully participate in the event as a team member, unencumbered by responsibility for the agenda. They also value the interventions that a facilitator external to the group can make, and the sensitivity they can apply to interpersonal relationships in the team.

Second, it assumes that, although excellent team development can be done 'on the job', and may be a part of the total activity, most readers will associate team development with specific 'events'. These involve time away from the normal workplace and workplace activity, and provide time for reflection, closer association and an emphasis on the human processes in the team.

The third assumption is that the type of team development we are dealing with in this chapter falls in the middle area of a spectrum that ranges from, at one extreme, pure recreation, to the other extreme, which means going away from the workplace to do the same work activities the team usually does, but more intensively! In some organizations team building is perceived as going to a hotel or conference venue for one or two days, doing some recreational team activities, then enjoying the benefits of hospitality provided by the organization, ending perhaps with some motivational words from the senior manager and then back to work with a hangover!

A burgeoning industry of recreational providers can supply all forms of outdoor games and activities from laser shooting to falconry, from 'It's a Knock Out' team games to tank driving! The 'Awayday' option, however, is not without its payoffs: it provides a basis of shared experience that may 'bond' some team members; it recognizes that 'rest and recreation' strategies have a proven value in any number of situations; and recognition is a powerful motivator. The challenge, therefore, is to import some elements of the recreational option without sacrificing the true value of team development.

The fourth assumption is that, with the existence of so many models, techniques and theories concerning teams and personal relationships, we shall have to be selective in this chapter. The reading list at the end of the chapter will attempt to fill the gap; but to try to do justice to Transactional Analysis, Neuro-Linguistic Programming or Gestalt approaches in a single paragraph would be robbing some deep and eminent techniques of the space they richly deserve (see Hay, 1992, O'Connor and Seymour, 1993 and Clarkson, 1993).

STAGES IN THE TEAM DEVELOPMENT PROCESS

Figure 25.1 outlines the stages in the process of designing, delivering and evaluating a team development event. The first assumption mentioned earlier was that the services of a facilitator external to the team would be used. But even where the line manager decides to facilitate the event on their own, the same thinking and decision making processes are still relevant.

Initial contact with client

The purpose of the initial meeting is to establish rapport with the client, gain an initial impression of what the client is seeking to achieve and understand how they perceive the team and its situation. The initial contact may be the result of the client seeking advice, or the facilitator reacting to input they have received and offering support, or the organization 'sending in' help. This last situation may arise, for example, from a negative attitude survey or poor team performance, or the client's manager feeling that the team could be improved. Alternatively, the team may be performing well, but about to face a new work challenge or project, or feeling the need for reflection in order to build on its success.

In all these different circumstances the facilitator will be sensing the degree to which the client is committed to the event, and the extent to which their relationship will be successful. The facilitator will take the opportunity to assess all the circumstances presented, the business environment, and any data that can be absorbed about the nature of the team. This will mean that the facilitator should be using an active listening style, and should not be leaping to conclusions or presenting ready-made designs or solutions. The meeting should certainly cover most of the design considerations listed later in the chapter, and should also be used to find out what *389*

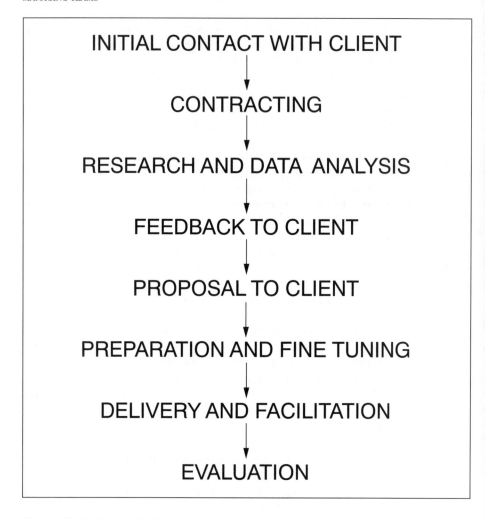

INITIAL CONTACT WITH CLIENT

CONTRACTING

RESEARCH AND DATA ANALYSIS

FEEDBACK TO CLIENT

PROPOSAL TO CLIENT

PREPARATION AND FINE TUNING

DELIVERY AND FACILITATION

EVALUATION

Figure 25.1   Stages in the team development process

previous team development experiences the client has had that may have shaped their views.

Contracting

The contracting stage could be a subsequent meeting, when both parties have had a chance to reflect on possibilities, or a further stage of the initial meeting. The former is preferable, but may not be logistically possible.

There are many views as to the role of the consultant. The generally accepted view is that the client knows what they want to achieve, and the consultant should know how to help the client to meet their objectives. Consultants who profess to know what the client wants to achieve (and tell them!) are exceeding their role, although they may help the client to modify

390

their expectations based on their specialist knowledge of what is possible. Cockman, Evans and Reynolds (1992) deal with the issues associated with the consultancy role in some depth.

The contracting stage provides the opportunity for agreement to be reached on achievable objectives, for confirmation of commitments on both sides (for example, to time and methodology) and for reaching consensus on what expenditure is acceptable for the agreed outputs. Both clients should come to an arrangement about the next steps (that is, research and data analysis) and the implications of the accepted techniques, and make commitments to dates and logistics so that team members can book their diaries and a suitable venue can be sought.

Research

There are a number of ways that data in preparation for team development events can be collected, from a full-blown attitude or opinion survey with full statistical analysis to a quick conversation with a member or two of the team. As mentioned above, the event may have been suggested as the result of data created by attitude surveys, performance or ranking processes, or by critical incidents. In these cases the facilitator should have access to the available data. The facilitator should also attempt to learn about the type of work the team is doing, how they are organized, and research any local jargon or norms that the team uses.

If the facilitator is to use some form of psychometrics to support the event, this can form an excellent basis for data collection and will allow the facilitator to build relationships with the team members individually. Chapter 20 indicates some of the instruments that can be used in teamwork, particularly the Myers-Briggs Type Indicator.

The general preference is to conduct face-to-face interviews with each member of the team, including the leader or client. This helps to build rapport with team members, establish the situation at first hand, encourage disclosure and create trust. It also serves to identify any anxieties or needs individuals may have which will affect the design of the event. For example, a common concern is that team members will be forced into a higher level of self-disclosure than they feel comfortable with, or that they have a fear of outdoor-type physical activities (water and heights being common phobias!). Reassurance can be offered where appropriate, and the general nature of concerns taken into account in the proposed design. It is also useful to check which members have any previous experience of team development, and what types they have experienced. This will prevent using an approach or activity that all or some have done before, and is one of the questions to include in any prepared list of questions. Some excellent examples of team interview checklists are included in several of the books listed at the end of the chapter (for example, Moxon, 1993, pages 99–101, and Harshman and Phillips, 1996). Such lists are not intended to be used slavishly during the meeting, but may be reviewed beforehand and kept in mind.

Key areas to probe in face-to-face meetings are:

- Feelings about the effectiveness of the team and its processes;
- Openness, trust and communication within the team;
- How the team handles change, conflict, and problems;
- How the leadership of the team is viewed;
- How clear are the roles of the team and its overall goals;
- How the team handles success and failure;
- And what changes would team members like to see in the team.

A good facilitator question is: 'If you had a magic wand, what three things would you change about this team?' The responses can be most revealing!

Confidentiality needs to be taken into account at all stages of preparation, and there should be a clear contract with the client and all team members about what is kept confidential and what may be divulged. Often the facilitator will contract to give generic feedback to the client without attribution, and encourage team members to 'open up' at the event. Most facilitators find that the team members, having brought up an issue in confidence beforehand, are more able to raise the topic in open session.

Feedback to client

Where the client is under time pressure, or the issues are reasonably clear cut, this stage can be combined with the next stage (the proposal itself). However, where the issues are complex, the data analysis detailed, and the feedback sensitive to handle, it may be better to have a separate meeting to allow time for both parties to reflect and do further planning. It would also not be prudent to approach the client with sensitive data *and* a detailed proposal, unless the facilitator knows the personality of the client so well that the way the client will react is totally predictable!

Proposal to client

The method of making the proposal will vary according to the culture of the organization, the personality of the client, the relationship and trust that have been established – or a combination of all three. At one extreme consultants may be asked to make a formal presentation to all team members, and have to defend every idea, or see their design proposals being torn to pieces! At the other extreme the client may have built up such a relationship with the consultant that they will be comfortable with a brief overview. Whatever the method, the consultant should be able to agree objectives for the event, articulate their design decisions (based on the design considerations later in this chapter) and agree methodology, the role to be played by the client and logistics (such as timings and venue).

Fine tuning and preparation

The consultant will use this stage to refine ideas based on the client's reaction to the proposal; skilled practitioners will make sure that a total rework is not a possibility! Then detailed preparation can start which may involve developing handouts and materials, visual aids, business games or simulations, management exercises, psychometrics, and so on. It can involve visiting the venue where the event is to be run and, depending on the contract, liaising directly with the venue staff and briefing them. Where outdoor activities are involved, it is necessary to check routes, materials and the competence of any staff involved.

A word of warning here! Most experienced facilitators have learned to build flexibility into their planned designs. Team development is dynamic and sometimes unpredictable, and the facilitator should be prepared to change tack to achieve the best outputs for the client. For this reason timings that are too detailed may be unrealistic and may straitjacket the facilitator on the day. Also it is wise to have a selection of alternatives in the kitbag! And skilled facilitators carry large kitbags – either literally, or in their minds!

Delivery

There is a section later in the chapter about facilitation which covers intervention style and the variety of approaches the facilitator can use in delivery. During the event itself there should be few surprises about the role the facilitator plays, if the contracting with the client has been effective. It is important that the client and the facilitator agree who does what; there is nothing more embarrassing than when the two are confused about their roles. For example, if it is agreed that the client will 'top and tail' the event they should have prepared themselves for this, perhaps with suggestions from the facilitator.

So far we have discussed the facilitator in the singular. If the group is large enough, or if the planned approach is complex or if the event calls for a mixture of skills or knowledge, or if syndication is to be widely used, it would require additional facilitators. As with the client, they will need to contract with each other about roles they play and how they will support each other. Sometimes one facilitator may be a learner, or junior in experience. Sometimes they may be someone with an additional role, say an HR adviser for the participating department. In these cases forming a contract beforehand is particularly important.

Evaluation

Most authors on the evaluation of training and development tend to use several levels of evaluation that include participant reactions, learning, changes in job behaviour and business results. 'Participant reactions' refers   *393* to the immediate reaction of participants to the event, usually gathered by discussion or questionnaire at the end of the event. Skilled facilitators tend to seek feedback at regular stages during the event. This is appreciated by participants, and ensures that the facilitator does not go off track because the participants are too polite to point it out.

'Happiness sheets', which sometimes seek to confirm that everyone had a good time and enjoyed themselves, have acquired, not always fairly, a poor reputation among evaluation professionals. A well-constructed questionnaire can give valuable and immediate feedback on the reaction of the clients to a training event, and act as an instrument of quality control in high-volume training situations. For team development activity, however, an oral and interactive approach is preferable and is more consistent with the nature of such activity.

'Learning' evaluation covers the increase in knowledge or data gained from a training event, and is highly measurable. Pre- and post-training tests are applied and the gain can be accurately measured. Team development events are not usually run with the primary intention of increasing the technical knowledge of participants, or of increasing their knowledge of behavioural theory, although the latter will probably happen. The knowledge to be gained is about other members of the team, their reactions and motivations. It would be difficult to devise a questionnaire that would accurately measure knowledge gains in this area, although there are some games that could reflect participants' general increase in knowledge of each other.

Some changes in job behaviour may be noticed during the event itself, in terms of how team members interact with each other. Whether this carries back into the workplace, however, needs to be subsequently explored. Many events close with individual participants articulating how they propose to, or are committed to, change their behaviour ('Things I will do differently'). As this is an open declaration, it can be monitored by the team itself back in the workplace. Alternatively the facilitator can contract to sit in on subsequent work meetings and comment on noticeable changes in behaviour. Sometimes the team will make a team commitment to change, develop new 'operating guidelines' or 'rules of engagement' and publish them. This has become something of a vogue, in the same way as corporate mission statements and values. It can be made a more worthwhile exercise for the team if they use their own words or images.

Team development can be expensive. It can take a number of key people away from their 'real jobs' for two or three days; it can involve heavy expenditure on hotel accommodation, food and drinks; and the use of consultants and their associated activities can incur high costs. It is therefore not unreasonable for senior managers to ask for justification of such expense in terms of improved business results. The problem is that it is extremely difficult to prove or demonstrate increases in business performance as a result of team development. Business results can be highly measurable in some areas, for example, sales or turnover, but fluctuations may be the

result of a variety of circumstances, of which team development may be one. To demonstrate that team development is more than an 'act of faith', some organizations allow their managers to make their own decisions about whether to run team events, with the proviso that the expense involved is deducted from their budgets. Those managers who are convinced of its value will see the expense as an investment, but will not be profligate. Those who are not convinced will watch their colleagues' business results with interest!

DESIGN CONSIDERATIONS

The nature of the team

Before attempting to design any event, the consultant or facilitator will need to gather key information about the team during initial discussions with the client and during the research stage. This will include the nature, size and maturity of the team. What are their key work processes and outputs? How many are there in the team? How long have they been together as a team? Are they an ongoing (organizational) team, or brought together for a project or *ad hoc* mission? What level of skills do they have? How interdependent are they in their work and how homogeneous in their skills? Where are they in the team development cycle (otherwise known as stages of group development – Forming, Storming, Norming and Performing – Tuckman, 1977)? How well do they know each other (at work and outside work)?

The team's previous experience

Unless the organization has a team development strategy and resources are shared equally, the chances are that the Pareto principle will apply and 20 per cent of teams will receive 80 per cent of team development! This can lead to the creation of team-building 'junkies' who take advantage of every variation of team building on offer! As mentioned above, some organizations allow their managers to spend in this area from their own budgets, so that it is seen as an investment, just like marketing or advertising, to increase business results. The 'junkies' must therefore be convinced of the value in increased motivation, morale and outputs. They do, however, represent a challenge to the event designer, who has to explore, as part of the research stage, what each team member has done before and attempt to use methods that have not been experienced already. This is to avoid unfortunate comparisons, to exploit the lure of the new and unique, and to avoid boredom. Perhaps this is the reason that HR and OD professionals are sometimes accused of indulging in fads and fashions!

The client's objectives

It is important to be clear with the client about the real objectives of the event. Hidden agendas can be time bombs, and it is very important to   *395* develop a level of trust with the client that allows them to be totally open. If the client wants an event purely for 'rest and recreation' that is perfectly acceptable, but may require a different style of facilitation. If the client is seeking a cathartic experience with plenty of openness and expression of feelings, the facilitator will need to have experience and competence in this area, and may question whether the client understands the implications and risks.

To avoid hidden agendas, it is wise to confirm the objectives with the client and distribute them to participants with their joining instructions. Here is an example of some core objectives agreed with the client for their team development event:

- Review how the team is working together
- Get to know each other better (motivation, skills, preferences)
- Build basis for effective working relationships
- Identify strengths and improvement areas for the team
- Review future business plans, outputs and accountabilities
- Create a vision for the future success of the team
- Agree values and operating principles for the team.

Additional, or alternative, objectives could be:

- Explore differences and similarities in Type (MBTI)
- Celebrate success and recognize our strengths as a team and as individuals
- Have some fun and relaxation together!
- Discuss our business strategy and agree detailed plans for next year.

Design principles

There are certain conventions which apply to the design of learning events which are appropriate to team development. Adult Learning Theory (see Knowles, 1979) provides some basic design principles for adults in learning situations. These include the following:

- Build on previous experience of participants
- Allow for maximum participation, and learning by doing
- Focus on current, existing problems rather than abstract concepts
- Check with participants on what they are learning and experiencing, and be prepared to change direction to meet their needs
- Recognize that people learn at different rates and in different ways
- Build in variety of techniques and activities
- Allow for feedback to participants from facilitator or team members
- Avoid lectures! Ten to fifteen-minute theory inputs are sufficient (if needed at all!).

This emphasizes the need to offer participants experiences that they may not meet in their normal work situations, and use the resulting behaviour for analysis and feedback. The Kolb Learning Cycle (Kolb, 1984) offers four stages in the experiential learning process:

- Concrete Experience (an activity, exercise, simulation or task)
- Reflective Observation (reflect on experience, debrief, give feedback)
- Abstract conceptualization (develop general principles and relate to theory and research)
- Active Experimentation (preparing to try new behaviours in next activity).

The learning cycle can apply to any learning situation, and is particularly relevant to team development which includes a series of group tasks or exercises, and especially to outdoor development. To gain the most from experiential learning it is important not to skip stages, especially reflection and conceptualization; here the role of the facilitator is to apply the discipline and provide theoretical input or models. Both stages can be difficult and uncomfortable for participants; in organizational life there is unfortunately not enough time given for reflection before moving on to the next task or activity. Beware team development providers who offer a series of tasks and activities without any opportunity for debriefing or feedback!

Another basic design principle in team development is to follow the time sequence – Past, Present, Future. This means that the first part of the event should be devoted to dealing with past experiences, past feelings, and reflection on what has happened before that may still be affecting current behaviour. This can have the effect of allowing people to 'complete on the past', draw a line, and move on. It allows old conflicts and disagreements to be buried, old successes to be resurrected and enjoyed, and people to get their feelings out of the way. This is important for new teams who may be carrying a lot of 'emotional baggage', and who should be allowed to dump it.

The Present phase should deal with current team performance and relationships, with the use of psychometrics, team exercises or group discussion. In this phase the facilitator supports the learning with interventions that point up behaviour and feelings that the team may not have noticed or may be reluctant to deal with.

The Future phase leads up to the end of the event, and has the effect of encouraging team members to look forward to future challenges and successes, leaving the event hopefully feeling optimistic and reinvigorated. The sequencing of Past – Present – Future provides a logical flow to the event, and gives the team members a sensation of constantly moving forward.

The last consideration in the design of team events is the need to maintain pace and energy levels. The old precept for instructors about not lecturing after lunch holds good for team facilitators. At low energy times, schedule periods of high activity, an exercise or lively discussion, or use energizers or physical breaks to revitalize the team. Be prepared to introduce these when energy flags or the team becomes stuck, as long as it is not used to avoid conflict or uncomfortable situations (see University Associates, 1983 and West, 1997).

The style of the event

During the initial stages of contracting, the discussion should cover the respective roles to be taken by the client and the facilitator. Will the leader want to lead or chair the event with a degree of formality, perhaps wishing to maintain control and demonstrate leadership? Or will they prefer to allow the facilitator to drive the bus, with the client as active passenger? Or will the client prefer to be totally passive, listening and observing, and not taking sides? Experience shows that the central position is sought by most leaders who prefer to free themselves from their working role, and give themselves a democratic voice.

The consultant will also need to form a contract about the depth of interventions. Roger Harrison (1970) recommends that group facilitators 'intervene at a level no deeper than that at which the energy and resources of the client can be committed to problem solving and to change'. Reddy (1994) identifies five levels in what he describes as the 'Iceberg of Group Dynamics'. Above the surface are Level 1 (Content, that is, the work to be done) and Level 2 (Overt Group Issues such as interactions, task and interpersonal conflicts). Below the surface are Level 3 (Covert and Core Group Issues, such as membership, control, power, competence and friendship), Level 4 (Values, Beliefs and Assumptions) and Level 5 (Unconscious, similar to the 'unknown' pane in Johari's Window – see Luft, 1961).

To go below the surface, the facilitator needs the willing agreement and commitment of the client and all team members, and the competence, knowledge and skills to undertake such psychological deep-sea diving. Many team development events have failed badly where the facilitator has taken the participants to a level of self-disclosure to which they had not given permission, or to which the client has contracted, but without consulting team members. Unless team members are consulted and clearly give permission, it is unethical and unprofessional to allow peer pressure to pull them into areas they do not wish to reveal or explore. Sometimes such behaviour is rationalized using the argument that there is 'no gain without pain', and that they will 'feel better' for the catharsis. In an organizational setting, however, there is an obligation on the management to safeguard the physical and psychological well-being of its staff, and protect them from psychological malpractice. This can be made particularly worse by organizations that use such training or events as precursor to promotion or as a corporate 'rite of passage'.

The concept of ensuring voluntary participation is especially important in the case of outdoor team development. The spectrum of activities commercially available ranges from what approximates to the rigour, exertion and danger of SAS or Royal Marine training, to the use of the outdoors to provide some background to problems or situations not likely to be encountered in the workplace. Assuming that participants understand and have chosen the level of arduousness and intensity to which they are committing themselves, there are some major benefits to be gained from outdoor team development as a form of experiential learning:

1 As the tasks involved are usually totally different from what team members usually do at work, they can be directed towards *team process* rather than *work content*.
2 Traditional learning usually emphasizes theory or application. 'Learning by doing', especially in the outdoor context, is a powerful technique, and increases the intensity of the learning experience.
3 Outdoor activity gives more opportunity to mix elements of intellectual and physical challenge in the exercises, so that individual strengths and skills can be viewed and valued in the team. Unexpected skills and knowledge can sometimes be revealed, which increase the self-esteem of the individual and their standing in the team.
4 The shared experience can break down the normal barriers and create opportunities for 'bonding' that would not usually occur. Sharing a tent or bivouac, wearing outdoor clothing, and cooking and eating together in the outdoors, is an experience that can be remembered and acknowledged back in the office.
5 In these unusual circumstances, mistakes are more readily made, more readily accepted, and more readily reviewed and learnt from. These are often lessons for the team to take back to the workplace.
6 As participants are 'all in the same boat' – sometimes literally – they are more likely to disregard their normal organizational roles and identities, and display their individual talents.
7 Memories and visual images of the learning situations can be carried back into normal working life and mentally replayed when similar team process scenarios occur. This can apply as much to a 'walk and talk' or 'stroll with a purpose' around the Cotswolds countryside, as a night spent on top of a snow-capped mountain!

If outdoor development is not competently handled, it can present far more physical and psychological risks then 'conventional' team development. There has been a great deal of discussion recently about the safety aspects of adventure and outdoor training to ensure that trainers have the necessary competence and knowledge and, in some cases, qualifications. This should apply to competence in handling group dynamics as well as first aid and the use of outdoor equipment.

Facilitation of event

Facilitation styles can vary according to the nature of the team, the level of intervention and the basic methodology used. Heron (1989) identifies six Intervention Categories (grouped into Authoritative and Facilitative sections) as follows (see Table 25.1).

Bentley (1994) writes of 'the facilitation spectrum' which ranges from 'gentle intervention' to 'forceful intervention', moving from 'doing nothing' through Supportive and Persuasive behaviours to Directing.

As in the discussion of levels of intervention earlier in the chapter, the issue is about the situational appropriateness of style rather than global rules of correctness. Another important aspect to consider is the style range of the facilitator, their comfort in moving out of the preferred style, and whether it is more effective to use the principle of 'horses for courses' in the selection of consultants. It emphasizes the need for effective contracting to ensure a good match between task, team and situation, with the skills of the facilitator. This is one reason why line managers tend to use consultants or facilitators, as they cannot offer the repertoire of facilitative styles or access to the vast variety of method of facilitating teams.

Specialists in team development will be expected to be competent in at least one of a number of basic methodologies, (for example, psychological testing, Gestalt, NLP, Transactional Analysis, or Behaviour Analysis). They will have a wide knowledge of models and theory of group dynamics. They will also be expected to have knowledge of creative team methods such as brainstorming, metaplanning and Nominal Group Technique; analytical processes such as Force Field Analysis, SWOT and Kepner-Tregoe; grouping techniques such as buzz groups, pairings, syndicates, triads and fishbowl. They will usually have experience and competence in the use of exercises, simulations and games. There are many books on the subject (see Milson, 1993, Newstrom and Scannell, 1991 and Silberman, 1996). The facilitator

Table 25.1
Facilitation styles – intervention categories

Authoritative	Facilitative
1 *Prescriptive* Giving advice, offering opinions, evaluating performance	4 *Catalytic* Encouraging self-directed problem solving, eliciting information
2 *Informative* Giving information, imparting knowledge, offering interpretation	5 *Supporting* Giving positive feedback, encouragement and acceptance
3 *Confronting* Being challenging, giving direct feedback	6 *Cathartic* Encouraging release of tension, expression of feelings and emotions

should also have knowledge of a range of Icebreakers and Energizers (West, 1997 and University Associates, 1983).

SUMMARY

Team Development events are usually facilitated by specialists rather than line managers themselves to give them full opportunity to participate.

There is a sequence of activity for team events which includes contracting, design, delivery and evaluation.

Contracting is essential to the success of the event, both with the primary client and team members.

The design of the event depends on the nature of the team, their needs and experience.

There are some conventions about designing such events which take account of adult learning and experiential learning principles.

There are various levels of intervention (organizational, team and individual), which need to be agreed in advance and matched to the needs of the team.

Facilitation styles vary and need to be contracted.

Facilitators need a broad repertoire of facilitation styles and wide knowledge of theory, techniques and activities.

REFERENCES

Bentley, T., *Facilitation: Providing Opportunities for Learning*, McGraw-Hill, Maidenhead, 1994

Clarkson, P., *Gestalt Counselling In Action*, Sage Publications, London, 1993

Cockman, P., Evans, B. and Reynolds, P., *Client Centred Consulting: A Practical Guide for Internal Advisers and Trainers*, McGraw-Hill, Maidenhead, 1992

Harrison, R., 'Choosing the Depth of Organizational Intervention', *The Journal of Applied Behavioural Science*, 1970, **6** (2), 181–202

Harshman, C. and Phillips, S., *Team Training: From Startup to High Performance*, McGraw-Hill, New York, 1996

Hay, J., *Transactional Analysis for Trainers*, McGraw-Hill, Maidenhead, 1992

Heron, J., *Six Category Intervention Analysis*, 3rd edition, Human Potential Resource Group, University of Surrey, 1989

Knowles, M., *The Adult Learner: A Neglected Species?*, Gulf Houston, 1979

Kolb, D., *Experiential Learning*, Prentice Hall, Englewood Cliffs, NJ, 1984

Luft, J., 'The Johari Window', *Human Relations Training News*, **5**, 6–7, 1961

Milson, C., *Team Games for Trainers*, McGraw-Hill, Maidenhead, 1993

Moxon, P., *Building a Better Team: A Handbook for Managers and Facilitators*, Gower, Aldershot, 1993

Newstrom, J.W. and Scannell, E.E., *Still More Games Trainers Play: Experiential Learning Exercises*, McGraw-Hill, New York, 1991

O'Connor, J. and Seymour, J., *Introducing Neuro-Linguistic Programming:*

Psychological Skills for Understanding and Influencing People, The Aquarian Press, London, 1993

Reddy, B.W., *Intervention Skills: Process Consultation for Small Groups and Teams*, Pfeiffer & Company, San Diego, 1994

Silberman, M., *The 1996 McGraw-Hill Team and Organization Development Sourcebook*, McGraw-Hill, New York, 1996

Tuckman, B.W. and Jensen, M.A.C., 'Stages of Small-group Development Revisited', *Group and Organisational Studies*, **2**, 419–427, 1977

University Associates, *The Encyclopaedia of Icebreakers*, University Associates Inc, San Diego, CA, 1983

West, E., *201 Icebreakers: Group Mixers, Warm Ups, Energisers and Playful Activities*, McGraw-Hill, New York, 1997

RECOMMENDED READING

Bailey, A., Hunter, D. and Taylor, B., *The Facilitation of Groups*, Gower, Aldershot, 1996

Bourner, T., Martin, V. and Race, P., *Workshops That Work: 100 Ideas to Make Your Training Events More Effective*, McGraw-Hill, Maidenhead, 1993

Bramley, P., *Evaluating Training*, Institute of Personnel and Development, London, 1996

Clark, N., *Team Building: A Practical Guide for Trainers*, McGraw-Hill, Maidenhead, 1994

Heron, J., *Group Facilitation: Theories and Models for Practice*, Kogan Page, London, 1993

Heron, J., *The Facilitators' Handbook*, Kogan Page, London, 1993

Hirsh, S.K., *MBTI Team Building Program*, Psychologists Consulting Press, Palo Alto, CA, 1992

Jaques, D., *Learning in Groups*, Kogan Page, London, 1992

Leigh, D., *A Practical Approach to Group Training*, Kogan Page, London, 1991

Megginson, D. and Pedler, M., *Self Development: A Facilitator's Guide*, McGraw-Hill, Maidenhead, 1992

Mill, C.R., *Activities for Trainers: Fifty Useful Designs*, University Associates, San Diego, CA, 1980

Schein, E.H., *Process Consultation: Its Role in Organisation Development Vol. 1*, Addison-Wesley, Reading, Mass, 1988

26 Using management games

Chris Elgood

Is there any point in having a chapter about 'games' in a book about teams and teamworking? Teams have goals, and teamworking is a means of reaching those goals, so everybody concerned with the subject must have sought ways in which the relevant skills could be practised and improved. He or she will have tried to create an artificial environment which offered some or all of the following benefits:

- Dangers associated with a 'real' team activity could be avoided
- Costs associated with a 'real' team activity could be avoided
- Time associated with a 'real' team activity could be saved
- Individual features of teamworking could be isolated, studied and practised
- Interventions by tutors or coaches could be made.

A person devising such a situation may not have called it a game. Words like 'exercise' or 'training session' or 'simulation' may have been preferred. But that is a semantic difference, for 'game' is almost indefinable. The very same activity can be described differently because of the attitude taken towards it. People will commonly say 'How about a game of chess?' Yet chess at a high level is a test of reasoning, foresight, strategy and mental skill. So this chapter assumes that every serious student of teams and teamworking is knowledgeable about management games – whatever he or she calls them.

A specialist in management games has a certain expertise in creating 'non-real practice situations', and may be able to answer the question: 'If I want an environment in which people can grasp such-and-such a concept or practise such-and-such a skill, what is the best way of acquiring it?' This chapter presents some examples of necessary concepts and skills, with 'devices' – or whatever title is preferred – which help people to acquire or develop them.

UNDERSTANDING THE OBJECTIVE AND BEING COMMITTED TO IT

Most people today would probably agree that this approach is necessary if a complex activity is to go well. But other approaches have been used in the past. Armies and Navies have employed a teamworking technique based on precise distinction between skills and on repetition of well-learned actions under threat of punishment! 'Obey the orders you are given', was the concept, 'and leave the rest to the generals!' If team membership was not sufficiently attractive to win recruits, they used techniques like the press-gang.

For those who see a common understanding of the objective as a better tactic than blind obedience, The Four Letter Word Game is an excellent device for examining what it means and how to achieve it. This one has been popular for a long time, in many forms. A small group of people are given a sealed envelope with verbal instructions that go something like this: 'In the envelope are a number of letters, each written on a small piece of cardboard. You may take as long as you like to decide the method you will use for this task, but from the moment you open the envelope you may have only two minutes in which to make as many four letter words as you can, using the letters in the envelope.' The exercise takes a different course each time, but common developments are:

1   Different people have different understandings about the objective, don't realize that this is the case, and argue from different premises, and
2   Different people have different ideas about the value of the activity and therefore show different levels of commitment.

Frequently the instruction to 'make words' causes confusion. Does it mean that the letters in the envelope should be set out as in 'Scrabble'? If so, then a letter can only be used twice at most (in a vertical word and a horizontal word) and the number of words that can be 'made' is very limited. Or does 'make' just mean thinking of a word and writing it down? In that case a great many words can be made. Each group member attaches an image to the instruction 'make words' and assumes that image to be the natural one, or the only one possible. It does not cross his or her mind that another person has interpreted the instruction quite differently. The exercise demonstrates very clearly how easy it is for team members to form different ideas about 'What we are trying to do', and how these different ideas lead to different and sometimes conflicting actions.

One lesson is concerned with 'What we are trying to do' and the other with 'Why we are trying to do it'. The exercise can reach the point when the question arises 'What constitutes a word, anyway? Are foreign words allowed? Obscene words? Proper names? Can one use a letter more than once in the same word?' The group may then split into those who 'want to do a good job' and those who feel that the whole exercise is pointless. There is obviously a lack of agreement about the importance of the activity: about how much it matters. Is it a meaningless game – in which case it is inappropriate to exert much effort – or is it a serious learning experience which will improve teamworking skills? If it is the latter, then some hard work on the details is justified.

Bringing these problems into the open leads the team to consider helpful behaviours. If these human characteristics are a natural hazard that besets effective teamworking, how can they be countered? The Four Letter Word Game creates awareness. It directs attention to a danger, and a danger once realized can be tackled constructively.

COMMUNICATION

All aspects of teamwork require communication, so subjects like 'leadership', 'delegation', 'planning' and 'problem solving' would all include it. Can it be studied on its own? One primary characteristic can certainly be so studied – the fact that the words we speak derive from some imagined situation in our own minds. This makes communication subjective and unreliable.

What actually happens in the communication process is that a 'sender' has a mental image of an event that he or she hopes to bring about – through the agency of another person. To communicate a clear picture of the present situation, the desired action and the expected future situation, the sender has to choose words. If the words are accurately transmitted, and the sender says 'the green steel box', then the receiver hears 'the green steel box'. But the trouble with words is that they are no more than symbols. They don't carry all the context that caused the sender to choose them, and the receiver interprets them according to his or her view of the world. So there maybe a misunderstanding, and after the event one person says to another 'Oh! Is *that* what you meant by "the green steel box"?'

It is a salutary experience to discover how little of the concept that is in our minds we actually put across by the use of words. We tend to think that, because we all speak the same language, communication is easy. That is certainly not the case. It can be argued that the common language increases our tendency to assume that we understand each other, and to conceal the fact that we often don't.

It is not hard to invent a game in which one person or group is required to give instructions to another – and then watch as the receivers of the message get it disastrously wrong. A useful exercise is 'The Sentencing Exercise' and is based on brief descriptions of 'crimes' committed in an imaginary country. One group member is given the role of Lord Chief Justice and uses five 'cases' to illustrate his or her views about sentencing policy, saying, for instance, 'I would fine the man who was guilty of *this* £5 000, and   *405* here are my reasons.' Later, the listeners are asked to adopt the role of local magistrates required to administer the policy that has been described to them – and consider five new cases. Their judgements can then be compared with those that The Lord Chief Justice would have made. The variances are huge, and in the debrief it becomes apparent that The Lord Chief Justice is operating with a set of values and assumptions that have only been understood by his staff in the most superficial manner. Interpreting any policy requires an understanding of why it was defined. What values were used? Without such knowledge one is unable, in cases of doubt, to decide that *this* is more important that *that*.

The armed forces have struggled with communication problems for centuries, and a 'drill' often used is to prefix an order with an intention, defining 'What we are trying to do'. It provides a reference point when the detailed plans run into trouble. It makes it possible to reason '*This* is what we are trying to do. What is the best we can do at the moment to achieve it?'

LEADERSHIP

While leaderless groups are often used as a means of studying group dynamics, the fact of organizational life is that teams have leaders. A convincing consensus solution does not always emerge, and somebody has to accept responsibility for making the decision. Therefore studying leadership is a fundamental part of studying teams. The idea of management games is that those taking part should learn from their in-game experience, and the nature of that experience is determined not just by the 'game' itself (rules, data, imaginary situation, and so on) but by the manner in which it is run. There can be a huge difference, for instance, between telling a group of players to act as equals, and appointing one of them as the leader, responsible for the outcome. 'The value of "T"' is an information-sharing exercise, with items of data given on separate cards that are handed out to group members. If all the data and instructions are integrated, the answer to a problem will emerge. One way of using this exercise is to select one person as the leader, ask him or her to leave the room, and then distribute the cards to the remaining members. The leader can then be called back, told the nature of the problem very briefly, and required to start working on it. It simulates the situation of a person appointed to a position of leadership knowing little about an environment about which his or her staff know rather more. A person in that position will show the behaviour that he or she considers appropriate for a leader. This may or may not allow for appearing ignorant in the eyes of the team. In this exercise the leader who is prepared to admit ignorance and ask for help will usually be given the right answer. The one who tries to find out 'what is going on' without admitting ignorance will soon be in deep trouble.

Another way of using the 'setting-up' of an exercise to modify the experience which participants will encounter can be illustrated through The Symbol Game. The team is given a pack of cards on each of which is a selection from a set of twelve symbols. It is rather like a party game: the tutor or facilitator has to choose a personal symbol and the team has to work out which it is by showing different cards and asking 'Is your symbol on this card?' The conditions established might be that the task is 'To devise and operate a standard system'. The appointed leader has to elicit the views of different team members, summarize the alternative methods, reach a decision as to which method is best, and ensure that all team members can operate it. The tutor or facilitator retains the right to 'test' any team member, and the rules say 'If the chosen team member fails the test then the team leader is fired – because it is his/her job to ensure the competence of all staff.'

THE COMMUNICATIVE CLIMATE

The 'technical' skills of communication – the ability to use words accurately and the ability to sense when concepts are being misunderstood – are of little use if communication is just not welcome. Relevant knowledge may be possessed by *anyone* in the group and the whole group should have the benefit of it. Without this, some key element necessary for a good solution may be overlooked. Ensuring that all members – even those of the lowest status – speak up when they have something to offer is not easy. Such people watch what happens to those who do speak up, and make judgements in their own minds about 'How I am going to be treated if I make this particular point – which I am not quite sure about anyway?' Sometimes the conclusion is that: 'In this group, expressions of doubt and uncertainty seem to be unwelcome. Those who offer them are severely put down. Nobody else knows that I have these doubts, so I will just keep quiet.'

An exercise likely to create such a situation is the Card Display problem. The task of each group is to duplicate at their workstation a display of playing cards set out in another room. They do this by sending observers to memorize what they see. It is not too difficult to get the identities of the cards and their position relative to each other right. What many people don't realize is that some cards (for example, the sevens) are not symmetrical in design – the extra heart, spade, club or diamond can be in the top half of the card or the bottom half. The card can therefore be 'the wrong way up'. There have been many cases when a team has been eager to declare the task finished but one member has noticed this fact and is wondering 'Is it part of the exercise or not? Dare I stop these eager people from saying "Finished" – and involve them in extra work – when I am not sure of my ground?' The danger is specially acute if the team has an appointed leader who happens to be one of the action-oriented brigade whose instincts are to go for quick results, then move on to the next task! Sometimes a declaration of 'Finished' is followed by conclusive proof that several mistakes have been made.

MAINTENANCE AND MORALE

There is always potential conflict between the need to obtain results with reasonable speed, and the need to maintain interest, commitment and satisfaction within a team. There are always some members whose skills are specially relevant to the task in hand and others whose skills are peripheral to it, or irrelevant. How much time is to be given to meeting the needs of the latter group when doing so will delay results? Is it better to shorten the time for which they will endure idleness and frustration (by leaving things to the 'experts' to make sure the job is done quickly) or is it better to alleviate that idleness and frustration by attempts to explain things to them and keep them involved? If the idleness and frustration continue too long, or are too severe, such people may 'switch off'. That can mean that when some point is reached at which they really could contribute to the work, they miss the opportunity because they have lost track of what is going on. At worst, they leave the group.

The Fig Tree Game offers a means of studying this problem and suggesting useful forms of behaviour. Like many such exercises, the basic idea is quite simple and can be found dressed up in different words under different proprietary titles. It is a logic puzzle, in which there are five imaginary people each with four attributes. The task is to deduce, from a range of clues provided, which attributes match which person. There are at least three logical ways to tackle it.

The Fig Tree is the sort of problem which seems adapted for single-person working, or perhaps for two people together. It is not a natural task for a team approach, but using it as such will dramatically illustrate the problems of motivation and morale. Typically, progress is driven by different ideas in turn. Adherents of one method will hold the floor for a time, explaining their ideas and taking the whole group through their early workings. Then they will run into trouble, or they will lose the attention of their listeners, or both. Adherents of another method will then take over and have the same experience. For each member of the group motivation will move upwards or downwards depending on apparent progress or the opportunity for personal involvement. The experience reveals the effect of what may be called the 'mini-motivators' or 'immediate rewards' which influence the commitment a person offers from moment to moment. These are comparatively small bonuses like 'Knowing what is going on', 'Being able to contribute', 'Increasing understanding', 'Making visible progress' and 'Building upon the views of each other'.

RECOGNIZING, USING AND DEVELOPING HUMAN RESOURCES

An excellent game for studying resource utilization can be put together by collecting diverse, easily scorable tasks and challenging a group to achieve maximum points (by successful task completion) in whatever time is available. The emphasis here is on internal group organization, so the tasks themselves do not have to carry any special learning content. They must have just four characteristics:

1   Each task must offer some form of challenge – to the intellect, to manual dexterity, to knowledge or to concentration and accuracy
2   It must be possible to complete each task in a relatively short timescale
3   With a few reservations, each task must be easily and objectively scorable
4   The range of tasks must be as varied as possible. The ideal is that every group member should find something that allows him or her to demonstrate skill and have a chance to shine.

The ideal sequence of events – what the facilitator hopes will happen – begins with an assessment of the different tasks and of the skills and abilities that each group member brings. What sort of a task is each one? How important is it in terms of the score attached? Is it a task for one person or a small group? Who feels able to tackle it? Is it a proper use of the skills and abilities of that person or would he/she be better employed elsewhere? Once the activity begins, some person has to take responsibility for monitoring progress and, if necessary, shifting resources from one task to another. Equally, each member ought to have some awareness of what others are doing, and how they are progressing.

The mistakes commonly visible are exactly those that beset organizations in 'real work'. There is rarely any detailed review of the contributions that individuals could make: any review, that is, carried out on a serious basis before the tasks themselves are made known. When that moment arrives, there is generally a 'grabbing' process in which people stake a claim for attractive work. It does not always turn out as planned! For example, any person making a clear claim to expertise is likely, having landed the task, to be entirely ignored by everyone else. The attitude appears to be 'He said he could do it, let him get on with it' – this in spite of the fact that the person is in obvious difficulty. People will also demonstrate the common human failing of fastening upon something that seems achievable and forgetting all else. They seem to use their preoccupation as an excuse for withdrawing from the group, and they often allow their determination to override logic. When running into problems, they just work harder and harder without any thought of giving up the task and doing something of more value to their team. It can be extremely difficult for the team leader, in an exercise of this sort, to prevent the team fragmenting into a collection of dedicated individuals and acting in exactly the opposite manner to that required.

UNDERSTANDING HOW IT ALL FITS TOGETHER

The form that people call to mind most frequently when Management Games are mentioned is probably the business simulation in which playing teams   *409* run an imaginary company. They receive a written description of it, including a list of 'Decision Variables' that they are allowed to change, and they make decisions in a sequence of weeks or months or years about 'What the company shall do'. They write their decisions on a form, or enter them into the computer, and in due course receive back a Profit/Loss Account, a Balance Sheet and various other documents.

Business simulations can be simple, or highly complex. In the latter case their authors often include the most sophisticated elements of business economics, and quite reasonable claims are made that the device will teach this, that or the other technique. The means by which teams interact with each other and with the controller are also extending: the Internet has become an option. However, if players of such simulations are asked about them five years after the event, two statements will predominate. They are:

> 'I learned how the different functions of an organization fit together', and:
> 'I learned a lot about working with others in a team'.

The first of these responses is entirely natural and understandable, for almost all such simulations integrate the marketing and production and financial functions to get a bottom-line result. It is almost impossible to take part in such an event without realizing what happens if you don't forecast sales reasonably accurately, or you make too much of the wrong product, or you fail to order enough materials, or you price yourself out of the market.

The second response is interesting, because the devices commonly used for studying teamwork are the shorter type described earlier in this chapter and they often emphasize an individual feature of teamwork. It is somewhat unusual for a facilitator whose roots are in the sociological field to use a genuine business simulation for such study. This may be because such a simulation would take too long, or it may be because the difficult aspects of business economics are seen as irrelevant. Whatever the reason, substantial simulations are not used extensively for studying teamwork, and an opportunity is being missed. A notable and illuminating exception is the fact that the original work behind Dr Meredith Belbin's concepts of teamwork started by examining behaviour in such a context.

The length of time taken by substantial simulations may, in some cases, increase the opportunities for studying teamwork because it brings in other factors that will never arise in a short session. Some such simulations (for example, National Competitions) are played on a weekly basis and can therefore extend over several months. Difficulties then arise over gettting the team together for meetings, and coping with the absence of important members through sickness or holiday or assignments away from the organization. The VENTURE competition run from Bradford University invites entrants to get a team together as the board of directors of the imaginary company. It supplements the repetitive quantitative decisions with Agenda Items demanding a decision between limited allowed actions. If the Chairman of the Board is away overseas messages are sent by phone, fax and e-mail about what he wants done in regard to the latest crisis. Alternatively, the team members left at home take matters into their own hands and confront the Chairman with a *fait accompli*. These are genuine teamworking issues.

IS THE LEARNING TRANSFERABLE?

Applying lessons learnt in games and simulations is always a controversial area. Whether it happens or not depends largely on the legitimacy of the learning situation as perceived by the individual participant. In this respect the method certainly has detractors. A common charge is that, because of the 'non-serious' nature of games and simulations, any behaviour displayed within their boundaries bears no relation to what the person concerned would do in 'the real world'. The charge is most frequently made with regard to those games that use abstract materials – even playthings – or situations that are remote from the real work of the participants.

A helpful way to tackle this issue is to disregard the physical materials used and concentrate on the situation that is created for the participant. This is a fundamental concept, because the participant is not being asked to learn lessons from the materials themselves, but to learn from the total situation and the way people behave within it. What skills and abilities does it demand? What qualities are necessary for success? One suitable component task for the exercise about team organization described above is finding the volume of an irregular object and, although many different objects would work well, one often used is a yellow plastic duck. This object does not itself represent serious learning. But the situation created demands imagination, creativity, lateral thinking, determination and accuracy. What method is to be used? Probably, after discussion, the group concerned will decide on the displacement of water. How is it to be measured? What measuring instruments are available? What size are they? How are they calibrated? It may be quite hard to lay hands on something suitable, so what substitutes can be found? Well, spirits are sold in quantities of one sixth of a gill – so there is one way of measuring small quantities of liquid. How many millilitres (the measure in which the answer is required) does one sixth of a gill equate to? Does anybody have a conversion scale in a diary? Who can we ring up to find out? How accurate does the measurement have to be? The smaller an object, the harder it is to measure accurately, so perhaps the group should make several experiments and average the results. Have the experiments been done accurately? If, for instance, it has been necessary to hold the duck underwater, does the measurement include the water displaced by the finger that held it? The point being made is that the materials don't have to be serious and work-related provided the behaviour made necessary by the task is relevant. A big advantage gained if one can grasp this concept – and communicate it to participants – is that one avoids the need to build highly complex and fictitious games and simulations that look *outwardly* like work. There is much to be said for using everyday materials – including playthings – because everybody immediately knows what they are. One does not have to waste time by explaining what the materials represent, and in what ways they *do* represent the reality simulated and in what ways they *don't* – for they are bound to fall short in some respect!

There will always be participants who find it difficult to accept that their own behaviour in a 'game' represents fair comment upon their real selves. This is a natural reaction and ought not to worry the facilitator too much. If people are given time to think through the issues, and alleged lessons are not underlined in an aggressive manner, they will usually come to accept the idea in time. The responses of colleagues who know them in both game and 'real' situations is evidence enough that personal habits carry over. Group members are frequently told by their colleagues 'That is *exactly* what you do normally!'

RECOMMENDED READING

Elgood, C., *Handbook of Management Games and Simulations*, Gower, Aldershot, 1997

Fripp, J., *Learning through Simulations*, McGraw-Hill, Maidenhead, 1993

27 Turning teamwork into knowledge creation

Ronnie Lessem

Over the past ten years, a group associated with City University Business School's Management MBA programme has developed a distinctive approach to team, alongside individual and organizational, learning. In the context of what is simultaneously an academically based activity and an organizational change programme, we have integrated managerial and group learning with organizational knowledge creation. In the UK our partners have been Anglian Water and Ford Motors, the City Corporation, IBM (Insurance), Lloyd's of London, J. Sainsbury and the Surrey Police Force. In the Arab Middle East our partners have been TEAM, the largest management and engineering consultancy in the region. The focus has been on the development of teamwork, over and above individual performance, and upon cultural change as opposed to merely managerial development.

The key to this change process has been what we term our 'developmental trajectory', which extends from 'preparatory' to 'ordinary' to 'extra-ordinary' to 'mastery'. The acronym we use for this is 'POEM'. The 'preparatory' activity, within the context of the Management MBA, is confined to modular courses – such as Service Management, Organizational Dynamics and the Knowledge Creating Company – which will not be referred to explicitly in this chapter. An 'ordinary' project is undertaken by groups within an action learning context, directed towards improving teamwork within a work unit. An 'extra-ordinary' one, moreover, involves the development of self-organizing groups and organizational learning. The final 'mastery' project is aimed at developing the organization, through its duly socialized groups, as a knowledge-creating company. This chapter describes the developmental process – from ordinary teamwork to masterly knowledge creation – which extends over the course of two years.

PROJECT 1: ORDINARY ACTION LEARNING, DEVELOPING TEAMWORK

The action learning process

Action learning takes off, within a development programme such as ours, from where the courses of instruction leave off. Three so-called action-centred projects constitute the heart of the process, the development of each being normally undertaken individually, within the context of a work-based group, or a 'learning set'. Such action-centred learning is both a social and a mental process. Such a mental process, for which the individual learner, the learning set and the group facilitator are ultimately responsible, involves an interplay between action and reflection.

This specific model of the learning process, as illustrated in Figure 27.1, is in fact a particular application of classical scientific method (1) (see Lessem, 1993, Chapter 3). Faced with a problem (survey), a group uses its general understanding (hypothesis) of the situation in order to decide on a strategy and means of implementing it. It goes into action phase (test) when trying to put ideas into practice. This is followed by a process of evaluation (audit) whereby the results expected are compared with what has occurred. The incorporation of the learning cycle as a whole into the team's approach to management is identified as a 'control' process. This process is undergone within the context of a 'learning set'.

The learning set

The group context for action learning is the so-called 'set'. This 'learning set' provides a focal point for reflection, while the 'project' is a focus for action. Such a small learning group is a source of challenge and support, a source of shared reflection upon individual action. It is through the 'set' that the scientifically based learning cycle is socially channelled. Group members therefore learn with and from each other, by supportive attacks upon real and menacing problems. As Revans (see Lessem, 1993) has intimated, such a set, with its facilitator, serves to provide:

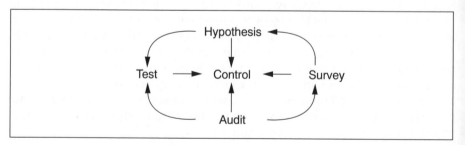

Figure 27.1   Action learning

1   An exchange of Information, that is of ideas, advice, contacts, hunches, concepts
2   Interaction between set members, offering each other support and encouragement as well as challenge and critical appraisal
3   Behavioural change resulting more often from the reinterpretation of past experiences than from the acquisition of fresh knowledge.

A production manager, for example, who 'thought' that marketing meant 'bribery and lunches' would never be able to take in fresh information about it until he or she came to 'feel' differently about the subject. Only when he or she had reinterpreted past experiences would it be possible to think and subsequently 'act' differently. From a practical perspective then, typically action learning-based 'set meetings' are expected to provide the following:

1   An opportunity for members to *seek each other's help* in carrying out the project
2   An external *source of pressure* upon members to play their individual projects in getting the group project moving
3   A source of *progress planning and review*
4   The occasional provision of formal *inputs*
5   Through reflection, the gaining of *insights*
6   Mutual encouragement and *support.*

The role of the 'ordinary' set facilitator

The facilitator, within the context of the first group project then, has a specifically 'ordinary' role to play. This can be divided between four major functions:

1   *Scheduling* a minimum of four set meetings during the course of an eight-month project, for each of three projects, including a final review meeting
2   *Structuring* the project, and thereby the meetings, to follow the four major steps of establishing the aims and practical context, creating hypotheses followed by appropriate theory, taking action, as well as finally reflecting, evaluating and internalizing the effects
3   *Stimulating* the project-based progress of each individual within the group, while enabling members within the set to support and challenge each other
4   *Ensuring* that each individual member – as well as the group as a whole – develops knowledge, skill and personality-based competencies.

Criteria for project evaluation

The first project then is set within an 'ordinary' functional context. As such the following criteria for evaluation apply: *415*

AIR

1 Identify what needs to be **A**chieved, the constraints that the group needs to **I**nvest in overcoming, and the **R**esources to which access will be needed

SHARE

2 **S**urvey the practical business context in which a problem/opportunity is lodged, and the managerial skill and self on which the project will draw.
3 **H**ypothesize, that is establish the general and particular theoretical base for, primarily, the group's knowledge development, and, secondarily, the skill and self-development of its members.
4 **A**ct, that is apply the newly acquired competencies to the problem/opportunity at hand, documenting the way in which the group has experimented in each case.
5 **R**eview the results of the team's actions, drawing out the specific lessons learnt for each of the three sets of competencies.
6 **E**valuate the whole action learning process, drawing out general conclusions and recommendations with respect to business performance, organizational know-how and corporate identity.

REView

7 Relate the team's project **Re**sults – knowledge, skill and self-development – to **Vi**sible improvements in members' performance and in departmental results.

The outcome of the ordinary project

Ultimately, the first, ordinary project should result in a demonstrable improvement in the group's performance, both individually and in the work team's performance as a whole. We now turn from ordinary to extra-ordinary group processes.

PROJECT 2:   EXTRA-ORDINARY SELF-ORGANIZING NETWORKS, DYNAMIC LEARNING

The dynamic learning process

A second project, to the extent that it follows the developmental trajectory, requires of the group, set within the context of an emergent self-organizing network, the kind of emotional resilience and conceptual ability that DYNAMIC LEARNING warrants. Specifically, group members need to develop significant self- and political awareness, a sensitivity to changing individual and organizational processes, and an ability to cope psychologically, politically and commercially with such a dynamic environment.

Within such a dynamic learning process the group needs to be able to reflect upon its own 'mental models', and modify them according to personal and interpersonal need. The learning set and facilitator play an important role in that respect, helping to reflect back such models to the group participants. Such complex learning moreover, organizationally set in the context of so-called 'self-organizing networks' in which the group is lodged, serves to encourage open conflict, authentic dialogue, and the public testing of assumptions. At the same time informal political networks function to undermine the hierarchically-based *status quo*. Therefore the most important learning that groups do flows from the trial-and-error action they take in real time, and especially from the way they reflect on these actions as they take them.

Where this extra-ordinary approach (Figure 27.2), pioneered in Britain by Ralph Stacey (1993), parts company from the ordinary action learning, championed by Reg Revans (see Lessem, 1993), is in its emphasis on emergent processes, and on self-organizing networks. Continuing success for Stacey flows from tension with people, socially and politically, and with the market environment, commercially and technologically. Moreover such a managerial approach involves not simply building on existing strengths but intentionally steering away from equilibrium, provoking conflict and learning.

It is with all these 'extra-ordinary' tensions – both within the manager and in the organization without – that the second project is concerned. Whereas the 'ordinary' project then, is contextualized within a learning set, the 'extra-ordinary' one is also set within a self-organizing network, and is likely to incorporate significant organizational dynamics.

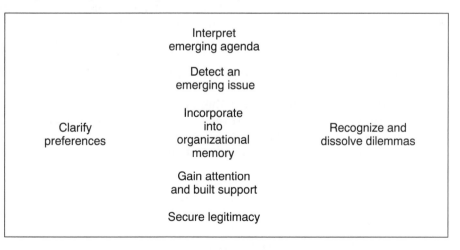

Figure 27.2 Dynamic learning

A chaos theory of organization

In the extra-ordinary second project therefore, the emphasis shifts from team members' job-related performance in the context of their immediate work group, to the group's role evolution in the context of a whole network of which it forms an emerging part.

While the immediate work group member continues, therefore, to undertake a project as a learning set, it is the emerging network surrounding it, within the organization, that now occupies pride of place. In this way the extra-ordinary group discovers and creates the long-term futures of its organization as an integral part of a process incorporating a network of associates. It is the facilitator's role, alongside the members of the learning set, to directly recognize and indirectly improve such a process of emergent networking.

Containing anxiety

The key control parameter, moreover, in facilitating such learning for Stacey (1993) – thereby moving the group between what he terms the stable and unstable zones of behaviour and into the space for novelty – is the level of the team's anxiety and the degree of its containment. Group leader and participants can, regressively so to speak, be returned to the 'ordinary' stable zone by re-erecting the containing structures and thus reducing the level of anxiety. At some key intermediate level, though, there is enough challenge and contention existing to provoke group members into some kind of exploration. However, this is only likely to arise if there is enough emotional containment of that anxiety to prevent team members from being submerged by defensive-aggressive behaviour. At such critical points of 'anxiety containment' members can avoid both the rampant fears of the unstable zone and the rigidly defensive behaviour of the stable one. It is the 'extra-ordinary' facilitator's role then, to play a part in providing such containment.

If, as a direct result, relationships within the 'set' have the quality of trust and compassion, if for Stacey (1993) they are based on empathy and even love, then they operate as effective containers of anxiety. Given such high-quality interconnectedness a group can contain the anxiety and stay at the edge of chaos.

The second way of containing anxiety without abandoning the edge of chaos is provided by honest self-reflection, that is when members of a group jointly reflect upon the system they constitute. The third way to contain anxiety is through the quality of facilitation and the way in which power is exercised. Specifically then the facilitator avoids authoritarian behaviour and exhibits a capacity for articulating issues and posing insightful questions. In this way, moreover, enabling conditions are established for role evolution, and the facilitator's role is to foster such a climate within the learning set.

The role of 'extra-ordinary' facilitator

A set facilitator in the second project, therefore, engaged in following the 'developmental' trajectory, is involved in such activities as:

- Giving feedback on self-perceptions
- Serving as a role model for 'extra-ordinary' development
- Supplying mental, emotional and behavioural support and challenge, as well
- Providing conceptual frameworks for modelling group work and management processes.

More specifically, tolerance for ambiguity, openness and frankness, patience, a desire to see others learn, and the ability to empathize are desirable facilitator attributes.

Criteria for extra-ordinary learning

The non-linear 'extra-ordinary' criteria for evaluation, finally, are very different from the linear 'ordinary' ones:

AIR

1 Detecting and selecting an emergent project issue
   - What significant issues or opportunities are simultaneously emerging from the depths of the business or organization, and from the work group itself?

SHARE

2 Survey – gaining attention and building support
   - What important team project is arising, addressed at resolving what dilemmas, who will be joining forces with the group, and who will become a sponsor?
3 Hypothesis – interpreting/handling the emerging agenda
   - What conceptual approaches to managing complexity is the team acquiring, and how is it being reflected in business and organizational emergent strategies?
4 Act – clarifying preferences
   - How has the group been involving the emerging project stakeholders, with what resulting kind of involvement in political/ learning processes?
5 Reflect – undergoing action and learning
   - What experimental actions have been engaged in by the group, yielding what kind of benefits, followed by what kind of reflection on the results?
6 Evaluate – gaining legitimacy and backing

- How has the group, and its network of project associates, engaged with the formal authorities to legitimize initially experimental activities?

REVIEW

7 Incorporate outcomes into organizational memory
- To what extent have the actions taken combined with the insights acquired led to the evolution of the group's role in the organization?

The extra-ordinary project outcome

Ultimately the extra-ordinary project two should result in the group's role evolution, as well as that of its constituent members – set within the context of an emerging network – and in the parallel development of a new product or process, service or system, organizationally.

PROJECT 3: LEADERSHIP AND MASTERY – TRANSFORMATIVE LEARNING

Re-authoring your self

Whereas the 'ordinary' project concentrates on improved team performance, and the 'extra-ordinary' one on its role evolution, the so-called 'transformative' project is aimed at completely 're-authorizing' team-and-organization. Such a 'masterly' group is able to accommodate and harness tensions within its self, within the organization, and within society at large, through the pursuit of a higher 'knowledge-creating' cause.

Therefore, whereas a similarly ordinary business improvement team is working towards continuous improvement, while a self-organizing network is oriented towards a more broadly based change management, a so-called 'knowledge-creating group' is working towards integrated product, process and organizational renewal. In fact individual members of the group, in this knowledge-creating case, are each oriented towards their pursuit of truth, goodness or beauty, with a view to providing utility.

To develop such a transformative orientation is our ultimate objective, insofar as we are managerially focused upon gaining mastery rather than merely acquiring a master, and organizationally upon knowledge creation rather than merely upon its administration.

The knowledge-creating company

A knowledge-creating company, according to the two Japanese researchers Nonaka and Takeuchi (1995), is one which continually recreates itself through developing new knowledge and converting it into new products and services. Such activity, moreover, is fostered by 'transformative' learning.

Such a pursuit of truth, goodness or beauty – with a view, moreover, to creating utility – is fostered on our programme through the third project, whereby group members individually and the team as a whole collectively build up, and upon, their own perspectives on the world. Yet these perspectives remain localized, as Nonaka and Takeuchi emphasize, unless they are articulated and amplified through social interaction, that is by a 'field' or self-organizing network in which group members collaborate to create a new concept. At the centre of this field, moreover, lies a knowledge-based vision, and the enabling conditions for its realization. We start with what we call 'socialization' (Figure 27.3).

Socialization/Internalization

Such a 'social' field is created, at least initially, through the learning sets, which serve to foster continuous dialogue, and appropriate 'interaction rhythms'. In order for a group of learners to start the process of knowledge development, they first need to build up mutual trust. This takes place through *Socialization* among the learning set members. A key way to build such mutual trust is to share original experience. Such a sharing is fostered through self-development in the context of others, and duly improved on during the ordinary project.

The tangible improvements resulting from the first project serve to combine social interaction, conventionally set within the context of human or customer relations, with the achievement of the desired practical results, or 'business' benefits, through *Internalization.*

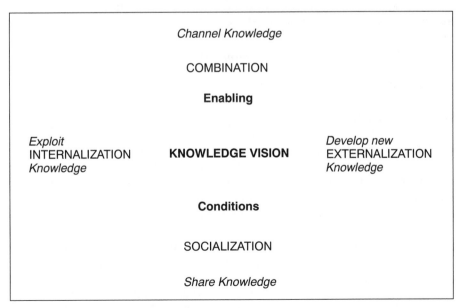

Figure 27.3 The knowledge-creating process

Externalization/Combination

Direct understanding of other individuals relies on shared experience that enables members to 'indwell' others and to grasp their world from 'inside'. When such collective indwelling, altogether, is turned inside out, this brings about an *Externalization* of the internal worlds, that is 'originality'.

Subsequent explicit sharing of mental and physical rhythms among learning set members, with a view to product and process development, may drive socialization towards *Combination*. Such combination is represented by knowledge created in an interactive field that is crystallized into some concrete 'form' such as a product or a system, which serves the purposes of business development in the extra-ordinary MMBA project.

Combination/Internalization

As would-be masters, at this point, team members test the reality and applicability of concepts put together along the way. Such prolonged experimentation needs to be followed by justification. This is a process of final convergence and screening, whereby a group judges whether the knowledge created is truly worthwhile for the organization and the society. Justification determines the 'quality' of the knowledge. Standards arising may include cost and profit, a product's contribution to a firm's development, as well as such criteria as adventure, romance and aesthetics.

Through a third project then, a new product or service concept created, crystallized and justified in the organization is integrated into a whole network of organizational knowledge. At the same time the emerging member's self-concept is deepened, as well as that of the group as a whole, and is broadened through their becoming 'the stories we are', something with which the mastery project is intimately involved.

The stories we are

The poetics of learning

For the Canadian Professor of Literature, William Randall (1994), learning is making – making sense, making a life, making ourselves. Learning for him then, in the context of 'the stories we are' is synonymous with self-creation. The 'poetics of learning', in our context therefore, is concerned with how individuals and groups, as well as organizations, story and re-story themselves. Such stories, moreover, are incomplete: lives and careers are still unfolding, mysteries yet unresolved, open books for whose endings we can but wait and see. It can also imply that a group, as well as its individual members, are 'legend-ary'.

Personal and interpersonal history, in that legendary context then, is profoundly purposeful, that is intricately 'plotted'. Each event in the group's work and life is therefore novel, and as a result charged, actually or potentially, with significance. Every group member then, during the course of the group's mastery project must build – starting with the most natural territory of his or her own life – a work, an opus. Such a legendary project serves to resolve the tension between the determined and the undetermined dimensions of the individual's and the group's individual, as well as their organization's, existence. In that context groups create, through re-storying themselves, what the organization does likewise, through its knowledge-creating processes. How each team carries this out – that is, in what proportions these knowledge-building or self-making elements are blended – is one of the things that make people and enterprises unique.

Unfolding plot

A story, a group's life story, its developmental trajectory, unfolds. The greater the *energeia* inherent in its beginning moreover, the more pregnant with possibilities the initial 'germ' of the story. Narration locates itself in the past in order to allow itself forward movement, as if a story's own future were a vacuum into which it is steadily sucked.

Storying for Randall like 'autopoetic learning', that is self-making for individuals or groups, involves four stages which can be likened to our developmental trajectory. First, as a *protagonist* the group is inside the story, acting and reacting in the present, unable to see the whole story or even any story.

Operating by reflex, such a group – through its members – acts on the move. For all intents and purposes, its group life is the plot, as close to raw existence as can be. As *Narrator*, second, the group and its members are more outside their story psychologically, thereby engaging in action and reflection.

Through such conscious action learning the team has greater control over its work and life as a story. As *Reader*, third, the group is now outside its knowledge-creating story even more, not controlling it so much as monitoring it, recognizing it, discovering its meaning. Finally, as *Authorizer*, the 'masterly' group creates the story, their novelty.

The author-ity of the facilitator

Poetry in motion

As trainers become facilitators of such individual and organizational mastery, they use stories, or indeed parables, all the time. They use these to instruct and to provide insight; they work within, are constrained by, and contribute to the unfolding stories of particular individuals, groups and organizations. As such, as motivators and mentors therefore, they are involved in enabling individual managers, and ultimately their individual organizations, to create and recreate the stories of their work and lives, products and processes. As such they are involved, indirectly if not directly,   *423* in enabling such individual companies to become unique knowledge-creating enterprises.

In fact, to entertain a story on how a team or an organization holds together – past, present and future – is by implication to entertain a theory on how a life holds together within it. The larger the stories swirling about in the world around the individual, or group, the more uniquely they shape their stories in turn. Each soaks in their plot lines through their pores, their point of view, their conflicts, their morality, their modes of characterization, their themes, their knowledge-creating spiral, their atmosphere.

Attaining mastery

From re-storying to knowledge creation

In effect the more unstoried existence the team, and its members, is enabled to transform into experience, and the more untold experience they are able to express, then the more powerfully and profoundly can self-creation proceed. Moreover, the more artistically coherent and ethically satisfying the story a group can live and tell, the more emotionally fulfilled they will feel. In other words, the more aware of the stories the group is, then the more power it has in relation to others, that is the more confidently it can critique the several larger stories in which the forms of its self-telling originate.

Criteria for evaluating 'mastery'

Retracing our steps, finally, the 'ordinary' project, rooted in cognitive and behavioural psychology, was directed towards action learning. Thereby team members become like classical scientists, and teamwork was oriented towards performance improvement. The second 'extra-ordinary' one, rooted in psychodynamic psychology, was oriented towards dynamic learning, and oriented towards self-organizing networks. Thus group members become like quantum scientists. Now in the third 'mastery' project, team members become like artists and authors, who in turn form teams that become part of a knowledge-creating company. Set within the context of such a developmental trajectory the members, and the teams of which they become a leading part, following in the footsteps of the heroes and heroines as well as the journeys set within myths of old, are judged according to the following criteria:

AIR

0   Opening Out
- To what extent has the group adopted the 'learning faith', thereby becoming committed to lifelong learning set within the context of members' emerging vocations?

- To what degree has the team adopted a knowledge-creating cause, on behalf of the organization?

1 The Call to Adventure
- What has been the nature and scope of the team's heroic journey, over the course of its life and work in general, and over the past three projects in particular?
- To what extent has it enabled the surrounding organization to engage in such a journey?

SHARE

2 Survey: The Role of Protectors
- What has been the part played, during the development programme, by 'protectors', that is by colleagues, adjacent groups, and surrounding networks?
- How extensive was the process of socialization, whereby a learning community has been established around the group, aimed at business and organization development?

3 Hypothesis: The Road of Trials
- To what extent have the seminal ideas and experiences that have been acquired over the three projects been explicitly incorporated into the group's mindset?
- To what degree has the learning undergone been incorporated into the 'knowledge network' of the team and surrounding organization?

4 Action: Death of the Old/Birth of the New
- To what extent, and in what way, have aspects of the group's self-concept been discarded as destructive, in favour of other self-concepts newly adopted, as creative?
- How effectively has the group internalized its learning within a wider network, with a view to exploiting such new knowledge commercially and/or organizationally?

5 Reflection: Forging a New Union
- How explicitly has a new union been forged between the team's newly established role and its recently reconceived and self-organizing network?
- How methodically has the team combined its learning and development with that of others, thereafter converting knowledge into new products/services or processes/systems?

6 Evaluation: Penetrating the Depths
- To what degree has both personal and interpersonal, group and inter-group insight been improved, in the light of current developments in the marketplace, with technology, and in society?
- What is the nature and extent of the enabling conditions for organizational learning and knowledge creation that the group has helped to establish around itself?

REVIEW

7 Uncovering the Vision
- To what extent has the emerging group/network become a creative force in the business/organization, having journeyed through the ordinary and extra-ordinary towards mastery?
- What is the nature and extent of the knowledge vision that the team has helped to both realize and also actualize within and around the immediate work group?

CONCLUSION

The journey to mastery, undertaken by a group, is inevitably interrupted by the 'chaotic' flow of an organization's life. Group members will therefore be periodically seconded, transferred, promoted, or even retired from the business at either expected or unanticipated moments. On some occasions, therefore, new members are brought into the group, along the journey's way, while on other occasions the group is reduced in size, from say six to four members. This need to be accepted is normal for the organizational course during these turbulent business times.

That having been said, the broad pattern of learning and development, from single (action-centred) to double (dynamically-oriented) to triple (heroic) loop proportions, should not change. In the process the group's orientation will need to change from one of 'ordinary' continuous improvement, to extra-ordinary business development to 'masterly' organizational knowledge creation.

REFERENCES AND RECOMMENDED READING

Lessem, R., *Business as a Learning Community*, McGraw Hill, London, 1993
Lessem, R., *Management Development Through Cultural Diversity*, Routledge, London, 1998
Lessem, R., with Palsule, S., *From Management Education to Civic Reconstruction: The Evolving Ecology of Organizations*, Routledge, London, 1999
McGill, I. and Beatty, J., *Action Learning*, 2nd edition, Kogan Page, London, 1996
Stacey, R., *Strategic Management and Organisational Dynamics*, Pitman, London, 1993
Stacey, R., *Creativity and Complexity in Organizations*, Berrett Koehler, San Francisco, 1996
Nonaka, I. and Takeuchi, H., *The Knowledge Creating Company*, Oxford University Press, Oxford, 1995
Randall, W., *The Stories We Are*, Toronto University Press, Toronto, 1994

Part IV
TEAMS AND TECHNOLOGY

Introduction to Part IV

The chapters in Part IV reflect the fact that in the current business environment technology plays a large part in the way that teams operate. Technology has not only affected the way in which organizations function and collaborate together, but also has enabled teams to work in ways which were undreamt of a few years ago. This section examines the technologies involved and provides examples of the effects on organizations, team utilization of technology and the ways in which technology provision teams have adapted to changing requirements.

In his chapter on making the most of new technology, Robin Hirsch examines the way in which modern technology gives more freedom and flexibility but changes established organization structures, creating new challenges for team leadership and personal identity. Topics that are covered include: the effects of new technology; fax, e-mail and the Internet/intranets; groupware; limitations of technology; video conferencing; language and translation.

One of the areas where technology has influenced teamworking is Computer-Supported Cooperative Work (CSCW). Chris Hutchison traces the history of cooperative work and defines what CSCW is. Using three case studies, he shows how CSCW has been applied within organizations and the lessons learned.

The chapter on virtual teams by Chris Hutchison looks at the way in which small companies with no corporate overhead can compete with larger organizations by using technology to source expertise worldwide on a project-by-project basis. He explores the concepts of virtual organizations, a virtual office and virtual teams, together with the planning skills, leadership and team development required.

Introducing new information systems into organizations that operate in a multi-team environment can be fraught with problems. Managing the people aspects, expectations and cultural change is a clear requirement. Roger Stewart describes an approach to the involvement, using soft systems workshops, of user department teams in the design, testing and implementation of an IS system in a community health trust. Its success in gaining user–team ownership of the new system and the easing of the operational cultural change is discussed.

The other side of this coin is the effect on teams that supply and maintain technology and application systems due to organizational change. Pat Keane in his chapter shows that the provision of information technology to organizations affects not just user department teams, but also the working practices of the IT provision teams. The London Borough of Richmond upon Thames has undergone many changes in recent times and this has been reflected in the way the IT Division has been required to change its structure and its methods of operating. This chapter traces the teamworking changes, successes and failures, within the IT division.

28 Making the most of new technology

Robin Hirsch

Modern technology makes it possible to build teams within organizations or between groups of organizations regardless of physical distance between the participants. It encourages task-focused, self-managing teams and 'virtual companies'. Standard software and groupware enable teams to share data and work systematically together, and encourages the inclusion of outside experts. Nevertheless, face-to-face meetings are still necessary for informal bonding and developing shared goals. Videoconferencing can help members to exchange information, but is no substitute for meeting to work together. The biggest obstacle to international team building is not the limitation of technology, but the lack of common languages and culture. Technology can mitigate this, but not remove it. In summary, technology gives more freedom and flexibility but disregards organization structures, creating new challenges for team leadership and personal identity.

THE EFFECTS OF NEW TECHNOLOGY

Technology as an enabler

Before the Second World War, the idea of a single team located in diverse geographical locations was almost unthinkable. However, the work done by Allied code-breakers and scientists working on the development of the atomic bomb was often carried out in laboratories separated by significant distances. The enabling factor was that they had shared goals, and reasonably well-demarcated areas of responsibility, but did not need to share information on a daily basis. Their main output, calculations and formulae, could be sent by telegraph or post, and only rarely did they need to meet. But, even then, one of the reasons for the success of the Manhattan Project was said to be the increased synergy achieved by bringing the team physically together.

In the 1980s, however, the spread of facsimile transmission (fax) and then electronic mail (e-mail) made geographically separated teams more common. CAD-CAM enabled designs to be transmitted from research centres to manufacturing units. Document transmission systems meant that newspapers such as the *Financial Times* and *International Herald Tribune* could be published in multiple locations by cooperating editorial teams. In the 1990s, it is normal for teams to work from the locations which suit them, not to cluster in one place to do their work. This applies to teams that design software, automotive vehicles and fashion goods, publish newspapers and magazines, manage financial funds or international companies, supply management consultancy and many other services. Some teams are formed simply to carry out a specific project or work on particular tasks, and may bring expertise from outside their own organizations as needed. On a larger scale, consortiums or joint ventures may form 'virtual companies' without employees other than those on secondment.[1,2,3]

Breaking barriers to competition and culture change

The fact that teams need not come from only one region or country accelerates the breakdown of barriers to competition in a wide range of goods and services. It was a significant factor in breaking the stranglehold of the unions in the UK newspaper publishing industry and led to the development of large software and computer service industries in Ireland and India serving European and US markets. Such teams typically have little tradition behind them and are relatively keen to try new methods and tools and accept new organizational paradigms. Hierarchical thinking is difficult to sustain and such teams tend to be more informal than is normal in their own society, less protective of their own cultural heritage.

This trend is forced on all international teams working with American or 'Anglo-Saxon' clients and managers, but it applies even more in the free-wheeling world of the Internet, which adds a Californian dimension to styles of personal address and the use of English. It was amusing to see a German manager finding out the first names of his staff, in preparation for a presentation in English to a Dutch company, in which first names would be the norm. He had worked with some of these staff for years before the presentation! Afterwards, the manager switched back to the formal mode of address in German (Sie), but the younger staff continued to use the informal (Du)

[1] Peter Drucker's article, 'The Coming of the New Organisation', refers to people participating in 'multiple task-focused teams'.

[2] Charles M. Savage describes 'virtual' or 'task-focusing' teams and the development of the 'virtual enterprise' in his book *5th Generation Management*. He refers to Peter Drucker's article in that book.

[3] Such companies are common in management consulting, and a good example of one which was founded by a specific consortium is Creative Star, to develop and operate a smart card revenue collection system for the main (competing) bus and rail companies of Hong Kong.

version with one another. In the author's experience, French, German and Mexican managers all use a more informal and direct style of writing on the Internet than in a fax or letter.

While some non-Americans are initially uncomfortable with this informality – and it helps to realize this – it leads to closer relationships more quickly than would normally be the case. What can then happen is that members of international teams may develop closer relationships with the other members of the team than with many of their colleagues in their own offices. People who regularly work in teams from other countries start to feel themselves to be an élite, with the advantage of a more open approach to alternative processes and ideas, but also with some danger of becoming rootless and alienated from their own culture.

Technology as an exclusive membership badge

The possession of new technology tools, shared by team members, but not by the majority in the organization in which they work, has a significant effect in binding team members together, and encouraging the team building process. When the Host Group, part of Diageo, introduced e-mail in the 1980s as part of the drive towards the 'paperless office', they were aware of other companies which had found a marked reluctance among senior managers to adopt the new technology. They therefore provided e-mail at first only to top managers, as part of an executive information system. The more progressive managers took to the system well and found their productivity increasing as information flowed more quickly. This news was carefully leaked around the organization, stressing the élite status of the system. Soon, the next level of managers were clamouring for it, and those less quick to adapt to it were spurred on to use it before their subordinates received the new tool. Soon, it was in use throughout the company.

A similar experience was noted among a group of senior managers from the world's major metro railways who were starting a worldwide benchmarking programme. The Mass Transit Railway Corporation of Hong Kong and Imperial College's Railway Technology Strategy Centre discovered the benefits of e-mail and passed on the information to the other participants. The Paris and London team members obtained Internet addresses, the first senior managers in their organizations to do so, while the Berlin and Tokyo members opened up personal accounts on AOL or other service providers as a stopgap measure until their companies developed their own facilities. These managers are now looked on almost as Internet experts in their own organizations. Within the team, members without e-mail gradually found themselves isolated, receiving information late or being omitted from mailing lists. The combination of 'technology pull' by leading-edge practitioners and 'standards push' by the mainstream group can thus lead to lagging members falling out of the fully functioning part of the team.

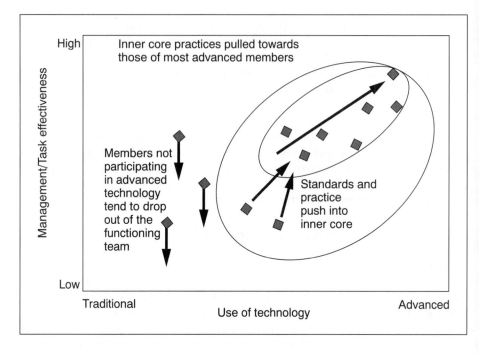

Figure 28.1 Technology effects on team members

FAX, E-MAIL AND THE INTERNET

Information exchange and communication

E-mail engenders enthusiasm because it enables much faster communication than fax. An international exchange of airmail letters may take up to two weeks. A letter is a relatively formal document with a signature, and it is often realized to be (at least to some extent) legally binding. So it is carefully considered, discussed internally, reviewed and revised before being sent off. It then takes up to a week to arrive if sent by post, a day or two if sent by courier. When it arrives, the recipient realizes that this is a document requiring relatively careful consideration . . . and so on. Within an organization, documents can take several days in the internal post. It was well known in ITT headquarters in Brussels in the 1970s that, because of tight security within the building, the fastest way to get a document from the second to the executive floor was not to try to take it oneself, but to send it by courier!

A fax may be in the form of a memo or letter, but it still carries a signature, and will often be reviewed in the same way. Letters and faxes pass through the internal post system, though some senior managers have their own fax machines. However, anyone who has tried to send off draft documents by fax to the members of a sizeable government committee or international team will know that it can tie up telephone lines for a long time. Only relatively few high-tech organizations can instantaneously send many duplicate faxes to different addressees. Often, addressees' fax machines run out of paper or their lines are engaged. So merely the sending of a fax to all members may take several hours. With an international team, some members may already have reached the end of their day and gone home. At the quickest, their response will be a day later.

E-mail has traditionally been used more for internal than external use and in some societies is not legally binding – for example, there is never a signature on the document other than an electronic one. It therefore carries the implication that the message is more in the form of a draft suggestion, request or idea. It is action-oriented, not an encouragement towards a carefully considered, reflective approach. It is usually sent to another manager during the course of the day with the assumption that a reply will be sent the same day. Even where it is an external message via the Internet or over the network of Compuserve, AOL or another of the Internet Service Providers, it carries these same informal, real-time associations.

As Table 28.1 shows, it can be quicker to send a message by e-mail to the other party than it is to speak with them on the telephone, especially if their extension is often engaged or they are frequently in meetings. Huge volumes of e-mail messages can be sent easily and quickly. A team's addresses are almost always in each member's electronic address book. Groups and sub-groups can be selected by highlighting a single name, sending a message to all of the members simultaneously. But information overload can easily become a problem, and many a manager rues the despatch of ill-considered messages which once sent, cannot be recalled.

File transfer

The other advantage that e-mail enjoys over fax is the ability to send and receive files and jointly work on documents. It has made it realistic to telecommute, work from home or other remote locations – including a hotel room on the other side of the world. In one example, a request for a proposal from an important client was received by post only the day before the deadline for submission, because it had gone to the wrong location in the organization. A rush meeting was called at around midday, at which all team members were briefed by the team leader: they agreed the workflow and roles in the preparation of the proposal and the broad parameters of the proposal itself. One member then stayed in the office to prepare the first draft, while the others went off to meetings. He sent the draft by e-mail in the late evening to two others who reviewed it, put in their particular parts of the document and sent it in the early hours of the morning for review to the two senior members of the team. These started work on it at about eight and were able to prepare a final version in time to take it to the client's office before the deadline at 10 a.m.

Table 28.1
Timescales for communication methods

Communication method (2-way)	Fastest time	Average time
Airmail letter	6 days	14 days
Courier	4 days	8 days
Fax	1 day	3–4 days
E-mail	10 minutes	1.5 days
Telephone	5 minutes	0.5–2 days

Internet, intranet or remote access?

Another use for file transfer is in updating larger teams such as sales forces or service teams by downloading to their personal computers the latest information that they need to know – such as inventory availability, order lead times, price databases, work schedules, and so on. This does not have to be over the Internet: it can be done by polling the organization's central computer. Typically, in the evening a salesman uploads future diary schedules together with orders or literature requests, and downloads from the central computer information needed about clients to be seen the next day. Within companies, this sort of information is increasingly being exchanged via intranets, which allow the same Internet browser and access controls to be used for internal communications and for obtaining external information from sites on the Net. The use of this standard interface means that users need less training and less homogeneity in their software and hardware, which in turn implies that teams are quicker to form and can become productive at the earliest oportunity. It also improves productivity by automating the provision of answers to Frequently Asked Questions, or FAOS as they are called on most websites.

This is another advantage of an intranet: information may be obtained directly without human intervention from different sources within and outside the company. As Figure 28.2 shows, it encourages lateral 'peer to peer' communication and the trend of breaking the organization up into smaller units, each with accountability for informing other units about the data, products and services for which they are responsible. Because information is given directly, rather than through a chain of command, information users have more points of contact with information suppliers. More units are recognized as part of the team directly supporting the salesforce or the customer. Accountability between the members of this team are clearer, with less intermediate suppliers to blame for information bottlenecks. Some of these information suppliers may also interface directly through the Internet with the customers themselves.

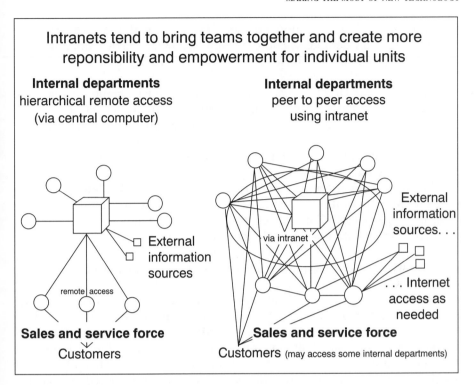

Intranets tend to bring teams together and create more reponsibility and empowerment for individual units

Internal departments
hierarchical remote access
(via central computer)

Internal departments
peer to peer access
using intranet

External
information
sources

via intranet

External
information
sources. . .

. . . Internet
access as
needed

remote access

Sales and service force
Customers

Sales and service force
Customers (may access some internal departments)

Figure 28.2   Remote access and Inter/intranet

STANDARD SOFTWARE

The growth of standard software environments, packages and groupware is having profound effects on the nature of teams and teamwork. The IBM-compatible PC running on DOS and then on Windows, and the domination of mid-range computers by UNIX, both led to standard interfaces for different software packages. This put an end to the days when programmers of proprietary hardware controlled software development, and separate Information Systems teams and Business User teams. Now, integrated multi-disciplinary development teams are increasingly run by business managers with a realistic understanding of the potential of software to effect the process changes they want.

Standard software makes project-focused teams more effective

Simply using standard packages enables teams to function better as groups. It has long been obvious for organizations to standardize on packages for word processing, spreadsheets, business presentations and databases, but it now applies equally to international, multi-organizational teams. Due to Microsoft's domination of the PC market, any major competitor has to offer the facilities to exchange files easily with Microsoft packages, just as Apple   *437*

TEAMS AND TECHNOLOGY

and others are forced to support diskette exchange with the standard Intel-based PC. In UNIX databases and development tools, Oracle's dominance is similar, the position of Sybase and Informix mirroring that of Lotus and Novell.

Microsoft's and Oracle's lead, however dangerously monopolistic it is, helps to set standards for teams from disparate environments. It has also created a standard currency for software development people and their skills. These individuals can therefore live a much more mobile life, either as freelance contractors or as employees moving from company to company. Companies benefit too, by employing people only for the duration of a project, knowing that the existence of such a pool of skilled labour permits sharp reductions in the time to assemble and train teams for the development of new systems. This places ever greater demands on such workers to learn to assimilate quickly and smoothly into teams.

Standard software changes the roles and composition of teams

The proliferation of high-level applications packages such as financial, manufacturing and human relations systems works in the same way. As Tom Peters said in *Thriving on Chaos*, 'New flexible manufacturing systems and the decentralized availability of the information needed for fast product changeover are leading to the wholesale adoption of cellular manufacturing, which essentially concentrates all the physical assets needed for making a product in a self-contained configuration which is tailor-made for team organization.'[4] He mentions how the supervisor moves from a rule enforcement role to that of facilitator, selling ideas to and from team members rather than transmitting management directives downwards and thinking for the members.

The role and membership of technology development teams change at least as much. Assembling standard packages with a reasonable fit to business needs is normally better than writing systems from scratch or customizing them heavily, which involves more input from business users and less from internal IS resources. Increasingly, external consultants join the team to assist in package selection. This should introduce more objectivity and provide a fresh look at the critical success factors, key performance indicators and business processes of the company. Unfortunately, most large consultancies have dedicated teams to sell and implement the leading packages, so their objectivity has to be questioned carefully. This makes the selection and definition of the roles of the expanded team a highly sensitive task.

Most leading applications packages require considerable work to be done to set the parameters of the packages, specifying internal rules and inter-

---

[4] Tom Peters' books have been so popular because of the number of suggestions that he gives in implementing management methods for the new technological age. An integral argument is the need for smaller, customer-focused, 'self-managing' teams and management units.

faces. The team will need extensive support from the software supplier or their partner consultants to do this. It is a critical process because the way in which the package is implemented will have a significant effect on the way the company operates. There are dangers:

1 There may not be enough managers or in-house team members with the strategic overview and business vision to ensure that the way in which the package is implemented fulfils the present and future needs of the company.
2 The primary interest of the software supplier or consultants may be to minimize their own cost or risk, or to sell more consultancy, rather than to put the client's needs first.
3 The external consultants may create jealousy in the organization by their high cost relative to that of core employees, and lead to the loss of those employees working on the team.

The first two of these issues have been dealt with by Glaxo and others by using a high-level consultant from a third, unrelated firm to represent the client's interest on the team. This reduces the conflict of interest for the partner consultancy or software supplier, and enables them to concentrate on achieving a rapid implementation. The third firm is given the task of managing the process so that the business needs are met and the implementation fulfils the contractual commitments made for it.

In a complex implementation, other services firms may be needed for downstream products and services such as networks, infrastructure services and training. This puts pressure both on management to give the team and each of its members clear goals and accountabilities, and on the team to relate to the different parties in different but effective ways.

The third issue, that of the motivation and loyalty of core employees whenever new technology is introduced, is always difficult. A legal agreement by the software supplier and consultancies not to poach in-house staff will afford short-term protection, but the development of a more mobile labour force is universal, and therefore other measures are needed in the medium term. Good career and salary planning will help, together with the regular practice of extensive cross-training for staff, and a credible commitment to continue to invest in further new technology. What is important is that these elements must be in place with a successful track record before the start of the systems implementation, or employees will consider them to be nothing more than empty words.

Version standards and procedures

Whether the systems involved are sophisticated financial packages or PC office suites, for technology to have a positive effect on team productivity, members of the team should share a common standard for package versions and communications protocols. Should all files be exchanged using a par- *439* ticular brand of software and a particular version of it (say, Excel 4.0)? Do all members have the latest version of that or other brands? If the answer to either of these questions is no, the team leader or central facilitator should announce which version is to be used as standard throughout the group, and which alternatives are acceptable. Just as the latest version of Lotus files can only be opened by the latest version of MS Office and vice versa, so most software products are forward compatible (earlier version files can be read by later versions) but not usually backwards compatible (later version files cannot be read by earlier versions). Forgetting such limitations leads to inefficiencies and frustration between team members, while being sensitive to them builds gratitude and positive responses.

A technology help desk can help to overcome failures by individual team members, as a recent experience illustrated: a delegate team had been scheduled to give a presentation to an international meeting, but was unable to come. One of the consultants to the team had brought his laptop computer and, as usual, checked his e-mail daily from his hotel room. On the second day, he received a Powerpoint file from the absentees which they asked him to present on their behalf. Unfortunately, the file was the latest version, which he could not read, and to compound the problem, the host company's standard was Lotus and Novell, not Microsoft. However, the host company's Information Systems Department operated a technology watch machine to test the latest software packages, so before the end of the conference the presentation was printed out and issued to all of the other delegates. Without the technology watch programme, the effect of the absentees' failure to observe the team standards would have been the complete loss of the presentation.

GROUPWARE

Many of the difficulties in ensuring that different packages communicate with one another can be resolved by the use of groupware packages such as Lotus Notes. This package enables forms and documents to be set up to recognize and read the output from multiple packages and package versions. Of course, the same limitations apply as in the above anecdote: if a major software supplier brings out a new version of their package, the groupware will continue to work satisfactorily only if the users keep on upgrading to the version with the latest translation facilities.

Standard software changes the nature of teams simply by its very existence, while groupware is designed specifically to alter the way teams work together. Groupware acts both as a facilitator between software application packages and as an organizer for information and people. In its role as facilitator, it supports the use of multiple software packages; in its role as organizer, it structures support for communications and information retrieval, the sharing of expert resources and the execution of tasks. There are many definitions of groupware, but for our present purposes it can be described as software which facilitates the working of people in a group or team.

Groupware offers more than just communication between different software. It can also include workflow and scheduling functions, organize marketing and sales contacts, and enable customer tracking and project reporting to be made more systematic and effective. However people find, track and share any sort of information, they can be brought to work in a more productive and interactive manner with one another through the systems, procedures and the ease of communication which groupware brings. Agenda items from meetings may be followed up, individual to-do lists and team progress milestones monitored, customer behaviour and service support tracked. One of the more exciting features is the alert function which automatically refers events outside desired parameters to users and to more senior management as appropriate.

Workflow is one of the most obvious technologies for changing the way teams work. There are a number of packages specifically designed for analysing and restructuring workflow or Business Process Re-engineering, while Lotus Notes and most leading financial and business systems offer workflow as an integral part of their package. In operational workflow systems, events trigger the automatic distribution of tasks to the units required to deal with them. For example, an incoming payment would be sent to the receivables department; if the sum were large enough, it would advise the Financial Controller, take the customer off credit hold, permitting orders to be placed again and simultaneously communicate the situation to the relevant salesman. The system thus treats all these people as a single team working off the same data. Internal tension due to one department thinking another is slow to inform them of events will be eliminated by the system's guarantee to all parties of keeping them in the picture and alerting them if pre-set parameters require it.

Computer Integrated Telephony, or CIT, includes specific workflow routines. It provides a set of scripts for the telephone operator to say and actions to do, dependent on the replies of the person on the other end of the line. It can be used for customer conversations, both outgoing sales calls and incoming enquiries, and to support service people in the field. For cold sales calls, it may be integrated with automatic dial facilities timed to get the next prospect on the line just as the last one is dealt with. The scripts are beneficial in lowering the uncertainty of not knowing what to say, but this technology has less impact on the internal working of such sales teams than in other forms of workflow. Very high productivity is achievable, but often with high levels of stress unless the system is very well implemented.

Like e-mail, groupware generates huge quantities of information and leads to far higher intensity of communication. At its worst, groupware can be a bureaucratic timewaster, tracking events of little importance and demanding constant feedback responses from busy people who become so dedicated to running the system that they are prevented from getting on with work *441* that really adds value to the organization. Some systems are set up with such standardized and structured data that they prevent the team from changing the way they look at the world and their own processes. According to Ovum Ltd's report 'Ovum Evaluates Workflow', 'most workflow systems are so inflexible that a poorly designed one is worse than none at all'.

At its best, groupware can help to identify best practice and turn it into procedures which allow even poor performers to come up to the standard of the best, and help the best performers to use information and communications resources even better, enabling them to carry on the process of continual improvement. Just as bad use of groupware leads to rigidity, so well-designed groupware systems are highly adaptable: forms, reporting protocols, the organization of information resources and expertise can all be designed for the balance of structure and flexibility which best suits the needs and preferences of the people involved.

LIMITATIONS OF TECHNOLOGY

As we have seen, groupware and standard packages can be excellent in enabling companies to put together new teams of people and use them in a highly efficient way, but the effectiveness of such technology is very dependent on how well it is implemented.

E-mail can play a very powerful role in speeding up communications and bringing people together, but it carries the dangers of all informal communications – that it can arouse negative as well as positive emotions in more immediate ways than either letters or faxes. The same rules of good behaviour in face-to-face communication apply to e-mail, but with the additional caution that because one cannot see the other person's body language, the scope for adopting a false tone and misunderstanding the nuances of what is being said are much greater.

Because of its informality, e-mail is good for communicating some emotional contact, but face-to-face meetings still remain vitally important. Only if team members can see one another can they evaluate the effects on their colleagues of what each person has just said. For people from some cultures, such as the Japanese, it is particularly necessary even where there are no cultural differences within the team, but for international teams the danger of culturally based misunderstandings adds an extra potential difficulty.

'Real' meetings enable team members to deal not only with the task in hand, but to enjoy the more informal contacts and cultural exchanges which enable the task-oriented functions to be fulfilled harmoniously. Apparently unimportant activities such as smiling, eating and drinking together, laughing at one another's jokes, enjoying a boat or cable car ride or game of golf, can make all sorts of work-related decisions easier. The best and most harmonious teams are usually those who have worked hard together to achieve deadlines and difficult tasks. Without the opportunity to do this in physical proximity with one another, there will always be the danger that one has not one team, but as many sub-teams as there are working locations.

VIDEOCONFERENCING AND CONFERENCE CALLS

Videoconferencing can provide some informal and non-verbal communication, but even after 15 years, this medium is still relatively limited. It works effectively between two parties (each of which may be a group of people) but becomes more difficult to handle with larger numbers, more than five on either side of the video link, or with more than one link. Voice conference calls are effective with up to about five parties in all, but require good discipline and a positive attitude among the members. For both voice and video, a chairman or compere is needed to allocate airtime to each participant as appropriate. Another key success factor is to prepare the topic and agenda very well and circulate papers (electronically, no doubt) prior to the meeting.

Despite these difficulties, the advantage of videoconferencing is often the discovery of underlying factors which were not previously recognized as an issue. This is facilitated by the presence of functional experts who were not previously involved. A videoconference is an excellent way to introduce such outsiders into the team on a consultancy basis, thereby creating a layering of the team into core members and associated specialists.

Data conferencing allows charts and pictures to be shown and is invaluable as an addition to audio conference calls, but it integrates badly with videoconferencing. The time and concentration put into switching from the faces of the people to the data and back detracts from the concentration on what is being said. Because of the relatively poor quality of the image with current levels of technology, most people need to look more carefully on a video link to pick up non-verbal signals than in a face-to-face meeting, when the normal observation of other team members takes place subliminally. However, it must be said that the technology is improving all the time, so this may well change in the next few years.

One of the greatest disadvantages of videoconferencing and conference calls – and of all voice communication – is their more demanding requirement for a single common language. In written communications translators can always be used, which slows communication down, but does not prevent it. E-mail, on the other hand, enjoys a peculiarly favoured position: even managers whose English is not that fluent and who would never initiate their own letters or faxes in that language are often ready to correspond by e-mail. They may well participate in a single-language meeting satisfactorily, relying on non-verbal clues and repetition, but the same managers tend to be reluctant to join a videoconference. Conscious of the cost and pressure of time, they fear that the demands on their language skills may be too great and that they may be required to give an instant response before they have really understood what has been said.

The other problem with videoconferencing at the time of writing this is *443* the cost. It costs almost as much to arrange a 60–90-minute videoconference between London and Hong Kong as it does to fly one person between the two cities. Videoconferencing is cost-efficient if the traveller's time is strictly limited or charged out at a high rate, but the other benefits of business travel, such as that of seeing the situation at first hand or making unexpected discoveries, should not be ignored in the equation. The cost should not be overstated: equipment and software costs are dropping rapidly, and telecommunication prices are going down in line with the increasing pressure of global competition.

A recent breakthrough in cost was due to voice and video exchange over the Internet. The cost of the camera and microphones is low, and the communication cost is only that of a local telephone call. It does have drawbacks:

- The time delay between speaking and the interlocutor hearing the words is much greater than with a normal videoconference line.
- With current technology, the cameras are suitable only for one person rather than a group.
- Capacity limits to volume on the Internet make it difficult to rely upon achieving the desired real-time links at a predictable time.

The advances in technology in the next few years are likely to reduce or remove some of these drawbacks, but the capacity to handle the huge growth of traffic on the Net may always be in doubt.

In summary, videoconferencing and audio conference calls supplement other means of bonding teams together, but the advantages of non-verbal communication in videoconferences are not as significant as early suppliers expected. However, such conferences can command the full attention of team members, and the preparation of the event forces the team to concentrate more clearly on the issues. In terms of the social development of the team structure, the need for a strong chairperson or compere works in the opposite direction to other technology developments, which encourage the trend towards self-managed teams without a hierarchical structure.

LANGUAGE AND TRANSLATION

Shared background and communication materials of high quality are an obvious aid to team building. The exchange of training videos can help to broaden support in each company participating in the team. In international teams, the ability to dub or sub-title videos is an essential technology for such an initiative. This raises the importance of mastering language difficulties, without which multilingual teams cannot function.

Dictionaries on disk or CD-ROM are useful aids for e-mail; automatic translation software can provide first drafts of written communications; and simultaneous translation is valuable in helping delegates at conferences; but there is no adequate substitute for learning languages oneself. For example, even when one has simultaneous translation, the personal bias or emotional tone of a particular translator can create misunderstandings and problems between team members. Even the act of putting on earphones creates a barrier between oneself and the speaker, which is why so many delegates at international conferences listen to the translation with only one ear.

Fortunately, in the field of interactive computer-aided learning, progress has been such that the time taken to learn languages has been sharply reduced, especially for English, the international business language used as the official language of most multinational companies. This gives English speakers a built-in advantage in teamworking.

One disadvantage of people having learnt their English through a short computer-aided course, is that they may think they speak the language better than they really do. This is not exclusive to technology-based learning. On the eve of my first business trip, my boss, an old hand in NATO and EEC committees, warned me: 'Be careful with the Dutch. They speak excellent English, but they don't always understand it.' The same can apply to all non-English language groups speaking the language regularly. It is also as well for native English speakers to remember that the English spoken in the corridors of the EU in Brussels and Strasbourg is a very different dialect from the English spoken in the UK, the USA, Australia or India – and the British should not claim that their version is always right.

For new members of specialized teams, there is frequently a whole vocabulary to be learnt. In organizations like the EU, UN or NATO, the demand for standard phrases for simultaneous translation and the accepted work processes of the bureaucrats is quite a barrier to newcomers. The same applies to jargon in every advanced technological area, and is made worse from the speed of progress and the lack of vocabulary to describe new phenomena. The Internet itself has such a jargon or dialect, which can only be expected to grow, and has certainly been used in the past to distinguish experienced Net workers from newcomers, and make it difficult to join a team on an equal basis. Nevertheless, as a higher proportion of business people – and their children – use the Net, the barrier that different English dialects make to participation in Internet-based teams will become insignificant.

CONCLUSIONS AND LOOSE ENDS – THE EFFECT ON TEAM STRUCTURE AND INDIVIDUALS

Technology makes far larger and more geographically dispersed teams possible. It allows tasks to be broken up into constituent parts and documents to be transferred from one to another. It breaks up traditional ways of thinking and working and allows the formation of fluid teams and virtual companies, enabling easy movement of people from team to team. It can lead to a greater identification with other members of a multi-organization team than with one's fellow employees. While every team tends to have *445* some sort of a leader, this fluidity means that accepted authority structures are no longer appropriate. It creates a greater demand for leadership, but a leadership based on influence, not structure, the ability to convince and to engage interest, enthusiasm and loyalty, not the ability to control.

Controls, performance monitoring and systematic procedures will continue to exist and to be strengthened, but dictated by the nature of the work and the computer systems which make teams more productive, not imposed by titular bosses. Hewlett Packard and Digital Equipment are examples of companies which have long attempted to transmit to individuals and teams the need to agree their own goals and to monitor themselves against key results rather than being externally assessed.

HP was quite extraordinary in the 1980s in Germany in their operation of flexible working hours on a trust basis, without any time clocks or registration system – but it worked. We believe a key reason was this use of self-motivating teams. However, if the mechanisms are inadequate for ensuring that their goals are congruent with others and with the business aims of the company as a whole, such teams may underachieve, play internal politics and escape budgetary controls. Activities which do not add value to the company proliferate and can lead to the extinction of the company, as happened to Digital Equipment in the early 1990s. In such circumstances, no technology can protect the organization – good management alone can restore the situation (usually with substantial reduction in personnel, as in Digital's case).

For the individual, too, technology offers flexibility and freedom, decision and information support. It will become easy as never before to slip into virtual participation in a virtual team of a virtual organization. The challenge will be to keep a sense of identity and both a corporate and personal sense of direction, to know the degree to which one shares the goals, aspirations and value systems of the different teams to which one belongs. Setting priorities for one's loyalties, time and resources becomes more complex than ever before.

Part of the challenge will also be to remember how to interact with other people. Many high-tech companies already have virtual offices, where the individual's office is no more than an e-mail address, and most people work in whatever building is most convenient at the time. This can be wonderful for personal productivity, but it can also lead to the practice of sitting all day at a computer, communicating exclusively by e-mail, and meeting other team members every few months at a conference of carefully crafted presentations. Some people then carry on social interaction exclusively over 'cyberspace', without any face-to-face business with real people for weeks on end. In these conditions life itself can become virtual.

REFERENCES

Drucker, P., 'The Coming of the New Organisation', *Harvard Business Review*, 1988, **66**(1), January–February

Peters, T., *Thriving on Chaos*, first published in the USA by Alfred A. Knopf, Inc., New York, 1987, UK paperback by Pan Books Ltd.

Savage, C. M., *5th Generation Management*, Digital Press, Burlington, Mass., 1990

29 Computer-supported cooperative work

Chris Hutchison

First gaining recognition as a distinct field of study in the early 1980s – though with a 40-year prehistory reaching back to Vannovar Bush's conception of the 'memex' as 'a large, shared, structured information base' (Greif, 1988, p. 15) – Computer-Supported Cooperative Work (CSCW)[1] is an emerging set of tools and technologies (often called 'groupware') concerned with enhancing the role that the computer can play in the support of groupwork (Greif, 1988; Greenberg, 1991; Baecker, 1993). We can generally regard Group Support Systems (GSS) and Electronic Meeting Systems (EMS) as cognate fields (Jessup and Valacich, 1993). Stating more precisely what CSCW is, however, is a slightly more contentious matter (Baecker, 1993, p. 1).

In this chapter we define, describe and discuss CSCW by not only examining the technologies that enable people to work together more efficiently, but also, and more importantly, by understanding that the way in which people *actually* work has an effect on the design of those very technologies. The focus will consequently be as much on human factors issues, including team behaviour, as on the groupware itself, and it is this concern that has motivated the selection of case studies presented in the section on Case Studies.

CSCW AND THE NATURE OF 'COOPERATIVE WORK'

The term 'cooperative work' has, itself, a long history in the social sciences. First used by economists in the early 19th century[2] to designate work involving multiple actors, it was formally defined by Marx as 'multiple indi-

---

[1] The term was coined by Irene Greif and Paul Cashman in 1984.
[2] For example, Andrew Ure, *The Philosophy of Manufactures*, London, 1835, and Edward Wakefiled, *A View of the Art of Colonization*, London, 1849.

viduals working together in a planned way in the same production process or in different but connected production processes'. The term has been widely used with this meaning – 'cooperative work' as essentially monolithic, hierarchically organized, top-down activity – throughout most of this century.

The term 'cooperative work' is today becoming less well-defined, however, its meaning rendered problematic with the emergence of further concepts such as collaborative work, coordinated work, articulation work, collective work, groupwork and teamwork, reflecting new uncertainties and lack of consensus on how to describe the accomplishment of multi-actors tasks. For Ehn (1988), for example, *all* work, to the extent that it depends on others for its successful performance, is essentially cooperative; for Sørgaard (1987) it is characterized by being non-hierarchical, non-specialist, and relatively autonomous, while Howard (1987) doubts that any real work situation is properly 'cooperative' in that sense. For Strauss (1985) and Gerson and Star (1986), cooperative work requires 'articulation work': distributed work normally involves numerous constituent tasks to be undertaken, typically asynchronously, by numerous individuals coping with often unanticipated local contingencies, and the final coordination of the whole may consequently require 'local situation actors [to] "fiddle" or shift requirements in order to get their work done . . . We argue here that such articulation is not extraneous to requirements analysis, but central to it' (Gerson and Star, 1986, p. 259).

What constitutes a 'group' for 'groupwork' is no clearer, with definitions both broad and narrow. Narrowly, 'a group is defined as a relatively closed and fixed ensemble of people sharing the same "goal" and engaged in incessant and direct communication' (Bannon and Schmidt, 1991, p. 51); yet the same authors go on to note that:

> The notion of a shared goal is murky and dubious . . . The cooperative process of decision making in a group is a very differentiated process involving the interaction of multiple goals of different scope and nature as well as different heuristics, conceptual frameworks, etc.

How much more difficult then to define the team in teamwork. The design of the Physician Workstation (described in 'Designing for Information Sharing'), for example, had to acknowledge that, although in a broad sense the shared goal was care of the patient, the stakeholders in the system, ranging from surgeons to nursing staff to technicians to administrative and accounting staff, each had their own specific roles and agendas which, while converging on individual patient records, rendered problematic the notion of 'groupwork'.

One might consider also that the accomplishment of work tasks in offices typically involves the participation of both people and artefacts, including machines. Artefacts may have an important symbolic function, and the understanding and use of an artefact by actors may be different from its *449* intended or ostensible purpose. The 'complex sheet' described by Suchman and Trigg (1991), and further discussed in 'Designing for Practice' later in this chapter, mapping the movements of passengers and baggage for an airline were clearly being used in five different ways to express five different types of meaning; only by observing the subtle interactions between actors and the paper sheets would computerization of the procedure have been possible. Furthermore, office workers may frequently communicate with one another only indirectly, via their machines. By this, we mean not only overt dialogue by means of, for example, e-mail or electronic bulletin boards, but also a less obvious form of communication through the sharing of electronic documents: the databases, texts, images and diagrams, spreadsheets, and so forth, which convey meanings between members of groups. Bearing that observation in mind, Hutchison and Rosenberg (1994, p. 109) avoid the concept of a specifically human 'group' in favour of viewing the grouping of people and computers '*in toto* as a *distributed knowledge-based information processing system* accepting inputs from and outputting to its environment'. From that perspective, they argue, there is little sense in distinguishing that part of the information processing which is executed mechanically and that part which is executed by human beings. This issue is discussed in more detail in the Case Studies section with regard to a shared electronic 'whiteboard'.

The role of the shared artefact in groupwork is highlighted by Sørgaard (1989) who offers the analogy of two people carrying a table:

> Two ways of co-ordinating co-operative work can be identified. One is by explicit communication about how the work is being performed. Another is less explicit, mediated by the shared material used in the work process. A simple example is the way two people carry a table.... the two people can follow each other's actions because the actions get mediated through the shared material. This co-ordination is not necessarily explicit ... The pattern of co-operation is not fixed, it is often defined by the actors.

The 'complex sheet' discussed in the section 'Designing for Practice' illustrates how a shared artefact is used as a dynamic communication medium between actors.

The issues raised in this discussion of cooperative work mean that, although its technologies suggest CSCW to be a subdiscipline of computer science, as a *research* field it gives great importance to dealing with 'soft' questions about *people* and how they work together on tasks. CSCW is consequently an interdisciplinary field that draws together researchers from such disparate intellectual communities as psychology, sociology, linguistics and conversation analysis, artificial intelligence, organizational theory, ethnography and interaction analysis. Thus, Baecker (1993, p. 2), for example, cautions that

technical brilliance is not enough. Many groupware applications created to date have failed [...] despite what may appear to be elegant technology. Even more so than with conventional single-user systems, groupware can only be successful insofar as *it is responsive to the social and organizational context in which it is embedded.* (My italics)

We will present, later in this chapter, overviews of studies that highlight the importance for groupware design of some of the disciplines listed in the previous paragraph: conversation analysis for a viable model of group interaction, interaction analysis for requirements capture, and ethnography and artificial intelligence for integrating and analysing mutliple data sources in distributed teams. Next we shall consider the more general issues of what CSCW actually is.

WHAT IS CSCW?

Definitions abound, but most agree at least that CSCW marks a paradigm shift from the human–machine coordination of the solitary worker to human-to-human communication, collaboration, and coordinated problem solving within a shared digital workspace. CSCW is therefore, in its broadest sense, an umbrella term for those human-to-human activities that take place within a framework defined by the convergence of telecommunications and computing, and which thus includes electronic mail ('e-mail'), text-based conferencing (for example, USENet and mailing lists), collaborative hypertext systems (for example, intranets as repositories of 'organizational memory'), and real-time conferencing via text, speech, whiteboards, video, or some combination of these. A now classical taxonomy of CSCW categorizes groupware according to whether it supports interaction in real time ('synchronous') or not ('asynchronous'), and whether that interaction is between individuals in the same location or geographically dispersed locations. This is summarized in Figure 29.1, with examples of each.

Helpful as this grid may be as a typology, it poorly reflects current directions in research and groupware design. Further useful distinctions have therefore been made (i) between those technologies which support the work of large numbers of individuals – such as e-mail and mailing lists – and those designed specifically for the coordinated activities of small groups, that is, team, and (ii) between groupware that supports the management of the work *process* and that which supports the management of the work *content* (Dyson, 1992). Figure 29.2 attempts to capture the orientation of current research into groupware design – increasingly the focus is on the coordinated work of small groups in real time.

The purpose of this chapter, however, is to concentrate less on the technologies than on the nature of group behaviour which the technologies are designed to support. The following case studies have been chosen both to exemplify the multidisciplinarity of CSCW as a research programme and also to highlight the importance, in groupware design, of how people actually work. The first study shows how a collaborative ideas generation system was salvaged through the application of conversation analysis to develop *451*

	SAME TIME	DIFFERENT TIMES
SAME PLACE	Face-to-face interaction e.g. electronic meeting system	Asynchronous interaction e.g. shared database
DIFFERENT PLACES	Synchronous distributed interaction e.g. teleconference with shared whiteboard	Asynchronous distributed interaction e.g. e-mail and other messaging systems

Figure 29.1 Groupware time–space matrix

an authentic model of interaction. The second shows how interaction analysis was crucial to an understanding of how important artefacts may be as vehicles for communication between group members. The third study illustrates how data gathered from an ethnography of actual clinical practice led, through the implementation of a knowledge-based system, to the design of a system that managed different types of information flowing from a distributed heterogeneous team.

CASE STUDIES

Designing for conversation: the Cognoter (XEROX PARC)

The first case study exemplifies support for generating synchronous work content in small groups, and its initial implementation highlights the problems that can arise from designing software without first observing how teams actually behave. The Colab project (1991) was an attempt to provide computational support for the groupwork of between two and five people working together in the same room. The project combined a specially designed room comprising technologies that included networked computers, video facilities and display screen ('Liveboard'; see Elrod et al., 1992) with an elaborate model of the meeting process that the room tried to support. Users are able to share displays by projecting the contents of their own screens either onto the Liveboard or onto another user's screen (Figure 29.3).

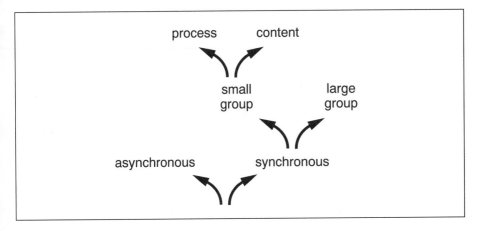

Figure 29.2 Directions in groupware design

Cognoter is a multi-user idea organizing software tool developed for the Colab that was designed to support small design teams in the creation of plans or outlines. It sought to achieve this through the implementation of a three-part process of brainstorming, organizing the ideas into sequences and groups, and evaluating them, much as would the team in a non-computational environment with a whiteboard. The basic unit in the interface is an icon with a short title and annotation. Icons would be created individually in a personal 'edit window', and displayed in shared 'item organization

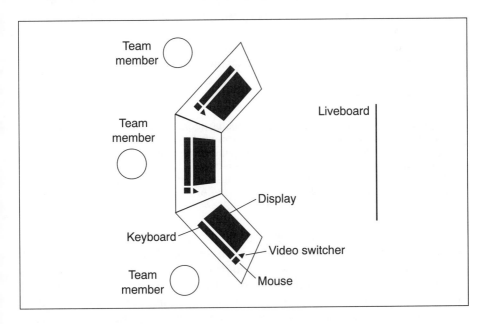

Figure 29.3 The Colab (based on Tatar et al., 1991, p.186, Figure 1)   *453*

windows' on the 'Liveboard' where they could be organized in groups to any level of nesting.

When the software was tested with trial groups, problems arose. In the first group trial it was found that individuals worked alone in edit windows without talking or sharing screens, and finally gave up the system to work together with notepad and pens. The second group used the video link to look at the screen of whoever was typing at the time, thus foregoing the flexibility to be able to generate and share ideas concurrently and having 'to spend quite a bit of effort negotiating who would type next' (Tatar et al., 1991, p. 189). Both groups, although experienced computer users, eschewed use of the Liveboard, finding it impossible to work with.

The problems were of two kinds. The first (reported by the second group) was with regard to what could, and could not, be seen on the Liveboard: talk was not well coordinated with display – since each user had a separate and individually tailorable screen, talk about items in one might not map easily into objects in another or on the Liveboard. The second problem concerned mistaken reference: when several events (mouse clicks, screen switches, icon creation, by different participants) are happening simultaneously, a question such as 'Who did that?' could (and did) lead to misinterpretation and to what appeared to be unjust accusations. That editing of items was done in private editor windows and only the results, anonymously, broadcast to the Liveboard also lessened the sense of work being done collaboratively. As the authors note, 'It is as if the person, rather than making a bid for the floor, had simply dropped out of the conversation in the same way they have to when recording information in traditional media' (p. 199). The result was that the system, far from facilitating group work, actually disrupted it.

The diagnosis was that Cognoter embodied an inappropriate 'parcel-post' model of conversation, in which it is assumed that one utterance is terminated and sent before the next is begun. 'The starting point of the interactive model of conversation', by contrast,

> is the observation that conversation does not consist of one person making a complete utterance while the other person waits passively. Both participants are active even when only one is actually speaking. Thus people nod, complete or reshape another's phrases, and say 'uh-huh' . . .
> . . . conversation is distinguished . . . by the amount of work to ensure understanding that is done within the time frame of the actual communication . . . (Tatar et al., 1991, pp. 192 and 195)

Speakers frequently look, mid-utterance, for confirmation from their hearers that they are being understood, and often add clarifications or change tack while speaking in response to subtle vocal or gestural cues from hearers. In this way, in face-to-face conversations, ambiguities and mis-reference are generally avoided. The 'parcel-post' model implicit in the textual component of Cognoter thus frustrated the 'collaborative work of holding a conversation' (Tatar et al., 1991, p. 193): not only is it not responsive to contextual cues, but also is a feature of asynchronous rather than of real-time inter-action. The problem was exacerbated by the way in which the Liveboard was being used: in face-to-face talk, a whiteboard might be actively used as a prop *within* a conversation (in various ways annotating the talk) as well as containing items that the conversation is *about*; (see the discussion of artefacts in the first part of this chapter and section on 'Designing for Practice'). The icons recorded on the Liveboard, however, were able to serve only the latter function, hence writing to the board was in a sense 'stepping out of the conversation'.

The software was consequently redesigned, as Cnoter, to address the problems observed. First, editing an item – previously private and hence tantamount to a withdrawal from conversation – became a shared activity, with the edit window simultaneously displayed on all screens, thus giving everyone visual access to items while they are being created; users were now even able to contribute collectively in the creation of items. Second, window positions and shapes were standardized across all machines so that users could now rely on unambiguous positional information for resolving the uncertainties of reference. These modifications, together with speeding up the rate at which changes are propagated to other's screens and to the Liveboard, resulted in a more usable system.

The main lesson learned from the group trials was that 'system designers must draw on and reason about social science results such as the interactive model . . . many of the serious problems in Cognoter stem from the culturally prevalent, easy-to-make assumption that communication consists of bits of verbal or textual material passed whole from one person to the next' (pp. 207 and 206). Only by observing how groups really converse could the system be redesigned to support authentic team work.

Designing for practice: the workplace project (XEROX PARC)

An example of the emphasis on distributed synchronous work process in small groups is the study by ethnographers Suchman and Trigg, who begin from the premise that 'work practice is fundamentally social . . . in that any activity, whether characterized by conflict or cooperation, relies on a foundation of meaningful, mutually intelligible interaction' (1991, p. 209). The computerization of systems for collaborative working should conse-quently, they argue, be based on a detailed observation and lucid understanding of actors' actual work practices 'in settings designed by the participants themselves, over time, rather than contrived by the researcher for purposes of the analysis' (p. 211). When those work practices involve the routine use of artefacts then, to the extent that these 'constitute active elements in the organisation of the relationships of people to each other and with their environment' (Akrich, 1987, p. 1), systems design must take these artefacts and their uses into account.

Part of Suchman and Trigg's three-year study of work in an airport as 'situated activity' took place in an airline operations room. Each of the five *455*

'Ops Room' staff had responsibilities relevant to getting aircraft to and from gates, and to transferring passengers and baggage between aircraft, the activities chunked each day into eight one-hour blocks called 'complexes'. The information required to manage the work of a 'complex' was present both online and, updated as circumstances changed, on paper documents called 'complex sheets'. The use of the sheets, as artefacts having a key function within the routinized work practices, suggested 'interaction analysis' as a fruitful research method insofar as it focuses 'on the joint definition and accomplishment of the work at hand, through the organization of interaction and the use of supporting technologies and artifacts' (Suchman and Trigg, 1991, p. 210).

Their study of team behaviour then, for CSCW design, involved them in making video recordings of the Ops Room staff during the course of their normal work, and subsequently annotating, transcribing and analysing the video records. The use of video records was deemed important in so far as participants' gaze, facial and bodily gestures, and body positions would reveal salient aspects of group interaction with each other and with artefacts that would not be captured by audio recording alone.[3] The research team dealt with the problem of capturing the complex activities that work involves by constructing four types of record:

1   Setting-oriented records, recording with stationary camera and microphone the coordinated activities of all employees within the Ops Room
2   Person-oriented records, attempting to understand the work from each individual employee's point of view, including the use of a mobile camera in tracking the use by ramp crew members of the 'complex sheet'
3   Object-oriented records, tracking a technology or artefact, for example tracing a 'complex sheet' from the time it is first generated, as an empty matrix, through its markup and highlighting by Ops Room members, to its filing and possible eventual recovery by auditors
4   Task-oriented records, simultaneously recording the activities of distributed individuals – for example, Ops Room staff and gate crews – working towards a common goal.

The video records could then be reviewed by both employees and researchers, with the former drawing attention to items that might otherwise elude the analysts. In a similar study, Jordan and Henderson (1995) note:

This gives some idea of how participants structure the event, i.e., where they

---

[3] Jordan and Henderson (1995) also note that 'Observers have frequently reported that they have seen such [actions] even though on replay it is clear that none occurred ... Errors of this sort are invisible in a paper-and-pencil record because there is no opportunity to go back and re-examine what happened. In contrast, a tape segment can be played over and over again, and questions of what is actually on the tape versus what observers think they saw, can be resolved by recourse to the tape as the final authority.'

see significant segments as beginning and ending; it also gives information on troubles that may be invisible to the analyst, on resources and methods used by participants to solve their problems.

Among the problems arising from the use of the paper 'complex sheets' as initially designed and as intended for use were that, for example, while showing projected movements of passengers and baggage between aircraft they were not designed to show movements of aircraft themselves, hence they made no allowance for unanticipated gate swaps. Further, they were designed to cover only one 'complex' at a time, hence did not lend themselves to noting activities that spanned two 'complexes'. Also, they were ostensibly to be filled in and read as in principle fixed projections of an hour's activities, even though in reality changes might need to be made after a sheet had been distributed to ramp and gate crews.

Activities that might span two one-hour blocks – an aircraft arriving at one gate in one complex and departing from a different gate in the following complex, for example – would therefore present problems for using the sheets as discrete hourly schedules. The staff consequently devised an informal system of annotation to show gate swaps across complexes. Other forms of annotation evolved to manage various contingencies as they arose.

The system of annotation was one that had evolved naturally out of situated work practices as an informal response to actual circumstances. Thus the Passenger Planner – the employee responsible for liaising with ticket and gate agents inside the terminal – had devised a coding for indicating a gate 'swap' across 2 complexes. When flight 909 came in to gate 18 during complex 7 and was moved to gate 14 to depart as flight 1018 during complex 8, for example, the Passenger Planner indicated this with a '18/14' on the complex sheet, then updated the online information on the airline computer and radioed the gate agents to modify their own copies of the complex sheet.

The authors observed that, as artefacts embedded in routinized work practices, the sheets served five different purposes for the Ops Room staff:

1 As a representation of intended movements of people and baggage
2 As a template to be completed, with whatever information is available at that time, and distributed each day to ramp crew and gate agents
3 As a dynamic medium for making notes on events as they happen (for example, unanticipated gate changes)
4 As a physical record, at the end of a complex, of what actually happened
5 As a dynamic 'model' of movements on the ramp and at gates, conveying on-the-job information between Ops Room staff and ramp and gate crews.

Suchman and Trigg went on to consider the actual functions and the short-comings of the paper complex sheets (for example, that counter to the   *457* purpose for which they were initially designed, they may bear annotations that span two complexes) and to conceive of possible modifications to address these shortcomings. Clearly, replacing the paper sheet with a computer-based representation would have had the advantage of enabling the Ops Room staff to instantly propagate modifications and changes to the complex to the various crews' computers. But because the uses made of the paper copy, that effectively it was being continually 'redesigned' by its users, the design of a computer-based system had to be based on the understanding that development of artefacts with which people work goes hand in hand with development of work practices and that it is ways of working that give technologies shape and significance.

Designing for information sharing: 'ethnographic workflow analysis' (Hewlett-Packard Laboratories)

The Physician Workstation Project exemplifies distributed asynchronous collaborative work, the heterogeneous group composed of physicians, physician-assistants, nurses, laboratory technicians and administrative personnel, collectively having the goal of patient care but each having a specific role, with specific subgoals and professional agendas, within the larger framework. The issue under discussion is one of managing and integrating data from multiple points of view; this study shows how ethnography, for requirements capture, and artificial intelligence, for integrating and analysing multiple data sources, together led to the design of a system that allowed all users access to patients' up-to-date health maintenance record.

Fafchamps (1991) describes 'Ethnographic Workflow Analysis', a design methodology for 'modelling information-related work practices and for deriving specifications for the design of information systems to support these practices' (p. 709). She describes a 'minimal conceptual framework' for data collection and analysis that is sufficiently generic and engineering-independent that they 'do presuppose technological solutions, yet they are understandable to designers unfamiliar with social science research' (p. 711). The framework is shown schematically in Figure 29.4.

Fafchamps identifies five techniques for data collection (p. 711):

1 *Thinking aloud*: professionals describe what they are doing as they are doing it
2 *Guided tour*: individuals are asked to give a guided tour of their work space, both private (for example, their office) and shared
3 *Structured observations* to record meetings, face-to-face and phone interactions
4 *Written artefacts*: formal and informal (for example, reports, stick-on notes) are collected and the professionals' descriptions of these artefacts are recorded

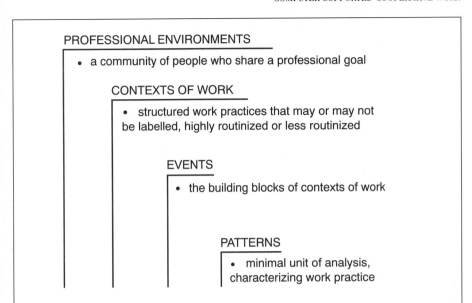

Figure 29.4   Conceptual framework (based on Fafschamps, 1991, Figure 1)

5 *Focused interviews*: to explore specific aspects of work that cannot be satisfactorily captured through other techniques.

Themes analysis and coding techniques – based on the tracing of recurrent topics of verbal interaction and of recurrent patterns of behaviour – were used to identify patterns in the data that helped map out standard routines or processes, atomic information-related behaviours, sequential procedures, interactions (including cross-departmental) between professionals, inter-actions with and attitudes towards objects (for example, a document, a database, and so on), baseline job descriptions, possible communicative breakdowns (for example, unsanctioned entries in patient charts), and so forth. On the basis of an analysis of the data, a set of functional specifications were developed and a Patient Status display and a Patient Details display were built.

The application programs underpinning the Patient Status display dynami-cally drew together data from multiple databases within the clinic so as to enable the user to view patient data through a single abstract data model: active problems, active medication, current labs, physicians involved with a particular patient, and so on. A 'knowledge server' was able to interpret the data from several sources (in this case, lab result and medication record) to, for example, be able to post an alert on a patient's cholesterol result as borderline high and to generate a reminder that the patient is on hydrochlor-othiazide which can exacerbate an elevated cholesterol level.

The Patient Details display, designed on the basis of an ethnographic analysis of attested medical queries and physician behaviour, presents the   *459* physician with more patient-specific information: the user is able to select particular items – changes in dosages, potential complications of therapy, and so forth – and use the 'Show details' button to bring current information to the screen.

CONCLUSION

CSCW is as much concerned about understanding group behaviour and actual work practices as about designing technologies to support group-work. The studies presented above have drawn attention to the specifically human and ergonomic issues implied in groupware design. Among the lessons learned are that it is necessary to understand work practice and role of artefacts, and to understand that effective use of technology depends on successful translation between its conception (the idealized 'design scenario') and the reality of those for whom it is designed.

REFERENCES

Akrich, M., 'How can technical objects be described?', Paper presented at the Second Workshop on Social and Historical Studies, Twente University, The Netherlands, 1987

Baecker, R.M., *Readings in Groupware and Computer-Supported Cooperative Work*, San Mateo, CA, Morgan Kaufmann Publishers, Inc., 1993

Bannon, L.J. and Schmidt, K., 1991, 'CSCW: Four Characters in Search of a Context', in J.M. Bowers and S.D. Benford (eds), *Studies in Computer Supported Cooperative Work: Theory, Practice, and Design* (from Proceedings of the First European Conference on Computer Supported Cooperative Work, 1989), North-Holland, Elsevier Science Publishers B.V., pp. 3–16, Reprinted in Baecker (1993), pp. 50–56

Dyson, E., 'A Framework for Groupware', in D. Coleman (ed.), Proceedings of Groupware '92, San Mateo, CA, Morgan Kaufmann Publishers, Inc., pp. 10–20, 1992

Ehn, P., Remarks in panel discussion on 'CSCW: What does it mean?', in *Proceedings of the Conference on Computer-Supported Cooperative Work (CSCW '88)*, New York, ACM, 1988

Elrod, S., Bruce, R., Gold, R., Goldberg, D., Halasz, F., Janssen, W., Lee, D., McCall, K., Pederson, E., Pier, K., Tang, J. and Welch, B., 1992, 'Liveboard: A Large Interactive Display Supporting Group Meetings, Presentations, and Remote Collaboration', in Proceedings of CHI 92, pp. 599–607

Fafchamps, D., 1991, 'Ethnographic Workflow Analysis: Specifications for Design', in H.J. Bullinger (ed.), *Human Aspects in Computing: Design and Use of Interactive Systems and Work with Terminals*, North-Holland, Elsevier, [from Proceedings of the 44th International Conference on Human Computer Interaction, Stuttgart, September 1–6, 1991, 2 vols., pp. 709–715

Gerson, E.M. and Star, S.L., 'Analysing Due Process in the Workplace', *ACM Transactions on Office Automation Systems*, 1986, **4**(3), 257–270

Greenberg, S., *Computer-Supported Cooperative Work and Groupware*, New York, Academic Press, 1991

Greif, I. (ed.), *Computer-Supported Cooperative Work: A Book of Readings*, San Mateo, CA, Morgan Kaufmann Publishers, Inc., 1988

Howard, R., 'Systems Design and Social Responsibility: The political implications of "Computer Supported Cooperative Work": A commentary', *Office: Technology and People*, 1987, **3**(2).

Hutchison, C.S. and Rosenberg, D., (1994), 'The Organisation of Organisations: Issues for Next Generation Office IT', *Journal of Information Technology*, **9**, 99–117 (special issue on 'Organisational Perspectives on Collaborative Working')

Jessup, L.M. and Valacich, J.S., *Group Support Systems: New Perspectives*, New York, Macmillan Publishing Company, 1993

Jordan, B. and Henderson, A., 1995, 'Interaction Analysis: Foundations and Practice', *The Journal of the Learning Sciences*, **4**(1), 39–103. Also on the WWW at: http://lrs.ed.uiuc.edu/students/c-merkel/document4.HTM

Sørgaard, P., 'A Cooperative Work Perspective on Use and Development of Computer Artefacts', 10th Information Systems Research Seminar, Vaskivesi, Finland, 1987

Strauss, A., 'Work and the Division of Labour', *The Sociological Quarterly*, 1985, **26**(1), 1–19

Suchman, L.A. and Trigg, R.H., 'Understanding Practice: Video as a Medium for Reflection and Design', in J. Greenbaum and M. Kyng (eds), *Design and Work: Cooperative Design of Computer Systems*, Hillsdale, N.J., Lawrence Erlbaum Associates, pp. 65–89, 1991

Tatar, D.G., Foster, G. and Bobrow, D.G., 1991, 'Design for Conversation: Lessons from Cognoter', *International Journal of Man-Machine Studies*, **34**(2), 185–209

RECOMMENDED READING

Pendergast, M., Aytes, K. and Lee, J.D., 'Supporting the Group Creation of Formal and Informal Graphics During Business Process Modeling', submitted to Interacting With Computers, 1997

Rosenberg, D. and Hutchison, C.S., (eds), *Design Issues in Computer-Supported Co-operative Work*. London: Springer-Verlag

30 Virtual teams

Chris Hutchison

On 4 May 1996 Jessica Lipnack posted a request to the Learning-Org mailing list (learning-org@world.std.com) with the question: 'Does anyone know of a mailing list devoted specifically to virtual teams? With Jeff Stamps, I am writing a book called *Virtual Teams*, due out from John Wiley & Sons in Spring 1997. Please send me e-mail if you know of such a thing.'[1] She followed up with a 'current working definition':

> A virtual team is a group of people with common purpose communicating across boundaries on interdependent tasks.

This elicited a response two days later.[2]

> Well, this definition does not seem to distinguish *virtual* teams from any other organization. *All* organizations are:
> - groups of people
> - with common purposes
> - communicating across boundaries
> - on interdependent tasks
>
> The term *virtual*, unless you're just using it as a buzz word to gain interest, would seem to require a steep decrease in 'face to face' communication and/ or some electronic infrastructure or 'world' within which the work is done and wherein the one contributor's work is immediately visible to others in this 'world' construct.

The respondent, John Galt, was clearly right to question the initial definition, just as he was right in worrying that 'virtual' might have been used here 'as

[1] The posting can be accessed at: http://world.std.com/~lo/96.05/0086.html
[2] John Galt's response can be accessed at: http://world.std.com/~lo/96.05/0118.html

a buzz word to gain interest'. The word 'virtual' has in the past few years been appearing before numerous more familiar terms: the expressions 'virtual reality', 'virtual classrooms', 'virtual organizations', 'virtual teams' and 'virtual offices' all would seem to be drawing attention to the observation that the individual may be interacting with people and artefacts that need no longer be physically co-located with the individual himself. There is, at the same time, a slightly unsettling trend towards applying the adjective to almost any vaguely plausible object or activity. In other words, the word has become 'fashionable' and hence susceptible to overuse and imprecise meaning. Thus in the same year in which Howard Rheingold published *The Virtual Community* (Rheingold, 1994), an account of social groupings created and maintained electronically in 'cyberspace', there was published a book entitled *Virtual Playhouse* (Price, 1994) in which 'virtual' seems to have the much looser meaning of 'digital' or 'multimedia'.

This chapter outlines some of the issues arising from, and perhaps peculiar to, the notion of 'virtual' teams. Under what circumstances have they emerged? How does the notion of the virtual team relate to that of the 'virtual organization'? What are the problems in managing, motivating, and coordinating virtual teams? How can the knowledge generated by successful virtual teams be captured, stored, and reused as a corporate asset? And how can virtual teams capitalize on the emergence of new information and communication technologies? To set the scene, I shall first question some of the common assumptions underpinning the classical notion of 'organization' and then, in the following section, distinguish three precise senses in which there would probably be broad agreement that the term 'virtual team' is being used appropriately.

REAL AND VIRTUAL ORGANIZATIONS

For most of us, the standard model of organizations is still one of local employees gathering for certain hours during each day in office or factory premises. Yet at the present time, with the increasing globalization of business and industry, and in light of the opportunities offered by modern information and communication technologies, the very notion of what constitutes an 'organization' is open for discussion. What, after all, is an 'organization'? One might take as a starting point a standard definition such as the following: 'Organizations are social arrangements for the controlled performance of collective goals' (Huczynski and Buchanan, 1991, p. 7). So far as it goes, the definition is uncontentious. Organizations are collections of people who interact with each other as a group for the purpose of performing tasks that are set and monitored by the organization itself; moreover, membership of the group is controlled within and by the organization. But this definition makes no claims for the existence of some entity over and above a 'social arrangement' of the personnel who constitute its membership. Nor is reference made to, for example, the physical and conceptual paraphernalia that support the activities of the personnel as a   *463* cohesive goal-oriented body: the premises and their geographic location, the office furniture and office technology, the allocation of tangible and intangible resources, the flows of information through and beyond the personnel, and so forth. Should these be considered part of the organization? If not, why not? Would the organization still exist as *just that organization* were significant change made to any part of the physical and conceptual infrastructure? The classical notion of resources as proprietorially tied to a clearly bounded, self-contained business entity is being questioned. In their 1995 book, *Agile Competitors and Virtual Organizations*, Goldmann, Nagel and Preiss define, in contrast, a virtual company as one where

> complementary resources existing in a number of cooperating companies are left in place, but are integrated to support a particular product effort for as long as it is viable to do so . . . Resources are selectively allocated to the virtual company if they are underutilized or if they can be profitably utilized there more than in the 'home' company.

And what about the information that flows in and out of the organization? Is that a defining part of the organization? If so, at what point does that information shift from being external to being internal to the organization (assuming that question makes any kind of sense)? Lipnack and Stamps (1997) observe that most types of business involve people working on a routine basis across classical organizational boundaries. 'Supply chain management, marketing, product development, sales, quality improvement, and change management are just a handful of activities that require virtual teams to work over walls and across borders', they note.

And if the organization has boundaries, where do they lie? If, for example, an important element of the organization's activities is the transport of parts into the factory and of products out of the factory, then should the trucks and the roads on which they travel be, for operational reasons, considered part of the organization? 'External' circumstances, such as the 1992 and 1997 lorry drivers' actions in France or security alerts on the London Underground at rush hour, can patently have an at least short-term effect on the behaviour and decision making of the organization. Is it then possible to draw a line demarcating something that clearly is the organization from everything else that clearly is not? The answer must be 'no'. In light of the webs of interconnectedness and ambiguity suggested earlier in this chapter, the classical concept of the organization is no longer sustainable and business can no longer afford to behave as though it were. Although the idea of 'virtual organizations' is not new, a new version of the concept is emerging as the classical model breaks down. New implementations of virtual organizations are exploiting the capabilities of information and communication technologies, of the World Wide Web (WWW), and of intelligent agent technologies, in breaking out of the essentially 19th-century mould of the monolithic, self-contained corporation, towards a more flexible, more fluid and more responsive entity.

Ursula Huws (1994), in a report commissioned by the European Commission's Employment Task Force as a follow-up to the *White Paper on Growth, Competitiveness, and Employment*, sees information and communication technologies transforming the nature and location of work to the extent that

> the concept of the office... as a fixed, geographically-defined space has become redundant. Instead of being defined in terms of the buildings it occupies, an enterprise will increasingly be defined as a network of relationships, held together on the one hand by telecommunications networks and, on the other, by a variety of different types of contractual arrangement. The term 'virtual enterprise' has been used to describe this development.
>
> (Huws, 1994, p. 6)

The core unit of the 'virtual enterprise' is the virtual team, and it is to the conceptualization of the virtual team that we must now turn.

WHAT IS 'VIRTUAL' ABOUT 'VIRTUAL TEAMS'?

What is it that makes a 'virtual team' virtual? There is probably no reason why in principle 'a group of people with common purpose communicating across boundaries on interdependent tasks' should require the support of electronic information and communication technologies. Empires were built and wars were won throughout history by networks of virtual teams with a common purpose, and with a communication infrastructure no more sophisticated than the light beacon and the horseback rider. But empires were built generally with little sense of urgency. In today's competitive global economy it is almost inconceivable that a team of geographically dispersed workers could be viable without the support of computers and communication networks. Indeed, it can be argued (as I shall, later in this chapter) that it is the technology that has, in some degree, not merely facilitated but in fact created the contemporary notion of the virtual team. In that light, three conceptions of the virtual team can be discerned.

In the first case, members of the same organization may work together towards a common top-level goal by communicating and coordinating their work electronically rather than face-to-face; in this case team members are likely to be geographically remote from one another. Teleworking, for example, enables the formation of virtual teams whose members may never need to meet in the flesh. Consider, by way of illustration, a law firm with offices in London, New York, Los Angeles and Sydney, which – for, say, a Hong Kong client – might continue working around the clock by electronically moving current information across time zones. A radical extreme of this form of organization is what Spigai (1994) calls 'Shamrock' corporations, an organizational paradigm of using full-time, temporary, contract, part-time, freelance and highly flexible employees in a diverse organizational structure. If supported by groupware for sustained distributed collaborative work, then this overlaps with CSCW (see Chapter 29 in this book).

465

In the second case, employees of different organizations may work together, in the same place or more often remotely but more or less in real time, towards a goal to which each organization contributes some part of the whole; the team is 'virtual' in the specific sense that it has been assembled, possibly on a short-term basis, for the purpose of accomplishing some task in which the collaborating organizations have a common interest. Most virtual teams of this kind are brought together for a specific project, then disbanded. Co-development of the CHRP (Common Hardware Reference Platform) by a coordinated virtual team involving employees from IBM, Motorola and Apple could be considered an example of this.

One of the more interesting features of this form of virtual teamwork is that it enables small companies, with no corporate overheads, to compete with larger organizations by exploiting developments in networking, telecommunications, and workgroup software to source expertise worldwide, and form and re-form on a project-by-project basis. A freelance software developer, for example, might assemble a time-limited virtual organization for a particular project by employing experts from their respective fields: specialist programmers, a graphic designer, a technical writer to produce professional product documentation, a quality systems expert to ensure standards compliance, professional trainers to produce training materials, a Web publisher to provide Internet presence, a marketing consultant to help sell the product, and so on. The team will typically be disbanded on delivery of the product.

The third sense of the term is similar to the second in that it may involve the collaboration of different organizations in a single large project, but with typically a clearer partitioning of the whole into more or less bounded subtasks involving particular kinds of expertise. 'Collaboration' may be largely sequential, diachronically distributed over a significant period of time, rather than concurrent; but features of virtual team work are still prominent. The construction industry is an example of this kind of collaboration, with each organization (surveyors, architects, builders, and so on) responsible for more or less self-contained tasks that nonetheless need to be coordinated along a time line.

We might add to the foregoing examples the observation that sometimes virtual teams may emerge spontaneously rather than being assembled by design. Toffler (1990, p. 184) highlights the emergence within organizations of 'colonies' of 'numberless, unofficial, suppressed, or underground groups that get things done in any large firm when the formal organisation stands in its way. Each brings together a unique, discrete body of knowledge – organised outside the bureaucracy's formal cubbyhole structure'. By way of a personal example (Hutchison and Rosenberg, 1993), a computer manufacturing organization we studied found there was a significant number of intermittent faults in a third-party vendor's tape-drives. Since attempts at repair by the field engineer on customer site did not solve the problem, the faulty units were brought into the manufacturing organization for testing in their diagnostic laboratory. Vendor participation in the diagnostic process was also required, as there was not sufficient information available from the field engineer as to the system behaviour at the time of breakdown. Most of the tests yielded negative results: no faults were found in the tape-drives tested. The established practice was to return the units to the Spares section, put them back into customer systems, where they would eventually break down again, come back to the diagnostic unit and the cycle would then repeat itself at great expense and inconvenience to the manufacturer, the original vendor and the customer. In this particular case, however, an informal collaboration between the diagnostic engineer and an engineer from the vendor organization led them to interpret failure as evidence of a possible inadequacy in the testing procedures themselves. It was therefore possible to expand this cooperation in order for both parties to sharpen up their testing and quality procedures. The end result of this collaboration by an emergent virtual team was that the vendor organization became an important repair centre within the manufacturing organization.

How, and why, do virtual teams arise? In each of the above cases it is not uncommon to discern the following pattern of features:

1   *Costs*: corporate overheads, as noted earlier, disadvantage larger organizations *vis-à-vis* lean virtual organizations. A push for lower costs and higher productivity has prompted many companies to abandon traditional one-employee-one-desk office space in favour of either 'hot desking' or, in many instances, 'no desking', with employees and contract workers being issued with laptop computers, mobile phones and pagers, and with individuals working from their cars, homes, or customers' offices. In doing so, the foundations for 'virtual' teamwork are laid.

2   *Globalization*: bringing new products to global markets may not only involve 'dispersing' the organization (for example, through outsourcing or through the export of its manufacturing base to countries with lower labour costs or significant internal markets) but also tapping the best brains for projects regardless of their geographic location (Geber, 1995). Such external expertise implies *de facto* virtual participation in the project team.

3   *Flexibility*: the members of a team may therefore be made up of intra-organizational employees, partners, suppliers, sub-contractors, and so forth, who will typically work together in a more flexible and responsive manner than the traditional corporation.

4   *Enabling technologies*: the team members have access to information and communication technologies to support distance working by geographically dispersed teams. Both information and knowledge (see later) can be stored and accessed on public networks such as the Internet/World Wide Web, which in turn generates valuable new and reusable intellectual assets for the organizations(s) involved.

5   *'Knowledge management'*: a consequence of virtual teams using electronic group collaboration tools to support team work is that the   *467*

content and processes of coordinated work can be more easily captured, organized, stored, and later reused by others for other projects.
As the work of most industries comes to depend increasingly on information and knowledge as corporate assets and strategic resources,
'knowledge management' and 'organizational memory' assume ever
greater importance.

6 *Organizational consequences*: virtual teams are changing the nature
of the organization, putting networks of expertise at the centre of
productive work. Traditional bureaucratic hierarchies are being challenged and replaced by flatter, more heterarchical structures.

Yet new forms of organization give rise to new problems. Prominent among
these is the management of virtual teams that, by virtue of their dispersed
nature, are potentially more difficult to monitor and coordinate than collo-
cated, face-to-face teams.

MANAGING VIRTUAL TEAMS

Ursula Huws (1994) notes that

the introduction of teleworking can improve the productivity and efficiency of
existing enterprises, thus enabling them to compete more effectively on world
markets and increase their market share

and in particular that

it can open up the possibility for new forms of collaboration, or synergistic
'tele-partnerships' between SMEs, enabling them to pool information in a highly
cost-efficient way and compete effectively with much larger organizations

(Huws, 1994, p. 3)

Yet these 'new forms of collaboration' can in turn give rise to new problems
of team management. Kelly and McGraw (1995) conducted an extensive
study of the general management issues associated with the virtual office,
virtual teams and telecommuting. Their proposed solutions to common
management challenges were subsequently validated by a survey sent to 52
managers, more than two-thirds from large companies with above 1 000
employees.

Over half of the respondents to the survey identified adequate planning
skills as the key factor in managing virtual teams: effective goal setting,
action planning, and distributing plans were seen as extremely important.
The corollary of this was that managers felt good leadership to be crucial
in motivating, facilitating and inspiring virtual teams as effectively as if they
were traditional office workers. A different view of the leadership issue is
offered by Lipnack and Stamps (1997), who observe that the leadership role
is often devolved to, and distributed across, the team itself: 'invariably the
diversity of technical and management expertise required in cross-boundary

work means that most members take a leadership role at some point in the process. In virtual teams, shared leadership is the norm'.

Correspondingly, in this looser organizational structure in which remote workers assume greater personal responsibility for their work regime and may work in more diverse ways than their office-bound peers, managers stressed the importance of a corporate culture and strategic vision that places a higher emphasis on the achievement of goals, rather than on the specific methods used to accomplish them. 'Managers must forsake traditional "eyeball management" and learn to evaluate work based on performance and productivity. Management's role will have to shift from a "steamroller" approach in which employees are told how to do work, to a "snowplow" approach in which the manager becomes the facilitator and enabler of work' (Kelly and McGraw, 1995, 'Controlling'). And elsewhere in the report: 'employees who are aware of the overall direction of the organisation are often in the best position to identify how they can best contribute to the success of the organisation' (Kelly and McGraw, 1995, 'Planning').

It was recognized, however, that not every individual has the personal qualities for virtual team membership. Since access to co-workers for assistance and moral support is significantly reduced for the teleworker, managers particularly looked for self-motivation, with a high level of job knowledge and skills, ranking these above such factors as flexibility, organization skills or aptitude as a team player. An emphasis on self-motivation and self-monitoring does not nevertheless obviate the need for the team manager to communicate frequently and continually with team members to monitor performance, provide feedback and evaluate work outcomes.

So far, we have considered only the relationship of the manager to the individual virtual office worker, yet clearly the effective unit of the virtual office, as of the traditional office, is the team rather than the individual. However, a dispersed team membership gives rise to unique problems in management and coordination. Research from MIT has shown that likelihood of face-to-face collaboration between individuals is directly related to distance, and that people are unlikely to collaborate very often or very closely if their primary work spaces are more than 15 metres apart (see Figure 30.1 below).

Kelly and McGraw note that while 'it is not easy getting a team to work well together in the traditional office environment, it becomes much more difficult as individuals are separated by time and space'. Team building and team coordination have therefore to be a high priority. The first obstacle to achieving a 'sense of team', they point out, is the problem of isolation. Of five possible 'team-building approaches used with virtual teams' that were presented to managers in the survey, over half the respondents favoured the option of involving virtual office workers in all group activities, either in person or via conference calls, as the primary approach to building an effective team. 'One example frequently used by managers', the authors *469*

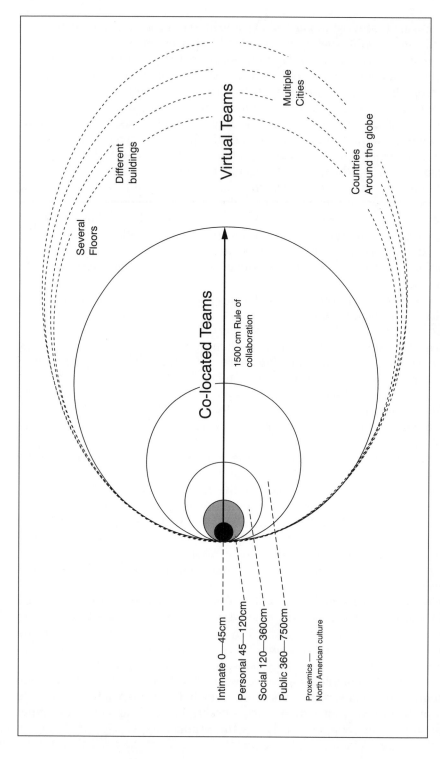

Figure 30.1 Distance vs. likelihood of collaboration (from Lipnack and Stamps, 1997)

note, 'is to set a weekly team meeting using a teleconferencing system, in which all off-site team members dial in and participate.' Another approach was 'to schedule important review sessions using videoconferencing facilities usually available within large organisations'. This was also felt to be of great importance in ensuring 'employee visibility', which was another key issue for managers when the virtual team members are dispersed geographically, remote both from each other and from an office-based manager.

Gould (1997) draws attention to the parallel team management issue of 'project visibility', in which team members 'knew what they were doing on an individual basis, but they weren't always sure where their pieces fit into the whole puzzle'. For Lipnack and Stamps (1997), therefore, maintaining a sense of common purpose is necessary: 'Virtual teams are more dependent upon having a clear purpose than face-to-face teams. Because they operate outside the bounds of traditional organizational life without bureaucratic rules and regulations to guide them, they must rely on their common purpose to stay in tune.'

Yet clearly more is involved in the building of effective virtual teams. 'The management challenge of maintaining a team that is highly effective becomes harder when some of the members are not physically present during the working day. A manager is responsible for the coordination of the workgroup in order to ensure that the team goals are met and each employee coordinates their activities with the other team members' (Kelly and McGraw, 1995, 'Coordination'). While for most managers the favoured approach was to establish clear objectives for all team members and to routinely monitor progress at both the individual and team level, many also felt that the optimal solution was to concentrate on managing the process rather than the people. Recognizing that working in relative isolation from other team members encourages the emergence of a 'personal work style' that might be curbed in face-to-face coordinated work, there was some enthusiasm for a standard Management by Objectives technique that 'primarily focuses on the results achieved and less on the techniques utilized to accomplish the goal' (Kelly and McGraw, 1995, 'Summary').

TEAM KNOWLEDGE MANAGEMENT AND 'ORGANIZATIONAL MEMORY'

'Dialogue knowledge'

A natural outcome of team work is experience and knowledge. In this and the following sub-section we turn from team work management to team knowledge management.

Gundry and Metes (1996) point out that much of the knowledge now accessible to businesses is a by-product of people actually working together. Workers frequently learn how to solve problems through the very act of tackling those problems. 'Knowledge about work', they therefore argue, 'can   *471* best be acquired (learned) through work itself'. They identify as of particular value what they call 'dialogue knowledge', which

> is entailed in what people communicate to each other in the course of their work. It comprises formal and informal communication and includes any accompanying materials. Modern collaboration tools, and especially computer conferencing, allow what people write and send to each other to be stored, and that stored material becomes a rich base from which people can acquire knowledge.
>
> (Gundry and Metes, 1996, 2.6)[3]

That accumulated work-embedded knowledge is quite different from published company information (for example, on intranets) and its management – knowledge management – is very different from more traditional information management. Having knowledge, for example, means that 'one can generate new appropriate statements about a subject, not just reproduce the statements that were received' (Gundry and Metes, 1996, 2.3.), and therefore a knowledge-based system that captures the ratiocinative and problem-solving strategies that were successfully used in previous projects can effectively be regarded as a virtual team member that surrogates for real human beings. In essence, it may be regarded as a solution to questions such as:

> People are leaving the company with a lifetime's experience. How can we capture and re-use that?

and

> How do we start learning from our experiences and help our people stop repeating others' mistakes?

Since the core concern of this section is *team* knowledge management, however, the more relevant questions to be addressed may be:

> We had a team that did a successful proposal for aerospace five years ago. Why did they make the decisions they did? How did they deal with the customer? What made the team tick?

and

> We're involved in an exciting project with four other companies. How can we all learn how these virtual teams click?[4]

Teams by their very nature generate through their working together a great

---

[3] References are to the numbered sections in Gundry and Metes's paper, published online at: http://www.knowab.co.uk/wbwteam.html

[4] The questions are all taken from Gundry (1996), Section 1: 'The Need for Knowledge Management'.

deal of potentially valuable knowledge; yet, both because it is distributed over a number of individuals and because it is embedded within their continuous interaction, that knowledge is more intractable to capture by the knowledge manager than that of the individual worker, particularly in view of the fact that little of it may normally be recorded. In traditional methodologies for team knowledge management, only explicit and formal task elements of a process are documented – the 'what' of a process – while failing to capture 'the dynamics, uncertainties, insights, interactions and deliberations' that made the process successful: 'Much of the hardest-won and highest value operational information about the process still resides in the heads of people who were personally involved, and remains uncaptured, unshared and unapplied by others' (Gundry and Metes, 1996, 3.1). In consequence, team members in later projects of a similar kind need either to spend time with someone who was involved in the previous project or to co-opt that person on to the new team.

Gundry and Metes describe a methodology for knowledge acquisition and organization, using the very same conferencing tools as are used to support the work to capture the process knowledge as it is dynamically created: a well-designed electronic workspace, used systematically as a forum for managing the work process, becomes itself a record of the team's activities. Recounting a case study, the authors note that while for the original team members 'the electronic workspace helped them progress their work and remain connected to their colleagues, without continually having to travel'; for a new team the electronic record became a valuable documentary resource in helping them to repeat a previously successful task.

The essence of the methodology lay in restructuring the knowledge implicit in the computer conference records through hyperlinking: topics or issues which might be distributed through a number of documents (dialogues) can be accessed via the hyperlinks that provide a top-level conceptual organization.

The use of computer-mediated communication for supporting team work and capturing dynamic knowledge is developed still further in a number of projects of which BICC was a major partner. The 'virtual meeting room', described below, provided a multimedia forum for electronic meetings as well as a mechanism for recording the content of those meetings. Subsequent projects such as CICC have explicitly addressed the issue of constructing an 'organizational memory' – the 'People and Information Finder' – that gives team members access to relevant expertise, both human and documentary, to support virtual team endeavours.

The virtual meeting room

The BICC Multimedia Communications Group (MMCG) has considerable experience, through EC-funded projects, of developing virtual environments for distributed team work. An early development of the DIMUN project (Leevers, 1993), under the European RACE programme, was the virtual *473*

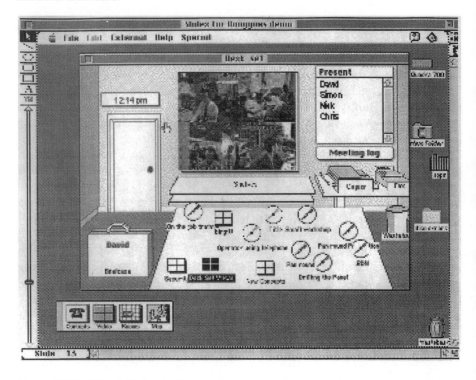

Figure 30.2   The virtual meeting room

meeting room as a component of a broader electronic framework for supporting multimedia communications with both people and data.

When customers, designers and factories are located in different countries, real-world meetings on a regular basis become difficult. The virtual meeting room provides intuitive access to voice, video and data communications to geographically dispersed team members: virtual teams constituted on the basis of a shared task enter a room by 'knocking on the door' (clicking on a door icon), at which point the standard image of that room appears on their computer screen (see Figure 30.2). (Any one person may have a 'global village' map of perhaps a dozen meeting rooms to which he has access for specific purposes or activities.) Individual team members are represented in the room through a multiway (4, 9 or 16 frame) video window; all members share the same view of the room. Guests can be invited into the room by selecting their 'multimedia business cards'.

Items in the room can be 'picked up' by clicking on them; documents can be displayed on a shared whiteboard; named mouse-pointers identify each participant as he 'redlines' shared documents. At the same time, the bounded room metaphor emphasizes the privacy and confidentiality aspects of the meeting as much as the feeling of telepresence.

The methodology described by Gundry and Metes for capturing process knowledge is enabled within the virtual meeting room in the form of a ten-minute recycling buffer in which an audio, visual and data record can be held – effectively, electronic minute-taking. And because the shared visual metaphor encourages all participants to 'build consistent and compatible mental models' they are likely to 'use the same language to describe their interactions' (Leevers, 1993), thus increasing the likelihood of consensus and coherence of descriptions.

The People and Information Finder

Follow-ons to the DIMUN project were other application pilots, VirtuOsi, BRICC (Broadband Integrated Communications for Construction) and CICC (Collaborative Integrated Communications for Construction) which give shared online access from diverse locations to all the design and administration information for specific projects; in the case of the BRICC and CICC pilots, a construction project. Presenting people and electronic documents in an imaginary 3D landscape, the 'People and Information Finder' (PIF) was designed to help team members in locating the right person they need to talk to about a problem or the information they need to solve it. The role of the PIF is shown schematically in Figure 30.3 below.

The PIF is accessible to team members remotely via the World Wide Web, such as in the example shown overleaf, where a navigable virtual reality 'Reference Factory Landscape' allows users to share a common mental

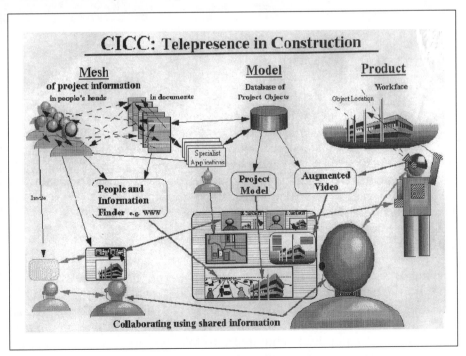

Figure 30.3 Accessing people and information

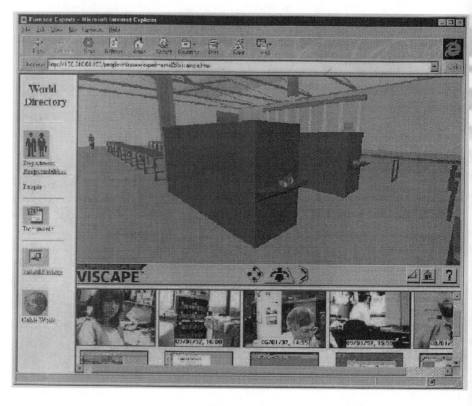

Figure 30.4 The People and Information Finder

model of the factory (top frame) and access via video link the relevant expert personnel (bottom frame).

In accompanying 'nearest neighbours' concept helps define more clearly the notion of informal teams and collaborations: each member will nominate his six most important contacts with respect to a current project. These 'neighbours' are then represented by regularly refreshed video snapshots on the member's WWW homepage (see Figure 30.5). Thus the team has permanent access both to immediate team members (the 'nearest neighbours' scheme) and to up-to-date relevant information (the PIF).

CONCLUSION AND SUMMARY

The concept of the 'organization' is changing from one of a static *place* of work to a dynamic, quasi-organic process model that places the accent on goals and outcomes. At the heart of the 'virtual enterprise' is the virtual team, a unit defined not in terms of location or organizational parentage, but in terms of its aptitude and ability to take on those goals and deliver those outcomes. The successful management and operation of the virtual team is in turn, by its nature, ensured by supporting information and com-

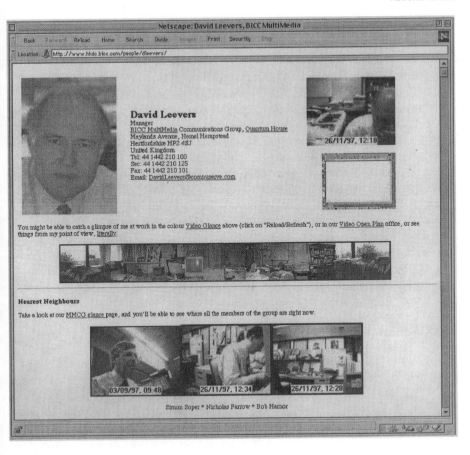

Figure 30.5 Virtual teams and nearest neighbours

munication technologies; and, in the use of these technologies, organizations are also able to build electronic records of team knowledge that can serve as immediately accessible resources for future projects.

REFERENCES

Geber, B., 'Virtual Teams', *Training*, April 1995, pp. 36–40

Goldman, S., Nagel, R. and Preiss, K., *Agile Competitors and Virtual Organizations*, New York, Van Nostrand Reinhold, 1995

Gould, D., 'Leading Virtual Teams', *Boeing Manager Magazine*, May 1997

Gundry, J. and Metes, G., 'Team Knowledge Management: A Computer-Mediated Approach', published at http://www.knowab.co.uk/wbwteam.html, 1996

Huczynski, A. and Buchanan, D., *Organizational Behaviour*, 2nd edn, London, Prentice Hall, 1991

Hutchison, C.S. and Rosenberg, D., 'Conflict and Co-operation in Knowledge-

Intensive Computer-Supported Co-operative Work', in S. Easterbrook (ed.), *CSCW: Cooperation or Conflict?* Springer-Verlag, 1993

Huws, U., *Teleworking: Report to the European Commission's Employment Task Force (DGV)*, European Commission publication #V/1697/94-EN, 1994

Kelly, B. and McGraw, B., 'Successful Management in the Virtual Office', Published electronically at: http://allison.clark.net/pub/kmcgraw/guide/telgdl.htm, 1995

Leevers, D., 'A Virtual Environment to support Multimedia Networking', talk given at a Unicom Seminar on Collaborative Work, July 1993

Lipnack, J. and Stamps, J., *Virtual Teams: Reaching Across Space, Time and Organizations With Technology*, Chichester, John Wiley & Sons, 1997

Price, J., *Virtual Playhouse*, Indianapolis, I Haydn Books, 1994

Rheingold, H., *The Virtual Community: Finding Connection in a Computerized World*, London, Secker & Warburg, 1994

Spigai, J., 'Project Management', paper presented at XTMAN IV, University of Maryland, College Park, MD, cited in Kelly & McGraw, 1995

Toffler, A., *Powershift: Knowledge, Wealth and Violence at the Edge of the 21st Century*, New York, Bantam Press, 1990

RECOMMENDED READING

Byrne, J.A., 'The Virtual Corporation: The Company of the Future Will Be the Ultimate in Adaptability', *International Business Week*, 8 February 1993, 36–41

Clemons, E.K., Row, M.C. and Miller, D.B., Rosenbluth International Alliance: Information Technology and The Global Virtual Corporation, in J.F. Nunamaker jr. and R.H. Sprague jr. (Hrsg.): *Proceedings of the 25th Hawaii International Conference on System Sciences*, Vol. IV, Los Alamitos, Cal., 1992, 678–686

Davidow, W.H. and Malone, M.S., *The Virtual Corporation: Structuring and Revitalizing the Corporation for the 21st Century*, New York, 1992

Miller, D.B., Clemons, E.K. and Row, M.C., 'Information Technology and the Global Virtual Corporation', in S.P. Bradley, J.A. Haisman and R.L. Nolan (eds), *Globalization, Technology and Competition: The Fusion of Computers and Telecommunications in the 1990s*, Boston, Harvard Business School Press, 1993

31 Information systems and cultural change

Roger Stewart

Replacing information systems in an organization is not just a matter of updating the technology and replacing old systems with new ones, but involves operational changes and the way people work. The culture of the organization will change and the management of these changes will to a large extent affect the success of the new system. Many of the current information systems analysis and design methodologies bring the users of the existing systems into the design process to ensure that their requirements are understood and incorporated into the new systems. An important result of this process is to give the users a sense of ownership in the new system and the new ways of working.

In a multi-team environment, where each team has its own information system that supports its tasks and provides specific databases of information, and there are information and functional links between the teams, replacing existing systems can be extremely complex. In addition to the technological problems, the understanding of each team's culture, its values and norms of behaviour and its way of working must be understood and catered for in the design and implementation of the new system.

This chapter describes an approach used by the author to multi-team involvement in analysing and designing an organization-wide information system in a community health trust.

BACKGROUND

Wandsworth Community Health Trust (WCHT) provides primary and community care services in close association with general practitioners, social services, voluntary organizations and other local health and social care organizations. The services provided are diverse and include: district nursing, health visiting, chiropody, physical and learning disabilities, family planning and community child health services. Each of these areas operates as a team and, with administration and the information systems department, forms the area for which a new information system was being designed and implemented. The teams having different responsibilities and aims had developed their own individual cultures and values while subscribing to the overall aim of the Trust to provide community care. The multi-team environment was therefore complex, with some clashes of priorities and values.

The current information systems were developed over a period of years and on different computer platforms. They had significant technical and operational problems: for example, the existing portfolio of applications were disparate and essentially single team-based, they exhibited little connectivity, produced minimal management information and did not support the future business objectives. It was therefore decided to replace these systems with a new second-generation, person-based, integrated system that would facilitate the planning and delivery of integrated multi-agency care within a community setting. To achieve this all teams had to be involved in the analysis and design process.

The objectives for the new system were established during a detailed audit of user teams and organizational requirements, and encompassed the needs of different stakeholders including management and general practitioners. An example of identified needs for a particular stakeholder can be seen in the requirements of the clinical care providers: care assessment/ planning and delivery; caselist management; increased sharing of up-to-date patient information across professions and disciplines; multi-disciplinary teamworking.

WCHT approach

An early decision was taken to source the information system as a package from a third party, the final selection being the Reuters Template Healthcare system. This product required some tailoring in terms of functionality and screen design and therefore a prototyping approach involving the user teams was adopted. Pilot sites from different areas of the trust examined the system for functionality and ease of use, and recommended changes. When satisfied with the system, a full roll-out of the system would be undertaken and parallel running ceased.

The project was controlled using an approach based on PRINCE, a CCTA project management methodology. Part of this was the risk identification and planning process for the business case and technology implications. However, it was realized that the project involved not only procedural changes for the users but also cultural changes such as multi-team working and the management of team expectations. In addition to normal risk analysis techniques and cost benefit analyses, soft risks and people problems would need to be dealt with as one of the project's objectives was to 'facilitate change' within the trust and to recognize the changing models of service delivery.

Soft systems analysis workshops, as described below, were seen as a complementary process to the work of the prototyping teams, developing organizational learning of the impact on cultural and social changes engendered by CISP (the new information system) and of the associated changes in working practices. The workshops were intended to identify key operational issues from the different teams and resulting actions required to manage the change. These issues would form part of the risks to be managed, critical success factors to be monitored and measured against, and used to develop a sense of joint ownership of the system and service processes between the healthcare teams, internal information systems staff and Reuters, the software suppliers.

SOFT RISK MANAGEMENT APPROACH

The Soft Systems Methodology (Checkland, 1981, 1990) was developed to analyse a complex 'messy' situation, characterized by human values, emotions and different perceptions of the situation by the involved parties, in order that some kind of organizational change process could be adopted to improve the situation. A main facet of the methodology is its close involvement of the analyst with the people in the situation.

Soft Systems Analysis is usually linked with an Information Systems project in the context of developing a single or suite of applications. In many cases Checkland's seven-stage model (1981) is used to develop a set of conceptual models and derived information flows that are used in conjunction with more structured approaches, such as in SSADM and Multiview (1990), to create Data Flow Diagrams (DFDs) and Function Event matrices. In the case of Wilson (1990) it was used to compare information transformation processes generated by the Soft Systems Methodology (SSM) with those present in an existing IT system in order to establish the changes.

The situation at WCHT was somewhat different in that an information Systems package provided by Reuters was being tailored using a prototyping approach to meet specific requirements. The benefits of the prototyping approach were perceived to come from involving the users in the iterative and interactive development of the system. This made sure, as certain as is possible, that the system would be appropriate for its operating environment, generating a sense of 'ownership' by the user teams, a primary requirement of the Health Trust. A key part of the implementation of the system was to identify and manage the cultural and operational changes that this new system will entail. It is for this reason that the 1990 SSM version with the stream of Cultural Enquiry was seen as providing a basis for workshops during the implementation phases.

WORKSHOP APPROACH

As the primary use of Soft Systems analysis in the CISP project was to identify the cultural issues involved in the implementation of the IS system, rather than the initial development of the system itself, an approach which combined IS prototyping and soft analysis was developed. This is shown in Figure 31.1.

The version of Checkland's Soft Systems Methodology upon which this approach was based contains two parallel streams of analysis, a Cultural

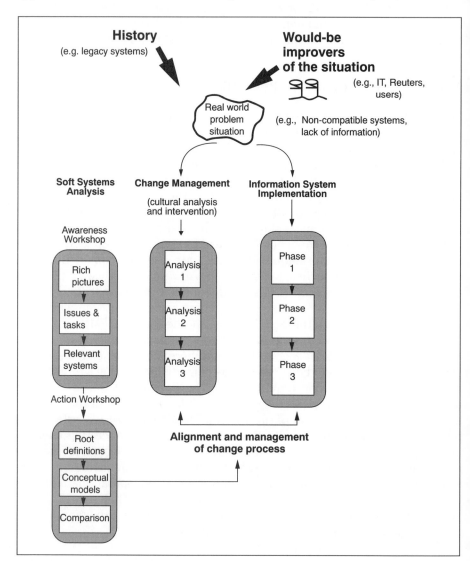

Figure 31.1   CISP and SSA approach

Stream of analysis and a Logic-Based Stream of analysis (based on the original Checkland seven-stage model).

1   *The Cultural Stream of analysis* – It was proposed to use the concepts underpinning the Cultural Stream of analysis to identify those areas in culture and operating procedures that needed changes as a result of prototyping the system in the pilot sites. It was also intended to suggest functional changes that could be made to the new system. It was primarily a process of alignment between the users and what they did and will do in the course of their jobs, and the Information System. It is similar in concept to the strategic alignment process in Business Process Reengineering.

   Analyses 1 to 3 in Figure 31.1 refer to the Checkland methodology where Analysis 1 considers the nature of the 'systems' intervention, examined in terms of 'Client(s), 'Problem Owner(s)' and 'Problem Solvers'. Analysis 2 is the Social System analysis where the 'Roles', 'Norms', 'Values' and their interactions in the problem area are examined. Analysis 3 is a 'political' analysis of the processes by which differing interests reach accommodation and how power is expressed in the problem area. The ways in which this type of cultural analysis is normally used vary according to the nature of the problem area under investigation and the type of organization. The approach envisaged at Wandsworth did not try to accomplish these analyses separately but used these ideas to establish what needed to be managed, from a human perspective, in implementing the IS system within the pilot areas.

2   *The Logic-Based Stream of analysis* – This was split into two as shown in Figure 31.1 and run as separate analysis workshops as described in the next sections of this chapter. The workshop results were fed into the cultural stream of analysis and into the risk analysis and prototyping phases of the project.

Awareness workshop

The purpose of this type of workshop was to consider the problems currently faced in each of the user teams and the impact of implementing the Information System in the pilot areas. This information could then be used to identify, for example, stakeholder expectations, problem drivers, cultural drivers and critical success factors. Each workshop had representatives of a selection of user teams, for example, family planning, administration, IT, undertaking the first three stages of the Logic-Based Stream of analysis. This is shown in Figure 31.2.

An explanation of each stage was given to the workshop attendees followed by a practical session in which the user teams applied the technique. For example, the first stage was to draw a rich picture on a flip chart. This   *483* was a diagrammatic representation of how they saw their situation, including what they did in the performance of their job, the problems they faced, conflicts with other jobs and people in the Trust and what they believed should happen after implementation of the new information system. Stage 2 followed, which involved listing problem themes that they saw in the rich picture, and again writing these on a flip chart. Stage 3 was to name on a flip chart relevant systems that could deal with these problem themes. Each team then placed their flip charts on the walls, explaining them to the group as a whole, and then discussed them as a group. One benefit of this approach was that team problems were made explicit and cross-team learning occurred. A subsidiary aim of the Awareness Workshop was to develop a sense of ownership of the new IS system by not just identifying the requirements of change in operation but also an attitude of how to get the best out of the system.

Summary findings of each stage were collected and formed the basis for subsequent analysis. This information gathered from the stages was used to feed into the cultural analysis and the management of change process. Figure 31.2 shows examples of the main links between the SSA stages and the elements that can comprise the change management process. Examples of the type of information gained and what it was used for now follow.

Rich pictures

The rich pictures gave an holistic picture of how the workshop attendees saw the situation in their pilot sites. The pictures included the people

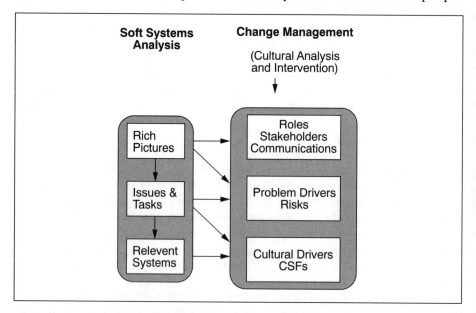

Figure 31.2 Awareness workshop model

working in the area, what they did, what information they needed to do their jobs and what the current IS system provided. It also provided the structural elements of people's jobs and their relationships to the environment, the tasks or processes they undertook and the problems that they encountered in the pilot running. This technique, unlike more traditional structured analysis techniques, enabled soft information, such as people's feelings, conflict between individuals and between teams, to be depicted. The information gained in this way was subsequently used in role analyses, comments on the key stakeholders and their expectations being met or otherwise, the communication requirements and problems that had been experienced.

Issues and tasks

Each team examined their rich picture, which is their perception of what happens in their area, and produced a list of tasks that they were trying to achieve and a list of issues or problems they experienced. These were then clustered into groups of related tasks and their associated issues. These clusters were subsequently examined for the information requirements and compared to the information provided by the IS system. Where the tasks and information requirements identified as a result of the soft systems analysis were satisfied by the existing and new prototyped IS system, there was confirmation that the system would be appropriate for the users' needs. Where an important task was missing it was identified as a required IS system change and fed into the project management process.

The issues will reflect the operational and cultural needs. Again where the comparison to the prototyping phase showed there were no discrepancies, then there were no changes needed to the cultural and operational procedures. Where issues were not dealt with it indicated that cultural or operational changes were required. The clusters of issues forming the Problem Drivers (operational changes) and Cultural Drivers (attitude changes or cultural constraints such as user Norms and Values) needed to be further investigated, and were placed as risk areas into the project management process.

Relevant systems

The Problem Drivers and Cultural Drivers indicated from the previous analysis were classified in two ways. Those that required simple changes were compared to the risks and associated contingency plans in the existing project plan. Where these were not covered they were given a name and plans constructed for the implementation of the changes. Critical Success Factors were identified to monitor the progress of the changes. Although no important omissions were identified and only minor changes to the project plan were noted, important problems identified would have been the subject of the second type of workshop, the Action Workshop.

Action workshop

The format of this type of workshop is similar to the Awareness Workshop in that an explanation of each stage is given to the workshop attendees, followed by a practical session in which each attendee uses the technique. Verbal explanations are given to the group as a whole and discussed. The summary findings of the comparison stage are collected and form the basis for an action plan. This process is shown in Figure 31.3.

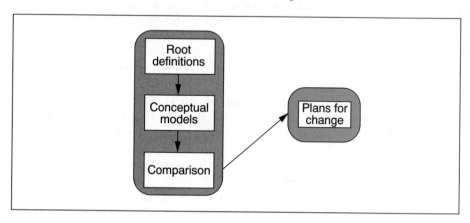

Figure 31.3 Action planning cycle

It was hoped that most cultural and operational changes would be handled by the Awareness Workshops and subsequent actions, and this turned out to be the case. However, there may have been some changes that were more extensive. These would have been 'named' and would have prompted Action Workshops to develop an action plan. The process is as follows. For the named area of change a root definition, or statement of what the system has to do, is constructed, and conceptual models of the activities involved developed. A comparison to what happens at present reveals those changes required to put this culture or operational change into practice. The agreement of these changes and subsequent implementation can be the subject of an intervention meeting with involved parties.

As in the Awareness Workshop these changes can be input to the risk analysis process and critical success factors identified.

WCHT RESULTS TO DATE

Four Awareness Workshops were run for the areas of Information Management and Technology, Family Planning, District Nursing and Child Health. The workshops of the three care areas were mixed groups involving teams from administration, nursing, clinical and IT personnel, with some having direct experience of prototyping the CISP system. Although the subject of each workshop was their particular care area, by including teams from other areas a sharing of perceptions on the situation and discussion on common problems enabled organizational learning to be gained. The techniques involved in the workshops worked extremely well. The workshops did, however, produce some unexpected results.

The purpose of the workshops was explained to the participants in the following manner: 'As a result of the prototyping and in your working experience, how well does the CISP system meet your needs, and what needs to be managed in the change process.' The response on the prototyping results was that generally it looked all right with some revisions. The overwhelming amount of information gathered from the workshops related to the problems they felt were important to resolve in the existing systems and the Trust as a whole. However, it also highlighted the high expectations of the new system held by individuals, and these would need to be carefully managed. Examples of the issues raised and their categorization are as follows.

Problem drivers

- Duplication of information
- Scattered and non-linked information
- Information held in multiple places
- Previously failed systems.
- Lack of information
- Failure of existing hardware
- Systems communication links
- Hardware and project delivery.

Cultural drivers

Access to staff, privacy and security of information

- People relationships
- Feelings of isolation
- Feedback on statistics and aggregated information to data providers
- Information seen as for management not for workers
- Broken management promises.

Critical success factors

Project delivery in terms of functionality and delivery timings

- The very high expectations of the CISP system addressing user needs
- Project benefits being realized
- Continuous involvement with the users.

Organizational issues

Space shortages

- No strategic direction information passed down the organization
- Telephone call handling
- Lack of funds.

As a result of identifying these issues, the problem drivers and cultural drivers were incorporated into the preventative action plans and contingency plans within the risk management process. The critical success factors were incorporated into the stage review processes and the organizational issues were fed back to the trust management.

It should be mentioned, however, that although the soft systems approach adopted concentrated on identifying the problems perceived by the teams in their own areas and within the Trust as a whole, there are many areas that were being handled very well and that the care provision to the public was very good. An impression that everything in the garden was sickly would be far from the truth, the aim being to make sure that, as far as possible, everything was done to ensure that the new information system supported the primary task of care provision to the community.

CONCLUSIONS

Cultural change management

Replacing and updating information systems in an organization in which multiple teams operate involves not just a technological change but also a potential change to the culture of the organization. Where teams operate as individual units providing different services, but are to an extent dependent upon other teams, then an analysis of the changes engendered by new ways of working is of paramount importance. This involves the understanding of each team's culture in terms of the ways in which they operate and the values and norms that prevail. Traditional techniques for the analysis and design of information systems (which concentrate on the functional aspects) need to be supplemented with a people-based approach that can encompass team and individual expectations. Without this there is a risk that the system, while being appropriate at an organizational and technical level, will not operate in the most effective manner, and team expectations of ways of working may not be met and their cultural values violated. There is also a danger that there will be a lack of ownership of the new information system.

An approach such as the one described previously, which combines in an interactive manner an analysis of the human aspects in the situation with the technological and functional analyses, will reduce the 'soft risks' in

488

a multi-team environment, facilitate organizational learning and develop a sense of shared ownership in the teams.

WCHT

The use of the soft risk management approach developed by the author and used in WCHT provided the following conclusions.

- Using an interactive workshop mode of analysis complemented the prototyping phases of the implementation of the CISP project in the identification and alignment of the cultural and social changes required to make best use of the information system.
- The workshops were highly interactive, well-received and produced a wealth of information. Comments from the participants indicated that they welcomed the chance to participate in the evaluation of the CISP system and the opportunity to express their thoughts on what was important in the cultural and operational changes to the organization.
- A sense of ownership of the new system was engendered in the user teams and developers.
- The information gained from the soft systems workshops addressed the human issues in a way that more traditional risk identification and assessment techniques do not normally manage.
- It achieved the effect of organizational learning by the sharing of perceptions about the problems and expectations of the user teams and developers, contributing to a shared ownership of the new system.

In summary it was seen to be a successful and worthwhile activity which will improve the cultural and operational changes in Wandsworth Community Health Trust.

REFERENCES AND RECOMMENDED READING

Avison D.E. and Wood-Harper, A.T., *Multiview: An Exploration in Information Systems Development*, Oxford, Blackwell, 1990
Checkland, P.B., *Systems Thinking, Systems Practice*, Chichester, Wiley, 1981
Checkland, P.B., Scholes, J., *Soft Systems Methodology in Action*, Chichester, Wiley, 1990
Wilson, B., *Systems: Concepts Methodologies and Applications*, Chichester, Wiley, 1990

32 IT teams in the London Borough of Richmond

Pat Keane

The author is employed by the London Borough of Richmond in the capacity of Head of IT. Over the last three years there have been many changes in the way the Borough operates and this has been reflected in the way the IT Division has been required to change its methods of working. Some of these changes have been as a result of legislation, others as a response to the demands of the market place and others as result of internal organizational change.

This chapter describes some of the changes, good and not so good, that have occurred and the way in which it is hoped teams will develop. Teamworking has always been a central part of the way IT has provided its services to its customers and various team structures have been tried. These have resulted in cultural changes and different ways of operating, and both have provided lessons about how, in addition to managing the technical change, the people aspects must also be carefully managed.

ORGANIZATIONAL BACKGROUND

The role of IT in local government is to support the business of providing services, often to the most needy of society, and in order to understand the context in which IT teams have been working a brief overview is given below.

The London Borough of Richmond is a local authority situated in the south-west Greater London area, and is unique in that it is the only London borough that spans both sides of the Thames. This brings its own problems in providing services. For example, service provision such as refuse collection has to be duplicated so that customers are adequately served. This makes the operational context somewhat complex. Politically the local council is overwhelmingly Liberal Democrat as are both members of parliament; the MEP is, however, Labour. Democratic control over the activities of the Council is exercised through 52 members elected every four years. The full Council deals with many of the important matters, but most detailed policy decisions are delegated to eight committees. A number of specialist issues are considered by sub-committees. All meetings are open to the public, although certain confidential items may be discussed in closed session.

Day to day management of the Council's activities is performed by its full-time officers. These are organized into 18 service delivery units headed by Chief Officers. The Council's most senior officer is the Chief Executive and Director of Finance. Strategic direction is set by the Executive Board that consists of the Chief Executive and three strategic directors. These have responsibility for elements of the council's strategy and a group of service units. This is a new structure that is still in a period of gestation. The electorate is highly literate and members are great joiners, resulting in large numbers of pressure groups and therefore much greater public consultation and interaction than in many boroughs.

Services for which Richmond, like any other London borough, is responsible include:

- Education from infant to secondary level as well as some further and adult education
- Social service provision from childcare to meals on wheels and care of the elderly or less able
- Recreational amenities such as swimming baths, playing fields and parks
- Library and arts-related services
- Refuse collection, street cleaning, street lighting and highway maintenance
- Public housing provision and the management and maintenance of some 5 000 dwellings
- Local environmental health and trading standards issues.

Those services are funded in part by the raising and collection of council tax, which accounts for some 40 per cent of the borough's income. The remainder comes as a grant from central government. The total budget for 1998 exceeded £135 million. By far the largest area of spending for the council is education which receives some 40 per cent of the budget. Social services is the next largest, accounting for some 30 per cent of the borough's revenue spending.

IT DIVISION

The IT Division supplies support services to the departments where, to a great extent, system ownership lies. The IT Division is responsible for the telephone and data networks, operating a support desk, training and traditional mainframe-based operations. A small team/group of staff, referred to as Business Development Analysts, act as internal account managers. This is a situation which has arisen due to the need to keep the 'techies', for want of a better term, away from the customers.

HOW THINGS WERE

One of the approaches used by the division to understand the business environment is Soft Systems Analysis. It is an approach that enables an analyst to tackle complex messy situations in which people have differing appreciations of the situation and of the problems to be tackled. One of its strengths is in incorporating the people issues by involving them in the design process of organizational change, thus building ownership of the structural, process and cultural changes. One technique used in this approach is a diagrammatic picture of the situation called a 'Rich Picture'. The technique is very useful in depicting soft and human perspectives, and is used here to show how we in IT were perceived, how we are perceived, and how we would like to be perceived.

In 1995, as the division prepared itself for what was termed Compulsory Competitive Tendering (CCT), it was realized that we needed to do some serious thinking if we were to compete with the private sector and retain the work with the in-house unit. Figure 32.1 shows the perception of the organization regarding the role and way of operating of the IT division at that time. As part of the process of serious thinking a firm of consultants were employed who carried out a quite comprehensive survey of 400 customers and organized some structured workshops with our own staff and again with customers. This added to our understanding of how we in IT were viewed.

At the time of this work, as indicated in Figure 32.1, the division was aptly named. Each service was in its own small team with a manager having responsibility for three or four staff. These managers had been employed for their technical skills rather than people skills, which meant that management practices, such as appraisals or disciplinary processes, were not dealt with in the same way, if at all, and members of these teams were very protective of their specialism while being envious of the other teams. The customers dealt with Communications, Operations, Help Desk, Training or the Development team, without necessarily realizing that they were part of the same division.

As a result, unless people communicated within the IT division, work was duplicated or, worse, forgotten, as it was thought that someone else was dealing with it! This didn't help customer relations, the reputation of the division or the people working in the division. Customers went to individual teams for services causing delay and duplication or, more often than not, encroached on each other's specialism, resulting in further resentment. Far from spurring teams on to outdo each other, the competitiveness was destructive rather than constructive.

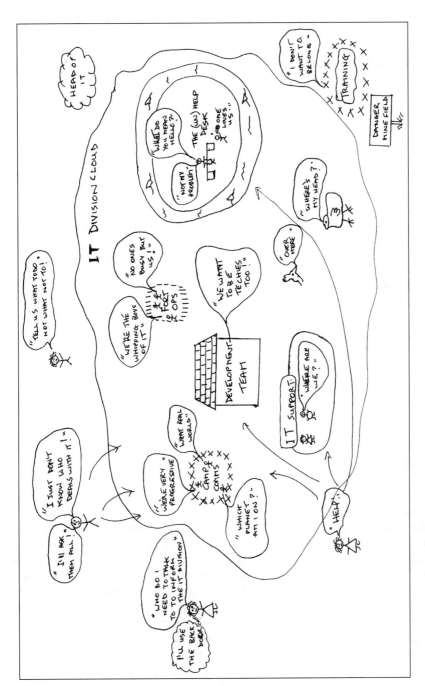

Figure 32.1 The old IT division

493

However, it should be pointed out that this way of operating was typical of the culture of the organization as a whole. Local government has in the last 15 years, been subject to quite stringent financial cuts. This has meant that the annual budget-setting round results in competition between the service heads, and has instilled a competitiveness between services that is reflected at all levels in the organization.

The barriers between the teams in the IT division were high and wide. The consultants' recommendations were that a matrix management style be adopted, that line management responsibility be taken away from the 'super techies', that a client /contractor split be introduced between those supporting the services and the business analysts, and that a quality and standards post be introduced.

This was a big upheaval for the division, with all jobs having to be re-evaluated and re-graded. In the event, after much negotiation, status was sacrificed but not income. This was probably the manifestation of another corporate cultural trait: avoid conflict at all costs. The result was that the consultants' recommendations were adapted to fit the corporate culture. The new structure was discussed at length, and those most affected involved in the decision making process – or so we thought.

HOW THINGS ARE

The outcome of the changes is depicted in Figure 32.2. From this you will see that we have been successful in creating a single pool of expertise from which support services are provided. This has been quite successful, as has the introduction of the account management role.

Customers are becoming used to being more disciplined in how they approach the division for services, and the division is better at responding to requests for support. Customers like the account manager role, which gives them someone to deal with who they feel has an understanding of their part of the organization. Some of the changes have been positive. The division has improved its reputation with some customers. Processes have been introduced to manage the work flow, the software supporting the help desk function has been upgraded twice, a business plan for the division has been developed, the use of technology within what is now the IT division has become proactive rather than reactive. This last point is important as the IT division is now beginning to evaluate and lead on new technology introduction rather than playing catch-up with the customers. Unfortunately not all the changes have been positive. Trying to encourage the 'super techies' to act as team members, or be part of the pool, has proved very difficult, and resentment is now aimed at these people. The issues are that those who have embraced the challenge of working in a team and exchanging skills feel that they are being put upon, and that the experts are distancing themselves from the operational delivery of the service.

The reality is that the 'super techies' have tried to retain the barriers between the services for which they are responsible while the team

494

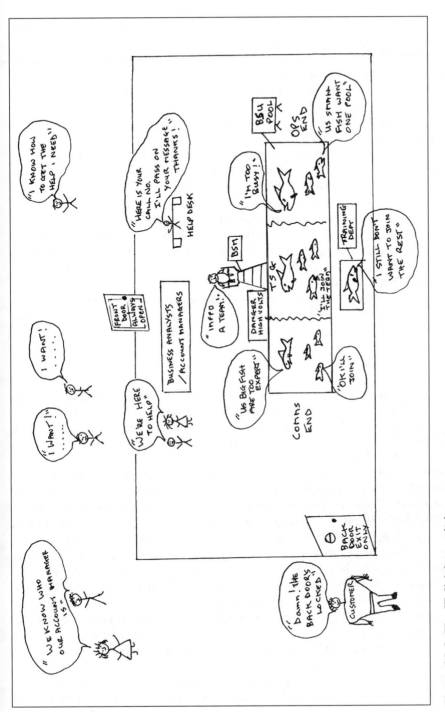

Figure 32.2 The IT division as it is now

members are trying to remove them. The team members feel unsupported, therefore, by these 'super techies' and have set up their own support mechanisms The result is that they are now questioning the need for these senior posts in the organization.

As you would expect of 'techies' a number of technology-based tools have been introduced to bring together people who are geographically separated. This again has had its ups and downs. Two tools are used, e-mail and a networked help desk package.

The e-mail has been very successful: communications are faster, information can be broadcast, consultation becomes easier and tasks can be turned around much more quickly. The negative side is seen in what I have recently seen referred to as 'flame-mail' – mail which inflames a situation. In one reported case an employee has successfully argued and proved constructive dismissal because of the way a manager treated him via e-mail. It does seem that people will be far more critical and less guarded when using this medium. In fairness the instances of our own flame-mail have been few, but they have been there.

The networked help desk has again been a real boon. The down side has been that some people feel that they can allocate work to others without consultation. This has proved more difficult to resolve.

Observations

What has been interesting is that it is those who were employed for very specific skills who seem to find it hardest to adapt to a new structure or take the initiative as far as the softer people skills are concerned. Those that seem better able to adapt are the more junior members of staff, the 'Doers' as they refer to themselves. The issue is probably that the heads of sections were the ones most affected by the reorganization. I suspect that they did not embrace the new structure because it was not adequately explained or sold to them, leaving them in a state of limbo. The 'super techies' have begun to work as a team in their own right and to develop a role and identity for themselves. This has proved easier than was expected. It is too early to say that the situation has improved dramatically. What has become apparent is that the 'Doers' did not understand the different role required of those responsible for the service. It is probably right that a 'Doer' has 12 help desk calls outstanding and a head of service only one or two. This needs to be communicated with more clarity. What is expected of the senior members of the support unit needs to be explained to the rest of the team. Figure 32.3 identifies where roles and responsibilities lie and how they relate to each other.

The 'Doers' are dealing on a day-to-day basis with tasks that are in the bottom left-hand quadrant of the diagram, the cash cow area in Boston Matrix terms, keeping work going at an operational level. This is vitally important in its place. The Principle Support Analysts (PSAs), those that have been referred to as 'super techies', are required to move the service

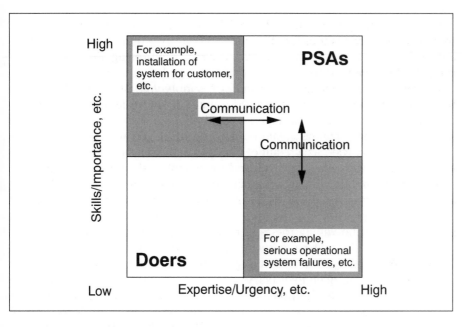

Figure 32.3   Roles and responsibilities

on to ensure the support infrastructure for such things as the telephones, Help Desk, operational printing, and so on, making sure these move forward and have investment. The shaded area of the diagram represents the overlap between the 'Doers' and the PSAs. So that things work well, communication when working in these areas between the Doers and the PSAs must be of the highest quality.

Working in a technical environment has proved very interesting. The term 'anorak' comes to mind. Quite often the 'techies', and in particular the 'super techies', are more interested in the technology than its application or the customers' needs. This is more apparent in such areas as IT, but seems to hold in other disciplines as well. This manifests itself in the attitude of wanting to move on to the next technology or project, having delivered 80 per cent of what the customer requires or applying one's own sense of priority or urgency to the situation, not the client's.

What also seems to hold true in our environment is that the more technically expert the person is, the narrower the vision and the greater the inability to work in a team environment. The technical skill seems to be honed at the expense of communication skills. This may be because the greatest emphasis in development is spent on keeping technical skills up to date at the expense of, or to the exclusion of, the soft people skills. It would seem that as technical people we deal with the 'hard' issues but not the soft people issues. It may be that we look for a technical solution, such as e-mail, to improve communications while ignoring the more obvious one of getting people talking.

Much of the difficulty the IT team have had with the change was, in hindsight, in moving away from a management style that was very prescriptive and directive to one that is enabling and empowering. People still stop at the problem without realizing they also own the solution. The challenge is to persevere with the coaching and not simply give in and do it yourself. The hardest thing to do is to stand by and see a job done not so well by those that should be doing it and learning, and not to take over. What is intriguing is that a similar dynamic is to be observed within local government on the meta level as a result of the change in government. The previous administration was very directive and prescriptive about the outcome and how to get there. The new government knows what the goals are – how we attain them is up to us. Best practice will be rewarded and a lack of enthusiasm dealt with by outsourcing. It will be interesting to see if central government will be willing to stand by and give local government the time to relearn the skills that have been stifled in the past.

Much has been said about changing the habits of members of the IT Division. It has also been necessary to train or educate the client. There are those who do not like the new procedures for allocating work and feel we have depersonalized the service. This on the whole is to the good. There were many instances of what we have come to call 'back-dooring', not using the correct channels but the personal contact. It still happens to a small extent but is now much more obvious and can be dealt with.

THE FUTURE

An illustration of the IT Division's future can be seen in Figure 32.4.

Work has already begun on building the team further and attempting to bring the 'super techies' into the team structure. In the public sector one cannot simply dismiss someone because they don't fit in. This has its good points. It does ensure that employees are fairly treated and that as managers we are obliged to look at our own skills of encouragement and communication before criticizing the team members. This probably sounds strange, given all that has gone before. The good side of this is that we have a good base on which to build. The new government has said that it will be less restrictive, and in fact is positively encouraging innovation in service delivery. This is an opportunity for the big fish: having been given the opportunity to develop their soft skills the hope is that they become part of the pool and spread their expertise to others.

As stated, work has begun on the team. A small group has been set up to look at opportunities for cross-training within the division so that skills are spread. The intention is not to create a clone, but that the key aspects of the post are learnt by others so providing back-up for each other. We are also beginning to introduce quality circles and action learning sets as methods of developing the soft skills. For the senior managers in the division the use of an external mentor/facilitator has proved very useful. It is also apparent that our new strategic directors have very definite views about corporate working which will change the culture of the organization. This is very positive for the IT division, which in the past has been working in isolation and without support from other parts of the organization.

Figure 32.4 shows how I would like the future to develop, with customers who use the proper channels and approach us for help in the preferred way, and team members all swimming in the same direction, feeling part of the team and wanting to be involved. There is a quotation that comes to mind: 'The snowflake is one of nature's most fragile structures, but look what they can achieve when they stick together' (attributed to Nancy Reagan).

The IT Division at Richmond has achieved much in the last two years. The lessons learnt are simple:

1 If you lower someone's status make sure they know why, that those around them know why and that they are at least resigned to the change and don't keep looking forward to the past.

2 Make sure that roles and responsibilities within the team are known and clearly understood by all members of the team. NASA have an interesting measure of ensuring understanding. If asked what he or she is doing, a cleaner at Kennedy Space Centre is expected to answer: 'Helping to keep the space shuttle in space,' not 'I'm sweeping the floor.'

3 In areas that are expected to deliver highly technical support services to an organization do not invest solely in technical development of people to the exclusion of the soft issues, which are just as important. A technical expert who cannot communicate with customers or colleagues is a very expensive overhead.

To some these lessons may seem obvious or common sense. Often such observations are common sense, but unfortunately they are not always common practice.

Figure 32.4 How IT needs to be

Postscript: Pulling it all together

Roger Stewart

This book is intentionally eclectic in bringing together different perspectives on teams and teamworking. They range from examining the effect of the environment in which teams operate through to specific techniques that can be used to understand and manage teamworking to make it more effective. This spread of perspectives is needed for the reason that in many cases teams are embedded in a complex situation involving different and sometimes novel organizational structures, alterations in work practices, the adoption of new technologies and the changing attitudes to work. It is therefore not surprising that often when faced with a team situation, even when a clear remit including quantitative and qualitative goals is available, it is difficult to know where to start and how to establish priorities for action.

The aim of this chapter is to provide an approach that can be used for deciding what needs to be done and managing the change process. The approach draws on examples from previous chapters to indicate how the techniques in question can be used as part of an integrated framework.

KEY STAGES

The approach, summarized in Figure PS.1, consists of five stages. It starts with an appreciation of the current situation to identify the areas that need attention, followed by a closer examination of the team in order to establish its current status. As a result of the information from the previous two stages the priorities for action can be decided and a plan constructed. The last stage is concerned with the implementation of the planned actions and managing the resulting changes. It is basically a refining process, starting with a broad understanding of the situation, concentrating and prioritizing on the actions needed to be taken and implementing them. Although shown

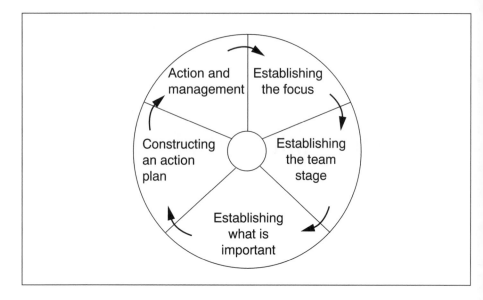

Figure PS.1 Team analysis and action approach

as a sequence of stages, iteration between them is often necessary as a greater understanding of what needs to be done is developed.

In the description of each stage examples of relevant techniques and models for gaining information relating to the situation are outlined; however, they are not exclusive lists. Team leaders will add to these from their past experience, and practice in using this approach will suggest other techniques and indeed may develop their own.

Stage 1: Establishing the focus

One of the dangers in establishing new teams, taking over the management of a team or in dealing with existing team problems is taking action without ascertaining what the situation is. The first stage of the approach is therefore aimed at providing a wide understanding of the situation in order to clarify what the team leader should be looking at and why it is important. The danger of precipitate action or just meddling is that the team leader may undertake courses of action without knowing the full picture. Dealing with some problems in isolation without fully understanding the interaction between the problems can make the situation worse or leave important areas untackled.

The first step for the team leader is to clarify his/her own role – that is, what am I supposed to be doing. This may be made clear in the team leader's remit, but in adopting an initial overall assessment of the factors affecting the team and the relationship of the team to its environment it is possible to start to find out in general terms what is required.

One technique is to use the model, as shown in Figure PS.2, to position the initial perception of the areas that need attention and start to ascertain where more information is required most urgently. Even during this broad stage of awareness of the problems other techniques or models may become apparent that will enable action plans to be defined. The model is layered, with the individual situated within a team, the team being part of an organization that operates within a market place. All these layers reflect different viewpoints or issues that can be examined.

The individual layers are used to guide a series of questions, examples of which are as follows.

Market layer

- What are the market drivers that are influencing the organization to structure in this way?
- What are the structural forms adopted by the organization?
- Do they work and what rate of change in the market is influencing the organization?
- What are the problems caused to the organization by the market?

The answers to these questions will indicate what effect the market is having on the organization and whether the organization is adopting structures and internal processes that are appropriate. In the chapter on flexible organizations by Valerie Garrow and Linda Holbeche there are examples of the actions organizations are taking and the considerations involved in their decisions. This is further developed by the chapter on the business environment by George Blair and Sandy Meadows, which discusses why teams are needed and the different types of teams that may be used. The information gained from this analysis can indicate problems caused by the reaction of the organization to its environment.

Organizational layer

- What emphasis is being placed on teamworking?
- What is the degree of empowerment?
- What are the relationships between the teams in the organization? For example, competitive, cooperative, isolated.
- What problems are occurring due to the structures in the organization?

This set of questions directs attention to the organization and the operating of teams within it. Problems, such as there is no common purpose within the organization, the culture of the organization does not facilitate good team working or that corporate values are different to teamworking, may be identified. The chapter on corporate alignment and cultural realignment by Nigel MacLennan deals with these issues. The prevailing culture and hierarchical structures in place within an organization may be in conflict with the structures and decision making processes adopted by newly formed *503*

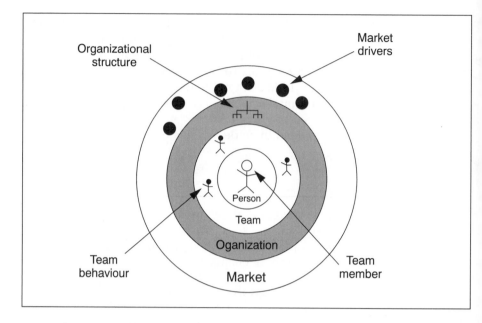

Figure PS.2 Team situational model

teams and transient teams. Examples of this are given in Tony Molony's case study (Chapter 8). As in the first set of questions a range of problems may be identified.

Team layer

- Is it a new team or an established team?
- Are the team's goals and objectives clear?
- Is the team achieving its objectives?
- Is the team operating as a team?
- If not, what are the problems and why are they being caused?

These questions relate to the specific team performance, first in establishing the status of the team and second in noting whether there are any immediately apparent problems. More detailed analysis of the team is carried out in Stage 2; however areas such as a high incidence of team member turnover – evidence that there is a high degree of intra-team conflict – failure to achieve initial goals and targets or consistent failure over a period of time to achieve these, all indicate problems with the team and its working. A team needs analysis, as discussed in the chapter by Leslie Rae, may be one of the actions considered at the planning stage of this approach. Communication, management style or team meeting problems may be seen and noted for subsequent action.

Person layer

- Are there individuals who are having problems working within the team?
- Is the right management style being used?
- Is the composition of the team in terms of skill mix or team roles causing problems?
- Are individual objectives supporting the team objectives being met?
- Are personal objectives being met?
- Is there conflict within the team?

At this lowest, but not the least important, level of questions the emphasis is upon the individual. It may be that in the earlier consideration of the team a high incidence of turnover was noted, and these questions may help to draw attention to why this has occurred. If individual needs are not being met, then the reasons why need to be examined. Chris Elgood discusses this area in his chapter on choosing, joining and leaving teams. Individual team members may be showing signs of stress and this can be attended to in the action planning stage. A range of problems relating to the team members will have been identified at this stage.

Although these four sets of questions relate to specific levels and have raised the awareness of what the problems are at each level, it is obvious that they are interrelated and at the very least each level will reflect the level below. In many cases it can be seen that problems may be clustered and are linked across the levels. Handling these problem clusters will often involve a series of connected actions at different levels within the organization.

A second model, the Team Formal Model, that can aid in the broad understanding of the situation is shown in Figure PS.3. It has been developed by the author from the Formal Systems Model discussed in the chapter on a systems approach to team effectiveness by Joyce Fortune. It has been used in many team based organizations, such as naval command and control, police and healthcare teams to examine the structural relationships between teams and the relationship of the team to its sponsor.

The model shows an organization that has multiple teams in operation each with a team sponsor who has initiated the team by stating the reason for its existence (the team purpose), planned its structure, provided the initial resources, set the objectives, empowered the team and monitors the performance of the team in relation to the organization's strategy and objectives. For example, it may be an international organization incorporating many smaller organizations within the main structure. Factors in the market place and environment may disrupt the functioning of the organization.

Similar to the first model, this can be used to structure a series of questions whose answers provide an understanding of the situation.

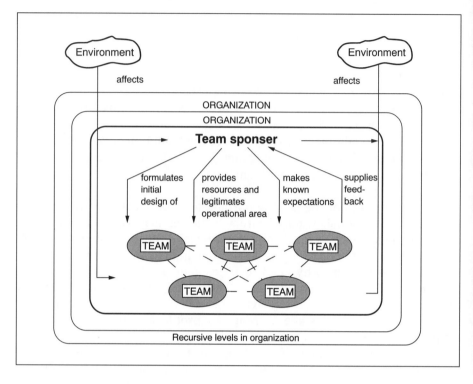

Figure PS.3 Team relationship model

- Was the initial design of the team appropriate to its purpose?
- Were sufficient resources made available?
- Are the team's objectives clear and achievable?
- Does the team have the power to achieve its objectives?
- What is the current relationship of the team to its sponsor?
- What are the team's relationship to other teams?

Problems may be identified in any of these areas – for example, if the team has been incorrectly structured to handle a project. Dennis Lock, in his chapter on project work discusses the types of structures that need to be adopted depending on the characteristics of a particular project. It may also be that there is conflict between teams, that is, responsibilities, non-cooperation, mutual dependencies not being met, and so on. If there are serious problems then it can be necessary to initiate a full failures analysis of the type outlined by Joyce Fortune.

The third area is not a model but an examination of the technology employed in the organization and by the teams – for example, technology needed by the organization to support the strategic business direction of the organization or the current operational activities. For the latter this

includes what technology the team is using or needs to operate effectively.

Again a set of questions, such as below, can be asked to clarify the problem areas.

- What technology is currently being used?
- Are there problems with it?
- Is it related to people issues?
- Is it a company-wide problem
- Does the market or organization require a particular technology?
- Does the team need additional software or training?

Several of the chapters in Part IV discuss the use and design considerations of technology and relate this to team construction and team working. The result of this analysis is to identify what technological problems exist for the team and its environment.

As a result of the three analyses the team leader has established a broad understanding of the problems that exist within the team, the team and its relationships to the organization and what is causing the organization to behave in the way that it does. To complete the identification of the problems that need to be dealt with, the current status of the team must be examined.

Stage 2: Establishing the team stage

The team may be newly formed or has been operating over a period of time; in either case the team leader needs to identify what the current status is. This stage examines the development and maturation cycle that all teams generally go through. It is based on the stages of the group formation model of Tuckman and Jensen (1977) which is still valid, even in the case of virtual teams. It is described in more detail in the chapter by Leslie Rae, but is shown here in Figure PS.4.

The stages are as follows.

Forming – where the individuals have not yet become a team. Members are trying to get to know each other and form some pattern of relationships.
Storming – this is the conflict stage in team development where team members try to reconcile individual and team demands. Conflict between personal goals, resistance to control and interpersonal hostility characterize this stage. The key issues that are discussed are team direction and management of conflict.
Norming – team members develop ways of working together and establishing rules in terms of norms of behaviour and team roles.
Performing – the team is now fully mature and is concerned with performance and achieving its objectives. It knows how to operate as a team.

Using this model as a basis by either observation of the team or by discussing with the team how they view their status, the team leader can determine what stage of development they have achieved and which stage they ought to have reached. A typical problem that may be deduced is that   *507*

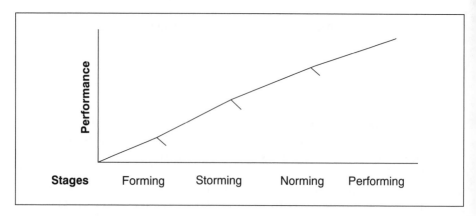

Figure PS.4 Tuckman and Jensen team development cycle

the team has not passed through all stages and is rooted in one of the first three. Knowing which stage in team formation they are at and where they should be highlights key problems, such as an inability to handle conflict.

A second method of clarifying team problems, that complements the above, is to monitor their behaviour. In the above model, in Figure PS.4, if a team does not mature through all of the stages but is stuck at a particular one, or indeed has fragmented, this presents one group of problems. Monitoring their behaviour for signs of counter-productive behaviour can also help to show more clearly the areas that need attention. The following four models are examples of team behaviour where, if detected early, actions can be initiated to counter the problems.

The anomic reaction model

This model parallels the 'forming' stage of team development. It covers the period from the restructuring of the organization and the definition of the new team, to the early period of operation. This involves setting the purpose of the team, its objectives, authority, resources, financial structure and the nomination of the personnel involved. Almost certainly this will necessitate incorporating new members into the team from other areas of the organization with new functions that were previously central responsibilities, for example, from finance or personnel. The team will then begin to operate and, if everything has been defined well and conducted with due consideration to the people involved, then this new 'social' system will perform as required. However, some initial counter-productive behaviour by the team may occur in certain danger areas. One such pattern of behaviour, the anomic reaction model, is described below.

Behavioural description – The team has been formed with the members coming from different areas of the organization. There is a degree of uncertainty as to exactly what they are meant to be doing and the scope of

508

their authority. This manifests itself in a continuous checking of work and decisions, both internally within the team and with other areas of the company. The level of communication of team members with previous formal and informal networks is high, showing a propensity to discuss previous activities. There is a reluctance to let drop past 'favoured' activities and a possible low commitment to, or understanding of, the new tasks. There is neither a full identification with the new team, nor an understanding of how this new appointment may serve individual members' long-term needs.

There are multiple problems in the above description and if any of them are apparent in the monitoring of the team, solutions must be found to change each one.

The intercon model

This parallels the 'storming' stage of team development and is when the team has been operating for a short period and its roles and responsibilities are clearer. Individuals are setting up the formal and informal positions within the team. Bonding between individuals and the forming of informal groups are taking place, and the way in which the team as a whole takes decisions is being established. This stage is characterized by the conflict that occurs and the strategies, overt and covert, that individuals and the team adopt to overcome the conflict. If a team does not formalize these strategies it will never develop its performance and, in the case of a serious problem or decision at a later time, it will not achieve consensus decision making and indeed may disintegrate.

Behavioural description – A great deal of conflict in evidence with team members establishing their identities and strengthening or rejecting individuals in their formal roles. 'Expert' and transient leaders are starting to be apparent. Informal alliances are being formed. There is a lower level of external communications that tend to be on role or task-required lines.

If this behaviour is apparent then appropriate conflict resolution strategies and actions must be put into place.

The team cult model

This parallels the 'norming' stage of team development and covers the period in which the team has developed as an entity and is performing normally. Members have been assimilated and old links to previous work areas have changed or decayed and new links established. The roles, responsibilities and authority of members have been clearly defined and strategies for handling conflict have been settled.

Behavioural description – This model examines the relationship of individuals to the team. Intra-team norms, work and social patterns have stabilized. A tightly knit society has developed with a 'clan' type of operation of close   *509* working ties and personal connections within the team and to other teams. A strong or charismatic leader may have arisen, with pressure on members to conform to the team. A team developed in this form can cause dissatisfaction and indeed some form of cognitive dissonance to individual members. Other problems may surface as a result of the formation of a strong team. For example, 'deindividuation' may cause a lack of self-recognition, 'groupthink' and 'group polarization' may run counter to an individual member's strongly held attitudes and beliefs. This can lead to disassociation from the team or indeed 'reactance' or rebellion.

There are several problems associated with this type of behaviour. Depending on which of the above problems is recognized then action, such as a management style change or opening up of the team to suggestions from outside, may be appropriate.

The team primacy model

This parallels the 'performing' stage of team development and occurs when the team is well-established and has been operating for a period of time successfully. There is strong cohesion in the team coupled with a high self-belief. It has been meeting its original objectives, although not without what it perceives as constraints on current and future activities imposed from higher in the organization. In the light of its success and the experience it has gained, the team believes that it knows best what should be done for itself and for the organization, and that it has the best expertise in the organization to achieve this. There are inherent dangers of estrangement of the team in this situation.

Behavioural description – This model examines the relationship of the team to the organization. The team has developed a strong identity, self-belief and self-importance bordering upon arrogance. It is very clear on how to run its activities successfully, the resources it should have, how it should be structured and demands the authority to define its own boundaries of operation. It perceives as interference, hierarchical and lateral organization attempts to control its activities by setting detailed objectives, goals and budgetary limits in areas where the team believes it knows best. The team feels that it does not have the power to follow its own strategies and is not being given the support or recognition warranted. This leads to some stormy external relationships. The belief of the team is that its activities are of prime importance to the success of the organization, and hence a 'primacy' or pre-eminent status should be attributed. The result of not obtaining this status is an alienation of the team to the organization. This team alienation is demonstrated by a resentment of the way in which the team is forced to operate, and frustration at the way in which members are required to apply their skills and knowledge without the discretion and autonomy they expect. The end product is an estrangement of the team from the organization and, from the senior management's perspective, counter-productive behaviour.

510

This is the most difficult of teams to deal with as it has been successful. Strategies to reintegrate the team with the organization, such as bringing them into the strategic planning process of the organization, can be adopted.

In summary with the combination of team stage analysis and team behavioural analysis, problems at a team level should now have been identified.

Stage 3 Establishing what is important

The first two stages are aimed at identifying where the problems lie in the team and its relationship to the organization. This was accomplished through a refining process from a broad awareness to specific behaviours of the team and team members. In this stage the purpose is to ascertain the priorities for action and is composed of two components. The first is a scoping technique for establishing the key operational constraints of the team and the main driving factors. The second component is a technique for prioritizing the problem areas.

Scoping team operating constraints

The purpose of scoping the team operational constraints and driving factors (in other words those factors which affect the performance of the team) is to provide a framework in which to understand what conditions the team is or will be operating under. For example, short decision time-frames, which is an *operating constraint*, means that the team must have: a clear structure for taking decisions; relevant information on which to take a decision and hence good communication; an appropriate management style. Goals and tasks are *driving factors* that will obviously be important to the way in which a team operates. Some of these are potentially problematic or are creating existing problems.

The technique used here for the scoping process is a combination of Construct Theory (Kelly, 1955) and multivariate mapping. The basis of construct theory is that people interpret their worlds, or the domains in which they are operating, by building individual or common sets of bi-polar constructs such as hot – cold, good – bad, fast – slow. These constructs are used as a guide for, and interpretation of, actions of individuals within a particular domain or set of events. In the context of team analysis a set of constructs can be elicited, either on an individual or group basis at a team meeting. These represent the factors that have most effect on the operation of a particular type of team. For example, the time-frame in which a decision by the team has to be taken, can be a prime determinant of performance. It can vary from seconds, as in naval command and control teams, to months, as in civil engineering design teams. A bi-polar construct for this would be DTF (decision time-frame) and it could be rated on a scale from 0–10 (short to long). A selection of factors and associated constructs, such as DTF, that are most important to the performance of a team can then be used as the *511*

Table PS.1
Construct theory: sample of factors

Factor	Bi-polar Constructs
Environment	This can be characterized at one extreme as very *rapid* change and the other as a *slow*-moving environment
Goals	From *unitary*, where all team members have identical primary goals, to *pluralist* where multiple individual goals exist.
Task	The nature of the task is very *focused* and singular, or there can be *diverse* and multiple tasks.
Decision Time-frame	Very *short* periods in which to make a decision measured in seconds, to long time frames measured in months.
Control	Where the predominant method of team control is *feedback* or *feedforward*.
Power	The power to influence or control the team is vested in the *formal* positions within the team, or *experts* who have transient power according to the circumstances.
Management	*Autocratic* to *consensus* decision making style of the formal senior team positions.
Culture	*Task*-oriented through to *people*-oriented

axes on a multivariate display to produce a map of key determining team operating characteristics as shown in Figure PS.5.

A sample of factors that might be important to a particular team are shown in Table PS.1

These are shown as in the left-hand circle in Figure PS.5. The right-hand circle shows the ratings on each of the operating constraints and driving factors as viewed by the team leader, team members or a consensus by the whole team.

If individual team members construct their own diagrams from their own perspective, they can be compared and the differences between them used to direct a discussion towards what is important to the team and what problems ensue from them.

Prioritizing the problems

From Stages 1 and 2 and the team scoping technique, a range of problems have been identified and it is good practice to build up a problem register as the different analyses have progressed. The problem now is to decide which ones to tackle first. The team leader can do this in isolation, with the team or indeed with other members of the organization. One thing for certain is that the team leader cannot do everything immediately.

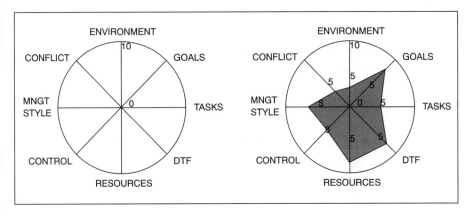

Figure PS.5   Team scoping diagrams

Figure PS.6 represents a simple technique for prioritizing the problems for action. The two axes are *Time* – the time it will take for the implementation of an action plan to take effect and *Impact* – the impact of resolving the problem on team performance.

Those problems that fall within the short time-frame and high impact box are those that should receive immediate attention and for which action plans should be developed. For those that fall within high impact and long time-frames, action plans should also be developed with the recognition that the benefits will not be realized quickly. Those that have a long time-frame and low impact should be noted but put on the back burner. The short time-frame low impact problems can be dealt with if there are few problems and the team leader has enough spare time. Those that have

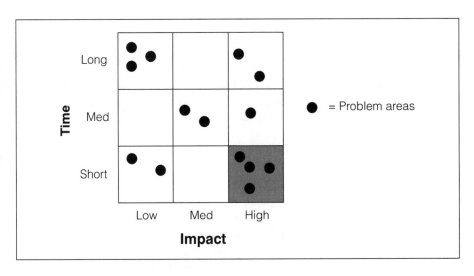

Figure PS.6   Change analysis matrix

medium impact or have a medium time-frame are difficult decisions and will depend on the circumstances but in any case are not the immediate worry.

As a result of this process of prioritizing the problems the team leader is now in a position to construct the related action plans.

Stage 4 Constructing an action plan

The result from Stage 3 is a prioritized list of problems to address. It is beyond the scope of this chapter to outline plans for all the possible problems, and indeed many of the chapters in this book provide guidelines as to what areas should be considered together with methods and techniques for dealing with the problems. Therefore, a useful classification of the areas that could be considered is suggested, together with indications of which chapters, in addition to those already mentioned, are applicable to these areas.

Structure

This area relates to the way in which organizations adopt structures to support their strategic direction, and the role that teams and teamworking play within the structure. Problems that have been identified may require changes in the culture of the organization or in the way that teams are constructed and empowered. Many of the chapters have already been mentioned, such as aligning the team mode of operating to the business, and the implications of the technologies employed. Further chapters that can help to provide methods and techniques that can be used in action plans to deal with problems are as follows:

> *Teams and the learning organization* (Julia Pokora and Wendy Briner) discusses the problem of experience being passed between teams and the approach to creating a learning organization.

> *Team selection, psychometrics and feedback* (Malcolm Crockford) covers the constraints and problems on forming teams in organizations, examines the use of psychometrics in teamwork and provides examples of psychometric instruments.

Process

This area relates to team processes that are common to all teams, such as, running meetings, developing team members' motivation and creativity. Problems that are identified in these areas must be dealt with by the team leader in order to achieve a high degree of effectiveness. The following chapters consider these areas and provide approaches to problems that can be built into action plans:

How teams learn (Alan Mumford) considers the characteristics of good teams, leadership effectiveness, balancing team tasks and learning, assessing learning skills in groups and improving learning performance.

Creativity in teams (Tudor Rickards) describes the MPIA approach to enable teams to discover new and unexpected ways of doing things, and to provide a way into a more reflective understanding of habitual behaviours in teams.

Managing stress for optimum performance (Jane Cranwell-Ward) shows how to recognize the stress symptoms and triggers and suggests strategies for dealing with stress.

Leading team meetings (Quentin de la Bedoyere) describes the process of good running of team meetings.

Motivating teams (Gisela Hagemann) introduces the concept of a super-team and describes the four conditions to make teams thrive.

Interaction (people, communication)

This area and cluster of problems is concerned with the interaction betwen individuals within the team. If the team is functioning as a group of disparate people rather than a cohesive unit, then performance is likely to be affected. The following chapters are concerned with three aspects that, if improved, will bring the team closer together:

Intra-team communication (Chris Moore) examines communication in teams, control and interpersonal relationships, outlines techniques for eliciting the quality of communication and group tasks for developing understanding and communications.

Managing teams assertively (Terry Gillen) describes three management styles and how to develop the assertive management style deemed to be the most effective.

Solving problems face-to-face (Quentin de la Bedoyere) outlines the LEGUP method for dealing with people problems, whether they are performance problems or personal problems.

Team development

There are a range of approaches and techniques for groups in the process of being formed into a team or teams that have problems. The following chapters describe a range of actions that can be taken to alleviate the problems:

515

Creating a team-based organization (Colin Hastings) examines the development of high-performance teams, preparing leaders, ensuring that the mix of job and team skills is correct and the role of senior management.

Using management games (Chris Elgood) indicates necessary concepts and skills in teams and provides examples of games that can help to develop these skills.

The superteam approach (Julia Pokora and Wendy Briner) examines the characteristics of a superteam and how to develop one.

Coaching and mentoring teams (Nigel MacLennan) describes the processes involved in helping the team and team members to develop into high achievers.

Designing and facilitating team development (Malcom Crockford) discusses the relevance of these type of events and provides a practical guide to the process by which team development events are designed, facilitated and evaluated.

Turning teamwork into knowledge creation (Ronnie Lessem) describes the POEM approach to the development of teamwork over and above individual performance.

Stage 5 Action and management

It is a trite phrase, but nonetheless true, that this stage depends on what you want to do. The stages involved in this approach are designed so that a team leader can gain a wide view of all the problems and, through a refining process, prioritize them into a list of key problems against which action plans can be developed and then implemented. There are two further actions that must be undertaken.

1   New problems will arise during the implementation period and hence the activity must be undertaken on a regular basis.
2   The team leader should monitor the effectiveness of the action plans and be prepared to modify them if required.

This is a framework of activities, not a prescriptive methodology, and therefore can be modified and added to in the light of the team leader's previous experience and knowledge of using this approach. After all, any approach is better than none.

REFERENCES

Kelly, G.A., *The Psychology of Personal Constructs*, New York, Norton, 1955

Tuckman, B.W. and Jensen, M.A., 1977, 'Stages of Small Group Development Revisited,' *Group and Organisation Studies*, **2**, 419–427

Index

519